CHRIS
PEARCE

The Story of an
AFRICAN
GAME

The Story of an

AFRICAN GAME

To Chris,
With best wishes and I hope
we will meet again in Cape
Town or Birmingham.
Regards
André Odendaal
Newlands, 14. 9. 2007.

ANDRÉ ODENDAAL

dp davidphilip

ABOVE   *Nelson Mandela was a keen boxer in his youth. He is pictured here during a training session in the 1950s.*
OPPOSITE   *Mandela as a 19-year-old student in the 1930s.*

FOREWORD

IN *LONG WALK TO FREEDOM* I recalled the values we were taught as pupils at Healdtown College in the late 1930s. The educated Englishman was our model; what we aspired to be were 'black Englishmen', as we were sometimes derisively called. We were taught – and believed – that the best ideas were English ones. In line with these ideas, sport, particularly cricket, was given a high priority. I enjoyed myself on the playing fields at Healdtown. The standards were high. Therefore, even while athletics and boxing became my favoured games, I have been aware for a long time of the mission roots of cricket in the Eastern Cape and the deep love for the game that developed in the African communities in that part of the world.

In addition to the early education I received at Healdtown College and Fort Hare University, another of the great influences on my life was my imprisonment on Robben Island. To my surprise, I have discovered in *The Story of an African Game* that Robben Island, too, has a direct relationship to the beginnings of cricket in the African communities. During our prison years, we drew inspiration from 19th-century anti-colonial resistance leaders such as Makana, Maqoma, Xhoxo, and Mhala, who had been imprisoned on the island a century before us. We did not know that one of the outcomes of their imprisonment was that the children of the latter three chiefs were at the same time studying in Cape Town and paving the way in making cricket an African game.

Professor André Odendaal has in different ways already made an important contribution to the preservation of our national heritage. He deserves credit for bringing to life the rich traditions and history of sport among black South Africans. During the apartheid era, black people were deliberately erased from history, and their experiences were negated. Now, as we enjoy the benefits of a hard-fought democracy, it is important to correct these exclusions. This book, focusing on one small aspect of our national life, shows just how big they have been.

Recently, I participated in the marketing drive for the ICC Cricket World Cup 2003, which our country hosted. The event demonstrated how cricket has captured the imagination of a whole cross-section of South Africans, young and old, black and white, men and women, in the past few years. It also showed how far our country has come in a short time since sports unity and political democracy in 1994. Once divided and seen as the exclusive preserve of a small section of the population, cricket, surveys have shown, now ranks second after football in popularity in our country. This book is sure to add to this popularity and the more inclusive culture that cricket is seeking to cultivate so that it can become a truly South African and African game in the future.

Mandela

N.R. MANDELA

CONTENTS

Acknowledgements

THE MAKING OF *The Story of an African Game* has been part of a long personal and intellectual journey, which is partly explained in the Notes on Author and Bibliography. It could not have happened without the inspiration and support of hundreds of people who have been teachers and partners on that journey. My thanks to them, even if I cannot hope to single them all out here.

To start with, I owe a debt to those who introduced me to the non-racial cricket set-up more than a quarter of a century ago, including Laughton and Millie Jacobs, Omar Henry, Rashid Varachia, Hassan Howa and those recorders of SA Cricket Board of Control history — Cliff Adams, Chummy Mayet, S.J. Reddy and Younis Agherdien — some of whose valuable papers ended up in my care. When I joined 'the Board', the Osmani, Khota and Wadee families in Lenasia took me in as one of their own. Ahmed Mangera, Faisel Kimmie and Paul Saville gave direction, and Sadick Emeran, Sainie Abrahams, Salie Green, Seraj Gabriels, Yusuf 'Tayoo' Jacobs, Ashraf Burns, Miley Emeran, 'Boeta' Behardien and Ismail Behardien, and the people at United became like family.

Over the years, I have shared many good times with diverse friends and team-mates at school, university, club and first-class level. They have helped me develop a deep understanding for this strange game.

During the writing of my Masters and PhD dissertations, and in my subsequent academic career, I benefited enormously from the friendship, skills and insights of colleagues at Stellenbosch University, Cambridge University, the University of Cape Town, the University of South Africa and, particularly, the University of the Western Cape.

My experiences in the liberation struggle fundamentally influenced and enriched my life, intellectual work and understandings of sport and history. The struggle was also a training ground for the life-long PhD in humanity course. I am indebted to the many wonderfully resourceful people who supported me, and created space for me, during the 1980s and 1990s. Telling this story with the particular imagination one finds here is only possible because of what I learned in those years.

It was during the tumultuous 1980s that I first met and played against Khaya Majola. Later, we worked closely together and became friends. He inspired me to start putting down this story on paper.

The Majola family have shared Khaya's enthusiasm and given invaluable support. My thanks to all of them, particularly Gerald, Cynthia, Vukile, Sipokazi, Tozie, Honey, Nomonde and Vuyo Majola, and Skumbuzo Oliphant. Milase Majola's front door was always open to me. Her character and resilience are a lesson to all.

Over the past few years, colleagues and friends involved in cricket administration in South Africa encouraged in important ways my writing and personal development. They include a broad range of people at the United Cricket Board of South Africa and the Western Province Cricket Association at executive, council and staff level — as well as members of the the Transformation Monitoring Committee, Provincial Monitoring Committees and the ICC World Cup 2003 Policy Committee.

The UCB Council endorsed this work and made possible its publication in the impressive format we see here.

Numerous others helped with information and contacts. Dan Qeqe, Haroon Lorgat, Krish Reddy, Ray Mali, Junior Sokhanyile, Bob Edgar and Devdas Govindjee, especially, gave me access to important information and material.

I also owe a particular debt to Graham Abrahams, Junaid Ahmed, Mogamad Allie, David Anthony, Norman Arendse, Peter Bacela, June Bam, Ngconde Balfour, Lyndon Barends, Mick Baskin, Willem and Carol Basson, Debbie Batzofin, Gary Boshoff, Arnold Bloch, Frank Brache, Henry Bredekamp, Nomonde Mbulawa, Alison Burchell, Colin Bundy, Laloo Chiba, Peter Chingoka, Bossie Clarke, Rodney Davenport, Chris Day, Ashwin Desai, Nabeal Dien, Nomsa Dlamini, Michael Doman, Clem Druker, Ashton Dunjwa, James Early, Hamza Ebrahim, Mohamed Ebrahim, all the family in Walmer Estate, Dave Emslie, Anton Ferreira, Sadie Forman, Greg Fredericks, Yusuf 'Chubb' Garda, Jakes Gerwel, Sada Govender, Urmila Govindjee, Albert Grundlingh, Peter, Ad and Walter Hain, Peter Heeger, Archie Henderson, Jocelyn Henderson, Denver Hendricks, Barbara Hogan, Mike Hutchins, Rodney Inglis, Shamiel, Shanaaz and Suleiman Isaacs, Eugene Jacobs, Ahmed Jinnah, Danny and Maxwell Jordaan, Anthea Josias, Donnie Jurgens,

Tsepo Kadi, Rahima Kara-Shaik, Ahmed Kathrada, Rose Kekana, Tim and Naledi Khumalo, Jeremy Kriekler, Robbie Kurz, Wolfie Kodesh, Chuck Korr, Robbie Kurz, Trish Lewis, Farah Lorgat, Richard Loring, Lynette Maart, Enver Mall, Gordon Metz, Niels Momberg, Solomon and Miriam Makhosana, Victoria Matshikiza, Kwedi Mkalipi, Diketho Modise, Grace Modiselle, Helen Moffett, Logan Naidoo, Mveleli Ncula, Braber Ngozi, Mtutuzeli Nyoka, Dougie Oakes, Brian O'Connell, Mary Odendaal, the late K.P. Odendaal, Jeff Opland, Imtiaz Patel, Khonaye Penxa, Thenjiwe Perhe, Larry Popkas, Flip Potgieter, Praba Reddy, S.K. Reddy, Sam Ramsamy, Cheryl Roberts, Christopher Saunders, Paul Saville, Bennie and Petra Schereka, Ameena Smith, Percy Sonn, the 'Spin Doctors XI', Louise and John Sprenger, Makhenkhesi Stofile, Rodney Swiegelaar, the late Uncle Ben Tengimfene, who died while this manuscript was being completed, Raymond Uren, Carol van Vuuren, Helene Volgraaf, Fuad Waggie, Mario Williams, Paul Weinberg, Busi Xhalabile and Phaki Ximiya.

My apologies to those I have left out of this long but incomplete list.

Thanks are also due to those responsible for getting this book into the shape it is. Shannon Copperfield was always available to put in an extra hour, no matter how inconvenient the time. John Young offered intelligent insights, which helped me greatly, and Robin Isherwood read the manuscript closely. Drusilla Yekela allowed me to use her map of Alice. Ivor Markman helped collect photographic material in Port Elizabeth. Staff at the various research libraries and archives were very helpful, especially Esther van Driel at the UWC-Robben Island Mayibuye Archives, Marius Fortune and Faiek Ariefdien and the other staff at the National Library of South Africa, Marion George at the Cape Archives, and Mike Berning and Jackson Vena at the Cory Library at Rhodes University. (Mike brought to my notice at the last moment the valuable 19th-century cricket photographs which have so livened up this book.) The Human Sciences Research Council are publishing partners in this project, thanks to Wilmot James, Garry Rosenberg and John Daniels. I could not have hoped for a better publishing and production team than Brian Wafawarowa and Jeremy Boraine at New Africa Books, designers Peter Bosman and Damian Gibbs, and the project management of Clive During and Cathy Bothwell at Integrated Publishing Solutions.

Finally, special thanks are due to Zohra Ebrahim and our children, Rehana Thembeka, Adam and Nadia. Zohra's intelligence, strength and love give me sustenance, while the warmth and energy of our children, and their inquisitiveness and sense of fun and wonder, are my greatest rewards in life. My family make me feel blessed and whole. They allowed me to work at all sorts of times, even (more than once) over Eid, Christmas and New Year holidays.

This book is dedicated to Khaya, our respective children, and all the young people of South Africa. May they learn from and be inspired by the remarkable history that follows.

ANDRÉ ODENDAAL
CAPE TOWN
23 MARCH 2003

INTRODUCTION

CRICKETERS OF ALL COLOURS in South Africa today know they can aspire to playing at the highest level of the game. They also take it for granted that they play together under one United Cricket Board and that their country has just hosted the ICC World Cup 2003.

This was not always the case. The current situation in cricket, reinforced by a democracy that emphasises equal rights for all South Africans, is relatively new. It is, after all, only since the UCB was formed in 1991 that all cricketers in South Africa have been playing together regardless of colour or creed. For more than one hundred years before that they were segregated into separate racial bodies, and there were no less than ten national associations formed between 1888 and 1991. At one stage six of these were operating at the same time, giving a whole new meaning to the words 'national' and 'South Africa'.

White cricketers excluded those classified 'non-white' from their clubs and competitions. Only whites could play official test cricket, and in 172 tests between 1888 and 1970 they played against 'white' countries only – England, Australia and New Zealand. This was in keeping with the logic of colonialism and apartheid.

The history of cricket in South Africa was about this racially privileged group of people. 'Non-whites' did not feature. This gave rise to the belief in many quarters that cricket was not a game played by Africans, and that they had no real cricket history or culture to write about. The facts seemed to speak for themselves. After all, everyone knew that blacks played soccer, that cricket required a cultivated environment and 'gentlemanly' discipline apparently absent from township life, and that blacks who did play cricket had been 'brought through' by the cricket 'development programmes' of the 1980s and 1990s. Popular wisdom had it that cricket needed to be 'taken to the townships', needed to be 'introduced' or 'sold' to black South Africans. And the record books bore out this view: there were no statistics pertaining to black cricket, no photographs, no famous names.

In short, if appearances were to be believed, there were no black cricketers.

The South African team singing the national anthem during the opening ceremony of the ICC World Cup 2003 at Newlands.

OUT OF AFRICA

The Story of an African Game sets out to show that this view of South Africa's cricketing history is not only wrong, but that it perpetuates one of the most insidious myths in sport. Far from being a game foreign to black South Africans, they have a cricket tradition stretching back 150 years, and cricket is truly an 'African' game.

Africans have played cricket for as long as whites have in South Africa. There was a flourishing and established cricket culture among African cricketers by the 1880s, the stronghold of which was in the Eastern Cape with its strong mission school system and distinctive pattern of colonial conquest and incorporation. The cricket tradition established there has persisted right up to the present, despite the systematic assault on the social, political, economic and human rights of black South Africans during the 20th century, particularly after the advent of rigid institutionalised apartheid in 1948.

Another little-appreciated feature of this history is that from its introduction to the mission schools in the 1850s, cricket among Africans grew to maturity along much the same lines as 'white' cricket did: the formation of clubs (1869 onwards); the first inter-town competitions (1880s); the establishment of leagues and regional associations (1890s); and the establishment of national organisations and tournaments (1900s).

Intended to instil the 'virtues' of the Eton playing fields, the game had a profound influence on the pupils in the mission schools of the Eastern Cape (which were still producing half of all African matriculants in South Africa as late as the 1940s), and they and their descendants in turn influenced it. For not only did they adopt this most Victorian of games, but they adapted it to their own context and, in the process, helped give it a distinctively South African and African character.

The cricketing culture created here has proved itself as durable as any of the other examples in the former British Empire: the Parsis in India; the descendants of the diverse

Broadening cricket's base in the 21st century: boys and girls play together in the UCB's mini-cricket programmes.

immigrants and transported transgressors in Australia; the indentured labourers and slaves of the Caribbean, who became masters of the game; and the conservative English-speaking white colonials in South Africa who tried to establish 'Little England on the veld'.

The Story of an African Game, coming 195 years after the first recorded cricket match in South Africa, finally sets the record straight and makes visible those cricketers who have for so long been ignored.

After *The Story of an African Game* people will no longer be able to say, 'But we didn't know.' And those who have struggled to be heard over the years will be able to say, 'Here is proof, here are statistics and facts.' Hitherto unknown details of cricket milestones at national and provincial levels, particularly in the Eastern Province, are chronicled. For the first time, the names of black cricketers who represented their country, albeit unofficially, are listed.

While cricket has always been regarded as a 'gentleman's game', this book also sheds light on its increasing popularity amongst women and their involvement from the earliest years.

Today, as South African cricket tries to reposition itself as a 21st-century game in an African context, and attempts to tap into the energies and imagination that drive the new democracy, the realisation is growing that the legacy left by black cricketers of the past can be a valuable guide to the future. That which was negated and derided in the past, has now become a source of inspiration and example.

The renowned South African writer, Peter Abrahams, reflecting on the 20th century from a mountain-top in Jamaica, observed: 'How an enslaved people come to be free, the institutions and patterns of association they fashion as part of the struggle for that freedom, usually determines the nature of that society.'[1]

He might have been writing about South African cricket when he penned those words. Without knowledge of the history described in this book, one will not properly understand where South African cricket is heading to in the future.

FOCUS ON A FAMILY

Another important purpose of this book is to pay a special tribute to Khaya Majola, one of the most famous of all African cricketers, who died prematurely from cancer on Monday 28 August 2000 at the young age of 47 years. Khaya's poignant last fight, and the faith he had that I would help to tell his story in a form that it deserved, made the task of writing this book doubly important for me.

This partly explains the narrative structure of the book. The period of the first one hundred years of the story, up until the 1940s, is recounted by focusing not on any one person or family, but on the broad social history and organisational development of cricket, using rare 19th-century African-language newspaper and documentary sources unearthed in the course of a doctoral dissertation. The focus shifts in the 1950s, and the half century following, to the Majola family, a family from New Brighton who have been at the forefront of cricket in the region and the whole country for 50 years. They are a family who, to black South Africans, are as famous as the Pollocks.

Eric Majola was a sporting legend in the 1950s and 1960s. A 'Bantu Springbok' in both rugby and cricket, he is still referred to by old timers as a fly-half in the same mould as Hansie Brewis, Keith Oxlee and the great Cliff Morgan of Wales.

Eric's eldest son, Khaya Majola, became one of the leading players in South Africa in the 1970s and 1980s, and also one of the top administrators in the 1990s. His contribution to South African cricket was recognised in 2001, when the long-standing national schools week — the Coca Cola Khaya Majola Week — was named after him.

Younger brother Gerald Majola also gained national honours in cricket and provincial colours in rugby. On 1 January 2001 he became Chief Executive Officer of the United Cricket Board of South Africa, responsible for the daily running of the game in this country.

There is an African custom that says, 'Umntu ngumntu ngabanyabantu' – 'a person is

Two famous cricketing families. Khaya Majola with Graeme Pollock in 1973.

Basil D'Oliveira, a key figure in the broader history of black cricket in South Africa.

a person through other people'. So, in telling the story of Eric, Khaya and Gerald Majola we also attempt to tell the story of their family, the particular community in which they lived and something of what they learned from and shared with other cricketers.

Being black people living in apartheid South Africa meant that the Majolas could not be delivered in the same hospital ward as white children. Could not live in the same suburb. Go to the same school. Have the same job. Enter the same cinema. Swim on the same beach. Sit on the same park bench. Glide stiff-legged and laughing down the same slide in a public playground. Enter shops through the same entrance. Use the same railway bridge. Travel in the same train compartment, or coach. Be served at the same post office counter. Join the same sports clubs. Play in the same sports team. Sit on the main pavilion at matches. Or be selected for their country to play in official test matches.

What was it like for those cricketers on the wrong side of the line under apartheid? How did they play and organise themselves? How did they relate their sporting activities to what was happening in the society at large, and what choices did they have to make?

With its focus on the Majola family from the 1950s to the present, *The Story of an African Game* attempts to answer some of these questions and to make 'real' this rich story, without losing sight of the broader social and political backdrop and overall organisational development of the game.

RACE AND TERMINOLOGY

This is the first book to detail systematically and acknowledge the long history of black African cricketers. While it focuses on Africans — defined at different times by those in power as 'Kaffirs', 'Natives', 'Bantus', 'Plurals' and (since democracy) 'black Africans' — it also touches in parts on the broader story of those defined as 'non-white' under apartheid.

Although segregation and, sometimes, political differences meant that African,

Gerald Majola, CEO of the United Cricket Board, in his playing days.

coloured and Indian communities often played and organised separately, there was also a constant interplay between them (and, indeed, white cricketers) from the very beginning. This was based on shared experiences of racial discrimination and, often, shared social values and political understandings. The broader, more in-depth history will be told fully in the soon-to-be-published official history of South African cricket.

Segregation, apartheid and ethnicity created boundaries, but these have always been porous. From the outset in the 1880s progressive-minded cricketers sought to build unity across racial boundaries. The complex and constantly changing set of relationships accompanying these efforts were always more nuanced and ambiguous than formal organisational affiliations and political alignments suggested.

Identities are fluid and ever-changing, but in South Africa they have tended to be frozen and defined according to 'race'.[2] It is, therefore, impossible to escape using these racial categories, even if one is not comfortable with them. For me, all South Africans are Africans, but here 'African' is used as both a noun and an adjective, and refers to the country's Bantu-language-speaking inhabitants. The word 'coloured',

referring to people of mixed race, is as often as possible decapitalised and used as an adjective, as in 'coloured cricketers' or 'coloured people'. The word 'black' is used to describe African, Asian and coloured people collectively. Words that now give offence – 'non-European', 'non-white', 'kaffir', 'native', 'Bantu', 'Boer', 'whitey', etcetera – appear in the text only in direct quotations or where the word became part of a standard term, as in Bantu Cricket Board or Native Congress. The use of some of these words also enables us from the vantage point of democratic South Africa to realise how crude racial definitions often were in the past.

In the old South Africa black people were often not given proper (or even basic) recognition. For example, it would not be unusual for a newspaper report of five people killed in a car accident to name them as Mr and Mrs Smith and 'three natives'. In keeping with this was the regular mutilation of African names in their spelling. Care has, therefore, been taken here to get the spelling of names correct, often with the assistance of old players. However, in some instances records give several versions of the same name; even the *South Africa Non-European Cricket Almanack*, the starting point for any historian of black cricketers, mangles

From 'invisible' African to media icon in a post-modern world. Star bowler, Makhaya Ntini, pictured here in a promotional brochure for a sports television channel.

African names. Africans also commonly had both English and indigenous names. Often the English name would be used in reports, while the person was commonly known by his or her African or clan names by friends and colleagues, as in Hamilton Mahonga John Masiza, Leander Fikile Siyo, or Steve Vukile Tshwete, who was also affectionately called Tshangana.

While this book provides a coherent narrative of African cricket for the first time, and outlines the unfolding organisational developments over a 150-year period, it does not claim to be the final word on the subject. It is simply one narrative from a particular perspective. There are still many untapped sources available and many histories that need to be written. These range from regional histories and biographies to studies of national organisational developments in specific periods, as well as a consideration of themes such as cricket and class, ethnicity and education. The inevitable omissions of names, events, and regions do not mean, as other authors of similar works have pointed out,[3] that less value is placed on the contributions of those who are not given centre stage in this story, or who get less attention than perhaps they deserve.

However, notwithstanding such omissions, I hope that *The Story of an African Game* has provided a base from which to demolish racist myths about Africans in sport, and that it has contributed a whole new body of knowledge to serve as a platform for further studies, thus deepening our insights and understandings of the past.

One of my aims in telling the story of black men and women who have played and followed this wonderful game in South Africa is to help deconstruct old colonial mentalities (on and off the field) and to give impetus to the process of transforming the racially-exclusive game of the past into a dynamic African and 21st-century phenomenon, operating comfortably within the context of democracy and changing patterns of global development.

Another objective is to contribute to a modern international culture of cricket, one freed of cloying nostalgia about an imperial past and which celebrates both the diversity of the game and the contribution made to it by those defined as 'the other'. Cricket has long since become an international (rather than a British) game, but we often remain fixed in the discourses and attitudes of a time long gone.

ABBREVIATIONS AND ACRONYMS

AGM – Annual General Meeting
ANC – African National Congress
APO – African Political Organisation
AZAPO – Azanian People's Organisation
BCCI – Board of Control for Cricket in India
BMIA – Becoana Mutual Improvement Association
EPBCB – Eastern Province Bantu Cricket Board
EPCA – Eastern Province Cricket Association
EPCCU – Eastern Province Coloured Cricket Union
EPCF – Eastern Province Cricket Federation
EPCL – Eastern Province Coloured League
EPCU – Eastern Province Cricket Union
ICC – International Cricket Conference
KZN – KwaZulu-Natal
MCC – Marylebone Cricket Club
NMMC – Nine Man Motivating Committee
NNC – Natal Native Congress
NOSC – National Olympic and Sports Congress
NP – National Party
NRC – Native Recruiting Commission
NSC – National Sports Congress

NUSAS – National Union of South African Students
OFS – Orange Free State
ORCNC – Orange River Colony Native Congress
PAC – Pan Africanist Congress
PE – Port Elizabeth
PMC – Provincial Monitoring Committee
SA&RWCA – South African and Rhodesian Women's Cricket Association
SAACB – South African African Cricket Board
SABCB – South African Bantu Cricket Board
SABC – South African Broadcasting Corporation
SACBOC – South African Cricket Board of Control
SACCA – South African Coloured Cricket Association
SA – South African
SACCB – South African Coloured Cricket Board
SACOS – South African Council on Sport
SACU – South African Cricket Union
SAIC – South African Indian Congress

SAICCB – South African Independent Coloured Cricket Board
SAICU – South African Indian Cricket Union
SANC – South African Native Congress
SANC – South African Native Convention
SANNC – South African National Native Congress
SANROC – South African Non-Racial Olympic Committee
SASA – South African Sports Association
SASSSA – South African Senior Schools Sports Association
SFW – Stellenbosch Farmers' Wineries
TCB – Transvaal Cricket Board
TIC – Transvaal Indian Congress
TMC – Transformation Monitoring Committee
TNC – Transvaal Native Congress
UCBSA/UCB – United Cricket Board of South Africa
UDF – United Democratic Front
UN – United Nations
USSASA – United Schools Sports Association of South Africa

ORGANISATIONAL STRUCTURES *of* CRICKET *in* SOUTH AFRICA

1890 – 2003

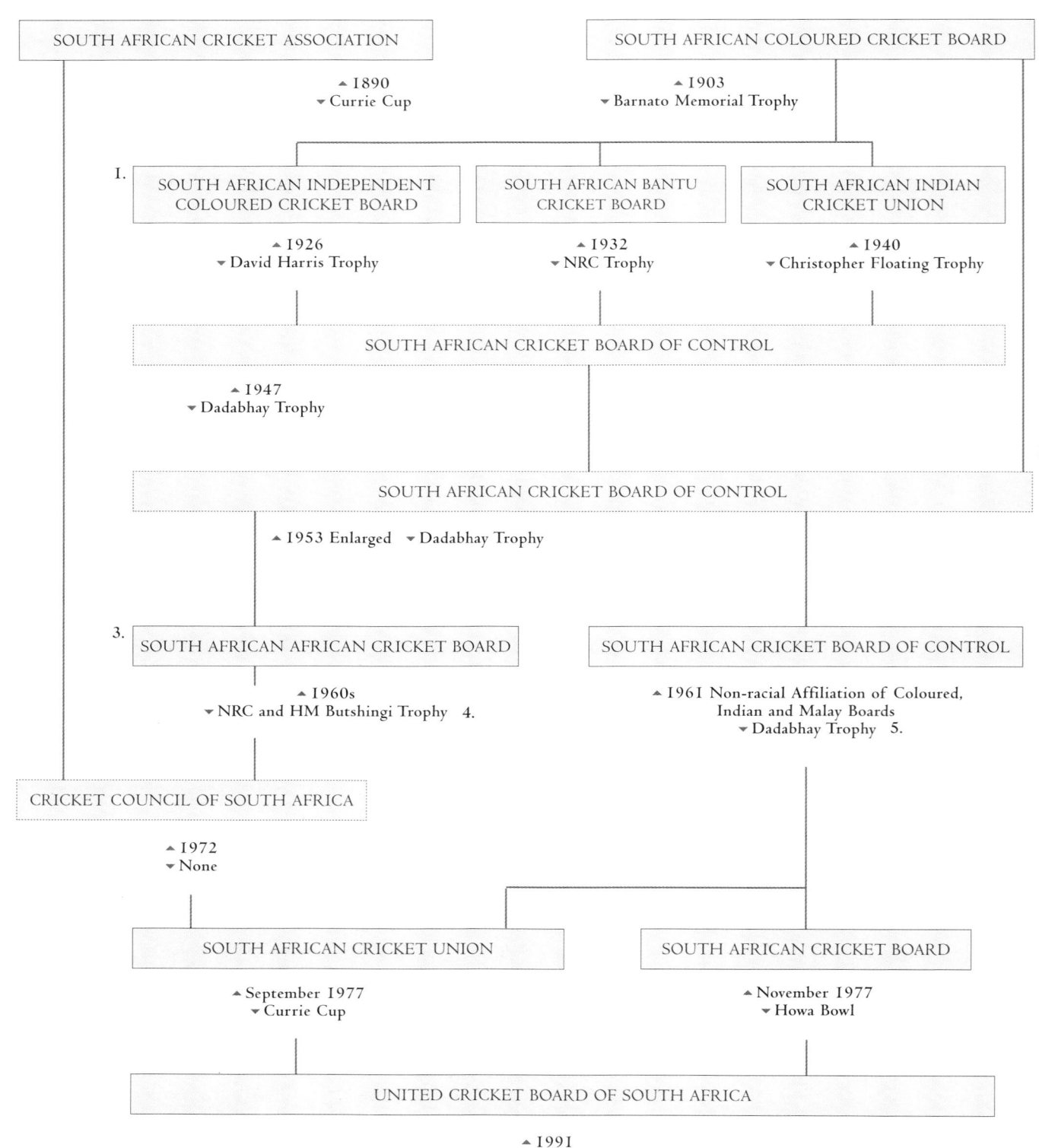

KEY AND REFERENCES

▲ Foundation date
▼ Premier competition
----- Umbrella body where
       affiliates maintained autonomy

1. The SA Independent CCB changed its name to South African Coloured Cricket Association (SACCA) in 1948
2. SACCB, the old mother body, was forced to change its name to the South African Malay Cricket Board (SAMCB) before it was allowed to join SACBOC
3. SABCB changed its name to the South African African

Cricket Board (SAACB) in the 1960s
4. In 1968/69 the NRC Trophy was replaced by the HM Butshingi Trophy named after the SAACB president.
5. The Dadabhay Trophy was later replaced as the major SACBOC trophy by the Stellenbosch Farmer's Winery (SFW) Trophy.

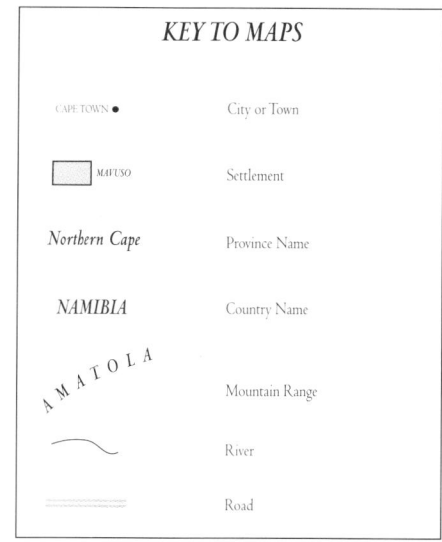

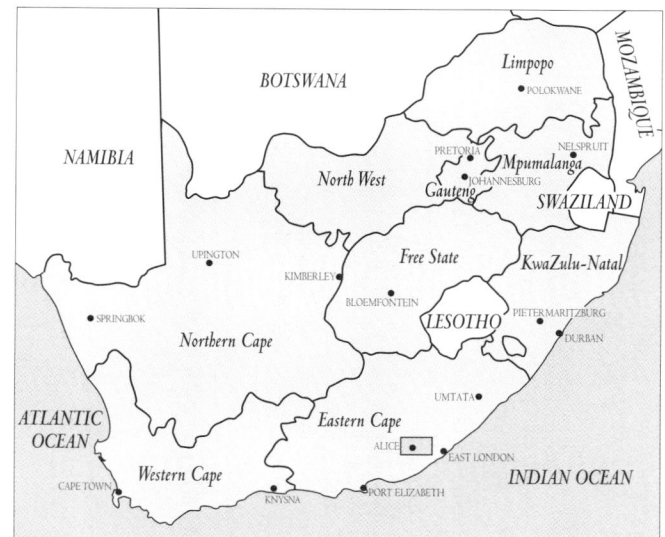

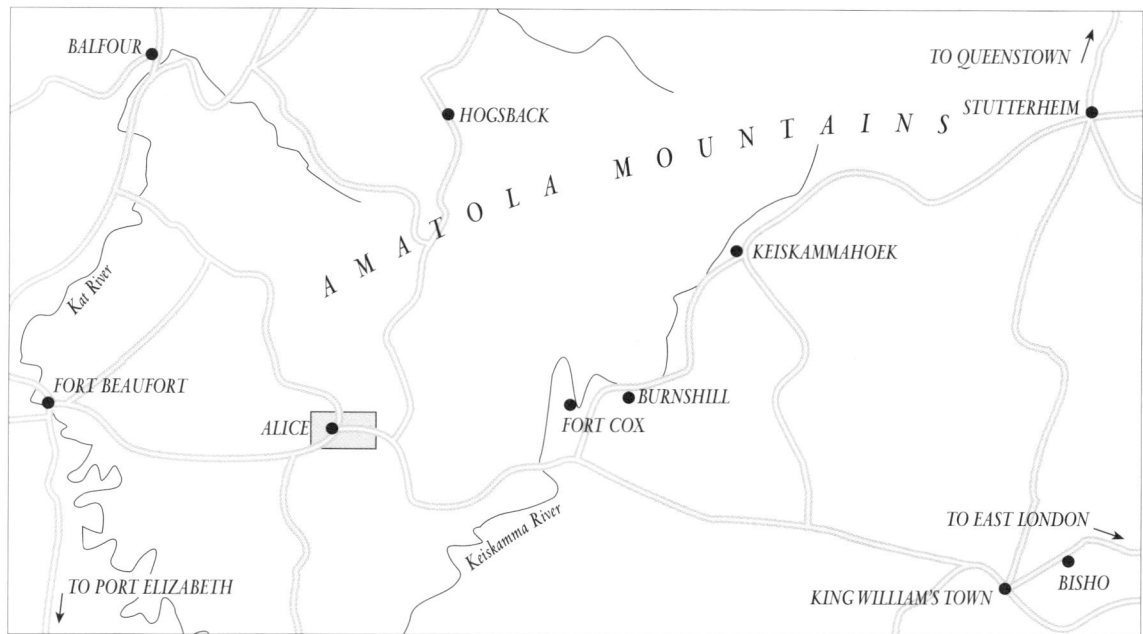

The Eastern Cape, heartland of African cricket in South Africa.

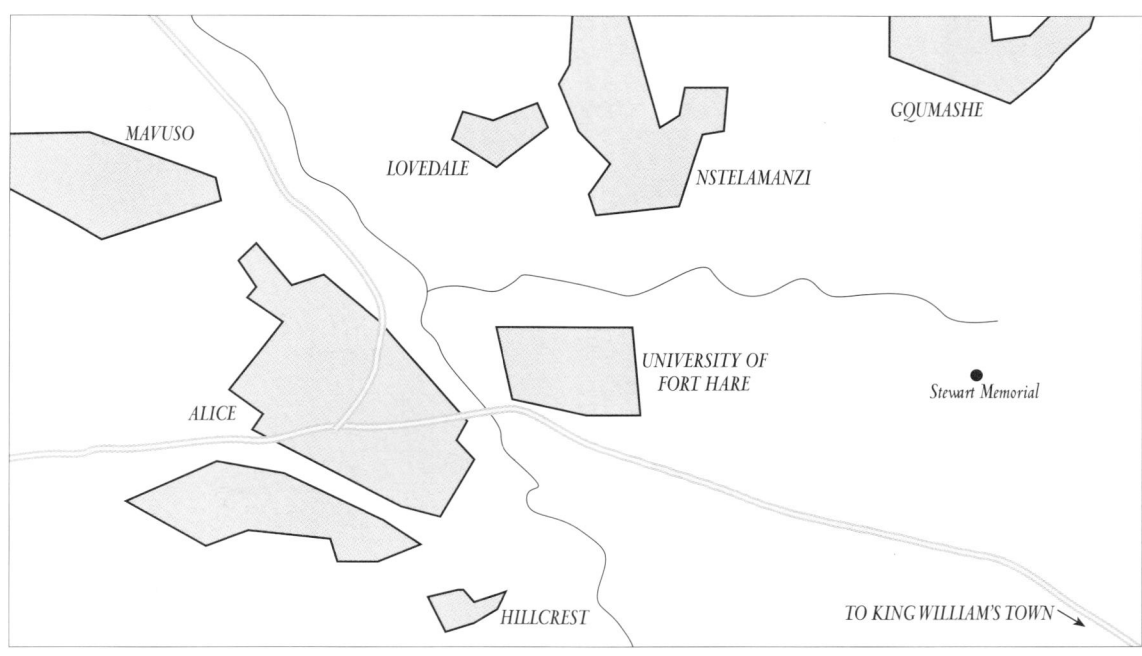

Alice, home of cricket nurseries Lovedale College and Fort Hare University.

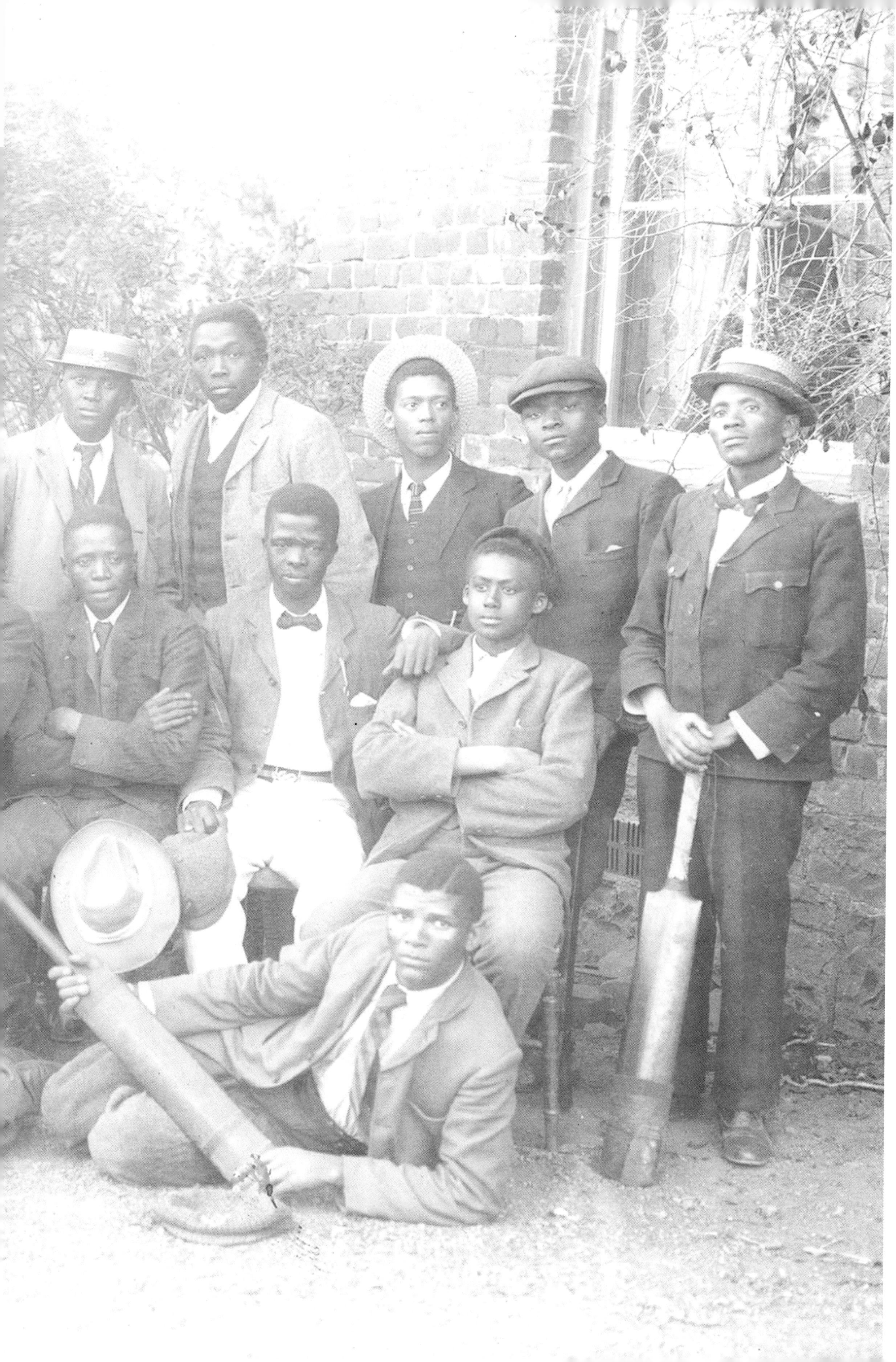

Part One

THE MAKING OF A UNIQUE CRICKET TRADITION (1850s–1900s)

The Indian prince, Kumar Shri Ranjitsinhji, came to personify the very style and grace of cricket
during its Victorian and Edwardian 'golden age'. Few know that in South Africa,
too, the sons of iinkosi (chiefs or 'lords') were among the pioneers of the game
in the mid-1800s.

Chapter 1

A GAME *for* PRINCES

———————————— ◗ ————————————

T HE PEOPLE BELIEVED THAT on a given day two suns would rise. As they arced over the Mountain of Calves, *Amathole*, they would collide. A day of darkness would follow. Then a new world, free of trouble and want, would arrive.[1]

This fantastic vision came to a young girl, refreshing herself at a river. It was announced and spread by her uncle, a 'seer' or religious man. The year was 1856. The place, Xhosaland.

The Xhosa people were demoralised. Recently defeated in battle, they were losing their land. The conquering British were slowly but surely subjugating them. To make matters worse, their cattle, the main measure of wealth and well-being in Xhosa society, were dying at the rate of 5 000 a month. A new disease, lung-sickness, a kind of pneumonia which caused an unpleasant choking death, was running rampant through herds. It had been brought from Europe in a cargo of Friesian bulls unloaded at Cape Town two years before.[2]

The Xhosa needed relief. And the prophecies of the girl, Nongqawuse, and her uncle, Mhalakaza, promised this. But, they were told, it would come at a price. First there had to be a kind of purification. All cattle had to be killed. Sowing and cultivation had to stop. Storage bins of corn were to be emptied and the contents scattered. All 'witchcraft' had to be abandoned.[3]

If the instructions of the forefathers were obeyed in this way, the rewards would be great:

The English then would all walk into the sea, which would divide and reveal a road along which they would march back to the place of creation, uhlanga, *where Satan would dispose of them and the [collaborating] Mfengu. A day of darkness would follow and then would come the new world. A grand resurrection of the ancestors would be accompanied by herds of new cattle emerging from below the earth ... New corn would stand in the fields to replace that which had been emptied from the corn bins. Along with the resurrection would come complete renewal for those who were alive. The lame, the sick, the blind would all be cured. The ageing or aged would have their youth restored. There would be no more care, no one would have to work. All their requirements, even household goods, would emerge from the ground new for their use.*[4]

There were many sceptics, but when Sarili, Paramount Chief of the Xhosa, decided in desperation to follow the instructions, hoping to reverse the tide of history, the people followed.

Quiet foreboding covered the land.

People waited in anticipation. The two suns did not arrive. Instead of a new life of milk and honey, there began to unfold, in the words of an eminent historian of this period, 'one of the greatest self-inflicted immolations of a people in all history'. He categorised it as 'the saddest and most overwhelming of all South Africa's many human tragedies'.[5]

Tens of thousands of people starved. Nearly two thirds of the population of 105 000 living west of the Kei River died or were displaced. To the east, an estimated 40 000 lost their lives.[6]

Contemporary observers noted the pitiful scenes. Bodies of the dead and dying dotted the countryside. Desperate to survive, people streamed to white farms and towns to beg for food and offer their labour. The independence of the Xhosa and the power of the chiefs were largely broken.

JOURNEYS OF A FATHER AND SON

This great tragedy of the mid-1800s gives us a graphic entry point into the history of cricket in South Africa, providing one of the most detailed early references of how the indigenous people came to play the game. The apocalypse also illustrates vividly how the advent of cricket in this country went together with major changes in how people lived and in the world as they had known it.

Through the individual examples of Chief Mhala of the Ndlambe branch of the Xhosa people and his 15-year-old son, we can see how the event did, indeed, bring the start of a new world, though far different from the one anticipated. Both had their lives radically disrupted. Both embarked on journeys that took them far away from the familiar comforts at the Great Place of the chief near modern-day East London.

Described as a 'great hater of the English', Chief Mhala had nevertheless tried to co-exist with the powerful foreigners for strategic reasons. Now, however, he was one of several chiefs brought before kangaroo courts and sent to the notorious Robben Island on trumped up charges. The process is uncannily reminiscent of the imprisonment of Nelson Mandela and his fellow freedom fighters almost one hundred years later. Mhala was court-martialled and found guilty on evidence which the Cape Attorney General at the time agreed 'would have failed to convince any who are strangers to South Africa' and 'could scarcely have been deemed conclusive'. The new colonial rulers wanted to make a political example of those opposing them. Governor Sir George Grey and the colonial officials decided to get Mhala and several other chiefs out of the way – even if this meant essentially twisting or disregarding justice. He was transported hundreds of miles away from his homeland, by boat, to be incarcerated on a cold island. The descriptions left by observers show something of the humiliation, terror and deprivation that accompanied the process.

When the soldiers brought him down to the beach, they put him under a crane, and told him they were going to hang him. They actually put a rope around him to frighten him, but an officer stopped them. When they got aboard ship ... Mhala suddenly gave three most dreadful yells ... the deposed chief was terrified at the appearance of the waves as they broke outside, and he fancied the sea was coming in upon him. This made him cry out for fear ... Mhala was very low-spirited, and sat on deck looking wistfully at the land that was once his own.[7]

One of Mhala's sons was also sent to Cape Town by Grey, but his was to be a different kind of journey.

Drawing on his experiences in New Zealand, Grey's plan was to 'civilise' the Xhosa and 'assimilate' them into the colonial economy and structures. After the cattle-killing, he could proceed forcefully with this 'dispersion and breaking down of the Xhosa social structure'. Amongst other things, he decided to set up a special 'Kafir College' in Cape Town to anglicise the sons of chiefs. He persuaded the chiefs of the western Xhosa and their councillors to allow their children to be given a British education there. Among those who agreed were Sandile, Maqoma, Mhala, Dundas, Xhoxho, Anta, Phato, Khama, Toyise and Tshatshu. Grey promised personally to look after the students and to return them home on completion of their studies.[8] Although the chiefs had previously resisted, they were now 'keen to come to terms'. They also saw the value of getting their sons skilled in the new ways, thus lessening their dependence on mediators such as missionaries. The children were in effect diplomatic hostages.

The first location for the new college was Bishop's Court in Cape Town (home, eventually, to Archbishop Tutu). Later the school moved to the former wine-farm, Zonnebloem, on the edges of District Six. The sites were chosen because they were 'within reach of the highest civilization in South Africa and yet separated from the contamination of the Town'.[9]

Grey boarded the HMS Hermes in East London en route to Cape Town in February 1858 accompanied by 35 'princes and princesses' from the main Xhosa clans and chiefdoms. There were only three girls, including Emma, daughter of Paramount Chief Sandile. Unknown to the Governor, all except one of the boys were 'lesser sons' because it was the duty of the eldest heirs to hand down the traditions of the tribe. Grey was also able to attract the sons of Sotho (Moshoeshoe) and Rolong (Moroka) chiefs.

The worst was expected of the 'little savages', as they were called by some. Their warden, the clergyman son-in-law of the Bishop of Cape Town, expected his new pupils to be 'a compound of the wild beast and of the spirit of evil, with passions uncontrolled, and full of that mixture of duplicity and cruelty which is generally considered the characteristic of those who for long years have sat in darkness'.[10] They created a sensation in Cape Town and were gawked at in church. Yet, to the surprise of their teachers, the new pupils soon 'turned out to be as intelligent as any similar group of English children and remarkably well behaved'. Their racist and chauvinistic superiors did not know that a tribal upbringing placed great emphasis on respectfulness to elders, a core value in Xhosa society, good manners and obedience. Soon there was a 'perfectly well-ordered school, containing many boys of exceeding promise'.[11]

*While the Xhosa chiefs were imprisoned on Robben Island in the 1860s,
some of their sons were being given a British education and learning to play
cricket across the bay in Cape Town.*

All the children had received a traditional upbringing. They might have been skilled in herding cattle and goats and proficient in stick fighting. Now, in foreign surroundings one thousand kilometres from home, these young Africans were to be turned into black Englishmen and women. They received a British schooling and instruction in Christianity, far removed from what their peers in Xhosaland were used to.

ETON IN AFRICA

Janet Hodgson, the historian of the college, has documented in visual, sensitive detail how the young people set out on their new lives, and how their 'African identities were soon submerged'. The first step in the acculturation process was to wear the correct dress:

They were fitted out in western clothing; the girls in flannel petticoats, dresses, aprons and shoes, and the boys in flannel shirts, duck or mole-skin trousers, caps and blucher boots. They were also introduced to all the paraphernalia of western living such as soap, scouring, blacking, wax candles and sheets, and their diet was comparable to any similar English boarding establishment.

Starch featured prominently on the menu and there was no attempt to provide familiar food such as sour milk or sorghum porridge. There was bread and tea for breakfast and supper, the main meal being taken mid-day. Meat was served six days a week, either roasted or stewed. Thursday was the meatless day with coffee being given as a treat to make up for the deficiency... The invariable vegetable was sweet rice, a mixture of rice, sugar and raisins to which cinnamon and borrie were sometimes added. Plum puddings on Sundays sounds a more appetising fare, except that it was a concoction of the usual ingredients: flour, suet, sugar and raisins.

The pupils were soon regimented into a strictly supervised routine, their day being ordered by the ringing of a bell. Their time was taken up by instruction and improvement and there was little room for play. The rising bell in winter was at half past six in the morning, in summer it was even earlier; but winter and summer through the boys began the day with a bath in the Liesbeeck River at the bottom of the Bishop's Court garden. [The girls] were spared this routine, being allowed to carry out their ablutions in the house.

The bell was rung at seven o'clock for morning prayers, followed by religious education until eight, when they had breakfast. They were then allowed an hour's run until school assembled at half-past nine. They had three hours of school in the morning and two in the afternoon with dinner and a short break in between. [The teacher] gave extra instruction to some of the pupils from four until six o'clock, after which they sat down to tea. There then followed an hour's Bible class. The retiring bell was rung shortly after eight o'clock and the candles were extinguished.

This was rather an early hour for the older ones as they were fond of learning their lessons in the evening, but [the teacher] did not dare leave them alone with the candles.

Their lessons were largely taken up with learning the three Rs and religious instruction. The boys were divided into three classes and the top group soon forged ahead. By the end of the first year they were tackling English grammar and composition and were able to do difficult sums in the first rules of arithmetic. They all had difficulty with English reading, however, and this continued to be their main weakness.[12]

[Soon] the curriculum was expanded to include Geography, English History and the elements of Euclid. Greek and Latin followed a few years later. [The system] being based on the time-honoured theory that Classics and Mathematics were the best instruments for training the mind.[13]

Religious instruction involved the teaching of the Lord's prayer, the principle parts of the Church catechism and Bible study ...

The children's education was not exclusively academic though ... they were required to spend half the day working at a trade. Besides the practical value of industrial training in teaching the pupils the 'discipline of honest industry', Grey hoped that their work might be the means of making the institution partly self-supporting. A start was made with carpentry, followed by tailoring and shoemaking ...[14]

Art classes and singing lessons were introduced as well: 'There had been no music in the bishop's chapel up to this time but Hymns Ancient and Modern now came into daily use at morning and evening prayers. The pupils showed a natural talent for art and music and blossomed under the new regime.'[15]

Every day, at Zonnebloem, as the sons of Maqoma, Mhala and Xhoxho went to school, they could see across the waters the island in the Bay where their fathers – who they were not allowed to visit – were imprisoned.

CRICKET OUR FAVOURED GAME

As at any British public school, provision had to be made for the healthy physical development of the children. For physical exercise, according to Hodgson, 'drilling' was introduced in the second year. Teachers reported that some of the older boys 'did not yield quite so cheerfully' to this discipline. 'The master felt that their aversion was due to their not understanding the object of the exercise, and that being tractable they would soon become reconciled to it...'[16]

Soon the sons of the chiefs were playing cricket as well. The college authorities introduced the game in 1861, and they reported 'a subsequent keenness for the game', which the college was happy to encourage.

By 1864, the year in which over arm bowling was finally legalised in England, Zonnebloem College had two teams. The first team played their first games away in Rondebosch in

The sons of chiefs, Zonnebloem College, Cape Town, 1863. Cricket became their 'favoured' game.

August 1864 and Wynberg in February 1865, probably against fellow church school Diocesan College (Bishops) and Wynberg Boys' High.[17] Both these schools became famous for sport. For example, Bishops has produced Herschelle Gibbs for the current South African team, and Wynberg, Jacques Kallis.

Closely linked to the British and colonial establishment, Bishops played a pioneering role in introducing rugby and cricket to South Africa. The headmaster from 1861 onwards was Canon Ogilvie, 'a stern disciplinarian', described by the Archbishop of Cape Town as 'a strong, manly Christian'. It was the Winchester-educated Ogilvie who introduced the 'carrying code of football' to South Africa.[18] His first project was to build buildings and then oversee 'the clearing of a new cricket field'.[19] Rugby was played on this field in June 1864, and it was probably also the venue when Zonnebloem played their first-ever away game two months later.

(Hodgson notes that a football was acquired for the Zonnebloem boys, too, but cricket remained the favourite.)

The little princes were, indeed, cricketing pioneers. According to Hodgson, quoting Hattersley, cricket was still in its infancy at the time, though becoming popular in the Cape thanks 'to its promotion as a fashionable form of recreation' by Sir George Grey's successor, Governor Wodehouse. Bats in use then were 'very unwieldy', 'fashioned out of a single piece of wood' and were 'of nearly uniform thickness throughout the length of the blade'. They cost 18 shillings. Balls went for eight shillings and sixpence. The college was happy to encourage the pupils to play. 'Whereas parsimony was the usual practice at Zonnebloem, expenditure on cricket equipment featured in the accounts as a regular and rather extravagant outlay', according to Hodgson.[20]

General view of the match

Shared histories. The native Parsis in Bombay depicted playing against English soldiers in 1878,
the same decade as the St Mark's mission side played against the Queenstown club.

When the college students went on a special ten-day out-ing to Stellenbosch in July 1865, the cricket kit went with them, even though it was mid-winter. Two of the pupils, Nathaniel Cohon and 13-year-old Walter Monde, docu-mented the experience in some of the earliest published writing in English by black South Africans. They travelled by train, which must have been very exciting as the Cape Town - Wellington route, the first railway line in Africa, had only been open for a little over a year and a half.

Cohon described this excitement:

We the Kaffir Students at Zonnebloem made ready on the Friday 30th June to go to Stellenbosch in a carriage pulled by a fire Horse, on Saturday the 1st July. At ten o'clock we went down to the Capetown station to go by a quarter to Eleven's train, Mr Daniel took down our things in his wagon to the station. I mean our mattresses and books, but we took our bats and stumps I mean (Wickets) by ourselves. We went in the Carriage the third-class one . . . A man rang the bell at a quarter to Eleven not a minute after that the other man the (Guard) Whistled. And the train moved slowly out of the station. . .[21]

Walter Monde continued with the story:

We arrived at Stellenbosch about one o'clock; and about half past one we had our dinner, and before dinner we saw some young men going to

play quoits, and we went to them and knew one out of them and we looked at them playing and thought they can play that kind of game pretty well, and then after we had seen them playing, we went into the house and had our dinner there in the hall, and after we had our din-ner, we went outside, and Stellenbosch people were very anxious to see us; a great many of them went out from their houses to look at us; and it seemed to us that they never saw People [meaning Africans] before, especially Malays and Hottentots, and we went on looking what kind of place it is, and I myself thought it was a pretty place full of trees along the sides of the Streets and water running along the sides of the Streets, and we went and saw the Dutch Church, and we admired it very much indeed, and I am sure it is the best Dutch Church that I ever saw in my life, and after going around the Town, we came back and saw the same young men that were playing quoits, but this time we saw them playing Cricket our favoured game and they kindly asked us if some of us would play, and we were very much obliged to them and some of us played with them, and when play was finished their Captain came and asked if we would like to have a match with them, we said yes we would try.[22]

The sons of chiefs at Zonnebloem trod where none of their compatriots had gone before. Lifted out of their familiar world for up to 12 years, they developed ideas and forms of consciousness which were new among their people. And, although their African identities would remain primary though more complex — they regarded Maqoma as being as heroic as Napoleon and the Duke of Wellington — these pupils did in many ways assume the identity of black Englishmen. The names they adopted emphasised the point: George and Jeremiah Moshesh, Samuel Moroka, Edward Dumisweni Maqoma, Edmund Sandile, Arthur Toyise and, spectacularly, Boy Henry Duke of Wellington Tshatshu. The game of cricket they so enthusiastically embraced was an essential part both of the high Anglican education they received and this new consciousness.

AN AFRICAN 'RANJI'

Chief Mhala's son, who was among the group of 35 who accompanied Governor Grey to Cape Town by boat in February 1858, was a prime example of how African identities were being reshaped at the time. He anglicised his name to Nathaniel Cyril Umhalla. He became literate, underwent a British education, adopted Christianity as his religion and visited Britain to study. He worked for the church as a teacher and then for the government as a civil servant. He also became an important public figure. In 1890 he helped to start the South African Native Congress, one of the first proto-nationalist political organisations in South Africa (formed 22 years before its successor, the modern-day ANC). Later in that decade he became first editor of one of the earliest independent black newspapers, *Izwi Labantu* or *Voice of the People*. Of relevance here is that Nathaniel Umhalla retained a lifelong passion for cricket.

Nathaniel Umhalla was about 15 years old when he went to Zonnebloem. His teachers described him as someone 'who had inherited considerable intellectual ability from his father'. He showed such 'exceptional talent' that he was permitted to attend a drawing class at the Cape Town School of Art. After eight years of schooling in Cape Town, he was sent in 1866 to St Augustine's Anglican Missionary College in Canterbury, England, to further his studies. Before going overseas, Nathaniel returned home for a holiday, and we are told that 'he resisted all his father's efforts to persuade him to become a heathen again, even refusing the tempting offer of being made a chief'. He spent two years in England, during which time his experiences included visits to St Paul's Cathedral and the House of Commons: 'He was said to have been much impressed with the debating skills of Gladstone and Disraeli, and to have become a firm believer in British democracy.' His 'piety, gentlemanly manners, diligence and

commendable progress with his studies' was commented upon in England.[23]

After his return to South Africa in December 1868, Umhalla became a 'catechist-teacher' and then assistant to Reverend Waters, the head of the St Mark's mission in the Cofimvaba district near Queenstown. The Anglicans reached deep into Xhosa society at St Mark's; the mission station had around 50 outposts and 30 schools, some up to 80 miles from its main location.[24] Umhalla clearly was an important figure here. An 'admirable' reader of English, he was headmaster and took the English and Xhosa services when Waters was absent.

Nathaniel Umhalla's love for cricket, learned at Zonnebloem, never abated. He no doubt played the game during his stay in Canterbury, and reports of his cricketing activities at home continued after his return. In November 1869 he participated in a Zonnebloem College reunion at St Mark's where 'several games of cricket' were played, as well as in an athletics meeting that included a 'ball throwing contest'.[25] Twelve ex-pupils attended, including Edmund Sandile. In November 1870, Umhalla played for the St Mark's side against the white Queenstown Club together with several other ex-Zonnebloem pupils, among them Arthur Toise, J. Benekazi and H. Xhoxho.[26]

The *Queenstown Free Press* reported that students at St Mark's and its outposts challenged Queenstown, the main town for a hundred miles. This created considerable excitement:

It was a novelty in these parts for our swarthy brethren to pit themselves against Englishmen in a game of skill — especially cricket in which Englishmen take credit for being the most proficient in the world, and it therefore did not surprise us to see such a throng of ladies, gentlemen, children and natives as were never on our cricket ground before, turn out on this occasion to witness the sport.[27]

Early in the morning of the match, the ground was 'decorated with bunting', tents were put up and 'refreshment booths were created'. The playing space was marked off with flags. The weather 'upon the whole was charming', and play started at 11.00 with Queenstown winning the toss and sending their 'swarthy opponents' in to bat. The *Free Press* reported that, 'Their play on the whole was creditable.' St Mark's managed 46, which in those days was sometimes enough to win by an innings. Nathaniel Umhalla, batting at number four, was joint top scorer with 12. Queenstown soon dominated. They knocked up 220 before being all out. The newspaper observed, 'Some of the bowling on the side of the natives was very good, and it was that swift round hand which we certainly think much fairer, and showing greater skill than the pitching of the ball practised by our men.' However, it continued that the bowling was 'irregular' and too many catches were dropped. Extras were second top score, and they included 11 wides and 38 byes. The best batsmen were Dowdle (60) and Fleischer (41). Former Zonnebloem student, J. Benekazi, took no fewer than six of the wickets.

With winning impossible, the Africans now 'made bold to play the unequal game; and well did they struggle'. When play ended the total was a respectable 112 for seven. Umhalla 16, Benikazi 17 and Nxitanama 18, helped by 25 extras, were responsible.

The Queenstown people were clearly impressed, particularly as the visitors, who lived a 'considerable distance apart', had not been able to prepare or play together for several months. Moreover, the spirit on both sides was good: 'There was no temper shown, no impatience, no complaints on the part of anyone; everyone behaved himself as a gentleman.'[28] A return match at St Mark's in January 1871 was agreed to.

Not everyone was impressed though. The *Free Press* noted: *Among the talk upon this unusual event we were surprised to hear some intelligent men, at least they call themselves such, shake their heads at it, and speak as though they thought the Europeans were bemeaning (sic) themselves in playing such a game. We cannot see it, and must attribute such feelings to the abominable prejudice which would raise impassable barriers between one race and another. Occasionally friendly games like that on Wednesday would, we are sure, promote kindly feelings between Kafirs and English, and from all we saw and heard of those native players we certainly think there was nothing derogatory in Englishmen playing with them.*[29]

Far from being inferior, the African players were in many respects more sophisticated than their white opponents, according to the *Free Press*. Not only did they have cultured bowling styles, and not only were they 'far removed from the raw Kafirs', they were also better educated and better travelled than the local cricketers: 'In fact, they are men, who as far as book learning goes, are far better educated than many

Nathaniel Cyril Umhalla. If someone must be given the epithet of an 'African Ranji', then this 'prince' of the Ndlambe branch of the Xhosa people is a strong contender. His cricket career stretched from the 1860s to the 1890s.

of their opponents. Several of them have been to England, and others have lived in Cape Town.'[30]

This is almost certainly the earliest detailed match report and scorecard that we have to show clearly how the love for the game and its Victorian protocols were taking root in the African soil among the ex-Zonnebloem students and other mission-educated people.

The headmaster at St Mark's was foremost amongst these cricket adherents. Umhalla was described as the most 'enlightened native' on the Anglican missions, but his white colleagues reported a 'defect which deterred him from being an earnest missionary to his brethren'. They thought that he might be better suited for a government position. He, perhaps, did not share the missionaries' repugnance for certain traditional customs.

After being charged with 'gross misconduct' soon afterwards, Umhalla moved to King Williams Town to become an interpreter in the magistrate's court there. This was described as 'an ill-paid post of great responsibilty'.[31] He became an important public figure and one of the pioneers of cricket in that town.

In 1883 Umhalla captained the Champion Cricket Club from King Williams Town in the first inter-town match against Ngqika Cricket Club from East London; it took place in mid-winter, on 24 May, Victoria Day, the public holiday to celebrate the birth of the Queen of England.[32] The following Christmas and New Year his team won the first inter-town competition for black clubs in the Cape Colony. On returning home, Champion CC challenged and beat the local Alberts Cricket Club, one of the earliest and best known white clubs in the colony.[33] In a return match against Alberts, who included four players who had just played in the Champion Bat Tournament – the premier competition in South Africa at the time – Umhalla top scored with 46 (run out) as Champions rattled up 142 for four in an hour and a half.[34] A newspaper report in 1889 described him as among the best players around and as someone worthy of consideration for a proposed 'Anglo-African' team to tour England.[35] In the mid-1890s, 30 years after first playing, he was still prominent as an administrator.[36]

The literature of cricket has documented the passion and flamboyance with which the Nawabs and Maharajahs in India took up the British game of cricket. Prince Kumar Shri Ranjitsinhji, the Jam Sahib of Nawanagar, owner of four castles, came to personify the very style and grace of cricket during its Victorian and Edwardian 'golden age'.[37] He is still remembered today as one of the game's greatest batsmen, and the abbreviation, 'Ranji', is enough to bring him instant recognition among fans of the sport with which he was associated. Neville Cardus, the Ranji of cricket writing, captured the magic that he evoked:

... when the Sussex men loomed in our view in Lancashire, we beheld them like unto a cavalcade out of the warm South; and if it was not headed by Kumar Shri Ranjitsinhji on an elephant panoplied with gold and diademed with rubies, then a boy's fancy must not be counted more closely related to truth than obvious facts and appearances. 'Ranji' cast his magic over all his team; we saw them in the glow of his Eastern splendour. And C.B. Fry was his Grand Vizier, the subtle adviser to the Prince, the Machiavellian logician who evolved a comprehensive statecraft of batsmanship from 'Ranji's' first and governing principle: 'Play back or drive'.[38]

The fact that young men of chiefly lineage in Africa also became enthusiastic adherents of cricket and supporters of the notion of benevolent Empire in the 19th century has never before received prominence. Nathaniel Umhalla may not have studied at Oxford, averaged 44.95 in test matches or lived a life of princely opulence, but if someone must be given the epithet of the 'African Ranji', then this 'prince' of the Ndlambe branch of the Xhosa people (a grandson of Ndlambe himself) is a strong contender.

Umhalla's dedication and love for cricket was to be emulated by thousands of students who followed him through the colonial mission-school system, and they came to love the game as much as any Englishman did. However, they were not simply cardboard imitations, as is so often wrongly assumed. This was powerfully demonstrated when

The Queenstown Free Press, 4 November 1870, with the historic match report and scorecard.

Umhalla himself became one of the first black citizens of the Cape Colony to be charged with treason after he refused to support the colonial war against the Ngqika Xhosa in the War of Ngcayecibi in 1877/78. The *Cape Times* newspaper commented, 'Deeper than his civilisation is his genuine Kafir nature.'[39]

In its own racist, twisted way, the newspaper was unwittingly pointing to an important truth about the whole class of 'school people' which was emerging from the mid-19th century onwards. While being receptive to new western ideas and customs, the 'school people' gave them a particular character and idiom, remaining close to their communities and deriving strength from their African identities and ideas. This applied in cricket as well.

TOP *Architecture of Empire. The students prepare for a day of festivities and sports on the Queen's birthday at Lovedale College in the late 1800s.* BOTTOM *St Peter's College in Adelaide, Australia, playing against the Aborigines from the Poonindie Mission in 1875.*

Chapter 2

MISSIONARIES *and the* GENTLEMEN CRICKETERS *of the* 1800s

A FTER THE CATTLE KILLING, the Xhosa lost their economic and political independence. The final phase of a 100-year process of systematic subjugation and incorporation into the expanding British-ruled Cape Colony unfolded. By the 1880s, after ten wars of dispossession, hundreds of thousands of Africans had become British subjects.

British rule had a disruptive effect on the conquered societies as a new system of administration was imposed upon them. The whole scale of politics in Xhosaland changed, and long-established social and economic practices were challenged. Thousands of people gave up old ways and went to look for work on colonial enterprises and farms. New towns set up by the British sprang up. Agents of imperialism such as missionaries, teachers, traders and farmers moved into the African territories, bringing the indigenous people into contact with alien ideas and institutions from Europe.[1]

Early resistance to missionary schooling subsided. Attendance rose from 2 827 pupils in 1856 to 15 568 pupils in about 700 schools in 1885.[2] More than one hundred mission stations, laid out like little English villages, dotted the landscape of what is today the Eastern Cape.

Lovedale College near Alice, established in 1841, became the most famous mission college. It was run by the Presbyterians, who also started the Tyume, Burnshill and Pirie missions in the Ciskei, as well as Emgwali amongst the Ngqika and Blythswood in 'Fingoland'. The Methodist church became the largest church among the Xhosa. It had a string of missions: Mount Coke near King Williams Town in Ndlambe territory; Durban, Newtondale and Healdtown among the Ciskeian Mfengu; Butterworth among the Gcaleka; Bensonvale in the Herschel district; Lesseyton near Queenstown; as well as Morley, Clarkebury and Buntingville near Umtata. St Luke's mission at Chief Mhala's kraal near East London, St Matthew's at Keiskamahoek amongst the Mfengu, St John's at Port St John's, St Mark's near Queenstown and the so-called Kafir Institution in the town of Grahamstown were Anglican institutions.[3]

At the Eastern Cape mission schools, as at Zonnebloem College, the emphasis was on encouraging people to forego customs which the missionaries regarded as uncivilised. Students were given a basic Western education and taught Christian doctrine in combination with British cultural values. They were also instructed in agriculture and trades and were encouraged to wear European clothes and build square houses. They were expected to denounce local customs such as initiation, polygamy and lobola, the transfer of cattle on marriage.

Cultural conversion, therefore, had to accompany the acceptance of the Christian religion, which threatened the whole fabric of Xhosa society. Traditional relations and authorities were undermined.[4] As one missionary put it:

The moment a Caffre becomes a convert, he comes into direct opposition to the institutions of his country. Circumstances occur almost every day in which he cannot obey his chief, or yield to the abominable customs in which very much of the chief's influence consists ... The pure gospel of the Son of God cannot prevail in Caffraria while Caffre institutions remain.[5]

SPORT AT THE MISSION SCHOOLS

The Oxford historian Headlam once wrote, 'First the hunter, the missionary and the mercenary, next the soldier and the politician, and then the cricketer – that is the history of British colonialism. And of these civilising influences the last may, perhaps, be said to do the least harm.' The fact was that these different strands of British influence could not be disentangled. They were all part of the same project of Empire.

Recreation became a matter of supreme importance at the mission schools because many of the amusements of tribal Africans were deemed 'incompatible with Christian purity of life' and had to be abandoned by those embracing the new religious ideas of the missionaries. Provision was, therefore, made for 'healthy exercise and the profitable employment of leisure'.[6] Drill became a regular feature on timetables and sports like cricket and football were introduced.

At a mission in Natal, an observer noted in 1857 that the skill of African boys in flinging assegais gave them an advantage over white boys at cricket: 'they rarely fail to strike down the wicket from a distance'.[7]

In September 1860 the Bishop of Grahamstown gave the earliest testimony of cricket at the St Mark's mission:

Before chapel there was a hearty game of cricket going on, with somewhat defective instuments, it is true, but with great earnestness and considerable skill. A bat and ball, kindly sent to the St Mark's boys by two young ladies in England, were much valued, and they had made a second bat themselves, but for wickets they used stones, as the ground was too hard for any wickets made by them. Sometimes the English word 'out' but more generally the Kafir 'ufile' ('He is dead') proclaimed the fall of an adversary.[8]

Early reports from Lovedale show very well the connection between religion, education, culture and sport at the time. In 1870 festivities were held to celebrate the founding of one of the earliest African Sunday School Unions. After a day and a half of church services and festivities the nearly 700 young people involved 'broke up into parties for various sports, among which the English game of cricket attracted many of the elder boys and young men'.[9]

On the Queen's birthday in 1877, all the pupils at Lovedale, in a typical way, had a day of sports in the fields.[10]

A missionary newspaper reported that there were five clubs around Lovedale in 1884. These were the 'European' club, the Oriental CC comprising students, the Brotherly United CC comprising those working at Lovedale, the 'location' club

called Gaika's Imperial CC, and the coloured club, True Blue CC. In February 1884, Brotherly United defeated the Lovedale white club's second team by an innings, scoring 133 against the 32 and 22 of their opponents. There were also teams in the adjacent rural villages of Ntselamanzi and Gqumahashe. The Lovedale clubs were said to be seeking matches against neighbouring towns.[11]

Lovedale and Healdtown became the main nurseries for African cricket over the years. Inter-college matches came to assume the same importance as they did at British public schools and the well-known local white boys' schools such as Queen's College, Dale College, Selborne College and St Andrew's College. In fact, Dale College, from King Williams Town, played against Lovedale in 1891 and was beaten by

*Cricket at Lovedale station, '1890s or earlier'. The first known
cricket action photograph of black cricketers in South Africa.*

15 runs.[12] The former, known for its sport, was for more
than a century a whites-only school. Today it has been identified as one of the centres of excellence where promising
young black players are given scholarships to pursue their
careers. In the context of South Africa's living memory and
its racialised history, the above result is hard to grasp, but it
is important in showing just how well developed the early
black cricket culture was.

Thousands of students went out from this heartland to
play and set up clubs. In Port Elizabeth, for example, ex-
Lovedalians challenged 'the rest' in 1884 and beat them
quite easily.[13]

The strong cricket tradition at Lovedale and the other
mission schools and colleges continued well into the 20th

century. An obituary for a Lovedale alumnus, Date Kwatsha,
published in the *Imvo Zabantsundu* newspaper in 1926
demonstrated this enduring Victorian approach to games
which African cricket players internalised at the new schools:

*He could not – from a cricket point of view – have arrived at a more
opportune period. Lovedale cricket then was at the height of its glory.
Those were the days of such giants as the Reverend Xaba, Mocher,
C. Mabona, D Haya, Niekerk, the Seti's etc. With patterns (sic) such
as these, his ever ready spirit was infected not only by their enthusiasm
but also by the high standard of cricket they played.*

*In 1912 he won his cap, and remained the mainstay of the Lovedale
XI until 1916 when he left school. During his college days, it is really
hard to say in which department of the game he excelled, as he combined
the wiles of a Barnes with the whirlwind tactics of a Jessop.*

St Matthew's and Healdtown players who had the misfortune to play against him in those — undoubtedly his best — days, have cause to remember Date to this day.

It would take up too much space to set on paper his many brilliant achievements in these inter-collegiate contests; but undoubtedly his two best performances were against the Saints: the first in 1915, at St Matthew's when he scored his only century; the second, towards the close of the second year, at Lovedale. In this latter match he not only scored 77 in his best style, but later in the day, sharing the attack with 'Mzalwana', speedily brought the Saints innings to an ignominious end for the meagre total of 29, as against Lovedale's 344 for five wickets. To this day I can still hear the lusty shouts of the students, 'Jija tole le Alert' [roughly: keep on stirring the milk, calf of Alert].[14]

Xhosa-speakers were also being introduced to cricket in informal ways outside of the educational institutions. For example, Africans were interested spectators at the cricket matches and horse races that were staged during the 1850s in the new towns springing up in the conquered African territories.

Reporting on one of the first 'postwar' cricket matches in King Williams Town in 1853, the *Grahamstown Journal* noted that most of the spectators were Africans.[15] A report of a race meeting in that town having been 'enlivened' on the fourth day by 'Kaffir races on horseback and on foot' also gives a good indication of the informal interaction starting to take place.[16]

In a similar vein, an early colonist gave details in his journal of a meeting in 1862 with a dishevelled farmer at an outpost, three days 'ride from the nearest town', who had been 'amusing himself by playing cricket with Kaffirs'.[17]

These stories show the impact that the incoming farmers, traders, government officials, missionaries and teachers had on the Xhosa people, and vice versa.

Cricket reports in Xhosa appeared regularly from the 1880s onwards.

CRICKET PART OF THE PROCESS

New forms of African consciousness and response emerged as a consequence of the subjugation of African societies and their incorporation into the Cape Colony. These were well illustrated by the missionary-educated 'school people' and an emerging new class of peasant farmers who started seeking involvement in the evolving colonial society and economy.

The peasant farmers learned new methods and started to produce goods for the market rather than for subsistence purposes. Those undergoing a western education became literate and began qualifying to become teachers, ministers, law agents, clerks, interpreters, blacksmiths, telegraph operators and printers.

These people developed into a distinct new elite class and self-consciously sought to develop the same skills and lifestyles as the middle class white colonists. They began to look for a place in the new economic and social order. They started demanding political rights for qualified black people in line with Christian and British liberal values which emphasised equality. They realised that the only way forward in this new common economy and society that was developing was for Africans to 'play the white man at his own game'.[18]

The political system in operation at the Cape at that time provided some outlet for these aspirations. The Cape constitution of 1853 made no colour distinction. A qualified, non-racial franchise was instituted, based on mid-Victorian liberal ideas. In order for British trade to flourish, the Victorians emphasised the importance of free wage labour, secure individual property rights based on a free market and a system of political representation.

Africans hoped that the Cape system would lead to progress and, eventually, their acceptance as full citizens.

They held it up as a model for the future, particularly as there was little pretence of social equality and virtually no political rights for blacks in any other territory, British or Afrikaner-ruled. Their aim was eventually to be assimilated fully into the evolving Cape Colony.

The whole constitutional approach of the new generation of political leaders was captured in a memorable poem by Isaac Wauchope from Port Elizabeth:

Your cattle [rights] are gone, my countrymen!

Go rescue them! Go rescue them!

Leave the breechloader alone

And turn to the pen.

Take paper and ink,

For that is your shield.

Your rights are going!

So pick up your pen.

Load it, load it with ink.

Sit on a chair.

Repair not to Hoho [the mountain stronghold used during war],

But fire with your pen.[19]

The 'school people' had developed into a distinct, well-established stratum of Cape society by the 1880s, thus paving the way for the process of political mobilisation that occurred in that decade. The first modern political organisations were formed. An independent African newspaper – called *Imvo Zabantsundu* or 'Native Opinion' – was started. Around ten thousand Africans registered as voters. In certain Eastern Cape constituencies, they were strong enough in numbers to return candidates of their choice to parliament. In others, they held the balance of power.[20]

This unique group of enfranchised blacks came to occupy a special position in Cape and South African politics. As the renowned author J.M. Coetzee has observed:

The cattle-killing may have marked the end of Xhosa military power, but it was by no means the end the Xhosa. With the hold of tradition broken, individual Xhosa were released to sink or swim in the colonial economy. Many sank, some swam ... From [the missionary institutions] for advanced education began to emerge a new Xhosa elite, 'Christian, articulate, model Victorian gentlemen in their conservatism, respectability and sobriety' ... Westernised by force as the Zulu never were, the Xhosa were to provide black South Africans with political leaders for the new age they were entering, including most of the founding fathers of the African National Congress ...[21]

The political developments were duplicated in other areas of life. Concurrent with the new politics, the newly educated leaders formed numerous social bodies as well in the 1880s,

including church, temperance, mutual aid, farmers, teachers, cultural and sports associations.[22]

Politics was only one of the whole range of day-to-day activities in the wider social sphere in which people were responding to new opportunities, and opening up the way for the future.

Sport was integral to this whole process of assimilation and mobilisation. It was one of the many aspects of British culture that the new elite enthusiastically adopted to promote their goals of ensuring the full participation of Africans in the new colonial society. Cricket, in particular, was taken very seriously, because it embodied a perfect system of ethics and morals for the Victorians. The main character in *Tom Brown's Schooldays* observed, 'But it's more than a game. It's an institution.'

'Yes,' said Arthur, 'the birthright of British boys, and young, as habeas corpus *and trial by jury are of British men.' 'The discipline and reliance on one another which it teaches is so valuable, I think,' went on the Master. 'It ought to be such an unselfish game. It merges the individual in the eleven; he doesn't play that he may win, but that his side may ... And then the Captain ... requiring skill and gentleness and firmness and I know not what other rare qualities.*[23]

CRICKET AS AN INSTRUMENT OF PROGRESS

Sport served an explicitly political function for the 'school people' from the beginning. It was seen as an integral part of the process of modernisation, and the early political leaders were almost invariably also leaders and members of the first sports clubs. Rank in this arena added to their status and showed their commitment to community development at a time when people were organising at every level, and were building a whole new framework of interrelated activity based on western models. Numerous examples will be given in the pages that follow.

The emergent black leadership was intent on using sport as an instrument of improvement and assimilation. By enthusiastically playing the most gentlemanly and Victorian of games, they intended to demonstrate their ability to adopt and assimilate European culture and behave like gentlemen – and by extension to show their fitness to be accepted as full citizens in Cape society. Through sport they could pay homage to the ideas of 'civilisation', 'progress', 'Christianity' and 'Empire' that were so precious to the Victorians and call for imperial concepts of 'fair play' to be respected. Through sport they could assert their own self-conscious class position.[24]

The Public Schools' ethos circa 1890. The Lovedale girls' school.

Dinner time at the boys' boarding school.

Campus: The main Educational Building at Lovedale.

The Lovedale cricket team, 1880s or 1890s.

Classroom.

*Conversion and change: a marriage of mission
people in a traditional setting.*

The making of black Victorians. Lovedale students at drill.

The epitome of Victorian gentlemen. The first English touring team to South Africa
under Major Warton, 1888/89. Imvo Zabantsundu *reported, 'It is singular*
that the sympathies of the Native spectators were with the English.'

Given the realities of life at the Cape it is not surprising that the new elite held these idealised values dear. Despite the obvious contradictions, they glorified things 'British' (the ideal) as against things 'colonial' (the reality). Thus, when the first English cricket side under Major Warton toured South Africa in 1888/89 the black sportsmen cheered them on against the local white sides in an obvious political commentary. In the report on the match against the King Williams Town-based Cape Mounted Rifles team, *Imvo Zabantsundu* noted, 'It is singular that the sympathies of the Native spectators were with the English.'[25] To rub salt into the wounds of the XXII of the CMR, they were thrashed by the visitors.

For the early players, the social activities connected with cricket were just as important as the actual games. Sports on public holidays such as Empire Day and Christmas were also almost inevitably followed by social functions. Here the aspiring black middle class could show off its elegance and education. The events differed little from those that catered for white bourgeois society. Often functions were held in the town hall, with the mayor or other dignitaries in attendance. A well-known historian, writing about Kimberley, has explained the ambience of such occasions. A splendid dinner was put before the guests. After this a programme of musical entertainment and speeches followed. It was begun with a toast to the Queen and ended with a rendering of God Save the Queen. Musical items included 'Oh, what can the matter be' and 'We shall meet again'. Finally the proceedings were brought to a close with speeches, hymns and a benediction.[26]

Sport and the related social activities were providing the new elite with a social training ground for participation in the changing society, and in typical Victorian fashion it provided both a personal and political lesson for them. In 1884 a paper extolling the benefits of sport was read before the pioneering Native Educational Association.[27] A member of the African Political Organisation (APO), speaking on the topic of a sound mind in a social body, emphasised just how closely sport and politics were linked:

Great lessons can be learned . . . on the cricket and football fields — two forms of sport of which our people are passionately fond. No one who is not punctual, patient, accurate and vigilant, can ever expect to become a consistently good batsman. Both batsman and spectators know that; and yet do we carry those moral lessons into our private or public life? Patient, of course we are: but are we punctual and vigilant: Often, a chairman of a Branch of the APO is half an hour late. Again, are we as watchful of our public welfare as the batsman is of every ball — even those which the umpire declares to be wide? If we were, much of our present trouble would have been forestalled.[28]

Through their education, as well as economic and religious activities, Africans were adapting to western ways and beginning to internalise many western values. A new kind of citizen was being produced here. And, as in the case of British public schoolboys and the white South Africans who followed their examples, sport became a defining passion for them.

Historians have noted in the comparative literature of Empire 'the extraordinary influence exercised by the public school ethos' in the colonies and the fact that it 'produced "gentlemen" on an almost industrial scale throughout the British Empire'.[29] V.S. Naipul, a winner of the Nobel Prize for literature, has observed that the celebrated cricket writer, C.L.R. James, taught by 'two generations of Oxford and Cambridge men' at Queens Royal College in Trinidad had in effect become a 'British intellectual' at age ten — this within living memory of his family having emerged from slavery.[30]

James himself remembered, 'Our masters, our curriculum, our code of morals, everything began from the basis that Britain was the source of all light and leading, and our business was to admire, wonder, imitate, learn.'[31]

Compare how close this is to what Nelson Mandela experienced a generation or two later at Healdtown in the Eastern Cape: 'The educated Englishman was our model; what we aspired to be were "black Englishmen", as we were sometimes derisively called. We were taught — and believed — that the best ideas were English ideas, the best government was English government and the best men were Englishmen.'[32]

There sprang from the 19th century South African roots described above a tradition of cricket as distinctive and durable as any of the other great international examples: the Parsis in India, the descendants of the diverse immigrants and the transported transgressors in Australia, the sons of indentured labourers and slaves in the Caribbean, who turned the tables to become masters of the game, and the conservative English-speaking white colonials in South Africa who tried to recreate 'Little England on the veld'. This tradition — more or less ignored or unknown until now — was denied full expression in the decades to come, but it was nevertheless to prove remarkably resilient.

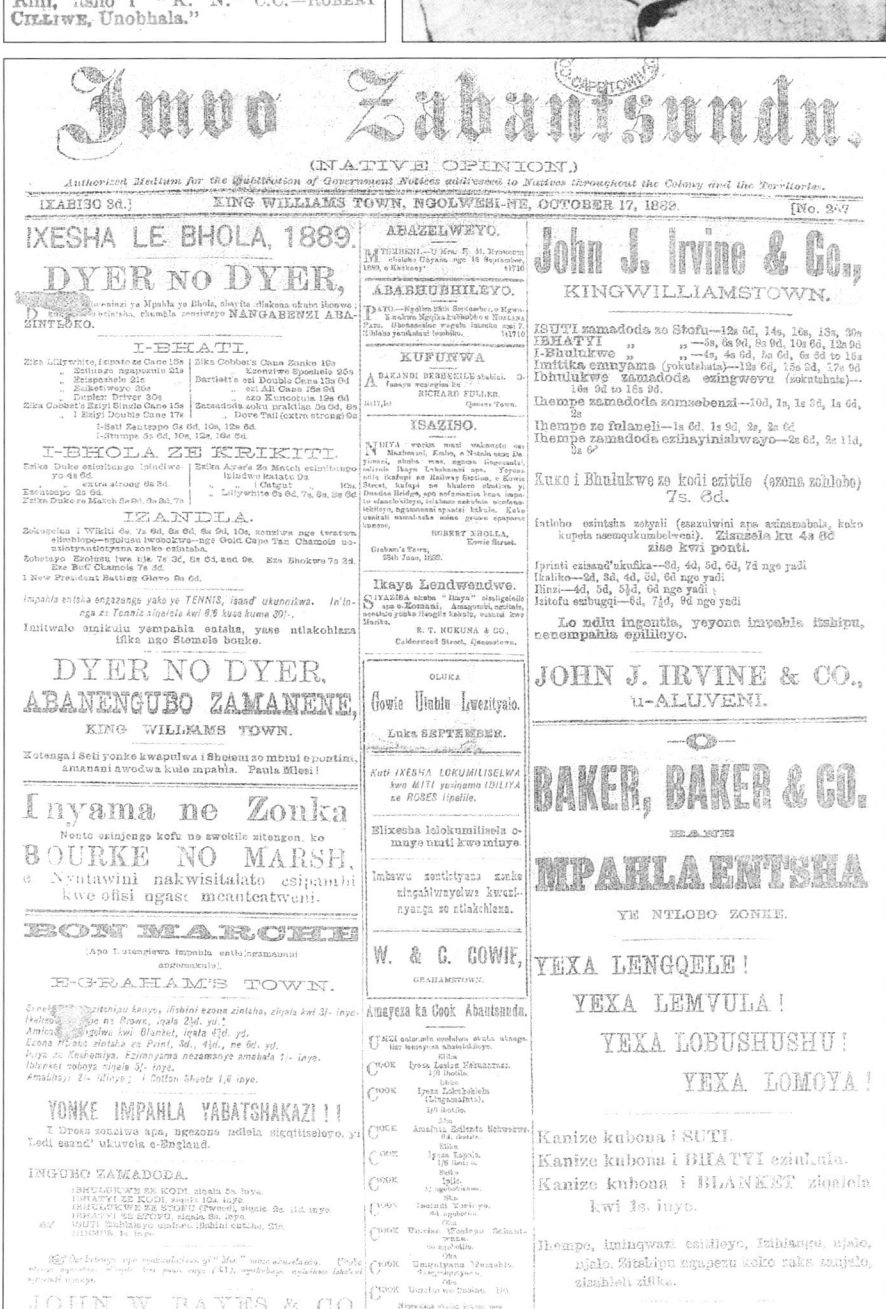

TOP LEFT *A letter to the 'sporting editor' in 1887.* TOP RIGHT *John Tengo Jabavu documented the development of cricket in his pioneering* Imvo Zabantsundu *newspaper, which was established in 1884.* BOTTOM *Adverts in Xhosa aimed at cricketers.*

Chapter 3

FIRST CLUBS *and* COMPETITIONS

———————————— ◉ ————————————

A S WE HAVE SEEN, cricket accompanied colonialism. The game came with British soldiers and settlers after the British permanently occupied the Cape in 1806, starting a century and a half of colonial rule in South Africa. The first recorded match in this country took place two years later in 1808, although the origins might even go back to the 1790s when the British were temporarily in control.[1]

However, organised sport as we know it did not emerge until much later. By the 1870s, only a few clubs existed in the bigger centres such as Cape Town, Pietermaritzburg and Port Elizabeth (including some formed by black sportsmen). No regional or national associations had been formed, nor were there any official leagues or competitions.

Then, from 1875 to 1885 a number of British sports became established in the various territories that we know as South Africa today. The first rugby, football, athletics, cycling, horse racing (jockey), golf and tennis clubs were formed, competitions were started, and sport started to become organised in the modern sense.[2]

The major cricket competition was the inter-town tournament for the Champion Bat started in 1876. This competition, like the early clubs, was for whites only. Black people were excluded and segregated in the traditional way. Despite this, black sports enthusiasts took to the British games such as cricket, rugby, athletics, boxing and tennis, almost as soon as they arrived on the shores of modern South Africa.

The development of black cricket closely followed that of white cricket in many respects; from its introduction into schools (1850s), to the formation of clubs (1869 onwards), to the introduction of inter-town competitions (1880s), leagues and provincial competitions (1890s) through to the formation of a national controlling body (1900s). Nowhere was this growth and enthusiasm more evident than in the Eastern Cape. A distinct tradition of sport developed in this region, and as clubs, competitions and regional and national associations for white players emerged to place sport on an organised footing in the 1870s and 1880s, the 'school people' in the Eastern Cape quickly and purposefully replicated the pattern.

FIRST CLUBS

The earliest known black cricket club was formed in Port Elizabeth in 1869. Reference to it is made in an article on one of the founders, Peter Rwexu, in *Imvo Zabantsundu*. He became a prominent Port Elizabeth community leader and spokesman.[3]

The next reference to a club is from Queenstown. Africans reportedly started playing there in 1871, together with the whites.[4] This seems entirely feasible given the historic match in 1870, mentioned earlier, between the white Queenstown Club and the St Mark's mission side consisting of Africans.

The attention then shifts back to Port Elizabeth, where another report mentions that Peter Rwexu, together with Messrs Ngcoza and Mqikela, formed the Fear Not Cricket Club in 1872. Rwexu, a wicketkeeper, apparently played for Fear Not for 22 years, through to 1894, by which time his and the other co-founders' sons were also playing for the club.[5]

Given the fact that Rwexu's name is mentioned in both Port Elizabeth reports, the possibility exists that they refer to the same event, and that the dates for the formation of Fear Not were confused. In any event, it is clear that the interest in cricket in Port Elizabeth at the time was growing because in 1876 another club, the predominantly coloured South End Cricket Club, was started, and reports indicated that it was an amalgamation of two already existing clubs.[6]

South End was a mixed area next to the harbour, which became a vibrant cosmopolitan community much like the famous District Six in Cape Town and Fordsburg in Johannesburg before it, too, was destroyed by bulldozers and the Group Areas Act at the height of apartheid in the 1960s. The South End Cricket Club survived for nearly one hundred years before amalgamating with other clubs under a new name in the mid-1970s.[7]

Port Elizabeth is already known in cricket history as the place where the first cricket club in South Africa (Port Elizabeth CC) was formed in 1859, where the first inter-town tournament for the Champion Bat took place in 1876, and where the first test match took place in 1889. Less well known is the equally important role it played in black sport. Besides the first cricket club mentioned above, Port Elizabeth was also the home of the first black rugby club, Union Rugby Football Club, formed in 1887, and was the venue for the first national cricket tournament, as we shall see below.[8]

Port Elizabeth, or *iBhayi* (literally 'The Bay'), provides a good case study to show how cricket became an integral part of black community life by the 1880s. The second oldest, largest and economically most flourishing town in the Eastern Cape, it had a relatively large and stable African population at an early stage. Already in 1878, people who had been born and resided all their lifetime in Port Elizabeth' were making representations to the government on behalf of the local community.[9]

The permanent and semi-permanent population had built good houses, and several churches and schools for themselves. They lived mainly in the town or three municipal locations set aside for Africans, namely Strangers, Coopers Kloof and Reservoir.

It was against this background that various new-style sport and community organisations and activities emerged in the 1870s. For example, in addition to the cricket clubs, the first black temperance body in South Africa was formed in the city in 1875 to oppose the use and distribution of liquor. It was called the Ark of Refuge Temple.[10] In 1877 local people established the Ethiopian Benefit Society for mutual aid and burial purposes. Peter Rwexu was chairman of the Benefit Society, and it was still flourishing in 1887 with more than £400 in the bank.[11] The growing local economic capacity was reflected by the fact that there were already seven black owned shops and a butcher in Port Elizabeth by the end of that decade.[12]

The secretary of both the templars and the Benefit Society was Reverend Isaac Wauchope, a prominent local figure for many years. It was he who coined the memorable 'shoot-with-the-pen' poem quoted in the previous chapter. Wauchope was one of the hundreds of black soldiers who died in World War One, when the troopship Mendi sank in the dark off the French coast. He is reputed to have gathered the troops on deck to sing hymns as the Mendi went down. Today there is a Mendi monument in their honour in New Brighton, on the corner of Ferguson Road and Avenue A.

During the 1880s, as Africans started mobilising politically on a regional level for the first time, Port Elizabeth once again took the lead. On 26 September 1882, local community leaders convened the first meeting of the *Imbumba Yama Nyama* in the city. The *Imbumba*, known as the South African Aborigines Association in English, was an explicitly political organisation. It aimed to unite Africans in political matters so that they could band together 'in fighting for national rights' in the same way the white Afrikaner Bond was doing.[13]

The *Imbumba* was the forerunner of various other proto-nationalist organisations, including the modern-day African National Congress, which was started in 1912. There were around one hundred members in Port Elizabeth, many of whom were also qualified voters.

The cricket clubs were an integral part of these community networks and activities. By the mid-1880s the number of African clubs in Port Elizabeth had grown to include the Fear Not CC, the Kreli Star Native CC (named after the Gcaleka chief Sarili, son of Hintsa), Imperial CC, Ethiopian CC and Fight Again CC.[14] They were followed by teams like Champion CC and Bakers CC.[15]

In Uitenhage, there was the Good Hope Native CC, founded in 1883.[16]

Following the white precedent, there were by now thriving African cricket clubs and regular competitions in almost all areas in the Eastern Cape.[17]

The first regular reports on black cricket are found in the missionary newspaper *Isigidimi sama Xhosa* (known in English as the *Kaffir Express*), which was published at Lovedale. In 1883 and 1884, *Isigidimi sama Xhosa*, edited at the time by a precocious young journalist, John Tengo Jabavu, placed various match reports in its columns. The first referred to the inauguration of contests between King Williams Town and East London on a home and away basis in 1883.

The first inter-town match between these rivals was held on 24 May 1883. Champions CC of King Williams Town took on Ngqika CC from East London. The King Williams Town team won, but when they went by train to East London for the return match in September the tables were turned.[18] From then on, matches between teams from these towns became regular features, played mainly on public holidays.

Reverend Walter Benson Rubusana, who was to achieve fame as a community leader, politician and translator of the bible into Xhosa, was one of the East London umpires in 1883. Special mention was made of how well he did the job. He was a founder member and president of the South African Native Congress and the only African ever to be elected to a legislative position in South Africa before democracy in 1994. During the 1913 general election, he was elected as a member of the Cape Provincial Council in the Tembuland constituency, when the large number of qualified black voters voted *en bloc* for him.[19]

Another notable participant in these historic cricket fixtures was the Zonnebloem-educated Nathaniel Umhalla, whose exploits were documented in Chapter I. He had only recently emerged from the traumatic experience of being charged with treason for refusing to support the colonial forces in the War of Ngcayecibi in 1877/78.

Ngqika CC was back in King Williams Town on Boxing Day and once again emerged as winners over the favoured local Champion CC. It was a hot day and there was a large crowd. According to the newspaper, *'langati lipume lonke iQonce'* – it was as if the whole of King Williams Town turned out. The ladies and old men brought along umbrellas to shade themselves and the visitors threw their hats into the air in celebration afterwards.[20]

The victorious East London were looking forward to playing Grahamstown in the same town on New Year's Day, meeting their opponents halfway on neutral ground, but due to a misunderstanding which led to some tension the King

Williams Town cricketers played their Grahamstown counterparts instead. East London was offered a game against a weaker local club and soon finished them off, 'so much so that we saw ourselves watching the King Williams Town and Grahamstown match without recognising that we had already played'. J. Malgas, captain of the visitors, wrote to the editor to express dissatisfaction about the attitude of the King cricketers.[21]

Various other inter-town contests were reported by *Isigidimi sama Xhosa*. Try Again CC from Grahamstown played the Fear Not CC from Port Elizabeth in Grahamstown in November 1883. Kreli Star from Port Elizabeth twice took on Good Hope CC from Uitenhage in April and May 1884. The venue in Grahamstown was the main (white) municipal oval, 'City Lords', rented for the day for a pound and a penny, matting included.[22]

Matches between clubs from the same vicinity were also reported, including Gaika CC versus Newlands CC in East London, Fight Again CC (Ntselamanzi) versus Never Give Up CC (Gqumahashe) in the Alice district, and Good Hope Native CC versus Ever Ready CC in Uitenhage.[23]

From the educational centres, *Isigidimi sama Xhosa* reported that Oriental CC (the workers) beat Occidental CC (the students) at the 'Kaffir Institution' in Grahamstown, and that the Fort Beaufort Club lost to the local Healdtown College. The low scores in this match – 34 and 36, and 55 and 38 respectively – were typical for the time.[24]

The *Isigidimi sama Xhosa* also attempted to foster the game by placing news of a century by 'Dr Grace' against Australia and giving advice on how cricketers could best protect their bats in hot climates, where they broke easily. The suggested remedy: *'uyifake kunye namafuta embizeni, uyibilise ke yonke lonto kunye'* ('You put it together with fat [oil] into a pot and bring everything to a boil together').[25] *Isigidimi sama Xhosa* noted that the educated and christianised 'school people', *'tina mpi imnyama igqobokileyo'*, had left behind the old tribal ways, but had not yet adopted the new, namely the cricket, lawn tennis, croquet, hunting and dancing of the English. It encouraged them to do so.[26]

The brilliant 24-year-old editor of *Isigidimi sama Xhosa*, John Tengo Jabavu, had taken on the job with the aim of 'educating the people to their rights under the Queen's sway', but he soon found himself frustrated by the paternalistic control of the missionaries at Lovedale. So he set up his own newspaper with the help of his black and white political allies. The first issue of *Imvo Zabantsundu* (*Native Opinion*) appeared on Monday 3 November 1884. Its appearance was a landmark occasion in the political history of South Africa, heralding the birth of an independent black press, a major step forward in the struggle for racial equality within the still-new colonial system. Jabavu and his weekly King Williams Town-based newspaper made an immediate impact as a vehicle for promoting the goals and publicising the activities of the new African elite. Within a short time, he could state without fear of contradiction that as the standard bearer of 'Native Opinion' his newspaper was now a power in the land.[27]

Imvo Zabantsundu soon revealed just how popular cricket was amongst Eastern Cape Africans. In the very first edition, Jabavu devoted his editorial notes to the game:

> To our Colonial English contemporaries, the playing of the game of cricket by natives would seem to be regarded as a strange phenomenum (sic); and already all sorts of guesses are indulged in as to the probable motives of the sons of Ham in taking to this English time-honoured pastime. 'Mimicry', 'travesty of civilization' and expletives of a like character have been hinted as the possible causes, but our countrymen have gone on the even tenor of their way without noticing their critics … the natives do not only mean to persevere in playing at cricket, but are resolved to proceed from conquering to conquest so far as the cricket world is concerned.[28]

Imvo Zabantsundu is still in existence today, though in a different guise. It is a goldmine of information on the history of African sport, perhaps the most important single existing archive. Week after week, month after month, decade after decade, for nearly 120 years now, its correspondents (including cricket administrators and volunteers from numerous areas) have detailed the unfolding evolution of the game in the African communities. While other newspapers also hold valuable information, it is unlikely that there is any other source on black cricket history as valuable as this.

Jabavu, the most influential black spokesman of his age in the Cape Colony, remained editor for nearly 40 years. Besides his many other achievements, he was a pillar of middle class social respectability in his community, becoming a Wesleyan church steward, templar and chairman of two of the sports clubs formed in King Williams Town, namely the Frontier Cricket Club and the Oriental Lawn Tennis Club.[29] Like most of his contemporaries, he developed a lasting passion for the game. During his editorship hundreds upon hundreds of cricket reports appeared in *Imvo Zabantsundu*, even during the winter. These were printed under the title 'Ibala labadlali' (sports field or 'patch of the players'). By 1887 he had appointed a 'sporting editor'.[30] The big Dyer and Dyer merchant house soon began placing advertisements directed specifically at African cricketers and clubs in his newspaper. In addition to tweed jackets and 'impahla yabafundisi — iminqwazi ne kolala, i makentoshi, njalo njalo' (clothes of priests — hats and collars, mackintoshes, etcetera, etcetera), cricket kit of every variety, as well as tennis racquets and nets were offered. There were special discounts for clubs, who were encouraged to send for price lists before making purchases.[31]

FIRST INTER-TOWN TOURNAMENT, 1884

The *Port Elizabeth Telegraph* was certainly not exaggerating when it observed in 1885 that 'cricket seems quite to hit the Kaffir fancy'.[32] By the mid-1880s, cricket was so well organised in the Eastern Cape that the first inter-town tournament for black clubs was held in Grahamstown in late December 1884.

In the letters column of that first issue of *Imvo Zabantsundu*, 'Umtandi-we-Cricket' (A lover of cricket) from Port Elizabeth suggested that 'the leading native clubs in the colony' such as those at Grahamstown, East London, Port Elizabeth, Queenstown, St Matthew's, Keiskamma Hoek and Lovedale should arrange a tournament in King Williams Town in the 'New Year's vacation'.[33] Jabavu enthusiastically supported this idea and said thought should also be given to a 'native eleven, consisting of those who distinguished themselves in the proposed tournament being equipped for a cricket campaign to England'.[34]

Grahamstown was chosen as the venue and East London (Ngqika CC), King Williams Town (Champion CC), Grahamstown (Fear Not CC) and Port Elizabeth (Ethiopian CC) sent sides.[35] The appropriately named Champion CC from King Williams Town, captained by Nathaniel Umhalla, emerged as winners after beating Ngqika by an innings, Fear Not by three wickets and Ethiopian CC by seven wickets. It was the first contest between teams from the two towns and the former were thrilled to beat the Port Elizabeth cricketers with their big reputations. Fast bowler Austin Ngcumbe was the star of the winning team, taking ten wickets twice and nine in the remaining game. The scores were very low, and the available scorecards show that in nine completed innings, the totals were under 50 in five cases and just over 50 in the other four.[36] The *Cape Mercury* commented that 'the play of the four teams is much alike', with their fielding 'much superior' to their batting.[37]

As we will see below, low scores were a feature of 19th-century cricket. Clearly it was a different game to what we know today. High scores were the exception rather than the

The 'City Lords' ground, Grahamstown, where the first African Inter-Town Tournament was held in 1884.

rule. In 1889, when a Cape Mounted Rifles XXII played the first English touring team in King Williams Town, only one of the local batsmen managed to reach double figures, thanks to the phenomenal figures of 15 wickets for four runs by Major Warton's main strike bowler, Johnny Briggs. Overall the Lancashire player took an unbelievable 294 wickets at fewer than six runs apiece on the tour, figures which 'have never been equalled and are never likely to be'.[38]

The organisation of the African inter-town tournament was a remarkable achievement if one considers the fact that white cricketers were holding only their third inter-town tournament in nearby Port Elizabeth in the same month,[39] and that white rugby players only organised their first inter-town tournament – also in Grahamstown – in the following year.[40]

Travelling away in those days obviously had its hazards. The winners had their horse impounded and damages of five pounds, ten shillings and a sixpence were demanded for its return. A local white attorney intervened on the team's behalf. Mr Wright, 'as if emulating [the generous hospitality of] the dark citizens, added to our score of good luck by exerting himself successfully without charge for the recourse of our stallion'.[41]

The first inter-town tournament marked the arrival of African cricket. The African players had now shown the aspiration and ability to organise competitions based on

similar inter-town tournaments for the Champion Bat, and for decades to come inter-town tournaments of different kinds would become commonplace.

Not only was there the excitement of organising the big inaugural event, but also a flurry of further activity in its immediate aftermath. Several challenge matches were played against white clubs in King Williams Town, Cradock and Port Elizabeth during the remainder of the season.

NOT MERE 'SCHEPSELS'

The 1884 black inter-town winners, Champion CC of King Williams Town, challenged Alberts, 'the leading European Club in this town', on returning home. At least four of the Alberts players – Schermbrucker, Leary, Byrne and Tully – had just participated in the white inter-town tournament in Port Elizabeth.

The result was 'a clear [first innings] victory for the players of colour'. They bundled out the white team for 55 runs and passed this total with only three wickets down, before being all out for 89. The bowling of Reverend Gawler, a teacher at St Matthew's, and Austin Ngcumbe was outstanding. The *Cape Mercury* commented that they sent down several maidens before Alberts got their first run and, 'the bowling of the two seemed to surprise the Alberts' batters, and it took them all their time to guard their wickets'.[42] The dismissal of the local star, Schermbrucker, for three and one triggered great excitement among the African players. Alberts scored 104 in their second innings and by the time Champion went in again it was already 17.45. When the second wicket fell it was dark and 'impossible for the batsmen to see properly', according to the *Cape Mercury*. Nevertheless, the game continued until stumps were drawn at 51 for seven.

Ngcumbe's final figures were four for 28 off 53 balls and seven for 47 off 100 balls. He was well backed up by Gawler who took six wickets altogether.

Commenting on other aspects of the game, the *Cape Mercury* said that 'the fielding of the Natives was sound, and their throwing was excellent, but their batting in most cases wanted defensive power'. Tshatshu (21) and Gawler (17) were the highest-scoring batsmen, and *Imvo Zabantsundu* commented tongue-in-cheek that they did better against 'the balls of those eminent local cricketers Schermbrucker and Leary' than vice versa.[43]

The Africans, moreover, were said to have gained the victory 'in the face of disadvantage': 'It was against the rules of cricket to allow players from clubs other than Alberts to bowl, nor was it fair to the Natives to change one of the Umpires without consulting the Champions.'[44]

The *Cape Mercury* said the match was significant 'to all those who take an intelligent interest in the progress of the country'. Evoking images of peace less than a decade after the last of the ten wars of dispossession, the newspaper said the game recalled an 'old song':

And men learn't wisdom from the past,
In friendship joined their hands;
Hung the sword in the hall;
The spear on the wall,
And ploughed the willing lands.[45]

The newspaper went on to comment that 'those who play together will not object to work together, and the manly fellows who donned the flannels last week will have a heartier feeling of respect for their dusky conquerors than they had before ...'[46]

Jabavu republished the above extract from the *Cape Mercury* with approval, though omitting this significant rider: 'But we should be sorry for their victory, if it were the means of puffing them up with conceit, by which we do not mean that they ought not to be filled with some honest pride that the first cricket match of any note that has taken place between the two races should result in an unmistakeable win for the Africans.'[47]

The delighted *Imvo Zabantsundu* editor added that such cricket matches were 'calculated to make the Europeans and Natives have more mutual trust and confidence than all the coercive and repressive legislation in the world'.[48]

In the return match, Alberts had the better of the game, winning comfortably on the first innings. Alberts knocked up 210 thanks to an undefeated century from Schermbrucker. No other batsman reached twenty. They then bundled Champion out for 48. In the follow-on innings the African batsmen showed what they were made of, hitting 146 for four in the hour and a half before stumps. Regular captain, Nathaniel Umhalla, top scored with 46, before being run out.[49]

The Port Elizabeth Africans followed this example by beating the white Cradock town club early in 1885. The African team also won the return match, scoring 71 and 69 against the single innings 45 of the country town. *Imvo Zabantsundu* exclaimed 'Bravo, Africans, Bravissimo' in its columns.[50]

Commenting on the win, despite a lack of experience and facilities, Jabavu declared:

It is enough to say that the contest shows that the native is a rough diamond that needs to be polished to exhibit the same qualities that are to be found in the civilised being, and that he is not to be dismissed as a mere 'schepsel', as it has been the habit of the pioneers to do so hereto.[51]

A few weeks later the Port Elizabeth Africans challenged the local Port Elizabeth CC to a match. The so-called 'native team' was a combined side, and its composition reflected the middle class aspirations of the players and their prominence in local community affairs. It consisted of Frank Makwena (captain), H. Pezisa, George Ross, Moses Foley, J. Morley, J. Mdana, T. Klaas, B. Christian, B. Swartbooy, A. Mabope and Paul Xiniwe. The local newspaper listed their employment details 'to show that those who engage in the ennobling time-honoured game of cricket have either worked or are working their way up the social ladder by hard, honest labour'. Except for Xiniwe of the Ethiopian CC, who was a teacher, the rest all worked for white firms in the city.[52]

After graduating from Lovedale, and starting to teach in Port Elizabeth, Paul Xiniwe became an important community leader. In 1884 he read a paper at the Native Educational Society in which he stressed that the time had come for Africans to sit in parliament. He was a member of the *Imbumba Yama Nyama* and went on to become a leader of the South African Native Congress. In 1894 he opened the Temperance Hotel in King Williams Town. This double storey building in the main Market Square cost £2 000. It was the first hotel for Africans in the Eastern Cape. Paul Xiniwe remained intimately involved with sport until his

King Wms Town
20/12/92

W. Anderson Esq.
Town Clerk
Sir
        I am directed
by our tournament committee
to apply for the use of the Town
Hall on the evening of the 27th inst
for a concert by the "Native Harmonic
Society" in aid of the tournament
fund.
        I am Sir
        Yours obediently
        Paul Xiniwe

Paul Xiniwe: prominent 19th-century political activist, entrepreneur and cricketer.

early death. In 1901, he was sporting editor of the *Izwi Labantu* newspaper, which was established in East London in opposition to Jabavu's *Imvo Zabantsundu* in 1898.[53]

Several of the other players were prominent in local affairs as well. The captain, Frank Makwena (or Mokuena in Sotho), a member of Fear Not CC, was vice-president of the pioneering *Imbumba Yama Nyama*. J. Morley of the Ethiopian CC was also a member of *Imbumba*. Makwena later started the Basuto Pioneering Trading Company.[54] As already noted, the veteran Peter Rwexu of the Fear Not CC, was chairman of the Ethiopian Benefit Society. George Ross and Moses Foley were well-known local spokesmen who started the African and American Working Mens Union (AAWMU) in 1891, together with two African Americans living in Port Elizabeth. The AAWMU intended to start black-run businesses and create jobs for people; it soon had over £3 000 in the bank from subscriptions. Ross was also the president of the Native Dramatic Opera Company in 1891, and he and Foley were members of the Port Elizabeth Debating Society.[55] Clearly the sportspeople were part of the local elite, tied together by a whole network of different activities.[56]

Women were part of these new social networks as well. At the helm of the Port Elizabeth Ladies' Croquet Club, formed in 1884, were Mrs Wauchope (secretary), Mrs Malgas (treasurer and umpire) and Mrs Rwexu (umpire). The elaborate constitution of this club was printed in the missionary newspaper.[57] The local women also became active tennis players. As we shall see below, it became common for sports clubs in Port Elizabeth in the 20th century to have so-called 'ladies sections' — the first known black women's cricket clubs were formed in Kimberley in 1909, when coloured women there 'set the pace in a highly commendable way' by forming The Daisies, The Ivies and Perseverance Clubs, and grouping themselves into a union under prominent local sports administrator, Mr J.S. Lackey.[58]

After beating Cradock's whites, Port Elizabeth's educated black middle class must have been buoyant going into the

IZIMISELO ZE KROKI.

Ndikutumela (utsho um'baleli wetu ose Bayi) imiteto ye kroki (croquet) ..ayilwa entlang....weni yamanenekazi eyayi sendiwini ka Mr. Wauchope nge 22 April 1884. Amanenekazi awayeko yayi ngu Mrs. Rwexu, Mrs. Malgas, Mrs. Wauchope, Mrs. Lwana, Miss Sakuba no Miss Nginda. Kwavunyelwana ngayo lemiteto ukuba ilungile. I Komiti inga ingabonakala e *Sigidimini* :—

I COMMITTEE.

1. Kuya kumiswa i Committee yokupata imicimbi ye Kroki, enje ngokwamkela amalungu, nokwenza amatuba okuhlanganisa imali yokuyixasa.

Amalungu e Komiti oba ngu :—

   1. *Mrs. Malgas*   Treasurer and Umpire,
   2. *Mrs. Rwexu*   Umpire,
   3. *Mrs. Wauchope* Secretary,
   4. *Mrs. Lwana*
   5. *Mrs. H. Lwana*
   6. *Miss Xali*   Collector,
   7. *Miss Wauchope* Collector,

2. Imali ehlanganiswa zi Collectors zoyinikela kwi Treasurer entlanganisweni ye Committee.

3. I Collectors zowabala encwadini zazo onke amalungu abateleyo, ziyahlule eyomnikelo we nyanga kweyo kungena.

3. I Treasurer yobala igama layo encwadini ye Collectors malunga nemali eyamkeleyo kuzo.

5. Umsebenzi we Secretary kukubala imicimbi yentlanga....e Committee, nokuhlanganisa amalungu e Committee, nokukangela incwadi ze Collecters abone abangeka batali.

6. I Umpires ziya kugcina ukuba kudlalwe ngokwe miteto. Zilungise amapike, zikangele kudlale amalungu odwa, nokuba kungadlal mntu ongeka yihlauli i Entrance fee (Imali yokungena.)

7. I Committee ingongezelela eunsini 1: .. unyula kwapakat' kwamalungu.

8. Imali yokungena iyakuba yi 2s elungwini—ihlaulwe ekuqaleni.

9. Imali yomnikelo wenyanga uyakuba yi tiki (3d) elungwini ihlaulwe ekuqaleni.

10. Ofuna ukupuma e *Krokini* akayi kuyibuyiselwa imali angaba ebeyihlaule.

11. I Committee ayibotshiwe ukwamkela wonke ubani ofuna ukuba lilungu.—Abantu abaya kwamkelwa ngabafanelekileyo (decent).

12. Inteto yabadlali iyakuba yete civil yembeko. Umntu oteta kakubi nabanye emdlalweni watetiswa zi *Umpires*, ukuba akavumi ukuva wobika e Komitini, iti ukuba iyabona imkupe.

13. Ikomiti inamandla okutenga impahla efunekayo ye Kroki.

14. I Treasurer yonika ingxelo entlanganisweni ze Committee ngemali eyamkeleyo, ngencito, nangemali eseleyo.

Constitution of women's croquet club, Port Elizabeth, 1884.

match against Port Elizabeth CC. However, they were annihilated, replying to the Port Elizabeth CC's 180 with a measly 13 and 11 for three. Godlonton and Ogden were the bowlers who wreaked the havoc. Christian (four wickets) and Pezisa (three) were the most successful African bowlers.[59] *Imvo Zabantsundu* lamented:

'Dirty' indeed was the licking received by a team of the Port Elizabeth Natives from the local European Club. We trust the return match will soon come off and leave the fair fame of Native cricketers vindicated. The explanation given by the defeated team is that they had challenged the second eleven of the Port Elizabeth Club, but to their utter surprise they found themselves in the field pitted against the eminent cricketers who beat the Colonial Clubs at the late Tournament in Port Elizabeth. On the sight of these illustrious knights of the willow they lost heart.[60]

The newspaper added that 'the thrashing administered to the local Alberts Club by the Natives the other day' apparently had a lot to do with the turnout of the top players.[61] Port Elizabeth CC was the oldest club in South Africa and reigning holders of the Champion Bat, the main competition in South Africa at that stage.

It is remarkable, looking back, that two of the top white clubs in the Cape Colony at the time played two of the top black counterparts, and that, notwithstanding the Port Elizabeth result, the standards between black and white cricketers were so even.

Newspaper reports from the mid-1880s show that African teams regularly played — and beat — white teams. The Champion fixture against Alberts became a regular one, and they also played against the Cape Infantry and the well-known local sporting school Dale College,[62] described as an invaluable nursery of cricket in W.M. Luckin's earliest history of the game in South Africa.[63] Champion beat Dale in 1887 and Lovedale College repeated the medicine in 1891. Teams from Alice, Queenstown and St Mark's also reported successes around this time.[64]

These matches were in line with paternalistic colonial practices, which allowed the odd encounter to take place across the colour line on special occasions, such as Christmas, New Year or Empire Day. It seems that the local black cricketers were also allowed to use the grounds of

Ladies at Cricket: Stuttaford's Staff v. Garlick's.

~ Garlick's ~   batting

Women were keen cricket followers from the start.
TOP *An early match between two elite department stores in Cape Town.*
CENTRE *Lovedale 'ladies' were schooled in the etiquette of sport, early 1890s.*
BOTTOM *A women's cricket team in Pietersburg, 1894.*

white clubs from time to time, most notably the Victoria Ground in King Williams Town and the Union CC Ground in St George's Park, which are mentioned in various reports.

Regular matches were played against coloured teams as well. In Port Elizabeth, for example, on Christmas Day in 1883, Fear Not took on a local Muslim or 'Malay' team, Star of the East. The latter won. The report noted that this was because the opponents came with 'nabafundisi bawo' (with their 'ministers' or imams). However, in the return game Fear Not won by the big margin of seven wickets. This time they had their lucky charm 'Mpinda' with them. Bill Swartbooi starred 'and his crippled father even cried because of his superb performance'.[65] In 1889, the Ethiopian CC played against both West End CC and South End United.[66]

According to the *South African Cricket Almanack*, published in 1969, African and coloured cricketers at one stage formed a Euro-African cricket association in Port Elizabeth.[67] But this relationship was never uncomplicated. In one instance, in the early 1890s, tensions were reported between African and coloured sportsmen because the latter considered themselves too 'high' to play with Africans. This contributed to the exclusion of coloured people from the pioneering African and American Working Men's Union, an organisation set up to uplift Africans economically and help them start businesses.[68] As so often happens, sport was reflecting wider patterns within the local communities. For most of the 100 years until unity in 1991, people actually played separately, showing that even among the oppressed the hierarchies and prejudices of a racially ordered society were present.

JABAVU CUP AND THE EXPANSION OF THE GAME IN THE EASTERN CAPE

A correspondent in *Imvo Zabantsundu* noted in 1888, 'It is admitted by all that King and Port Elizabeth have the most powerful Native elevens in the Eastern Province and up to the present day no fair conclusions have been tried between these two rivals.'[69] It is telling that these two towns also provided the dominant teams in the corresponding white tournament.[70]

After losing to King Williams Town at the 1884/85 tournament, the Port Elizabeth Africans turned the tables on their opponents in the 1886/87 encounter.[71] In 1887 they travelled to King for a game, but it is not clear what the result was. At the 1890/91 tournament, Port Elizabeth won again in a match 'to find the best side', after both had beaten Grahamstown and Kimberley. There was a large crowd of 'ladies and gentlemen' present.[72]

The idea of sending a combined side chosen from the best players at the inter-town tournament on a tour of England, first mooted by Jabavu in 1884, was discussed in earnest again at the time that the first British touring team under Major Warton toured South Africa in the 1888/89 season. A 'number of gentlemen from England' were apparently enquiring about the prospect. They wished to ascertain whether there was the enthusiasm and ability to make viable a 'tour through Great Britain' during the following English season starting in April. The conditions were demanding:

1st. Good character, total abstainers and generally intelligent;

2nd. Smart and athletic, good figure, with no deformity;

3rd. Must be willing to practise incessantly the next six months;

4th. All candidates required to prove their proficiency before being chosen, and to pass a committee of experts.[73]

These ideas fitted in with the 'exhibitions' of human traffic from the colonies in Britain in the 19th century. The Victorians, suffused with notions of Social Darwinism and the 'exotic other', specialised in the hierarchical classification and display of people from the colonies. Sarah Baartman, the Khoi women displayed naked as a freak 'African Venus' at circuses and other venues in Europe, was one example of this.[74] Here, it seems, were entrepreneurs seeking to cash in on this market, although not necessarily in such a crude fashion. But the African cricket players in turn were not passive objects, and they immediately showed an interest in using such opportunities to their advantage. *Imvo Zabantsundu* observed, 'There can be no question that the project will commend itself to the Native athletes, just as it has completely fascinated us. We trust that the various Kafir clubs will lose no time in arranging for an undertaking that is fraught with momentous issues for the native races of this country.'[75]

The view of *Imvo Zabantsundu* was that 'a tour to England would also afford our friends there the opportunity of realising the tone that European civilisation gives to the society of Africans'.[76] Letters came in supporting the plan and making suggestions on how to implement it. The idea was that a so-called 'Anglo-African' team could be selected after a tournament featuring the best players.[77]

The plans for going to England were not as fanciful as they may have seemed. The first Australian touring side to Britain in 1868 was a team of native Australians from the now extinct Werrunbrook people from Victoria. The Aborigines had a tough five months' schedule, playing no fewer than 47 matches, some watched by up to 7 000 people. (A Maori rugby team brought over on a similar tour in the 1880s were 'condemned to a programme of 70 matches that a galley slave would hardly have considered leisurely'.)[78]

According to Rupert Christiansen, who has written about the Aborigines tour, they were well treated, but 'remained a novelty' and were 'gawped at' by the racist Victorians:

The more educated justified their curiosity as scientific and wondered about their relative status in the Darwinian hierarchy and the family of races. The Sheffield Telegraph *reported that the Aboriginal team turned out to be 'a really fine body of men, of superior type for Australians, and in "build" and physique not only far removed from the low, Negro type of the genus homo, but able to "take their own part" with well-developed Europeans.'*[79]

The Aboriginal cricketers were the first Australians to tour England in 1868.

The Parsi community in Bombay, India, which had formed at least 30 clubs by the end of the 1860s, sent teams to tour England in 1886 and 1888. The 1888 tourists performed well and Dr M.E. Pavri, the 'W.G. Grace of the Parsis', took 170 wickets at measly cost.[80] Local fans were confident that an African team would also do well in England. 'N[ative] Cricketer' noted that Bobby Abel, the English test player and professional, who was a member of Major Warton's team, was about to go to India to coach among the Parsis. He said he had no doubt that 'the Natives of this country, with proper coaching, would thoroughly efface the best records of our friends in India'.[81]

Recent research shows that Major Warton's team itself was briefed about the interest Africans had in cricket before they left England for South Africa in 1888. The possibility of the English playing an African team here was raised with them.[82] Unfortunately none of these plans was realised. It took six more years before the first (all-white) touring team left South African shores in 1894.

One interesting possible spin-off of this debate was that the well-known cricketing personality, Paul Xiniwe, actually took an African choir to England in 1891. During its successful tour, the African Native Choir, as it was called, gave a performance for Queen Victoria at Osborne.[83]

The African inter-town tournament continued to be held regularly into the 1890s, apparently on a two-yearly basis. The reports, notices, scorecards and correspondence published in *Imvo Zabantsundu* over the years constitute a history begging to be written up in a separate study. The newspaper's illustrious editor donated a cup, the John Tengo Jabavu Trophy, as the prize for these regular tournaments. There were also bat prizes. In 1886/87, for example, William Seti won the bat presented by Colonel Bayly for the best average (24).[84] In 1890/91 the best batsman received the Reverend Gawler Bat and the best bowler the Foley Bat.[85]

In 1892/93, when King Williams Town were the hosts, the local organising committee wrote to the town council 'with the object of ascertaining whether it will be pleased to allow us to hire the [white Victoria] municipal Cricket Ground, at as moderate a sum as possible for at least ten days during the Tournament'.[86] The Town Clerk took six weeks to reply, and the answer was negative on account of 'all the space being taken up by the various local clubs'. The influential Paul Xiniwe 'for the sec' appealed directly to the Mayor and Town Council:

We interviewed several of the prominent cricketers in town and they invariably stated that those days are vacant, that they are arranging to go up and play up-country during the holidays; and in fact that even if they had fixtures for that time they would waive them in order to allow us our tournament space. Therefore, gentlemen, under these circumstances we beg you to reconsider your decision and grant us the ground for our tournament to which we have already invited teams and incurred expenses — of course not anticipating any difficulty as the ground was granted us on a previous occasion.[87]

*Paul Xiniwe (back row, second left) and his African Native Choir, which performed for
Queen Victoria in traditional dress at Osborne, 1891.*

Xiniwe got his way. Permission was granted and the tournament went ahead as planned.[88] He invited the mayor to 'preside over our concert', which was a special fundraiser for the tournament held in the City Hall.

In 1899, shortly before the Anglo-Boer South African War, Robert Mantsayi (secretary) put out a notice informing cricketers that the Jabavu Cup Tournament that year would be held in King Williams Town[89] and the 'Jabavu Cup Board' was still functioning in 1910. The president was G.W. Tyamzashe and the office bearers and auditors were almost without exception prominent politicians.[90] Mantsayi and Tyamzashe were also long-standing members of Jabavu's Frontier Cricket Club.

The Eastern Cape inter-town tournament served as a launching pad for subsequent national tournaments and organisation, particularly after formal contacts were established with Kimberley, where there was a well-developed sporting culture in the black communities (see Chapter 4).

In addition to the main inter-town tournament, teams from big and small centres alike regularly travelled to, and hosted, other towns for matches.[91]

On 2 January 1888 Port Elizabeth hosted the Kimberley 'native team' for the first time. The visitors were described as being 'charming, decent and civil gentlemen', young men who were liked in every respect. The highly respected Peter Rwexu, described as a 'renowned PE citizen', welcomed the team. He was regarded as 'the best choice for such duties' and once again 'the crowd applauded him'. Mr R. Christian put the Kimberley side up at his home. Mrs Wauchope supplied the bedding for the visitors. The 'countless others' who contributed were also thanked.[92]

The match was played at the white Union CC grounds. It cost a sixpenny to sit on the pavilion. The wind was howling through the trees on St George's Park, doing justice to Port Elizabeth's nickname of the Windy City. But this 'did not disturb the proceedings. The black community of Port Elizabeth and the surrounding areas fully supported the game.' Moreover, 'For the first time in the history of matches in the area married men brought their wives and single men brought their partners.' The reporter, 'Nkosi', said this needed to be applauded 'as it is a symbol of change in our communities'.[93]

The Parsi team which undertook the first Indian tour to England in 1886.

That these events were great social occasions was demonstrated by a report in the 1890s which showed that the King Williams Town team travelled by sea in the new Dunvegan Castle liner for their match against Port Elizabeth. A special farewell function was held at Paul Xiniwe's Temperance Hotel before the team left for East London to catch the boat. Fellow passengers included Prime Minister Cecil John Rhodes and his entourage.[94]

Cricket continued to grow in Port Elizabeth in the late 1890s and the first decade of the 1900s. Newspaper reports mention various new cricket clubs, including the Brotherly United CC, Wide Awake CC[95], Gaika CC, African Lion CC in the newly formed New Brighton township and the Cape of Good Hope CC in the neighbouring Korsten Township.[96] And, as we shall see below, the first national tournament was held there in 1898, and again in 1910.

These achievements are put into perspective by a report in 1915 that the local white league had 'not always flourished' and that it had at times 'fallen into abeyance' until 1896 when it was successfully restarted with an 'average of five clubs'. The main white clubs were Port Elizabeth CC,

Pirates, Uitenhage and Union. The latter won most of the early league competitions.[97]

Meanwhile the game was growing in other parts of the Eastern Cape too. Just one indication of this was the 15 fixtures played by Jabavu's Frontier Club of King Williams Town in the 1895/96 season. Frontier played local rivals Champion CC and 'Buffalos' three times each. They also played the local white Alberts Club twice, winning once and losing once. In the other games they beat St Matthew's College, 'Junior Champ' from East London, Forward CC from Debe Nek and Queenstown. The only other loss was to the strong Gaika CC from East London. The final results for the season were played 15, won nine, drawn four and lost two.[98]

In Queenstown, another major centre that participated in the inter-town tournaments, the main clubs in the 1890s were Pioneer CC and Komani CC.[99] The Komani officials, Reverend Samuel Mvambo (President) and Richard Nukuna (Treasurer) were prominent political figures, the latter president of the local *Iliso Lomzi* or Native Vigilance Association.[100]

By 1908 there were eight clubs playing in the East London Native Cricket Union, namely Gaika, Willows, Champion,

Rising Star, Lily White, Five Great Powers, Naughty Boys and Never Despair. The president was the well-known Dr Walter Benson Rubusana and 52 people attended the annual meeting that September. The report said the Union was waiting to hear from the secretaries of the Jabavu, T.B. Burnham King and Barnato Trophy Boards as to when the next tournaments would be held.[101]

Later that season, East London did, indeed, play against Alice, King Williams Town and Queenstown for the T.B. Burnham King Cup under the auspices of the Border Native Cricket Union. The tournament was held from 26 December through to 2 January in King Williams Town and the hosts were unbeaten in their three matches, trouncing the holders Alice by an innings and 104 runs. *Izwi Labantu* noted approvingly that 'King Williams Town is remarkably sportsmanlike in its friendly concessions to native cricketers and we were agreeably surprised to observe the amicable relations existing between the Europeans and the natives who were allowed the use of the Pavilion and grounds for this important fixture'. The cup, described as 'of chaste and handsome design', was presented by Dr Rubusana.[102] The following season East London were the hosts and King Williams Town retained the Cup.[103] This new tournament showed the increasingly organised nature of cricket in the Border region going into the 1900s.

There was also a Border Native Cricket Tournament for the McCallum's Presentation Cup at the time. The participating teams in 1908 and 1911 were Gaika CC from East London, Border CC from Stutterheim, Try Again CC from Cathcart and Kaffrarian CC from Queenstown.[104]

Cricket reports came in from what today would seem the unlikeliest villages and *dorpies* (small towns): Stutterheim, Cathcart, Tylden, Bolotwa, Whittlesea, Dordrecht, Burgersdorp, Molteno, Adelaide, Alicedale, Cookhouse, Somerset East, Richmond, Aliwal North and Herschel, as well as towns in the Transkeian Territories.[105] In 1890 Aliwal North hosted a tournament of teams from Johannesburg. There were two black clubs in Burgersdorp at this stage, Millionaire CC and Labour On CC – you will not find any today, among any section of the population. Examples from

Dr Walter Benson Rubusana, first president of the Border Native Cricket Union and prominent church and political figure in the late 1800s and early 1900s.

the Transkei include reports on the Imfecane CC in Butterworth in 1889[106], the Pondomise CC in Tsolo in 1896[107] and the match between the Prince Victor CC and the Civics CC, ('*i 1st XI yama Ngesi*'), in Mount Frere in 1900[108]. No part of the Eastern Cape was untouched. There are hundreds of reports in *Imvo Zabantsundu* and *Izwi Labantu* in the late 19th and early 20th century to show that cricket was not only the favourite sport in the African communities of the Eastern Cape, but indeed an integral part of their lifestyle.

Moreover, not only the 'excuse me' types, slavishly copying British manners, played. The most assertive and dynamic personalities and politicians of the time were involved. James Dwane (vice-president of the Frontier CC, together with Paul Xiniwe in 1895)[109] broke away from the Anglican Church to form the Order of Ethiopia. Another religious separatist leader, Reverend Jonas Goduka, who formed his own Ethiopian Church in protest against the paternalism and racism of white missionaries, was also involved in his home district of Herschel.[110] The point has been made before: the cricketers and 'school people' were not cardboard Englishmen, but a new generation leading Africans into the future.

THE OTHER GAME

While cricket was by far the most popular sport, the aspiring black middle class also took, to a lesser extent, to sports such as tennis, croquet, football and rugby. In a paper on 'Natives in Towns', presented to the United Missionary Conference in 1888, Reverend Elijah Makiwane stated that in 'almost all the towns [of the Eastern Cape] there are cricket clubs which are in a more or less thriving state, and at Port Elizabeth and a few other towns, there are also croquet and lawn tennis clubs'.[111] Rugby took root in the 1890s. More unusual was the report, also in the 1890s, of the horse races held by the Queenstown Africans on the local showgrounds. Meshach Pelem, a prominent politician, won the one mile pony plate with his 'Little Wonder' and gained a place in another race with another horse.[112]

Rugby, or *Mboxo* (the thing that is not round) established itself in a lasting manner in Port Elizabeth and the Eastern

Cape – today this is the only region in the country where it has a popularity rivalling soccer amongst Africans.

As in cricket, the first black teams were probably institutional, based at Lovedale, Healdtown and the Kaffir Institution. Located in Grahamstown and run by the Anglican Church, the latter was a sister school to the white St Andrew's College, which started playing the game as early as 1878. According to tradition, it was the St Andrew's headmaster, Reverend Mullins, who introduced rugby to the black community.[113]

The first adult rugby club was the Union Rugby Football Club, which was formed in Port Elizabeth in 1887. According to records collected by rugby historian Braber Ngozi, the club was started by 'kitchen boys who learnt their rugby from whites'.[114]

This could only have been part of the story. Among those involved were leading figures in the local Native Vigilance Committee through which the local elite of voters (totalling 274 in 1891), ministers and educated people represented African opinion in the town.[115] The headquarters of the club were at Kwampundu, the present Mill Park, where Grey High School is located.

The games were played at Dubula, where the provincial hospital now stands. At first Union's opponents were local coloured rugby teams, which formed themselves into a Port Elizabeth Coloured Rugby Union in 1892; but in 1894 a second African club, Orientals, was formed, followed by the Morning Star, Rovers, Frontier and Spring Rose Clubs.[116]

Union and Orientals became the strongest teams, and their matches were modelled on the rivalry between the main white clubs, Crusaders and Olympics.

Contests between different towns in the Eastern Cape were taking place well before the turn of the century. Sometimes challenges would take place via the press, as when Grahamstown challenged towns such as East London and King Williams Town in the columns of the *Imvo Zabantsundu* in 1899. *'Velani makwedini ase ma Xhoseni'* ('Come on, show yourselves, young boys of Xhosaland'), the Grahamstown correspondent teased.[117]

By 1904 the level of organisation and enthusiasm had reached the stage where the first inter-town tournament could be organised in Port Elizabeth. Teams from both Grahamstown and East London participated.

An Eastern Province Native Rugby Union was formed in 1905. The first EPNRU president was Tobias Mvula. The secretary was R.R. Booi, an employee of the Union Castle Shipping Company.

The inter-town fixtures were continued under the new union and were played over a period of several weeks. After first round play-offs in the various localities, the winning local teams went on to play against other towns in the second round, leading to a final in Port Elizabeth for the Wynne's Cup. In 1906 there were nine teams playing for the Wynne's Cup: the 1905 champions Oriental, Union and Rovers (all Port Elizabeth), Zebras Football Club (Uitenhage), Lions Football Club (Cradock), and Wanderers, Winter Rose, Lily White and Eastern Province Football Club (Grahamstown). The following year, they were joined by the Tigers Club from Somerset East. Founded in 1895, Tigers acquired their first jerseys after the South African War and chose the colours of the Union Jack – red, white and blue – in honour of the victors.[118]

The aim of the Eastern Province Native Rugby Union was clearly regional, but it does not seem to have been able to cover the whole of the vast area of present day Eastern Cape. For example, in 1908 the Queenstown-based Winter Rose Rugby Football Club, which was not a member of the EPNRU, played no fewer than eight games, indicating that there were a number of rugby networks operating in the region.[119] Later, various other 'provincial' units based in East London, Queenstown, Aliwal North and Alice would emerge.

Meanwhile, coloured rugby players were playing in separate competitions. By the time of Union there was a smoothly functioning Eastern Province Coloured Rugby Football Union based in Port Elizabeth. It was probably founded in the late 1890s, when the first 'coloured' Eastern Province teams were picked.

The champion teams in 1912 were West End and the predominantly Muslim Red Crescent Club, who met in the final at the prestigious St George's Park grounds.[120] In the same year the EPCRFU combined with the EP Coloured Cricket Board to organise a special dance in the Town Hall to raise funds for the families of local fishermen who had died in a fishing disaster.[121]

Clearly, the Eastern Cape rugby players were respected members of their local communities, closely tied to what was happening there, and they were not without means, as the EPCRFU's balance of £251.24d in 1913 indicated.[122] But here, too, we see early patterns of segregation which would be re-enforced by legislative decree and lived experience in later years. Although, according to Booley, 'tradition has it that the first Eastern Province team [in 1898] contained blacks as well', team lists and photographs in the early 1900s show that the coloured and African players organised themselves separately.[123]

Black and white cricketers, Great Brak River, 1899.

Chapter 4

CRICKET BECOMES *a* NATIONAL GAME

B Y THE 1890s CRICKET was being played by black people throughout Southern Africa. This expansion laid the base for the formation of a South African Coloured Cricket Board in 1903. Besides the Eastern Cape, with its pioneering educational institutions, Kimberley and Cape Town were the other strongholds in the early days. The game also took root in the modern-day Free State, Gauteng, Natal and even Basutoland (Lesotho) and Bulawayo in Rhodesia (Zimbabwe), where those accompanying the conquering British 'pioneer column' as clerks, missionaries, interpreters and teachers formed the Loben CC in 1898, named inappropriately after Lobengula, vanquished Chief of the Matabele. In 1901 the Loben CC played ten matches and won them all, according to the secretary, R.H. Sioka.[1]

As noted in Chapter 3, sport became increasingly organised from the 1880s onwards. These developments coincided with the rise of sport as a mass leisure activity in Britain in the late 19th century. As a result of the industrial revolution, towns and cities grew. New forms of leisure appropriate to these crowded environments emerged among the English. Cricket, rugby and football became popular sports that appealed to larger audiences.

A similar process occurred in South Africa. The discovery of the rich diamond and gold deposits from 1870 onwards attracted thousands of fortune hunters from throughout the world. People streamed into the interior. Industrialisation took off and cities and towns grew. Kimberley, and then Johannesburg, became big names in the global economy. The discovery of fabulous wealth in the African soil also revived waning British involvement in the region. This led, in turn, to the Anglo-Boer South African War and the incorporation of the conquered territories into a single British colony – the new Union of South Africa – in 1910. National sporting associations were formed in line with the wider process of economic and political integration that was occurring, generally preceding the formal political unity.

Among those who converged on the new mining centres in the late 19th century were many missionary-educated 'school people' and artisans from the Eastern Cape and Cape Town, where cricket had been played for some time. With their unique educational qualifications they generally occupied the most sought-after and best paid jobs available to black people. They also assumed a position of social dominance and leadership among the increasingly cosmopolitan communities in the new industrial centres where members of many different chiefdoms were conglomerating. As with the mission stations of the Eastern Cape, the ideas of 'progress' and 'civilisation' remained important to the 'school people', who took the lead in starting new choral, church, mutual improvement and sporting associations.[2]

Duncan Makohliso, for example, who was prominent in Eastern Cape politics, started a tennis club in Bloemfontein while working on the construction of the railway line to the north.[3] The Eastern Cape influence could also be seen in the contests inaugurated between teams from that region and rapidly developing centres like Bloemfontein, Johannesburg and Kimberley from the late 1880s onwards.

Circa 1900. Black children having an informal game of cricket near Aliwal North, which was a popular cricket venue and important stopover on the railway from East London to Johannesburg in the 19th century.

KIMBERLEY

Kimberley soon became one of the most important sporting centres in Britain's South African colonies and the adjacent Boer republics. By 1888 cricket organisation among Africans had developed to the extent that Kimberley sent a team to play against Port Elizabeth for the first time, and in 1890 it started competing in the inter-town tournaments.

The African population in the town was over 8 000 in the 1890s. Among them were a 'considerable number of educated natives'. It was noted that 'they come principally from Lovedale, and belong as a whole to the Fingo and AmaXhosa tribes. Three of them are employed as clerks, and several others as messengers, in the Post and Telegraph Department at good salaries. Many others find employment in the stores from five pounds to six pounds per month.'[4]

Brian Willan, biographer of the famous writer and activist, Sol Plaatje, has written in detail about the sports activities of the educated class in Kimberley. Confident about their future progress in this 'supremely British' and rich town, they started numerous churches, clubs and societies which operated as part of a 'network of regular activities and involvement'.

There were two clubs for the Kimberley Africans. They were the Duke of Wellington CC (known simply as 'Duke') and the Eccentrics CC. Each ran several teams. The local derby would be a big social occasion, and was often held as the main entertainment on Christmas Day. Reflecting the cosmopolitan urban environment, the local African cricketers also played against Indian, 'Malay' and coloured teams such as Good Hope, Oddfellows, Primrose, Red Crescent and United.[5]

According to Willan, 'Anybody who was anybody sought to become involved in running the club even if they did not actually play the game.' That is how the upwardly mobile Tswana-speaking Plaatje, brought up on a German mission station, became joint secretary of Eccentrics CC in 1895. The president was a post office employee, Boyce Skota, 'a very religious and real upright Christian gentleman, whose son later became Secretary-General of the ANC. The vice-president was Basutoland-born Patrick Lenkoane. Legendary for his sense of humour, he was described as 'one of the leading citizens among his people'. The captain was T.J. Binase who had a reputation as 'a ladies man and as a musician'. The local Methodist and Anglican ministers were both honorary officials. The latter was J.J. Jabavu, brother of the famous John Tengo.[6]

The level of organisation in Kimberley was such that a Griqualand West Coloured Cricket Union representing all black cricketers in the area was established in 1892 to regulate the contests between the various local clubs.[7]

Two years later a similar regional rugby board was formed.[8] The main African rugby club to participate was Rovers Native Rugby Football Club. The captain was an ex-Healdtown student, Isaiah Budlwana Mbelle (known universally as Bud). Opponents included Excelsior, Progress and the strong Universals and Violets Clubs, who tended to dominate the league.

There were three African tennis clubs, namely Blue Flag, Champion and Come Again. Women were members and played in the competitions.[9]

While black cricketers in Kimberley played together and formally adopted a policy of non-discrimination, the regional cricket body split in November 1895 when three clubs – Wanderers, Universals and Progress – broke away to form the Diamond Fields Colonial Cricket Union. They were apparently unhappy that an African, J.S. Moss, known as Mr Interpreter Moss after his job at the local magistrate's court, was appointed as vice-president. Isaiah Bud Mbelle wrote to the local newspaper condemning these attitudes. He described Mr Moss as 'a cultured and respectable native gentleman of whom any sensible community can be proud' and continued:

I could understand if the objection of the three clubs was based on the fact that a barbarous native, a street Malay, nay, even a stupid Cape Coloured man had been elected to such a post. As far as ability, education, and all other things – except an almost white (?) colour – are concerned, Mr Moss is far superior to any of the men composing the three clubs.[10]

Mbelle ended by saying that while 'natives and Malays have always allowed Cape Coloured people to fill the official positions' in the combined bodies, this was no longer automatically the case.

The split became permanent, but the GWCCU and the DFCCU did play each other on a regular basis.[11]

CAPE TOWN

Cricket was flourishing among the coloured Christian and Muslim communities in Cape Town at the time. The so-called Malay and coloured people of Cape Town became knowledgeable and proficient sports followers at an early stage. For example, there are references to 'gay' scenes at the horse races as early as the 1820s where '… Malays and Negroes mingled with whites, all crowding and elbowing, eager to get a sight of the momentous event'.[12]

This scene played itself out on Green Point Common, for centuries the main recreation space in Cape Town. The Bo-Kaap, or so-called 'Malay Quarter', was close by, and the inhabitants soon became passionate about the new games; there is no deeper tradition of cricket and rugby in South Africa than here.[13]

In Rowland Bowen's, *Cricket: A history of its growth and development throughout the world*, mention is made of a match between 'Hottentots and Africander (sic)' in the Cape Colony as early as 1854, which the 'Hottentots' won.[14]

One of the earliest visual records of a rugby match in South Africa – a painting by Otto Landberg – also features the majority of spectators wearing the distinctive koufeia (or fez), which was identified with the Cape Muslim community or 'Malays' as they were generically, and often incorrectly, labelled.[15]

Islam had been brought to the Cape by political prisoners and slaves from the East in the 17th and 18th centuries and had grown as a religion for those excluded from the mainstream of Cape society. According to an early Muslim political leader, Abdol Burns, Muslims constituted fully one-third of the population of Cape Town by the mid-1880s. This community had its own schools and institutions and distinct codes of behaviour based on the Koran. Islam was regarded not only as a religion but a way of life. Therefore, although the local Muslims became passionate rugby and cricket followers at an early stage, they adopted the new games on their own terms, giving them a distinctive character and meaning. The values of muscular Christianity and the British Empire attached to sport by the ruling classes and the church schools of the time obviously did not have the same relevance for Muslim sportspeople.

Teams were community based, often coming from one street, a family group or the *Jamaahs*, organised groups meeting for religious purposes, whose activities spread out into the social sphere as well. For example, people would gather for the *Mouled Jamaahs* to celebrate the birth of the prophet Mohammed, and groups would vie with each other in 'producing recitations in melodious tones' in praise of the prophet. First one group would present (*toekan*) and then others would reply (*jawap*). These were often big social occasions, lasting well into the night. Formal sports clubs and choirs emerged from these communal activities,[16] and the teams were predominantly (but not exclusively) Muslim. A local Muslim sports historian has explained why this was the case:

They also decided it necessary to organise on ethical and cultural grounds in order to keep the Muslims of the Cape together and also to bring unity amongst them. As most of the leading administrators were also the Imams of the congregation, they felt it was better to organise separately as they were mostly against the drinking habits of the other groups, especially over the festive season.[17]

The earliest clubs – like Ottomans in cricket and Arabian College and Hamediahs in rugby – indicated the links with the cohesive and well-established Muslim community in Cape Town. Ottomans Cricket Club, named after 'the great Ottoman Empire', was founded in 1892 by Abdullah Gamat, known as 'Boeta Plaat'. The Club had one address for over 60 years – 23 Pentz Street in the Bo Kaap – and 'only about four sets of officials' in its first century. For those who took on the responsibility of administration, it was a lifetime's commitment.[18] By 1888/89 the Muslim community was confident enough to organise a tournament for 'Malay' teams in Cape Town, in which sides from Port Elizabeth and Johannesburg participated. The following year Kimberley hosted the tournament. Cape Town won and were presented with the Glover Challenge Cup.[19]

Major R.G. Warton, who brought out the first English side to South Africa in 1889/90 vividly described the enthusiasm for the game amongst black cricketers in Cape Town at the time. 'On our way home we saw as quaint a sight as cricketers ever saw at Mowbray. Two or three cricket matches by Malays and Kaffirs, and hundreds of Malay women in their many-coloured costumes were there to do honour to their friends'.[20] Warton came across this scene coming back by coach from a Christmas lunch in Simonstown.

The English captain, Aubrey Smith, contributed his feelings in an after-dinner speech in Port Elizabeth a few days later:

Our visit, from all that I can see, is calculated to have so great an effect on the cricket of the Cape, not only amongst the white population, but even amongst the black. I noticed while driving through the suburbs of Cape Town that every spare patch of ground was used by the blacks to pitch wickets – or paraffin cans in some cases – in order to play cricket. I think it is not only here but wherever you go in the colonies you will find it is cricket which binds men together in the cause of sport and I hope it will always be so.[21]

The above two references, uncovered by Jonty Winch during recent research on sports unification in South Africa, add to what we know already: A 'Malay' team was actually given a fixture against the second English touring side, captained by W.W. Read, in March 1892. They lost by ten wickets, but Krom Hendricks took four wickets for 50 runs in 25 overs and L. Samsodien hit 55, one of only two South Africans to reach 50 on the tour.[22]

The *Cape Times* newspaper reported that 'this match caused great interest among the Mohammedan community, who showed their appreciation of the great honour accorded them by attending the match in large numbers, as did many Europeans'.[23] Samsodien 'showed himself no mean batsman and set about scoring in fine fashion, cracking the bowlers for threes and fours with the utmost contempt, and to the great glee of the spectators'. When the English openers Chatterton and Barton opened the batting the local team's

openers, Adams and Ariefdien, sent down five maidens before the first runs were scored. The *Cape Times* concluded that the 'Malay' team 'gave more trouble and showed better form than some teams of odds and ends the Englishmen have recently met'.[24]

Following this game, the local sportsmen articulated what the game meant to them in a letter to the press:

On behalf of the Mohammedan community of Cape Town we hereby sincerely thank the English cricket team for their kindness in consenting to play the Mohammedan team and we also congratulate our players for the fair stand they made against the professionals, considering the drawbacks they have as regards practice grounds etc. We hope that the local cricket teams will, in future, show a similar kindness in allowing us a better field to practise on.[25]

In 1894 Hendricks was included as a fast bowler in the final squad of 15 for the first tour to England by a South African side, but he was later omitted as a result of political pressure.[26]

The local Muslim sports enthusiasts also became colourful features of the whites-only establishment cricket and rugby scene. Often players took part in the practice sessions of local white clubs and visiting teams.

In his book on the 1905/06 MCC tour, Sir Pelham Warner described how, at practice, C.J. Nicholls, 'a young Malay with a fast left-hand action hit my middle stump nearly every other ball'.[27] Easily distinguished by their *koufeias* (or fezzes) and *liedtjies* (songs), they became passionate supporters of local white clubs and provincial teams. In rugby,

the teams which had most support were near the people's homes – 'Varsity, Villagers and Hamiltons' and it led to increased rivalry between the people of the city and those 'agter die Tol' – beyond the Tollgate at Woodstock. These were above all the people of Claremont, known to the people of the city as Tamaleitjiedorp. If Villagers lost they would say, 'Die ligte is uit in Tamaleitjiedorp.' And if Hamiltons lost ... the Malays of Claremont ... would say with delight, 'Vanaand is daar martial law in die Kaap.'[28]

The Muslim supporters became synonymous too with the historic Newlands cricket and rugby grounds. In those days, before the Group Areas Act and forced removals, many of them lived a stone's throw away, across the railway line. Sir Pelham Warner, describing the match between Lord Hawke's team and Western Province in December 1898, is again our reference:

On Boxing Day there was a crowd of over 8 000 spectators and the parade during the luncheon interval reminded us of an Eton vs Harrow or Varsity match. The bands of the King's Royal Rifles and the Liverpool Regiment played on the ground, while amongst the crowd there were a large number of Malays, many of whom are engaged as bowlers by the

W.W. Read's second English touring side to South Africa played against a 'Malay XVIII' in Cape Town in March 1892. Both Read (middle, fourth left) and George Hearne (middle, second left) commented on the enthusiasm and skills of the local cricketers, and the captain recommended that Krom Hendricks should be included in the first official South African team to tour England.

clubs in Cape Town. They could easily be recognised by their red fez. Some of them bowl well and their keenness is beyond doubt.[29]

In 1909, when Western Province beat Free State by six runs, 'amid a wild demonstration from the crowd' of several hundred, the press commented in strong terms on 'the booing of Smith, one of the umpires, at the close of play yesterday, the coloured element being the principal offenders'. Applause for the players the next day, however, made 'some amends', it was reported.[30]

The black spectators were accommodated in segregated enclosures. At cricket, it was in the 'Willows Corner', and at rugby behind the posts in the segregated south stand (or 'Malay Stand'), where they sat in 'rows of red fezzes above smart grey suits'.

In some cases, the Newlands loyalties and links were thicker than blood, making the apartheid of the white establishment that much more obnoxious in the long view. The Jacobs family from Claremont ran the cricket scoreboard at Newlands for three generations, and for more than 30 years

– from 1919 to 1953 – the legendary Gasant Ederoos Behardien (commonly known as Gamat) was the 'ballboy' for Western Province and South African rugby teams. According to rugby writer Paul Dobson, Gamat would inevitably appear at the tunnel 'elegant in his long white coat and red fez' to stir up a 'delicious pre-match excitement'.[31]

Doekums or 'Malay tricks' were meant to jinx the opposition, and this form of warding off bad luck for the home team became part of the Newlands folklore. Famous players like Bennie Osler, who carried a bag of *doepa* around with him on the 1931/32 tour to Britain, (and was injured in the one match he failed to do so), were known to engage in superstitious rituals attributed to Muslim custom.

Osler was reputed to have been very close to the Muslim community, regularly coaching local teams and even helping to establish the Cape Malay Choir Board. One observer has pointed out that he was also a representative for the United Tobacco Company and that his duties included attending local meetings to persuade players to use UTC products.

Gamat the subservient jester and Osler the famous benefactor were reflections, from different ends of the spectrum, of the unequal and paternalistic relations that characterised sporting contacts between black and white at the Cape.

White players sometimes helped coach black teams, or allowed them to use their fields, and the affinity which developed between the white cricket and rugby establishments at the Cape and the 'Malay' constituency was not paralleled anywhere else in South Africa. However, these contacts certainly did not challenge the racial order.[32]

A Western Province Coloured Cricket Board (WPCCB) was formed as early as 1890, but 20 years later the coloured Christian and Muslim cricketers were still playing in different unions based predominantly on religious and geographical considerations. One of the most important was the Cape District Cricket Union, formed in 1900. Clubs playing in its main competition, the Bailey Shield, were Eclectics, Hand and Heart, Oakdales, Polytechnics and Yorkshires. Leading officials, such as Matt Fredericks (president) and Stephen Reagon (secretary) were prominent members of the African Political Organisation, the most important early coloured political movement.[33] In 1911, there were also a City League, where Thistles led Sea Points, Saint Augustines and Crusaders on the log; a Claremont Union, with teams like Riverstones and Albions; a Woodstock Union, where St Phillips were the strongest team; and a Wednesday Union, where Rovers and West Ends dominated.[34]

The president of the Western Province Coloured Cricket Board in 1911 was the famous Dr Abdullah Abdurahman. Educated in Edinburgh, Scotland, he was the first black medical doctor in South Africa. The leading coloured politician in the Cape, he was the first president of the African Political Organisation and a city councillor for 40 years. Once again, we see here the value of cricket as a signifier of social status in the early years.[35]

Dr Abdurahman was a strong proponent of co-operation and unity on the sports fields. In 1912 the WPCCB announced that, 'We wish to draw attention to the fact that this Board is making a serious effort this year to bring all existing unions in the Peninsula into one union, and, if possible, by the beginning of next season.' Two mass meetings were called for this purpose. One, for players in the city centre, was in Buitengracht Street; the other was called for the Newlands Hall at the bottom of Palmboom Road.[36]

A current Western Province club which deserves special noting besides Ottomans, is St Augustines CC. Saints produced Basil D'Oliveira, while Paul Adams also became a member. Established in the 1880s, it too has long since celebrated its centenary. Whereas Ottomans represented the Muslim tradition, Saints — and other cricket clubs like Crusaders and St Phillips, as well as rugby clubs such as Temperance, Progress and Perseverance, whose names might have come straight out of John Bunyan's *Pilgrim's Progress* — were located in the social milieu of the coloured, Christian communities of Cape Town. A correspondent noted in 1914 that the coloured City and Suburban Rugby Union had impressive facilities, including a stand which could accommodate between 600 to 700 people, good dressing rooms, first aid facilities and a 'nicely kept refreshment stall' run by a 'very obliging lady and her daughter' who served cake and tea.[37]

Small wonder, then, that the Western Cape became a stronghold of 'non-white' and non-racial cricket and rugby in the 20th century. The sportspeople here were part of a long tradition. As city dwellers in relatively skilled occupations, they were relatively affluent. They took part in large numbers, and they had closer connections with white establishment sport than anywhere else in the country.

Less well appreciated is the fact that Africans also played cricket from the start in Cape Town, as the path-breaking exploits of the sons of chiefs in the first Zonnebloem College side in District Six in 1861, and Major Warton's comments above, demonstrate. In 1894 the racially-mixed Zonnebloem team, which totalled 155 for five, beat the St Mark's Recreational Society, who managed 92 in reply.[38] In the next season, the first and second teams took on Albion CC. Names like Falati, Mbali and Moroka were reminders of the College's distant origins.[39] In 1910 the mayor recalled a time when 'the College had the best cricket team in the whole Peninsula'.[40] By 1898 there were six African clubs in Cape Town, the most established being the Bantu CC, under the presidency of the well-known Reverend Elijah Mdolomba of the Wesleyan Church.[41] Mdolomba was also captain and secretary of the Wild Horse Cycling Club.

At that stage the African population in Cape Town, numbering around 10 000 out of 160 000 people, lived in Cape Town proper, but in 1903 the council began herding Africans into two 'locations' or barracks. One was at the docks and the other at Uitvlugt or Ndabeni near today's Pinelands.[42]

The superintendent of 'Docks location', situated in the Table Bay harbour where the famous Waterfront tourism destination now stands, wrote to the Port Captain in 1904 asking that part of the neighbouring commonage be used 'for a cricket ground, for the benefit of natives resident in this Location':

> At present the boys off duty are playing cricket in a very primitive fash-
> ion, and in a cramped space, viz the road inside Harbour Board area
> and outside Location Gates. A considerable amount of talent is being
> displayed but owing to want of space it cannot be cultivated.[43]

The location superintendent gave the assurance that he would take personal responsibility for any damages and 'also that passers by on the Green Point Road will be entirely free from molestation'.

In January 1904 'about 15 Malays ... attired in cricketing costume' entered the new Uitvlugt location to play a game against their African counterparts. Mixed matches such as these were not that unusual, as demonstrated by a contemporary newspaper report of a game in which the Ethiopian CC defeated the Rocklands CC comprising Muslim players.[44] But, this time, the visitors were summarily sent packing by the authorities. The strict standing order, endorsed by the assistant resident magistrate, was that 'all NCOs and men on duty in the Location will pay special attention to all Hottentots and others, especially females, and will on sight demand their identification cards, and if unable to produce one will at once be put outside the Gates'.[45]

A correspondent at the location wrote to the local *South African News* complaining about the way the players were 'incontinently ejected' by the police. The newspaper went on: 'Our correspondent asks "Is this location a gaol or a compound?" and in the light of the alleged occurrence the question is pertinent.' It recommended that those responsible be reprimanded if an irregularity had been committed.[46] None had been, in an official sense. The Western Cape was on its way to apartheid and the 'coloured labour preference policy', which would make Africans 'aliens' in the Western Cape.

The Uitvlugt location had five big corrugated iron huts, each sleeping about 500 people, and about 600 small iron shacks for families and small groups. It was surrounded by a six foot high barbed wire fence, with guards checking for identity cards.[47]

NATAL

Natal, like the Cape, was a British colony, but cricket did not take off among the Zulu-speaking people in the same way as it had in the Xhosa-speaking communities in the Cape. The reasons were twofold. Firstly, the Christian mission efforts in that region were dominated by American, Norwegian and German missionaries who did not actively encourage cricket.

The legendary Dr Abdullah Abdurahman, president of the Western Province Coloured Cricket Board and the African Political Organisation (known as the APO), the first major 'coloured' political organisation, early 1900s.

Secondly, and more significantly, colonial control in Natal was based on a system of indirect rule and segregation, which left old social conventions intact. Unlike the Cape, where people were forcefully integrated through conquest, Africans in Natal were governed indirectly through the protection of the chieftaincy and customary practices. A layer of British judicial and administrative machinery was placed on top of pre-colonial African institutions. Thus, this system 'utilised the existing distribution of power in Zulu society to achieve control and extraction of surplus'.[48]

Football dominated in Natal from the start. *Imvo Zabantsundu* commented in 1893 that football, which had not yet been introduced in the Cape, was preferred above cricket and tennis, the popular sports in the Cape Colony.[49] Nevertheless there are some cricket reports in the early *Inkanyiso lase Natal* (Light of Natal) and *Ilanga lase Natal* (Sun of Natal) newspapers.

The earliest reference is from the Anglican mission at Ekukanyeni in 1856, headed by the controversial John Colenso. A fiery critic of colonial policy, who later became the first Bishop for Natal, Colenso built a boarding school for the sons of chiefs 'who would conduct themselves as any young nobleman at Eton and Harrow'. This was even before Zonnebloem College in Cape Town was established. He noted in 1856 that Africans 'would make excellent cricketers and even now pitch and catch a light ball, as if they have been used to it all their lives'.[50] Ekukanyeni was established in February 1856 and by the following year observers were commenting on the considerable fielding skills of the Zulu pupils: 'They rarely fail to strike down the wicket from a distance.' This skill was attributed to their familiarity with 'flinging assegais'.[51]

Ekukanyeni did not last long and the Methodist mission at Edendale near Pietermaritzburg became the main base for cricket.[52] In December 1893, Edendale played against New Scotland, and the team list on this occasion reflected the fact that Edendale was home to one of the most affluent and influential Kholwa (believer or educated and christianised) communities in Natal. It included several surnames – Msimang, Mtimkulu, Xaba, Khumalo and Gule – which become particularly prominent in the politics and social life of that colony.[52]

Cricket was also played at the famous Ohlange Institute, founded by the Reverend John Dube, founding president of the ANC, but Adams College south of Durban became the main African cricket institution in the 20th century. Cricket was introduced here in the 1930s by Don Mtimkulu, who had a Masters degree from Fort Hare and studied at Harvard. The former (white) West Indian captain, George Copeland Grant, who played 12 tests in the 1930s, also later became a teacher and promoter of cricket at Adams.[53]

The 'non-whites' who showed the most interest in cricket in Natal were from the Indian community. Between 1860 and 1911, just over 150 000 indentured labourers from India came to work on the sugar plantations of Natal. They were followed by 'passenger' Indians from Gujarat, who paid their own way and started shops and businesses. These traders, with whom the legendary Mahatma Gandhi was closely associated in his 20 years in South Africa, combined with the small professional class of teachers and clerks to start the first community groups and clubs from 1889 onwards. The first clubs included Bluebells CC, Western Stars, Evening Stars and Greyville. In October 1894, representatives from ten clubs met to start the Durban Indian Cricket Union. In 1902 delegates from Pietermaritzburg and Durban formed the Natal Indian Cricket Union. Although this body was short-lived, cricket grew and by 1913 Natal Indian cricketers were playing in competitions with black cricketers from other parts of the country. Sport was so well organised in this community that a team of footballers and cricketers from Durban, known as 'Christopher's Contingent', went on a three-and-a-half-month tour of India in 1922. The well researched *Blacks in Whites, A Century of Cricket Struggles in KwaZulu-Natal* by Ashwin Desai, Vishnu Padayachee, Krish Reddy and Goolam Vahed, tells the story of the early years in detail.[54]

TRANSVAAL

The modern-day Gauteng and Free State were for large parts of the 19th century Afrikaner Republics, namely the South African Republic (ZAR) and the Orange Free State. The pattern of race relations in the Afrikaner Republics differed fundamentally from that in the relatively liberal Cape Colony and the segregationist British Natal – there were no pretensions about political, economic and social equality.

In the South African Republic (later Transvaal) the underlying principle, entrenched in the constitution of state, was that there would be *'geene gelijkstelling van gekleurden met blanke ingezetening … noch in Kerk noch in Staat'* (no equality between coloured and white inhabitants … either in Church or State). Similarly, in the Orange Free State relations between whites and blacks were conducted on a level of *'bazen tegenover dienstknechten'* (masters and servants).[55] Only whites could become citizens of the country and rigid social segregation was maintained. The indigenous groups had no political rights, and no claims to economic and social equality. Their main function was to provide labour – a position supported by the considerable British-controlled mercantile and mining interest, situated mainly on the Rand. Nevertheless, there were mission schools providing education to a small section of the black population. The numbers of pupils in schools in 1887 were 4 210 in the Orange Free State and 3 720 in the ZAR.[56] In time to come, these 'school people' would start seeking the same political and social rights as their contemporaries in the Cape.

A good starting point for the story of cricket in modern-day Gauteng is the discovery of gold and the establishment of Johannesburg in 1886. As already mentioned, large numbers of people from throughout the world flocked to the city of gold in search of opportunity. Among them were many mission-educated 'school people' and artisans from the Eastern Cape and Cape Town, where cricket had been played for some time already. They soon took the lead.

Reports of cricket in the black communities in Gauteng go back to at least 1890, when the Potchefstroom Native

*M.K. Gandhi (front row, fifth left) pictured with the Greyville Indian Cricket
Club in Durban in 1913. He criticized the exclusion of black spectators from
the Wanderers Cricket Ground in Johannesburg.*

Cricket Club played against Kroonstad Club in Kroonstad, a
popular venue for contests between teams from the ZAR
and Orange Free State because of its central location.[57]

In October 1893 Potchefstroom played Klerksdorp, pur-
portedly to celebrate President Paul Kruger's birthday on the
10th of that month. The day was probably a public holiday
then, just as it was for much of the apartheid period.
Reverend Bruno Kohler of the Berlin Mission Society forbade his black parishioners from playing, the reason given
that the minister's charges might misbehave themselves.
Clearly, the continental missionaries in the ZAR were not as
convinced as their English counterparts in the south of the
beneficial nature of the game.[58]

In 1896, ten years after the establishment of Johannesburg, the Indian cricketers there started the Transvaal Indian
Cricket Union. According to Desai et al, it became dormant
after a while, before being resuscitated again in 1930.[59]

In the same year, African players from the Morning Star CC
from Johannesburg travelled down to Aliwal North for a
Christmas tournament involving teams from that town, as
well as from Dordrecht and Burgersdorp.[60]

Over New Year in 1897/98, the Doornfontein Standard CC
played three matches in a few days. On 27 December,
Doornfontein Standard CC took on the Bloemfontein CC

at Kroonstad, winning by 'five runs and six wickets'. On
3 January 1898, they played the Ottomans CC 'of the
Malays' and again emerged as winners by three wickets. The
next day Doornfontein beat Elandsfontein Diggers CC by
an innings and 59 runs.[61] It was one of the strongest clubs
around and the president was A. Daniel, the secretary
J.W. Mguli and the captain T.G. Kwaza.[62]

In October 1898 the African clubs in Johannesburg
formed a union as well. Mr E. Chake was secretary of this
'Transvaal Union'.[63] No further details were given, but we
know from newspaper reports that there were around ten
'native' clubs in Johannesburg in 1898, including the
Johannesburg CC, Jubilee CC, Grand Zodwa CC, Progress
CC, Progressive CC, Morning Star CC, Herschel CC, Five
Great Powers CC, Doornfontein Standard CC, and the
Elandsfontein Diggers CC from Germiston.[64] Some of these
clubs had more than one team. Outside Johannesburg, there
were clubs like the Don't Care CC from Klerksdorp and the
Wanderers CC from Potchefstroom.[65] We know of their
existence because the Transvaal cricketers regularly sent
reports of their activities for publication in *Imvo Zabantsundu*
and later *Izwi Labantu*.

In the Transvaal black people were not encouraged to play
the game. Even after the British assumed control following

*The Wanderers Pavilion, one of the grandest buildings in early Johannesburg, built especially for the
first English tour by Major Warton's team in 1889, but black people were not allowed
to enter the strictly 'whites-only' ground.*

the Anglo-Boer South African War, a rigid system of social
and political segregation and discrimination existed. Laws
forbade blacks from walking on the same pavements as
whites and they were not even allowed to watch sports
matches where whites were playing.

The British High Commissioner, Lord Selborne, criticised
this situation in a speech in 1909:

*I will only ask the white men to consider whether they have ever
calculated the cumulative effect on the Natives of what I may call
the policy of pin-pricks. In some places a Native, however personally
clean, or however hard he may have striven to civilise himself, is not
allowed to walk on a pavement in the public streets; in others, he is
not allowed to go into a public car, or to pay for the privilege of watching a game of cricket; in others he is not allowed to ride on top of a
tram-car, even in specified seats set apart for him; in others he is not
allowed to ride in a railway carriage, except in a sort of dog kennel; in
others, he is unfeelingly and ungraciously treated by white officials.*[66]

Mahatma Gandhi complained about this sport discrimination too. And when a local newspaper suggested that a
special 'enclosure should be set aside for respectable and
decent Asians' at the Wanderers Stadium, Gandhi rejected
the proposed concessions as more unacceptable than the
existing outright exclusion:

*... character and education distinction are not made in respect of
Europeans. All that can be reasonably expected is that those who apply
for admission be suitably and cleanly dressed. Nor will the suggestion*

*that a portion of certain stands be set aside for Asiatics meet with
favour. So long as prejudice is allowed to influence the deliberations of a
sporting community, so long it is better that we do not have any right on
entry at all, than that such right should be reorganised in a limited and
niggardly spirit.*[67]

New African clubs to emerge in Johannesburg in the early
1900s were Cush CC, Pioneer CC, Braamfontein CC, Try
Again CC , Yinindaba CC, Fear Not CC and Head of Lion
CC based at Glen Deep mine.[68]

When Braamfontein CC travelled by train in November
1907 with an entourage that included whites to play Cush CC
at Klipspruit Location, they arrived at 10.00 and were met
by a welcoming committee of Cush CC ladies, including
'Mesdames' Sontongo and Msane, before the captains tossed
at 10h30.[69] It is tantalising to wonder whether or not these
women were in any way associated with Enoch Sontonga,
composer of *Nkosi Sikelel' iAfrika*, and the early ANC leader,
Saul Msane, whose granddaughter, a friend and contemporary of Walter Sisulu, still lives in Soweto.

In December 1911, the Fear Not CC 'of the City and
Suburb, Johannesburg' challenged the top Kimberley
African team, Eccentrics CC. They arrived 'by the midnight
train' on Christmas Eve and played on Christmas and Boxing
Day. It was reported that the result of the match

*was expected with considerable interest in native sporting circles in
Transvaal and Griqualand West, where they wished it to be decided at*

Street scene in Johannesburg at the start of the 20th century shows not only segregation between black and white but also emerging class differences among black people.

the wickets whether gold or diamonds was the toughest mineral ... On reference to the score below it will be seen that the pebble came out of the affray with its reputation for sheer hardness unsullied.[70]

This was clearly a hometown report because the Johannesburg players did not do badly. In reply to the 175 all out and 199 for four of Eccentrics, Fear Not scored 124 and 123 for three. The number of runs here were unusually high for those times.

More research needs to be done on the early Transvaal history, but it seems that the Indian and African Unions formed in the 1890s had gone out of existence or been absorbed by other bodies by 1911. Oral testimony by one of the early cricket stars, Piet Gwele, and the report quoted above, indicate that Africans and coloureds were playing together under the City and Suburban Union at this time. There was also a Transvaal Coloured Cricket Union based in Vrededorp by 1911, which appears to have been a predominantly 'Malay' and coloured body.

The office bearers elected at the annual general meeting in 1909 were Mr Minnaar (president), Hadjie Gafeldien Abrahams (vice-president), G.Z. Sallie (chairman), Hadjie

Abdol Samaar (treasurer) and George Manuel (secretary). Six clubs, some with as many as four teams, were affiliated, namely Progress, Fair Players, Ottomans, Borders, Pirates and Brotherly United from Pretoria. They competed for the Shahabodien Cup.[71]

ORANGE FREE STATE

In the Orange Free State, too, cricket was being played early on despite the rigid political system and discrimination in operation there.

As we have seen, Kroonstad played against Potchefstroom as early as 1890, while in the same year, Royal CC of Rouxville travelled to Aliwal North to participate in a tournament there.

During the Easter weekend of 1894, a team from Aliwal North played against the Oriental CC in Bloemfontein.[72] In November of the same year, cricketers from Venterstad were reportedly run into jail in Bethulie for not having 'official passes'.

The issue led to press comment, *The Friend* newspaper describing the actions as 'mean'. *Imvo Zabantsundu* said the incident made the Free State government 'look blacker than it really is as regards the treatment of subject races'.[73] The magistrate unconvincingly denied the affair.[74]

Venterstad also features in the other occasional cricket reports for this early period. In 1899 the Alberts CC from that town travelled to Norvalspont on the banks of the Orange River to play the Orange CC.[75]

Further reports mention St Peter's School in Bloemfontein playing St Patrick's in 1900 after being bought '*impahla ye bhola*' (clothes or kit) by the Reverend Rose.[76]

The Inspector of Locations was not impressed by this kind of encouragement. He preferred black youngsters being forced to work rather than being given a liberal education. He commented, '... you see them daily down here practising gymnastics and white people to teach them. I think,' the Inspector continued, 'work is about as good gymnastics as Natives could get...'[77]

By 1907 there were seven cricket clubs in Bloemfontein, while tennis, golf and football were also being played. Oriental, captained by J.B. Gwayi, was reported to be the strongest club in the city, and matches with white teams apparently also occurred.[78] Universals, Occidentals and Orientals were the three predominantly coloured clubs.[79]

In 1909 the Bloemfontein Town Council rescinded a decision to allow business people to start a skating rink in the local Waaihoek township. Local residents and ministers said the innovation would be morally undesirable and would 'possibly lead to immorality'. Some local whites felt 'it would disturb the whole domestic arrangement of the town, as their servants would always want to be at the rink'.[80]

Describing social conditions in Bethulie in the southern Free State in 1911, the resident magistrate wrote that 'Natives go in for tennis, football and cricket whilst nearly all the younger population attend school. Nearly all are church goers.'[81]

Cricket was also being played in the Rolong enclave of Thaba Nchu and in Basutoland. In 1906 Try Again CC from Mohalie's Hoek lost heavily to Quithing's Mangan CC, after J. Lepotane and A. Moalasi scored half centuries.[82]

At Thaba Nchu, teams drawn from a prosperous, highly politicised land-owning elite played against their white neighbours, who were possibly missionaries and British soldiers granted land in the area after the Anglo-Boer South African War. Commenting on these matches which the Africans won more than once, the *Tsala ea Batho* newspaper, financed by the local elite, commented that while whites held themselves socially aloof in order to command respect from blacks,

the fact is no Natives respect their European neighbours as much as the Baralongs at Thaba Nchu who twice beat the whites in fair games of cricket. In other parts, where the whites will not play them, the coloureds boast that the whites are afraid of them.[83]

The newspaper went on to suggest that South Africans could learn from India where the Mohan Bagan Club had recently beaten the East Yorkshires for the Football Association Shield.

Eighty thousand spectators had attended and the absence of racialism was noticeable, both on the part of the Indian spectators and the whites who 'took the affair good

Children playing in an informal game of cricket in Basutoland (Lesotho), early 20th century.

humouredly'.[84] In the article, entitled 'Colour and sports', *Tsala ea Batho* also noted that the South African government had prohibited 'bioscope shows' in the townships of the sensational boxing championship fight in which Jack Johnson knocked out the great white hope 'Gentleman Jim' Jefferies in a brutal contest filled with racial overtones in San Reno, Nevada, to become the first black world heavyweight champion. This was the first known instance of film censorship in South Africa. According to the newspaper, this action had 'greatly depreciated the white man's prestige in the locations'.

Evidence provided in this chapter shows that cricket was played in black communities throughout South Africa by the end of the 19th century and black sportspeople were showing an intelligent interest in the development of sport internationally. Moreover, the inter-town tournaments for Africans in the Eastern Cape from 1884 onwards, the irregular 'Malay' inter-town tournaments, starting in Cape Town in 1889, and the formation of the first 'provincial' organisations, had laid the foundations for increasing co-ordination on regional and national levels.

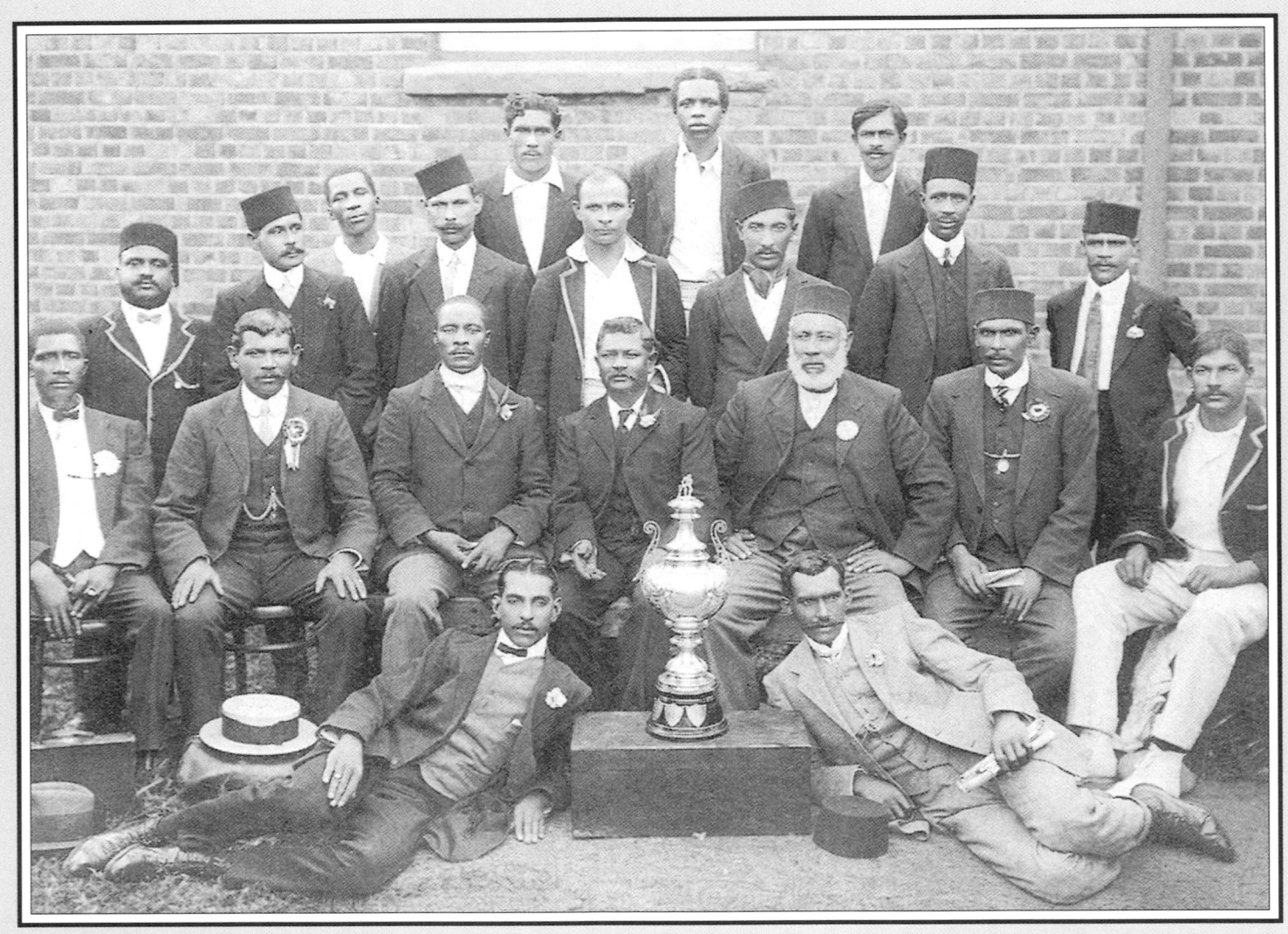

South African Coloured Cricket Board officials posing with the Barnato Memorial Trophy during the inter-provincial tournament in Kimberley, March–April 1913. The only identified representatives are those from Natal, namely the captain, R. Bhugwan (seated, right); Albert Christopher (second row, fourth left); the manager, S. Emamally (second row, right); and A. Haffajee (back row, right).

Chapter 5

THE FORMATION *of* NATIONAL CRICKET *and* RUGBY BOARDS

K IMBERLEY TOOK THE LEAD in the formation of the first national sports organisations in South Africa. Both the cricket and rugby associations – for both black and white – were started in that city.

The whites-only South African Rugby Football Board was first to be established in 1889, prompted by the need for a co-ordinating structure to settle disputes and differing interpretations of the rules between the different centres. The first president was Percy Ross Frames, one-time chairman of De Beers Consolidated Mines.[1]

The South African Cricket Association (SACA) was formed early the next year on 8 April 1890. The first meeting was held at Glovers Athletic Bar. The chairman was W.M. Hopley from Western Province, who later became a judge.[2] Clearly cricket was following the example of rugby, and this included the social stature of its office bearers.

The successful first tour to South Africa by an English team in the previous season provided another powerful impetus. Known as Major Warton's team, the English tourists were captained by Aubrey Smith, who later became a famous Hollywood actor. Prior to their departure, Sir Donald Currie, owner of the Union Castle Shipping Company, held a banquet for the team on board his SS Garth Castle. He gave Warton a cup to give to the South African team which 'excels most against the visitors'.[3] The cup, named after the donor, was awarded to Kimberley, who in turn 'decided to offer it to be competed for by other centres'. The main cricketing centres were now encouraged to form provinces and join together in one controlling body.

Sir Donald Currie also gave a trophy for rugby. This time the presentation was held on his Dunottar Castle, in 1891, and the recipient was W.E. Maclagan, captain of the first British rugby team to visit South Africa. Griqualand West were again awarded the trophy, and the same pattern as cricket was followed.[4]

WHITES-ONLY SACA

The South African Cricket Association was for whites only. In keeping with the general practice in South African society, black cricketers were excluded from its clubs, competitions and representative sides. The segregated SACA was happy to run cricket in the 'traditional' way.

Closely linked to the colonial and British establishments, SACA initiated regular contacts with other 'white' countries that formed part of the British Empire. Between 1889 and 1970 it organised 41 series involving 172 test matches, all against England, Australia and New Zealand. Until the 1990s South Africa never once played against India, West Indies, Pakistan or Sri Lanka.[5]

The Currie Cup was SACA's main domestic competition until the body disbanded in 1977. According to Christopher Merrett, this competition was 'primitive in format' until after World War One, and 'generally played at one venue and until 1903/04 often contested on a challenge rather than league basis'. For more than 80 years, until the 1970s, no black players were allowed to participate in the Currie Cup.

Though white paternalism allowed for the odd sporting encounter with blacks, social segregation was the norm. Whites had no intention of relaxing the barriers. Some mixing may have occurred in mission teams but clubs remained strictly segregated. This was also the case until the mid-20th century in other colonies such as Kenya, Nigeria and Ghana.[6]

In fact, in Britain's African and Asian possessions, clubs were built on a notion of exclusivity which went far beyond the sports field. Here the club served as a symbol, not only of social status, but also of political domination, as the well-known historian Jan Morris has pointed out. It was developed as an enclave of power and privilege in an alien setting. Its members were patently different from the unadmitted millions. More than anywhere else, the club was where the imperialists celebrated their Britishness, authority and imperial lifestyle.[7]

The social exclusivity of the Victorians in the colonies went hand in hand with the most prejudiced feelings of cultural superiority, not only towards black colonial subjects, but also towards others in the dominant white strata. Afrikaners and Jews, for example, were for a long time not welcome in many clubs.

Writer John Buchan said the Afrikaners had none of the 'qualities of courage, honour and self-control' that defined sportsmen and the British national character. The Boer was 'seen at his worst' in sport. He was 'without tradition of fair play' and he was 'soured and harassed by want and disaster'.[8]

Yet, despite this snobbery and the long rivalry between English and Afrikaner, reflected most starkly by the Anglo-Boer South African War, integration between these two groups on the sport field increased in the 20th century. As English and Afrikaner combined on a political level to keep out the *swartgevaar* (black peril), Afrikaners became influential in South African sport, and old social barriers began to fall.

Black people, however, were affected in exactly the opposite way. The paternalistic treatment they sometimes received in social and political life grew into a rigid system of segregation in the 20th century. In the process, the contradictions in the ideologies of sport and imperialism became more and more apparent. While on the one hand they supposedly represented 'fair play' and liberal ideals, on the other they entrenched racial domination and class divisions in practice.[9]

Black cricketers could not hope to play for white clubs and provincial or national teams, and they were regularly discriminated against. An outstanding example of this was the exclusion of Krom Hendricks from the first South African team to tour England in 1894. He had impressed against the English in the match against the Malay XVIII in Cape Town in 1892 and after that the English tour captain, W.W. Read, advised, 'If you send a team [to England], send Hendricks; he will be a drawcard and is to my mind the Spofforth of South Africa.'[10] F.R. Spofforth, known as 'The Demon', was the first great Australian fast bowler to wreak havoc against English teams.[11] George Hearne confirmed that the parallel was not exaggerated: 'A Malay named Hendricks was very fast indeed. In our last match against the Malays, the wicket was very bad and we didn't like facing the man at all. I was captain during the match and everyone began to ask me to let somebody else go in his place ... The balls flew over our heads in all directions...'[12] When the time came to pick the first South African team to go to England in 1894, Hendricks's name was among the nominations sent in to the selectors by the major centres, but he was omitted on the basis of colour.

New research by Jonty Winch has shed interesting new light on this episode. According to Winch, Transvaal newspapers and cricketers strongly advocated his inclusion, but this suggestion was met with stiff-upper-lip disapproval in Cape Town. The *Cape Times* suggested he go along as the 'baggage man' in order to ensure that there 'could be absolutely no objection to Hendricks on account of his being a Malay'. An insulted Hendricks replied, 'I would not think of going in that capacity.' He also pointed out that he had not been asked about his availability and that he was not in fact 'Malay', but Christian, with a father 'born of Dutch parents in Cape Town' and a mother from St Helena.[13] The response of South Africa's top batsman, A.B. Tancred, to Hendricks's statement was revealing of white attitudes:

Well, after his impudent letter, I should certainly leave him out. If he wants to go on the same footing as the others, I would not have him at any price. As baggage man they might take him and play him in one or two of the matches when the conditions suited him. To take him as an equal would from a South African point of view be impolitic, not to say intolerable ...[14]

A letter writer in *The Star* remarked that if South Africa was going to lose they should 'at least take a licking like white men'. The 'moral effect' of including Hendricks would be bad. 'Therefore … it is imperative that the line be drawn sharp, straight and unbroken between white and coloured.'[15]

Some enlightened whites, such as H.G. Cadwallader, secretary of SACA, supported Hendricks, but the English establishment at the Cape was comfortably aligned to the drawing-the-line cricket racists. After consulting with the Cape Prime Minister, Cecil John Rhodes, William Milton, the president of the Western Province Cricket Union and chairman of the selectors, vetoed Hendrick's inclusion in the team. Milton played rugby for England and captained South Africa at cricket. A close associate of Rhodes, he became Secretary for Native Affairs, and later Administrator of Southern Rhodesia.[16] Milton also saw to it that Cadwallader, who had been favoured to manage the team, did not get the job. He was furious that the SACA secretary had 'placed the WPCU in a very embarrassing situation' by sending a letter to the press in support of Hendricks. The plucky Cadwallader nevertheless followed the tour as a journalist. 'Very little went right for the tourists in England' and he never missed the opportunity to remind the selectors of their mistake.[17]

The Krom Hendricks saga of 1894 entrenched segregation in South African cricket and confirmed that the English political and sports establishments were responsible for this, and not the apartheid government of the Afrikaners, a myth perpetuated by some journalists even today. From the beginning, and in the apartheid years, the buck stopped with the white SACA itself. The English-speaking cricket establishment chose not to accommodate black cricketers in its ranks and operated comfortably within the system of white domination and racial segregation from the start.

SACA's decision before its first overseas tour in 1894 established the pattern for the future and, although Hendricks subsequently had some games for a white club, he was later also excluded from the prestige fixture between 'Mother Country' and 'Colonial Born'. The lines had been drawn.

Many other examples of discrimination against black cricketers in the late 19th and early 20th centuries exist. As we have seen, cricketers were arrested in Bethulie for not carrying passes, prohibited from watching white cricketers play in the Transvaal, ejected from 'locations' earmarked for other racial groups, and regularly discriminated against when it came to the use of municipal facilities.[18]

In 1885, after beating the local white team, Africans in King Williams Town were temporarily barred from the pavilion at the Victoria Ground, which they previously had been allowed to use.[19]

In 1897 a match in Stutterheim had to be suspended 'owing to the conduct of the Town Council who, without assigning any feasible reason, deliberately refused to allow the coloured cricketers (some of whom, by the way, are ratepayers) to play on the town commonage'. The local club, 'composed of a respectable and well-behaved section of the Native residents, in the division, consisting of teachers, public servants, agriculturists, storemen etc', protested vociferously saying the matter affected not only the community concerned, but the 'Natives' of the Cape Colony generally.[20] One of the members said he could not credit 'that such treatment was practised in what is a British colony, to British subjects of a respectable standing, who through a fault, or otherwise, of Nature's design, are black'. He said this was 'one of those questions that greatly affect the Government of the country, to say nothing of complicating and unsettling the Native mind and rendering it more difficult for them to understand the arts of the government of the white man'.

The writer continued that this was a violation of 'the ancient statute called Magna Carta' by the local missionary and his 'clique' on Council, who were afraid that 'someone's servants might go and play the game and neglect their work'. He reminded readers that the Masters and Servants Act was there to punish any real offenders.[21]

This hostility to black middle class advancement and leisure activities was shared by many white colonists. The resident magistrate of Adelaide recommended in 1908 that a law should be passed to force Africans to understand that 'work is no crime'. He said that the educated Africans 'sole idea is to copy the European with white cricket coat and trousers, he is great at tea-meetings, cricket and tennis parties, but he thinks that to do an honest day's work is far beneath his requirements'.[22] The message was clear: blacks should not aspire to social equality. Their proper role was to be a labouring class. Restraints such as those mentioned above became the norm under apartheid and were to frustrate the ambitions of black sportsmen.

KIMBERLEY TAKES THE LEAD

But black people did not accept the role set out for them by the dominant classes. Within years of the white SACA and SARFB being formed and the whites-only Currie Cup being started, they began making plans for their own national organisations and competitions. Kimberley was again at the centre of things as black sports leaders tried to emulate the example of their white counterparts.

ABOVE LEFT TO RIGHT *Sir Donald Currie; Percy Ross Frames, first president of the white South African Rugby Football Board; A.B. Tancred, best SACA batsman in the first decade of international cricket and the first player ever to carry his bat in test matches, also a strong upholder of the colour-bar in cricket; SACA captain, selector and administrator, Sir William Milton who vetoed the selection of Krom Hendricks for South Africa, setting in concrete the racial segregation that would mark the 87-year history of the whites-only SACA.*

The 'diamond city' was an economic growth point and, centrally located, it had regular contact with black sportspeople from different regions. The various communities in Kimberley played together in mixed local leagues, and they had watched from close up as white sportsmen set up national bodies and competitions. They had access to the patronage of powerful mining interests. And, as Willan has explained, they were bullish about the future, invigorated by the air of this 'supremely British place'.

By 1888 organisation among Africans in Kimberley had developed to the extent that a team was sent to play against Port Elizabeth for the first time, and by 1890 cricketers from Kimberley started participating in the inter-town tournaments for both Africans and 'Malays'. Black cricketers were clearly starting to reach out across regional boundaries.[23]

In 1892, within two years of Griqualand West winning the first Currie Cup trophy, a Griqualand West Coloured Cricket Union representing all black cricketers in the area was established to regulate the contests between the various local clubs.

Two years later a similar regional rugby board was formed.[24] It is interesting to note that the rugby board used the word 'Colonial' rather than the more conventional 'Coloured' in its title. This is the first recorded instance of a

The Currie Cup, premier trophy of the white South African Cricket Association.

specifically non-racial approach to sport in South Africa. In 1894, it was specially noted in the Xhosa columns of the *Imvo Zabantsundu* newspaper that the Rugby Union did not discriminate on the basis of '*bala, luhlanga, lulwimi, nalunqulo*' (colour, nationality, language and religion).[25] By the following year the cricket board had reconstituted itself in a similar way, replacing 'Coloured' with 'Colonial' in its title.

The secretary of the GWCRFU was the 25-year-old Isaiah Bud Mbelle, described as 'a man of immense ability and wide-ranging talent'.[26] He was typical of the new generation of educated intellectuals and sports leaders. Educated at Healdtown, he taught before becoming the first African to pass the qualifying examination for the Cape Civil Service. A speaker of no less than six languages, he was appointed as Interpreter in Native Languages to the Northern Circuit of the Supreme Court in Kimberley. His salary of £25 per month reputedly made him the highest paid African government employee in the colony.[27] He later became Secretary-General of the ANC and Mbelle's sister married Sol Plaatje, the famous journalist, writer and political figure. Their marriage across traditional ethnic lines, which caused unhappiness in family circles, was yet another example of how the younger generation of western-educated, urbanised

I have the honour to be,
Sir,
Your Obedient Servant,
Isaiah Budlwana Mbelle
Box 39.
Colesberg.

The Secretary for Native Affairs
Cape Town.

Isaiah Budlwana Mbelle (standing, right), first secretary of the South African Coloured
Cricket Board, pictured with fellow cricket administrators, Sol T. Plaatje (standing, left)
and Patrick Lenkoane (seated, right). The fourth person is not identified.

and christianised intellectuals was crossing old boundaries and shaping new directions.[28]

Clearly determined to emulate the example of the white cricket and rugby players with their South African boards and Currie Cup competitions, the well-connected Bud Mbelle and his fellow black sports administrators in Kimberley initiated plans to start national rugby and cricket bodies and competitions.

FORMATION OF THE SOUTH AFRICAN COLOURED RUGBY FOOTBALL BOARD

Imvo Zabantsundu reported in July 1897 that black rugby administrators had persuaded Cecil John Rhodes, the arch imperialist and symbol of Kimberley's new wealth, to present 'all the Coloured Sporting People of South Africa with a Silver Cup, valued at Fifty Guineas, for Competition amongst themselves on the same lines as the Currie Cup'.[29]

The GWCRFU sent out a notice calling on clubs and 'Unions (if any)' in 'the various towns and districts' to send delegates to a meeting at the Savona Café in Kimberley on 19 August 1897. The aim was to form a South African Coloured Rugby Football Board (SACRFB).[30] The meeting was held one day after a team representing the GWCRFU left for a tournament in Cape Town where they were due to play seven matches. The turnout was disappointing. Only local people attended, although Bud Mbelle was requested by the Port Elizabeth Union (consisting of the Rovers and Union Clubs) and African clubs from Johannesburg and King Williams Town to represent them by proxy. Nevertheless, J. Joshua of the Progress Club, seconded by Bud Mbelle, proposed that the new SACRFB be formed, and the motion was carried.

Robert Grendon from the Excelsior Club in Beaconsfield was elected as the first president of the SACRFB. Educated at Zonnebloem College in Cape Town, Grendon was a teacher at the Beaconsfield Public School. He later taught at the famous Ohlange Institute in Natal, founded by John Dube, first president of the South African Native National Congress (later simply the African National Congress), and became editor of the congress newspaper, *Abantu Batho*.[31]

Bud Mbelle was voted in as the SACRFB secretary and D.J. Lenders and E. Heneke as auditors. The former was a foreman at a local 'Harness and Saddlery', while Heneke was a 'boiler' at De Beers, and secretary of the B (or Coloured) Section of the South African League, a pro-British imperialist organisation formed to support Rhodes's adventures in Southern Africa. Lenders later became a prominent politician

and president of the national rugby and cricket board. He was vice-president to the legendary Dr Abdullah Abdurahman in the African Political Organisation (APO). The leaders of the new rugby board were therefore respected figures within the emerging black educated and political elite.[32]

In keeping with the convention of the time, the SACRFB decided that 'an influential local gentleman' be asked to become a patron of the Board. The person chosen was William Pickering, brother of Cecil John Rhodes's closest friend and sole heir. Pickering later became secretary and a director of the De Beers Company.[33]

BARNATO MEMORIAL TROPHY

At the same time as the rugby developments were happening, Bud Mbelle, on behalf of the Griqualand West Coloured Cricket Union, persuaded Colonel (later Sir) David Harris of De Beers and also a member of the Cape Parliament to donate an expensive trophy worth 100 guineas to black cricketers. On 1 November 1897, Harris informed Bud Mbelle that following his request, he had consulted with Mr Solly Joel and said, 'I have this day ordered from England a suitable silver trophy, and on its arrival I shall be glad to hand it over to the Griqualand West Colonial Cricket Union, as a Barnato Memorial Trophy.'[34]

The trophy was to be in honour of mining magnate, Barney Barnato, who had recently committed suicide by jumping off an ocean liner at sea. Born 'dirt poor' in the East End of London as Barnett Isaacs, this uneducated Cockney was a street-fighter and magician before striking it lucky on the mines. He adopted his stage name and became fabulously wealthy when he sold his share of the Kimberley mine to Rhodes's De Beers Company for more than £5 million.[35]

John Tengo Jabavu welcomed the news in an editorial in *Imvo Zabantsundu*:

The coloured sportsmen of Kimberley have had another turn of good luck. Some time back we announced that they were the fortunate recipients of a Cup from Mr Rhodes, and we then made observations on the manifest duty of millionaires to the aboriginal inhabitants, which were so appreciated by our contemporaries as to be widely commented upon. We then showed the amount of good that comparatively small gifts to Native causes were from those whom Providence has made the stewards of His bounties embodied in the mineral deposits of Africa. It is a satisfaction to us to learn that the remarks then made have come before the representatives of other millionaires ... We add our thanks ... It cannot be too strongly insisted upon that ... any money spent on the amelioration of the Natives is money well spent, and such as will be repaid with interest to the community in times to come. Sport is one way of increasing the wants of our people and making it obligatory to them to work to supply those wants. But as we have before said it is not the only way; and it would be well if the moneyed ones of the community recognised that the Missionary agencies among the raw material played no small part in rendering Natives effective citizens, and therefore a source of wealth to the country.[36]

The cricketers now had a cup as rugby had. However, for reasons that are not clear, they did not, as rugby did, follow up by forming a national board at the same time.

Nevertheless, the Kimberley-based officials now started planning for the first rugby and cricket tournaments. Rugby's first Rhodes Cup Tournament took place in August 1898 in Kimberley and the first Barnato Cricket Tournament was held in Port Elizabeth a few months later, over New Year.

FIRST RHODES TOURNAMENT

The newly formed SACRFB decided to hold the first of 27 Rhodes Tournaments in Kimberley in August 1898. Bud Mbelle was instructed to inform the rugby fraternity of the plans and to send them the constitution once the committee appointed to finalise it had done so. He also had to see that the Rhodes Cup, which 'has been ordered from overseas', was acquired. When it arrived it was 'on two separate occasions exhibited to the public'. Bud Mbelle, meanwhile, was working hard travelling to and corresponding with other areas in order to ensure that they set up provincial associations and affiliated to the new national board. When the SACRFB met again in May 1898 there were representatives from the Western Province, Eastern Province and Transvaal 'Coloured Unions', in addition to the GWCRFU, and all had paid their registration fees. These had also been the four constituent unions of the white South African Rugby Football Board (SARFB), formed a few years earlier in the same city. The development of sport in South Africa among both black and white was clearly influenced by broader patterns in the historical development of the country as a whole.[37]

The inaugural Rhodes Cup Tournament, organised by the South African Coloured Rugby Football Board in Kimberley from 20 to 27 August 1898, was a roaring success. Advertisements for the tournament were placed in the local *Diamond Fields Advertiser* and 'spectators rolled up in good numbers'. The mayor was in attendance to present medals to the winners and the South African rugby international, Chubb Vigne, was one of the referees. Western Province won all three of its matches to win the tournament.[38] The four team lists reflected the sporting demographics of the different participating regions: from the coloured/Muslim composition of

the Western Province and Transvaal teams, to the African names of the Eastern Province squad and the fully mixed Griqua XV. The aim of the SACRFB was clearly to organise all those rugby players excluded from the whites-only SARFB. This was a significant achievement, predating formal political co-operation along inter-racial lines by nearly a decade; for it was only in 1907 that the South African Native Congress and the coloured APO held their first formal joint conference.

FIRST BARNATO TOURNAMENT

The success of the rugby tournament perhaps galvanised Bud Mbelle and others into organising the corresponding tournament for the summer game. Early in November 1898, notices went out calling cricketers to a tournament in Grahamstown.

The organisers invited seven centres, who were encouraged to form regional teams including players from surrounding towns. Invitations went to Kimberley, Cape Town, Johannesburg and the main Eastern Cape centres: Port Elizabeth, Grahamstown, Queenstown and King Williams Town.[39]

It was also announced that during the tournament a cricket board would be elected to 'administer the Barnato Memorial Trophy which cost around 100 guineas'.[40]

The notice pointed out, too, that the white Currie Cup tournament would be in Port Elizabeth over the Easter weekend, indicating the self-conscious mobilisation of the excluded black cricketers along the same lines.[41]

East London people were upset that they did not get a separate invitation. They said that one club from East London would defeat all those in Grahamstown combined. Moreover, Grahamstown was 'not known in tournaments; it was cut off a long time ago'. East London had an abundance of players and Kimberley would not even see the sun set against them. Uitenhage, which did not get a separate invitation either, had previously beaten both Kimberley and King Williams Town. What right did Kimberley have to exclude them?[42]

It was explained that East London needed to combine with King Williams Town to form Southern Border and Uitenhage with Port Elizabeth to form Eastern Province.

The critics also asked how, if all the towns could not come, would cricketers be able to elect a representative board. Moreover, there were complaints that the invitations were too late, but *Imvo Zabantsundu* encouraged them not to let these questions derail preparations for the tournament.[43]

The historic first Barnato Tournament finally took place from 28 December 1898 through to 5 January 1899. Although Grahamstown was originally chosen as the venue, Port Elizabeth ended up hosting it.

Newspaper reports give some indication of the arrangements. Only one game was played every day, which was probably because the facilities of a white club had been secured. Only on the last day were there two fixtures, while a three-day break was taken over the New Year. It was agreed that accommodation would be provided by the host town. However, the visitors were expected to fend for themselves regarding meals. Gate takings, it was also rather grandly decided, would be shared after expenses had been deducted.[44]

The first match of the historic tournament was between the home team and Griqualand West. The first official Eastern Province side batted first, in the following order: Mtshutshisa, Mabelana (also the wicketkeeper), Nyusela, Dalaza, Busakwe, Fiti, Rune, Haya, Ngcoza, Phu and Maloni. They were bowled out for 80. Dalaza scored no fewer than 55 of the runs. Griquas replied with 108, with Phu taking four of the first six wickets to fall. Rune had the next best return of three wickets. After the home side managed 99 runs in the second innings, with twenties from Fiti and Maloni, Griquas needed 72 to win. They passed the score with five wickets down.[45]

Imvo Zabantsundu's correspondent was scathing about the performances of the home side in the tournament. He wrote that even though they had done well in the recent inter-town Tengo Jabavu Cup, they played 'in a disgraceful manner'. Indeed, Port Elizabeth fared extremely poorly, losing every one of their matches. Queenstown and Southern Border both beat them by four wickets.

The fifth team in the competition, from Western Province, emerged as winners, beating Southern Border in the decisive match against the run of play. Batting first, Western Province collapsed dramatically to 27 all out in their first innings, with Buhlungu taking eight wickets. Southern Border followed with a healthy first innings of 145, with E. Koti 40 not out. Then, Western Province rallied to post 219 in the second innings. Kenny and A. Hendricks both registered sixties. With victory in sight, Border collapsed to 64 all out. Their downfall came after the Cape Town team identified a weakness against slow bowling and switched to spin.[46] Abdul and

Daniel J. Lenders, vice-president of the APO and president of the SACRFB.

T. Hendricks, with eight and six wickets apiece, did the damage.

The Western Province slow bowlers, described as 'unplayable', also put Griquas to the sword in a six-wicket victory, and the team was 'by far' the best, according to *Imvo Zabantsunu*. The incomplete placings given by the newspaper were as follows:

	P	W	L	D
Western Province	3	3	0	0
Griqualand West	3	2	1	0
Southern Border	2	1	1	0
Queenstown	3	1	1	1
Eastern Province	3	0	3	0

The two other centres expected to play, Grahamstown and Johannesburg, did not in the end participate, even though a Transvaal Board had been formed in October. Even the cricketers in Bulawayo in Rhodesia (Zimbabwe) had hoped to come.

As with rugby, the composition of the teams in the first Barnato Tournament reflected both the inclusive goals of the early black cricket administrators and the local specificities of the game in each area. Western Province had mainly Muslim players; Griquas were mixed between Africans and coloureds. The Eastern Cape teams were made up of Africans.

Two things were clear from these demographics. Firstly, so-called 'non-European' players were determined to work together. Secondly, from the first inter-town tournaments to Mbelle's initiative regarding the Barnato Cup to the organisation of the first tournament in Port Elizabeth, African administrators were in the forefront in the early moves towards cricket unity.

FORMATION OF THE SOUTH AFRICAN COLOURED CRICKET BOARD

A national board was not formed at the tournament as intended, but the black cricketers were apparently looking forward to the next Barnato Tournament in Cape Town, amidst concern among some in the Eastern Cape that the Jabavu Cup tournaments would be negatively affected.[47] However, before the next season could get under way, the Anglo-Boer South African War broke out, in October 1899, putting paid to any further plans for the next three years.

Participating teams and officials from the Western Province, Eastern Province, Griqualand West and Natal at the South African Coloured Cricket Board inter-provincial tournament for the Barnato Memorial Trophy, Kimberley, March–April 1913.

Within months of peace being declared in May 1902, E.D. Makula, designated 'Secretary Pro Tem' of the Griqualand West Colonial Cricket Union sent out the following notice:

BARNATO TROPHY TOURNAMENT. I am directed to inform, through Press, all Cricket Centres that a Tournament re above Trophy will take place in Kimberley during Christmas and New Year holidays. All sportsmen interested are kindly requested to take up and communicate with the undersigned for particulars.[48]

Discussions were resumed about further tournaments and the establishment of a national board on provincial lines.[49] However, the proposed 1902 tournament failed to take place.

In February 1903, Mr S. Mtoba, apparently newly appointed as secretary of the Griqualand West Colonial Cricket Union, based in the Malay Camp, a 'dynamic mixed area' in Kimberley, sent out a notice on behalf of the Union. It informed all centres interested in a tournament during December 1903 and January 1904 to contact Kimberley in writing so that a board could be established in time for this.[50]

This time the efforts of the organisers were successful. By the end of 1903 there was a new constitution for the South African Coloured Cricket Board and it was announced that the first tournament would be held in Kimberley in April 1904. Affiliation would be two pounds two shillings and the board would be 'governed by a general body' consisting of the president, secretary (who would be resident in Kimberley) and 'two representatives from each State, Colony, or Province affiliated to the Board'.

The new SACCB made it clear in clause 25 of its constitution that 'this Board does not recognise any distinction amongst the various sporting peoples of South Africa, whether by Creed, Nationality or otherwise'. This was an obvious reference to the racial policies of the white cricket body and the governing classes in general. Furthermore, the SACCB decided to 'adopt the rules of the [white] South African [Cricket] Association' in its general administration of the game, underlining its desire for unity rather than re-inventing the wheel.[51]

For every tournament, a meeting would be called in the host city to discuss arrangements and to elect a secretary to 'conduct the business of such tournaments and meeting'. It was agreed that 'in no case' would the trophy be competed for more than once in two years, and another condition was that at least three 'representative teams' from the affiliates had to participate.[52]

The founding members were, it would seem, Eastern Province, Griqualand West and Western Province, with Transvaal joining in 1904.[53]

The next tournaments for the Barnato Trophy were in 1904 in Kimberley, 1906 in Cape Town, Easter 1910 in Port Elizabeth and 1913 in Kimberley again. Western Province were regular winners. In 1910, however, they failed to take part in the tournament, and in their absence Griquas won the title. Dr Abdullah Abdurahman, president of the Western Province Coloured Cricket Board and the APO, handed over the Trophy at 'a gathering of a large number of sportsmen and friends' held at the Seamen's Institute near the harbour, which is today the South End Museum. 'He warned the men not to give all their time to sport – and he hoped to hear that the winning team … have all joined the APO on their return to Kimberley, for a good sportsman generally makes a good politician.'[54] He was backed by a contingent of APO leaders, which included Daniel Lenders.

It was agreed that the absent Western Province were the strongest cricketers and, in keeping with the political tone of the evening, one of the APO leaders explained why:

The reason for that is very clear: in the Western Province the coloured people were permitted to witness the best cricket played in the Colony, and also the matches between the English and Colonial teams; whereas in the Transvaal those sources of improvement were shut to the coloured people, for no coloured man was permitted to witness a match either between the best colonial teams or the English cricketers. [55]

The reason why Western Province did not play in 1910 was probably religious, and also linked in a lingering way to the 'Native-Malay vs Coloureds' split in Kimberley in the 1890s, which led to the formation of the breakaway Diamond Fields Colonial Cricket Union from the GWCCU.[56]

In 1912, the APO newspaper commented that there was currently a move afoot to make the SACCB 'truly representative'. The newspaper added:

We regret, however, to learn that those responsible for the movement are encountering some opposition on the part of a narrow-minded section of Coloured cricketers whose grounds for objection … is based on religion, and other absurd notions. [57]

The paper warned that a board that did not embrace 'every section of the Coloured players' would not have credibility as a national organisation.

The immediate problems seem to have been solved and Western Province once again participated and won in the Easter 1913 tournament in Kimberley.

Detailed records of the 1913 tournament exist, which allow for an assessment of SACCB cricket at the time, but they will only be touched on briefly here. Natal were participating for the first time. Its team consisted of Indian players only and costs came to the princely sum of ninety pounds and 15 shillings. They were proudly kitted out in blazers presented by their unions – 'green body with gold braid' – together with a hatband from the manager. However, they came last in their first tournament behind Western Province (eight points), Griquas (five), and Eastern Province (two), failing to win a match.[58]

Africans were still participating, but whereas they formed the majority of players in the 1898 Barnato Tournament, they were now very much in the minority. There was only one team (compared to three out of five in 1898) from the Eastern Cape. Moreover, Eastern Province, which had been mainly if not entirely African then, now seemed to consist mainly of coloured players. The team was Abrahamse (top of the batting averages at 32.4), J. Davids (top score of the tournament with 127), T. Davids, Jalil, Johnson, Kafaar, Liberty, Maininka, May, Situngu, Solomon (best bowler with figures of 82-20-195-22) and Watson. Griquas, however, had at least three Africans in F. Ntchoko, who averaged 25.3 with the bat, J. Kakazela and G. Makoti.[59]

The 1913 tournament was the last held for eight years. World War One broke out, deeply affecting South African life. The SACCB and the SACRFB more or less went into limbo. Establishment white sport was similarly affected at this time as thousands of young men went off to fight. No Currie Cup rugby tournaments were held between 1914 and 1920 and no test matches were played between 1912 and 1921. The consequences for black rugby players were even more serious than for the cricketers: the SACRFB only organised its first post-war tournament in 1928, 14 years after the previous one.[60] It took a shocked sporting world a long time to recover after the guns fell silent in 1918.

Parts One and Two of *The Story of an African Game* have set out to show that ground that was deemed fallow actually teemed with life. Africans were playing cricket on a large scale more than a hundred years ago, and the myth that cricket and other games like rugby are new to black people can once and for all be laid to rest. Not only is there a history, as this book sets out to illustrate, but it is a well-documented history.

Furthermore, the way cricket developed in the black communities in this early period closely followed the path taken by white cricketers, and, as we have seen, the enthusiasm and playing standards in the Cape often matched those of the white cricketers. The yawning disparity of the later 20th century resulted from the intensification and institutionalisation of racism, political oppression and economic exploitation in the modern South African state, leading to the decline of the black (especially African) middle class and the frustration of its ideals.

When modern South Africa was created at Union in 1910 the new whites-only constitution brought the formal colour bar instead of greater opportunity. The black elite protested vociferously at the restriction of their rights. They claimed that there could never be peace without justice in the long term. A.K. Soga perceptively warned in *Izwi Labantu*:

'Equal rights for all South of the Zambesi' is the motto that will yet float at the masthead of the new ship of state which has been launched under the Union, and no other will be permanently substituted while there is one black man of any consequence or self-respect in the country, or any white man who respects the traditions of free Government – so help us God.[61]

A South African Native and Coloured Delegation was sent to London in 1909 in what turned out to be a futile bid to persuade the British Parliament not to ratify the constitution for the new Union of South Africa until the discriminatory 'colour-bar' clauses in it were removed. The delegation marked a high-point in the history of African political mobilisation, and paved the way for the formation of the South African Native National Congress (later African National Congress) in 1912.[62]

It is instructive to note which heavyweight politicians were delegated to go to London. The names show how closely the formation of a national freedom movement was linked to the development of cricket in South Africa. The leader of the delegation was ex-Prime Minister, W.P. Schreiner, who was the most vocal white opponent of a discriminatory Union, and soon to become president of the South African Rugby Football Union. Schreiner spoke no fewer than 61 times during the debates in the Cape Parliament in an attempt to block the new Union constitution.

The delegation also included Matt J. Fredericks, general secretary, APO (and president of the Cape District Cricket Union); Dr Abdullah Abdurahman, president, APO (and president of the Western Province Coloured Cricket Board); Dr Walter Benson Rubusana, president, South African Native Congress and South African Native Convention (and president of the East London and Border Native Cricket Unions); John Tengo Jabavu, president, Cape Native Convention, editor of *Imvo Zabantsundu* (and president of the Frontier Cricket Club and donor of the Jabavu Cup for inter-town competition); Thomas Mtobi Mapikela, Orange River Colony Native Congress (ex-Healdtown College and patron of cricket in

The South African Native and Coloured Delegation to London to protest before the British Parliament against the new South African colour-bar constitution, 1909. It demonstrated how closely the formation of a national freedom movement was linked to the development of cricket in South Africa. (Back row, left to right) Thomas Mtobi Mapikela, Orange River Colony Native Congress (and ex-Healdtown College and patron of cricket in Bloemfontein); J. Gerrans, representing Bechuanaland Protectorate chiefs, Daniel Dwanya (brother-in-law of Paul Xiniwe), representing Gqunukwebe chiefs; Daniel Lenders, vice-president, APO (and president of the South African Coloured Rugby Football Board and Diamond Fields Colonial Cricket Union). (Front row) Matt J. Fredericks, general secretary, APO (and president of the Cape District Cricket Union); Dr Abdullah Abdurahman, president, APO (and president of the Western Province Coloured Cricket Board); William P. Schreiner, M.P. and ex-Prime Minister of the Cape Colony (and future president of the South African Rugby Football Board); Dr Walter Benson Rubusana, president South African Native Congress and South African Native Convention (and president East London and Border Native Cricket Unions); John Tengo Jabavu, president, Cape Native Convention, editor of Imvo Zabantsundu *(and president of the Frontier Cricket Club and donor of the Jabavu Cup for Inter-Town competition).*

Bloemfontein); and Daniel Lenders, vice-president, APO (and president of the South African Coloured Rugby Football Board).

If ever the importance of sport in the lives of black South Africans was demonstrated, the delegation showed this.[63] And the fact that Isaiah Bud Mbelle became Secretary-General of the South African Native National Congress in 1917 underlined the point.[64]

After Union in 1910, the integrationist ideals of the black elite were to become increasingly frustrated both on the field of sport and in the wider political arena. Black people were systematically discriminated against and many of their rights were removed as the colonial system hardened into rigid institutionalised apartheid.

Hamilton Mahonga John Masiza, secretary and vice-president of the South African Bantu Cricket Board, 1932-1941, and president, 1941-1954.

Chapter 6

AFRICAN CRICKETERS
go their OWN WAY

———————————————— ◖ ————————————————

HEREAS EARLY BLACK POLITICAL and sporting groups had from the start demanded integration and equality, the 1920s and 1930s brought about a deepening of segregation. As South Africa developed into a modern nation-state after Union in 1910, it became increasingly stratified along racial lines, leading eventually to the rigid, legalised apartheid that would cause such pain and shame in the second half of the 20th century.

The old South African Coloured Cricket Board (SACCB), known universally as the Barnato Board, started breaking up after World War One. Separate racial bodies were established for coloureds (1926), Africans (1932) and Indians (1941). The old SACCB mother body became virtually defunct before being resuscitated again in 1945 and changing its name to the South African Malay Cricket Board in 1953.[1]

The decision to form the South African Bantu Cricket Board for Africans took place at a meeting in East London in January 1932.

The inter-town tournament for the Orpen Cup – a continuation of the inter-town tournaments started in the 1880s – was held in East London over the Christmas/New Year period as per tradition. The hosts played against King Williams Town and Kimberley. Regular opponents Port Elizabeth, Fort Beaufort and Transkei did not enter 'owing to the depressed conditions'.[2]

In the early 1930s the world was plunged into an economic depression, and South Africa experienced the full force of it. The 'poor white' question became a national political issue as Afrikaners lost their wealth and their land in large numbers. Black South Africans were similarly affected, but they were cut off from power and their suffering remained invisible. Over the next few years newspaper reports regularly mentioned that cricket plans were thwarted by the Depression.

At the close of the East London tournament 'a representative informal meeting' of representatives from the 'cricket centres' was convened by Hamilton Masiza from Kimberley, the city that had initiated the first national Barnato Tournaments and Board in the 1890s and 1900s, from which African cricketers were now breaking away. Masiza was, in fact, still the Barnato Board secretary.[3]

The cross-section of people included H.B. Piliso, representing the NRC Union in Transvaal, C. Xabanisa and A. Mbuli (Transkei), H. Ben Mazwi and Julius Mtyobo (North Eastern Border), D.S. Mtyongwe, S.M.B. Tapa, E. Tshefu, C. Gcilishe and G. Xiniwe (Border), Frank Miya and F.H.M. Zwide (Eastern Province), J. Malangabe (Western Province) and A.Z. Mazingi (Basutoland – modern-day Lesotho).[4]

The meeting unanimously decided to form the SABCB with Messrs Piliso, Masiza and Malangabe as acting president, secretary and treasurer respectively.[5] The Cape-born Piliso was a clerk and headman at Crown Mines and later at the Modder B mine. He was well connected with both William Ballenden and H. Wellbeloved, the chief municipal and Chamber of Mines officials dealing with Africans, and was clearly part of the leadership strata in Johannesburg. In 1934, when the Prince of Wales visited South Africa, he was a member of the local preparatory committee, together with future ANC president,

H.B. Piliso, first president of the SABCB, 1932-1941.

Dr A.B. Xuma.[6] Piliso's deputy, Hamilton Mahonga John Masiza, was trained as a school teacher and became principal of the United Mission School, No. 2 Location, Kimberley. The son of a church minister, he was born in Somerset East and educated at Grahamstown Public School, Healdtown, Lovedale and Fort Hare. His curriculum vitae stressed that he was also conductor of 'the famous choir of Abantu-Batho Musical Association' in Kimberley. Like Piliso and many of his mission educated contemporaries, he was also a member of the multi-racial Joint Councils, established in the 1920s to promote good race relations.[7]

The new SABCB was part of a pattern in South African sport. Not only was the Bantu Board further splintering the virtually defunct Barnato Board, but new national associations were formed by Africans in soccer, rugby and athletics as well in the 1930s.

The reasons for African sportspeople organising separately from the 1930s was linked directly to the growth of urban segregation. The 1923 Native Urban Areas Act led to the stricter enforcement of urban segregation. As separate African townships became the norm, area-based clubs became increasingly racialised.[8] Another reason was the gradual emergence of a more assertive African nationalism which stressed African self-determination; these political developments were echoed in sport by complaints that African sportspeople were not getting a 'fair deal' under coloured leadership.[9]

Another point these groups had in common was that they were mainly sponsored by the mining industry. Both the cricket and rugby boards started organising Chamber of Mines provincial tournaments and both awarded Native Recruiting Corporation (NRC) trophies to the winners.

It is noticeable that while the fountainhead of cricket and the concentration of players was in the Eastern Cape, the first SABCB officials came from the big centres of Johannesburg, Kimberley and Cape Town. This became a pattern in the next few decades. The whole locus of African sport shifted to Johannesburg and the Transvaal province, by now firmly established as the economic powerhouse of 20th century South Africa.

INAUGURAL SABCB INTER-PROVINCIAL TOURNAMENT, 1933

The first Chamber of Mines inter-provincial tournament was planned for the end of 1932 in Johannesburg. Organising it was difficult because of the Depression, *Umteteli Wa Bantu* reported. Nevertheless, the organisers in Johannesburg attempted to go ahead. Transvaal and Kimberley confirmed their participation, but Eastern Province sent a telegram at the last moment explaining that they would not make it.

D.M. Denelane, secretary of the Transvaal Bantu Cricket Union, who worked as a headman and chief clerk at the Robinson Deep Gold Mine, put a notice in the paper saying that the tournament was 'definitely cancelled owing to the inability of all the centres to play'.[10]

The cancellation was a blow to the organisers. Denelane said, 'Arrangements for the hospitality and the grounds have been made and it will be a great disappointment to all those who worked so hard to make the tournament possible.'

The plan now was for Transvaal and Griquas to play a series of friendly matches over the Christmas weekend. But this also fell through. Eventually the 'picked team' was challenged to a match by the local City and Suburban Coloured Union affiliated to the original Barnato Board.[11]

In December 1933, however, the organisers pulled it off. Reports came in from around the country about preparations in the different centres. Trial games between composite teams from the Transvaal western and eastern districts were held at

Crown Mines and Van Ryn's Deep[12], while Eastern Province sent in their team list and put together a large contingent to go up to Johannesburg by train.[13]

What was described as the 'All Union Bantu Cricket Tournament' finally got underway at the Bantu Sports Club grounds in Johannesburg on 23 December. A large number of cricket enthusiasts turned out to watch. Five provinces participated. Matches were two days each and played 'under rules governing the European Curry [Currie] Cup tournament'.[14]

The host province, Transvaal, soon showed its superiority. After making heavy weather of winning against Western Province – collapsing to 42 for seven before reaching a meagre target – they comfortably won the rest of their matches. The victory margin against Eastern Province was an innings and 56 runs. They also thrashed Border who replied to Transvaal's 213 with 98 (after an opening partnership of 65) and a paltry 14. Captain Titus Majola, who took six wickets for six runs, was responsible for the mayhem. After one of the other games, his bowling was described as 'unplayable'. (Incidentally, the serving president of the Transvaal Native Rugby Union at the time was R.P. Majola,[15] while E. Majola also turned out for the Transvaal cricket team. This was not the famous Eric, father of Khaya and the current UCB CEO, Gerald, and it is not known yet if the Johannesburg Majolas were family.)[16]

The Eastern Province team included names such as the brothers Johnson and Lloyd Marwanqa, Walter Ntshekisa and the young Wilson Ximiya, a leading player and administrator for the next 30 years. The scorer, W.W. Jabavu, a member of the famous Jabavu family, was responsible for the newspaper reports and photographs used on this page.[17]

Runners-up Western Province achieved the highest team and individual scores in

D.M. Denelane, long-time SABCB secretary and treasurer, was also the president of the South African African Football Association in the early 1930s. Chief Albert Lutuli, later president of the ANC and Nobel Peace Prize winner, was on his executive. (Back row, left to right) A.L. Putini, H. Khumalo (secretary), L.B. Msimang, D.T. Msikinya.. (Front row) T.H.D. Ngcobo, D.M. Denelane (president), E.D. Msimang, A.J. Lutuli, H.L. Msimang (vice-president).

Women spectators at the first SABCB inter-provincial tournament in Johannesburg in December 1933. (Left to right) Mrs M. Piliso, G.E. Sidzumo, and M.M. Mayeza, described as 'well-known visitors'.

Another sign of women's growing involvement in sport. Women tennis players at the Bantu Sports Club in Johannesburg, 1934. (Back, left to right) Jane Oliphant, Martha Molefe, Eva Solomon. (Front) A.D. Pretorius, Mabel Solomon.

Queenstown representatives in the Border team, (left to right) J. Ben Mazwi, J. Mtshobo and the provincial captain, M. R. Masabalala.

Prominent cricket figures from Eastern Province in the early 1930s. LEFT TO RIGHT *Batsman Johnson Marwanqa, provincial president Andrew Pendla, and bowler Walter Ntshekisa.*

the tournament in their match against Griquas. Their 367 for four declared included centuries by D.M. Fongqo (121) and S. Mdlwana (105). The captain and manager, Walter Mama, declared himself satisfied with his team's performances as, besides himself, the team had consisted of young players selected 'more in the nature of an experiment' than anything else.[18]

Eventually the tournament ended without the final fixture between Transvaal and Griquas being played owing to the 'lapse of time'. The final standings were: Transvaal (15 points), Western Province (11), Eastern Province (seven), Border (six) and Griqualand West (two).[19]

Before the teams returned home, a 'well-attended' reception was held for them at the Bantu Men's Social Centre, the

Western Province 1933. (Back row, left to right) Don T. Mtimkulu, M.B. Liphuko, A. Matshikwe, S. Bam, E. Matshikwe, D.N. Mbali. (Middle row) S.M. Fongqo, P.K. Petu, P. Walton Mama (captain), S.M. Ndlwane, C.S. Mbali. (Front row) S.S. Msengana (score-keeper).

Eastern Province 1933. (Back row, left to right) J.K. Adams, E. Fuzani, R. Dlepu, Johnson Marwanqa, W. Ntshekisa, Ed. Nakani, M. Matyalana. (Middle row) C. Ngesi (captain), A.F. Pendla (manager), Ed N. Dubu (vice-captain). (Front row) China Manana, S.T. Ntshekisa, T. Jantjes, Lloyd Marwanqa.

Border 1933. The players in this photograph were unamed, but the squad was Reginald Solomon (Stutterheim), G.E. Xiniwe (KWT), M.J. Pitoyi (Macartney), G.R. Mtati (EL), P. Sono (EL), A.J.D. Gitywa (EL), Rascoe Siyo (EL), M.R. Masabalala (Queenstown), J.D. Ben-Mazwi (Queenstown), H. Mgudlwa (Queenstown), Slingby Mgudlwa (Cala).

The Transvaal team, captained by Titus Majola, which won the first SABCB Chamber of Mines tournament. The players in this photograph were unamed, but the squad was Titus Majola (captain), Charles Ngengebule (vice-captain), E.M. Matyalana, F. Roro, S. Zozi, P. Malete, E. Masiza, N. Habana, E. Majola, L. Seti, Geo Barnabas. (Reserves) J. Mpiliso, J. Adams, M. Xiniwe, W. Ngcelwana, T. Kota.

main social venue for the educated middle classes in Johannesburg. The fine trophy donated by the Chamber of Mines was on display and 'much admired'. H.B. Piliso acted as chairman and with him was Mr H. Wellbeloved, Chief Native Adviser to the Chamber of Mines, who 'welcomed the visitors to the Rand'.[20]

Wellbeloved seemed to be ever-present at the sports events in Johannesburg. On one other occasion, Piliso described him as having 'endeared himself to the Native people', *inter alia* by organising the NRC Trophy for inter-provincial rugby. Wellbeloved, in turn, said, 'It is my wish that the Natives indulge in sport more and more. The Natives have had it hard without their tribal feuds for the Depression alone has been a stroke.'[21]

The new SABCB and its main competitive structures clearly rested on the patronage of the Chamber of Mines.

Home Bachelors Cricket Club from Ndabeni and Langa in Cape Town, 1930.

Chapter 7

CRICKET *in the* PROVINCES

THE RESULTS OF THE first tournament seem to have been a fair reflection of the playing standards and strength of African cricket in the country by the 1930s. The rural and urban Eastern Cape and the Transvaal were where the numbers and strength lay, with the cities of Cape Town, Bloemfontein and Kimberley providing pockets of support. News reports from throughout the country in *Umteteli wa Bantu* in 1932 give an indication of the activities in each province.

In the Border, for example, ten teams were playing in the leagues of the Gompo Cricket Union servicing the East London area. Gaika CC were the A Division champions and the others were Swallows CC, Brotherly United CC, Peelton CC, Tembu CC and Willows CC. The B Division was made up of Transkei CC, Head of Lion CC, Black Buffaloes CC and Wide Awake CC.[1]

In Port Elizabeth, there were more than ten clubs in 1932. New Brighton had two teams in the league, and the other clubs were St Cyprians, Wide Awake, Gladstone, Fight Forever, Fear Not, Home Lads, Albany and Hard Catch.[2]

In Cape Town, the African clubs had been affiliated to the Metropolitan (Coloured) Cricket Union until 1928 when five clubs decided to combine to form a new Western Province Bantu Cricket Union. They were Home Bachelors, Oriental, Far East, Wanderers and Great Powers. They felt they were not getting a 'square' deal both on the field of play and in administrative matters. Mr B.M. Cebindevu was the first president and Mr Nyangiwe was the first chairman.[3]

In Kimberley, there were six clubs in November 1932, including Dukes, Ottomans, Red Crescents and the newly formed Excelsior, based at Green Point. They played under the original Griqualand West Colonial Cricket Union formed in 1894. (Coloured clubs in the city had broken away to play under the Diamond Fields Colonial Cricket Union.[4]) The Kimberley team went by train to play in the 1932 intertown tournament in East London, stopping over en route for games at Bloemfontein, Burgersdorp, Molteno and Queenstown.[5]

Orange Free State, Natal, Basutoland and North Eastern Districts were granted affiliation at the inaugural SABCB meeting in East London in 1932, but they did not attend the first tournament.

In the OFS, six teams played in the league of the Bloemfontein Bantu Cricket Union, namely Orientals, MCC, Good Hope, Occidentals, Fair Players and the nearby district of Thaba Nchu. Bloemfontein teams also played against Kroonstad, Aliwal North, Kimberley and clubs in Johannesburg in that year.[6]

When the Good Hearted Club from Kroonstad 'inaugurated' its new mat with a match against Good Hope six hundred spectators watched. News reports from the town revealed that Kroonstad had a dynamic social life at the time. They mention a dance in the Location Hall with the Midnight Follies playing, an exhibition boxing match and much political activity, including the affairs of the Advisory Boards, the ANC and the Industrial and Commercial Workers Union (ICU).

The latter had become the first mass organisation ever in the 1920s and its purpose was sometimes explained as 'I see you, white man'.[7]

The African cricketers in this province still seemed to be with the old Barnato Board at this stage. During the run-up to the NRC tournament, the well-known Thomas Mapikela, one of the founders of the African National Congress, was on a committee, together with the 'Native Location Manager' and several other Africans, trying to raise funds for a planned Barnato Tournament.[8]

Although Natal did start participating in the NRC tournaments, there were very few reports of cricket from that province in *Umteteli wa Bantu*. The Natal sports reports usually related to soccer and, in fact, Zulu-speakers from Natal were also prominent in the competitions and boards in Johannesburg. Nevertheless, Natal did start participating in the NRC cricket tournaments. In 1938 the tournament was held in Durban. Natal came second under the captaincy of Don Mtimkhulu, principal of the well-known Adams College.[9]

But the strength of cricket had definitely shifted to the Transvaal by the 1930s. Johannesburg was now firmly established as the economic hub of South Africa and as migrant workers flocked there from all parts of the country a large African urban population started developing. Fixture lists for Sunday 20 November 1932, publicised in the newspapers, showed that there were no fewer than 24 league games involving 48 teams, played mostly at the different mines. (See block on facing page.)[10]

Former students and migrants from the Eastern Cape formed the backbone of this process, both on the playing and administrative side.

The mines sponsored not only the inter-provincial competitions, but also the local leagues. In the *Umteteli wa Bantu* newspaper, financed by the Chamber of Mines, cricket reports from throughout the country were prominently placed next to the latest ructions in the ANC — where a conservative Dr Seme was being challenged by younger opponents — and safety advertisements aimed at 'mine boys'.[11]

For the mines, cricket was part of a marketing strategy and a way of maintaining a stable workforce. For the black players it meant the transplantation of the Eastern Cape traditions, the maintenance of social cohesion amongst migrants from that region and the growth of the game on a national level.

There was also a Saturday league, centred around the Bantu Sports Club, with six teams, including St Peter's College where Oliver Tambo taught before taking up law.[12] The BSC

comprised nine acres of land, with soccer and cricket fields, tennis courts, a clubhouse and an embankment that could seat 5 000 spectators. Situated on old mining land just south of the Central Business District, this was the only recreation area for Africans in Johannesburg proper.[13]

The full-time manager of the club from 1934 was the theatrical Dan Twala, who became legendary in Johannesburg as a soccer official and community worker. Trustees included prominent cricket and soccer personalities like H.B. Piliso, D.M. Denelane, T.T.P. Majola and Richard Msimang. As Cecile Badenhorst has explained in a well written doctoral dissertation, the Bantu Sports Club was one of the few 'unrestricted' African meeting places in Johannesburg and became 'more than a sports club':

Picnics, socials, music shows, musical competitions, choirs, jazz evenings and dances were organised. On Sundays members [of which there were over one thousand] could listen and dance to 'radiogram music' on the Club verandah. The BSC also housed a small library and ran a night school to teach literacy to members.

The Club boasted a pavilion with showers and a large room which was rented out for social functions. A kiosk sold refreshments to spectators and players using the two fields and six tennis courts. On the fields, teams played soccer every Saturday and Sunday ... these same fields hosted cricket, hockey, war dance practice, brass band practice, and any other sport. Boxers trained on the verandah of the Clubhouse. Although women could join and participate in BSC games and clubs, few did. Among the BSC women tennis was popular. The Club also had a successful women's hockey team, where 'girls give vent to animal spirit'.[14]

In its heyday, the Bantu Sports Club hosted 12 000 people at its soccer matches. The club and the more exclusive Bantu Men's Social Centre in Eloff Street extension — both started with funds raised by local missionaries and liberals, working with the City Council and mining groups — were the main social facilities for the Johannesburg black elite in the 1920s and 1930s.[15]

In the recently published biography of Walter and Albertina Sisulu, *In Our Lifetime*, there is a description of their 'glittering' wedding celebration at the BMSC in the early 1940s. The Merry Blackbirds jazz band provided the entertainment and the guests included ANC president, Dr A.B. Xuma, Nelson Mandela and Anton Lembede.[16]

Cricketers operated within this social milieu and cricket in Johannesburg was on solid foundations. *Umteteli wa Bantu* reported in 1937 that there were '50 to 100 clubs playing today from Randfontein to Nigel'.[17]

TRANSVAAL BANTU CRICKET UNION - FIXTURES SUNDAY 20 NOVEMBER, 1932

MANGENA CUP – FIRST LEAGUE:

TEAM	vs	TEAM	VENUE
West Springs	vs	Never Despair	Geduld
GGMA	vs	Van Ryn Deep	VR Deep
New MCC	vs	SACC	Modder East
Never Give Up	vs	Brakpan	Brakpan
Van Ryn Deep A	vs	USOB	New States
Sub Nigel	vs	Modder Bee	Modder Bee

WITWATERSRAND CUP – SECOND LEAGUE:

TEAM	vs	TEAM	VENUE
Never Give Up	vs	Never Despair	Wit Deep
GGMA	vs	Hard Cash	State Mines
Hard Cash A	vs	SACC	State Mines North
Sub Nigel	vs	ERPM	Nigel Shaws
Shaw's XI	vs	Modder Bee	New Modder
ERS	vs	Brakpan East	Geduld
Home Defenders	vs	Van Ryn Estates	Van Ryn Estates

NRC CRICKET LEAGUE – SENIOR SECTION:

TEAM	vs	TEAM	VENUE
Hard Cash	vs	Summer and Jack	Roodepoort
MCC	vs	Randfontein Estates	Randfontein
BSC Stone Breakers	vs	City Deep	Johannesburg
West Rand	vs	Independent B	West Rand
Deep	vs	Willows	Springfield

NRC CRICKET LEAGUE – JUNIOR SECTION:

TEAM	vs	TEAM	VENUE
Hard Cash A	vs	City Deep B	City Deep
Willows B	vs	Randfontein Estates B	Nancefield
OCC A	vs	Fear Not B	Langlaagte
OCC B	vs	Busy Bees B	Crown Mines
Simmer B	vs	Fight for Ever B	Simmer
Randfontein Estates A	vs	Rand Sweeper	Chris Shaft

Sport scenes from the Bantu Men's Social Centre in downtown Johannesburg around World War Two, reflecting the self-confident new urban generations of the 1930s and 1940s. With patronage from the mines, Transvaal won six of the nine Chamber of Mines inter-provincial cricket tournaments up to 1950.

Chapter 8

GOLDEN PROVINCE *of the* 1930s *and* 1940s

———————————— ⬤ ————————————

FROM THE ORGANISATIONAL AND competitive bases sponsored by the gold mining industry in Johannesburg, Transvaal won six of the first nine Chamber of Mines inter-provincial tournaments, before taking a back seat to Western Province and Eastern Province in the 1950s.

The winners of the NRC Trophy up to 1950 were as follows:

1933/34 Transvaal in Johannesburg

1934/35 Transvaal in Port Elizabeth

1935/36 Border in East London

1936/37 Border in Cape Town

1938/39 Transvaal in Durban

1940/41 Transvaal in Port Elizabeth

1946 Transvaal (venue not known)

1947/48 Western Province at Rubusana Park in East London

1950/51 Transvaal in Kimberley[1]

In addition to the African provincial tournaments, the Transvaal Africans played regularly against Indian and coloured clubs and provincial sides.[2] A pioneering Johannesburg Inter-Race Board was formed in 1936. The Inter-Race Board started an annual inter-race league with the Bernard L. Sigamoney Trophy at stake. The Africans showed a high level of competitiveness, winning the title in 1938/39 and being joint holders in 1940/41.[3]

The long-standing Transvaal captain Frank Roro was the outstanding African player of the 1930s and 1940s. Born in Kimberley in 1908, he was introduced to the game by the well-known Hamilton Masiza. In 1931 he came to Johannesburg where he played for the Randfontein mine team 'until the veteran player Robbey Brooker decided he must play for his team, Crown Mines'.[4] Between 1934 and 1951 (Roro pronounced like the Afrikaans *goggo*) scored over 3 000 runs for the Transvaal Bantu team, which he captained from 1938 onwards. This total included 20 centuries. His top provincial score was 228 versus the Transvaal coloured team. His highest league score was 304 versus Main Reef. Altogether, the 'Dusty Bradman', as he was reputedly called, scored over 100 league centuries, with an average of well over 100 per season.[5]

Lawrence Mvumvu, the veteran Soweto player and administrator, played with Roro and was hugely influenced by him. He recalls:

He was on the quiet side, soft spoken. At no time would he boast about his talent. Instead he was keen to help those who needed help. He was humble and dignified. I admired everything he did. He was graceful and unique when he was batting or bowling his off-spinners. He was as good as Eric Rowan or Bruce Mitchell, maybe even better. He played on atrocious wickets, but kept playing straight and his shot placings were outstanding. He was very hungry for runs, and could bat for very long periods in difficult conditions and still managed to look graceful and fluent at all times. Watching Frank play cricket and the way he helped introverted and shy teenagers like myself made me realise that cricket was going to be my game.[6]

By the 1950s the Johannesburg Inter-Race Board had no fewer than nine affiliated groups playing under its auspices. These were the Transvaal Coloured Cricket Union, the Transvaal Bantu Union, Witwatersrand Indian Cricket Union, City and Suburban Independent Cricket Union, North Eastern Transvaal Bantu Cricket Union, Eastern Transvaal Indian and Coloured Cricket Association, Western Transvaal Indian Cricket Union, Eastern Transvaal Indian Cricket Union and Northern Transvaal Indian Cricket Union.[7]

Reports on the Transvaal inter-race competition emphasised the inter-racial harmony that existed, and the need to do away with racial distinctions in future.

The formation of the North Eastern Transvaal African Board in the 1940s reflected the expansion of the game amongst Africans. Starting with a second place in 1948/49, this team regularly did well at the African inter-provincial tournaments, including being champions in 1953/54. In 1952/53 it won the Transvaal inter-race trophy. Eric Fihla and Julius Mahanjana were star batsmen and the opening bowlers, Gidi and Mashinqana, were regarded as the fastest seen since Majola and Masiza in the 1935 Chamber of Mines tournament.[8]

Mr Denelane was the solitary patron of the Inter-Race Board, Piet Gwele and Charles Ngengebule were the life vice-presidents and H.M. Butshingi was one of the vice-presidents.

Piet Gwele was one of the legendary figures of cricket. Born in Tsomo in the Eastern Cape in 1891, he settled in Kimberley with his parents at an early age and became a diamond digger. In the 1910s he moved to the gold mines in Johannesburg, working as a clerk. It was reported that 'he played for the "Coloureds" as there were no Africans playing the game'.[9] He started the Dobson team and was 'co-founder' of the Transvaal Bantu Cricket Union, which he also captained. Gwele's fielding abilities were legendary and gave rise to a Xhosa cricketing term which is still used today. When someone does badly in the field, they will say '*Yagqoboza nakwu Gwele*' (literally, 'it burst through also with Gwele'), implying that even the great man dropped the odd catch and had an off day.[10]

'Oom Piet' Gwele, Transvaal provincial captain and long-time president, one of the legends of African cricket, 1930s-1950s.

Known universally as 'Oom Piet', Gwele's career and character showed how cricket was welded into the lifestyle and identity of the black elite of the mid-20th century, and how they were proudly middle class and conservatively 'African' at the same time. In one tribute to him, the writer explained:

'Oom Piet' taught the mineworkers, some of them very raw indeed, the value of sport and the interpretation of the old adage, 'A sound mind in a sound body'.

Although he was cricket personified, Mr Gwele never gave free reigns (sic) to social intercourse between man and boy. This was brought about by his strict enforcement of his tribal rites. Many a player that found his way into his cricket eleven had to go through the popular Xhosa's university of manhood.[11]

This 'father of African cricket' remained president of the Transvaal Bantu Cricket Union until 1953. With his health failing, and the union not having held its annual awards event or AGM, he was finally voted out of office and replaced by Moses Nyangiwe, formerly president of the Transvaal Rugby Union and vice-president of the South African Rugby Board.

'Already the trains travelling between George Goch and Randfontein and between Pimville and Faraday Stations are being used as lobbies by several caucus groups', reported the editor of *African Sports*, Robert Resha, in the build-up to Gwele's controversial removal from office.[12]

Although he walked out of the meeting while the votes were being counted, peace was soon restored. 'Oom Piet' soon afterwards gracefully agreed to a special testimonial match in his honour. It was between the combined Transvaal and North Eastern Transvaal Africans XIs and the Transvaal Indians at the Natalspruit Ground. Speakers from 'the various sports organisations of South Africa' paid tribute to him and he was presented with an illuminated address and a gift of ten guineas. Robert Resha who, incidentally, became a prominent ANC leader and one of those charged in the famous Treason Trial of the 1950s, described this as 'the highest tribute ever to be paid to an African sportsman in this country'.[13] The players joined in the royal send off. Replying to the 237 for nine declared of the Transvaal Indian team, the combined African team notched up 165 for one, with Julius Mahanjana 81 not out.

The 'dusty Bradman', Frank Roro (back row, third right), pictured with the trophy-winning Crown Mines club side.

Besides people like Piet Gwele and Frank Roro there were many other larger-than-life characters who devoted decades of their lives to cricket, showing the deep grounding and love for the game in the African communities. There are several examples from the time of the first board and first tournament in the early 1930s. Hamilton Masiza, convenor of the inaugural meeting and first secretary in 1932, was SABCB president going into the 1950s. F.H.M. Zwide, a century maker for New Brighton and an Eastern Province delegate in 1932, was still involved as SABCB president in the mid-1950s. W.B. Ntshekisa was one of the top players in the Eastern Province in the 1930s and his younger brother, Samson was still at the top, aged over 50, when the first multi-racial cricket with whites was played in the 1970s. D.M. Denelane, first secretary of the Transvaal Bantu Cricket Union and one of the few Transvaal-born cricket leaders, was secretary and then treasurer of the SABCB in the 1940s. At one stage he was also president of the national Football Association, with Chief Albert Lutuli as one of the executive committee members. There are many other examples.

With a national organisation, regular provincial tournaments, 50 to 100 clubs in the Transvaal, and the game deeply established in the Eastern Cape, African cricket was clearly flourishing on the eve of World War Two.

Cricket remained the most popular game among the black middle class. T.M. Mweli Skota's *African Yearly Register*, the who's who of South African black life, listed as many as 69 people who mentioned an interest in sport. Of these, 44.5 percent described cricket as their favourite sport. Tennis players (30 percent) and footballers (22.4 percent) – including both rugby and soccer – followed.[14]

The international anti-apartheid activists, Robert Archer and Antoine Boullion, whose 1982 book on sport and racism was for years a standard work, saw these statistics as indicating that the black middle class elite followed white society in ascribing class attributes to sporting activity. 'This surprisingly marked preference for cricket is a clear sign of this, for as we have seen cricket was explicitly a "gentleman's game" with gentlemanly values.' At that stage, they pointed out, sport still 'expressed the values of a novel and attractive way of life, which (until the 1940s) held out hopes of assimilation and progress'.[15]

Indeed, so confident was the South African Bantu Board that it was now seeking international competition. At its fifth annual conference, in April 1937, the meeting resolved that 'avenues be explored to find a way of winning recognition from the South African Cricket [Association] and the MCC so that possible games could be arranged'.[16]

Cricket and rugby shared the same base and the same mission and middle class tradition.
Advertisements aimed at black sportsmen (and their wives) in the 1930s.

Chapter 9

ONGOING RUGBY *and* CRICKET CONNECTIONS

───────────────── ◉ ─────────────────

RUGBY AND CRICKET maintained their close connections in the 1930s and 1940s. Both sports fed off the same base and the same mission and middle class tradition in the African communities. Following the example of cricket, football and athletics, African rugby players broke away from the South African Coloured Rugby Football Union in 1935 to start the South African Bantu Rugby Board. Like its cricket counterparts, the Bantu Rugby Board also started running its own regular inter-provincial tournaments. These, too, were sponsored by the Chamber of Mines and were for the Native Recruiting Corporation (or NRC) Cup.

The Eastern Cape, and especially Port Elizabeth, was once again very much in the forefront of these moves. It was local administrators who formed a committee to discuss the formation of a South African Bantu Rugby Board early in 1935. Further discussions followed at the inter-town rugby tournament in East London. The Board was formally launched in Port Elizabeth later in the year while the inter-provincial cricket tournament was being held in the city. The Port Elizabeth people were undoubtedly taking advantage of the fact that sport administrators from various parts of the country were due in the city. This showed at once how tightly knit the African elite of the time was, and how inter-linked the organisation and interest in the middle class games of rugby and cricket were amongst Africans.[1]

The first president of the South African Bantu Rugby Board was J.M. Dippa of Port Elizabeth. He later became Native Welfare Officer for the Municipal Native Affairs Department in Bloemfontein. The secretary was Halley Plaatje from Kimberley. Also prominent in cricket administration, he was the son of Sol Plaatje, and the nephew of Isaiah Bud Mbelle, one of the driving forces behind the first national rugby and cricket bodies around the turn of the century.[2]

The first inter-provincial tournament to be organised by the new SABRB was held in Kimberley in 1936. At stake was the new NRC Cup. Eastern Province and Transvaal shared the honours after the final ended in a goalless draw. The other teams were the newly established Northern Eastern Districts Union, with its headquarters in Aliwal North, and the home team Griqualand West. For some reason Western Province, Border and Natal did not take part, even though Border had defeated Natal only the month before in a game in East London attended by 4 000 people.[3]

This was the first of 28 inter-provincial rugby tournaments to be held in the next 38 years up to 1974. The inter-provincial tournaments involved a grinding schedule of matches over a period of one week. Sometimes teams played more than one match a day, particularly after a knockout competition for the Parton's Cup was added to the league format for the NRC Cup.[4]

Transvaal did not dominate in rugby in the same way it did in cricket. Rather, Eastern Province was consistently the champion province, winning eight of the tournaments between 1936 and 1953.[5] The news reports of the 1940 inter-provincial rugby tournament in East London give a good indication (as in cricket) of the ambience of these events and the level of organisation required in staging them.

Eastern Province Bantu Rugby Board team and provincial champions, 1947. (Back row, left to right) W. Tsotsi, M. Ngcelwane, M. Mvakwendlu, Z. Katiya, M. Zinto, G. Snyman, J. Daniels. (Standing) F.W. Mtyobo, F. Bacela, M. Titi, E.J. Mboya, M. Manana, M.Y. Meintjies, H. Mjekula (vice-president). (Seated) M. Madolo (chaplain), C.M. Singapi (secretary), A.R. Daniels (captain), A.B. Ntsinga (manager), A.Z. Lamani (vice-captain), A.A. Moyake (president). (Front row) G. Matthews, M. Yili, C.B. Manana, Div. Tshangana.

Considerable effort went into preparing for the tournament. The Eastern Province team was selected after trials involving teams from Grahamstown, Uitenhage and Port Elizabeth. Similarly, the Border team included 'many students from the Native colleges of the Ciskei'. The cost of organising the tournament was put at £200. Because of the war the Board decided not to send round the customary subscription lists for financial assistance, but depended instead on gate takings. The usual enthusiasm for sport, and its social importance, was once again underlined: each of the six teams, consisting of squads of 25 players, played every day for a week and they were also entertained at a 'reception and dance' held in their honour in the East Bank location.

Power relations in the wider community were once again in evidence:

When the Mayor opens the tournament at 2.30 p.m. today, with him will be the Native Commissioner, Mr D.G. Hartmann, the manager of Urban Native Affairs, Mr R.C. Cook, and the secretary of the [white] Border Rugby Union, Mr H.W. Webb. There will be a separate entrance to the grounds for Europeans.[6]

The white officials said that the local council 'had always had the welfare of the natives at heart ... They would also be pleased to hear [that] ... the chairman of the Native Affairs Committee was quickly recovering after his serious illness (Applause)'.[7]

It would only be in the 1950s that black cricket and rugby players started challenging more aggressively this sort of paternalism and discrimination.

Prominent Eastern Province rugby players from the Union RFC in 1934, namely the captain, A.F. Magaba (left), and fly-half, China Manana (right), who also played cricket for Eastern Province.

Eastern Province, provincial rugby champions 1953. (Back row, left to right) L. Mokonenyane, R. Maduba, G. Nkongo and J. Thomas. (Standing) C.B. Manana (manager), C. Nonganga, G. Mgubela, A. Makwela, W. Maboza, D. Dunjane, G. Noqoli (captain), M. Zinto, C.S. Kapi. (Middle row) E.K. Majola, M. Mokonenyane, L. Yose, M.N. Solilo (vice-captain), G.K.R. Xotyine, D.S. Kondile, S. Malie. (Front row) D.P. Williams, M. Mpolongwane, W.G. Mona, N.M. Singapi, E.W. Pandle.

Halley Plaatje (left), first secretary of the South African Bantu Rugby Board in the 1930s, was the son of Sol Plaatje (centre) and nephew of Isaiah Bud Mbelle, first secretary of the SACCB, started around the turn of the century. On the right is brother Richard Plaatje.

*The 1950s heralded in a new era of inter-race co-operation in cricket,
going with a determination to start providing equal opportunities
and international exposure for black cricketers.*

Chapter 10

SACBOC *and the* MOVES TOWARDS NON-RACIALISM, 1947-1959

———————————————— ⬤ ————————————————

B
Y THE 1940s, BLACK cricketers were divided on the national level into four different racial bodies. The old South African Coloured Cricket Board (SACCB), or Barnato Board, formed in 1902 for all 'non-white' cricketers, was virtually comatose. It had not organised an inter-provincial tournament since 1932. Older spokespeople sometimes made statements protesting it was not dead, but this was more a reflection of the loyalty of some provincial affiliates who could not find a home in the other organisations than of the reality. In the early 1940s three of these — Western Province, Transvaal and Griqualand West — started to resuscitate the old Barnato Board. In December 1945, they got it on its feet again by organising the first Barnato Tournament in 13 years in Cape Town.[1]

The South African Independent Coloured Cricket Board (SAICCB), which had broken away in 1926, probably because of religious differences between Christians and Muslims (and perhaps dissatisfaction in the Cape over the permanent headquarters being in Kimberley), organised its own tournaments with the Sir David Harris Trophy as the prize. The SAICCB was for Christians only, and it was also common for its clubs to apply the 'pencil test' to its members. This meant that dark-skinned people (with hair types that a pencil could not slide through) were not welcome as members.[2]

The South African Bantu Cricket Board, as noted in a previous chapter, catered for Africans-only from 1932 onwards.

The South African Indian Cricket Union, formed in 1940, was the last of the ethnic unions. The first president was S.L. Singh, also a founder member of the South African Soccer Federation. Advocate Albert Christopher, who qualified at Lincoln's Inn in England and participated in passive resistance campaigns with Mahatma Gandhi, presented the Christopher Floating Trophy for the Indian provincial tournaments.[3] Perhaps because of their small numbers, Indian cricketers did not support the formation of different ethnic boards. However, they went ahead after trying unsuccessfully to revive the Barnato Board in 1938. The SAICU had difficulty establishing a national presence. Natal and Transvaal, where the majority of the Indian population lived, were the strongest provinces. Each won four tournaments between 1941 and 1958. Other provinces struggled to find the five clubs which were the minimum qualification for provincial affiliation.

The Indian administrators, relatively well resourced and influenced by the passive resistance campaigns of the 1940s, which presaged the mass defiance of the 1950s, were perhaps the most forward-looking in the country.

In January 1945 the Indian Union decided at a meeting in Durban that attempts should be made to set up a new co-ordinating South African Cricket Board of Control. After two years of negotiations, a body by that name was formed in July 1947, commonly known by its acronym, SACBOC.[4] The founders decided that SACBOC would be a federal body. The respective ethnic affiliates maintained their separate identities, but agreed to join forces to hold so called 'inter-race' tournaments and promote the interests of black cricketers. All the existing black bodies joined SACBOC. (Initially the old SACCB or Barnato Board was excluded, but when it agreed to give up its historic leading role and change its name to the South African Malay Cricket Board it was accepted.)

The first president of the new federal structure was Bob Pavadai of the Indian Union.

The African administrators enthusiastically supported the formation of SACBOC. At the historic meeting in 1947 to form SACBOC, the South African Bantu Board was represented by the president, Hamilton Masiza, and the secretary, D.M. Denelane. Mr Masiza became one of the SACBOC vice-presidents.

The enthusiasm of the African Board for the new directions was well demonstrated by the secretary, Mr Denelane. In a special message to fellow cricketers in 1947, he congratulated those seeking inter-racial unity and emphasised, moreover, that 'we should no longer have teams comprising separate races'. He continued, 'We do not want three or four Transvaal teams to play against three or four Natal teams all based on racial separations,' and said he was 'looking forward to the time when individuals will have the right of choosing to play for whatever club they wish. This is what the non-European world is crying for ...' According to Denelane, the Inter-Race Cricket Board set up in Johannesburg in the mid-1930s had 'exceeded all expectations' and shown this was the way to go.[5]

The new arrangements in cricket related to broader developments in society. In 1948 the National Party won the whites-only general election, inaugurating the era of formal apartheid. Long-standing discrimination was extended and legalised in a way that was unique in world politics. Deepening apartheid soon gave rise to its antithesis: a powerful national movement in favour of democracy and non-racialism in South Africa.

In 1949, the ANC adopted a new Programme of Action which rejected traditional moderate (and unsuccessful) methods of protest such as petitions and deputations to the authorities, and proposed the use of direct action through boycotts, strikes and civil disobedience in a 'mass struggle for national freedom'. The ANC joined with other pro-democracy Indian, coloured and white groups in order to ensure a broad campaign against apartheid. In 1955 the Congress Alliance adopted the Freedom Charter which spelled out a new democratic vision emphasising that 'South Africa belongs to all who live in it, black and white'.[6]

Once again, both the application of apartheid and the intensification of resistance against it had a direct bearing on developments in sport. From the late 1940s onwards, racially compartmentalised black sports bodies, including those in cricket, rugby and soccer, sought to establish unity amongst themselves. They began to seek international contacts, and to protest against discrimination much more forcefully than they had before.

These developments in sport were in many ways similar to the multi-racial co-operation happening at a political level in the Congress Alliance during the 1950s.

During this decade, the various racial bodies started selecting national teams for the first time. The spur in cricket was SACBOC's decision to start national inter-race cricket tournaments. The first one was held in Johannesburg at the famous Natalspruit grounds at Easter in 1951. Each federation chose a national team to participate.

In the same year the first of more than 20 rugby 'tests' between the South Africa Bantus and the South African Coloureds was played in front of 15 000 spectators in Port Elizabeth.

These 'tests' between the various 'non-white' bodies became regular events. They generated great enthusiasm and big crowds turned out to watch them. It is clear from the names Bantu Springboks and Coloured Springboks, as well as the colours and badges in both rugby and cricket, that black sportspeople were both imitating and aspiring to the test status enjoyed by white Springbok teams. The African rugby team's badge was a map of Africa with a jumping springbok in it. The badge of cricket's federal body, SACBOC, was a direct imitation of the white SACA's springbok head.

As co-operation between black cricketers deepened, they also started negotiating with international associations for reciprocal tours. Cricket reached out to India, Pakistan, Kenya and the West Indies. In 1951, SACBOC secretary, Rashid Varachia, travelled to India to tie up a 12-match tour, including three 'tests', but this never materialised.[7] SACBOC president Bob Pavadai believed that greater unity was the only way of ensuring that 'our vision of placing the Non-European cricket on an international pedestal will be reached'.[8] Rugby sought contact with the New Zealand Maoris and Fiji. This was part of a broader move by black South Africans for international recognition and opportunities.

Several sportsmen went abroad and met with success from 1948 onwards. The best known of these were the weight-lifter,

Dressed against the cold, delegates of the different racial bodies meet to discuss the formation of a new co-ordinating body for cricket, SACBOC, sometime between 1947 and 1951. With backs to the camera are the acting secretary, Rashid Varachia (left) and acting president, Bob Pavadai (right) from the SAICU. Facing the camera are (left to right) E. Khamisa (SACCB), G.S. Davies (SACCB), A.E. Docrat (SACCB), H.M. J. Masiza (SABCB), D.M. Denelane (SABCB), Rev B.L.S. Sigamoney (SAICU) and J.P. Abrams (SACCA).

Ron Eland, who represented Britain at the Olympics, and Jake Tuli who made history when he won the Empire fly-weight title in 1952.[9]

Given the chance to travel by his brother's employer at American Express, Tuli defeated the experienced British and Empire champion, Teddy Gardner, in a bout in Newcastle. He campaigned overseas until 1958 before returning permanently to South Africa and settling down as a respected member of the Orlando community in Soweto.[10]

Many sportspeople were to follow in the footsteps of Eland and Tuli in seeking opportunities that were not available to them at home. Those who met with significant success included Steve 'Kalamazoo' Mokone and Albert Johanssen (soccer), David Samaai (tennis), Winty Pandle, from Port Elizabeth, and Goolam Abed (rugby league), Cecil Abrahams and Basil D'Oliveira (cricket), Precious McKenzie (weight-lifting) and Papwa Sewgolum (golf).[11]

In 1956 the non-racial South African Table Tennis Board became the first black organisation to be recognised ahead of the whites-only body when it was made a member of the International Table Tennis Federation. Not surprisingly, this move caused a sensation and led to the apartheid government issuing its first formal sports policy forbidding inter-racial contests.[12]

Gradually, black sportspeople were moving in the direction of demanding equal opportunities on the playing field.

In 1956, SACBOC organised a historic tour to South Africa by the Kenya Asians. The tourists had six players with experience of first-class cricket in India and Pakistan, including Shakoor Ahmed who had represented Pakistan in England two years earlier. They played three three-day 'test' matches and nine games against provincial opposition. The visit was reciprocated in 1958 when a South African team captained by Basil D'Oliveira toured East Africa.[13]

In 1958 a new era in cricket dawned when SACBOC decided to become a united non-racial body. The historic decision was taken on 27 January 1958, after the fourth and final inter-race tournament in Cape Town. At a meeting of all the affiliated national bodies it was decided that racial forms of organising should be abolished in SACBOC.[14]

Henceforth all cricketers would fall under one provincial body and one national body. 'The struggle for integration on the cricket field is now over,' wrote one journalist. 'The result is a precedent for other sporting bodies which are debating the same problem. National cricket teams will be selected on merit not race.'[15]

In the rest of *African Game* we trace the story of cricket from this period of the 1950s onwards by following the progress of one player and his family, namely Eric Majola from New Brighton. Unfolding organisational developments merge

Inter-racial co-operation in sport in the 1950s was a reflection of the broader co-operation occurring in the Congress Alliance in politics.
The South African Bantu and Coloured Springboks line up before the historic first rugby 'test' match
at Green Point Common, Cape Town, 1951.

The South African African Football Association team versus the South African Coloured team at Wembley
Stadium, Johannesburg, 26 September 1953, during the Golden Jubilee celebrations of the South African
Indian Football Association. W. Msomi is the player with the ball. The Africans won 7-4.

with biography and family narratives to give an intimate insight of how black and African cricketers experienced apartheid and responded to it in the dark years after 1948 when racism became formal state policy in a way that was unique in the world. By focusing on the micro details like this, an intimate picture of African sport emerges, illuminating the personal ambitions and characteristics of individuals, the nuances of how cricket was played at different levels, the impact of the game on many different areas of life, and the broader influences that in turn shaped it. Exciting connections and rich narratives inform us how things worked at the level of the family, local community, clubs and province, and we get a close up view of the historic inter-racial matches and co-operation of the 1950s.

The remarkable Majola family from New Brighton township in Port Elizabeth, who are probably as well known in the black communities as the famous Pollock cricketing family from the same city, have been in the forefront of national cricket developments for over 50 years.

Eric Majola was a sporting legend in the 1950s and 1960s. A 'Bantu Springbok' in both rugby and cricket, he is still referred to by old timers as a fly-half in the same mould as Hansie Brewis, Keith Oxlee and the great Cliff Morgan of Wales.

Eric's eldest son, Khaya Majola, became one of the leading players in South Africa in the 1970s and 1980s, and also one of the top administrators in the 1990s. Picked for 'South Africa' by two of the ten national boards referred to in this book, he went on to have a distinguished first-class career of three-day matches spanning 17 seasons. In the process he set up a record second to none – the most first-class matches ever, the most first-class catches, the second highest number of first-class runs, and the fifth highest number of first-class wickets. He became one of a select group of three all-rounders in a period of two decades who made over 2 000 runs and took over 200 wickets. After dying prematurely of cancer, his contribution to South African cricket was recognised in 2001 when the long-standing national schools week – the Coca Cola Week – was named the Coca Cola Khaya Majola Week.[16]

Younger brother Gerald Majola also gained national honours in cricket and provincial colours in rugby. On 1 January 2001 he became Chief Executive Officer of the United Cricket Board of South Africa, responsible for the daily running of the game in this country.

There is an African custom that says, '*Umntu ngumntu nga-banyabantu*', ('a person is a person through other people').

Boxing champion Jake Tuli, guest of honour at the Indian versus African game at Natalspruit, Johannesburg, 10 October 1954. Shaking his hand is Rev Bernard Sigamoney and standing next to him are boxing promoter Jack Bennet and Dan Twala. At the back are linesman Moothoo and officials Bob Pavery and Sydney Siphanya.

So, in telling the story of Eric, Khaya and Gerald Majola, this book also attempts to tell the story of their family, the particular community in which they lived and something of what they learned from and shared with other cricketers.

Being black people living in apartheid South Africa meant that the Majolas and others classified as 'Bantu' could not be delivered in the same hospital ward as a white child. Could not live in the same suburb. Go to the same school. Have the same job. Enter the same cinema. Swim on the same beach. Sit on the same park bench. Glide stiff-legged and laughing down the same slide in a public playground. Enter shops through the same entrance. Use the same railway bridge. Travel in the same train compartment, or coach. Be served at the same post office counter. Join the same sports clubs. Play in the same sports team. Sit on the main pavilion at matches. Or be selected for their country to play in official test matches.

What was it like for those cricketers on the wrong side of the colour line under apartheid? How did they play and organise themselves? How did they relate their sporting activities to what was happening in the society at large, and what choices did they have to make? By telling the story of an African game through the experiences of a family that has been at the coal-face for five decades, the aim is to bring alive and make more interesting than any straightforward organisational history could ever do the amazing and still little-known history of those who played on the dusty township fields during the dark days of apartheid.

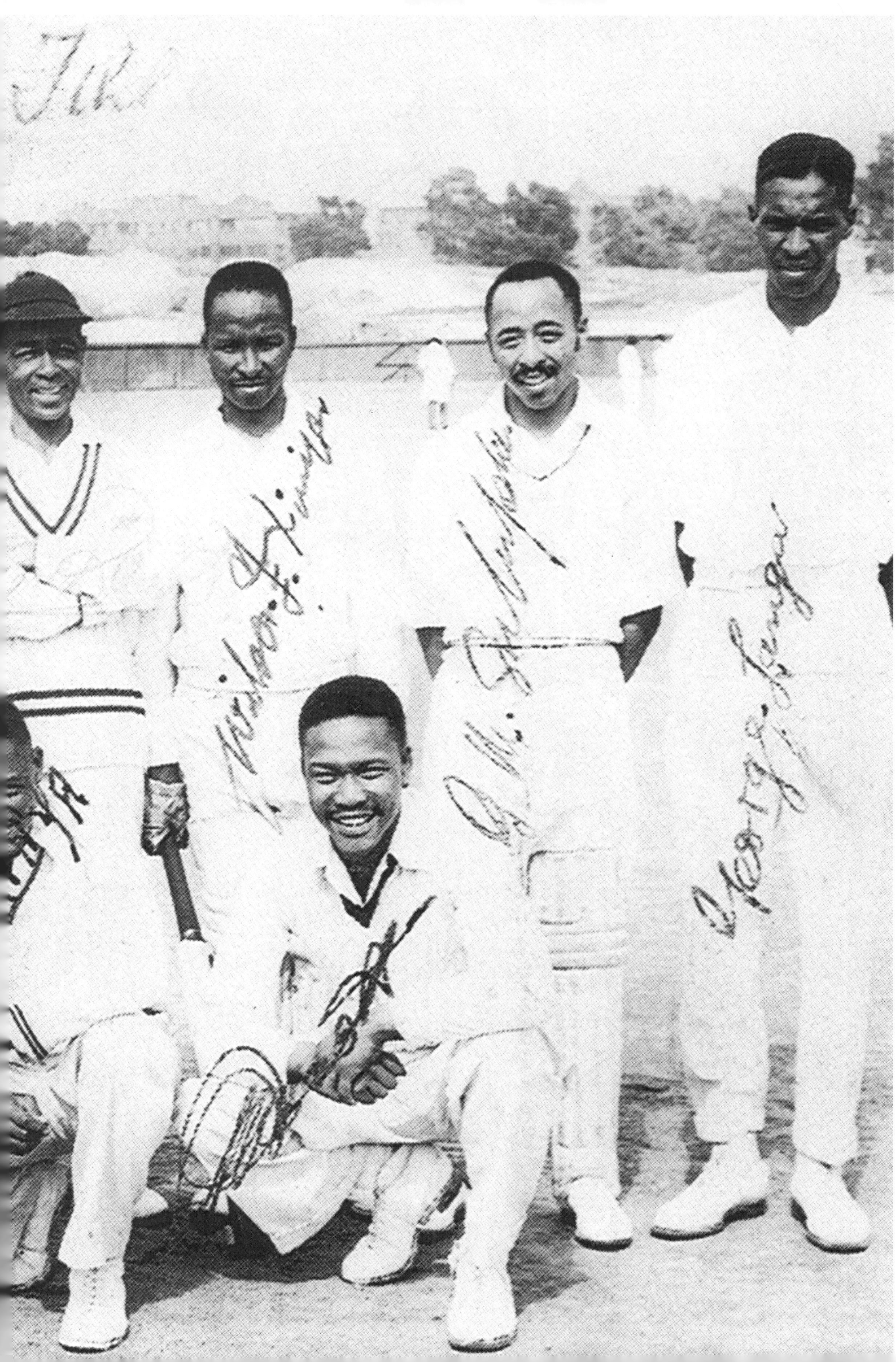

Part Four

ERIC MAJOLA AND THE BLACK SPRINGBOKS OF THE 1950s

Eric Khululekile Majola (also known as Kholekile or 'Kokkie'), one of the best African cricket all-rounders of the 1950s and 1960s, and 'still regarded by most African critics as South Africa's best fly-half since the days of Hannes Brewis', according to a 1959 newspaper report.

Chapter 11

CLAN

━━━━━━━━━━━━━━ ◉ ━━━━━━━━━━━━━━

ERIC MAJOLA LIVED IN NEW BRIGHTON township. To get there, you have to drive eight kilometres from the Port Elizabeth city centre. It has several hundred thousand inhabitants, but there is no signboard indicating where to turn off. Even eight years after democracy. It is the ugly child hidden from view, a typical South African picture.

Take the Grahamstown road. Put on your flicker at the quaintly named Deal Party Estate. Straight down through the factory area. Cellar Master. Bonnita. Other names that don't appear in television ads. Then you make two lefts and enter over a strangely crooked little S-bend bridge.

New Brighton is rough and energetic. On the first corner of Ferguson Street, a pulsing, two-kilometre-long artery, is the landmark Engen service station. It belongs to the famous sports personality, Dan Qeqe, who also has a stadium named after him in nearby Zwide. It seems there is always a car filling up here.

Even before you get to the garage, you see the signs of life. 'Iinkomo, iigusha, iinkuku zikoapha.' The advert is painted in big, hand-daubed letters on a large-blocked concrete wall. It says there are cattle, sheep and chickens available here. Next to Uncle Dan's garage, two little outlets beckon to customers. One is Fernando's Chicken House and Taverna. The other is Pinky Hair Design, with a telephone and fax number writ large. The claims of these establishments seem somewhat extravagant.

Across the way, on the right-hand side of Ferguson Road, stretches the old Railway compound, now converted into rough flatland. It is walled in behind murals and up-to-date graffiti: 'Don't fight families with Aids. Fight Aids.' Tattered plastic bags fly restlessly from the barbed wire above the asbestos segments.

On the left-hand side of the road is a thin stretch of houses called Thembalethu, 'Our Hope'. This is a middle class area, built in the 1960s. The neat houses at once proclaim their difference from and their belonging to this environment.

Dan Qeqe lives in the house next to his garage. In the adjoining plot, diagonally behind him, is number eight Ferguson Road, the home of the Majolas. I enter the driveway, where two other cars are parked. It is separated only by a thin row of trees from the giant PPC cement factory, which dominates the skyline around these parts. The cement factory looks like a futuristic film-set painted in grey and rust. Even on this Sunday morning, the tall concrete tower is emitting a steady smoky-white plume.

This driveway was the children's cricket pitch, I am told straight away by the welcoming party. The small garden is lawned. On it are a few neat clumps of flax and an array of bulbs which will bring colour when summer arrives. The pathway is polished, triangular red and black, in an old-fashioned way.

I am ushered into a small lounge to meet Mrs Milase Majola. She is the family head, having raised five children on her own since the death of her husband some 30 years ago. On the wallpapered walls, around the clock, are certificates and a trophy which tell of a lifetime spent in the Girl Guide Movement, and in service of the community. There is also a certificate from eldest son Khaya and his wife Nosiseko to the 'number one mother in the world'. On the TV set stands a small bust of Nelson Mandela. The kind you could pick up easily on any street a few years ago, but which are now scarce.

I can already sense the discipline, the steady politeness and sense of identity that went into shaping the sporting family whose story I am writing about.

The house is a buzz of activity in Xhosa and English as Milase starts talking into the tape recorder. I have chosen an inopportune time to come. There is an important church gathering today. Like so many times before, she is in charge of catering.

But this does not put her off. She enthusiastically launches into the family history.

Eric was born in 1930 and lived all his life in New Brighton, except for his two years studying for a teacher's diploma at Healdtown College near Fort Beaufort in 1950 and 1951.

Eric's family on his father's side originally came from Natal. They were from the Ndlovu clan, which means elephant in Zulu. His grandfather, John, moved down with his employer and eventually ran a blacksmith's business in Commercial Road 'as you came into town from the New Brighton side'.

Eric's father's name was Mvula ('rain'). He and his brothers worked in the family business, and later in various factories 'as PE grew'.[1]

The Ndlovus lived in the mixed-race township of Korsten, comfortable with its different patois. Here the family name was changed to Oliphant, Afrikaans for *ndlovu* or elephant. This was a common practice in apartheid South Africa. Bureaucrats who were not bothered, gave you a convenient name, as happened with the Ndlovus, according to Skumbuzo Oliphant.[2] Or people changed their names themselves to escape bureaucratic complications in a racialised society which discriminated most against Africans. People were forced to be creative to avoid obstacles in the cities and changing one's name was a way to get around the restrictions of the system. Coloured people, for instance, were not subjected to the pass laws. That is how it came to pass that many families got different names, like the Zulu Mthimkulus (Big Trees) who became Grootbooms.

But Eric, whose second name was Khululekile ('freed from bondage'), used neither Ndlovu nor Oliphant for a surname. He became a Majola, adopting his mother's maiden name instead. He grew up in the home of his maternal grandmother, Ellen Majola, at Block 11, White Location, one of the older parts of New Brighton.

Known as Mamsukwini, after her clan name, grandmother Majola was one of the first midwives in New Brighton. Dressed in her familiar white apron and white *doek* (scarf), she was apparently a 'well-recognised' figure in the township, someone to whom doctors would refer people.

Eric was born out of wedlock. This is the reason why he lived with Mamsukwini. In Xhosa custom, a child born out

Confident as young Madibas in their suits. Eric Majola and Dan Qeqe as young men.

of marriage belongs to the mother's family. When his mother, Emily, eventually married his father Mvula Oliphant, the other children took the name Oliphant and moved out with their parents. But Eric stayed at Mamsukwini's house and also kept his mother's name, Majola.

Mamsukwini's grandchildren still live in the modest brick house at Block 11 where Eric grew up. Today its backyard is swollen thick with corrugated iron extensions. Family members reaching adulthood, generation after generation, have needed their own space. Otherwise the street is more or less as it was then.[3]

Milase's family history also confounds conventional South African explanations of identity. Her maternal grandfather was a Scottish missionary called Griffiths and her grandmother a Sotho woman. That is why some of the Majolas are so fair-skinned, she explains. 'Look at this photo of Eric's funeral,' she says, pointing to a faded cutting from the *Weekend World* newspaper, where a grief stricken Milase is being supported by her mother.

Grace Shai married Wallace Moyake from Grahamstown and their daughter Milase was born there in 1932. A few

Growing up with the game. Eric and Milase Majola's eldest son, Khaya, batting in the garden at home.

years later the Moyakes moved to Port Elizabeth. They settled in Walmer Township before being forcibly relocated to 249 Dubula Street in New Brighton around 1938.[4] Milase was 'community educated' at churches before going to Molefe Higher Primary School and St Matthew's College near the village of Keiskammahoek outside King Williams Town.

Dan Qeqe met Eric Majola when he moved from Fort Beaufort in 1946 to school in Port Elizabeth. It was the start of a life-long friendship. They studied together at Newell High, played rugby together for Spring Rose and Eastern Province, courted together, became pillars of the community together and, eventually, neighbours, with their back doors connected. A photograph of them in their youth shows them to be confident, physical, snappily dressed and as handsome as a young Madiba in his suit. Any mother-in-law would have loved them.

Eric was one standard ahead, in Grade 2, when Dan arrived in Port Elizabeth in 1946. Dan remembers the cricket games that were played 'right through the year with this soft ball' between the White Location and the Red Location. 'Then we started schools cricket at Newell High.

This chappie was a star from the word go. I still have a picture of him in shorts and white tackies. Grey Mgubela was another star who played good cricket'.[5]

A number of the players from Newell went to Healdtown with Eric and earned provincial colours there. When they came back to Port Elizabeth in the early 1950s they joined the New Brighton Cricket Club.

Of Eric's rugby, Dan recalls:

Let me start with him when we were playing inter-classroom matches at interval ... we used to take our blazers and turn them around ... Man, big chaps wanted to tackle this chap. He would dummy you. He would dodge you. Hey, the chappies were cross. They said, no, they're going to get this bugger. They never got him.[6]

But, although Eric showed talent at an early age, it was only when he was at Healdtown College that he started playing rugby seriously. He immediately became a star. When he returned to Port Elizabeth after completing his studies, 'it wasn't long and he played for the province'. Dan summed up his fly-half play as follows:

He was an intelligent fly-half in all respects ... He had an eye on territorial advantage ... He was also an accurate kicker ... He was so sure of his drop kicking ... Even if it's a sharp angle. He was sure he would make a drop goal. And, again, he was a student of rugby. He knew when to give his centres. He knew when to grubber kick. He knew when to punt ahead. And you would find sharp flanks very, very bitter to get him. No, not with Eric, he would damage them to pieces.[7]

Milase met Eric when she was a student at St Matthew's and he was at nearby Healdtown. 'We would meet as home-boys and home-girls going to college on the same train.' Then they both started teaching together at Pendla Primary School, which later changed its name to Johnson Marwanqa. She explains, 'We were at the same school and he would walk me back to my home in Dubula Street every afternoon. One day he said, "We can walk and walk and not drop each other off," and that was that.'[8]

Eric and Milase had their first child, Eldridge Khaya Majola, in May 1953. They married the next year and moved in to their own house at 17 Mtika Street, close to Newell High School. Khaya was followed by his brother Tozie in 1956 and sister Nomonde early in 1958. Mongezi Gerald Gaylor Majola, who was to become the CEO of the UCBSA, arrived in 1959, and Vuyo in 1962. A sixth child, Julius Majola, the son of Eric's grandmother's brother, Mncedi, and therefore a 'brother' in African culture, also grew up with the family. He was Tozie's contemporary.

The Mtika Street building is still there, but today it houses the New Brighton Islamic Centre. It is just a few

Sports stars, teachers and respected members of New Brighton social set in the 1950s.
Photographs from the Majola family album. Eric (left) and friends at the family home.

hundred yards from eMlotheni Memorial Park. This is where political gatherings were held during the apartheid years, and where the remains of six struggle heroes were reinterred in 1998.

Vuyisile Mini went to the gallows singing freedom songs after being sentenced to death on trumped up charges. The plaque at eMlotheni remembers him and the others of the 'first detachment of the glorious people's army (Mkonto we Sizwe) butchered by the apartheid forces' in two sets of hangings in November 1964 and July 1965.

People still recall how, after the remains were brought down from Pretoria, a convoy of vehicles met them outside the city limits and escorted them back to their final resting place at home. In New Brighton, it seems from the Majolas, you are never alone.

In the late 1950s, the young Majola family moved to a house in Avenue E, Roseville, where they remained for ten years or so before the final move to 8 Ferguson Road.

The Roseville house was big. It was next to the railway line and formerly occupied by a white family. Gerald remembers the big playing area they had. And how they used to get 'amapetya – what you call it in English, marbles', from the white kids across the road.[9] These must have been the traders or officials who were forced to leave when the Group Areas Act was promulgated in the early 1950s. Later, one of the few black doctors in Port Elizabeth, Dr Siyolo Nyoka, and his family moved in as neighbours. His son Mtutuzeli, who became a doctor too, is a former

president of the Gauteng Cricket Board and member of the executive committee of the United Cricket Board. He grew up with the Majola boys and remembers with a sense of awe how they excelled at sport.

The house in Avenue E is a few hundred metres from the Red Location, where the children started their schooling at Jarvis Gqamlana Primary. This is the oldest part of New Brighton, built just after the Anglo-Boer South African War with red zinc materials taken from the English concentration camp for the Boers at Uitenhage. It is a ragged, working class area, with those same red materials, nearly faded to rust after more than ninety years, still the only protection. Uncle Johnny Makgatho, the local representative in the provincial parliament, says, 'If you have not been to Red Location, you have not seen poverty.'[10] When we drive past a solitary Jersey cow stands amid the ubiquitous plastic and decay.

Red Location is the place where the Spring Rose Rugby Football Club and the New Brighton Cricket Club originated. It is also the place where the famous Defiance Campaign was launched in Port Elizabeth in 1952. Today, the new representative Port Elizabeth Council is busy with plans to restore it so that a proud history can be preserved.[11]

While the Majola family have become well known in the bigger world – in the city, the province and the country – it is true to say that for five decades the centre of their world has been the few square miles of New Brighton township where their homes, schools, churches, clubs and sports fields were located.

ABOVE LEFT *Milase Majola with peers from New Brighton.* ABOVE RIGHT *Milase with the Majola children, (left to right) Tozie, Vuyo, Khaya, Gerald and Nomonde.*

Eric Majola (left) and Milase Majola (right) at a local function.

New Brighton had a distinctive tradition of politics and struggle.
Residents walking to work during the 1957 bus boycott.

Chapter 12

COMMUNITY

———————————————— ◉ ————————————————

THE MAJOLAS LIVED IN a township that was vibrant and making history. New Brighton came into being in 1904 when Africans in five inner-city locations of Port Elizabeth were forced out of town, victims of one of the first major attempts at urban segregation in the Cape Colony. Following a pattern that would become familiar in South Africa during the 20th century, just over 20 000 residents were pushed into new settlements on the edges of the town, the pretext being that Africans were a health hazard. New Brighton was intended as the official new location, but it was slow to grow. People voted with their feet, preferring to set up house in Korsten, which was closer to the city, yet outside municipal limits and, therefore, municipal control.[1]

However, by the 1930s Korsten had become a 'huge, rack-rented, shanty village arousing considerable official disapproval'. In the late 1930s the municipality started building houses in New Brighton and evicting and rehousing people from Korsten there.[2]

'Trucked under police surveillance with luggage, dogs and cats they were driven across the Dassie Kraal, another multi-racial area at the time, to the [segregated] New Brighton', a former resident remembers.[3]

By the end of World War Two New Brighton accommodated 35 000 people of a total African population of 42 000 in Port Elizabeth. According to historians, New Brighton was different in some ways from other major South African townships. Inhabitants lived in 'tidy rows of bungalows' and most workers lived with their families. There was not the controlled environment of single sex hostels, compounds or barracks found in Johannesburg and Cape Town. Official restrictions were also not as heavy as elsewhere: 'there was no curfew, no pass regulations, no registration of employment and even domestic brewing was allowed'. The population was largely homogenous, 95 percent being Xhosa-speaking.[4]

Jimmy Matyu has written a book about Jabavu Street in New Brighton in those days:

[The first residents] were impressed, especially with the water tap to each home, the outside flush toilet shared by two families, the fenced off yards, the street lamps. There were trees to beautify the environment . . .

He remembers it as a happy place:

Everybody knew everybody. The neighbourhood was a close-knit unit. Families used clan names to identify each other. They shared problems . . . buried their dead at simple but touching funerals. The hearse was a donkey cart. They held weekend all-night parties such as stokvels *and jam sessions and weddings too . On Christmas Day . . . homes were attractively decorated inside . . . Jabavu Road was friendly, and easily absorbed newcomers. But it was made clear hooliganism was out. It was for this reason that those who were said to come from eGoli [Johannesburg] were regarded with suspicion.[5]*

The 1946 census listed only 200 black professionals in the city. They were mainly teachers, ministers, traders and, strangely, policemen and soldiers. At that time there was only one black doctor and no black lawyers or legal workers. By virtue of their work and economic status, the Majolas and Qeqes would as teachers have been part of this small professional elite in New Brighton.

Most of the African population worked in manufacturing industries and local commercial firms or as dockers, railway workers and domestic servants. Port Elizabeth is one of the oldest industrial centres in South Africa and for a long time the economy depended mainly on the port and the leather industry. In the 1920s South Africa's emerging motor industry moved there. Ford opened a factory in 1923,

Eric Majola at the Johnson Marwanqa school.

followed by Volkswagen in the 1940s, and General Motors (now Delta Motor Corporation). The motor industry has had a major impact on the city to this day.[6]

The negative side of life in New Brighton was the high level of poverty and disease. By 1949 the city had one of the highest tuberculosis rates in the world, together with East London. The population grew rapidly over time, leading to the creation of Zwide, Kwazakhele, Motherwell and other adjoining townships.[7]

From the late 1940s onwards, political resistance started manifesting itself significantly when the city council began implementing stricter controls. Local politics had a particular local style of 'crowded meetings, and massed street processions through the city centre ... [as well as] the preference for direct action as opposed to lobbying and negotiation'. Port Elizabeth soon became a stronghold of the liberation struggle, influencing in important ways the course of South African politics.[8]

In 1952, when Eric Majola was 22 years old and had just been selected for the national cricket squad, Port Elizabeth was in the forefront of the famous Defiance Campaign against unjust laws. In a meeting at New Brighton, Nelson Mandela announced that people would flout apartheid laws, go into whites-only facilities and offer themselves up for arrest. He was the Volunteer in Chief. Two months later 28

volunteers walked into whites-only areas of the New Brighton station to start the campaign, while a crowd of supporters sang 'Senzeni na, thina sizwe Afrika' ('What have we done, we the African people'). They were carted away in police vans. More than 2 000 were arrested in Port Elizabeth, around a quarter of those arrested nationwide.[9]

In October 1952, a few months after the Defiance Campaign, riots erupted in New Brighton after police shot three people, killing one of them. Angry crowds went on the rampage. Three whites were killed and property was destroyed. Several other township residents died as well. Ray Mali remembers walking towards the township on that day and seeing billowing smoke in the distance. 'I knew straightaway there was trouble.'[10]

Similar violence broke out in East London as 'an anger that had long been held in check was unleashed'.[11] The government answered with greater repression, and South Africa was on its way to the outlawing of opposition, the Sharpeville massacre, the Soweto uprisings and the covert state terror of the 1980s.

Leaders who would become famous names in the liberation struggle came to the fore in Port Elizabeth at this time. Among them were Raymond Mhlaba, James Njongwe, Caleb Mayekiso, A.P. Mati, Frances Baard, Govan Mbeki, Wilton Mkwayi and Vuyisile Mini. Raymond Mhlaba, who ended up

Politics had a particular local style in Port Elizabeth, which Raymond Mhlaba has written about in his memoirs.

More than 2 000 people were arrested in Port Elizabeth during the Defiance Campaign in 1952, around a quarter of the figures countrywide.

spending a quarter of a century in prison with Nelson Mandela, recalled in his memoirs how unusually close the political struggles were to ordinary people in Port Elizabeth. 'We went to find people where they lived and worked and socialised.' The ANC would be prayed for in the local churches and in turn activists 'had to know everything that happened in their streets'. They made sure they 'diarised' and participated in funerals, weddings, rituals and initiation ceremonies of township residents. They would also go to the civic centres where young people trained for boxing, wrestling and weight-lifting. And, 'sometimes we played rugby with them'.[12]

The well-known sports personality and coach of Eric Majola's New Brighton Cricket Club, Wilson Ximiya, was on the Action Committee for the 1949 bus boycotts, together with Mhlaba and other local leaders. However, Mhlaba found during the Defiance Campaign, for instance, that people like teachers and nurses could not join, although they generally supported the ANC, because they feared losing their jobs. This would probably have applied to Eric and Milase Majola as well.[13]

Another feature of 1950s politics, which undoubtedly influenced sports developments, was the non-racial nature of the struggles. New Brighton residents, for example, demonstrated against poor services in Schrauderville and against the

removal of coloured people from the voters roll in 1953. Mhlaba lists numerous coloured, Indian and white activists who helped shape this non-racial ethos of the ANC.[14]

Port Elizabeth remained one of the strongholds of resistance in the country – and one of the places where oppression was at its worst – for the next 40 years. It was from here that the first people hanged in the 1960s for opposing apartheid came; where Steve Biko was beaten to the point of death in 1977; where the Goniwe Four and the PEBCO Three were abducted and brutally murdered; where Simphiwe Mtimkulu was poisoned with thalidomide and then made to 'disappear'. It was also the place where internal mass organisation in support of the exiled African National Congress re-emerged in the late 1970s via union activities and the formation of the Port Elizabeth Black Civic Organisation and other community groups. This was a major step towards the formation of the United Democratic Front (UDF) which changed the face of South African politics in the 1980s, consolidating the majority behind the broad aims of the exiled ANC, and taking the country in the direction of the democracy that finally arrived in 1994.[15]

The Majolas and other sportspeople of New Brighton played and administered their games from the 1940s onwards against this unfolding social and political backdrop.

A local sports club outing at the 'Non-Europeans-only' St George's Strand beach outside Port Elizabeth in the 1950s. Milase Majola (centre) and members of the ladies' section busy with the catering.

Chapter 13

CLUBS

———————————— ◗ ————————————

I N RUGBY, IF YOU were from the Red Location, 'even if you were not born there', it was compulsory to play for Spring Rose. 'Wherever you came from, Cape Town or wherever, you cannot be another club, you must be Spring Rose. That was the spirit those days', explains Dan Qeqe.[1]

So Eric Majola joined the Spring Rose Rugby Football Club. It was one of the main clubs playing under the auspices of the New Brighton Rugby Union. Others included Union, Butcher Birds, Oriental, Fabs and St Cyprians RFC.[2]

Gary Baines, one of the historians of New Brighton, noted that these clubs had 'sizeable memberships' and that their rivalry 'could reach intense levels'. He also confirms Dan's story:

The biggest drawcard and best supported match was that between Spring Rose and Union RFCs from the Red and White Location respectively. Rival spectators adorned in their club colours — Spring Rose's green and gold and Union's white — would take up positions on opposite sides of the field in the New Brighton Oval which was situated between the aforementioned areas. These 'grudge' matches would quite often end with … fisticuffs and free-for-alls involving spectators from both sides.[3]

The classical definition of the home derby would be stretched to the limit as 'supporters from one side would flee to their residential areas hotly pursued by opponents …' This is how old residents, perhaps with a touch of nostalgia and exaggeration, remember things. But there is no denying the passion that there was for sport in New Brighton. It was an important part of community culture. And, although 'often a signifier of "respectability" and class positions', historians have noted that sport in New Brighton had a wide appeal which transcended cleavages between the educated elite and working class people, leading to new patterns of popular culture and rooted social institutions.[4]

SPRING ROSE RUGBY FOOTBALL CLUB

When the black residents of Port Elizabeth were forced out of town to the new segregated settlements of New Brighton and Korsten in the early 1900s, sports clubs quickly became established there. By 1908 the African Lion Cricket Club had been established in New Brighton, while the mixed area of Korsten had the Cape of Good Hope CC. In rugby Orientals became the Korsten Club and Spring Rose the New Brighton Club, though the latter club's meetings continued to be held 'in the open air' in town.[5]

Spring Rose, named after the area from which most of its founding members had come, is still in existence today. It will be holding its centenary celebrations in 2007 and the Majola family have been active club members for more than five decades, showing again how rooted sport is in the black communities, and how it has been part of family and community cohesion for many years.

The Club was formed in 1907 by players from the Spring Grove area near Bedford. They were joined two years later by an influx of players from Grahamstown. Meetings used to be held in the open air in the Donkin reserve opposite the old King Edward Hotel in the city centre, and the driving force was William Xayimpi Tube. After starting in the second league in 1908, Spring Rose won the Wynne's Cup for the first time in 1914 under the captaincy of Samuel Ngene.

World War One and the influenza epidemic of 1918 severely disrupted the club. 'Many players left and others died', leaving the club in 'a hopeless position'. The recovery was slow, but Spring Rose won the Barney Miller Trophy for six years in a row between 1927 and 1932. The stars in those years were players like W.B. Ntshekisa (after whom a street is named in New Brighton), Ben and Pullen Ngxizela, J. Cintso, S. Mbali, J. Lukwe, M. Dweni and the captain, Ben Stungu.[6]

Spring Rose never managed the same level of domination again until the 1950s when Eric Majola, his brother, Skumbuzo Oliphant, and Dan Qeqe were playing. Union and Orientals were apparently the strongest clubs in the 1930s and 1940s. From 1951 onwards Spring Rose became a force again under the captaincy of Willows Nyangayibizwa. It 'achieved the honour of being recognised as one of the best rugby clubs in the country', according to a club brochure. Top players produced by Spring Rose included Winty Pandle, who later played rugby league in England, Grey and Chinky Mgubela, Matthews and Dai Mokonenyane, Themba Salamntu, Wilfred Khovu and Peter Mkata. Between 1959, when the club celebrated its Golden Jubilee, and 1962, Spring Rose were the top team three years out of four in the Sloans Trophy competition.

But, after winning in 1961, it was relegated to second position for not paying its subscriptions.[7]

NEW BRIGHTON CRICKET CLUB

In winter it was Spring Rose and rugby. Summer meant cricket for the New Brighton Cricket Club. For an unbroken 50 years, the Majola family have been leading members of New Brighton and its successor, United CC, which was formed in the 1970s when New Brighton amalgamated with two other clubs, as we shall see below.

Wide Awake Cricket Club, winners of the Runners Cup in 1948/49, one of many cricket clubs in New Brighton. (Back row, left to right) G.J. Leta, D.S. Mini, D. Mtyambo, F.N. Ntsangani. (Middle row) P. Ntshla (secretary), F.N. Msila, C.S. Tshete, K. Kumkani, C. Mncwabo, P.M. Rawana, E.B. Mali (vice-president). (Front row) R. Ntsundushe, W. Mpondo (treasurer), S.A. McMpondo (captain), F. Naka (president), R. Kildasi (vice-captain) Khaya Majola Room, St Georges Park, Port Elizabeth.

Cricket was played from the start in New Brighton. The *Izwi Labantu* newspaper reported the existence of the African Lion Cricket Club as early as 1908 and the New Brighton Cricket Club was established in 1917. By the 1920s it was already a force, with two teams in playing in the league. The Johannesburg-based *Umteteli wa Bantu* carried a report of a match in 1928 against St Phillip's from Grahamstown in which Johnson Marwanqa featured prominently.[8] He was described as one of the 'stars of the Bantu cricket world'[9] and was clearly a prominent local figure because a street in New Brighton, as well as the school the Majola children attended in the 1960s and 1970s, were named after him.

When Eric played for New Brighton in the 1950s there were just under ten Port Elizabeth clubs competing against each other. They were New Brighton, Albany, Hard Catch, Fort Beaufort, Victoria East, Rock of Ages, Wide Awake, Home Defenders and MCC (comprising 'home-boys' from the Middledrift area). These clubs made up the Port Elizabeth sub-union, which together with Uitenhage and Grahamstown constituted the Eastern Province Bantu Cricket Board.

The magazine *African Sports* reported in 1953 that Fort Beaufort and New Brighton were the top clubs and 'greatest rivals of Port Elizabeth since 1946'. It said, 'Both have stars and stalwarts that can measure up to any standards.' While Fort Beaufort had won a thrilling final in the 1952/53 season, New Brighton boasted Eric Majola and Wilson Ximiya, 'the only Springboks this end':

In addition they have an array of batsmen — from number one to 11 — each capable of a century and more. There is the powerful L[ent] Maqoma, the polished hard-hitter, with C[hina] Manana, the daredevil hurricane batsmen, and several others. Fort Beaufort on the other, has Stofile, Tengela, Nkohla, all-rounders of no mean ability.[10]

New Brighton again reached the final in 1953/54, when their opponents were Wide Awake CC, who had strong players like Mpondo, Fihla and Yoyo.

Eric Majola was clearly a star of the local scene. Besides scoring the only century in the league that season – 125 versus Albany CC – he also returned figures of seven for 20 against Victoria East, eight for 16 against Rock of Ages, five for 25 against Albany and five for 21 against Fort Beaufort.[11]

His long-standing team-mate and fellow opening bowler, Lent Maqoma, was a member of the Xhosa royal family. He was referred to in the press as '*the Isikhulu Tshawe*'. He was also a gifted saxophonist and became the first principal of the Johnson Marwanqa School.[12] Other talented cricketers playing with Eric at New Brighton included wicketkeeper batsman Matthews Mokonenyane, Themba Salamntu, Grey Mgubela and his brother Chinky Mgubela, 'the best left-hand batsman playing on African fields'. Most of them were ex-Newell students. Under the renowned and 'very strict' player/coach, Wilson Ximiya, they became a top team and it wasn't long before they made it to the Eastern Province tournament sides.[13]

Wilson Ximiya was an opening batsman who had played for Eastern Province way back in the first inter-provincial tournament in 1932. As an opener, it was reported, 'He has the essential defensive stodgy, straight bat that removes the gloss and wearies the attack.' He sometimes took a while to find his feet, but 'fortunately once in he cracks the bowling with impunity from side to side'.[14]

While working as a clerk on the mines in the 1940s, Ximiya played for the Transvaal Africans in inter-race competitions against other unions on a regular basis. After returning to Port Elizabeth, he became a community leader and one of the most influential sports personalities in the city. He and Eric Majola were the first Eastern Province players to be awarded national colours. *African Sports* commented, ' … he requires no introduction – he is on the lips of every sportsman the Union over.'[15]

Wilson Ximiya, who briefly worked as a 'municipal headman' before becoming an insurance broker, was also known for the sports columns he wrote for many years. African sport results did not appear in the weekend editions of local newspapers in those days, but the mid-week column he and a handful of other correspondents wrote ensured that township sport was covered.[16]

The love for cricket in the African communities was well reflected by the name he gave his son, Walcott Weekes Phakamile Ximiya – after two of the 'three Ws' of West

Cricket at the New Brighton Oval in the 1950s. Opening batsmen Cossie and Grootboom go out to start the Port Elizabeth Bantu Cricket Board innings against the Gompo Cricket Union from East London, framed by a host of keen spectators.

Indian fame. Today W.W.P. Ximiya, who spent many years in exile as an ANC cadre, is on the executive of Border Cricket, underlining once again the enduring tradition of cricket in African communities. Another son, Winky, became a promising businessman based in Johannesburg.

According to Ray Mali, Wilson Ximiya was responsible for overturning the dominance of Fort Beaufort in the Port Elizabeth leagues. He decided they needed to be countered by spin. That is how Eric, a top-order batsman and a useful bowler, who started off bowling fast, switched to spin. 'After that New Brighton cleaned up in the competitions.'[17]

The following newspaper report of New Brighton winning the championship in 1959, by 'Sotewu' in *Imvo Zabantsundu*, gives one a vivid feel of the Port Elizabeth club cricket scene in the 1950s, and the dominant role of Eric Majola within it:

Though New Brighton CC have never been weak, and have won the Knock-out trophy times out of number, the Grand Challenge Trophy has always eluded them. This season, the most enjoyable for many a

*Wives and partners of the New Brighton Cricket Club players celebrate
yet another championship win in the Majola home, 1960s.*

*year, they won this premier Trophy by beating Victoria East CC by ten
wickets in a match where the bat was predominant...*

*Although winning the toss, NBCC sent VECC in to bat at 9.15.
After six overs, Majola, NBCC captain, must have had visions of
Peter May's error of judgement in the fourth Test of the MCC tour of
Australia, for Zantsi and M. Tom set about the bowling in such a
hurry that in four overs, they had scored 17. It was not until an hour
had elapsed that Zantsi spooned a catch to Mosia off M. Majola ...*

*Thereafter there was not much resistance as E. Majola mowed the
side down with his vicious off-breaks ... Majola E. took eight wickets
for 25 and [his cousin, Mthetho] Majola two for 18. The pitch was
definitely not for fast bowlers, it was 'perspiring'.*

*Ximiya and Mokonenyane opened so confidently against Masuthu
and Mafu that the first wicket fell at 33 when Mokonenyane was run
out after the batsmen had attempted an impossible second run. At one
time it appeared that the opening batsmen would pass the VECC total
of 81. Two minutes before lunch C. Mgubela was bowled by
Masuthu at 46. Meanwhile Ximiya was batting with all the confidence and his cuts past gully were a treat. Zantsi (twice) and Ntete
dropped catches which might have changed the course of the match.
Ximiya was eventually bowled by Masuthu at 65 with his score at 29
made in 90 minutes.*

*The stage was set for the immaculate Eric Majola to pulverise an
already tiring attack. In 70 minutes he hit 48 before being caught at*

*cover from a skier off Masuthu but the score then was 134. He hit a
glorious six off B. Tom who conceded 17 in that over ...*

*Besman returned the best analysis of five for 30 in his 10.4 overs.
With L. Maqoma, Majola took the score from 70 for four to 129 for
five Maqoma scoring 22 mostly from drives. Mokonenyane was the
only other batsman to reach double figures, 16, but the NBCC side
were all out for 144 at 3.36.*

*Bent on forcing the pace to try to snatch an outright win, as a draw
would not help them, VECC changed about their batting order. When the
two Toms rattled up 12 in the first two overs, it appeared that they
would reach a substantial total to enable them to declare and force a win.*

*Majola's perspicuity was seen when he brought on two completely new
bowlers, Oliphant and Mosia. Oliphant had B. Tom caught at point at
26 and then accounted for two other wickets at a cost of 25...*

*E. Majola got the stick when he was hit for 14 in one over but came
back to bowl Phange who was last man out. He took two for 34 whilst
M. Majola bowled remarkably accurately to take four for five runs.
VECC were all out for 93 in 91 minutes, but set NBCC the easy
task of scoring 30 runs in 39 minutes.*

*E. Majola and R. Mosia hit off the runs in 5.2 overs, Masuthu
conceding 20 and Besman 11. Within 20 minutes the match was over,
with Majola 24 not out and Mosia eight not out. A crowd of well over
200 spectators was treated to a fine display of good batting though
some of it was rather scratchy.*[18]

LADIES' SECTION

No history of sport in the black communities of South Africa would be complete without recording the important role played by women.

As we saw in Chapter 3, Mrs Rwexu, Mrs Wauchope and others were prominent in hosting the first Kimberley cricket team to visit Port Elizabeth in 1888, and they had their own croquet club.

Both Spring Rose Rugby Football Club and New Brighton Cricket Club had active ladies' sections in Eric and Milase Majola's time during the 1950s and 1960s.

Milase's interest in sport started at home. Her father played cricket, rugby and golf 'and had even liked fishing'. As a child she would accompany her mother to matches:

We used to follow these mamas. If Union had red and white jerseys, they would put on red and white attire or scarves. We as young girls would follow up these ladies and the smart ones and the ones who sing well and join them singing. They would sing in encouragement. I used to like Easterns. I remember there was this young gentleman, the way he played, we admired him, and we would chant 'Mona, Mona, Mona' every time he ran (laughter). It was the only place we could go – to the fields – to enjoy the afternoon.[19]

Like her mother before her, she became heavily involved in the ladies' sections of the local sports clubs.

Many girls grew up with sport as part of their lives like this. Peggy Mali recalls a childhood in Cape Town in the 1950s and 1960s when she and her brother always accompanied her father to cricket. Wakeford Bali Lubulwana was a primary school principal in Langa and a Western Province rugby and cricket player. He believed in discipline. The children could not sneak off if they were bored, or cover for each other, because at dinner that night the game would be discussed and they would be expected to have followed it. W.B. was 'old school tie' and Peggy's inheritance from her grandfather reflects this upbringing; it is a piano which her daughter Linda, the chief chorister of the national youth choir, still plays.[20]

Enrolling as a Sunbeam Brownie at the age of seven, Milase Majola also developed a lifelong involvement in the Girl Guide movement, eventually representing South Africa at international events. She explained later in newspaper articles that, 'It was a natural choice when I was young. There were no other recreational opportunities for blacks ...' She believed there was no better base for young people than Guiding principles. 'I was a shy child. I used to be called a cry baby but today I can speak in public without fear.' And the Guides were also 'the only movement in the country that provided contact with all races'.[21]

Milase Majola also remembers how sport provided an outlet from the strict discipline at St Matthew's College, where she trained to be a teacher. It was one of the few ways she and her friends could get out and speak to boys. 'We always watched the inter-college games against Fort Hare, Lovedale and Healdtown, even if it was games like soccer, which we were not really interested in.'[22]

At these girls schools, women would be socialised into their role as 'ladies', who were expected to behave in certain ways in the patriarchal society in which they were growing up. When Milase studied at St Matthew's things had not changed much from 1885 when a Miss Lucas instructed the girls 'in all the duties of domestic life, such as washing, ironing, sewing, cooking and baking' for 'fixed hours' every day.[23] Referring to the 1950s, Anne Mager has noted:

The curriculum at Lovedale and other mission schools prepared girls for a life of servitude and domestic labour, reinforcing colonial values and gender stereotypes. The home and mother-craft syllabus included instructions on how to wash a hairbrush and comb and clean silverware, the subject of hygiene was 'taught from a book compiled in England and based upon a life as remote as the moon' ... The widely used Laundry and Housewife Primer advised the students on appropriate shoes – 'in the country, very strong ones and lighter type for town wear', warning that 'fancy feathers never wear well'. Several pages of the slim volume were devoted to the setting of tables in the manner appropriate for breakfast, supper, dinner and afternoon tea as well as the correct method of waiting at table.[24]

The strict Victorian injunctions taught at St Matthew's and other mission schools were often broken, as when young women became pregnant before marriage, and in 1945 there was a student riot against conditions at St Matthew's, but this education did set the pattern for women's participation in sport. The newspapers of the time reported women playing sport, but their role was generally more a support one for the men.

Spring Rose had a ladies' section with its own 'chairwoman', secretary and treasurer and male member of the club executive. Usually this was Mr Yaya, the club vice-president. Milase remembers how, at the regular meetings, generally held at members' homes, he would report on 'what the players are going to do and what they need'. The women would strategise on how to address these needs. 'We were kept busy by Mr Yaya.' There were a wide range of activities, besides watching and shouting support. The games were on Saturdays and often there would be Sunday 'socials' or so-called 'tea parties' in one of the halls, T.C. White, Hoza or Centenary. The ladies' section of the one club would be

The students and teachers at St Matthew's College for girls
during Milase Majola's time, circa 1950.

'Man, we were strong!' The Spring Rose Rugby Football Club Ladies' Section, 1959. (Back row, left to right) Mrs U.N. Ximiya,
Mrs H. Kulati, Mrs G. Funde, Mrs K. Qupiwe, Miss M. Phandle. (Middle row) Mrs E. Mama, Mrs E. Kuhlane,
Mrs E. Nozewu, Miss E. Ntlanganisela, Mrs P. Ncalu. (Front row) Miss N. Siwisa, Miss D. Tub,
Mrs A. Rwairwai, Mr W.M. Yawa, Mrs. R. Qeqe, Mrs E. Ximiya, Miss S. Boqo.

responsible and invite the others. Mostly there would be music and dancing. Then 'I used to enjoy singing with the Duru family'. Other times there would be beauty pageants and awards functions. 'We started having a Miss Spring Rose and then (laugh) a Mrs and Mr Spring Rose. One year I was Miss Spring Rose and my sister-in-law was Mrs Spring Rose. It was a family thing.'

For these functions, catering needed to be done. This was a major part of the ladies' section's responsibilities. Tournaments would be a 'busy time'. During Easter rugby tournaments, for example, when the Spring Rose Clubs from Grahamstown and Cradock and other teams came, the women would run 'shifts'. Some would come in early to make breakfast. Others would work till late at night to serve supper. Special light meals would be prepared before a match. 'We would also try to watch in between and there would be arguments about who could take off and when. It was fun.' Every year the clubs had special end-of-season outings to the beach. The women would work through the night preparing for these, cooking meat, making *roostercookies* and dumplings. People were taken to the 'non-Europeans Only' St George's Strand beach just outside Port Elizabeth in busses, trucks and cars. Hundreds would come. Old people, families 'as a whole', children. An elderly person, like Mr Yaya, started the day with a prayer. Then 'there was time for the beach and time to play'. Mr Lamani was a sports organiser and he would bring things like hockey sticks and balls. The children enjoyed themselves.

Sewing was another task. 'I think I used to be one of the targets,' says Milase with a laugh. 'My husband would collect all the ragged jerseys and make me sew them up. So that was part of the fun'.

She recalls, 'We were very smart, we even had blazers. Ours had one button and the men two buttons.' These were specially made. Tailored blazers. And then 'you had your caps, you know, with pom poms'. Spring Rose started the trend of having blazers for the ladies' section, 'then all the other groups followed'.

The ladies' section also had its own netball team. They would play in the morning and go and watch the men in the afternoon. The women also travelled with the team to other towns. For example, when Swallows in East London celebrated an anniversary the ladies' section made a flag for the event and went up as a team to support them.

Milase sums up:

Sport was part of the community, which is very lacking today. That's why you find these girls drinking so much. They have nothing to look for. Because

we were busy. As young ladies we would sit and discuss our uniform. We used to have black trousers. Then we said the men have grey trousers. Why not have grey skirts? We were serious you know. So we went in there. It was fun. Eric was wearing his greys and blazer and I was wearing mine. We were kept very busy. We were kept on our feet. Even the teams. The spirit was very high. The players knew they were well watched. So they must do their best on the field. There were big crowds, lots of people.[25]

Studies have confirmed that sport had become an important part of social life in the black townships by the middle of the 20th century. In a survey conducted in East London in the late 1950s and early 1960s by Professor B.A. Pauw, half of those interviewed expressed an interest in rugby and virtually all these claimed to belong to a rugby club. The under-35 group and those with an educational qualification of standard five and higher were the most enthusiastic, but interest extended along the whole spectrum of residents. The involvement of women in sport was becoming more common too. Although only 12.5 percent of East London women interviewed expressed an interest in sport, some were actually members of the local rugby clubs.[26]

In a strongly patriarchal society, where rugby was a 'man's game' and 'women belonged in the kitchen', women did not have the same freedom to play and follow sport as men. When they were involved it was inevitably in support roles, such as recruiting, washing, catering and cheering.

The historian Rachidi Molapo has noted this for Cape Town as well. He interviewed Mr M. Faku, an old stalwart of the Mother City Club, who recalled that the club started a ladies' section in 1968: ' We never used to hire any ladies for washing our outfit after the match. We used to collect all the smelling jerseys and took them to our ladies' section and had them washed up.'[27] These activities reinforced the 'place' of women in life. But, as Milase Majola's testimony indicates, some women felt this involvement brought them greater social opportunities and freedoms too. In fact, the Western Province Rugby Union was encouraging clubs to start women's sections at the time because women were ' bound to the kitchen at the moment'.[28] This theme is still touched on today. In the ninetieth anniversary brochure of Spring Rose Rugby Club, Eado Suka, the netball co-ordinator, commented:

We have moved away from 'the role of women in the kitchen', and to asserting ourselves as women in other arenas, sport being one such arena. This movement needs our endorsement and dedication to make everyone understand that we are serious about sport.[29]

We can see here that, as in any society, the sports clubs reflected the dynamics of community life, from class and social status to racial distinctions and gender roles.

Pin-ups and participants: redefining gender stereotypes in the 1950s. ABOVE LEFT *A model featured by the African Sports magazine, 1953.* ABOVE RIGHT *Joyce Taukobong plays an overhead smash during the 1959 Transvaal Tennis Union Championships in Orlando, Soweto.*

BORN TO BAT AND BOWL

Sport, predictably, played a significant part in the lives of the Majola children too. Eric was at the height of his career, playing for Eastern Province and the national African team in both rugby and cricket in the years between 1953, when Khaya was born, and 1962 when the last-born, Vuyo, arrived. When Eric was not practising, playing or coaching there were the social activities. The neighbours and closest family friends, like Dan Qeqe and Wilson Ximiya, were prominent sports personalities as well.

The children's mother was a big influence. As recounted above, Milase was actively involved in sport. As teachers, she and Eric believed in the character-forming qualities of sport, and were able to actively apply these to their family. They also kept a strict rein on their children. A friend of Khaya remembered that even after he had left school, he and his friends had to join a youth club to find a way past the strict parental discipline.[30]

In later years, when Milase became a community worker and recreational officer, the children would go along and play table tennis and other indoor events at the regular community events she organised in the War Memorial Hall.[31]

In a society where their colour meant automatic disadvantage, the Girl Guide mother and school teacher father were determined still to give them a 'respectable' middle class upbringing and keep them out of the ghetto. Sport was a way of doing this.

All four of the sons went on to play provincial sport, and Khaya and Gerald emulated their father in also achieving national honours.

Khaya recalled, 'From my first breath I lived the game [of cricket].'[32] He was soon tagging along and being groomed by his father. His mother remembers making him his own special white cricket trousers when he was 'only a tickey high'. At matches he would have to be chased off the field because he used to follow his father and the players across the boundary rope.

Milase remembers it was sport from morning to night, particularly with Khaya who was the eldest and identified as the protégé who would follow in the footsteps of his father:

Khaya would walk out the front door with this bat that was bigger than him. His father would have to go and throw balls to him. A few minutes later the little Khaya would come in crying. I would scold Eric for being too strict. But it wouldn't be long and the toddler would be dragging the bat outside again, and the process would repeat itself. Eventually I gave up.[33]

Khaya and his brothers confirm what a hard taskmaster Eric was. 'Khaya had to do everything right all the time.' If

Men and women playing rugby on the beach during a club outing, St George's Strand, Port Elizabeth, 1959.

he played across the line or made a mistake Eric would give him a '*hot klap*' ('hard smack'). And all the attention was focused on him. 'We would always have to bowl to my father and Khaya. Sometimes we would be woken at five in the morning to go and bowl at the fields next to the railway compound. It was made clear to us that he was the talented one.'

Tozie recalls that Khaya would spend hours hitting a ball wrapped in women's pantihose stockings suspended from the trees next to their 'pitch' at home. While the other brothers would watch and play soccer in the neighbourhood, cricket was the only game for Khaya. He 'never got close to soccer at all'. Partly it was because his father disapproved:

My father didn't like soccer. Not that he didn't like soccer as a sport, because he used to take us to watch [the white, professional] PE City, but he had a problem with dagga smoking and soccer ... we joined the club ... but Khaya was never interested. Khaya would play his cricket in the yard here... [34]

Khaya would go with his father when Eric went to round up team-mates in his Opel car to ensure that New Brighton fielded a full team. And that is how he started playing matches. When the team was short Khaya would be roped in. His first experiences were playing with the adults. [35]

After the games Eric's friends and fans would come to the house. Everyone had to get something to eat and drink.

'He would make me take even the last piece of bread to feed them. When we were beaten it would be all quiet.' [36]

The Majola boys played regularly with the children of Eric's team-mates. Khonaye Penxa, Nceba Ngxabazi and Fezi Ben Mazwi would walk all the way from Yokwe Street and past Red Location to the Majola's big house in Avenue E to play against Roseville represented by Khaya, Tozie and the Ximiya children. Here, in the big garden, they would take on the identities of their adult heroes. [37]

Everyone wanted to be Eric Majola. But Khaya would have none of this. 'I am Majola and that is final', he would say. And if anyone didn't fall in line with this, he would walk off in a huff with the balls or bats.

That is how Mveli Ximiya became Phakamile Lubambo and how Khonaye Penxa became Diki Lupondwana. Khonaye is still known today by the nickname coming from that time.

As the friends became teenagers, Diki became the more 'cool' Dixi Cola and then, in adulthood, just Cola, with a strong K and an A at the end in the Xhosa pronunciation. To this day 'Cola' Penxa can still imitate the way Eric Majola used to run, with 'arms down rather than elbows up'. [38]

'That,' recounts Milase, 'is how the children grew up – around rugby and cricket.'

The 'Big Four' of Eastern Province cricket, according to African Sports. *(Left to right)*
Lent Maqoma, Matthews Mokonenyane, Eric Majola and Chinky Mgubela, 1954.

Chapter 14

CHRISTMAS *in the* CITY

———————— ◗ ————————

URING THE 1950s ERIC MAJOLA BECAME A STAR at provincial and national level in both cricket and rugby. After matriculating in 1949 and studying at Healdtown in 1950 and 1951, he went straight into the provincial sides.

Besides his impressive league statistics, there were soon indications of talent on the broader stage. For example, he took seven for 27 and scored 92 when Port Elizabeth trounced Grahamstown in one inter-town sub-union match.[1] In the same season he scored 107 playing for the Eastern Province Bantu Cricket Union against the Eastern Province Coloured Cricket League. His bowling figures were five for 48.[2] Against the Eastern Province Indians he took four for 44. And so on.

In January 1954, *African Sports* declared that Eric Majola was 'about the best all-rounder that Bantu cricket has at the moment'. The magazine described him as 'small built, shy, happy-go-lucky' opening batsman who:

... in his carefree manner faces every bowler as just another he has seen before. He is warm before he comes in; and once in, displays all-round spectacular and well-timed drives, hooks and pulls. He is as difficult as [his opening partner] Ximiya to dislodge ...

He is, at the same time, the fastest opening bowler we can boast of in this area. He has a beautiful smooth run of about 20 yards that ends in a fast inswinger to bamboozle any opening pair. He does not end there but he switches on with the old ball to deliver artful, well flighted and sharp turning spins. He has captured numerous wickets for next to no runs ...

In fielding he is the non-pareil of excellence. He fields anywhere and everywhere and, in all places, excels. It is no small wonder because he is an ace at wicketkeeping — what an all-rounder![3]

Every second Christmas, going on into the New Year, the South African Bantu Cricket Board organised its inter-provincial tournament at a centralised venue in one of the major cities in the country. Eric appears to have played in most of the 1950s tournaments, which were held in Kimberley (1950), Cape Town (1952), Durban (1954), at home in Port Elizabeth (1956) and in Johannesburg over Christmas in 1958.

Eastern Province did not win one of the first 11 NRC tournaments organised by the South African Bantu Cricket Board between 1932 and 1954. However, after this lean streak, the province won both the twelfth and thirteenth tournaments in 1956 and 1958 respectively.[4] The last win, Gordon Qumza reported, proved 'beyond doubt that EP is far superior to all the other provinces ... their batting and fielding made other provinces look like kindergarten boys'.[5]

The 1950 tournament was held in Kimberley from 25 December to 4 January 1951. The local organisers calculated that the tournament entailed 'catering for at least eight provinces involving housing, feeding and accommodation of a little over 100 cricketers'. They calculated that a budget of £360 was needed, broken down into £30 per province, £52 for cricket mats and £50 for sundries.[6] Hamilton Masiza and his team approached the municipality for help. After the tournament the first ever national side was elected to participate in SACBOC's inaugural inter-race tournament in Johannesburg over Easter. Wilson Ximiya and 19-year-old Eric Majola were the Eastern Province players selected for the national squad, although Majola does not seem to have actually played in any of the matches.

At the December 1952 tournament in Cape Town, which involved 'ten days of continuous cricket without a break', the home team, captained by Pat Cossie, took the honours. Matches were played at the City and Suburban Grounds in Mowbray, generally reserved for coloured sportspeople. Majola was one of the stars. The *African Sports* magazine reported that 'in Mowbray ... he was the talk of the town where he stood the test of various accurate, immaculate and faultless bowlers'.[7] *Imvo Zabantsundu* commented that his batting and bowling 'is of such a quality that he "makes" the side'.[8] At the end of the tournament, Majola made his debut for the national team against a mixed Western Province Federation team and, thereafter, played in the Inter-Race Tournament in Johannesburg over Easter.[9]

The 1954/55 inter-provincial tournament held in Durban was well organised, thanks to the 'fine arrangements' and support by the local city council, which made a budget of several hundred pounds available. North Eastern Transvaal emerged as winners, with the host province ending as runners up for the second time in a row. There was not a 'functioning league' in Natal at the time and the team consisted mostly of students living in University of Natal accommodation in Wentworth. The make-up of the Natal team in 1956 was 'four Zulus and ten Xhosas', as well as two Indian medical students, who played for the Varsity XI affiliated to the Durban and District African Cricket Association.[10] North Eastern Transvaal was consistently one of the top teams in the 1950s, but the province experienced difficulties because of 'strife' between location and mine teams. The mines, for example, took players out of tournaments to play friendlies on the Orange Free State goldfields.

This problem affected both the Transvaal boards. In 1953, a new Mine Workers' Cricket Union 'obviously opposed' to the North Eastern Transvaal Bantu Cricket Union was set up with its headquarters at the ERPM mine. Mr H.H. Zibi, president of the NETBCU, said it would isolate African players from 'their brothers' development in matters sporting' and 'inevitably create enmity'.[11] Moses Nyangiwe, president of the TBCU, said his union had similar problems, and that they went back to around 1948. The problem was probably linked to the growth of rigid apartheid thinking at the time. He said, 'The Chamber of Mines Compound Managers Association say that segregate the Mine Natives from the Location natives and you shall have peace in sport.'[12]

African Sports explained:

In the past, cricket in the Transvaal has been the monopoly of the mining industry. The best players came from the mines and sports fields and equipment were also provided by the mines. But the employment of welfare officers and sports organisers in the mines after the war, led to some mine clubs disaffiliating from the TBCU...[13]

Moses Nyangiwe appealed to the mines to change their policies and to local cricketers not to treat sportsmen on the mines as 'enemies' because they had been 'forced into the position in which they find themselves'. He added:

I firmly believe, and have no doubt that sportsmen throughout the wide, wide world will bear with me, that sport is one field where men of different races and nations meet on an equal plane and it is therefore no wonder that members of the cricket union are stunned and puzzled by the separatist attitude of the Gold Mines in attempting to divide African from African — all in the name of sport.[14]

Clearly, apartheid thinking was behind these moves and the two unions were weakened by the drain of mine clubs and resources. Some mine clubs resisted the trend but standards started slipping as 'they get no encouragement from the mines' and did not have enough equipment. It was also noted that the standard of the mine competitions dropped as well. 'The players have nothing to aspire to except to play for the mines that employ them.'[15]

The TBCU now tried to encourage township cricket. It was noted in 1954 that town teams were 'improving fast' and that 'the townships are taking to cricket much more seriously than they have ever done before'. Furthermore, 'Young men and boys from the high schools are being recruited.'[16]

The top teams in the Transvaal first division, and joint winners of the Sugar Cup in 1952/53 were Dobsons XI from Roodepoort and Orlando Brotherly CC of Orlando township. Luipaardsvlei Estate, spearheaded by George Langa, 'that great and fast double-swing arm bowler, whose length has the consistency of a machine', won the Gwele Cup. Other first division clubs included Pimville, Western Native Township, Village Main, Jabavu Old Boys, Randfontein Estates, Orientals of Crown Mines, captained by Frank Roro, and Rand Leases, 'who for many years have dominated the cricket scene in the Transvaal'. There were also reserve and third division leagues. A team from the famous music recording company, Gallo (Africa) Industries, was entered here.[17]

This change in long established organisational and sponsorship patterns in the 1950s was probably one of the main factors for the poor state of cricket in the Transvaal into the 1960s and 1970s. Nevertheless, for those who think that the much vaunted development programme of the late 1980s first 'introduced' blacks to cricket in Gauteng, the 1930s statistics provided in previous chapters and this 1950s survey show that the wheel had already been invented long before.

The 1956 inter-provincial tournament was in Port Elizabeth, home turf of Eric Majola. The SABCB headquarters were at this time in New Brighton as well, with a prominent local figure, F.H.M. Zwide, as president. He was a school principal who later had a township named after him.

Another local educator, Pat Cossie, was the SABCB secretary. Originally from Cape Town, he led Western Province to victory in the 1952 Chamber of Mines Tournament, before being transferred to Port Elizabeth, where he played at league level and became involved in cricket and rugby adminstration for many years.[18]

F.H.M. Zwide was only the fourth SABCB president in 24 years. After H.B. Piliso (1932-1941) and Hamilton Masiza (1941-1954), I.D. Mkize from Cape Town took over in August 1954, serving only a short term. Mkize was also a school principal and one of the most prominent schools in Langa today bears his name. Harrison M. Butshingi from Johannesburg became the fifth president in 1958, holding the position through to the early 1970s, before being succeeded by Ashton Dunjwa (Western Province) and Moses Nyangiwe (Transvaal) respectively.[19]

Eastern Province were winners at home in 1956, with Majola having an exceptional tournament. Against Natal he scored 51 and took five for 22; against Transvaal it was 67 and five for 14; against OFS 46 not out and five for 32; against North Eastern Transvaal he took two for 18; and, finally, against Midlands he was back to the regulation fifty (56) and bagful of wickets, this time ending with four wickets for one run.[20]

Eastern Province successfully defended the title in Johannesburg over Christmas/New Year in 1958/59. The team went up to Johannesburg by lorry. Vice-captain, Dan Qeqe and his younger brother owned a GMC truck. The latter operated it while Dan was still teaching. It was the beginning of what would be a very successful business career. 'All the guys were in the back,' Dan recalls. 'It was a nice trip. There were clowns amongst the chaps. They kept us laughing all the way.'[21]

The 1958 champion team consisted of J. Ngubelanga (captain), Dan Qeqe, Eric Majola, A. Savahl, Selby Mbekeni, M. Mashinqana, S. Besman, D. Lupondwana, N. Mokonenyane, Vakele Skundla, M. Mokone and Wilfred Khovu. They won each of the seven games played in the two-week period by an innings. The batting was very strong and only one team managed to score 100 runs against them in the first innings. The scorecards underlined Eastern Province's dominance:

Against Midlands, Eastern Province scored 382 all out in 214 minutes on the way to winning by an innings and 217 runs.

Against Orange Free State they scored 304 for eight wickets in 150 minutes and won by an innings and 156 runs.

Against Transvaal they scored 297 all out in 194 minutes and won by an innings and 123 runs.

Against Border they scored 329 all out in 131 minutes and won by an innings and 105 runs.

Against North Eastern Transvaal they scored 219 all out in 192 minutes and won by an innings and 78 runs.

Against Natal they scored 206 for five declared in 130 minutes and won by an innings and 15 runs.

Against Transkei they had their only poor batting performance, scoring only 79 for six declared on the Western Township Oval which 'with its long grass on the outfield curtailed the scoring rate'. Still they won by an innings. Transkei were bundled out for a paltry 24 and 31 all out. Eric Majola returned figures of five for ten.[22]

Majola ended up as the third highest wicket-taker after Besman (31) and Mashinqana (29). His statistics were 52.7 overs, 166 runs and 24 wickets.

Those were the days of eight ball overs and in the tournament Eastern Province bowled a total of 326.7 overs, with as many as nine members of the 14-person squad turning their arms over.

Each match lasted for a day and a half, or a total of 12 hours, but not once did Eastern Province need the four hours on the second day.

Imvo Zabantsundu reported that the fielding was of a high standard. Lupondwana took some 'remarkable' catches in the slips, while Qeqe at cover, Skundla at point and Savahl at third man 'saved many a boundary'.

Batting-wise, Eastern Province scored a total of 1 726 runs for 59 wickets at an average of 29.2 per wicket. The reporter noted, 'Even when their star bat E. Majola failed to get among the runs, Mbekeni, Besman, Mashinqana and Savahl would get them in double quick time.' Majola scored 189 runs in four innings for an impressive average of 47.2. This performance put him marginally behind Qeqe in the averages (237 runs in five innings for an average of 47.4). Besman scored 233 runs but in seven innings and at a lower average of 33.2. Majola's best game was against Orange Free State when he scored 45 and had match bowling figures of nine for 50.

The final log was as follows, with the same top three as in the previous tournament in Port Elizabeth:

Champions. The Eastern Province team that swept the boards at the 1958/9 inter-provincial tournament in Johannesburg.
(Back row, left to right) M. Mashiqana, D.L. Lupondwana, S. Besman, D. Dlepu, N. Mbete, M. Majola, S. Mbekeni.
(Middle row) M. Mokonenyane, J. Ngubelanga (captain), T. Orleyn (manager), D. Qeqe (vice-captain),
E. Majola. (Front row) W. Khovu, V. Skundla. (Absent) A. Savahl.

	P	W	L	D	Pts
Eastern Province	7	7	0	-	35
North Eastern Transvaal	7	5	2	-	25
Transvaal	7	3	2	2	21
Border	7	3	3	1	17
Midlands	7	3	3	1	17
Transkei	7	3	3	1	17
Natal	7	1	5	1	8
Orange Free State	7	0	7	0	0

The tournament was covered in great depth by the *Imvo Zabantsundu*, and the reports give a revealing insight into both the playing and administrative situation under the SABCB. The SABCB's lack of resources and difficulties in organising cricket on a national level, as well as the situation in various provinces comes through in these. [23]

'After a lapse of a full ten years', Border, 'doyen of the cricket in the Forties', resumed her membership of the SABCB by 'liquidating all her arrear subscriptions'.[24] (Incidentally, Border rugby was also in conflict with the national body and this led to court cases which the province lost.) Gompo (East London), King Williams Town and Ntselamanzi near Alice were said to be the strongholds of cricket in this province. Gus Toyana, father of the current Easterns player, Geoffrey, was in the Border team.[25]

Transkei was participating as a province for the first time, but five of its members had played for other provinces before. U. Mayekiso (ex-Natal) was the best batsman with 308 runs in 14 innings at an average of 34.2, including a top score of 166.[26]

The Transvaal team in the 1958 tournament included famous names such as George Langa, Samson Ntshekisa and Sydney Hashe. Mokuena and Edmund Ntikinca scored centuries, with the latter totalling 448 runs in 12 innings at an average of 49.7. However, the team underperformed, coming third.[27] Once again their neighbours, North Eastern Transvaal, did better, ending as runners up.

Western Province, tournament winners in 1952, did not participate for the second time in a row. *Imvo Zabantsundu* reported that 'events which happened at the close season in Cape Town last year make sad thinking'. There was apparently a 'deadlock within the officials'. Dissatisfaction was so high that the famous Ben Malamba and others left to play in the coloured leagues in the province. It was noted that Hlubi Mvinjelwa and his executive 'will have to pull up their socks'.[28]

A similar situation applied in Griqualand West. Not only did the province fail to send a side, it also did not fulfil its fixtures in the inter-race games in Kimberley and several 'prominent' cricketers left to join the 'Indian Union'. In addition, it was reported, 'there will soon be a legal battle within the GWBCU'.[29]

From this it can be seen that the situation in some of the provinces left much to be desired. Judging by the scathing remarks about the tournament organisation itself, the national board was also beset by problems.

Imvo Zabantsundu published article after article criticising the organisers and the Johannesburg-based national leadership. It described the tournament as 'one of the worst ever sponsored by the South African Bantu Board'.

Pat Cossie, secretary of the South African
Bantu Cricket Board, 1954 onwards.

To make matters worse, the Christmas in Johannesburg was not a memorable one. 'While wives and families of players enjoyed Christmas pies and turkeys at home on Christmas Day, players in Johannesburg went without meals'. They had to see to themselves. Those who did not venture out onto the streets of Johannesburg stayed indoors playing cards – without food.[30]

'All is not gold that glitters in Johannesburg,' Qumza concluded, and declared that future tournaments should be held only in Eastern Province, Border and Western Province, the only provinces worthy of staging these events, his reason being that they 'shoulder most of our national sports bodies' and also 'have the biggest sports following'.[31]

There were clearly strains of provincialism at work here. The reporter claimed that in meetings the Johannesburg people or 'people from the Cape now resident in Johannesburg' made 'the biggest noise', but failed conspicuously to carry out plans.

On the other hand, the Transvaal officials were at the forefront of criticism of Eastern Province for not yet

Travel arrangements were haphazard and the distances from the place where the players were quartered to the grounds delayed the start of matches. Players had to travel 16 miles to get to Natalspruit, Fordsburg and Western Township.

Grounds were not prepared and Pat Cossie, the SABCB secretary from Port Elizabeth, 'was seen busy lining the pitch a few minutes before the start of the tournament'. Qumza complained also that some fields were too small, that mats were not put down in time, that there was an absence of gatekeepers, that teams had to get their own umpires and that the tournament reception in an Orlando hall, which consisted of 'eight ladies and about twenty players', was a flop.

Finally, the meals provided were poor. 'That players should have only porridge for breakfast, snacks for lunch and hard porridge strewn with tomato gravy for supper was preposterous. Meat was a rarity and so was tea, despite a donation from one tobacco firm.'

having submitted a financial report for the previous tournament in Port Elizabeth. Eastern Province's participation in the tournament was questioned and they were eventually given three months to account for the more than £50 outstanding to the board.

There were reportedly 'some ugly scenes' at the SABCB AGM and the 'vociferous' inputs and 'bad language' from Transvaal caused the chair to issue several warnings.[32]

The SABCB assistant secretary, Lennox Mlonzi, who was from Transvaal, indicated that a motion would be put at the next meeting in East London that 'all SABCB officials be resident in one province'.

This, indeed, does seem to have happened because officials in the Transvaal more or less took over the running of the SABCB during the 1960s with Harrison Butshingi (the president) and Mlonzi (the secretary and treasurer) at the helm.[33]

"It was the African version of the Englishman's cricket on the village green" . . .

Africans' village green cricket festival

— by — C. S. Morgan

WHILE sitting in the steamy heat during a dull spell in the Border-Eastern Province friendly cricket match at East London, I recalled the last game I had seen up in the cool, green hills under the Pirie Mountains' forested slopes.

It was the African version of the Englishman's cricket on the village green: Black men playing in one of the lively marathon cricket tournaments which have been held every Christmas in parts of the Ciskei Native rural areas for the past 50 or 60 years.

Four or five locations put up two or three XIs each, and they all play one another two or three times in the course of the week from Christmas Day to New Year.

All matches are faithfully scored, and the team which finishes up with the most wins carries off a cup which has been presented by a local trader or some other well-wisher.

Very often the batsman with the highest aggregate and the bowler with the best analysis also receives a trophy to take back to his home in the kraal, or to East London, Port Elizabeth, Cape Town, Johannesburg, or wherever he works during the year.

Tradition

These tournaments are a tradition which draw Ciskei men from the cities to their homes in the country every year at Christmas.

Clad in the usual white cricket uniform, the city slicker and the perennial kraal dweller are hardly distinguishable, and they are both subject to the cheerful barracking of the partisan clumps of spectators sitting or reclining around the irregular boundary.

Among the spectators I saw were many well-dressed women and schoolgirls, as well as men, women and children who obviously seldom left their kraals.

One group had a lunch basket and bottles of soft drinks were being passed around. The women burst into chanting song now and again for the benefit of their team out there on the field.

One or two raggedy men who had obviously had a little too much kaffir beer wandered amiably around, and they looked no more out of place than their White brothers in the same state around a city cricket field.

"Gibisela!" or "Posa!" someone would shout at a tardy fielder or a bowler who seemed to be wasting time. Those words mean approximately "throw", and that is undoubtedly an approximate description of some of the startlingly unorthodox styles of bowling one saw in action.

I saw nothing, however, which I would readily condemn as being outside the definition of bowling. It certainly did not disturb either of the typically casual umpires on duty.

Up went a bail for a catch and a fielder raced to get under it. "Bamba imbumba!" was the cry that went up—"Catch that ball, man!"

He got it and the unlucky batsman who lingered a moment at the wicket was left in no doubt about what he had to do.

"Puma, puma!" shouted the supporters of the fielding side. ("Out you go.")

Even less like Lord's were other cries one heard now and again, such as "Kauleza!" (Hurry up) or "Vuka!" (Wake up).

Formalities

But for all its derision at times, there was no doubt that the crowd was as keenly interested in the sport as any White Test crowd, and it certainly did not laugh at any of the somewhat quaint formalities observed on the field.

One was the drill when the fielding side went out to toil. They lined up on the pitch like a platoon section ready for drill, and were sent off one by one from there to their allotted places in the field by their captain.

Another was the honour shown to the opposing captain by the fielders when he went in to bat. They gathered around the wicket and clapped him to his place.

Quaint but pleasing.

The wicket was a cleared patch of more or less level veld, and it was certainly showing wear when I saw it. It was being used from about 8 in the morning to 7 at night, seven days in a row. Often two matches are in progress at the same time, with their fields overlapping.

Old carpets are often used as mats at each end of the wicket. In the game I watched there were no bails.

The whole scene really made a deep impression on me. Here, I thought, is some of the real spirit of cricket.

And what a cricket ground, with the dark green mass of the Pirie Mountains rising steeply a thousand feet above the veld a mile away.

Later, back at the huts lyn Valley not far away lyn Valley not far way, where the trout waters of the Buffalo River drain out of the Pirie range, I met an old African labourer who told me through an interpreter that he had taken part in the Pirie tournaments until he became too old to play.

Missionaries

As a boy he had been taught his cricket by another African, but where that man had learned his cricket he did not know.

Nobody has been able to tell me definitely how these people first became interested in cricket, but they must have been coached originally by the missionaries who laboured in these valleys last century.

I know that they have been playing cricket at St. Matthew's Mission, in the Keiskama River valley, on the other side of the Pirie mountains, ever since the mission was founded.

Mr. Bryce Ross, of King William's Town, and son of the Rev. John Ross, who established in 1830 the famous old Ross' Pirie Mission near the cricket field I saw, tells me that he remembers that cricket was a favourite game for the Africans around the mission when he was a boy living there 50 or more years ago.

Today, apparently, cricket is only played in most of the locations once a year — at these Christmas tournaments. They seem to be a part of the fine Christmas spirit out there.

I asked the old labourer: "Why is it that you people always like to play cricket at this time?"

He thought a moment and then replied with great dignity: "It is a good thing to play cricket at Christmas. There are a lot of bad things a man can do at Christmas if he does not play cricket."

He knew his people, and I knew what he meant.

"Bamba imbumba" (catch that ball) shouted the woman watching the game. And when the fielder caught it, they shouted, "Puma, puma" (out you go).

Dr. R. T. Bokwe, the African district surgeon at Middledrift 20 miles away, told me afterwards that the Christmas tournaments undoubtedly keep the young men out of mischief—dangerous mischief like their vigorous stick play which causes broken heads which the doctor has to mend, and often also fatal injuries.

Dr. Bokwe said that when he first arrived in the area 20 years ago, he was so impressed by the spirit of these Christmas cricket tournaments that he presented a cup for the one held at Middledrift.

"The pitches," he said, "are generally hastily prepared by those at home, and are by no means easy wickets. The carpets cover a lot of pot holes. But play goes on smoothly, and with relatively few accidents.

"Many players go into one tournament from another the previous year without having had any practice in between. I think that goes for the great majority of players, as the pitches are prepared just before the tournaments.

Donations

"In my area we are usually first reminded that a tournament is about to take place by being handed a subscription list for donations to meet expenses. This is generally subscribed to by traders, Government officials and the public in general."

He summed up: "There is no doubt that cricket is the most favoured game in these rural areas and would, with encouragement, some day displace the usual stick fights. As it is, hardly any stick play takes place in the cricket-playing areas."

In the old days, when the White and Black races treated each other with more respect in these parts, cricket matches between White and Black teams were not unusual. The Africans living close to the towns attained a high standard of ability.

The Rev. Bruce Gordon, of King William's Town, recalls the annual fixture which the local Alberts Cricket Club had on the town's main ground against an African XI called the Frontier Cricket Club. He still has the score card of the match played in 1895.

Chapter 15

CHRISTMAS *in the* COUNTRY

———————————— ◉ ————————————

A T CHRISTMAS TIME, PARTICULARLY if there was not an inter-provincial tournament on that year, Eric Majola would often go to the rural areas to participate in the special tournaments held there.

Milase complained that she would be left behind with the family in Port Elizabeth. She and the children would in turn usually participate in the festive season 'socials' organised by local clubs.[1]

Eric had a cousin in Port Elizabeth who played for Wide Awake CC, which comprised mainly players from Middledrift. He himself had played a little for Wide Awake before settling down with New Brighton. 'Time and again they visited this Middledrift' at Christmas time, according to Dan Qeqe.[2]

One year, they had an accident on the way. The lorry in which the cricketers were travelling overturned near Grahamstown in the early hours of the morning. A star sportsman, Willie Komani, who played provincial rugby at a young age, was killed in the accident. Eric, who 'worshipped this chap' ran several miles to Grahamstown to find help.[3]

The Christmas tournaments, held in villages all over the Eastern Cape, were part of a popular tradition stretching back to the 19th century. An unusual news report from the *Evening Post* in January 1954 vividly describes the atmosphere:

While sitting in the steamy heat during a dull spell in the Border-Eastern Province friendly cricket match at East London, I recalled the last game I had seen up in the cool, green hills under the Pirie Mountains' forested slopes.

It was the African version of the Englishman's cricket on the village green: Black men playing in one of the lively marathon cricket tournaments which have been held every Christmas in parts of the Ciskei Native rural areas for the past 50 or 60 years.

Four or five locations put up two or three XIs each, and they all play one another two or three times in the course of the week from Christmas Day to New Year.

All matches are faithfully scored, and the team which finishes up with the most wins carries off a cup which has been presented by a local trader or some other well-wisher.

Very often the batsman with the highest aggregate and the bowler with the best analysis also receives a trophy to take back to his home in the kraal, or to East London, Port Elizabeth, Cape Town, Johannesburg or wherever he works during the year.

These tournaments are a tradition which draw Ciskei men from the cities to their homes in the country every year at Christmas.

Clad in the usual white cricket uniform, the city slicker and the perennial kraal dweller are hardly distinguishable, and they are both subject to the cheerful barracking of the partisan clumps of spectators sitting or reclining around the irregular boundary.

Among the spectators I saw were many well-dressed women and schoolgirls, as well as men, women and children who obviously seldom left their kraals.

One group had a lunch basket and bottles of soft drinks were being passed around. The women burst into chanting song now and again for the benefit of their team out there on the field.

One or two raggedy men who had obviously had a little too much 'k' beer wandered amiably around, and they looked no more out of place than their white brothers in the same state around a city cricket field.

'Gibisela!' or 'Posa!' someone would shout at a tardy fielder or a bowler who seemed to be wasting time. Those words mean approximately 'throw', and that is undoubtedly an approximate description of some of the startlingly unorthodox styles of bowling one saw in action.

I saw nothing, however, which I would readily condemn as being outside the definition of bowling. It certainly did not disturb either of the typically casual umpires on duty.

Up went a ball for a catch and a fielder raced to get under it. 'Bamba imbumba!' was the cry that went up – 'Catch that ball man!'

He got it and the unlucky batsman who lingered a moment at the wicket was left in no doubt about what he had to do.

'Puma, puma!' shouted the supporters of the fielding side. ('Out you go.')

Even less like Lord's were other cries one heard now and again, such as 'Khawuleza!' ('Hurry up') or 'Vuka!' ('Wake up').

But for all its derision at times, there was no doubt that the crowd was as keenly interested in the sport as any white test crowd, and it certainly did not laugh at any of the somewhat quaint formalities observed on the field.

One was the drill when the fielding side went out to toil. They lined up on the pitch like a platoon section ready for drill, and were sent off one by one from there to their allotted places in the field by their captain.

Another was the honour shown to the opposing captain by the fielders when he went in to bat. They gathered around the wicket and clapped him to his place.

Quaint but pleasing.

The wicket was a cleared patch of more or less level veld, and it was certainly showing wear when I saw it. It was being used from about eight in the morning to seven at night, seven days in a row. Often two matches are in progress at the same time, with their fields overlapping.

Old carpets are often used as mats at each end of the wicket. In the game I watched there were no bails.

The whole scene really made a deep impression on me. Here, I thought, is some of the real spirit of cricket.

And what a cricket ground, with the dark green mass of the Pirie Mountains rising steeply a thousand feet above the veld a mile away.

Later, back at the huts, Lyn Valley, not far away from where the trout waters of the Buffalo River drain out of the Pirie range, I met an old African labourer who told me through an interpreter that he had taken part in the Pirie tournaments until he became too old to play.

As a boy he had been taught his cricket by another African, but where that man had learned his cricket he did not know.

Nobody has been able to tell me definitely how these people first became interested in cricket, but they must have been coached originally by the missionaries who laboured in these valleys last century.

I know that they have been playing cricket at St Matthew's Mission, in the Keiskama River Valley, on the other side of the Pirie mountains, ever since the mission was founded.

Mr Bryce Ross, of King William's Town, and son of the Reverend John Ross, who established in 1830 the famous old Ross' Pirie Mission near the cricket field I saw, tells me that he remembers that cricket was a favourite game for the Africans around the mission when he was a boy living there 50 or more years ago.

Today, apparently, cricket is only played in most of the locations once a year – at these Christmas tournaments. They seem to be a part of the fine Christmas spirit out there.

I asked the old labourer: 'Why is it that you people always like to play cricket at this time?'

He thought a moment and then replied with great dignity: 'It is a good thing to play cricket at Christmas. There are a lot of bad things a man can do at Christmas if he does not play cricket.'

He knew his people, and I know what he meant.

Dr R.T. Bokwe, the African district surgeon at Middledrift 20 miles away, told me afterwards that the Christmas tournaments undoubtedly keep the young men out of mischief – dangerous mischief like their vigorous stick play which causes broken heads which the doctor has to mend, and often also fatal injuries.

Dr Bokwe said that when he first arrived in the area 20 years ago, he was so impressed by the spirit of these Christmas cricket tournaments that he presented a cup for the one held at Middledrift.

'The pitches,' he said, 'are generally hastily prepared by those at home, and are by no means easy wickets. The carpets cover a lot of potholes. But play goes on smoothly, and with relatively few accidents.

'Many players go into one tournament from another the previous year without having had any practice in between. I think that goes for the great majority of players, as the pitches are prepared just before the tournaments.

'In my area we are usually first reminded that a tournament is about to take place by being handed a subscription list for donations to meet expenses. This is generally subscribed to by traders, government officials and the public in general.'

He summed up: 'There is no doubt that cricket is the most favoured game in these rural areas, and would, with encouragement, some day displace the usual stick fights. As it is, hardly any stick play takes place in the cricket-playing areas.'

In the old days, when the white and black races treated each other with more respect in these parts, cricket matches between white and black teams were not unusual. The Africans living close to the towns attained a high standard of ability.

The Reverend Bruce Gordon of King William's Town, recalls the annual fixture which the local Alberts Cricket Club had on the town's main ground against an African XI called the Frontier Cricket Club. He still has the score card of the match played in 1895.[4]

This graphic colonial narrative of an African game captures well the long tradition and passion for cricket in the Eastern Cape – and how Africans internalised it, adapted it to their particular social context, and gave it a particularly South African character.

The village Christmas tournaments also demonstrated again the social value and deep meaning of sport in South African society, particularly the close linkages between city and countryside at a time when urbanisation was still a relatively new phenomenon for most South Africans. As rurally-based, poor people migrated in increasing numbers to growing cities to look for work in the 20th century, they formed protective social networks in these new environments.

A so-called 'home-boy' tradition evolved amongst Africans. People from the same area would remain in touch and socialise together in the cities, affording each other security in what they often found to be very difficult urban environments.

It was common for migrants from certain areas to join specific clubs. One could tell affiliations from the club names. The Tembu RFC in East London, for example, represented Thembu migrants from Glen Grey and Cala. Ndlambe migrants gravitated towards the Swallows RFC and the Gqunukwebe from Middledrift played for the Black Lions. In Cape Town the rugby and soccer clubs had tell-tale names like Transkeian Lions, Zulu Royals, Natal Wanderers, Basutoland Happy Lads and Bechuanaland Swallows. In the 1950s people clearly still had strong links with their places of origin.[5]

On the other hand it was common for townspeople who had lived for a long time in the cities to have their own clubs. Thus the Mother City Rugby Club was formed in Langa, Cape Town, and its members would often hold themselves apart from the newcomers.[6]

This 'roots' phenomenon was evident in Port Elizabeth as well. This was the reason why the bosom friends, Eric Majola and Dan Qeqe, who went to school together, played rugby together, courted together, and eventually became next door neighbours, joined different cricket clubs.

It was almost predetermined that the city-born Eric Majola would play for New Brighton Cricket Club and that

Dr Roseberry Bokwe, son of the famous Lovedale composer and minister, John Knox Bokwe, and graduate of Edinburgh University, who presented a trophy for the village cricket tournament at Middledrift in the 1930s.

Dan Qeqe would join Fort Beaufort Cricket Club with its kinship ties to the area he had come from as a schoolboy. Besides New Brighton, all the clubs in Port Elizabeth were based on this 'home-boy' principle. Wide Awake and MCC were from Middledrift, Home Defenders from the Gqunukwebe areas in the Ciskei, Hard Catch from Fort Beaufort and Rock of Ages from Mxelo near Alice. Finally, the Albany, Victoria East and Fort Beaufort Clubs took the same name as the districts their players came from.[7]

141

Migrants from the town to the city formed clubs based on 'home boy' affiliations. The Fort Beaufort Cricket Club in Port Elizabeth, which produced many prominent administrators, was one such example. FBCC executive committee members in the late 1960s. (Back row, left to right) Dan Qeqe, T. Mankayi, H. Madikane, H. Tancu, Ray Mali, Wilfred Khovu, S. Made, E. Nkayi. (Front Row) T. Bawana, A. Mali, A. Xaba, Silas Nkanunu, J. Mali, R. Quphe.

While scholars have written about the value of sport and the 'home-boy' tradition in the cities, they have not fully understood the 'pull' in the other direction. For many city dwellers the Christmas tournaments 'back home' in the rural home were occasions not to be missed. One newspaper commented in 1955 that, 'A significant fact about these tournaments is that many a man who works in the urban area, be it in Johannesburg or right down in the Western Cape, will sacrifice all he has to take part in these tournaments.'[8] Four years later the same correspondent noted, 'There has been a string of arrivals of men from the big centres during the past week. All have come to play in these tournaments.'[9]

Special boards were established to run the tournaments. The one that Eric regularly played in was probably the tournament run by the Ntaba-ka-Ndoda Cricket Board at Qanda near Middledrift. The villages which took part in 1959 were Burnshill, Mxumbu, Cildara, Mnqesha and Qanda.[10]

Besides the Pirie and Middledrift-based matches described above, several other boards ran fixtures. One of them was the Zondeki Cricket Board at Izeli, founded in 1939 by the grandfather of South Africa's international cricketer, Monde Zondeki. Then there was the Mbeka-Mkupa Board and the Nongwane Cricket Board under G.M. Fanti-Qaqa from East London, which held its tournament at Mngaba. *Imvo Zabantsundu* observed, 'These [tournaments] are not a thing of yesterday ... [and] the management is beginning to take the form of town sports.'[11]

Captains and 'in most cases the entire executive' of a board came from the 'town dwellers'. 'The fellow who works in town commands respect because of his nearness to the game. Expression of this is the fact that he is the man who sees cricket and can make use of the experience.'[12]

The pull back towards the rural areas at this time of the year was so strong that many cricketers declined invitations to play in provincial tournaments to participate instead in

Cecil Zondeki, grandfather of South African international player, Monde Zondeki, at the village cricket ground in Peelton near King Williams Town. His father was the founder of the Zondeki Cricket Board in 1939.

the village tournaments: '… the grand old men of the village and the diehards and sponsors regard it as a sign of disrespect should a son of a certain village go and fulfil engagements not run in one's village.'[13]

The reporter, Gordon Qumza, disapproved of the way the village games systematically undermined inter-town and inter-provincial cricket. He said they were 'tribalistic' and went on to complain of perpetual organisational problems: 'Year in year out reports indicate that money gets lost after a tournament. Financial statements are never submitted. This is because a treasurer is resident in Cape Town, the president in Johannesburg, and the secretary in East London. Hush hush arrangements are made.'[14]

Moreover, while one of the social aims may originally have been to keep the young educated, Christianised Africans away from traditional stick fights and drinking over the Christmas period,[15] Qumza complained that 'immorality and drunkenness' were disturbingly common. 'What game

can be shown by a drunken player, and what decision can a drunken umpire make?'[16]

Perhaps Qumza was being overly puritan, but there is no doubt the tournaments were big social occasions. He observed that all the boards held receptions for players on Christmas Eve. For those 'who defend their village' there were also presents donated by the 'Grand Old Men of the Village'. Competition was so keen that betting odds ranged from 'a sheep to a cow'.[17] This practice gave rise to the name of *Amacala eGusha* (Sides of a Sheep) for these tournaments, generally pronounced as *Macal' eGusha*. It became traditional for the winning team to get a sheep as a prize. The sheep was then slaughtered and braaied as part of the occasion.

Today these *Macal' eGusha* tournaments are still held regularly in the rural areas of the Eastern Cape, particularly in the towns and villages around King Williams Town and Fort Beaufort (see Chapter 39).

*The Eastern Province Cricket Federation mirrored the inter-racial co-
operation of SACBOC on the national level in the 1950s.*

Chapter 16

CRICKET CO-OPERATION

———————————— ⬤ ————————————

ERIC MAJOLA MADE HIS way into the top flight at an interesting point in the history of black cricketers. SACBOC had just been formed as an overarching national umbrella body to encourage unity and co-operation between the different black cricket associations. These were the South African Indian Cricket Union, the South African Coloured Cricket Association, the South African Bantu Board and the old 'Barnato Board', reconstituted as the South African Malay Cricket Board in 1953.

The formation of SACBOC energised cricket and opened up new opportunities and approaches. Going with the more assertive politics of the 1950s as the Mandela generation came to the fore, black sportspeople started challenging white control, co-operating with each other across racial divides and seeking international contacts and opportunities.

The situation at provincial level reflected the new dynamics. While the Eastern Province African team continued to participate in the NRC tournaments of the Bantu Board, it also competed on an 'inter-race' level with the other provincial entities and, indeed, joined with them to pick united Eastern Province teams.

As part of greater national co-operation between the 'non-white' cricketers, the Eastern Province Cricket Board of Control was formed in 1948. It consisted of four bodies – the EP Bantu CU, EP Indian CU, the EP Coloured Cricket League (affiliated to the SA Malay Cricket Board or 'Barnato Board') and the EP Coloured CU (affiliated to the SA Coloured Cricket Association). They played against each other twice every season. The games were at the New Brighton Oval and the Adcock Stadium. The inter-race board was the forerunner of the later non-racial EPCU and EPCA. The president for 13 years was Nagin Umley of the Indian Union. He was a businessman from a prominent South End family, who ran a clothing outfitters shop. A founder member of the Eastern Province Indian Cricket Union in 1936, and its president on and off from 1943 to 1959, Umley also played in all the Christopher tournaments between 1942 and 1953. Between 1949 and 1951 he was president of the national body. He deserves to be in any Eastern Province cricket Hall of Fame.[1]

The treasurer and secretary of the Inter-Race Board were also from the Indian Union, indicating that it largely saw to the administration. Wilson Ximiya was vice-president in 1953/54. Ximiya was also secretary of the Eastern Province Bantu Cricket Union. His close friend W.B. Ntshekisa was the treasurer. This former star player was 'a staunch member of the church' and 'an ordinary worker', who ended up running a small cafe next to the New Brighton Oval.[2] His younger brother, Samson, was one of the mainstays of the Transvaal team in the 1950s. The president of the EPBCU was Mr F.H.M. Zwide, the school principal who also became president of the national body.

The Eastern Province team playing in the 1950 inter-race games was J. Stofile, S. Koom, D. Mbengashe, C.B. Manana, D.F. Titto, J. Tuswa, B. Nkhola, J. Ngubelanga, J. Gqomose, J. Maqubela, E.V. Gonomo, W.K. Gobe, M.T. Stofile, W.P. Ximiya and J.G. Ningi.[3]

The Eastern Province Cricket Federation team, 1954, the first 'mixed' provincial team since the days of the Barnato Board in the early 20th century. (Back row, left to right) S.V. Coopoo, T. Morgan, I. Nordien, E. Baderoen. (Middle row) W.F. Ximiya, N.V. Coopoo (captain), ~~~, C. Mgubela. (Front row) E. Majola, M.G. Dollie, A. Peerbhai.

Officials of the Eastern Province Cricket Federation, representing the different racial provincial boards, 1956. (Back row, left to right) A.L. Dwesi, A. Hendricks, D. Williams. (Middle row) J. Ismail, A.M. Johnson, N.V. Coopoo, A.G. Abrahams, C.A. Parker, V.M. Moodaley, A.S. Mpondo. (Front row) R. Wilson (asst. secretary), N. Williamson (vice-president), S.M. Siwisa (vice-president), J. Reddy (patron), N.P. Umley (president), S.J. Reddy (secretary), N. Baboo (vice-president), R. Daya (treasurer), P.S. Vandeyar (vice president).

Cricket in the province was flourishing to the extent that an annual publication, *Cricket Souvenir*, was published in Port Elizabeth in December 1950 and again in December 1951. The magazine, edited by J.J. Reddy, who presented the trophy for the local inter-race competition, was the precursor to the now famous *South African Non-European Cricket Almanack*, published in 1953, 1955 and 1969 by his son S.J. Reddy and Domodar (Damoo) Benny Bansda from the 'Hill' region of Port Elizabeth. The *Cricket Souvenir* and the *Almanack* were two of several efforts to start sports magazines for the growing black sports market in the 1950s. Robert Resha, who became a prominent ANC leader in exile, and who was one of the 156 people charged in the notorious Treason Trial of the 1950s, became editor of *African Sports.* This magazine was based in Johannesburg. It survived for nearly three years and regularly covered cricket. The Reddy's were pioneers in the sports journalism field and today the tradition is being continued by S.J.'s son, San Reddy, a familiar face on South African television screens in his role as news anchor for e-tv.

Another EPCBOC innovation in the 1950s was the introduction of a league championship between the winning clubs from the different unions. The champions who played in the first year of the competition were Union CC (EPCCL), Orientals (EPICU) and Majola's New Brighton (EPBCU).[4]

In 1954 a combined Eastern Province team was selected from the different boards for the first time in the modern era to play what was dubbed a 'goodwill' game against a similarly united Western Province Federation team. Instead of talking unity, the different Western Province affiliates picked a single team, loaded them into a truck and gave 'practical expression to unity and brotherhood which is the cornerstone of sport', according to the Robert Resha in *African Sports.*[5]

The staging of the first 'Inter-provincial Federation match' was described as 'the most historic event in South African

Nagin Umley

———

cricket' by the *South African Non-European Cricket Almanack.*[6]

Wilson Ximiya, Chinky Mgubela and Majola were the African representatives chosen for the Eastern Province mixed team. The last two were responsible for a minor scandal. After the Eastern Province captain, E.V. Coopoo, won the toss and elected to bat, his top-order batsmen were nowhere to be found. The game was held up for half an hour as cars and bicycles 'had to search for them high and low in the vicinity of the Livingstone Hospital'. The reporter covering the match said 'this was highly irresponsible and disgraceful for players of their standard'.[7]

The combined Western Province team won both games by an innings. It also played three other games against local opposition before going on to Durban. Majola's best figures in the three games he played were five for 52 and three for 59.

This 'goodwill tour' gave impetus to the idea of forming one national body based on provincial affiliations.[8] For example, the Eastern Province Inter-Race Cricket Board changed its name to the Eastern Province Cricket Federation around this time as members soon found the 'stigma of racial identity' in the name 'Inter-Race' outdated.[9]

The next big combined match was when the united Eastern Province team took on the visiting Kenya Asians in November 1956. The visit created great excitement in South African cricket circles. The head of the local organising committee summed up the sense of history when he wrote in the brochure that 'Port Elizabeth is agog with excitement at the visit of the first Official Overseas Cricket Team to tour South Africa'.[10] The president of the SABCB, Mr Zwide, said the barriers 'of what had recently been thought impossible' had been broken.[11] During their five-day stay in Port Elizabeth the visitors had a social event organised for them every day, including the welcoming cabaret dance in Humewood, a civic reception at the Muslim Institute and a 'smoker' given by the Aryan Sports Club. Later, local cricket enthusiasts chaperoned the

Eastern Province Cricket Federation team for the historic clash versus Kenya Asians touring team, 1956. (Back row, left to right)
T. Morgan, S.D. Raga, S.V. Coopoo, R. Wilson, A. Hendricks, F. Abrahams (12th man). (Front row) S. Mbekeni,
E. de Kock, C. Mgubela (vice-captain), S.M. Siwisa (manager), I. Nordien (captain), E. Majola, S. Baderoon.

tourists on their journey to Cape Town, stopping over to visit the Cango Caves on the way.[12]

Despite this hospitality, the Kenya Asians beat the combined Eastern Province team by an innings in the two-day match played at the white Union Cricket Club grounds. The organisers had applied to use St George's Park, but this was turned down. It was the tourists' first chance to play on a turf wicket in South Africa, and two thousand spectators were there to see the game start in 'brilliant sunshine'.[13]

The Eastern Province team was I. Nordien (captain), Chinky Mgubela (vice-captain) S. Mbekeni, E. de Kock, E. Majola, S. Baderoon, T. Morgan, S.D. Raga, S.V. Coopoo, R. Wilson, A. Hendricks and F. Abrahams (12th man). It was managed by S.M. Siwisa.

The Kenya Asians scored 240, with S. Coopoo returning the best bowling figures with three for 26. Eastern Province 'collapsed dismally' in both innings to be bowled out for 76 and 89 runs respectively. B.A.L. D'Cunha had match figures of seven for 21. He was one of six tourists with experience of first-class cricket in India and Pakistan.

Another, Shakoor Ahmed, had represented Pakistan in England in 1954.

The Kenyan tourists swept through the provincial opposition winning seven of their nine matches with two draws. However, they lost the first two three-day tests against a strong South African side, led by Basil D'Oliveira. The third rain-interrupted test was drawn.[14]

Despite the one 'coloured' affiliate refusing to participate in the match against the Kenya Asians because of continuing sensitivities around the status of its mother body, the SACCA, which did not want Barnato (or 'Malay') affiliates to use the term 'Coloured', Eastern Province was in the forefront nationally in terms of co-operation between black players from various associations. Where other provinces were often unable to duplicate the SACBOC federal model at provincial level, the Eastern Province Cricket Board of Control operated actively from as early as 1948 to promote inter-race co-operation. This co-operation finally led to the formation of the new united non-racial Eastern Province Cricket Union (later Association) in September 1961.

'Port Elizabeth is agog with excitement at the visit of the first official overseas team to tour South Africa.' Signatures and
photographs of the Kenya Asians team in a youthful Devdas Govindjee's autograph book, 1956.

South African Cricket
BOARD OF CONTROL

S.A. Coloured Cricket Association.
S.A. Indian Cricket Union.
S.A. Bantu Cricket Board.
S.A. Malay Cricket Board. (BARNATO)

Souvenir Programme

Second Biennial Tournament
Johannesburg = Easter 1953

Chapter 17

CRICKET SPRINGBOK

───────────────────── ● ─────────────────────

IN 1951, THE FIRST EVER South African team was selected by the Bantu Cricket Board. Black cricketers had long aspired to play at international level, and now they were taking the first step. History was made as the various components of SACBOC chose sides to play against each other at the first SACBOC Inter-Race Tournament, which was held in Johannesburg over the Easter long-weekend.

The SA Bantus played against the SA Indians in the first match of the historic tournament. They got off to a flying start, beating the strong SA Indian team on the first innings. The Africans were first to bat and scored 258 runs. They followed this up with 110 in the second innings. The Indian team put 184 on the board in their first turn at the crease and just avoided outright defeat by hanging in at 157 for nine wickets at the close.[1]

The legendary Frank Roro scored 116 in the historic match. It was the only hundred of the tournament. His average of 48.00 was also the highest of the week. He was already 53 years old and this tournament was to be his swansong. Going back to 1934, he had scored over 3 000 runs for the Transvaal Bantu team, including 20 centuries and a top score of 228 versus the Transvaal coloured team. His place in history was assured.[2]

There were several other good performances by African players in the game. Sam Ntshekisa took nine for 101 and George Langa seven for 119.

In the second and final match against the SA Coloureds, Langa was again in top form taking nine for 77, while the young Ben Malamba had match figures of eight for 153. Thanks to this bowling, the SA Bantus restricted the strong SA Coloureds team to scores of 170 and 198. But they were not able to rise to the batting challenge. They managed 124 in the first innings, with captain Roro again on form scoring 66, more than half the total. In the second innings the Africans did better to get 148, thanks to 40 from Eric Fihla and all-rounder Samson Ntshekisa's 31. However, they fell short by 96. Basil Waterwitch's 12 wickets, including eight for 32 in the first innings, had much to do with this.

The matches were played at the famous Natalspruit grounds, the so-called 'Mecca of Non-European sport', which the Indian community of Johannesburg had procured in the early 1930s. From that decade, when it hosted the All India Football team in the 'first non-white international to be played in South Africa', through to the early 1970s, Natalspruit was the premier venue for a multitude of sports, especially professional soccer, which used to draw crowds in excess of 20 000 in the 1960s. In the late 1940s it was also the venue for large Passive Resistance rallies. As one writer put it, 'The history of Natalspruit is the history of non-whites and their bitter struggle for survival in sport.' The end came when the ground was zoned exclusively for the use of Indians by apartheid planners and eventually expropriated by the South African Railways.[3]

Yusuf 'Chubb' Garda (who later played for SA Indians) watched that first tournament as a child. He recalls Natalspruit at the time. The changing rooms had small 'enclosed corrugated iron stands that took the team'. There were three overlapping fields and sometimes the fielders in the different matches would be 'in close proximity to each other'. But this would not have been the case during the national tournament. The adjoining City and Suburban ground, designated for 'coloureds' only and separated by a zinc

Eric Majola: sports icon of the 1950s.

fence, was probably used, or else only one game a day was played. Garda remembers the elegant Roro's 'wiry body' and shots off the back foot.[4]

Only three teams, rather than the hoped for four, participated in the first tournament. Because of tensions between the two national 'coloured' bodies, namely the old SACCB or 'Barnato Board' and the SACCA, which had broken away from it, SACBOC had set as a condition for the former's affiliation a name change to the South African Malay Cricket Board. At first, the Barnato group refused, but by the second tournament in 1953, they had joined the fold on those terms.[5]

The 1951 national team, the first ever selected by the Bantu Board, needs to be remembered. The players who got onto the field were Frank Roro (captain), Eric Fihla, George Langa, Julius Mahanjana, L. Mafongosi, Ben Malamba, C. Msikinya, Sam Ntshekisa, C. Scott, Green Sulupha and Wilson Ximiya, the veteran from Port Elizabeth, who had participated in the first SABCB inter-provincial tournament way back in 1932.

The *South African Cricket Almanack* also listed 21-year-old Eric Majola and four others – Sydney Hashe, H. Mawu,

Selby Mbekeni and Wesley 'Zorro' Mzondeki from Soweto – as having been in the tournament squad. Whether or not they were with the team in Johannesburg during the tournament is not clear.

Majola made his debut for the national team in December 1952 in Cape Town, when a side to play a Western Province Federation XI was picked after the Chamber of Mines inter-provincial tournament. Although Frank Roro was available and had played in the tournament, the selectors opted to look to the future. He was replaced as captain by S. Voss of Transvaal. The Africans were badly beaten, losing by ten wickets. The *Sun* newspaper reported that 'a feature of the match was the brilliant strokeplay of the openers of the Bantus'. Eric Fihla (49) and Julius Mahanjana got the team off to a good start, but at 94 for three the spinners were brought on and the Bantu Springboks subsided to 154 and 103 all out (when Wilson Ximiya top scored with 18 in his final match for the national team). With Lobo Abed leading the run chase, the Federation team scored 243 to win easily.[6] Majola opened the bowling and batted number three on debut, but he did not have a successful match, scoring 14 and one, and bowling six overs for 23 runs without taking a wicket.[7]

Majola was in the starting lineup for the 1953 Inter-Race Tournament, which was again held in Johannesburg. H. Mshumphela and various other non-playing survivors of the 1951 squad also made their appearances. However, the team failed to maintain the promise showed in the first tournament. They lost both matches, starting a pattern of being the wooden spoonists. Altogether, the Africans lost ten of the 12 matches they played in the 1950s, with two draws. Often the defeats were by big margins (see scores in block overleaf). This contrasted strongly with the rugby 'tests', where the Africans won more times than they lost (see scores on page 161). The strongest cricket sides were the Indian and Coloured sides who each won two tournaments.

In 1955, the SA Indians bowler, A.F. Walter Stevens, bowling pace and then switching to leg spin and googlies in his second spell, took all ten wickets for 57 runs in the SA Bantu's second innings. This game became known as Stevens' match and his ten wickets and match figures of 14 for 98 were the best ever recorded in SACBOC competitions.[8] Majola missed the 1955 tournament after making himself unavailable for Eastern Province in the preceeding provincial tournament, which served as a trial.[9]

In 1958, he was in the team again for the tournament in Cape Town, notching up his only notable achievement for the national side, a score of 48 against the SA Malays. The Malays just scraped home by three wickets after collapsing to 64 for eight in their second innings against hostile bowling from George Langa and J. Nyamakazi.[10]

The captain of the national African team in the last two tournaments was Julius Mahanjana from North Eastern Transvaal. He was known by the nickname 'Genius', 'because he excelled in all sports'. Born in Middledrift in the Eastern Cape, he grew up in Modder Bee township in Benoni, where his father worked. Mahanjana's parents were stern disciplinarians, insisting that their children

Julius Mahanjana of North Eastern Transvaal, national captain, 1955-1958.

Japhta Mahanjana, North Eastern Transvaal and Natal, another of the three brothers who played for the SABCB national team.

Frank Roro, captain of the SABCB national team in 1951, shows off the bat presented to him by SACBOC for scoring the only century of the first Inter-Race Tournament.

took their studies and sport seriously.[11] Julius's two brothers, Justin (1953) and Japhta 'Super' (1955, 1958), also played for the national team.[11] Julius Mahanjana, A.I. Jeewa (SA Indians) and Goolam 'Lobo' Abed were the only players to play in all four inter-race tournaments. (Abed showed up the nonsense of racial classification when he represented both the SA Indians and the SA Malays.) Ben Malamba was selected for all four, but pulled out due to injury in 1958.

When SACBOC finally managed to get international opposition in the form of the Kenya Asians in 1956 and a reciprocal tour of East Africa in 1958, George Langa and Ben Malamba – who shared the distinction of being a double cricket and rugby Springbok with Eric Majola – were the only representatives from the Bantu Board to be chosen for the combined national team captained by Basil D'Oliveira.

Both players performed outstandingly on the higher level. During the 1956 series against the Kenya Asians, Malamba was the top wicket-taker on both sides, taking 16 wickets at an average of 15.25 each. He also took the most catches, 'turning a few half chances into brilliant efforts'. The tall Malamba, born in Cape Town and educated in Natal, bowled off and leg cutters at a lively medium pace'. He was also a hard-hitting batsman. He 'scored some hectic runs with great enjoyment, bringing much delight to the spectators'. One of his shots landed on the roof of the pavilion at Hartleyvale in Cape Town.[12]

In East Africa in 1958, Malamba broke his finger in the third match and missed the rest of the tour. However, George Langa, nicknamed 'Ouboetie' (big brother) by his team-mates, had an excellent tour. A naggingly accurate medium pacer like Malamba, he ended second on the tour averages with 26 wickets at a miserly 9.65 per wicket. His best return was five for 21 against Tanganyika in a match played on a 'jute mat' in Dar-es-Salaam.[13]

ABOVE *SABCB national team, 1953 inter-race tournament.*
(Back row, left to right) ---, H. Mawu, G. Langa, C. Ngengebule,
S. Mbekeni, S. Ntshekisa, P.S.A. Gwele. (Middle row) F. Roro,
G. Mahanjana, S. Voss (captain), E. Fihla, S. Hashe. (Front row)
G. Sulupha and D. Msikinya.(Absent) A. Mshumpela, B. Malamba,
W. Mzondeki, E. Majola

RIGHT *SABCB national team, 1951 inter-race tournament.*
(Back row, left to right) B. Malamba, M. Sokopo, S. Ntshekisa, Julius Mahanjana, F. Roro (captain),
W. Ximiya, G. Sulupha, G. Langa. (Front row) L. Mafongosi, C. Msikinya, C. Scott.

SOUTH AFRICAN BANTU CRICKET BOARD MATCHES, 1951-1958[14]

1. SABCB vs SA Indian Cricket Union, Natalspruit, Johannesburg, 1951

Draw. (Won on first innings.)

SABCB 258 (F. Roro 118, I.A. Timol 4/44) and 110 (D. Msikinya 37, I.A. Timol 4/33)

SAICU 184 (A. Dinath 69, S. Ntshekisa 5/52, G. Langa 3/46) and 157/9 (G.H.M. Docrat 52, S. Ntshekisa 4/49, G. Langa 4/73)

2. SABCB vs SA Coloured Cricket Association, Johannesburg, 1951

Lost by 96 runs.

SACCA 170 (L. Maclons 60, C. Meyer 52, G. Langa 5/50, B. Malamba 4/68) and 198 (C. Meyer 65, G. Langa 4/27, B. Malamba 4/85)

SABCB 124 (F. Roro 66, B. Waterwich 8/32) and 148 (E. Fihla 40, S. Ntshekisa 31, B. Waterwich 4/44)

3. SABCB vs Western Province Cricket Federation XI, Mowbray Sports Grounds, Cape Town, 30-31 December 1952

Lost by 10 wickets.

SABCB 154 (E. Fihla 49, G. Voss 25, S. Bardien 4/29) and 103 (W. Ximiya 18, S. Raziet 5/48)

WP Federation 243 (G. Abed 66, G. Langa 4/61, B. Malamba 4/75) and 17/0

4. SABCB vs SA Indian Cricket Union, Johannesburg, 1953

Draw. (Lost on first innings.)

SABCB 121 (D. Msikinya 34, M. Garda 3/21)

SAICU 214 (G.H.M. Docrat 53, S. Ntshekisa 6/102)

5. SABCB vs SA Coloured Cricket Association, Johannesburg, 1953

Lost by 10 wickets.

SACCA 199 (B. Waterwich 49, S. Ntshekisa 4/56) and 46/0

SABCB 92 (E. Fihla 17, R. Simon 7/50) and 148 (S. Hashe 35, B. Waterwich 4/34)

The SACBOC Springboks departing for their historic tour of Rhodesia, Kenya and Tanganyika in 1958. The African representatives, George Langa and Ben Malamba are standing at the back (first and second left). Next to them are M. Bulbulia, S. Raziet, E.I. Jeewa, B. D'Oliveira (captain), J. Neethling, B.D. Pavadai (manager), G.T. Abed (vice-captain), A.I. Deedat. (Front, left to right) O. Williams, C. Abrahams, E. Petersen, S. Solomon, A. Abed.

6. SABCB vs SA Malay Cricket Board, Johannesburg, 1953

Lost by 9 wickets.

SABCB 105 (B. Malamba 36*, E. Fihla 31, E. Petersen 6/41) and 98 (Julius Mahanjana 33, E. Petersen 4/24)

SAMCB 163 (A. Freeman 79, G. Langa 7/51) and 42/1.

7. SABCB vs SA Indian Cricket Union, Johannesburg, 1955

Lost by an innings and 89 runs.

SAICU 341/7 (S. van Haaght 73, S. Mbekeni 4/118, B. Malamba 3/82)

SABCB 127 (Julius Mahanjana 41, W. Stephens 4/41) and 125 (J. Khumalo 48*, W. Stephens 10/51)

8. SABCB vs SA Coloured Cricket Association, Johannesburg, 1955

Lost by 7 wickets.

SABCB 56 (S. Mbekeni 18, R. Simon 4/22) and 147 (Julius Mahanjana 49, H. Lakay 5/27)

SACCA 161 (L. Herman 61, J. Ndlovu 4/38, J. Nyamakazi 3/46) and 47/3

9. SABCB vs SA Malay Cricket Board, Johannesburg, 1955

Lost by 7 wickets.

SABCB 104 (J. Khumalo 33, E. Petersen 6/28) and 116 (J. Khumalo 38, A. Rubidge 6/50, E. Petersen 3/28)

SAMCB 144 (G.T. Abed 37*, B. Malamba 4/38, T. Gidi 3/54) and 77/3

10. SABCB vs SA Coloured Cricket Association, Cape Town, 1958

Lost by an innings and 38 runs.

SACCA 221/8 (B. D'Oliveira 102, E. Ntikinca 5/62).

SABCB 95 (Julius Mahanjana 34, B. D'Oliveira 4/20) and 88 (Japhta Mahanjana 25, B. Eriksen 4/15)

11. SABCB vs SA Indian Cricket Union, Cape Town, 1958

Lost by 72 runs.

SAICU 102 (Parsuramen 29, J. Nyamakazi, 4/22, G. Langa 3/21) and 213/7 (A.I. Deedat 100*, G. Langa 4/59)

SABCB 112 (J. Nyamakazi 28*, M. Bulbulia 6/30) and 131 (Japhta Mahanjana 65, A. Variawa 3/27)

12. SABCB vs SA Malay Cricket Board, Cape Town, 1958

Draw. (Lost on first innings.)

SABCB 162 (Japhta Mahanjana 57, E. Majola 48, G. Abed 3/14) and 124 (S. Mbekeni 42, M. Connelly 5/43)

SAMCB 222 (G. Abed 102, J. Ngubelanga 4/28, S. Mbekeni 3/58) and 64/8 (G. Langa 2/17, J. Nyamakazi 3/32)

The Bantu rugby Springboks versus the Coloured Springboks, Green Point Track, Cape Town, 1959, in front of a large crowd. The defence spreads out as scrum-half, S. Mawing, dive passes.

Chapter 18

RUGBY STAR

———————————— ◉ ————————————

WHILE THE DIMINUTIVE Eric Majola achieved prominence as a cricketer, he became a legend in rugby. *Imvo Zabantsundu* asserted in 1959 that not only was Eric Majola 'one of South Africa's best [cricket] all rounders', but he 'is still regarded by most South African critics as South Africa's best fly-half since the days of Hannes Brewis'.[1]

Peers described him as a mercurial player in the same mould as the great Welsh fly-half, Cliff Morgan.[2] Former Minister of Sport, Steve Tshwete, compared him to another famous contemporary, Keith Oxlee. Today he is still readily remembered by rugby lovers as a maestro in the pivot position.[3] In Manie Booley's book, *Forgotten Heroes: History of Black Rugby, 1882-1992*, he is described as one of the greats of the game.[4]

During a holiday visit to the Montagu Springs, I asked former provincial cricketer and non-racial sports follower, Mogamat Galant, if he remembered Eric Majola. He responded in the patois of the ex-slaves in Cape Town, *'Wat praat jy? Die ou was a genius.'* ('What are you talking about? This guy was a genius.')[5]

Galant remembers going as a boy with his older brother to watch the SA Bantus play the SA Coloureds at the Green Point Common in Cape Town in 1961. A crowd of 10 000 watched Majola win the game for the Bantus. Galant laughs: 'To this day we still tease Igsaan Schreuder who played centre that day about letting Eric Majola through.'[6] Current national selection convenor for cricket, Omar Henry, also has vivid memories of watching Majola as a boy in the games at Green Point.[7]

Rugby did not achieve the same level of inter-race co-operation as cricket in the 1950s and 1960s. This was mainly due to entrenched racial attitudes in the Coloured Board. Nevertheless, regular 'test' matches were played. They generated huge interest, as this newspaper report of the 1959 'test', quoted by Manie Booley, conveys:

A South African side of Africans, selected after the recent inter-provincial tournament at Queenstown, met a South African side of Coloureds, chosen after the Rhodes Tournament in Cape Town.

Coloureds, in Springbok green and gold, took the field first at Green Point Stadium, Cape Town. A great cheer arose from the ten thousand spectators. Then the African Springboks, all in black, trotted on to an even greater cheer. This was the sixth test between Coloureds and Africans [since 1950]. A hush descended at kick off. From the start the play was of a high standard: brilliant long runs from the full backs, a lot of burly bustling from the forwards and some classic passing movements by the backs. First score came from C. Fredericks, the swift Coloureds' player from Griqualand West. He made a break, kicked ahead, dashed through a crowd of bewildered Africans, and was over. The kick failed. That made it 3-0 to Coloureds. Three minutes later Africans' fly-half, E. Majola from EP, got the ball from the lineout, steadied himself and banged over an effective drop-kick: 3-3.

The Africans' best movement came early in the second half. A wild rush by the forwards made a big hole in Coloureds' defence. Plaatjie gave the ball to Madikane, who gave it to Maqanda, who gave it back to Plaatjie, and he was over. Majola converted, the score was 8-3, and the Africans' supporters thought that they had already won.

The rugby Springboks with their distinctive badges at a reception. Wing three-quarter, Baba Jali (left), with Milase Majola (second left), flank forward, Mbulelo Twaku, and an unidentified supporter (right).

But the subtle Coloureds' backs still had their part to play. First I. Neethling of Boland went tearing down the left wing, kicked ahead, recaptured the ball when the Africans' full back miss-kicked, and plunged over. A missed conversion made the score 8-6.

Then Fredericks came through for his second try of the game. Once again he kicked ahead at the end of a passing movement, followed up, and dived over: 9-8. Coloureds held on to that one-point lead until the end.[8]

What the report does not mention were the 'loud complaints' about the referee Basardien and touch judge (who had initially been picked to play for the Coloured team). They were accused of blatant cheating in both of the tries against the Africans. Fredericks's first try, after Majola had allegedly pushed him into touch, led to a stoppage in play while irate spectators were cleared from the field.[9]

When the teams next played in Cape Town, in 1961, the African Springboks got their revenge, winning in front of another large crowd. These regular 'tests' against the Coloured Board and the two bodies evolving from it, SARU and the Federation, continued into the 1970s. In the 23 matches

The Eastern Province team that participated in the 1960 Chamber of Mines tournament in East London.

South African African Rugby Board Springbok team, 1961. (Back row, left to right) S. McDonald, H.M. Madikana, H.C. Lebakeng, B.N. Malamba, E. Rula, J.M. Mbiza and B. Phillips. (Middle row) C. Mvinjelwa, G.M. Mashinqana, F.J. Mtyeku (captain), C.M. Scott (manager), E. Majola (vice-captain), M.H. Bafana and S.M. Mjo. (Front row) C.M. Twaku and S.B. Jali.

played between 1951 and 1969, the Africans won 10, lost nine and drew three. One result is still unknown. The strength of African rugby in the 1950s and the 1960s is further underlined by the fact that six of the above defeats were by three points or less.[10]

Given the racial hierarchies in South Africa, it is often assumed that Africans are the sporting Cinderellas in South Africa, but these results and the 19th century cricket scoreboards described earlier in this book show that they proved themselves time and again as exciting sportsmen over the years.

In 1960, when a contest was organised to find the South African 'non-white' provincial champions, the Eastern Province Africans beat the Western Province Coloureds 9-6 in front of 12 000 people in Cape Town to take the title.[11]

In the same year, to celebrate the golden jubilee of the Port Elizabeth African Rugby Board, a combined Eastern Province Federation team took on a SA Federation XV at the opening of the new £20 000 Woolfson Stadium in New Brighton. Eastern Province beat what was the rest of South Africa 14-6 'as Majola once again wove his magic and the home team ended as winners'.

As in cricket, the African Board organised regular inter-provincial rugby tournaments – the one held in Port Elizabeth in 1961 was the twenty-first in 26 years. Eastern Province were always one of the strongest provinces, winning eight of the first 14 tournaments between 1936 and 1953. Eric was in the 1953 team that retained the Parton's Cup in

Eric Majola a mercurial player in the same mould as the great Welsh fly-half Cliff Morgan.

East London. In the process, according to *African Sports*, it gave an emphatic reply to the question of why most Springbok players came from Eastern Province.[12] Dan Qeqe recalls that there would be eight or nine teams participating and 'good rugby venues' would be Port Elizabeth, East London and Cape Town. Places like Queenstown and Umtata were also sometimes used. After these tournaments, the Bantu Springboks, with their black colours and badge depicting the African continent with a Springbok in it, would be chosen.[13]

Veteran journalist and activist, Govan Mbeki, writing in the often-banned 'struggle' newspaper, *New Age*, reported that the 1956 tournament schedule in Port Elizabeth 'was upset by half a day' when Native Affairs Department officials demanded that the 300-odd players 'had to straighten out their passes under the provisions of Section 10'. An official said, 'It is just a formality to comply with the regulations.' Security Branch members booked into the same compartment as players from Transvaal and North Eastern Transvaal on the train journey to Port Elizabeth. Mbeki described these actions as '... another act of humiliation born of South Africa's racialist laws'.[14]

This is not the place for a detailed history of Eastern Province and African rugby, but there was clearly a richness and romance to the game at this time that deserves to be recounted. No one contributed more to its making than the diminutive Eric Majola.

SOUTH AFRICAN BANTU/AFRICAN RUGBY BOARD 'TESTS', 1951-1978[15]
AFRICANS' SCORE SHEET

Year	Versus	Venue	Result	Score
1950	SA Coloured	Showgrounds, PE	Won	08 - 03
1951	SA Coloured	Showgrounds, PE	Won	16 - 03
1951	SA Coloured	Green Point, CT	Drew	06 - 06
1952	SA Coloured	De Beers, Kimberley	Drew	03 – 03
1952	SA Coloured	Sydenham, PE	Lost	03 – 05
1957	SA Coloured	Showgrounds, PE	Lost	11 – 18
1959	SA Coloured	Green Point, CT	Lost	08 – 09
1959	SA Coloured	Western Township, Jhb	Drew	03 – 03
1961	SA Coloured	Green Point, CT	Lost	08 – 11
1963	SA Coloured	Green Point, CT	Won	09 – 03
1965	SA Coloured	Green Point, CT	Lost	12 – 14
1965	SARF Federation	City Park, CT	Won	20 – 06
1965	SA Coloured	BRU Grounds, EL	Lost	06 – 08
1966	SARF Federation	Paarl	Lost	08 – 11
1966	SARF Federation	Woolfson Stadium, PE	Lost	06 – 24
1967	SARF Federation	Paarl	Won	08 – 06
1967	SARF Federation	KwaFord, PE	Won	18 – 06
1967	SARU	Green Point, CT	Won	08 – 06
1968	SARF Federation	Woolfson Stadium, PE	Not available	
1968	SARU	Woolfson Stadium, PE	Won	22 – 09
1969	SARU	Green Point, CT	Lost	19 – 40
1969	SARU	Woolfson Stadium, PE	Won	09 – 08
1969	SARF Federation	Woolfson Stadium, PE	Won	14 – 08
1970	SARF Federation	Woolfson Stadium, PE	Drew	03 – 03
1970	SARU	Green Point, CT	Lost	06 – 17
1971	SARF Federation	Athlone, CT	Won	10 – 03
1971	SARF Federation	Woolfson Stadium, PE	Won	13 – 06
1972	SARF Federation	Woolfson Stadium, PE	Lost	09 – 18
1972	SARF Federation	Athlone, CT	Lost	11 – 16
1973	SARF Federation	Athlone, CT	Won	14 – 12
1973	SARF Federation	Mdantsane, EL	Won	16 – 13
1974	SARF Federation	Mdantsane, EL	Lost	03 – 10
1974	SARF Federation	Goodwood, CT	Won	21 – 13
1974	British Lions	Mdantsane, EL	Lost	56 – 10
1975	SARF Federation	Johannesburg	Lost	09 – 12
1975	SARF Federation	Woolfson Stadium, PE	Won	18 – 12
1976	SARF Federation	Newlands	Lost	06 – 13
1976	SARF Federation	Goodwood, CT	Won	18 – 03
1976	SARF Federation	Woolfson Stadium, PE	Lost	09 – 17
1977	SARF Federation	Woolfson Stadium, PE	Lost	09 – 15
1977	SARF Federation	Paarl	Lost	15 – 22
1978	SARF Federation	Paarl	Won	10 – 06

Part Five

KHAYA MAJOLA AND NEW DIRECTIONS FOR AFRICAN CRICKETERS (1960s-1970s)

TOP *Eastern Province African Cricket Board fast bowler, Mtutuzeli Masuthu, sends down a ball in a club match between Hard Catch and Victoria East in 1969. The umpire is Jackson Malawu Mali and the batsman, Pontawuri Dlepu.* BOTTOM *Harrison Butshingi, SAACB president (left), and Lennox Mlonzi, secretary (right), talking to their SAACB legal representative, Nation Madikizela (centre), during a court hearing in 1967. J. November is standing.*

Chapter 19

AFRICANS *on* THEIR OWN AGAIN

───────────────── ⬤ ─────────────────

THE NATIONAL INTER-RACE tournaments came to an end when SACBOC decided to become a united non-racial body. On 27 January 1958, soon after the fourth and final tournament, SACBOC held a historic meeting of all its affiliated national bodies in the library of the Cape Town City Hall. The stalwart administrator, Reverend Bernard Sigamoney, proposed that racial forms of organising be abolished in SACBOC. He was seconded by the young Hassan Howa, who would become an icon of the non-racial struggle during the next three decades. After five hours of heated debate the motion was accepted by 12 votes to none, with the Malay Board abstaining. The coloureds, Africans and Indians decided to push ahead.[1] The national boards were given three years to disband and get their affiliates in the provinces to merge with their various counterparts.

In February 1961, a combined Eastern Province team travelled to Cape Town to play Western Province in what was described as 'the first-ever match played on non-racial lines'. Green Point Common was the venue and the home team won by the huge margin of an innings and 165 runs.[2]

The practical act of finally reconstituting SACBOC occurred in August 1961. It now moved from being multi-racial to non-racial. A few months later, in December 1961, SACBOC organised its first tournament on an inter-provincial basis in Johannesburg.

Eastern Province immediately followed the national lead. On 15 September 1961, the month after SACBOC restructured, the Eastern Province Cricket Federation convened 'the historic meeting where the clubs, formerly affiliated to the four racial units, affiliated directly to the [new] Eastern Province Cricket Union'. The Federation transferred all its assets to the new union.[3] Nagin Umley, who became president, declared, 'We are proud to record that all cricketers in the Eastern Province now play and enjoy their cricket on a completely integrated basis under the auspices of one cricket union.'[4]

To begin with, the Africans were part of the new set-up, and a few African players participated in the first SACBOC inter-provincial tournament held in Johannesburg over the Christmas/New Year period in 1961/62. The president, Harrison Butshingi, wrote in the tournament brochure, 'We have shown the world that we, the Non-White sportsmen of South Africa, are a unified group, and that we entertain no racial barriers in our ranks. May this example spread far and wide, and convince even the critics who look askance at this project … sportsmanship knows no colour, creed or race.'[5]

The fact that Butshingi signed the message as president of the SA Bantu Cricket Board, while others did so as provincial representatives, indicates that although Africans were part of the decision, they had not yet formally affiliated to the new SACBOC. There was clearly uncertainty on the part of Africans about the move. *Imvo Zabantsundu* carried an article in March 1961 headlined, 'What will happen to Bantu fears?'[6] At the time of the tournament the SABCB secretary, Lennox Mlonzi, was quoted as saying he was against unifying. One of the reasons Mlonzi advanced was that 'Indians are too highly placed for Africans'. He said, 'It is not practical to seek federation for Indians, because they are placed on a higher social as well as economic plane by the laws of this country.' He apparently subscribed to the views of the recently formed Pan-Africanist Congress which encouraged Africans to organise separately as whites and Indians would otherwise dominate. Mlonzi said he had plans for 'organising [African] cricket for better days'.[7]

But Mlonzi's position was at this stage still an unofficial one, and Africans participated in the SACBOC tournament. Eric Majola, Dicky Lupondwana and Wilfred Khovu were in the Eastern Province team under captain Pat Smith. The rest of their team-mates were Alphonsus and Phillip Snyman, A. Samsodien, G. Connelly, Neville Francis, Maurice Wilson, Yusuf Davids and Terry Hendricks.[8]

The only other African player in the five participating teams was George Langa, representing Transvaal. Since making his mark in the first inter-race tournament and the historic East African tours, he was recognised as one of the stars of cricket in that province.

During the course of the following year, the secessionist tendencies within the SABCB gathered strength. At a 'private' AGM held some time in 1962, a decision was taken to continue with the old racial tournaments, starting with an event in Welkom that December. The unadvertised gathering was organised by Mlonzi and the Johannesburg-based leadership of the SABCB. Apparently, 'no report of this meeting appeared in any of the newspapers read in the Cape'.[9]

The press reported that Eastern Province was not invited to the meeting because it had joined the integrated EPCU. 'Sotewu', the cricket writer of *Imvo Zabantsundu*, was highly critical of the politics behind the new moves. He described the movers as 'reactionaries' and asked:

Why do Mlonzi and Co rake up old bones which were better left buried and forgotten? Here again factors other than cricket have entered into the picture. The 'apartness' in some people is so strong that they are prepared to mislead a whole nation. The inferiority from which they suffer they infect into others under the guise that Africans will not get a square deal.[10]

'Sotewu' said it was a known fact that 'in cricket Africans are miles behind all the other races'. They had generally been wooden spoonists in the different competitions. Therefore, he asked, 'Why must they be favoured with selection? They must earn selection.'

When SACBOC organised its second tournament in Port Elizabeth in December 1963 the local African cricketers were still flying the non-racial banner. African stalwarts, Pat Cossie and Wilson Ximiya, who was the EPCU vice-president at the time, were on the organising committee under EPCU president Nagin Umley. The committee managed to organise

a successful event despite being given 'very short notice'. This time around Majola and Dan Qeqe, who was vice-captain, were the only Africans in the EPCU team – and, in fact, in the entire tournament.[11]

Qeqe had recently left teaching to go into business. An advert for his garage in the tournament brochure shows to what extent the early sportspeople had to depend on themselves to organise their sport. The opening function was held in the Moslem Institute in Kempston Road on Christmas Day. There was also a mayoral reception and a dance at the grandly-named Alabama Luxury Hotel during the fortnight-long tournament.

For some reason, the unified Eastern Province did not participate in the 1965/66 SACBOC tournament held in Durban.[12] Perhaps it had something to do with the sentiments expressed some years later by William 'Billy' Ross, the long-serving secretary, that, 'It is my forthright opinion that the Board has not played the game with Eastern Province in many respects.'[13]

In the same year, the Eastern Province Cricket Union 'found it necessary' to change its name to the Eastern Province Cricket Association. This had to do with the fact that the white body was also known as the EPCU and claimed that name.

EPCA teams participated again at the 1967/68 and 1969/70 SACBOC tournaments, but now there were no Africans playing. Organisational divisions between Africans and other black cricketers had become fixed again.

While representatives of the South African Bantu Cricket Board had voted for non-racial unity at the conference of national bodies which decided to reconstitute SACBOC in 1959, the SABCB did not in the end join SACBOC in its new format. Instead, it continued to organise separate Chamber of Mines tournaments as in the past and started rebuilding the SABCB. Tournaments were held in Kimberley in 1963/64, Umtata in 1964/65 and Johannesburg in 1965/66. By that season Eastern Province were 'back into the fold', together with Transvaal, Western Province and Transkei. The Border Cricket Union reaffiliated in April 1966, bringing the number of affiliates to five.[14]

As part of this reorganisation, the Bantu Board had by 1964 changed its name to the South African African Cricket Board, as the word 'Bantu' (meaning, ironically, people) had long since acquired derogatory connotations. It was taken over as official terminology for Africans by the race-obsessed apartheid government, so those at the receiving end decided to use terminology of their own choice, already long in use by political groups opposing apartheid.

The EPCA team for the second SACBOC inter-provincial tournament held in Port Elizabeth over the 1963/64 New Year period.
(Back row, left to right) R. Meyer, T. Hendricks, C. Houlie. (Middle row) R. Wilson, M. Wilson, A. Douglas, D. Haynes, M. Kara.
(Front row) C. Jeptha, E. Majola, P. Snyman (captain), G. Hendricks (manager), D. Qeqe, G. Connelly, N. Francis.

The EPCA organising committee for the 1963/64 tournament. (Back Row, left to right) B.P. Cossie, M. Loonat,
R.G. Doraswami, R. Bhana. (Front row) W. Ximiya, W. Yon, N.P. Umley, G. Hendricks, N. Baboo.

LEFT TO RIGHT *Harrison M. Butshingi (SAACB president, 1958-1970s).
A.B.C. September. Leander Fikile Siyo. Wilson Ximiya.*

Besides the issue of leadership, the main reasons given for the continued separate path of the SAACB was the way SACBOC demarcated its new provincial boundaries. At least three affiliates of the old national bodies had to exist in an area for that area to get provincial status. This meant that in areas where African cricket was strong, but other affiliates were weak or non-existent (for instance in the Orange Free State and parts of the Eastern Cape where there were four African provincial bodies, namely Transkei, Midlands, Border and Eastern Province), African cricketers could not be adequately catered for, according to the Board.[15] The low number of Africans involved in the first two inter-provincial tournaments highlighted the point.

The re-constituted SAACB was not in a healthy state by the mid-1960s. In 1965/66 there was not a quorum to hold an AGM because provinces had not paid subscriptions. This was a serious cause for concern. It was probably the first time that this had happened; between the founding of the Board in 1932 and 1965, no less than 32 AGMs were held. The president, Harrison Butshingi, noted that the formation of non-racial provincial bodies under SACBOC had 'contributed to disorganisation of our Provinces, and as a result the standard of Cricket has deteriorated tremendously since 1958'. The executive decided to 'embark on a country-wide organisation with a view to resuscitate cricket in the provinces'. A.B.C. September led a delegation to Griqualand West in December 1966 and in January and February 1967 the president and secretary visited no fewer than eight provinces. Liaison officers were appointed in the provinces and money was raised from 'patrons and sympathisers'.[16]

During its national roadshow, the SAACB took stock of the position in the various provinces. Eastern Province claimed the highest number of players, 840, and said there was a broad 'following' of 20 000 people out of an estimated total population of 120 000 (which probably referred to Port Elizabeth only). Cricket was being played in three out of six schools and there were 14 clubs and 20 teams overall. Border, with 24, claimed the most clubs, but they all consisted of single teams. Midlands, with its headquarters in Queenstown, had 11 teams and 200 players, and Transkei six clubs and 80 players. The Eastern Cape figure of 45 clubs, low as it was, far surpassed the other regions.

In addition, ten Border schools were reported to be playing, more than the rest of the country combined. This figure must have included the traditional cricket-playing nurseries in the Ciskei of which Lovedale and Healdtown were the best known. Outside the above two provinces, only two cricket-playing schools in Queenstown and one each in Johannesburg and Transkei were listed.[17]

In the Transvaal province the number of clubs had shrunk dramatically from the peak of over 50 in the 1930s. North Eastern Transvaal claimed 12 single-team clubs and Transvaal seven clubs with ten teams totalling 200 members.

Western Province counted nine clubs and 500 players and there were four clubs apiece in Bloemfontein and Kimberley.

Cricket in Natal, played mainly at the University of Natal and Adams College in the past, had apparently collapsed completely. Lennox Mlonzi reported, 'I wish to state categorically that Natal is completely out of the picture. We tried to trace many cricketers but their whereabouts were not known. We were informed by some Indians we met that there was not even a single African club there.'[18]

It was from this weak base that the SAACB tried to set out on its independent path again. The president was Harrison Butshingi from Johannesburg. Known by the clan name Hlangamandla (eat very much), he worked at Gallo Africa,

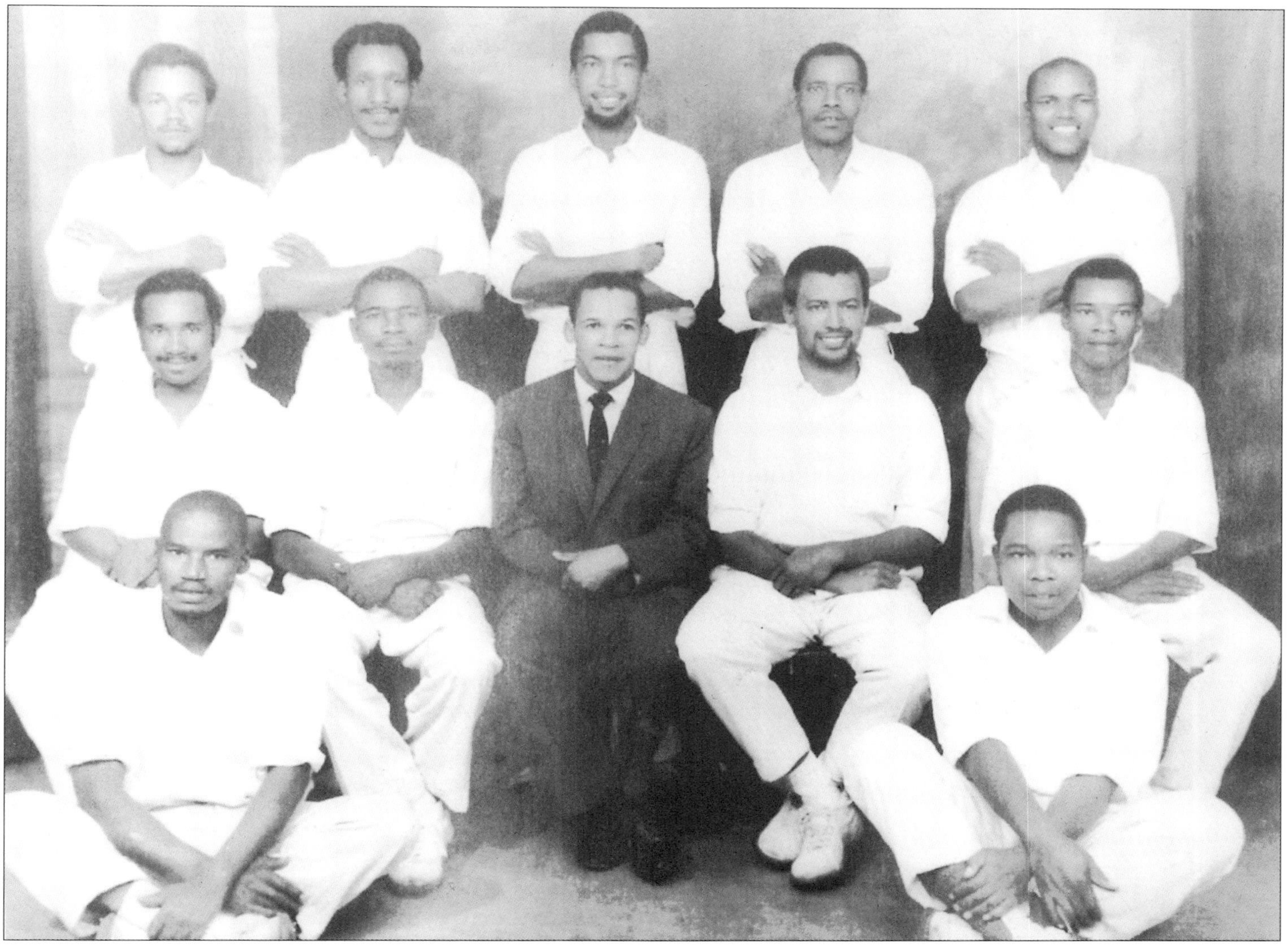

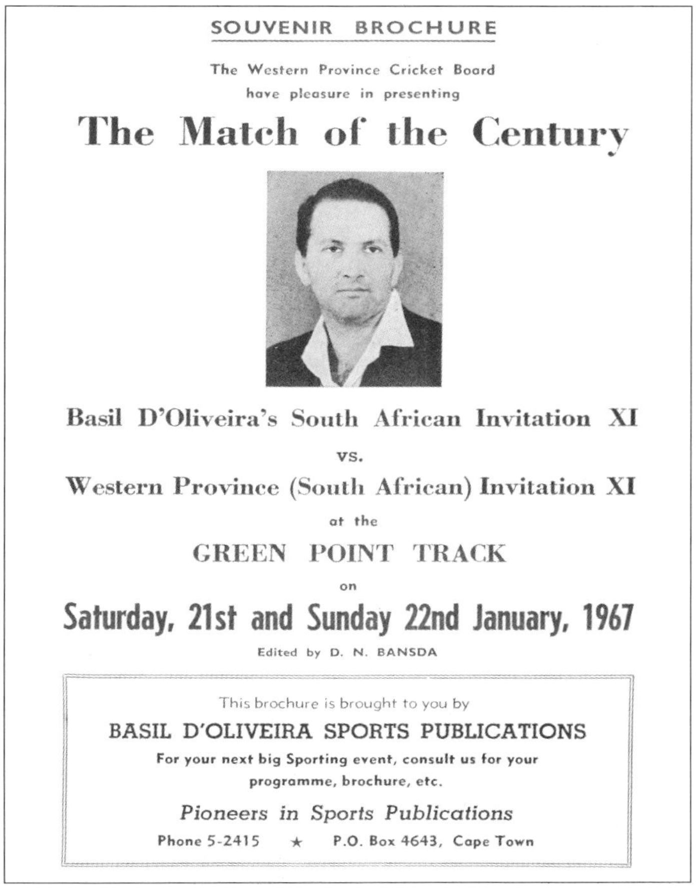

SOUVENIR BROCHURE

The Western Province Cricket Board have pleasure in presenting

The Match of the Century

Basil D'Oliveira's South African Invitation XI

vs.

Western Province (South African) Invitation XI

at the

GREEN POINT TRACK

on

Saturday, 21st and Sunday 22nd January, 1967

Edited by D. N. BANSDA

This brochure is brought to you by

BASIL D'OLIVEIRA SPORTS PUBLICATIONS

For your next big Sporting event, consult us for your programme, brochure, etc.

Pioneers in Sports Publications

Phone 5-2415 ★ P.O. Box 4643, Cape Town

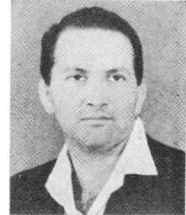

ABOVE *The 1967 SAACB team versus SACCA. The players represented Western Province, Eastern Province, Border and Transvaal, but all originally came from the 'black cricket belt of Border' as indicated below. (Back row, left to right) G. Mashinqana (Alice), S. Masuthu (Alice), Z. Mbatani (Fort Beaufort), G. Sihawa (Alice), W. Magitshima (Fort Beaufort). (Middle row) V. Sikundla (Fort Beaufort), G. Zibi (Peddie), A. Dunjwa (Alice), A. Mbatani (Fort Beaufort), G. Roji (Fort Beaufort). (Front row) E. Ntikinca (Fort Beaufort), T. Magodla (Middledrift).*

LEFT *The invitation matches organised to celebrate Basil D'Oliveira's selection for England provided some players with limited national exposure at a time when there were no longer inter-race games.*

EPCA team for the fourth SACBOC inter-provincial tournament, 1967/68. (Back row, left to right) Yunus Agherdien (umpire), Devdas Govindjee, Alec Douglas, Alphonsus Snyman, Philip Snyman, George Langson, Ronnie Haynes, Stanley Hendricks (selection convenor). (Middle row) Terence Hendricks, Maurice Wilson (captain), Colin Ryan (manager), Faried Abrahams (vice-captain), Armien Abrahams. (Front row) Surendra Vaghmaria, Neville Francis, Jaysukh Vaghmaria, Rubin Kistin.

the music recording company. According to Ashton Dunjwa, who succeeded him after a long term, he was a keen punter who 'went to the race-course every Wednesday'. Lennox Mlonzi, or 'Gcwanini', similarly served as secretary from the 1950s right through to 1977. Originally from Cala in Transkei, he worked for BP, who later transferred him to Umtata, where he eventually retired. He was a senior steward in the Methodist Church. Mlonzi, who doubled up as treasurer for a long time, was clearly the power around which the African Board revolved; he and a coterie from Johannesburg effectively ran the organisation. According to Dunjwa, the headquarters were in Soweto and at one stage 'the entire Executive of this Board was from the Transvaal, much to the objection of other provinces, particularly Western Province'.[19]

Former national cricketer, J.S. Bendile, 'B.A.', was vice-president in the mid-1960s, while Leander Fikile Siyo from East London held that position in 1969. Mlonzi's understudy as secretary in 1967 was A.B.C. September, a teacher who lived in Mofolo North, followed by L.J. Moholo. Other members of the national executive in 1967 were Ashton Dunjwa, V. Masabalala, N.T. Botile, W.D.D. Makhohliso and S. Nkosi.

Two years later the last three had been replaced by Moses Nyangiwe and the Port Elizabeth stalwart, Wilson Ximiya.[20]

The rise of Cape Town-based Dunjwa and Fikile Siyo from East London showed clearly that the SAACB tried to broaden its unhealthily narrow leadership base during this 1960s reorganisation. According to the former, most of the significant administrators and players in the Transvaal and Western Province at this time were in any case actually from the Eastern Cape, and most were ex-Healdtown and Lovedale students.[21]

Harry Oppenheimer and several other whites served as patrons of the SAACB, maintaining the long linkage between the mining houses and black cricket and rugby players since the presentation of the Barnato Trophy and Rhodes Cup in the 1890s.

As part of its efforts to revitalise African cricket, the SAACB once again tried to follow the path of the discarded inter-race matches of the 1950s. The opportunity was provided by a group of dissidents from the South African Coloured Cricket Association (SACCA) who had broken away from SACBOC at Easter 1964 and, like the Africans, resumed the coloureds-only Sir David Harris tournaments.

Eastern Province African Cricket Board team, 1968/69. First winners of the H.M. Butshingi
Trophy. (Back row, left to right) R.S. Mpinda, G.M. Mashinqana, L. Zulu, H. Tancu, N. Mzina,
T. Mavata, T. Williams. (Middle row) S.S. Mgengo, W. Khovu (captain), A. Mbatyoti (manager),
B. Mabonga (scorer), Winky Ximiya, P.X. Siko. (Front row) R. Mbilini, H. Njenje.

A match between a national African team and a SA Coloured XI was organised in Johannesburg over Easter in 1967.

Eight years after SACBOC had decided to go non-racial, it was still struggling to get everyone on board. According to Christopher Merrett, the breakaway SACCA group claimed support in Kimberley, the Boland, Durban, Pietermaritzburg and Johannesburg (City and Suburban). Inter-provincial tournaments for the Harris Trophy were played at Kimberley (1964/65) and Durban (1966/67).[22]

In 1968 a SACCA supporter wrote to the Prime Minister denouncing the non-racial sports movement. He took the attitude that SACBOC was playing politics and even reported it for breaking the Group Areas Act, complaining that the Queens Park Ground at Vrededorp in Johannesburg was in a white area but used for multi-racial soccer and cricket.[23]

The SAACB invited each province to nominate its two best players for the national team as trials could not be held. The match was played in Johannesburg. However, it was rained off after only three overs had been bowled.[24]

Eric Majola, now aged 37, was not in the 1967 team. He seems to have stopped playing provincial cricket around the mid-1960s, but he was still going strong in 1969 when, aged

39, he led New Brighton to the top of the local league. A new generation of players had emerged since 1958, with Edmund Ntikinca the only survivor from that tournament. The line-up was G.M. Mashinqana (EP), G.M. Masutu (EP), Z. Mbatani (Victoria East), G.G. Sihawu (Border), W.V. Magitshima (WP), G.M. Zibi (WP, vice-captain), A.M. Mbatani (Transvaal, captain), G.L. Roji (Transvaal), E.M. Ntikinca (Transvaal), T.H. Magodla (WP) and A.A. Dunjwa (WP, manager).[25]

In 1968, the SAACB tried to organise a second 'test' against the Coloureds. However, it did not materialise. Lennox Mlonzi said it was called off because 'arrangements started late'. 'Sotewu', the long-standing cricket correspondent for *Imvo Zabantsundu* welcomed the news: 'Not by any imagination could matches of this splinter group be regarded as fully representative.'[26]

The only other national level cricket in the 1960s was when two African representatives were included in Basil D'Oliveira's South African Invitation team which played three matches against composite sides in 1967. They were the 'fine attacking batsman', Gladman Roji, and Dai Mokonenyane from the New Brighton Cricket Club.

New Brighton Cricket Club, Port Elizabeth, 1968/69. Winners Championship Trophy. (Back row, left to right) C.T. Orleyn (Delegate), W. Nyati, B. Ntsele, W. Penxe, D. Mokonenyane, M. Tisani, Winky Ximiya, V. Mankahla. (Middle row) T. Oliphant, E. Majola (captain), S. Kapi (president), C. Attwell, T. Ndoyana. (Front row) S. Oliphant, W. Xotyeni.

Mokonenyane's elder brother had played scrum-half with Eric Majola for Spring Rose. He himself was a carpenter and provincial rugby lock forward.[27] Small wonder that the programme for the 'Match of the Century' against a Western Province Invitation XI described him as 'a fast and strong built bowler, who gets a tremendous pace off the pitch'.[28] These games were meant to stimulate interest amongst black cricketers and they showed that the boundaries between the SAACB and SACBOC were still fairly porous.

SACBOC eventually drew the coloured breakaway group back into the fold, but it was not as successful with regard to the African Board. The SAACB set four conditions for getting together with SACBOC again. SACBOC informed the SAACB in 1969 that it could agree to three of these, but it could not accept a 'Point C' (which is mentioned but unfortunately not explained in the minutes of the SAACB AGM).[29]

The African Board organised further Chamber of Mines inter-provincial tournaments in Queenstown in 1967/68, Port Elizabeth in 1968/69 (when Eastern Province won again at home), Germiston in 1969/70, and Welkom in 1970/71. The last tournament was held in Soweto over New Year in 1974/75.

Although the SAACB continued as a separate body, contact on the provincial level between African and coloured

cricketers did not stop. Dan Qeqe explained that clubs like New Brighton and Fort Beaufort would play special matches every season against winners in the SACBOC leagues.[30] Ray Mali, who was vice-president of the Eastern Province African Cricket Board between 1969 and 1972, confirms that the local African clubs played regular games at Gelvandale and other venues against SACBOC clubs until the end of the 1960s.[31]

There are also reports of regular games, described as 'trials' by the newspapers, between the Eastern Province African Cricket Board team and the Eastern Province Cricket Association team, usually before the respective provincial tournaments. For example, in November 1967, both A and B sides played against each other at the same time at the Woolfson Stadium. The Africans lost badly in both cases. In the A game, the EPCA scored 307 versus 129 and 91 to win by an innings. The usual captains, Dan Qeqe and China Attwell were both unavailable. In the B game the margin of victory was six wickets.[32]

In December 1969, the Africans again fared poorly, scoring only 140 and an unfinished 125 in reply to the EPCA's 303 for seven. Neville Francis was dropped five times on his way to scoring a century. Only Thoba Williams, 'who enjoys his cricket best when he has to fight with his back to the

Fort Beaufort Cricket Club, Port Elizabeth, 1968/69. Winners League and Knock Out competition. (Back Row, left to right) C. Mali, T. Matyana, C. Qeqe, H. Tancu, D. Mama, E. Williams, H. Njenje. (Middle row) A.B. Mali (life president), W. Khovu (captain), C. Xuba (president), D. Qeqe (vice-captain), S. Nkanunu (delegate), J.M. Mali. (Front row) T. Bleki, Z. Stofile.

wall', emerged with any credit, scoring a gritty 42 not out.[33] In the second innings Ndoda Mama scored 41.

The Eastern Province African team in that match was Mama, M. Zulu, Phakamile Lubambo, Winky Ximiya, L. Zulu, Thoba Williams, Dai Mokoenyane, S. Mpinda, Tommy Mavata, Hambile Njenje and Bruce Mahonga.

However, these contacts were made more difficult as apartheid control tightened in the 1960s. The permit system was used to enforce urban segregation more rigidly. Members of one racial group had to have permits to enter segregated townships designated for another. The 1969 *South African Cricket Almanack* confirmed this situation: 'The only racial unit which still exists in Port Elizabeth is the Port Elizabeth African Cricket Board, which seceded from the controlling body due to restrictive pressures of the authorities.'[34]

While Africans remained in a separate body at provincial and national levels, by the end of the 1960s historically African and coloured communities were closer here than in, say, the Western Cape – and this would again become evident in sport and politics in the 1970s and 1980s.

The 1969 *Almanack* also makes the interesting point that at one stage SACBOC clubs in the Eastern Province 'regularly participated' in matches against so-called 'European' clubs as well. It mentions that fewer than eight different

white clubs in Port Elizabeth had played against black sides in the past. The dates and circumstances are not elaborated on.[35]

However, the 1960s will be remembered as the decade in which African cricketers chose a separate path from other black cricketers who, at that time, were embarking on an increasingly politicised challenge to the white cricketing establishment, which history would reward with success in the long term. After being part of the decision to form the non-racial SACBOC, Africans stayed out and Lennox Mlonzi later referred to the decision to unite as 'the time of sabotage' against Africans.[36] While the decision by the Butshingi/Mlonzi leadership to go it alone may have had some merit, it was to take African cricketers down a path fraught with political complexity, and history has so far not judged this choice kindly. Because of apartheid, South Africa was speeding towards the dead-end alley of deep conflict; at this moment the SAACB and its leaders chose the path of collaboration with the white establishment rather than defiance.

In the late 1960s several major developments occurred within South African cricket, and these led to the reshaping of the narrow confines within which the African Cricket Board operated.

How the satirical British magazine, Private Eye, *portrayed the controversial D'Oliveira Affair in 1968, which led to the isolation of the white-only SACA from international cricket.*

Chapter 20

NEW ALLIANCES *and* OPPORTUNITIES

───────────── ⬭ ─────────────

INTERNATIONAL PROTESTS AGAINST APARTHEID sport grew in the 1960s, particularly after the D'Oliveira Affair in 1968. Basil D'Oliveira, the South African cricket star who captained the SACBOC team in the 1950s, went to England in the early 1960s to pursue opportunities closed to him at home. Defying the odds, he was picked for England soon afterwards. With a tour to South Africa in 1968 in the offing, the question was would he be selected and would he be accepted in South Africa if he was. Political debate intensified as the tour approached. It shot to fever pitch when D'Oliveira was first omitted from the tour party and then included after one of the players selected withdrew because of injury.

South Africa's Prime Minister, B.J. Vorster, responded in scathing terms: 'It's the team of the anti-apartheid movement. We are not prepared to accept a team thrust upon us – it's a team of people who don't care about sports relations at all.' A conservative MCC, which by some accounts had been playing 'footsie footsie' with Vorster and the whites-only SACA, had no option but to call the tour off.[1]

White South Africa, already expelled from the Olympic movement, now faced complete isolation in sport, and it dawned on the South African government and white cricket officials that something had to be done to prevent this. The result was the multi-national sports policy, whereby the government tried to win acceptance without making any fundamental changes to its apartheid policies.

The white cricket establishment tamely fell in behind this. Without challenging the government, the SACA tried within the confines of the new policy to reach out to the African Board and SACBOC. Basically the idea was to co-opt them, to show to the world that there was progress, but not to challenge apartheid in any fundamental way.

In 1969 Mr Jack Cheetham, president of the SACA, declared that future Springbok sides would be chosen on merit. At the same time, he announced a R50 000 grant by the SACA for 'assisting the development and advancement of non-white cricket'.[2]

The offer was made without prior consultation with SACBOC and SAACB. The former rejected it out of hand because it 'sought to perpetuate colour differentiation'. However, the African body accepted the offer and started working more closely with SACA.

In April 1969, the 'first-ever coaching course of Africans in cricket' was held in Port Elizabeth at the same time as SAACB gathered in the city to hold its AGM. SACA sponsored the course, which was run by South African spinner, Atholl McKinnon. The opening of the course 'was blessed by the presence' of SACA president, Wally Hammond, his predecessor, Arthur Coy, and white EPCU president, Billy Woodin.[3]

With R50 000 in the bank, Harrison Butshingi and Lennox Mlonzi approached the SACA Trust in 1970 about the possibility of an African schools week based on the lines of the annual Nuffield Week for white provincial schools sides. Started in 1940, with a grant of £10 000 from Lord Nuffield, the

Senior SAACB administrators pictured with members of the SACA Trust when the Trust announced the grant of R3 000 for an African schoolboy tournament in 1970. (Left to right) A.A. Dunjwa, J. Passmore, W. Moholo, J.P. Duminy, H.M. Butshingi, E. Carter and L. Mlonzi.

Nuffield Week had been a nursery for top-class cricketers for many years, producing many Springboks including Ali Bacher, who was captain of the national side at the time, and great players such as Graeme Pollock, Barry Richards and Mike Procter.[4]

The SACA Trustees, John Passmore, Edwin Carter and Dr J.P. Duminy, former principal of the University of Cape Town, decided that of all the initial requests for funds, this was the best one. They gave the go-ahead, and the first week was planned for Bloemfontein because of its central location. However, it was discovered that the city did not have a single cricket ground for Africans. The week was almost cancelled, but John Passmore jumped in and, working with a local committee, hurriedly rearranged the tournament for Cape Town in January 1971. This led to the week being named after him.[5]

The 17-year-old Khaya Majola, then in Standard 8 (or Grade 10 in today's terms) at Cowan High, was selected for the Eastern Province team for this first week. Pat Cossie from Newell was responsible for getting the team together. Other members included the captain, Charles Notoza, Billy Jaggers, Pilot Mashicila and the late Sidima Dwesi, who was a promising off spinner. Gerald Majola, then 11 years old, was taken along as scorer.[6] The white EPCU covered the costs of the kit.[7]

The Eastern Province Passmore team was chosen from schools playing in a regular schools league. Port Elizabeth was probably one of the few places in the country where sport was organised to that extent. Still, Khaya Majola and his friends learned the game more from his father than at school. Khaya attended first the Jarvis Gqamlana Lower Primary School and then the Johnson Marwanqa Higher Primary School in New Brighton. Although there was some cricket at Johnson Marwanqa, there was very little organised sport at primary level. Nevertheless, as the local *Evening Post* newspaper reported later, by the time he got to Standard 4 Khaya was already 'a star in Port Elizabeth'.[8]

It was only when Khaya went to Cowan High School that he started playing inter-school matches. There were six schools that played against each other. Cowan would challenge Newell High, Loyiso High, Tech, Kwazakhele High, where brother Tozie studied, and Kabah from Uitenhage. Newell was probably the best-known African school in Port Elizabeth, with a reputation for its sporting tradition. One of South Africa's top business personalities, Saki Macozoma recalls that this was an important reason why his parents sent him there in the 1970s.[9]

By his teens in the late 1960s, Khaya was starting to get used to the publicity. 'Nearly every week I would be in the paper for scoring a fifty or taking wickets.'[10] He was playing for both the school and New Brighton Cricket Club, who his father captained to the age of 40.

For Tozie Majola, living in the shadow of his elder brother, the Kwazakhele/Cowan games were a chance to get even: 'It was Khaya against Tozie and people were coming to watch. He used to get nervous batting against me. I used to take advantage of that.'[11]

Their father remained a hard taskmaster as he grew up. Khaya remembered how once, even after scoring an undefeated 50 for New Brighton, his father gave him a hiding for not winning the game. 'It came to the point that I hated cricket,' he recalled.[12]

Hate it or not, Khaya was poised for a career in the top level of the game — of course, within the parameters determined by the all-pervasive system of apartheid. The Passmore Week was the first rung on the representative ladder.

Nine teams played in the first Passmore Week, with Khaya's Eastern Province side beating Border in the final. Khaya screws up his face distastefully thinking back on that week: 'The standard was awful. Some of the guys couldn't even play the game.'[13] Indeed, John Passmore confirmed this: 'At the first week the situation was farcical with fielders, for example, doing cartwheels in the field. They had no idea about cricket.' The facilities were very poor and the dress was described as 'ill assorted'.[14] However, the white SACA kept a stiff upper lip in its annual report saying the tournament '…went a long way towards encouraging cricket in our Bantu community' and 'with a little technical "know-how", some of the players would make good cricketers'.[15]

Khonaye Penxa, Khaya's friend from the Yokwe Street versus Rose Village days, was then at boarding school at St John's College in Umtata, and played for Transkei in that first tournament. He remembers the excitement of travelling down to Cape Town by train and the 'lots of fish dishes' they got in Cape Town. 'It was nice.'[16] The teams were accommodated at St Louis Roman Catholic School in Langa, while the officials were housed in the Langa Community Centre. The cricketers slept on mattresses on the floor.[17]

At the end of the week Khaya Majola was picked for the first-ever South African Schools team to play a Western Province African XI. Z. Mbekeni was captain. The main prizes went to Billy Jaggers of Eastern Province (best cricketer), Stanford Somyo of Western Province (best batsman) and Peter Somyo of Border (best bowler).[18]

The white establishment came out in support. Local private schools lent equipment to the Western Province team. The mayor hosted an event and Ali Bacher, incumbent

Khaya Majola.

captain of an isolated SACA Springbok cricket team, put in an appearance together with John Waite (manager) and some members of the Transvaal team.[19]

The second Passmore Week was held in Johannesburg in 1972. A five-year sponsorship of R2 500 per annum from SA Breweries had made possible the continuation and 'permanent establishment' of the Passmore Week. Again, Khaya remembers Ali Bacher being present as part of the tournament organising committee. Lennox Mlonzi was the 'main guy in charge'.[20]

Khaya was once again in the champion side, but this time it was for another province, Border. Khaya performed brilliantly as vice-captain of Border. Journalist Thami Mazwai described him as 'the outstanding bowler and one of the leading batsmen'. He scored two centuries, the only batsman to do so, and also knocked up scores of 86 and 72. As a bowler he also took wickets 'to the tune of five for eight and four for four', the Port Elizabeth *Evening Post* reported.[21]

Passmore tournaments followed in Soweto (1973), Langa (1974), New Brighton (1975) and Mdantsane (1976) and became a permanent part of the cricket landscape until 1990.[22]

'Khaya Majola is following in the footsteps of his father. At Lovedale where he is training
to be a teacher, he is about the best they have. He is coach, player and trainer.'

Chapter 21

LOVEDALE TRADITIONS BATTERED *but* INTACT

---◆---

THE REASON WHY KHAYA played for Border at the second Passmore Week was that he had left Cowan High School in Standard 8 to enrol for a primary school teachers' diploma at the famous Lovedale College in 1972. He spent two years at Lovedale. Situated on the outskirts of the town of Alice, just across the Tyume River from the University of Fort Hare, the college has been described as the *grande ecole* of mission schools in South Africa. Both it and the town, which is some one hundred miles from Port Elizabeth, were famous for their role in African education.

Established in 1841 by Scottish missionaries, Lovedale College was the most important black educational institution in Southern Africa until Fort Hare (initially known as the South African Native College) was started in 1915. Countless African leaders were educated at these two institutions and the neighbouring Healdtown, St Matthew's and Fort Cox. The importance of these Ciskeian educational institutions could be measured by the fact that as late as the 1940s, they were still producing more than half of all the African matriculants in South Africa.[1]

The strong cricket tradition at Lovedale and the other mission schools and colleges, described in Chapter 1, continued well into the 20th century. It was strengthened by the formation of Fort Hare, which became one of the main nurseries for African sport. Archer and Boullion have noted that 'one of the first acts of the students ... was, without prompting from the staff, to lay out football and cricket pitches under the direction of one of their number'.[2] The initiator was Hamilton Masiza, who later became president of the South African Bantu Cricket Board. According to the official historian of the University, 'Sport has never been overdone ... Studies took first place and no one came to college just for the game.' Nevertheless, Archer and Boullion continue, the Fort Hare graduates were 'trained to be leaders, a Christian and intellectual elite for whom accomplishment in sport was a component part of Western civilisation'.[3]

A longstanding sports master recalled that the annual inter-college athletics competition 'for years produced the best athletics performances amongst Africans in the country'.[4] Football teams toured to Johannesburg in the winter holidays and cricket remained ever popular. Secretaries of the Fort Hare Cricket Club in the 1930s included the famous writer A.C. Jordan (father of Pallo, a minister in the first cabinet of a democratic South Africa) and W.M. Tsotsi who went on to become a leader of the Non-European Unity Movement.[5]

The missionary school tradition came to an end in the 1950s when the government took control of African schools as part of its Bantu Education policy. Rigid segregation and apartheid ideology were forced onto institutions with a proud (if flawed) history. 'The missionary colleges were ravaged,' according to the historian Anne Mager. She described the practical effect of this take-over at Lovedale. Students from outside South Africa were no longer admitted. Coloured and Indian students were excluded. The library was closed. Students were 'discouraged from reading outside of their prescribed

*A long inter-college tradition: Healdtown's athletic team from the 1930s, with the principal,
Rev A.A. Wellington and the trainer, Don Mtimkulu, also a provincial cricketer.*

works'. Transkeian, Ciskeian, urban and rural students were kept in separate dormitories. A stop was put to literary and debating societies. Time after class was taken up by manual work. Scripture filled most of the curriculum. Industrial training was stopped.[6]

Fort Hare, the training ground of African leaders, became a 'bush college' and famous teachers such as Professor Z.K. Matthews were forced out. However, despite the havoc wrought by Bantu Education and radical apartheid social engineering in the 1960s, the college sport traditions and rivalries were still strong during Khaya's time in the 1970s.

Many prominent figures in the new democratic South Africa cut their sporting teeth in this environment. Ray Mali was both cricket and rugby captain at Lovedale in the late 1950s. He remembers the inter-college games against Fort Hare, Healdtown, St Matthew's and Fort Cox, the agricultural college at Middledrift. The students also played against local clubs such as Gaika from Fort Beaufort, Five Great Powers from upper Gqumahashe, Never Give Up from lower Gqumahashe, and Conquerors and Fight Again from Ntselamanzi. For Fort Hare, there were even trips to Port Elizabeth, Grahamstown and King Williams Town for games against clubs there. In those days, the predominantly white National Union of South African Students (NUSAS) had a branch at Fort Hare and they organised an annual match between Rhodes and Fort Hare. Once, in the early 1960s,

Fort Hare went on a national tour, taking in Cape Town, Kimberley, Johannesburg and Durban.

Never Give Up and Fight Again were amongst the clubs mentioned in those early news reports in *Isigidimi Sama Xhosa* in 1884. Seventy five years later, Magadu Balfour, the father of Minister of Sport, Ngconde Balfour, was one of those playing for Fight Again. Ray Mali, who sometimes turned out for Conquerors, remembers playing against him.[7] Minister Balfour himself played cricket and rugby for Lovedale. He also gained provincial honours for Victoria East, while studying at Fort Hare at around the same time as Khaya Majola.

Ray Mali remembers tossing the coin in the match against Fort Hare. The opposing captain was Krish Mackerdhuj, long-time sports administrator and South African ambassador to Japan. A gregarious character, Mackerdhuj was universally liked. Ray remembers his flamboyant hairstyle and smart white shoes that earned him the nickname 'Texas'. He played for Fort Hare for six years and was captain for three. A team-mate recalls, 'If we wanted to go to bioscope on Saturday afternoons, we'd tell the captain to bring on Krish and he'd soon clean up with his mixture of offies, leg-spinners and googlies.'[8]

Other notable sports activists to study at Fort Hare were the poet and founder of SANROC, Dennis Brutus, the first secretary of a non-racial SACBOC, Ramakrishna 'Rammy'

Despite the introduction of Bantu Education, the old college sports traditions and inter-college rivalries continued into the 1970s.
TOP *University of Fort Hare.* BOTTOM LEFT *Healdtown Institution.* BOTTOM RIGHT *Lovedale College.*

Doraswami and prominent Eastern Province cricket administrator, Raymond Uren. Their presence at Fort Hare was a reflection of the relatively cosmopolitan era before the apartheid rulers banned non-Africans and, increasingly, non-Xhosa speakers from the University.

Ray Mali ascribes being made captain of Lovedale to the two young men sitting on either side of him in class, Chris Hani and Njongonkulu Ndungane. Hani told him that they were going to make sure he became captain and Ndungane helped this famous organiser with the lobbying. The latter is the Archbishop of Cape Town today and still watches regularly at Newlands.

In her book, *The Ochre People* (1963), Noni Jabavu, granddaughter of John Tengo, captured the atmosphere of college sport in the 'heartland' of black cricket at the time. While visiting family in South Africa from England, where she was then living, she went to Fort Hare one afternoon to watch tennis:

We reached the crowd and 'Old Man' began to introduce me to friends. They scrambled up, cutting short their animated conversations. One of them gave me his seat which I was glad to drop into. A strenuous silence descended. They were polite young people and I again had to take the initiative in order to put them at ease, and thought, no wonder generations prefer to keep their own company; I was finding it exhausting behaving as a senior towards the young. Had my reactions atrophied because of the 'lack of ritual of that life overseas'?

... They were watching a singles match, the last of the afternoon, which Kehle was pleased we had arrived in time to see for it was a contest between the best of all student tennis players, not only of Fort Hare, but of Fort Cox, Lovedale, Healdtown, St Matthew's and other great institutions in the Eastern Cape, breeding grounds of aficionados of sports and athletics. Adjusting my spectacles and getting my bearings, I was attracted by one of the players, a stylishly turned out young man in very short shorts that set off the light brown of his legs, like a fashionable Frenchman in summer in Antibes.

'That is Makalima,' my cousin said. He was another of those we call 'red-complexioned' at home, brown-haired, grey-eyed. As if that were not enough he had also the physique of a Greek figurine – for he was small. When his supporters rooted for him he acknowledged with the engaging smile of a bashful, dark, golden, confident Hermes.

However, his less striking opponent played a subtler game; a man called Hani, I was told. He had a curious gait, reminiscent of the South American professional, Segura. His fellow students who had seen Hani play a hundred times were not reconciled to the figure he cut either, for they talked among themselves about his extraordinary, painful-looking movements.

How can a chap play this tennis, walking and running like that?

I told them he was in good company, one of the champions of the world functioned under the same disability.

Segura? How! He looks stiff like Hani, this non-elegant – 'eli qhi-talaekunxibeni'? They were incredulous, but delighted to hear that their colleague's tennis was thrilling to me. I did not say that merely to flatter. Hani's placings were astute, his ball found remote spots, was delivered over the net with hair's breadth precision and a style the more scintillating because of the contrast with his awkward movements. He held his watchers spellbound. They forgot about the irruption in their midst and I was glad; it gave me the chance to see them as they really were.[9]

Noni Jabavu then described the ethos and character of this college sports setting:

They mostly talked in English. I knew, of course that they came from all over South Africa but had forgotten how vividly at Fort Hare you saw the tribes welding into a new nation. You had only to listen to the exclamations and shouts. Their various English accents gave you a sense of the vast spread of South Africa. There were the clipped, sharp Sutho of Basutoland and the Transvaal; the stacatto and glottal-stopped Chwana – from Bechuanaland and the Orange Free State; mellower silky Zulu – from Natal; soft sophisticated Western – from the faraway Cape Peninsula, Capetonians; and, of course, the abrupt and masculine Xhosa tones of locals of the Eastern Cape and Transkeians. You could even detect the different gestures.

I listened to comments on the play cast in satirical quips, in private jokes which had to be explained to me; I saw a young woman's finger raised in exclamation, a young man beside her leap up and reel in ecstasy like an umbhayizelo dancer, because of a successful backhand smash stroke at the net; heard remarks that illuminated attitudes which I had forgotten could be modified by the regions people came from, up and down the country. A series of rallies got under way. Everyone became entranced, only breaking out of their pleasure by moaning, grunting; squeaks that sprang from different languages and their tonality. A rally collapsed with a point to Makalima, upon which a young man rose, his eyes twinkling like a bird's; and he prepared to 'give a speech' as a big person might.

'Friends, Romans, countrymen, lend me your ears', he started in English, then slipped into a torrent of congratulations in Afrikaans mixed with English. Applause. His audience obviously loved the campus clown for his burlesquing tradition. The next service began. Another rally ... The ball streaked, almost invisible; necks craned; tension mounted, until another young man jumped up unable to contain himself and thrust the first one down by the shoulders, crying, 'Man, what justice can you do to this piece of tennis? Away with you. Allow me, friends, to take the floor.' His oration ... shed still more light on the complexity of current student humour for he played on a different set of assumptions. They were recognised as he linked the game with political issues – Verwoerd, inevitably; the forthcoming truncation of their normal study courses under the Bantu Education Act. He touched lightly on the existing ambivalence towards 'emancipated women', and I was

told, amid laughter, that the pretty girl besides him was his fiancée and a leading college feminist. When the match ended and we all went home, dusk falling, I realised that the sport acted like a catharsis. It helped release some of the pressures, 'iifrustrations' about the future that everybody was faced with. The rebellion masquerading as laughter was frightening and tempted me to remember only the laughter.[10]

Chris Hani did study at Fort Hare around this time, but it is not clear that the player in this description is in fact him. While neither Ray Mali nor Sobizana 'Bizo' Mngqikana, South Africa's current ambassador to Turkey and a national rugby player at the time, believe it was him, Krish Mackerdhuj remembers that Hani was a tennis player and often came to watch the cricket team playing.[11]

Nevertheless, the deeply rooted culture of sport at the Eastern Cape colleges described here is confirmed in Jabavu's book. Mveleli Ncula, the present chief executive officer of the South African Rugby Board, remembers, 'We were very disciplined. You did not have time to get into trouble. There was only work and sport'.[12]

Ncula grew up in Alicedale and learned the game in 40-strong street games. He studied at Healdtown, but was forced to leave school early and become a petrol pump attendant because his family could not afford school fees. As a 21-year-old he won a scholarship to Lovedale, and after that he went on to study at Fort Hare. He too was captain of both the college cricket and rugby teams. He remembers the practices. There were no nets. An old man from one of the nearby *lalis* (rural villages) used to come in and prepare the pitch.

Like Ray Mali, Mveleli Ncula also lost several teeth opening the batting against one of the adult clubs on a poor wicket. In a surprising deviation from the usual stiff discipline, the schoolmaster took him to hospital via his own home and gave him a stiff tot of brandy to ease the pain.

Sometimes Mveleli played rugby and cricket games on the same day, and sometimes he and his fellow students earned pocket money turning out for the adult clubs on the weekends.[13] How many tougher, more thorough apprenticeships could there be in cricket?

The inter-college games were big occasions, much enjoyed by those participating. According to ex-Healdtonian, Solomon Makhosana, a senior Western Province administrator and one-time UCB executive member, several thousand people attended. There would be a whole day of different sports, culminating in the first team rugby match on the field with its surrounding terraced banks. Alumni would come from far and wide to watch.[14]

Raymond Uren and Krish Mackerdhuj remember the food:

When you played at Fort Cox, an agricultural college, the food was delicious. Roast beef, big chickens, you could eat as much as you wanted. If you felt like more there were these bells on the table you could ring. And all this went with ice-cold amasi, *the traditional sour milk. When we had to field after lunch, we could hardly bend down.*[15]

Healdtown, on the other hand, provided real boarding school fare. It would be a plate of mealies and a smaller one of beans with hard brown bread and sour milk, they remember. Makhenkhesi Stofile, premier of the Eastern Cape, and a long-time sports administrator and activist, is another who has vivid memories of his Fort Hare student days in the 1960s and 1970s:

Matches between Fort Hare and Healdtown were a big thing. When I was there, they had beaten us regularly. In 1969 we decided this is going to end. When we arrived for the game, all the girls had been locked away at the hostels. We beat them 28-0. That night at the university we had a film show and all the girls were there.

In the 1970s the cricket matches were big events. Before that, rugby and athletics were the big contests. Lovedale had Khaya, that Mashacila guy and others from the EP Passmore side. They messed us around too much.[16]

Khaya Majola was late in applying for a position at Lovedale. In his interview, the principal, a Mr van der Merwe, asked if he played cricket and rugby. When the principal became aware of his pedigree, he was accepted together with a number of his talented peers from Port Elizabeth.

Majola, born into sport, took to his new environment like a duck to water. An article by the well-known journalist Thami Mazwai, written in 1972, gives insight into the young prospect's talent and ambition at the time: 'Like father like son. Khaya Majola is following in the footsteps of his father. At Lovedale where he is training to be a teacher, he is about the best they have. He is coach, player and trainer.'[17]

Khaya's two-year sojourn in Alice, a place regarded as a fountainhead of African intellectual thought and also a rural heartland of black sport, made a significant impression on him. He loved to go back in later years, helping with major sports development initiatives.

In the 1990s Majola played a leading role in developing a new cricket oval at Ntselamanzi near Alice. It was a special moment in his life when Pakistan played there in 1995 in the first of a series of invitation games involving various international sides.[18] Ray Mali and Ngconde Balfour were among the ex-students from the area present as well.

When Khaya coached the Soweto Cricket Club in the 1990s, he used to take the club to play in Alice. 'You will not know how to play cricket if you don't know how people play cricket in Alice,' he told the players.[19]

Ashton Dunjwa, SAACB president and the 'ambassador' for the Ciskei Bantustan in the Western Cape (right), watches as C.B. 'A! Zanoloxolo' Zimema is given his certificate of office as representative of the Hlubi tribe by the Paramount Chief S. Zimema, 1972.

Chapter 22

PART *of the* 'SYSTEM'

———————— ◉ ————————

N HIS 1972 ARTICLE on Khaya Majola, Thami Mazwai reported, 'The shy Majola told me he just wanted to do all his father did. He said he was no longer keen on rugby, but wanted to concentrate on cricket. The young man's goals were clear: "I want to play first-class cricket." '[1]

By this time it seemed this dream might just become a possibility. New avenues were opening up for African cricketers, and Majola was rapidly coming to the fore as a player with special talents.

At the end of his first year at Lovedale, aged 18, he graduated to senior provincial cricket. Back home for the holidays, he was picked for the Eastern Province team to play in the African provincial tournament held in Welkom between Christmas and New Year. Eastern Province was captained by Wilfred Khovu, who became better known as a provincial rugby captain for the successful KWARU side. Eastern Province, Border, Transvaal and Western Province were the strongest sides at the tournament. On the first day, Eastern Province beat Border, who promptly packed up and left for home, according to Khaya. He won the man-of-the-match award, scoring 'around 50'. The final was against Transvaal. They were ahead on the first innings, but became complacent in the second. Eastern Province bowled them out for under 50 to win.[2]

This senior provincial tournament in Welkom, like the Passmore Week recounted in earlier chapters, was sponsored partly by the SACA Trust, and reflected both the closer relationship developing between the African SAACB and the white SACA as well as the concrete benefits beginning to flow into African cricket as a result.

After the approaches by the white SACA following the D'Oliveira affair in 1968, the African cricket board and the white administrators were in regular contact. In the 1970s these contracts developed into a close alliance. With first the 1968/69 MCC tour and then the Springbok tour to Australia in 1971/72 cancelled because of apartheid, both the white cricket body and the government increased their efforts to reach out to black cricketers. This lead to the first formal meeting of the three national bodies controlling cricket in South Africa, in Johannesburg on 30 April 1972.[3] The white and African bodies here created the umbrella Cricket Council of South Africa. SACBOC, led by Hassan Howa, attended but refused to be part of the new council. It was dissatisfied with its federal (multi-national) rather than unitary composition.

The white body hoped that the new Cricket Council of South Africa would ensure its re-admittance to international cricket. And, indeed, SACA was working actively with its allies, such as Colin Cowdrey and Billy Griffith, the MCC secretary, to achieve this objective.[4]

On the other hand, SAACB had decided at its 1972 AGM in Queenstown to enter into the alliance so that it could get concrete benefits for players with parlous resources and facilities. The secretary, Mr Lennox Mlonzi explained:

The African people support the stand of Mr Howa's organisation in principle. It would be stupid of anyone in this country who is not white to dismiss the demands made by Mr Howa's Board. We would look stupid as Africans in this country to say we did not stand with Mr Howa's group in what they are demanding . . . the only difference between Mr Howa's group and

(Left to right) Harrison Butshingi (president SAACB), Boon Wallace (president SACA) and Hassan Howa (president SACBOC) at a meeting in Cape Town to discuss the future of South African cricket, 1973.

ours is that whilst we appreciate their demanding these things — we cannot afford to wait and fold our arms and say that we will not play cricket until the laws of the land are changed.[5]

Ashton Dunjwa underlined this point:

We do not want to be unrealistic. We are sensitive to what is going on in this country . . . but let us remember this Government may be in power for the next 25 years and we are not going to fold our arms and not play cricket.[6]

A new trend to actively promote the government's new 'separate but equal' policy of multi-national sports via business, the mines and the newly-created 'own affairs' Bantu Administration Boards was also becoming evident.

The mines, with their well-developed facilities, started putting significant resources into the development of African sport, and a number of champion athletes emerged in the 1970s and 1980s, including Humphrey Khozi, who was by international standards an outstanding middle-distance runner.[7] During the 1968 tournament, the 130 participants were housed in the 'hostel' in Thembisa, a township with many Xhosa-speaking migrant workers.[8] The 1972 senior tournament was held at the Harmony Gold Mine in Welkom in the Orange Free State, which had two turf pitches. Eastern Province fast bowler, Tsepo Kadi, remembers meeting Khozi there and being housed in the

mine compound. 'We used to shower with the miners and ate the miners food. It was *inyama ye hashe* (horse meat),' he jokes.[9]

In 1973 the government started a Bantu Sport and Recreation Fund to push forward its sport agenda. Big business slotted effortlessly in alongside it. Donations were made by Old Mutual, Rembrandt's Anton Rupert, the Argus Group and Anglo-American. Harry Oppenheimer said the launch of the fund was an important initiative. 'Many things could be achieved, not only in sport, but in housing and education, by co-operation between business and government,' he added.[10]

Actively supported by the Minister of Bantu Affairs, Punt Jansen, and the new 'own-affairs' Bantu Administration Boards, which had taken over the running of the townships from local councils, the SACA formed action committees for the development of African cricket in each province. The 'EPCU Bantu Liaison Committee' under S.K. Anderson, which was described as very active, noted that the Administration Board 'in particular' had given cricket 'a considerable amount of assistance in the townships'.[11]

Chief Director Louis Koch was key to the process. On his advice the work was initially restricted to the Port Elizabeth townships only, and he provided a budget of R5 000 and identified the areas that should be concentrated on.

Two pitches and two nets were prepared at the Skosana School for the 1974/75 Passmore Week and the EPCU ran up a debt of R566.59 organising it. This led to the warning that the SACA should ensure that this amount was refunded and that 'future tournaments do not become a financial burden on the local European Cricket Union'. Some games were played at the grounds of white schools and 'Springbok and Eastern Province cricketers entertained the boys one evening'.[12]

Next came projects at Loyiso High School and fields in Kwazakhele, meant to serve two schools in the immediate vicinity and 'also the 8 000 single men staying in the adjacent hostels'. The pitches at Zwide and Woolfson stadiums were upgraded.

This self-conscious drive by government and white sports bodies would contribute to the growing politicisation of sport in the 1970s and to certain black sportspeople becoming identified as collaborators with apartheid policy. The career paths of the long-standing SAACB secretary, Lennox Mlonzi, and Ashton Dunjwa, president in the early 1970s, are illuminating examples. Mlonzi became a member of the Soweto Urban Bantu Council and Dunjwa the Ciskei bantustan's urban representative or 'ambassador' in the Western Cape.[13]

By 1973 Khaya had come to the notice of the white SACA hierarchy which was desperately seeking black cricket stars to parade before the world in order to preserve its international fixtures. John Passmore, who came to be known as the 'godfather' of African cricket, referred to his talents in a special address on African cricket in South Africa to the SACA AGM in that year.

It is useful quoting from Passmore's speech, as it gives an insight into the mindsets and conditions of the time:

At the very outset, I am ashamed to confess that less than four short years ago, although I had spent many years helping in various capacities to administer cricket in the Western Province, I was completely unaware that Africans either played or wanted to play cricket — and though I knew the Coloureds played, this was only because of the exploits of D'Oliveira, and my knowledge went no deeper than that.[14]

He continued that if Africans were to 'achieve cricketing status' and have the means to develop their cricket, white cricketers had to take responsibility:

We are bound to accept it for the simple reason that there is no one else who can do it. But before taking on that responsibility they had to be sure two basic requirements were met. They had to be sure that Africans genuinely wanted to play cricket. And the second requirement on which we should satisfy ourselves is their potentiality — for however enthusiastically the game is taken up, it would not last the course if it transpired there was no inherent ability.[15]

On the basis of his recent experience, Passmore was convinced the answer was affirmative in both cases, referring to a few talented cricketers to illustrate his point. He said names, however, were difficult to come by and, 'in view of the appalling and primitive conditions under which virtually all have to play, and, knowing that only good conditions produce good cricketers, one is surprised that any instances can be found at all'. But Khaya was one of these examples, brought to Passmore's attention by the mercurial Eddie Barlow:

Eddie Barlow, who coaches Africans once a year in East London, tells of a potential provincial player in Majola, one of a kombi-full of boys who came over 70 miles every day from Lovedale for their coaching.[16]

Barlow also referred to the reputation of Majola's father. When the author fished out this reference nearly 30 years later, Khaya recalled the event instantly:

Eddie Barlow coached us for a few days before he played in a match in East London. I remember that well. The reason he mentioned me is that I bowled him out. He would bat and offer us money if we got his wicket. I said I will get him every day. And that is what I did. I bowled him three days in a row. And each time I got a whole term's pocket money for that.[17]

As his reputation grew, Majola was invited to a special net practice at the Old Grey Club, where Graeme Pollock commented favourably on his potential.[18]

Derrick Robins (centre), sponsor of private tours to South Africa aimed at breaking SACA's isolation,
pictured with Australian and Pakistani internationals, Bruce Francis (left) and
Younis Ahmed (right) during the 1973/74 Derrick Robins tour.

Chapter 23

DERRICK ROBINS *and* INTERNATIONAL CONTACTS

———————————————— ⬤ ————————————————

IN 1973, AT AGE 20, Khaya was picked for the national African team, like his father before him. After SACBOC switched over to non-racial cricket at the end of the 1950s and the inter-race tournaments came to an end, the idea of coloured, Indian or African team went out of fashion. But now, as part of the government's new 'multi-national' policy the concept of separate racially-based national teams was once again being resurrected. The government gave SACA permission for a limited amount of mixing to take place at the top level. As long as South African teams remained segregated, they could play against each other, as well as international touring sides with black players in them.[1]

In a move billed as historic, an African combination, comprising Edmund Ntikinca and Edward Habane, played in the International Datsun Double Wicket competition at the beginning of the 1973/74 season.[2] A few weeks later an African eleven was selected to play against the touring Derrick Robins team. With the 1968/69 MCC tour and the 1971/72 Springbok tour to Australia cancelled because of apartheid, SACA gave approval to the plans of Joe Pamensky, Ali Bacher and other Transvaal administrators to start recruiting international invitation sides to help break the isolation. Derrick Robins was an entrepreneur and cricket benefactor who had settled temporarily in South Africa in his luxury Villa XI at Plettenberg Bay. In the driveway were his two Rolls Royces displaying the custom-designed number plates, DHR 1 and DHR 2. Robins brought several sides to South Africa during the 1970s.

Having already established his reputation as something of a prodigy, and having performed well at two Passmore Weeks and the 1972 senior provincial tournament, Khaya was pencilled in as an all-rounder for the national team, occupying the prime batting spot of number four. The England international, Don Wilson, then coaching for SACA, was Khaya's manager and coach. He recalled taking 'my charges off to the vocational training centre in Soweto for a full-scale practice', where 'Khaya Majola, a quickish left-arm spinner from Eastern Province, excelled on the matting'.[4]

The match took place on 20 October 1973 at the Moroka Jabavu Stadium in Soweto with 'its little blue grandstand and corrugated iron fence'.[5] It was the first time since the 1892 fixture between W.W. Read's English tourists and a Malay XVIII that black South African cricketers got the opportunity to play against a 'white' side from abroad.

The Robins team easily won a one-sided contest. The event 'gained big-billing in the media, but a village-green atmosphere prevailed' as the Robins XI cruised to 359 in little over three and a half hours.[6] English test players, John Edrich and Graham Roope, scored centuries. Coming on late in the innings, Khaya took two Robins wickets for 48 runs in nine overs. His victims were lower order batsmen, Ray East and John Lever. He also took a catch to dismiss West Indian all-rounder, John Shepherd, who was one of the stars of the Robins side.[7]

Given official permission to tour by the government, Shepherd and Younis Ahmed of Pakistan became the first black players to play in South Africa in a SACA-sponsored international side. The *South African Cricket Annual* ironically noted in its review of the tour that 'standing ovations [for these players] became the order of the day and in retrospect it is incredible that throughout the Robins tour there has been no single report of any spectator, official or player of whatever political belief being contaminated either during the match, or at a civic reception or social gathering'.[8]

In their turn at the crease, the African team answered with 139 runs. Coming in at number four, Khaya was stumped for seven runs. Ironically, this was the way he had got his wickets when bowling. The bowler was the little Australian spin wizard, Johnny Gleeson, who took seven for 33. According to Don Wilson, this moved 'our Bantu spinner, Majola, to suggest that he might pay a visit to Johnny's witchdoctor!'[9]

Gleeson's unorthodox wrist spin not only mesmerised South African batsmen throughout the tour, but also proved too much for the first-choice Robins wicketkeeper, Roger Tolchard. Because of Tolchard's 'inability to read the mesmeric Gleeson', the assistant tour manager, former England keeper, John Murray, had to take over.[10]

The SAACB team on that day comprised the following: Samson Ntshekisa (captain), George Langa, Sam Sonwabe, Zimasa Mbatani, Edmund Ntikinca, Edward Habane, Gladman Roji, S.M. Nontshinga, S.S. Msutwana, Sydney T. Mkubevana and Majola.

The team had the unusual experience of being offered financial incentives, which were extremely attractive at the time. King Corn offered the players R50 per wicket and R2.50 per run. The total that they earned came to R842.50

Unofficial SACA national captain, Eddie Barlow (centre), with Derrick Robins tourists, John Shepherd (left) and John Lever (right).

and the sponsors promised R3 000 for the next game in Port Elizabeth.[11]

At the after-dinner function, the veteran ex-England captain, Brian Close from Yorkshire, joked that he and his African counterpart, Samson Ntshekisa, had probably set a record for the oldest captains ever. Close was 42 and Ntshekisa, 'who does not know how old he is', was well over 50.[12]

When interviewed many years later, Majola was dismissive about the importance of the match, and insisted that this was not only because his ideological position had hardened. He said Ntshekisa was around 57 years old and he and George Langa had played with his father as far back as 1951. 'It was clearly a show for the government and the white cricket Board.'[13]

The *Rand Daily Mail* carried a special feature on the match. It was impressed with the team's potential. The headline read, 'Habane, Majola talented.' The *Mail's* Trevor Bisseker said that besides Edmund Ntikinca and Edward Habane, 'the African side has an exciting young left hander from Eastern Province in Khaya Majola'. He added that the two young players 'made the heart beat faster'. Both Bisseker and his colleague, Marshall Lee, commented on Majola's natural talent and 'feel' for the game.[14]

Minister Piet Koornhof was present. Speaking to the two teams, he said it was an important day for Soweto, 'for all the

Younis Ahmed batting against the SAACB team in Soweto. Zimasa Mbatani is the wicketkeeper.

He was supported by other progressive political organisations who said such multi-national matches helped to reinforce apartheid. Speaking at the Ahmed Timol memorial meeting in Johannesburg, David Curry of the Labour Party declared that South African blacks were not 'grateful' to the Derrick Robins team and its two black members:

We do not view your visit with gratefulness. We will not be used as the white man's tool for crawling back into world sport — if he wants to come back into world sport, let him crawl on his own underbelly, not on the backs of Blacks.[19]

This meeting was held to commemorate the second anniversary of the death of Ahmed Timol, who fell ten floors to his death while in Security Police custody. It took place despite a ban on 'open air meetings of a political nature'.

In a letter to the Robins players, the National Union of South African Students (NUSAS) echoed similar sentiments:

The white controlled press and white South Africans hailed your arrival in this country as a step forward. This it is, a step towards more sophisticated white domination . . . By coming to South Africa you are prolonging the agony of sportsmen who desperately want to play sport on an equal, non-racial basis. The longer international sportsmen come to this country and participate in racially segregated sport, the longer the racial situation in South Africa will prevail . . . We are not trying to bring politics into sport. That was done a long time ago by the South African government. We seek a situation . . . in which all may participate on an equal basis, without regard to colour. Those who compromise with apartheid sport are ensuring that politics will continue to determine who plays with whom, and under what conditions.[20]

NUSAS commented further:

That blacks have jumped at the opportunity to play the tourists is indeed sad, not because they thus have accepted the Government's 'multinational' sports policy — they certainly have not — but because it indicated a willingness and capability on the part of black sportsmen, that can only be realised by white handouts. All sportsmen in South Africa need international competition, but to play international sport on the Nationalist Government's terms is coming dangerously close to being co-opted.

As strange as it may seem, this was also the view of the young Majola who was playing in the match, as can be seen below.

Bantu peoples of South Africa' and South Africa itself. 'I hope it heralds a new day for African cricket,' he added. The white cricket establishment made a meal of the game and Derrick Robins said, 'Let's hope this is the first step for South African cricket on the long road to international cricket.'[15]

Robins's sense of history was perhaps heightened by other dubious acts of history taking place in the wider world. The headline of the *Rand Daily Mail* on the day after the match was, 'The Big Sweep', referring to the Israeli 'drive for Cairo' during the Yom Kippur War. The Watergate scandal, which was to lead to the resignation of Richard Nixon, was also covered.[16]

On the back pages, the news was about the impending retirement of Transvaal and white Springbok captain Ali Bacher, after 14 seasons. Bacher said he was confident, after the cancellation of the tours to England and Australia, that South Africa would soon be back in international cricket: 'I am optimistic about the future. In Dr Koornhof we have a Minister of Sport who is making a genuine effort for cricket. I feel the time has come for all cricketers, irrespective of colour to support him.'[17]

However, not everyone was impressed. Hassan Howa, president of SACBOC, strongly criticised the match and remarked that anybody who 'has the least consideration for his fellow man . . . cannot accept that this tour is in the interests of cricket'.[18]

'THE DAY HISTORY WAS FAST-BOWLED AT SOWETO'

By Marshall Lee (*Rand Daily Mail*, 23 October 1973)

In a way they were right, all those people who said Saturday's cricket match was an act of history. Certainly there'd been nothing quite like it. Anyway not on the playing fields of Soweto.

If I was in any doubt at all, that was removed at exactly 10.00 or thereabouts when 'Stagey' Msutwana ran, according to my count, 15 paces and let the ball go at opening bat, John Edrich.

'We've just seen a bit of history,' said someone. So I settled down to record it. And this is how history went down in my notebook. The times are not fictitious, but looking at my watch, any similarity with official time is purely coincidental.

10.02: The first run is scored. By Edrich. Claps.

10.08: The first LBW appeal. Turned down. Crowd delighted.

10.11: The first boundary. Edrich again, with a pull past square leg.

10.15: Crowd count shows 100 or so Sowetonians, 60-odd Whites, including police, Press and Bantu Admin.

10.16: The first bye.

10.17: The first full toss. 'Aaaaee, FIRST STOP!' shouts the crowd. The expression is a new one to Whites. It's loaded with Township imagery, for the ball, like an express train, reaches the batsman without a stop. On this alone my day would have been made. 'First Stop!' is one of the most imaginative contributions to the game since the box was invented.

10.24: The first wicket. Smith is caught behind. To be honest I was looking somewhere else.

Damn! History is happening a bit quick. The crowd are vociferous. Jubilation in outstretched arms.

10.25: Brian Close, the Robins captain, goes in. He hits a four first ball, another second ball. Ho hum.

10.30: Someone says: 'There's Dr. Koornhof's secretary.' It's Mr Hoek, secretary for sport. Looking around I see Mackay-Coghill and several other people I've never seen before.

10.35: Msutwana nearly gets Close. Bowls three really good ones. Worth recording. Otherwise the play is very crick-etish, sort of settling in. Time to look beyond the ground to Soweto lying there in boxes. Distance lends enchant-ment to the view. But even from close the stadium field is in goodish green condition. Someone has been doing a lot of hard gardening. I also like the mat. It's dark green.

10.43: Crowd erupts (as they say). The double-wicket Habane rolls and sprawls and hangs on to a catch from Close. 39 for two.

'My! these chaps are playing well,' says someone. (I think it was me.) You can feel the Whites' surprise. The fielding and bowling is good, beyond my expectations.

10.44: Now it's the Pakistani, Younis Ahmed. Good-looking and left-handedly aggressive, he carries run-making history in his sky-blue bat.

Dr Piet Koornhof, Minister of Sport of the National Party government, addresses the two sides during the match in Soweto in October 1973.

Actually it's bit unreal. Here we have a Pakistani facing a Xhosa with a blue bat in Jabavu, Soweto.

10.50: Derrick Robins joins Trevor Bisseker and me. He's in good form. Likes what he sees. And is kind of delighted to be part of all this epoch-making cricket. Talks cricket, etc.

11.00: The first hour up. And the first bowling change. Edrich, who has been 'hambering kahle' looks relaxed. I think it's all up for the bowlers.

11.03: Edward Habane comes on to bowl with a load of 'first stops!' So far of eight bowlers and batsmen on show, six have been left-handers. Odd, hey?

11.10: Younis lofts a mis-hit. Crowd raise their constant chatter to shouts of excitement. I'm going to run out of crowd adjectives, I can see it. On the bleachers, lines of Black schoolchildren in their black and white gym uniforms in the sun. Interesting.

11.15: Shouts of 'DOUBLE ENGEEN!' bring me back to the game. 'Double Engine', the 48-year-old George Langa, has come on. He swings his arm over twice before letting the ball go. The description is head-shakingly, laughingly apt. Neville Cardus and other lyricists could not have come up with the same.

11.16: The Double Engine's bowling collides with the blue bat. Four, six, four – 'Cleen bowled!!' 95 for three. Jubilation tremendous. Crowd cock-a-hoop. Visions of collapse, etc. Not to be.

11.25: Paul Winslow arrives and so does the hundred up. Now it's Roope and Edrich.

11.30: Note this well: on comes Khaya Majola, left-arm spinner. Every movement of his up to now has been pure cricketer. Even the way he hitches his shoulders and flicks the ball about before bowling. Whites turn to their neighbours and nod their approval. 'This is a good one,' they say. What's more he opens with a maiden. Tumultuous applause for this.

11.43: Edrich hits 4,2,4 for his 50. But 'Double Engine' is bowling like a machine. 'He can bowl exactly on the spot,' says one African. Edrich goes close to a fielder with a lofted hit.

11.50: Motorbikes broom-broom behind the stand. Blare of trumpets in my mind: 'It's the Mayor!' says someone and Dr Bensusan arrives.

11.58: Edrich hits two sixes in a row over the cars. It's a short square boundary and a short haul to his hundred.

12.00: The first individual hundred and the two hundred up.

12.10: Ntikinca, the other double-wicketer, comes on. Long overdue.

Edrich clobbers him but lifts his head to be bowled for 108. More whistles, cheers, shouts. It's 213 for four. Each wicket is worth R50 for the African team. So far that's R200 from the sponsors.

12.24: Roope's 50. For me a mixedly impressive knock.

12.26: By my clock – lunch. Down to the blue and white marquee and its potted palms and cold meats and salads. Here White officialdom sits down politely in its suits and Cheetham smiles. There is much conviviality but no beer. And no seats for the Press, but I can stand and watch quite happily – all this gentility come to a picnic. Cricket does it superbly.

Of course, I have this thing about marquees. Blue and white striped ones especially. There is something upper class about them, you know. Shades of Joan Hunter Dunn, tanned by the Aldershot sun, Henley and Wimbledon. That sort of thing. Well, I lean up against a little of this feeling in a corner of the Moroka-Jabavu Stadium and think, tomorrow the tent will be let down. And how long will the hopes stay up?

1.15: Play resumes. Roope hits out.

1.25: Murray runs down the wicket and is bowled: 259/5. In goes John Shepherd, a very black Shepherd. The crowd acknowledge him and cheer his first single: 'Off the mark!' they shout, which amuses some Whites.

1.40: Roope hits one into the crowd. Much alarm and hand waving. Then more ecstasy. Majola catches Shepherd. It's straightforward but he does it with class.

1.42: Roope's hundred. Now he's got enough runs to hang himself. And soon he's out. Caught by Captain Sam running round near the boundary. The rest follow in some disorder, stumped by miles mostly.

2.20: Robins XI all out 359. R500 worth of wickets.

2.30: Meet up with Wilf Isaacs. Sit with him and Paul Winslow. Behind is Mark Henning.
On the 'White side' of the stand there are a number of cricketing personalities.

2.31: Lever, left-arm quick, bowls. Close has eight men in an umbrella behind the batsman. They probably haven't seen anything like it.

2.35: Crowd jubilant as ever over first four. Then Sonwabe is bowled all over the place.

2.40: Lee (no relation) bowls Mbatani. It's four for two wickets.

2.41: The minister, Dr. Piet Koornhof arrives. Nods at John Snow. Shakes hands in the 'Royal Box' and settles down. Mr. Lennox Mlonzi, round face aglow, sits next to him.

2.44: Ntikinca snicks and is gone. four for three. 'Oh dear, they won't get 20.'
In comes Edward Habane to join Majola. They've got 36 years between them, but put on 38 before Majola goes stumped off Gleeson. Habane looks assured and solidly superb. Drives, hooks.
'Oh, good shot!' exclaims Paul Winslow. Everyone is saying things like 'great shot!' The boy does look good.

3.15: Habane's out for 32. Caught and bowled Gleeson. 'He's unplayable on this,' says Wilf Isaacs. Gleeson promptly bowls the next chap. It's 55 for six. 'They'll at least have two knocks,' say I.

3.35: A mike goes onto the field followed by the minister and others. The players all line up to meet. Dr. Koornhof has a dark navy blue suit and brown shoes. And his speech is mellow with good-fellowness.
Full of 'my pleasure and my privilege' and he even talks of 'African' cricket and how Edward should go a very very long way (will he?) and that the 'African people' can be very proud of him.

He uses 'African' as though it is no bother. But I can't help feeling that for a cabinet minister he is making either a boob or history.
The crowd have received him warmly, but he spoils the impression somewhat at the end. He talks of 'your Bantu team' and a loud mutter of disapproval sounds in the stand.

4.30: Gladman Roji and his partner Msutwana send up the 100. It lets loose the loudest applause of the day. Ejaculation immense.
It is a shout of victory, nothing less! And for a while it looks as if the Englishmen will never get another wicket. Roji has a glad eye and Msutwana a propensity to cut. It is invigorating stuff.

4.45: I go for a walk around the ground with John Hobbs, whose name appears next after Sir Jack's in *Wisden's*. This walk is a very English thing to do, combining as it does a bit of watching with conversation.

4.55: The euphoria drops when the next wicket falls, 122 for seven. It's nearly over.
The smog of Soweto creeps over the skies. The photographers have packed up and the whole scene is bathed in a steamy Turnerish sun. Sam hits a four and a man effuses: 'That is one from heaven!'
But obviously in short supply up there, for suddenly the last man's in and out.
Drinking time.

6.00: The Cocktail Party. Much backslapping and bonhomie. And speeches awash with gratitude and thanks and good wishes. Speakers include Messrs Cheetham, Pamensky, Robins, Ames, Close, August, and the president of the [Transvaal] African Cricket body Mr. Nelson Mabula.
He was late in arriving and said, funnily enough, he had issued invitations to everyone there, but had forgotten to invite himself. So he got stuck at the gate with conscientious Blackjacks vetting the arrivals.
Anyway he makes up for that in a speech that went from Sir Henry Newbolt's 'There's a breathless hush in the Close tonight, Ten to make and the match to win' into a histrionic set of indigenous praises that left the Englishmen mystified and agog. Lord's was never like this. 'I'll tell you what it all means later,' says John Shepherd. And that is the question I'm left with after all this history. Just what does it all mean?

Edward Habane hits out for 'Black South Africa' during the International Datsun Double-Wicket Tournament
at the Wanderers in September 1973. Mike Procter is fielding at slip for 'South Africa'.

Khaya Majola with his mother and other family members before his departure. (Left to right) Skumbuzo Oliphant, Eric Majola's brother who also played for the Bantu rugby Springboks, Rev Dano, Dolly Oliphant, ~~~, Tozi Majola, Julius Majola, Khaya Majola, Mongezi Gerald Majola, Nobenguli Horo, Nomonde Majola and Milase Majola. (Children in front) Siviwe Oliphant and Vuyo Majola.

VISIT TO ENGLAND

A follow-up match between the Africans and the Derrick Robins XI was due to be held in the New Brighton Oval, the backyard of the Majola family, in November 1973. Unfortunately, heavy overnight rain led to the cancellation of the fixture.

Nevertheless, Khaya was by now firmly in the spotlight. He was invited by Derrick Robins to play for his side in England in the following northern summer, a clear indication that he was being groomed as a potential African star by a white cricket establishment desperate to unearth new talent.

Several other top South African cricketers — Clive Rice, Tich Smith, Rupert Hanley — were part of the tour. This would have been a rare opportunity for any youngster. For Khaya it was doubly so. Lennox Mlonzi, secretary of the SAACB, proudly declared that he would be the first African to play overseas. He was right, but only in the official sense because Nathaniel Umhalla and others had gone to England as early as the 1860s, and no doubt there were others who travelled and played in a private capacity after that.

Nearly 500 people, including the entire Johnson Marwanqa School, where he had taken over his father's teaching post, came to see Khaya off at the airport when he left for his three-week trip to Britain in mid-1974.[21]

The English journalist, Ian Hobbs, gave an indication of the newness of the experience for Khaya:

For this shy, soft-spoken schoolteacher, this week's visit is an unforgettable experience. He has played on turf pitches, used equipment of the best quality, showered and changed in luxurious dressing rooms and stayed in smart hotels. Above all he has kept the company of first-class cricketers who have been free with their advice.[22]

He shared rooms with Rice and Smith and was reported to have said, 'It feels like Clive, Tich and I come from the same house.'

The Robins's team played matches against Oxford and Cambridge Universities, and various county second elevens, as well as the touring Barbados Wanderers team from the Caribbean. Khaya played in all the games because he was being given the opportunity to learn. He remembers taking four or five wickets against the Barbados team. 'These guys could hit fast bowling so Clive brought the spinners on. The sixes were flying, but he kept me going.'[23]

The only press report in the Majola family album records that Majola scored 26 not out against Oxford University, coming in at number five with the score at 22 for three, 'in the process playing some graceful off-drives square of the wicket'. It also mentioned that he bowled nine overs 'with a smooth, flowing action'. His final figures were three for 34.[24]

At Oxford he faced Imran Khan and he bowled to stars like John Edrich, Bob Woolmer and Brian Close. He also turned out for a team called the Warwickshire Pilgrims. It must have been a memorable experience.[25]

Ian Hobbs was impressed with his performances, particularly the way he adapted to playing on wet turf wickets:

Consistently, almost studiously Majola was on the front foot. When asked why, he said that playing his matting-wicket shots in earlier matches, he had found himself aiming above the bounce of even short pitched balls.[26]

The whole of the Johnson Marwanqa School in Port Elizabeth was at the airport to see Khaya Majola off
when he became the first African cricketer selected to play abroad in 1974.

Majola with Norman Featherstone, Clive Rice and Derrick Robins during
one of the matches in England.

He wrote that 'Majola's shyness and modesty does not hide a burning ambition to play top-class cricket'. Basil D'Oliveira, who had coached in Port Elizabeth during the previous season and was described as a 'family friend' of the Majolas, said he was convinced of the youngster's future. 'If he can be kept away from matting and if he could stay here for two or three years, he would be bound to make the grade.' D'Oliveira also remarked that if Eric Majola had had 'my opportunities, you would have heard a lot of him'. He hoped Khaya would 'not miss out as well'.[27]

Khaya returned from England with the message that he 'dreams of playing one day in a mixed Springbok side'. He said, 'From what cricketers have told me, South Africa must have a mixed team to get back into test cricket. I hope it doesn't take too long'.[28]

His plans were to keep improving and, 'If things go well, I may perhaps be able to find a place in one of the county sides after a year or two. I would certainly not turn down a career in professional cricket if it was offered to me'.[29]

The English people he had met had been very hospitable and 'everyone has treated me as an equal'. However, while he hoped to return to play, he would not leave South Africa: 'I don't change that fast. I am used to the life in South Africa and I would not want to leave my family and my people.'[30]

RHODESIA AND OTHER OPPORTUNITIES, 1974-1977

The match against the Derrick Robins team in 1973 was an indication of a growing alliance between the white SACA and the SAACB, in opposition to the direction being taken by the non-racial SACBOC. Formerly part of SACBOC, the Africans had maintained their Africans-only composition and were now increasingly being seen as part of the system.

The SAACB's position was an awkward one. Although it tried to steer an independent political position, it took an increasingly contradictory stance and was compromised as political events unfolded in the 1970s.

The motivations for working with the SACA were greater opportunities for African cricketers. At the same time the administrators emphasised this did not mean supporting apartheid. When the prominent white administrator, Wilf Isaacs, travelled to London to testify against Peter Hain, leader of the anti-apartheid sports movement in Britain, SAACB secretary Lennox Mlonzi criticised him: '... we cannot be associated with him ... we are not against Peter Hain ...'[31] However, the reality was that the SAACB

became firmly embedded in the multi-national apartheid sports policy.

The SACA more or less started taking responsibility for African cricketers, making its plans in close consultation with government and the private sector.

As this co-operation grew, opportunities for the players increased. A busy 1974/75 season underlined the point. In addition to the season-opening Datsun Double Wicket competition and the by-now annual Passmore Week, the senior inter-provincial week was held in Johannesburg in December, the last of some 20 national tournaments played since the original South African Bantu Board was formed in 1933. The SAACB team also played a number of matches.

The national side selected after the inter-provincial tournament played some warm-up games in Johannesburg in January and then went outside of South Africa's borders for the first time when it undertook a four-match tour of Rhodesia (Zimbabwe). Strengthened by two English internationals coaching in Johannesburg, Don Wilson and Phil Carrick, the team was named the Eric Ellerine's XI after the sponsor. Three one-day fixtures against Rhodesian Country Districts, Midlands and Manicaland were followed by a 'test' at the Police Ground in Salisbury against a Rhodesian President's team led by national captain, Jackie Heron.[32]

After returning from Rhodesia the African team played a few matches against the Derrick Robins tourists and one against the strong International Wanderers side, led by Greg Chappell and including Ian Chappell and Dennis Lillee.[33]

The African team were also admitted into the Gillette Cup competition of the white SACA for the first time on the understanding that if they won their first round matches, they would not be able to proceed further in the competition. This strange situation was occasioned by government and SACA interpretations of the new multi-national sports policy, which aside from being politically insulting was riddled with ambiguity and contradictions.[34]

The last Africans-only team played against the SACA's Eastern Province at St George's Park in October 1976. The hosts scored 345 for two in 51 overs, with centuries from Graeme Pollock and Simon Bezuidenhout, before skittling out the SAACB team for 101.[35]

By this time, negotiations between the SACA, the SAACB and SACBOC had resulted in a historic agreement to play 'normal cricket' from club levels upward. This led to the disbanding of the South African African Cricket Board in 1977, after 45 years of existence, as we shall see below.

The SAACB Eric Ellerines XI that toured Rhodesia (Zimbabwe) in 1975 was the first black touring side to have left South Africa since SACBOC's East African tour in 1958. (Back row, left to right) Bridgeman Mokuena, Peter Bacela, Philip Carrick, Philip Njokweni, Sam Sonwabe, Gus Toyana, Edward Habane. (Front row) Edmund Ntikinca, Zimasa Mbatani (vice-captain), Don Wilson (captain), Eric Ellerine (managing director of Ellerine Holdings Ltd.), Ashton Duunjwa (manager), William Magitshima, Lennox Mlonzi (official).

MEMORIES OF THE 1975 RHODESIAN TOUR

In his autobiography, 'Mad Jack', tour captain Don Wilson, reminisced about SAACB's 1975 Eric Ellerine's XI tour to present-day Zimbabwe in prose exoticising indigenous Africans in a way that would have done Victorian myth-makers proud.[36]

At the end of February 1975, the first mixed-race side ever to leave the shores of South Africa headed off for a two-week tour of Rhodesia, with myself as captain and Phil Carrick in support – a trip that was trumpeted loudly as the first real breakthrough for African cricket. Eric Ellerine, a powerful man in a Johannesburg furniture business, had the foresight and financial clout to make it workable, and he received solid backing from the organisers, the South African [African] Cricket Board, part of the umbrella body, the Cricket Council of South Africa, who also embraced the South African Cricket Association. Mr Ashton Dunjwa, our tour manager, saw it as a stepping-stone to eventual merit selection in South African cricket, but we were criticised by Hassan Howa's rival [South African] Cricket Board of Control, who wanted immediate full integration and the priority development of African cricket and facilities.

The players were selected from all over the country, and we met up to be kitted out at Eric Ellerine's headquarters a week before departure. Some of the lads had never worn a tie in their lives, never mind a blazer, and the flight to Rhodesia was another first for many of them. Acquiring passports was also a complicated process involving several fairly restrictive government channels, but Ali Bacher cut a dashing swathe through the official opposition.

We were presented with a new bus at the airport on arrival in Bulawayo, but there was no driver, and none of our party held a license to drive – except the captain and coach, Wilson D! There was no option; I duly took on the chauffeur's job, which was the last word in role reversal in South Africa, where blacks traditionally ferry the white man around.

I impressed on the boys the importance of discipline and good behaviour and the need to uphold the true pioneering spirit; but then 'Fergie' Carrick and I were waylaid by Peter Carlstein and Jack Heron on the first night, necessitating a lie-in the following morning. I walked out into the hotel corridor at about 09h30, to hear all the other doors open simultaneously: the boys had not dared to venture to breakfast without us! That evening, we had a team dinner at which Fergie ordered prawn cocktail. That caused a commotion in the camp: they did not know what to order as they had never seen a menu, and were only used to 'mealypop' [sic], the staple

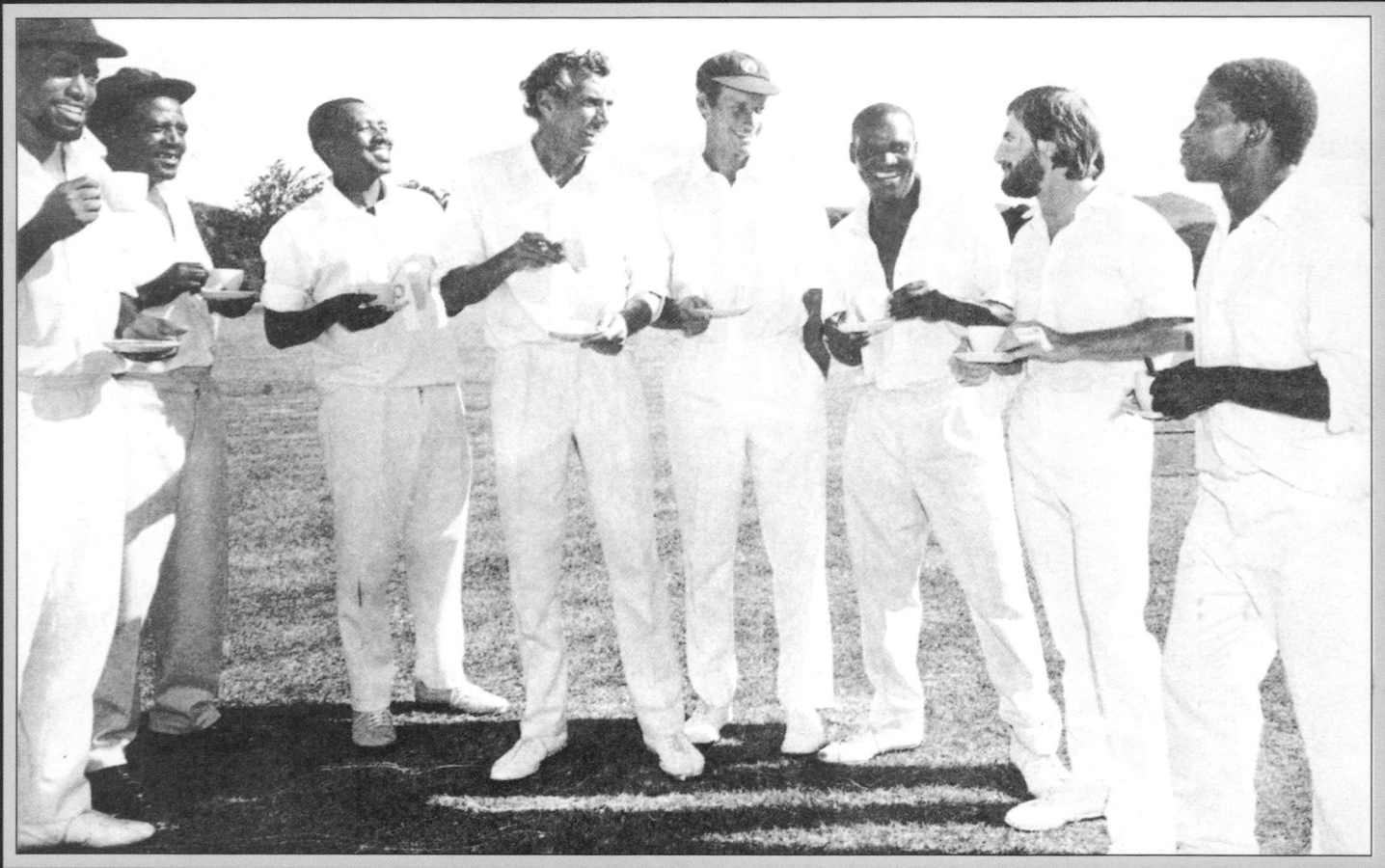

SAACB players posing with their opponents during the game against Manicaland. (Left to right) Zimasa Mbatani, Bridgeman Mokuena, Samuel Nontshinga, Don Wilson, Mike Griffith (Manicaland captain), Terry Wallace and Edward Habane.

diet of the townships. After being introduced to prime Bulawayo steaks and Fergie's *hors d'oeuvres* they demanded the same next morning at breakfast! These were amazing reactions for two Englishmen to witness, but they made us realise that we were indeed operating within a socio-cultural milieu so totally distanced from our own.

I decided that, in the first match against a Country Districts XI, we should field first in order to generate a feeling of togetherness, and our performance exceeded all expectations against opposition with Currie Cup experience on an easy-paced wicket. The fielding, led by Fergie who held four catches and trapped Ralph Ferreira lbw, was tremendously energetic, and we bowled them out for 222 and replied with 56 for three at the close: a thoroughly satisfying day's work. Our left-arm opener, Samuel Nontshinga, extracted some early bounce then whipped out the tail to finish with three for 35, but there was still, understandably, the odd blemish.

They wandered around in the field, chatting to one another from the opposite end of the pitch. Sam even went to sleep on a bench at third man after an opening stint in

extremely hot conditions, and I went absolutely berserk. He pleaded that I had told him to have a rest: 'Yes, but only from bloody bowling!', I bawled, almost tearing my hair out. It was a unique insight into the problems of attempting to nurture a cricket ethos from the bare basics. Unfortunately, we capitulated on the second morning for a meagre 104 and were forced to follow-on, although Fergie battled through the discomfort of a bruised toe in our second dig to strike a forthright 130 and earn a creditable draw.

In our next match, a one-dayer at Gwelo, we reduced a Midlands team to 127 for seven at lunch, but suffered thereafter from a hurricane knock of 103 by Brian Davison, latterly of Leicestershire and Gloucestershire, and then collapsed ourselves to 105 all out and defeat by 97 runs. The third fixture, against a fully representative Manicaland at Umtali Sports Club, followed much the same pattern. We were shot out for 82 and replied to 134 for eight declared with a more resolute 91 for five in a second innings which we used mainly for practice for the upcoming two-day clash on the Police Ground at Salisbury against a President's XI,

LEFT *Lennox Mlonzi, Boon Wallace, Ashton Dunjwa and Eric Ellerine cementing the alliance between SAACB and SACA.*
BELOW LEFT *Edmund Ntikinca, Sam Sonwabe, Edward Habane and Zimasa Mbatani sharing a light moment during the tour.*
BELOW RIGHT *The team getting ready for departure.*
BOTTOM *Back home: Ashton Dunjwa and Phillip Njokweni at 'the posh Diepkloof Hotel' after the team's return.*

It was to be the severest examination of the tour. Once again, we were indebted to Edward Habane, the boy with the big-match temperament, whose splendid undefeated 61 kept us afloat after I had put them in and seen Currie Cup players Martin Benkenstein and Jimmy Mitchell take us apart in an opening stand of 95. But our batting folded again second time around, and we returned to South Africa a chastened but wiser crew. Even though it was our first encounter with turf wickets, the batting had been worryingly brittle, a result more of lack of concentration that of poor technique. Yet there had been so many positive elements that it seemed churlish to dwell on a shortcoming of that nature; more important was that our players had experienced a level of competition that they had never seen before, something that they could take back to their townships in order to carry on our work from within.

SOUTH AFRICAN AFRICAN CRICKET BOARD MATCHES DURING THE 1960s AND 1970s[37]

1. SAACB vs SA Coloured XI, Natalspruit, Johannesburg, Easter 1967
Draw. (Match abandoned after three overs because of rain.)

2. SAACB vs Derrick Robins XI, Jabavu Stadium, Soweto, 20 October 1973
Lost by 222 runs.
DRXI 359 all out (G.R.J. Roope 110, J.H. Edrich 108, E. Ntikinca 3/71)
SAACB 137 all out. G.L. Roji 42

3. SAACB vs Derrick Robins XI, New Brighton Stadium, Port Elizabeth, 21 November 1973
Match cancelled due to heavy rain.

4. SAACB XI vs Patel's XI, Johannesburg, 5 January1975
Scores not available.

5. SAACB XI vs Crocodiles XI, Johannesburg, 7 January 1975
(British public schools touring team, including future internationals David Gower, Christopher Cowdrey and Paul Downton.). Scores not available.

6. SAACB tour to Rhodesia (Zimbabwe), March 1975
(Team known as Eric Ellerine XI included two English professionals, Don Wilson and Phil Carrick.)
Scores not available.

7. SAACB vs Rhodesian Country Districts, Bulawayo, 2 March 1975
Draw.
RCD 222 all out.
SAACB 104 all out (P. Carrick 130). Scores incomplete.

8. SAACB vs Midlands, Gwelo, 4 March 1975
Lost by 97 runs.
Midlands 202 (B. Davidson 103)
SAACB 105 all out. Scores incomplete.

9. SAACB vs Manicaland, Umtali Sports Club, Umtali, 6 March 1975
Draw.
SAACB 82 and 91/5
Umtali 134/8 dec

10. SAACB vs Rhodesian Presidents XI, Police Grounds, Salisbury, 8 or 9 March 1975
Lost by132 runs.
Scores not available.

11. SAACB vs Derrick Robins XI, Jabavu Stadium, Soweto, 12 March 1975
Lost by 132 runs.
DRXI 286 for 6 dec (F. Hayes 132. P. Njokweni 4/55)
SAACB 154 (S. Sonwabe 40)

12. SAACB vs Derrick Robins XI, Langa Stadium, Cape Town, 19 March 1975
Lost by 110 runs.
DRXI 230/9 (S. Nontshinga 4/60, P. Njokweni 4/58)
SAACB 120 all out (E. Habane 54)

13. SAACB vs Natal SACA (Gillette Cup), Kingsmead Stadium, Durban, 25 October 1975
Lost by 283 runs.
Natal (SACA) 361 for 2 dec (A. Barrow 202*, H.R. Fotheringham 128*)
SAACB 78 all out (G. Toyana 18. P. Henwood 5/30)

14. SAACB vs Derrick Robins XI, Soweto, 10 January 1976
Lost by 82 runs.
DRXI 202 for 4 dec
SAACB 120 (P. Chingoka 54, G.A. Cope 8/60)

15. SAACB vs International Wanderers XI, Soweto, 12 March 1976
Lost by 284 runs.
IWXI 331 for 7 dec (E. Ntikinca 5/62)
SAACB 47

16. SAACB vs Eastern Province SACA, St George's Park, Port Elizabeth, 16 October 1976
Lost by 244 runs.
EP(SACA) 345 for 2 dec after 51 overs (S.J. Bezuidenhout 114*, R.G. Pollock 102*)
SAACB 101 all out (M. Matyila 21)

SABCB/SAACB REPRESENTATIVES, 1951-1977

Bacela, Peter Vumile 1975

Carrick, Phil 1975 (guest appearances as English professional)

Chingoka, Peter 1975 captain, 1976 captain

Fihla, Eric 1951, 1953, 1955

Gidi, T. 1955

Habane, Edward 1973, 1975,1976

Hashe, Sydney 1953, 1958

Khumalo, J. 1955, 1958

Langa, George 1951, 1953, 1955, 1958, 1973

Ledimo, M. 1955

Mafongosi, L. 1951

Magitshima, William Velile 1967, 1975

Magodla, T.H. 1967

Mahanjana, Japhta 1958

Mahanjana, Julius. 1951, 1953, 1955, 1958

Mahanjana, Justin 1955

Majola, Eldridge Khaya 1973

Majola, Eric 1953, 1958

Malamba, Ben 1951, 1953, 1955

Mashinqana, G.Mbuzeli 1967

Masutu Mtutuzeli, 1967

Matyila, M. 1976

Mawu, H. 1953, 1955

Mbatani, A.M. 1967 captain

Mbatani, Zimasa 1967, 1973 1975 vice-captain

Mbekeni, Selby 1953, 1955, 1958

Mokuena, Bridgeman 1975

Mshumpela, A. 1953, 1958

Mshumpela, M. 1975

Msikinya, D. 1951, 1953

Msutwana, S.S. 1973

Mxoli, F. 1976

Mzondeki, Wesley 'Zorro' 1953

Ndlovu, Judas 1955

Ngubelanga, J. 1958

Njokweni, Phillip 1975

Mkubevana, Sydney T. 1973

Nonganga, Brian 1976

Nontshinga, Samuel M. 1973, 1975, 1976

Ntikinca, Edmund 1958, 1967, 1973, 1975, 1976

Ntshekisa, Samson 1951, 1953, 1973

Nyamakazi, J. 1955, 1958

Peter Chingoka, captain of the SAACB team in 1975 and 1976 is currently president of the Zimbabwe Cricket Union. Here he appeals for lbw against Alan Barrow of Natal in the Gillette Cup match at Kingsmead.

Roji, Gladman, L. 1967, 1973, 1975

Roro, Frank 1951, 1953

Scott, C. 1951

Sihawu, G.G. 1967

Sikundla, V. 1967

Sokopo, Melford 1951

Somyo, Stanford 1975, 1976

Sonwabe, Samson 1973, 1975, 1976

Stamper, Duncan 1975

Sulupha, Green 1951, 1953

Taleni, C. 1976

Toyana, Gustavus Gaxa 1975, 1976

Voss, S. 1953

Ximiya, Wilson 1951

Yengo, S. 1955

Zibi, Cannon 1958

Zibi, G.M. 1967 vice-captain

Wilson, Don 1975 captain (guest appearances as English professional)

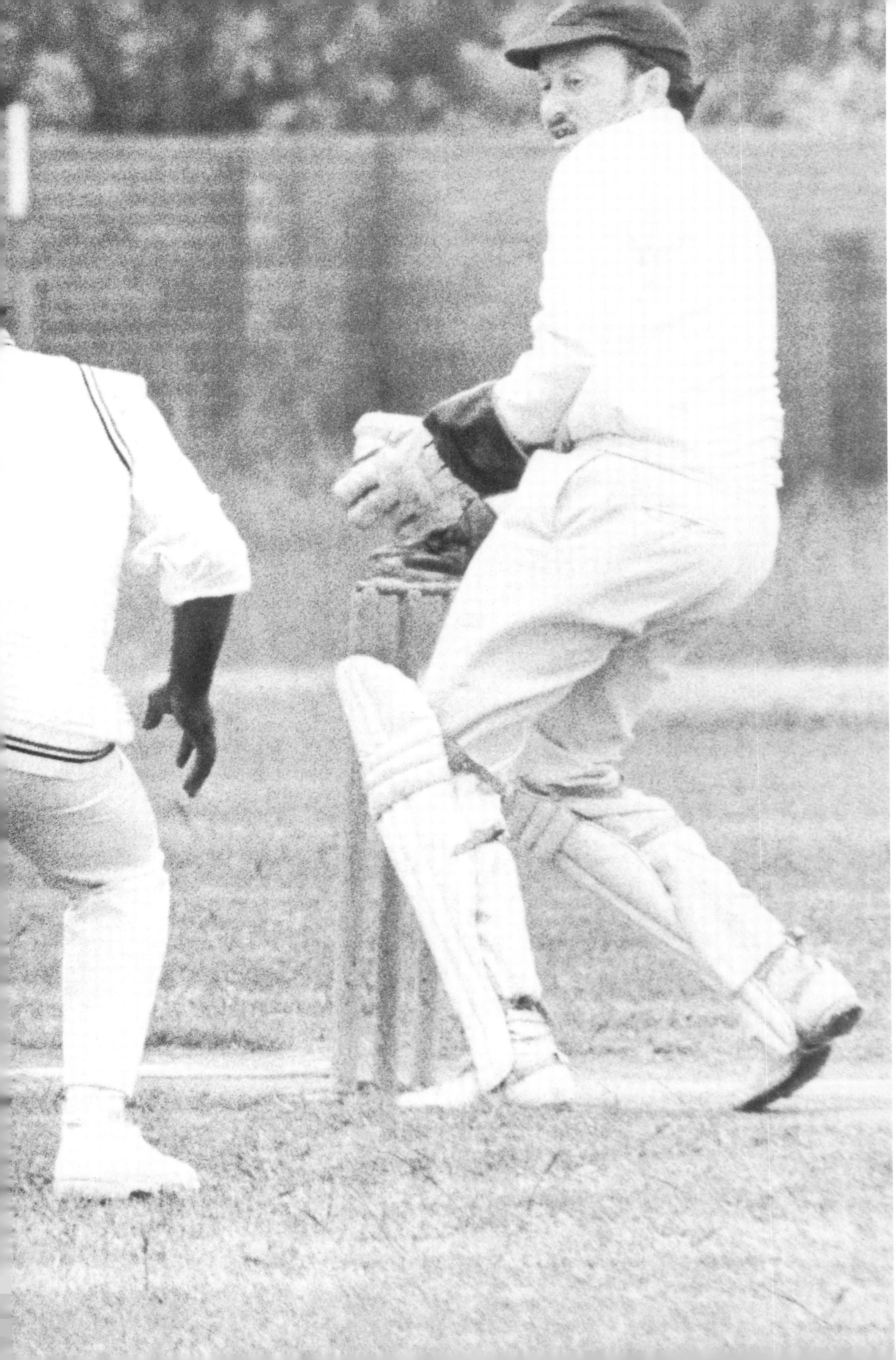

Part Six

NON-RACIAL STRUGGLES (1970s–1991)

'Facta non verba' *(Deeds, not words). KWARU led the move of Africans to non-racial sport in the early 1970s. One of the first KWARU executives (left to right) Vuyi Domkraag, Edwin Ncula, Dan Qeqe, Joseph Made, Royi Masoka, Baba Jali, Vuyo Kwinana, Silas Nkanunu, Dan Siwisa.*

Chapter 24

BREAKAWAY *from the* AFRICAN BOARD

———— ◗ ————

I
N THE EARLY 1970s resistance picked up again after a decade of intense repression and deepening apartheid. The Black Consciousness movement and its famous icon, Steve Biko, came to the fore. Workers flexed their muscles, starting with strikes in Durban in 1973. Mozambique and Angola became independent, giving hope to those seeking freedom in South Africa. On the sports front, the South African Council on Sport (SACOS) was formed in 1973 to unite under one umbrella those sports bodies opposing racialism and supporting non-racialism.

SACOS emerged from an *ad hoc* committee of eight sports organisations that was formed in 1970, following a decision by the Johannesburg City Council to ban the South African Soccer Federation from using municipal grounds 'because they played integrated soccer'. The grouping criticised the racialised permit system controlling the use of sports facilities and attacked white sports bodies for trying to co-opt black bodies into 'subservient affiliation'. Black sportspeople who were seduced by these offers were described as 'stooges and agents of apartheid'. The committee also called for South Africa's expulsion from all international sports federations.[1]

Three years later, in March 1973, the non-racial sports groups formally established SACOS at a meeting in Durban. Norman Middleton was elected president. Hassan Howa, president of the cricket affiliate, SACBOC, was made his deputy.[2] Like the Olympic movement, SACOS had five rings on its badge — but these were of a chain symbolising oppression rather than the five continents. This new umbrella body now started working closely with the exiled, London-based South African Non-Racial Olympic Committee (SANROC) and the Supreme Council for Sport in Africa to co-ordinate the campaign against apartheid sport.[3]

While the non-racial groups began to side openly with the goals of the banned liberation movements and to support moves to isolate apartheid sport, what remained of the Africans-only cricket and rugby bodies moved closer to the authorities, until eventually they were branded as sell-outs and collaborators.

The paths Khaya Majola and his siblings took from 1974 onwards reflected the new directions that sport was taking. They not only disassociated themselves from the Africans-only framework their father and other cricketers had been playing under since the formation of the Bantu Cricket Board in the 1930s, but also turned their backs on involvement with the paternalistic initiatives of a white cricket establishment trying to co-opt black cricketers as junior partners via the 'multi-national' policy of the apartheid government. Instead they threw in their lot with the ideologically non-racial SACBOC (but based predominantly in the coloured and Indian communities), which was demanding full equality for black South Africans on and off the sports field.

Milase Majola (second left) being supported by her mother Grace Moyake and sister
Amelia Rwairwai (right) at Eric Majola's funeral in June 1971.

THE CATALYST

This change in loyalties and thinking had been some time in
coming. Although Majola played for the African team in
1973 and toured England with Derrick Robins in 1974, he
had already started supporting non-racial sport as early as
1971, when the first breakaway from the African Board
occurred. The catalyst was, as it turned out, the unexpected
death of his father, in a car accident on 17 June 1971.

Eric was only 41 at the time. Milase recalls:

I was at school coaching indoor tennis. He put his head round the cor-
ner to say he was going out for a short while. I was wondering what
was keeping him when Rose Qeqe arrived to say Eric was in hospital
and I must come home with her. They wouldn't let me go to the hospital
and they didn't tell me anything until Dan arrived much later that
night to break the news.[4]

Nearly 6 000 people attended the funeral held in the
Edward's Memorial Church in New Brighton. It was
reported that, 'His closest friend and fellow player in rugby
and cricket, Mr D.D. Qeqe, bought a R225-public address
system' for the church in his memory. His school and various
sports clubs contributed over R1 000, a considerable
amount at the time. Mourners came from throughout South
Africa and Swaziland. They included old team-mates like
Ben Malamba from Cape Town, a double rugby and cricket
Springbok like Eric.[5]

Over 100 cars and a fleet of buses carried the mourners
to the cemetery. A guard of honour of Girl Guides lined
Avenue A, opposite the Bantu Social Centre, playing the
Last Post as the procession passed. At the cemetery the
church brass band 'played the funeral march to the grave'.
This was a society event in every respect, and *The World*
newspaper devoted a full page of its weekend edition to
the funeral.

A long list of people made
speeches. Those on the funeral
programme included Wilson
Ximiya 'representing home
clubs', Chief Lent Maqoma
from Johnson Marwanqa
School, Reverend G.B. Molefe of
the New Brighton Bantu School
Board, Lawrence Erasmus on
behalf of the 'Coloured community and sport', Nagin Umley on
behalf of the 'Indian community
and sport', national African
Cricket Board secretary, Fikile
Siyo for 'East London and SA Cricket', and Louis Koch,
Director of Bantu Affairs in Port Elizabeth.[6]

Erasmus, a former Coloured Springbok, claimed in his
speech that in his heyday Eric Majola was 'far superior to the
celebrated [British] Lions fly-half, Cliff Morgan'.[7]

What was noticeable about the speakers was that many
had affiliations to government structures. Koch was the
white bureaucrat in charge of running the New Brighton
township and implementing apartheid policy in Port
Elizabeth. Erasmus and Ximiya, both former sports stars,
were on the local Advisory Boards and Management
Committees which were to become totally discredited in the
1970s and 1980s. *The World* reported that Lennox Sebe was
also a speaker. He went on to become the notorious head of
the Ciskeian bantustan. Lent Maqoma, Eric's principal, later
became a minister in Sebe's cabinet.

It was ironic that this should be the case when, in many
respects, the funeral signalled a parting of the ways with the
old tradition of conservatism in African sport. Sport in
the African townships in Port Elizabeth split in two following the funeral.

Spring Rose and other clubs had been scheduled to play in
rugby fixtures that weekend. They asked the local board for
the postponement of these matches so that Majola's fellow
sportsmen could pay tribute to him. When this request was
turned down, the clubs went ahead regardless and attended
the funeral.

Feelings ran high. The officiating minister, Reverend D.M.
Zondeki, was aware of this. He lamented Eric Majola's
death at a time 'when his good influence and character was
needed to quell disturbances in African sport'.[8] In fact, it
proved to be the catalyst for a whole new era in the history
of sport in the Eastern Cape and South Africa.

KWARU LEADS THE WAY

When the Port Elizabeth African Rugby Board took disciplinary action against those who attended the funeral, ten of the 12 clubs in the first league broke away to form the rival Kwazakhele Rugby Union (KWARU). The new motto was 'Facta non verba' – deeds not words – and the crest was the sturdy rhinoceros. The Young Turks were led by Mono Badela, a journalist and vice-president of the PEARB. The initial reasons for leaving were dissatisfaction with the attitudes and perceived corruption and maladministration of the 'old-timers' like Norris Singaphi, head of the local Bantu Administration Board, and his lieutenants, Curnick Mdyesha and W.L. Dwesi. But the move soon assumed political connotations. After failing to get the SAARB to accept them as a separate affiliate, KWARU linked up with the coloured South African Rugby Union (SARU), which was moving in an aggressively non-racial direction to challenge the white, apartheid-supporting South African Rugby Board (SARB), and became one of the founder members of SACOS in 1973.[9]

Other African sporting bodies in the Eastern Cape subsequently followed KWARU in defecting from the African rugby and cricket boards to their 'non-racial' counterparts.[10] While the coloured-dominated rugby and cricket boards were delighted to get the first significant numbers of African players into their ranks, so giving content to their non-racial ideals, serious divisions arose in African sports ranks, bringing to an end the way that African sport had been organised since the formation of the Bantu cricket and rugby boards in the 1930s.

In Port Elizabeth, Majola's New Brighton CC and Dan Qeqe's Fort Beaufort CC followed KWARU into the non-racial ranks. The African cricketers apparently wanted to join the EPCA as a sub-union, but this line was not favoured by the EPCA:

During the last season we allowed some of the clubs [of the Eastern Province African Cricket Union] to play in our competitions, and we suggested several formuli for them to be completely absorbed in our Association. However, I have only come to one workable solution to the problem. We formed the non-racial EPCA 12 years ago and the African

Thoba Williams.

clubs seceded for valid reasons; now our doors are open to them, but they must come back to us as in the past as individual clubs and not as a sub-union, and these clubs must accept our constitution in toto.[11]

One of the clauses added to the EPCA constitution at this time was that anyone attending games 'arranged solely by white cricket bodies' would be 'sentenced for misconduct before the Disciplinary Committee'. Ex-players would also have their provincial colours withdrawn.[12]

Ray Mali, president of the EPACB at the time, remembers travelling down to Cape Town in 1971 with the current president of the South African Rugby Football Union, Silas Nkanunu, to join with SACBOC.

We wanted to join as an African entity, like KWARU, but were told we were racists. We explained that our cricketers were poor and had difficulty travelling. I'll never forget the rudeness. We joined anyway on SACBOC's terms.[13]

Some of the African clubs unfortunately folded in the process but Fort Beaufort and New Brighton forged ahead.

Dan Qeqe and later Wilson Ximiya became members of the provincial executive committee of the SACBOC-affiliated Eastern Province Cricket Association. Khaya Majola and stars like Thoba Williams and Thembisile Pono started making their mark in the non-racial (but predominantly coloured) leagues.

The Border African cricketers, who joined the non-racial Border Cricket Board followed the exit to SACBOC and SACOS ranks, while the Victoria East Cricket Board based in Alice and the Komani and District Cricket Board, with its headquarters in Queenstown, were later accepted *en bloc* as new provincial units.

KHAYA'S JOURNEY

While these ideological divisions and organisational realignments played themselves out, Khaya Majola found himself for a short while playing under two different national cricket controlling boards at the same time.

Although his club, family and friends in Port Elizabeth had disassociated themselves from the African Board in Port Elizabeth, the traditional Africans-only body was the only one operating at Lovedale while he was studying there in 1972 and 1973, so he kept on playing under the SAACB.

Khaya Majola (left) appealing in an Eastern Province limited-overs match against Transvaal in January 1975. The other players are (left to right) Keith Barry, Devdas Govindjee, Jausukh Vagmaria and wicketkeeper Glen Cuddumbey.

The EPCA executive committee, 1972/73 (Back row, left to right) D.D. Qeqe, W. Bougaard, E.L. Stoffels, P. Clarke, W.S. Hendricks. (Front row) M. Loonat, (treasurer), W. M. Ross (secretary), J. W. Marais (president), F. L. Erasmus (vice-president).

In the 1973/74 season, when he made his debut for the national SAACB team, he also made his debut for the EPCA under the SACOS-affiliated SACBOC .

When picked for the national African team to play against the Derrick Robins XI in October 1973, Majola did not want to play. However, the Lovedale authorities threatened to prevent him from writing his final exams for his teacher's diploma, only a few weeks away, if he refused.[14]

Khaya's dilemma increased when Derrick Robins offered him the opportunity to play in England in the 1974 off-season.

He was now no longer at Lovedale, and firmly committed to SACBOC's non-racial approach. He was reticent even though offers like this came once in a lifetime. Lennox Mlonzi flew down from Johannesburg to persuade him to go. What to do now? Dan Qeqe, who became like a second father to him after Eric's death, loaded him onto a plane and they went directly to Hassan Howa in Cape Town to talk the matter over. Hassan was very supportive. Let the youngster go and get the experience, then he could settle down in the SACBOC competitions when he returned.[15]

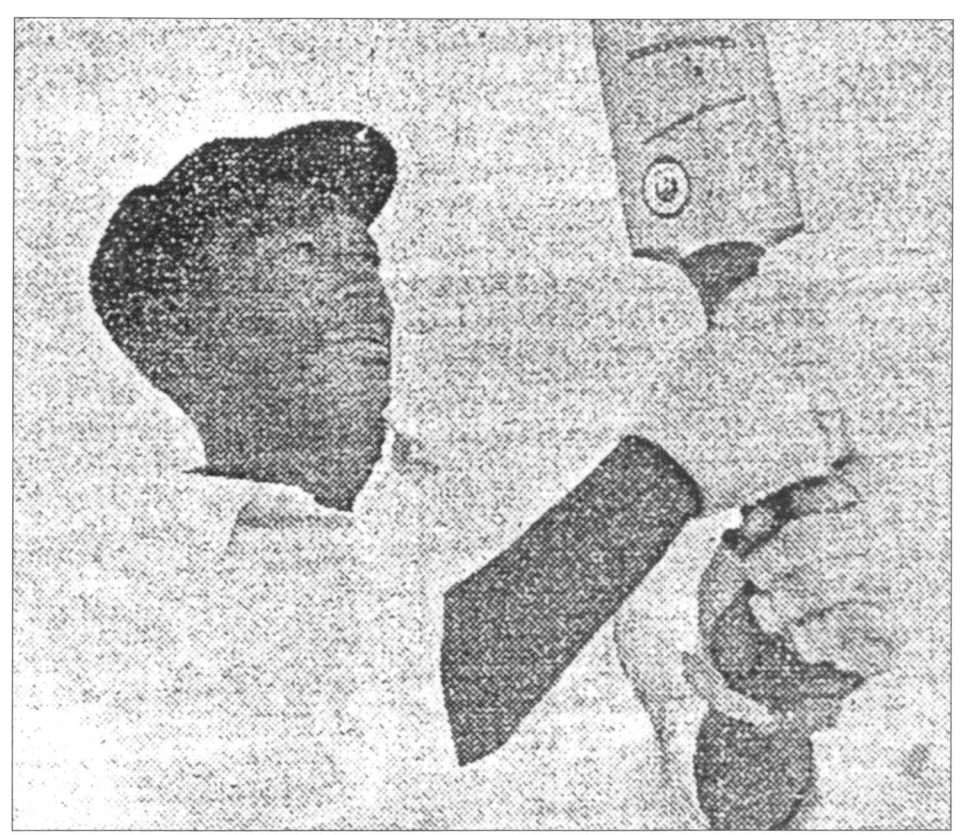

Dan Qeqe.

Majola actually made his SACBOC first-class debut just before his departure for England. It was in February 1974 against Natal at Curries Fountain, towards the end of the season. After having failed to win the Dadabhay Trophy, despite again having a strong team with West Indian professional Duncan Carter in it, the selectors, it was reported, 'have at long last decided that some of the regulars have had their last innings and it is time to build for the future'.[16] Majola and four other new caps — Fagme Abrahams, Jainudien Sandan, Clive Paulsen and Thembisile Pono — were brought in.

The Eastern Province captain in Khaya's first-class debut was the stylish left-handed batsman, Neville Francis. Eastern Province beat Natal by 15 runs, despite a Natal fightback of 236 runs in 86 overs in the last innings following a poor first innings 89 all out. Eastern Province scored 171 and 169 all out. Khaya did not make an auspicious start. Batting at number five, he was caught off the bowling of Baboo Ebrahim for three in the first innings and run out for a duck in the second. In the next, a drawn season-ender against Transvaal, he managed only one and one. While the runs eluded him, the young man's three catches in the Natal second innings and bowling figures of 29-4-56-3 in his first two games nevertheless gave a hint of things to come.

When Khaya returned from England Ali Bacher offered him a scholarship which would have given him the opportunity to live and play in Johannesburg, where the prospects were better for him than in Port Elizabeth.[17]

He was also invited to partner Edward Habane in the second Datsun Double Wicket Competition in September 1974 as a representative of the 'South African Blacks' side.[18] This event was one of the highlights of the post-isolation calendar for the SACA. It would have put him in star-studded company. The teams were Ian and Greg Chappell (Australia), Tony Greig and Keith Fletcher (England), Bev Congdon and Ken Wadsworth (New Zealand), Khalid 'Billy' Ibadulla and Younis Ahmed (Pakistan), Mike Procter and Brian Davidson (Rhodesia), Eddie Barlow and Barry Richards (South Africa) and John Shepherd and Geoff Greenidge (West Indies).[19]

But the young man with the big ambitions turned down these major opportunities coming his way. Basically, he felt he could not be part of an Africans-only set-up and the so-called multi-national policy of the apartheid government, which allowed limited mixing by separate racial sides at the top levels, but not integration down to club level. At a time when resistance to apartheid was growing and sportspeople were being challenged to make a stand, he decided to join the struggle for non-racial sport.

West Indian batting great, Rohan Kanhai, swings Cecil Abrahams to leg while batting for Transvaal against Western Province in Cape Town in the 1974/75 season.

Chapter 25

UPDATING WISDEN'S RECORDS

MAJOLA'S 1973/74 DEBUT season was only the third in which black cricketers were playing three-day matches. Since the formation of the South African Coloured Cricket Board way back in 1903, the different national bodies that came into existence had organised various inter-provincial and national competitions. These involved some 70 tournaments, an average of around one per year. For example, the SACCB itself organised 17 tournaments where the Barnato Memorial Trophy was competed for before it was dissolved to become part of a unified SACBOC in the 1960s. Then there were also the regular tournaments for the Sir David Harris Trophy (Coloureds), NRC Trophy (Africans) and Christopher Floating Trophy (Indians).

When these bodies came together under the umbrella of SACBOC in the 1950s, they started competing against each other on a national inter-race basis for the Dadabhay Trophy. In the 1960s, the format for the Dadabhay Trophy changed to a mixed inter-provincial rather than national inter-racial tournament. Altogether nine centralised Dadabhay tournaments took place between 1950 and 1969.[1]

But all the above-mentioned competitions had consisted of one- or two-day games played at centralised tournaments, never three-day matches. Thus they could not qualify as first-class according to international criteria. The only three-day matches played by black cricketers at this stage were the few games played by South Africa (SACBOC) in the reciprocal tours with the Kenya Asians in the 1950s.

Various factors prompted SACBOC to switch over to the three-day format for conventional first-class cricket in the 1970s. Firstly, the centralised Dadabhay tournaments had become too long, lasting as long as two weeks, and many players could not afford the time away from work. Secondly, the nature of sport and society was changing with travel, for example, becoming easier. Another strong factor was that as the non-racial movement grew in the 1970s and as international pressure on white South Africa increased, SACBOC started to seek international recognition from the ICC. If the non-racial body wished to get the same recognition as the white SACA, or supplant it, it would have to organise according to the traditional three-day format.

After an experimental season of two-day matches played at different venues in 1970/71, SACBOC introduced a home-and-away three-day competition in 1971/72, with the Dadabhay Trophy still at stake. It was decided that because of limited resources the competition would initially stretch over two seasons.

In the 1973/74 season, when Khaya Majola made his debut, the competition was further refined to be completed in a single season.

Altogether 216 inter-provincial three-day games were played under SACBOC and the successor SACB in the 21 years between 1971 and 1991. Four teams competed, namely Western Province, Eastern Province, Natal and Transvaal. All four teams played 108 games apiece.[2]

50: 11.45 (105)
100: 12.53 (173)

LUNCH 102 for 3 (1 - 1.43)
Tea 191 for 5 (3.40 - 4.00)

150: 2.55 (252)
200 4.13 (310)
250 4.53

CRICKET CLUB V

HOME CLUB   VISITORS

INNINGS OF   PLAYED AT

BATSMEN	TIME IN	TIME OUT	RUNS SCORED	MINS	50	100	150	HOW
1 DOUGLAS	10.00	1.00	3111124321111112121121211211 >> (1 short)	180				lbw
2 SNYMAN	10.00	11.23	132112023 >> (1 legbye)	83				ct. JAIRA
3 FRANCIS	11.25	12.13	4412 >> LUNCH	78				ct. m BULB
4 WILSON	12.15	1.11	1111114111112 >>	56				bows
5 D'OLIVEIRA	1.43	5.30	1114111121111121111421311113211141123221611134411422112211 11411112644242(138)211212221(150)266211662	115	3.38	5.00	5.32	e stpd SA
6 JACOBS	2.13	2.24	4 > Tea. St Chavel	11				C GARD
7 J.VAGHMARIA	2.26	4.07	14521112314 11 >>	81				C SAD
8 I.HENDRICKS	4.09	4.33	311 >>	24				C WADVA
9 J.GOVINDJEE	4.34	5.46	12114121111113(31)121322 4 >> 135 partnership	72				C AKHA
10 HOWLIE	5.48		1112					
11 T.HENDRICKS	5.52		11					

NOTE: Batsmen RUN OUT, or given out for OBSTRUCTION, HIT BALL TWICE, HANDLED BALL do NOT count as bowlers wickets

BYES 2343222
LEG BYES 111
WIDES 1
NO BALLS 111

TOTAL AT THE FALL OF EACH WICKET AND NO. OF OUTGOING BATSMAN									
1 FOR	2 FOR	3 FOR	4 FOR	5 FOR	6 FOR	7 FOR	8 FOR	9 FOR	10 FOR
38	66	102	119	128	196	216	351	366	
2	3	1	4	6	7	8	9	5	

MINS (83) 32 (48) 39 45 17 28 9/1 8/81 20 50 in 31 mins. 1st 100 in 50

Western Province were the provincial champions or joint champions in 14 of the 18 seasons of three-day games. Eastern Province won three times – in 1978/79, 1984/85 and again in 1985/86. Natal were joint champions with Western Province in one season and the only other outright provincial champions were Transvaal in 1974/75, when the great West Indian player, Rohan Kanhai, spearheaded their challenge and Abdul Bhamjee was captain.

In the 1975/76 season, the SFW Trophy (named after the sponsor, Stellenbosch Farmers Wineries) replaced the Dadabhay Trophy as the premier trophy. It was played for in one season only. From 1977/78 through to 1990/91 the Howa Bowl became the main competition.

Although not recognised at the time, these three-day matches of SACBOC (and the successor South African Cricket Board or SACB) were retrospectively declared first-class by the United Cricket Board in 1996.[3] They are therefore now officially part of South African and international first-class records. However, until recently, the full details were unavailable. Now, thanks to the work of retired school principal and current Natal selector, Krish Reddy, they are in the process of being finalised and published. When this task is complete the *South African Cricket Annual* and the famous *Wisden Cricketers' Almanack* will have to revise long-advertised records and integrate these statistics fully into the history of international first-class cricket. Some 450 players and 66 umpires, denied opportunities under apartheid, will be given long overdue recognition. This will also necessitate changes to the existing records of 41 players who have been officially recognised, including internationals such as Basil D'Oliveira, Rohan Kanhai and Omar Henry, who played under SACBOC and SACB as well as in first-class competitions elsewhere.

: 5.23   (380)
: 5.43   (400)

117

227
177
50

C. CLUB		
ON	19	
UT	BOWLER	TOTAL
slip	JAIRAM	42
on	MANACK	16
A	AKHALWAYA	11
♭	JAIRAM	18
2	JAIRAM	182
slip.	CHOTHIA	4
?k	MANACK	28
slip A	CHOTHIA.	5
A4A	JAIRAM	34
♭	out	5
♭	out	2
18	EXTRAS	25
3	TOTAL	372
1	FOR 9	
3		

dec.

TOP LEFT *An historic scorecard that has to go into Wisden. Basil
D'Oliveira's score of 182 against Transvaal in 1972/73 was the highest
under SACBOC until Rohan Kanhai surpassed it with 188 not out.*
ABOVE *Omar Henry (Western Province) catching Maurice Wilson
for a duck is another of the top cricketers whose
records must be revised.*
LEFT *Krish Reddy has systematically compiled the
SACBOC and SACB first-class scores.*

Basil D'Oliveira.

Chapter 26

DOLLY *and a* TIME *of* OPTIMISM

———————————————— ⬤ ————————————————

W HEN KHAYA MAJOLA started playing for the EPCA provincial side in 1974, there was an air of optimism and growth in the province. Records from annual general meetings in the early part of the decade give a good indication of this.

There were 27 clubs, playing in six different leagues, affiliated to the EPCA in 1970. The champions Hamediah, Stardust, South End United, Aryans, Lilywhite and Regents formed the first league and played ten games each.[1] Registration cost 50 cents per player and ten cents of this was sent to SACBOC as the national parent body. The president was Stanley Hendricks, who was succeeded in turn by J. 'Basie' Marais and Les Petersen. Billy Ross (secretary), Mia Loonat (treasurer and vice-president) and Wilson Ximiya (assistant treasurer) were other long-serving officials. Yusuf Lorgat became secretary in 1974, thereafter going on to become a long-standing member of the executive committee of the national board. [2]

Eastern Province fared poorly in the last centralised SACBOC tournament in the 1960s, so they started the new era and the new decade in the B Section. However, they emerged top in 1970/71 and were promoted to join the big three of Western Province, Natal and Transvaal in the premier competition from 1971/72, when the three-day matches were first instituted.

Then, in September 1972, Eastern Province pulled off a coup when Basil D'Oliveira, who had become a household name in world cricket after the infamous 'D'Oliveira affair', agreed to coach in Port Elizabeth.

D'Oliveira's two-season presence had an electrifying effect on the Eastern Province cricket scene. This is clearly shown by the EPCA official report for 1972/73:

There is no doubt that the presence of Basil D'Oliveira in the Eastern Province has been of tremendous significance to our cricket. Never before have we had so much spectator interest as well as other forms of interest in our cricket and our Association. As far as our EP team was concerned, never before have they so smartly taken the field, their fielding was excellent and their running between wickets an object lesson, the example set by Dolly himself. They really looked like a first-class team ... Basil's emphasis on physical fitness ... paid dividends.[3]

Indeed, D'Oliveira created a whole new dimension in the local game. He was brought to Port Elizabeth 'through a sudden break in the field of sponsorship' by the South African Bottling Company, the local distributors of Coca Cola.[4] He scored 182, then the highest-ever individual score in Board three-day games, against Transvaal, and the *Cricket Annual*, edited by S.J. Reddy, described this as 'one of the greatest seasons' for Eastern Province, even though they did not win the Dadabhay Trophy.[5] The provincial schools team, prepared by D'Oliveira, won the national schools tournament in Durban.

Meanwhile, the local municipality opened the new Adcock Stadium, Coca Cola sponsored an 'excellent' scoreboard, and plans to build a turf wicket were announced.

To top it all, the EPCA administrators were able to report that 'the cream of the African cricketers' had joined and were now available for provincial selection. This was the context in which Khaya Majola made his debut in February 1974. Eastern Province were cock-a-hoop and suddenly very much at the centre of the national cricket scene.[6]

The optimism noted at the provincial level was a sign of the generally upbeat mood of SACBOC in the early 1970s. Besides the new three-day, home-and-away format, and SACBOC's growing profile and confidence as the white SACA started being isolated, Hassan Howa could boast of the introduction of top overseas professionals, the inauguration of a B Section zonal competition, an under-19 tournament, a new, sponsored 50-over SFW Knockout Competition, the start of a new era of air travel for teams, and the organisation of special invitation matches to recognise the top players at a national level.[7]

The 'D'Oliveira affair' internationalised the South African cricket debate and Dolly's subsequent successful return to play domestic cricket under SACBOC emboldened the organisation. Part of its strategy was to start lobbying the ICC for recognition as 'the sole body representing South African cricketers'.[8] It also discussed with black cricketing countries – India, Pakistan and West Indies – the possibility of touring there, and New Zealand were reported to be on the way in 1973. Another initiative was to attract other top international players. Approaches were made to West Indian greats like Clive Lloyd, Charlie Griffith, Seymour Nurse and Rohan Kanhai to play under SACBOC.[9]

Griffith, whose fearsome pace caused some to brand him a 'chucker', formed one of the great West Indies pace bowling partnerships of the modern era with Wes Hall. On the recommendation of South African Lancashire League professional, Dik Abed, Griffith accepted an offer from the Natal Cricket Board and the South Coast Indian Sports Trust to sign on for 'a fee of R3 500 plus his airfare and accommodation'.[10] Dik Abed said he was on his way, but the visit of the outspoken West Indian, who had strongly criticised apartheid in his autobiography, never materialised.[11]

The first big-name foreign player to come was Rohan Kanhai, who played for Transvaal in 1974/75, helping the province to its one and only title under the captaincy of Abdul Bhamjee. His 188 not out against Eastern Province

that season was the highest-ever score in Board cricket, eclipsing D'Oliveira's 182.

The great West Indian's stay was not the most amicable, however. Sadick Emeran remembers him taking his lunch separately from others during a provincial game.[12] He lived in a five-star hotel in (white) Johannesburg and was seen to be aloof by some. During an end-of-season invitation game he refused to continue batting after his appeal 'for postponement to allow the wicket to dry' was turned down by the umpires. He stormed off the field and flew back to London within a day.[13]

According to Transvaal manager, Rafique Khota, he had an ' aloof, arrogant and aggressive' attitude to officials and 'did not participate in discussions before and after games in the latter part of his stay'. He also 'failed to meet' supporters who had travelled hundreds of kilometres from Ermelo to see him.[14]

Kanhai said the standard of SACBOC cricket was much higher than he had expected, but added that there was 'a crying need' for turf wickets and better practice facilities if the standards were to improve. He singled out Natal left-arm spinner Baboo Ebrahim, who had played in the Lancashire League the previous season, as someone 'who could hold his own in any form of first-class cricket'.[15] Kanhai also rated Devdas Govindjee, who at that stage was keeping Khaya Majola out of the EPCA team, as an excellent player.

When it proved difficult to attract other top international players, SACBOC lowered its sights and settled for West Indians playing as Lancashire League professionals. Duncan Carter (Eastern Province) Keith Barker (Natal) and John Holder (Western Province) were contracted. Holder later became an international umpire.

The first of the 'mini-tests' organised by SACBOC took place in November 1972 at the Adcock Stadium. Stellenbosch Farmers Wineries and Sedgwick Taylor sponsored a special two-day invitation match between Eastern Province, captained by D'Oliveira, and a South African Invitation XI. The match was drawn. The Invitation XI scored 163 and 114 for five in reply to Eastern Province's double Nelson 222. Top score in the match was Transvaal's Abdullatief 'Tiffie' Barnes's 59 not out. D'Oliveira did not

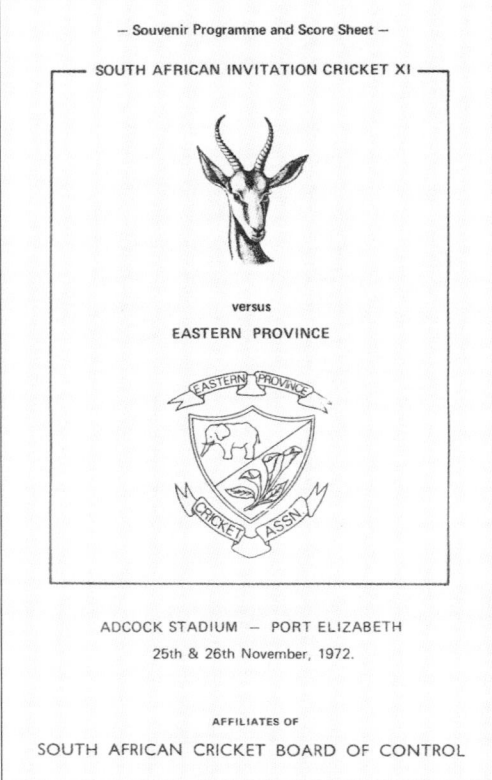

– Souvenir Programme and Score Sheet –

SOUTH AFRICAN INVITATION CRICKET XI

versus

EASTERN PROVINCE

ADCOCK STADIUM – PORT ELIZABETH
25th & 26th November, 1972.

AFFILIATES OF
SOUTH AFRICAN CRICKET BOARD OF CONTROL

*Duncan Carter from Barbados followed D'Oliveira as Eastern
Province's overseas signing.*

*The EPCA team coached by Basil D'Oliveira in 1972/73. (Back row, left to right) Devdas
Govendjee, Alec Douglas, Charlie Houlie, Alphonsus Snyman, Desmond Jacobs, Preston de Klerk.
(Middle row) Basil D'Oliveira, Maurice Wilson (vice-captain), Mia Loonat (manager),
Phillip Snyman (captain), Terry Hendricks. (Front row) Neville Francis, Jaysukh Vagmaria.*

star with the bat, but he did have bowling figures of four for 45 in the first innings.[16] He commented afterwards that the local players needed to show more discipline and concentration: they 'would concentrate for a while, then, whoosh, they'd swing and be caught.' Eastern Province had already made progress in this regard, he said.[17]

The next big match was in March 1973 between the Dadabhay champions, Western Province, and the Rest of SACBOC at the Green Point Stadium in Cape Town. This time Dolly was on song with an unbeaten century, which included four sixes. Ismail 'Morris' Garda also hit a blistering hundred to put the SA Invitation team in the driving seat. Nine down at the close, Western Province hung on desperately for a draw. The summarised scores were SA Invitation XI: 199 (Yacoob Omar 40, Rushdie Magiet five for 29) and 314 for seven declared (Morris Garda 106 and D'Oliveira 100 not out). Western Province: 221 (Rushdie Magiet 48, Alphonsus 'Bunny' Snyman three for 44) and 200 for nine (Saait Magiet 50, Ismail 'Baboo' Ebrahim three for 34). Garda earned a princely R231 for his performance, while D'Oliveira and Magiet took home R145 and R50 respectively.[18]

The next month, SACBOC organised the first North versus South game for the top players in the country at the new Lenasia Stadium in Johannesburg. Hassan Howa proudly noted that this is 'the first "Big" match we stage on turf'.[19] The reports underline the upbeat atmosphere prevailing within SACBOC ranks.[20]

It is interesting to note in these days of inflation that Mr Howa's airfare from Cape Town cost a grand R54. The cost of the SACBOC AGM came to under R500.[21]

The South team consisted of eight Western Province players together with Neville Francis, Jaysukh 'Yokes' Vaghmaria and off-spinner Clive 'Dimples' Langson from Eastern Province. They lost by six wickets to the North line-up from Transvaal, Natal and Griqualand West. Yassien Snyders of Griquas scored the only century. The scores were South: 268 (Ebrahim Isaacs 86, Rushdie Magiet 56, Solly Chothia four for 62) and 142 all out. North: 270 for seven (Yassien Snyders 103 not out, Ahmed Gabru 60, Solly Chothia 55, Gertjie Williams three for 78) and 146 for four (Yassien Snyders 73).[22]

Further North versus South matches were held at the 'Lenz' (now Lenasia) Stadium in 1974 and 1975. Both were drawn.

In 1974, the North again ended in a better position. The scores were North: 206 (Abdul Bhamjee 61, Yassien Snyders 49, Rushdie Magiet five for 42) and 189 for eight declared

The 1974 South Zone team. (Back row, left to right) A. Garda (umpire), V. Moodie, S. Conrad (captain), R. Magiet, E. Isaacs, A. Adams, A. Mangera (umpire). (Front row) G. Williams, J. Mahoney, C. Langson, A. Sonn, J. Vaghmaria and N. Francis.

(Snyders 69, Magiet three for 49). South: 137 (Joey Lambert 43, Solly Chothia two for 37) and 111 for five (Robbie van Graan 44 not out, Baboo Ebrahim two for 28).[23]

The 1975 fixture was restricted to the first innings due to rain. Batting first the North scored 248, with Aboo Manack 62 and Solly Chothia 43. Rushdie Magiet took three for 33. Lefty Adams's South replied with 228. Highest score was Ismail Timol's 45 and best bowling Manack's three for 34. It was during this match that Kanhai, captaining the North, stormed off the field. The official SACBOC report explained:

After a delayed start and after 15 minutes batting Kanhai refused to continue batting on a 'dangerous' strip. His appeal for a postponement for the pitch to dry was dismissed. Whereupon he took the law into his own hands by staging a walk-off. For the game's sake and the big crowd which came to watch, the umpires after lunch reluctantly yet sportingly agreed to resume the game. After the first day's play Kanhai withdrew from the match and returned to London 48 hours later.[24]

After three seasons, Chummy Mayet informed SACBOC that Transvaal would no longer be able to stage the 'mini-tests'. The reason given was that 'the players took advantage of the hospitality displayed', leaving 'huge phone bills'. The last game cost R4 000, and there was no return.[25]

Sponsors Stellenbosch Farmers Wineries, who contributed R60 000 to SACBOC in three seasons, stepped in to fill the breach in 1976. This time the season-ender was played on the picturesque Oude Libertas Ground in Stellenbosch between the provincial champions Western Province, captained by the current Rector of the University of the Western Cape, Brian O'Connell, and the Rest of SACBOC led by Tiffie Barnes. The Rest won easily by nine wickets

The 1974 North Zone team. (Back row, left to right) A. Bhamjee, Y. Snyders, M. Mangera, A. Jinnah, B. Ebrahim, E. Bhamjee, A. Barnes, A. Garda. (Front row) ~~~, H. Ayob, S. Chotia, R. Engelbrecht, Y. Omar.

thanks to another century by Morris Garda and ten wickets by Barnes. The scores were Western Province: 151 (Lawton Jacobs 50, Tiffie Barnes four for 23 and Baboo Ebrahim four for 51) and 167 (Viccie Moodie 55, Barnes six for 44). Rest of SACBOC: 312 (Garda 112, Solly Chothia 52, Willie Hendricks four for 50) and eight for one.[26]

After getting promotion to the Dadabhay Trophy competition, Eastern Province fared relatively well in the first five seasons up to 1975/76, playing 25, winning five, losing six and drawing 14. Western Province was the bogey team, as four of the six losses came against them. Eastern Province were marginally better than Transvaal and Natal with two wins to one loss and five draws.[27]

Eleven EPCA players made the various SACBOC invitation teams selected in this time. D'Oliveira and the veteran Bunny Snyman played for the Rest against Western Province in March 1973. Neville Francis, Jaysukh Vaghmaria, Dimples Langson, Devdas Govindjee, Thoba Williams, Desmond 'Bravo' Jacobs, Maurice Wilson and Imraan 'Ranie' Hendricks represented the Western Province-dominated

South in one or two of the three matches in 1973, 1974 and 1975. None of them played in all three.

Thoba Williams, the veteran fast bowler from New Brighton CC, was one of three Africans to play for the EPCA in the early 1970s. He made his debut in the 1973/74 season and made an immediate impact with figures of 124.3-36-256-20. His wickets came at an average of 12.80. They included a match-winning spell of six for 32 against Natal at Curries Fountain in February 1974, when he ended with nine wickets in the match. The other two African players, Khaya Majola and Thembisile Pono, made their provincial debuts in the same match, taking two wickets apiece.

Pono, also an opening bowler, made 15 appearances for Eastern Province in four seasons. Altogether, he took 43 wickets at an average of 18.30. His best return was six for 37 in the 1975/76 season, when he took 16 wickets. He was also useful with the bat averaging fractionally under 20, with a top score of 59. In 1976, Pono was the only Eastern Province player to play for the Rest of South Africa against

The North versus South mini-tests provided fresh incentives for SACBOC players. Former SACBOC president, J.S. van Harte, addresses the crowd in Lenasia in 1974, while the incumbent president, Hassan Howa, listens attentively.

Western Province after Francis, Jacobs and 12th man Govindjee withdrew after being selected.[28] Pono opened the bowling with Goolam Allie, returning a creditable 21-5-39-1 in a match in which spin and medium pace did the damage.

Left-arm spinner Devdas Govindjee, who played in the EPCA leagues for more than 20 seasons and was himself rated as one of the best players in South Africa by Rohan Kanhai, has described the strengths of some of the Eastern Province stars mentioned above. Neville Francis, known as 'Armpie', came in at number three and had 'no peers as a left-handed batsman'. From the Stardust Club, he was 'smoothly effective on the off side and devastatingly powerful on the leg side', amassing a large number of runs for Eastern Province. Jaysukh Vaghmaria, middle-order batsman from Aryans and a specialist close fielder, was 'lovely … to watch at the crease' and 'could glide, late-cut, square-cut and pull with great effectiveness'. All-rounder Bravo Jacobs, also a professional soccer player, was 'a natural sportsman who possessed all the strokes in the textbook'. Govindjee said he was a 'beautiful striker of the ball and the best runner between wickets I have seen'. The burly Maurice 'Nats' Wilson was also an all-rounder, who bowled off-cutters and could 'completely change the complexion of the game' in a few overs with his ability to tear any bowling attack to shreds. Finally, Ranie Hendricks from Good Hope, 'was an

economical fast-medium bowler and useful batsman with 'an ideal temperament for a cricketer'. He would score runs when they were most needed and was 'never ruffled', according to Govindjee.[29]

By the mid-1970s SACBOC had a strong profile in the country thanks to its charismatic president, the outspoken Hassan Howa. Never at a loss for words, he rubbed in the fact that until all cricketers in the country were given equal treatment, whites could forget about international competition. His condemnation of paternalistic white administrators and white hypocrisy made him a figure the establishment press loved to hate. Epithets like 'intransigent', 'hardline' and 'hot-headed' were routinely used to describe him, but he became a champion of the underdog.[30]

In 1974 Howa resigned as president after five years at the helm. He was replaced by the long-serving Rashid Varachia, who had had a spell as president in the late 1950s and early 1960s.[31] Varachia and the powerful Transvaal administrators had an uncomfortable relationship with Howa, whom they regarded as too hot-headed.[32] The new president had long before stated, 'We must think with our minds and not with our hearts. There has got to be more co-operation between White and non-White if we are to break the barrier that exists between us.'[33] Varachia's presidency was indeed to be marked by a very different style from that of his predecessor.

Offer ID: 2595495

Item ID: 36408482

Item Price: £0.15

Rejected by prescan

IS HE MR. CRICKET OR MR. CONTROVERSY?

Mr. Hassan Howa, boss of the non-racial South African Cricket Board of Control, is wellknown for his rigid no-apartheid-in-cricket stand. For some he is a hero and to others he is the "villain" who is holding South Africa from getting back into world cricket. What makes him tick? For the answer turn to Page 62 where he gives DRUM a frank interview.

'Normal cricket' enabled some SACBOC players to test their skills against international opposition. Here Natal left-arm spinner Baboo Ebrahim (right) is congratulated by SACA's Henry Fotheringham after taking six for 66 against the International Wanderers side captained by Greg Chappell in 1976.

Chapter 27

'NORMAL CRICKET' DISRUPTIONS

I N JANUARY 1976, following further negotiations aimed at unity, the national bodies, SACA, SAACB and SACBOC announced that they 'hereby adopt the principle that Cricket in South Africa be played on a normal basis under the controlling aegis of one controlling body in South Africa … and that "Normal Cricket" shall mean at this stage participation of and competition between all cricketers regardless of race, creed or colour in cricket at club level under one provincial governing body'.[1] It seemed as though the long-held goal of equality for black cricketers was taking a big step forward.

The provincial boards of the respective bodies were instructed to enter into dialogue to give effect to the resolution. A national co-ordinating structure, the Nine-Man Motivating Committee, was set up to oversee unity. Both the EPCA president, Les Petersen, and the white EPCU vice-president, Geoff Dakin, were members.[2]

The 'normal cricket' agreement created great excitement. The provincial affiliates in every province started making preparations for a single league competition at the beginning of the 1976/77 season. The Eastern Province club scene was radically reshaped. Several clubs amalgamated to ensure a strength versus strength scenario. For example, New Brighton amalgamated with Far East and long-standing rivals Fort Beaufort to form United. Lilywhite and Union in Uitenhage formed Lilywhite-Union. Albany, Aryans and Star Dust combined to form Pioneers. The 90-year-old South End CC was one of those to disband. These clubs were to be part of the combined premier league come September 1976.[3]

However, the normal cricket agreement was destined to end in failure. During the off-season, on 16 June, the Soweto uprisings began, fundamentally altering the course of South African history. As the country went up in flames, the concession of black and white being able to play cricket together on weekends while apartheid continued unabated in other areas of life seemed a triviality. Black cricketers started questioning the wisdom of proceeding. The stalling and ambiguous statements of government and the lack of sensitivity and commitment on the part of SACA's affiliates were the straws that broke the camel's back.

As late as October 1976, with the first round of league matches due to start throughout the country, the Minister of Sport refused to confirm that mixed cricket at club level would be allowed, although he had given cricket administrators indications that this would be the case. The first few weeks of the season were chaotic, with claims and counter-claims, and on-off-on-off situations throughout the country. Department of Sport officials stopped a match in Kimberley. The white Transvaal Cricket Union secretary refused to allow the national African player Edward Habane to play for the white Balfour Park Club.[4]

In the midst of the confusion, SACA president Billy Woodin upheld the government line: 'We and the minister agreed to club cricket matches between clubs of different races. We never agreed to multi-racial clubs.'[5] Trust was broken. Rashid Varachia and middle-of-the-line SACBOC and SACA administrators tried to hold the 'normal cricket' line, but the desired unity was to be elusive and unsustainable given the political situation and conservative white attitudes.

The EPCA was split down the middle by 'normal cricket', causing bitter divisions. The 1974/75 executive committee in happier times. (Back row, left to right) H. Petersen, J. Allison (assistant secretary), C. Peters (recorder), N. Ambraal, I. Bansda. (Front row) E.M. Lorgat (secretary), L.C. Petersen (president), M. Loonat (vice-president), R. le Grange (treasurer). (Absent) Y. Agherdien (match and registration secretary), W. Ximiya (assistant treasurer), C. Parker, A. Carels.

Rashid Varachia (front) leads the Nine-Man Motivating Committee to one of the numerous meetings with the minister of sport, Dr Koornhof. (Left to right) Les Petersen, Boon Wallace, Billy Woodin, Joe Pamenky, Moses Nyangiwe (partly obscured), Chummy Mayet and Pat Naidoo.

The executive of the new South African Cricket Union, established in 1977. (Back row, left to right) Selwyn Myers, Ferdie Gouws, Mark Henning, Neville Markham, Frank Brache, David Lewis. (Front row) Dennis Dyer, Rashid Varachia (president), Boon Wallace (vice-president), Joe Pamensky.

In the Eastern Province, Mr Les Petersen and his EPCA originally agreed to co-operate with the white EPCU and the Africans-only EPACB (which the Majolas and like-minded African cricketers had deserted in the early 1970s). They withdrew after the blunders of the early season. Vice-president Mia Loonat and more than half the EPCA players initially remained in the EPCU's leagues.

As a result of this split, eight of the EPCA's teams – Pioneers, Gemsa, Hamediahs, Regents, Suburban, Victorians, Violets and Dower – played under the normal cricket set-up. This left the EPCA with seven sides, namely Lilywhite-Union, Regents United, Thistles, Shatterprufe, Far East, Morning Star and United.[6]

United never actually got to play a game in the much-heralded new dispensation.

'We were lucky,' said Khaya. 'We drew a bye for the first round of games, then the unhappiness started.'[7] United and two or three other clubs withdrew immediately and started playing friendlies and 're-organising' EPCA players and clubs.

Raymond Uren remembers seeking out Yusuf Lorgat, one of the few remaining officials, and they went from club to club 'trying to pull them together'. They also worked with teachers, forming clubs in the educational institutions such as Gelvandale.

Some old EPCA clubs split. When nine of the 11 Regents first team players refused to go over, they formed a new club, Regents United. Feelings ran high and those leaving were accused of being led by 'a clique formed by a few uneducated members who were "eaten up" by the fantastic facilities that were offered'.[8]

The clubs who refused to join the 'normal' cricket played friendlies against each other and started reconstituting the EPCA. Raymond Uren became president, holding the position for eight years before being followed, in turn, by Lorgat and Ronnie Pillay. People in the provinces who did not support SACBOC president Rashid Varachia's stance started planning to retake SACBOC.

In September 1977, Mr Varachia formally took SACBOC and a minority of its players into the new unified South African Cricket Union. The African Board also joined SACU and dissolved after 45 years of existence. After being threatened with legal action if they used the old name[9], those SACBOC members who refused to join SACU formed the South African Cricket Board (SACB) in November 1977. The regrouping took place around the irrepressible Hassan Howa, who was elected the first SACB president. The new Howa Bowl became the premier competition. Vice-president, Sheikh Booley, also from Western Province, presented the Booley Bowl Trophy for the B Section competition.[10]

Club and provincial cricket in the Eastern Province was naturally severely disrupted by the on-off dramas in the so-called 'normal cricket' season of 1976/77. The EPCA lost some clubs and excellent cricketers to the EPCU. Most of the senior provincial players, eager to test themselves at the top

levels, had gone across to SACU. Jeff Frans became the first black cricketer to compete in Currie Cup A Section cricket when he was picked for the EPCU versus Rhodesia match in February 1977. Bravo Jacobs and Devdas Govindjee were also included in the 18-strong provincial squad. Other stalwarts who made the move were Imraan Hendricks and Garth Cuddumbey.[11]

However, many of the so-called 'defectors' started trickling back to the EPCA as the South African Cricket Board asserted its strength and those participating in the 'normal sport' set-up were ostracised by their communities. For some it also became clear that white cricketers and the government were not prepared to accept fundamental changes to the apartheid paradigm.

Monday, January 19, 1976

DAILY

Mixed cricket

The presidents of the three national associations at yesterday's historic cricket summit in Johannesburg were, from left, the president of SAACB, Mr Moses Nyangiwe, president of SACBOC, Mr Rashid Varachia and the president of SACA, Mr Bill Woodin.

Robins: don't let chance slip away

DURBAN — Cricketing philanthropist Mr Derrick Robins, welcomed yesterday's announcement of multi-racial cricket for South Africa as "tremendous news . . . absolutely magnificent."

"It's what I have been aiming at and driving for in my efforts for South Africa," Mr Robins said.

He congratulated the administrators but added: "Make sure it doesn't slip away. Turn it into something really concrete."

Natal captain, Barry Richards, said: "It looks promising. It can only be to the advantage of cricketers in South Africa.

"I would like to see them make this one as-

sociation work and if they can, it will be a major step towards international cricket."

The president of the Natal Cricket Association, Mr D. Dowling, exclaimed: "Best news I have heard for many a long day. Cricket can only go forward from now onwards."

Bob Woolmer, England and Natal cricketer coaching in Natal, said: "Mixed cricket is common in every other country except South Africa. It's what every South African cricketer wants . . . not only wants but needs."

The Minister of Sport, Dr Piet Koornhof, said yesterday that he was not in a position to comment on the resolution at this stage.

"I would like to have the resolution in front of me and to study it before I comment," he said. — DDC.

JOHANNESBURG—In one of the most dr. African sports history, it was decided yesterd. be played at all levels throughout the country ber this year.

At an historic meeting here, it was also decided to form a single body to administer cricket in South Africa.

The South African Cricket Board of Control, the South African Cricket Association and the South African African Cricket Board agreed unanimously that cricket in South Africa would be played on a "normal basis" under the aegis of a single governing association.

A resolution put to the meeting by the SACA president, Mr Bill Woodin, and seconded by the president of the African board, Mr Moses Nyangiwe, read: "SACBOC, the SAACB and SACA hereby adopt the principle that cricket in South Africa be played on a 'normal basis' under the controlling aegis of one united governing body in South Africa, the name composition and constitution of which will be agreed as soon as posible.

'normal cricket' shall mean at this stage participation of and competition between all cricketers regardless of race, creed or colour in cricket at club level under one provincial governing body."

It was also resolved that the three national bodies required their provincial authorities to have dialogue with their opposite numbers to give effect to the main resolution.

A nine-man committee, consisting of three members from each of the national associations, was appointed at the meeting to ensure that the resolutions taken yesterday were put into effect.

Delegates elected to the committee, with the SACBOC president, Mr Varachia, as convener, are: Mr Pat Naidoo, and Mr Matt Seegers, of SACBOC (the main body ruling Indian, Asian and Coloured cricket); Mr Woodin, Mr Wally Hammond and Mr Joe Pamensky, of SACA (which controls white cricket); and Mr Nyang-

iwe, Mr Lennix Mlonzi an., Mr Nelson Mabunu, of SAACB (black cricket's controlling body).

Asked if the committee would approach the government with its recommendations, the SACA secretary, Mr Charles Fortune, said this would be up to them to decide.

"The committee may decide to do nothing that is in the slightest variance with the government," Mr Fortune said.

Delegates after the meeting all agreed that it should be possible to work out and implement a programme within a year, and that October should be the target.

Mr Woodin was confident that the decision would mean a tremendous boost to the growth of cricket inside South Africa and to the country's chances of being readmitted to the international cricket Test scene.

"It is a step which must be recognised by the rest of world cricket," he said.

He expected no objections from white cricketers to playing with or against blacks.

Mr Varachia said: "We are not seeking any confrontation. We are just working for the good of cricket."

He was delighted with the outcome of the meeting. "It was more than we hoped for," he said, "and now we must move fast to bring it into effect."

Mr Nyangiwe added: "We have waited 20 years for this moment — th ; was when we last staged multi-racial cricket competitions."

He was optimistic that the new approach would mean vastly improved conditions for black cricket.

South Africa has been isolated from international cricket since 1970, but if the terms of yesterday resolutions are put int practice, it would appea that this country wou automatically qualify membership of the national Cricket national. — DDC-SA

United Cricket Club were flagbearers for the non-racial struggles and regular EPCA league winners. Pictured here is the 1987/88 double league and knock-out competition champion team captained by Mongezi Gerald Majola. (Back row, left to right) D. Maku, M. Jordaan, E. van Aardt, T. Kadi, S. Kruger, L. Coetzee, E. Jonklaas (umpire). (Middle row) A. Coetzee (vice-captain), W. Khovu (executive member), M.G. Majola (captain), D. Jordaan (chairman), K. Majola (executive member). (Front row) P. Mashicila, G. Sauls.

Chapter 28

UNITED WE STAND

———————————— ◗ ————————————

UNITED, CAPTAINED BY 25-year-old Khaya Majola, became the first league winners under the reconstituted EPCA in 1976/77. United were always a strong club. After amalgamation in 1975, it had as many as six teams. Two of these played in the eight-team premier league. Matches between United A and B, who informally called themselves the 'West Indians', often had a lot of needle. Over the years the club 'won everything available'.[1]

The press cuttings show the dominance of United in club cricket, and the key role played by Khaya Majola and his brothers. By December of the 1976 season Khaya had already scored two big centuries in four innings, 133 versus Regents United and 130 not out (and four for 18) against Thistles. His best bowling return that season was 6.1-2-20-7 against United B.[2]

In 1977/78 Khaya started his season with 60 and 101 versus Morning Star. Once again United won, but the league ended on a disappointing note when their nearest rivals Regents United and two other clubs were suspended for not having paid their players' levies. The *Cape Herald* described this as a 'pathetic anti-climax' to the season, but said the EPCA was right to have taken this action:

> Players must realise that to take part in the activities of a club costs money, and no club can survive unless players pay their way. Cricket is becoming as expensive to play as golf, what with bats costing R60, pads R40, gloves R20 and balls R16.'[3]

Khaya's younger brother, Mongezi Gerald, also known as 'Gailer', announced his arrival on the cricket field during the 1977/78 season. The 16-year-old schoolboy hit four half centuries for United, and could also boast bowling figures of seven for 21 against United B.[4] Mongezi was a pupil at Kwazakhele High until the 1976 student uprisings, before finishing his schooling at Uitenhage High in 1978. He played in the inter-schools matches for African schools, but did not make himself available for the African Board's Passmore Week. Instead, he played for the SACOS-affiliated South African Senior Schools Sports Association (SASSSA), shining as a cricket all-rounder and rugby fly-half, like his father.

In December 1978, Mongezi captained Eastern Province schools at the SASSSA cricket week held in George. He was selected to lead the South African Schools side, which included future provincial players such as Enver Mall, Eddie Harris and *Cape Argus* sports writer, Michael Doman. The schoolboys participated in the 1978/79 SACB B Section competition and became the first and last schools side to win it, beating a strong Western Province B team in the final. Mongezi also played for Eastern Province and SA schools in rugby, partnering Allister Coetzee, who went on to have a brilliant career for Eastern Province and SARU. Majola later named his son Allister after his half-back partner and bosom friend.[5]

Besides Khaya, Mongezi and brothers, Vuyo and Tozie, the latter a 12th man for Eastern Province, the United Cricket Club had a host of other notable members and it became a unique institution in non-racial cricket. All eight African players who represented the EPCA between 1973 and 1991 came from the club. They were the veteran Thoba Williams, who was still performing well for United in the late 1970s, Thembisile Pono and Tsepo Kadi, the formidable provincial opening bowling pair in 1977/78, Thembisile Bleki, Archie Mali, Mandisi Mali and Khaya and Gerald Majola. There was also a group of

Following in the footsteps of their father, Khaya (kicking here) and Mongezi (at fly-half), as well as 'brother'/cousin Julius, played rugby for Spring Rose and the KWARU provincial team. Younger brother Vuyo earned provincial colours from the Western Province Rugby Board. Mongezi also represented Tygerberg and PERU.

provincial cricketers from the former African Board, including Pilot Mashicila, Billy Jaggers, Hambile Njenje, Sidney Mgengo, Winky Ximiya, Brian Nonganga and Wilfred Khovu.

While the membership was primarily African and the club was based in New Brighton, many players from the adjoining coloured 'northern areas' joined, making United a model for non-racial co-operation. The Jordaan brothers – Danny, Maxwell and Andrew – started the trend of crossing the traditional divides between coloured areas and African townships, and players such as Sidney Kruger, Allister and Leon Coetzee, Mokshum Arondslaam, Greg Sauls and Eric van Aardt also became stalwart members. Danny Jordaan, who taught at Dower College, was to achieve prominence later as an African National Congress MP in the first democratic parliament, and as the CEO of South Africa's powerful bid to host the 2006 World Cup in football, defeated narrowly by 12 votes to 11 in favour of Germany after an octagenerian New Zealand delegate voted against the mandate. Danny became club president in the 1980s. He recalls that it was a deliberate political choice to join the club. The actively non-racial and political approach at United was very much part of the wider ferment in sport and community circles in Port Elizabeth at the time. KWARU and the Watson brothers were at the same time making national and international headlines. The Watson brothers and some other white players broke laws and ignored pressure from the police and cabinet to play at Kwazakhele, becoming heroes to township sports fans. Port Elizabeth, perhaps more than anywhere else, was defining

the direction of the non-racial sports struggle where it mattered – on the fields.[6]

In addition to the Majolas and Jordaans, there were three other sets of brothers who became well known at United, the Ximiyas (Winky, Dumile and Phaki), the Coetzees (Allister and Leon), and the Nyokas (Mtutuzeli and 'Bond', the latter an occasional cricketer only). Phaki Ximiya, who went into exile as an ANC cadre during the apartheid years, is today a South African schools selector and executive member of Border cricket. Winky became the first African to practise as a pharmacist in Port Elizabeth before entering the commercial world. Mtutuzeli Nyoka qualified as a medical doctor and became president of the Gauteng Cricket Board. His brother, sporting his trademark Lionel Ritchie haircut, has appeared as a lawyer in several high profile criminal trials.

Other team-mates of the Majolas at United who went on to distinguish themselves on a larger stage included Allister Coetzee who, at the time of writing, is the national under-23 rugby coach, and Douglas Maku, who is a national selector and has served on the Border and UCB executive committees.

Sometimes considerable passions were generated in the local club cricket as the abandoned game between United and their perennial rivals Regents United in 1981 indicated. The incident happened after the Majola brothers stood as umpires in the absence of official umpires. Mongezi gave seven wides, which counted four runs each in this limited-overs game. This upset the Regents players and when one said that for provincial players the brothers were acting like

The Majolas have been loyal members of Spring Rose Rugby Football club for 50 years. Here Khaya, Mongezi and Julius are pictured with their team-mates in the 1980 team, winners of the league and the Doug Morgan Cup. (Back row, left to right) L. Maneli, C.M. Zwide, T. Ludwaba, G.V. Piet, L.J. Fundani, M. Mlumbi, M.B. Mbula, S.P. Neer, M.J. Majola, V.V. Tsotsobe. (Middle row) V. Maliza (official), M. Klassen, M. Agherdien (coach/manager), Z. Yeye (captain), L.W. Jacobs (president), L. Mange (vice-captain), M. Sloti. (Front row) D. Watson, M.G. Majola, P. Mkata, D.B. Mtati, E.K. Majola.

idiots, an altercation broke out and the player in question had to receive medical treatment.[7]

In the same year United, with Khaya at the helm, organised the first floodlit night cricket match in the history of non-racial cricket in the city at Woolfson Stadium. Two invitation sides consisting of some of the best players in the province were selected, with Jeff Frans and Wilbur Fischer as the respective captains. Admission was 50 cents. The local newspaper reported that, 'The floodlighting was good, the weather perfect, the cricket exciting, and one of the best crowds to attend an EPCA game for a long time gave this occasion a gala atmosphere.'[8] Khaya took six for 21, but Frans's Good Hope/Albany invitation team still managed 134 in their 25 overs to win by 15 runs.

Through initiatives like these, and its performances on the field, United continued to be one of the top EPCA clubs in the 1980s. Year after year they excelled and won cups.

Danny Jordaan and Khaya Majola became the cogs around which United revolved. They were brought in by Dan Qeqe and Silas Nkanunu at the start and told, 'You will be on the executive.' That is how township clubs worked, Danny remembers. The seniors would say, 'You are going to be the

treasurer, you are going to do this, and that was that.' People had specific roles. While Danny was the speechmaker, Khaya was the organiser overseeing club preparations.[9] By the end of the 1980s Khaya, known by the nickname 'Meneer' (Afrikaans for Mister or Sir), was becoming Mr Sport in an administrative sense as well. He was seeing to the township facilities in his capacity as a full-time sports administrator for the local council and serving on the executives of United and Spring Rose RFC. He was also a rugby referee, the club and provincial cricket captain, a provincial cricket selector, and was increasingly involved in coaching.

Majola remained evergreen as a player too. As late as 1991 he was still starring in club cricket and playing for Eastern Province after a remarkable run of 17 seasons. In January 1991, for example, he almost single-handedly led United to an eight wicket win over Avalon in the premier division match at Woolfson Stadium. His first innings four for 34 was followed by 96 (out of 177) and then eight for 36, giving him match figures of 12 for 70.[10] However, he reflected that the standard of club cricket had sadly deteriorated over the years since the heyday of his father. 'There are now only two or three clubs here,' he said to illustrate the point.[11]

232

Chapter 29

THE HOWA BOWL

———— ● ————

AFTER THE DISRUPTIONS CAUSED by the 'normal cricket' disputes, provincial competition was slow to get going again. For 18 months, until SACBOC was replaced by SACB in November 1977, no first-class competition was held. When first-class cricket did get off the ground again, the standard was low.

The first EPCA game of the new era was against Western Province at Avonwood Park in Cape Town in November 1977, the first of the formal SACB inter-provincial matches.

The *Cape Herald* newspaper noted that Eastern Province and Transvaal 'have been worst hit by defections and there is good reason for making Western Province firm favourites'. The hosts and Natal, it reported, had been the former SACBOC affiliates 'least affected by the move to "normal" cricket' and were therefore the favourites for provincial honours that season.[1]

The first Eastern Province team of the new era was a young one with 'only four familiar names to followers of the game in the Peninsula'. They were the newly appointed captain, Wilbur Fischer of the Lilywhite Club, new vice-captain, Khaya Majola, the latter's club-mate Thembisile Pono, and Colin Moodaley of Regents United, who had played cricket in Cape Town as a student. The rest of the team was Manilal Kara (Lilywhite) Thembisile Bleki, Tsepo Kadi (United), Noordien Sain (Regents), Fagme Abrahams, Mallick Davids (Union) and Basil Booysen (Morning Star). Mongezi Majola was 12th man.[2]

In line with predictions, Western Province easily won by six wickets with a day to spare in a game which 'generally must have disappointed the SACB officials'. Both sides scored at under two runs an over for long periods in a low scoring game with 26 single-figure scores. It was a fast bowler's wicket, providing unexpected lift, and was probably unprepared. Thembisile Pono 'completely tied up' the Western Province batsmen with figures of 25-11-26-3 and 8.2-2-18-2. Saait Magiet took six wickets and wicketkeeper Braima Isaacs was involved in seven dismissals. The solitary fifty by Sedick Martin saw Western Province home.[3]

Local reporters noted that the new-look Eastern Province team seemed 'poorly balanced'. There had been a major drain of experience and 'few batsmen of note' were left.[4] It would obviously take time to replace stalwarts like Jainudien Sandan, Neville Francis, Maurice Wilson, Devdas Govindjee, Bravo Jacobs, Garth Cuddumbey, Imraan Hendricks, Steven Draai and Jeff Frans. In an attempt to remedy matters, special net sessions run by Ronnie Haynes and a trial match at the Adcock Stadium were organised ahead of the festive season double-header at home against Natal and Transvaal.[5] However, only two changes were made. Danny Jordaan, a left-arm swing bowler and middle order batsman who was then studying at the University of the Western Cape, and Vernon Malgas were brought in at the expense of Tsepo Kadi and Basil Booysen.

Eastern Province went into the Natal match on Boxing Day with only two players who were involved the last time the two teams had met in Port Elizabeth in December 1975. These were Majola and Moodaley. On the other hand an experienced Natal team was led by Yacoob Omar, who had scored 174 not out on that occasion.

The Natal line-up included Ray Rogers and Len Esterhuizen, white players from non-racial clubs in Chatsworth and Ladysmith respectively. (Later, the sons of the great English batsman, Denis Compton, Richard and Patrick, and Mike Hickson, also played for Natal. They all belonged to the famous Aurora Club, which defied government instructions for it to remain an 'own affairs' white SACA club, and which later went over to SACBOC's non-racial leagues.)[6] Rogers and Esterhuizen took 12 wickets between them as Natal predictably won by 72 runs, despite a creditable Eastern Province performance of 258 in the first innings. Danny Jordaan had a satisfying debut with figures of 22.3-9-53-4 in the second innings.[7]

After these two heavy outright defeats, Eastern Province came back to beat a 'woefully weak' Transvaal by 112 runs with a day to spare over the New Year. Tsepo Kadi had match figures of 26-11-50-8 as Eastern Province bowled over a raw Transvaal outfit twice for low scores.[8] Transvaal, the home base of Rashid Varachia, was particularly hard hit by 'normal' cricket. Less than one hundred players and only six teams remained, although the number grew again to 60 teams within five years.[9]

The match marked the debuts of two schoolboy all-rounders who would go on to make a big impact on South African cricket, namely Haroon Lorgat and Mongezi Majola. Lorgat, the 17-year-old head prefect of Woolhope High School, had a dream debut, top-scoring for Eastern Province in both innings, with 49 and 37 runs respectively. The latter innings included a six and six fours.[10] Majola got a duck on debut, but he was clearly destined for bigger things, captaining the South African Schools cricket team and playing fly-half for the South African Schools rugby team in the same year

The debuts of the two schoolboys showed that a new generation of Eastern Province players was now coming to the fore. This and the impressive fast bowling opening pair of Thembisile Pono and Tsepo Kadi, the experience and all-round savvy of Khaya Majola, and the gradual return of defectors to 'normal' cricket were to ensure a solid new core of players, which would once again make Eastern Province a force to be reckoned with.

The Eastern Province renaissance really took off when they beat the strong Western Province by 34 runs in their return fixture in January 1978. The visitors had quality players like Saait and Rushdie Magiet, Armien Jabaar, Braima Isaacs, Munsoor Abdullah, Charlie van Schalkwyk, Georgie van Oordt and Ebrahim 'Baby' Damon in their team, but

Majola (41) and Fagme Abrahams (83) put on 88 for the third wicket to put Eastern Province in front, and then the two African fast bowlers, Thembisile Pono and Tsepo Kadi, took eight wickets between them to ensure victory.[11]

Western Province, by virtue of one loss and one draw to Eastern Province's two early-season losses, nevertheless became the first SACB provincial champions.

As Mogamad Allie has written, 'This was the beginning of a pattern – a straight fight for Howa Bowl honours between Western Province and Eastern Province, with Natal and Transvaal following far behind.'[12]

In fact, the records show that in the first ten seasons of the Howa Bowl, the scorecard between these two provinces was exactly even over 20 games: nine wins for Eastern Province, nine wins for Western Province, one draw and one tie. Winning the Howa Bowl, which Western Province did seven times to Eastern Province's three, depended on these two teams' performances against the weaker Natal and Transvaal.

Eastern Province's first win in the Howa Bowl was in the following season, in 1978/79. One of the major reasons for this success was the return of experienced players who had been playing in the white leagues, including Bravo Jacobs, who took over as captain from Wilbur Fischer.

As early as January 1978 the newspapers had reported that Garth Cuddumbey, with a century against Rhodes University under his belt, Ashwell Frans, Neville Francis, Bravo Jacobs and Steven Draai had reapplied for affiliation.[13] When the new season started in September 1978 other stars like Jeff Frans, Imraan 'Ranie' Hendricks and Devdas Govindjee were also back in the fold, compelled by a combination of community pressure, white conservatism, growing polarisation and personal and political considerations. Only a minority of players remained in the formerly white leagues. These returnees provided a nucleus of experience which would make Eastern Province a cricketing force in the next few years.[14]

Cuddumbey, Draai, Govindjee, Hendricks, the Frans brothers and Jainudien Sandan were all in the 1978/79 squad, together with the cream of those who had remained in the ranks, like Khaya Majola, Fagme Abrahams, Wilbur Fischer and Haroon Lorgat.[15] After losing against Western Province in the opening game, Eastern Province managed three victories in a row by an innings, including the return match against the defending champions. Bravo Jacobs, with top score of 81 and figures of 6-1-7-4, and Majola with a second innings haul of six for 69 put Western Province to the sword to give Eastern Province a win by an innings and

The 1978/79 EPCA team, winners of the Howa Bowl. (Back row, left to right) Jainudien Sandan, Haroon Lorgat, Fagme Abrahams, Tsepo Kadi, Vernon Malgas, Jeff Frans, Steven Draai, Devdas Govindjee. (Front row) Garth Cuddembey, Desmond Jacobs (captain), Charlie Houlie (manager), Khaya Majola (vice-captain), Imraan Hendricks. (Absent) Wilbur Fischer.

The 1984/85 EPCA team, winners of the Howa Bowl, pictured after beating Transvaal outright at the Adcock Stadium. (Back row, left to right) G. Cuddembey, S. Kruger, A. Peters, M. Stallenberg (manager), D. van Vuuren (12th man), M. van Eyck, S. Draai, J. Sandan. (Front row) J. Frans (captain), K. Majola (vice-captain), M.G. Majola, A. Frans, H. Lorgat.

53 runs. When Natal beat Western Province after a match-winning 149 by Yacoob Omar, the road was clear for Eastern Province. The trophy was clinched with a five-wicket win and a haul of 15 points against Natal at Newcastle. Following identical first innings totals of 170, Natal reached 218 thanks to 91 by veteran off-spinner, Mustapha Khan. With nearly a day to bat, and the top-order firing, Eastern Province reached the total with only five wickets down.[16] Majola got another five-wicket haul, ending the season with 16 wickets at 9.56 runs per wicket.

It took another five years before Eastern Province repeated their Howa Bowl success again in 1984/85, but as indicated above, they remained the top team together with Western Province.

In 1982/83, Eastern Province got off to a flying start when they thrashed Western Province by eight wickets after the ever-consistent Steven Draai took ten for 67 in 33.3 overs. Log leaders after three games, they then dramatically walked off the field in protest against poor umpiring in the game against Transvaal in Benoni. Eastern Province were 93 for seven at lunch after being sent in to bat. Four of the wickets were lbw decisions. A fifth was a controversial run out 'which even some of the Transvaal reporters were said to agree was not out'. After lunch the team refused to resume their innings, ignoring the instruction of the EPCA president, Raymond Uren, to continue. The match was abandoned and Eastern Province forfeited the bonus points, returning home with no points to Transvaal's 14.[17]

Home-town decisions by local umpires were a perennial source of unhappiness in SACB cricket, but the Board did not have the funds to appoint neutral umpires.[18]

In another drama involving the team the previous season, six of the top players — Jeff and Ashwell Frans, Khaya Majola, Fischer, Govindjee and Hendricks — declared

Khaya Majola drives against Western Province in 1978 on the way to scoring 41. His partner is Fagme Abrahams (back to camera) and Braima Isaacs is the wicketkeeper.

themselves unavailable to play Natal in Pietermaritzburg and Transvaal in Benoni over the festive season. They were reluctant to travel by bus, including the whole of Christmas Day, and be away for nearly two weeks. Five substitutes were brought in and the under-strength team drew against Natal and lost to Transvaal. For the big home game against Western Province later in January the senior players were 'black-listed'. Instead of picking them or giving the original replacements — Jainudien Sandan, Ali Kader, Archie Mali, C. Sampson and Gedaya Abrahams — another chance, the selectors acting 'childishly', according to the *Evening Post*, replaced them with five other players. Eastern Province lost and Majola was not picked again that season, although some of the other 'rebels' were.[19]

Good Hope's number three batsman Zakie Hendricks became captain in February 1981 because Bravo Jacobs, a brilliant but maverick cricket and soccer player, had gone back to playing in the mainly white EPCU leagues. In 1982/83, Hendricks was replaced by Jeff Frans, who led the team for the next three seasons.

Despite the hiccup in Benoni, the Eastern Province provincial set-up was stabilised by the appointment of Frans. The new captain, together with new manager Mike Stallenberg and vice-captain Khaya Majola (who succeeded Frans in 1986/87) provided continuity of leadership and the province entered its golden period, reaching two limited-over finals and winning the Howa Bowl twice in the mid-1980s. The 'no nonsense' Frans, an experienced fast bowler from the Albany Club, was a tough-minded captain. In his 53 games for Eastern Province he took 133 wickets at 15.88 apiece. Stallenberg came from a rugby background and one of his favourite sayings were, '*So doen ons dit in rugby*' (That is how we do it in rugby). Observers noted that, 'While he may

Majola fielding for Eastern Province. Devdas Govindjee is the other player.

Eastern Province leave the field well satisfied at the end of play, having taken three Western
Province wickets for three runs, Zwide Stadium, January 1979.

A famous tie: Eastern Province came from behind to take seven wickets for 14 runs to tie the match against Western Province in November 1984.
ABOVE *Steven Draai gets Armien Jabaar lbw.*
OPPOSITE PAGE *Wicketkeeper Fagme Abrahams appeals as Seraj Gabriels is run out attempting the winning run. Goolam Allie is the other batsman.*

not be an authority on the game, there is nobody who can match his enthusiasm for seeing to the needs of the players.' Always 'smartly attired' in his Eastern Province jacket and 'setting an example to the players', he was a 'major force behind Eastern Province's success', according to Devdas Govindjee and other players.[20]

After coming second in 1983/84, the province won the Howa Bowl in 1984/85. They played consistently all season and even an unexpected loss to Transvaal in the last game could not deprive them of the Bowl. In a memorable match against Western Province in Cape Town in November 1984, Eastern Province came from behind to force a tie. Western Province were cruising at 107 for three needing only 122 to win when a sensational collapse followed. Six wickets fell in half an hour of drama to leave them at 117 for nine. Seraj Gabriels scored four runs off three balls to level the scores, but when Goolam Allie tried to take a quick single André Peters threw in splendidly to have Gabriels run out. Six leg-

befores in the innings, a last wicket run out and a tie! A more dramatic ending could not have been scripted.[21]

In the return match in Port Elizabeth, Eastern Province won comfortably after Khaya Majola took a career best of eight for 96.[22] He remembers that everything went just right on that occasion. 'It was one of those days where if a batsman missed, the ball hit the wicket.' That Western Province were the opponents made it doubly satisfying for Khaya. 'They were tough competitors and you had to fight all the way.'[23]

Majola had his best season ever taking 22 wickets at 12.40 with the veteran pace pairing of Jeff Frans and Steven Draai, and Ashwell Frans and Haroon Lorgat complementing him. The grizzly all-rounder Draai, a '100 percenter' and javelin thrower in athletics, was one of the finest new ball bowlers and deep fielders to play in the SACB. In his 48 matches for the province he took an outstanding 212 wickets at 11.82 apiece.[24]

According to Peter Clarke, long-time reporter of Eastern Province cricket, Garth Cuddumbey, the Majola brothers and to a lesser extent the rising André Peters 'virtually carried the batting' in the Bowl-winning season. Mongezi Majola was a revelation, scoring 231 runs at an average of 33. It was his first season in the team since his debut in January 1978. Much to his frustration, he had to wait several seasons before being picked again.[25]

Eastern Province again dominated in the 1985/86 season, winning both matches against Western Province and the title. A highlight was the win in Cape Town. Western Province were set a target of 311 in 240 minutes plus 20 overs and, although Faiek Davids (81) and Saait Magiet (61) boldly led the chase, they perished at 291 all out, 19 runs short.[26] Magiet missed part of the match because of the drowning of his younger brother, and an arm injury. Colin Cruywagen described the game in the *Cape Times* as one of the best Board matches yet seen at the Green Point Track.[27]

Eastern Province's solid season was reflected in the national statistics. There were several partnerships of over a hundred

and the 356 for eight declared against Natal was the highest score of the season. Haroon Lorgat topped the Howa Bowl batting averages with 417 runs from ten innings, including a hundred and three fifties, at an average of 41.70. Mongezi Majola was fourth in the list with 244 runs. Lorgat was also the fourth highest wicket-taker with 31 wickets at an average of 15.16. Fagme Abrahams's 15 dismissals were the highest by a wicketkeeper and between them Khaya Majola, Ashwell and Jeff Frans took 18 catches.[28]

Haroon Lorgat became one of the top all-rounders in SACB's history with career statistics of 2 813 runs (average 24.89) and 191 wickets (average 18.12) in 76 matches. The province also did well in the sponsored Benson and Hedges Trophy limited-overs competition in the 1980s, which unfortunately lasted for only three seasons. The tobacco company was the main financial backer of one-day cricket in England and South Africa (SACU) at that time. Its decision also to sponsor SACB, partly because of the growing political influence of this body, created some extra excitement in the otherwise drab routine of Howa Bowl fixtures.

The Eastern Province team taking it easy on tour.
(Back, left to right) Hammie Petersen (manager), Sydney Kruger.
(Front) Khaya Majola, Tsepo Kadi, Thembisile Pono, Ronnie Haynes.

Eastern Province team tour album. (Back, left to right) Danny Jordaan,
Sydney Kruger, Khaya Majola. (Front) Mongezi Majola
and Thembisile Pono.

Newspaper supplements, large marquee tents with generously loaded tables, and gold and silver medallions for the finalists created a big-match ambience.

In two of these games Eastern Province played against Western Province in the final. In 1982/83, they lost by 96 runs, managing only 59 in reply to Western Province's 155 for eight. The following year the trophy was shared after play was abandoned because of rain. Khaya top scored with 39 not out as Eastern Province reached 136 before the rain came.[29] In 1984/85 Western Province beat Transvaal to make it three out of three limited-overs championships.[30]

Eastern Province's Howa Bowl success in 1985/86 was their last. They gave Western Province a run for their money again in the following season, but from the 1987/88 season through to the final competition in 1990/91, Western Province won five, drew two and lost only one (by six runs) in matches between the teams.

Star all-rounder Haroon Lorgat was enticed to play for Transvaal (1986) and veterans like Steven Draai (1987) Jeff Frans (1988) and Garth Cuddumbey (1989) retired. Jeff Frans's two brothers, Ashwell and Edwin, also called it a day, but the family flag was kept flying by youngest brother Vernon, who made his debut in 1986. The only new African cap was Mandisi Mali who took a useful 52 wickets at 17.63 in 13 matches after his debut in January 1988. While new-generation players like André Peters, Clayton Kisten, Richard Dolley, Keith Miller and Mandisi Mali came to the

fore, there was not the depth in emerging talent to compare with the likes of Faiek Davids, Ismail Behardien, Yunis Thomas, Nazeem White, Shukri Conrad and others at Western Province.

Both Peters and Dolley served Eastern Province well after making their debuts in the 1982/83. Peters scored 1 870 runs at an average of 23.37 in 44 matches. An excellent fielder, he also took 32 catches. Dolley took 99 wickets in 35 provincial matches with his nagging medium pace and contributed a useful 1 150 runs at an average of 22.52.

In 1990/91 Khaya Majola, nearing retirement, made way as captain for Richard Dolley. But, fittingly, when the EPCA played its very last game against Transvaal in Lenasia in March 1991, Dolley was not available and Majola was at the helm again. He and André Peters were the only recognisable names remaining. The line-up, in batting order, was Roderick Yearwood, Elgin van Heerden, Cecil Finger, André Peters, Donovan Reid, Gary Paul, Peter Hufkie, Khaya Majola, Burton Forbes, Max Jordaan and Farouk Sarrahwitz. The hosts won by six wickets helped by a hat-trick from Abdulhack 'Jack' Manack. The Transvaal speedster had 100 first-class wickets to his credit by the age of 19 and altogether he took 197 wickets in only 40 games.[31]

All in all, Khaya Majola played for the Eastern Province Cricket Association for 17 consecutive seasons, building an unsurpassed record. His 85 three-day caps are the most attained by any player in the country. He also took the most catches (70), scored the second highest number of runs and captured the fifth highest number of wickets.

In his 85 matches he captured 216 wickets with his slow left-hand bowling at a cost of 3 515 runs at an average of 16.27. Vincent Barnes of Western Province with 287 wickets was the highest wicket-taker.

Majola took five wickets in an innings 11 times, with best figures of 41-4-96-8 against Western Province at Adcock Stadium in January 1985. He also had four six-wicket spells, including 25-8-29-6 against Transvaal in March 1984. In December 1986 he took five for 11 against the same opponents. The last-mentioned hauls were also on the notorious home turf at Adcock.

As a batsman, Majola scored 2 739 runs in 145 innings at an average of 20.51. His best season was in 1987/88 when he scored 417 runs at 41.70, including a career-best 80 against Natal at Khan Road Oval in Pietermaritzburg. Altogether he hit 11 fifties. Only Yacoob Omar of Natal scored more runs (3 055), although there were many specialist batsmen with higher averages.

Together with Mustapha Khan of Natal and Seraj Gabriels of Western Province, Majola was one of only three players to have scored over 2 000 runs and taken over 200 wickets in SACB's first-class matches.[32]

What kind of player was Majola? He started his career as a left-handed, top-order batsman who complemented his batting with orthodox left-arm spinners, and eventually became a genuine all-rounder, achieving considerable success with his bowling. Devdas Govindjee described him as 'graceful and patient' at the crease, 'showing wonderful temperament and a natural flair for the game'. He also had a safe pair of hands fielding in his favourite slip position. His strong temperament was often commented on by team-mates and opponents.

What about the Board's standard of cricket? Khaya would not to be drawn into 'us' and 'them' comparisons between black and white cricketers, or between his and earlier generations of players. However, he observed:

The pitches were generally poor and this was the biggest single factor affecting standards and the nature of SACB games. This ensured the bowlers inevitably dominated. As for the batsmen, it was often a case of Russian roulette. This is why the batting averages are so low. The games were often low scoring. The balls were unpredictable. You had to improvise and have guts. It was seldom a normal balanced game between bat and ball.[33]

Khaya's comments are borne out by the author's own experience of playing at Adcock Stadium in November 1985 for Western Province against an Eastern Province team which included Majola. The pitch was simply unprepared and unfit for play. It looked like it had not been touched since the end of the rugby season.

The scoreboard told the story. Only four players scored more than 30 in the four innings. There were 28 single figure scores, including eight ducks. The highest innings tally in the four turns at the crease was 152. So one big knock – Keith Miller's 61 – and an eighth wicket partnership of 40 between Khaya and Fagme Abrahams was always going to swing the game. Eastern Province scraped home by one wicket.[34]

This 'Russian roulette' unpredictability in batting scores is a pattern found throughout the two decades of SACBOB/SACB first-class cricket. As Vincent Barnes, SACB's top wicket-taker put it:

Most of the wickets available to us were underprepared. For me, as a bowler, it was great. But, for the batsmen, it was always a struggle. We never played at set provincial venues where the groundsmen could work on the wickets.[35]

Batting was more often than not about facing an obstacle course rather then honing skills and technique in a fair battle between bat and ball. A closer analysis of the statistics shows that the best scores were at the better grounds, like the Lenasia Stadium in Johannesburg, and the Natal pitches. Khaya liked playing away against Natal the most. 'They usually had good wickets and weren't all that strong,' he quipped.[36]

Because of the conditions, SACB standards were not high, in Majola's opinion. There were lots of reasonable players around, but he singled out only one as being a great one. That was Western Province all-rounder Saait Magiet. According to Khaya, 'He could do anything he wanted with bat and ball and he would have been a great at any level if he'd had the opportunity. He made cricket look effortless.' Magiet could hit a ball great distances. Khaya recalls that his bat was called 'Lucifer'.[37]

He was modest about his own talents, and did not want to make claims for other players besides Magiet. He also described Mustapha Khan as a tough competitor.[38] However, the overseas stars like Basil D'Oliveira, Rohan Kanhai and Duncan Carter were 'in a league of their own' in his estimation.

By common acknowledgement, the SACB standard of cricket had declined alarmingly by the late 1980s. Facilities remained poor, the Group Areas Act had broken up formerly stable communities and people battled to establish new sporting patterns, the virtual civil war and chaos in black schools meant that sport increasingly became a side issue, spectator interest declined and there were few incentives for the top players.[39]

EASTERN PROVINCE CRICKET ASSOCIATION CAPTAINS IN FIRST-CLASS MATCHES, 1971-1991[40]

1971/72	1975/76	1979/80	1983/84	1987/88
Phillip Snyman	Desmond Jacobs	Desmond Jacobs	Jeff Frans	Khaya Majola
	Zakie Davids		Steven Draai	
1972/73		1980/81		1988/89
Basil D'Oliveira	1976/77	Desmond Jacobs	1984/85	Khaya Majola
	No first-class cricket	Zakie Hendricks	Jeff Frans	
1973/74				1989/90
Arthur Douglas	1977/78	1981/82	1985/86	Khaya Majola
Neville Francis	Wilbur Fischer	Zakie Hendricks	Jeff Frans	
		Jeff Frans		1990/91
1974/75	1978/79		1986/87	Khaya Majola
Maurice Wilson	Desmond Jacobs	1982/83	Jeff Frans	Richard Dollie
Neville Francis		Zakie Hendricks	Khaya Majola	
		Jeff Frans, Steven Draai		

LEFT TO RIGHT *Basil D'Oliveira. Neville Francis. Wilbur Fischer.*

LEFT *Bravo Jacobs talking to his Natal counterpart, Jugoo Govender, Tills Crescent, 1980/81.*
RIGHT *Jeff Frans tosses while Western Province captain, Armien Jabaar, looks on.*

LIST OF PLAYERS WHO REPRESENTED THE EASTERN PROVINCE CRICKET ASSOCIATION IN FIRST-CLASS MATCHES, 1971-1991[41]

E. Abrahams, Faghme Abrahams, Fareed Abrahams, Ganief Abrahams, Gedaya Abrahams, M. Abrahams, S. Abrahams, C. Africander, I. Ajam, G. Barry, K. Barry, T. Bleki, B. Booysen, R. Bergins, D. Carter, G. Coericius, A. Coetzee, Garth Cuddumbey, Glen Cuddumbey, Z. Davids, G. Dolley, R. Dolley, A. Douglas, S. Draai, B.L. D'Oliveira, N. Ebrahim, H. Felix, C. Finger, W. Fischer, N. Francis, A. Frans, J. Frans, V. Frans, B.S. Forbes, S. George, D. Govindjee, G. Harrison, I. Hendricks, T. Hendricks, Z. Hendricks, C. Houlie, P. Hufkie, R. Isaacs, Desmond Jacobs, A. Jalil, A. Jordaan, D. Jordaan, M. Jordaan, A. Kader, T. Kadi, M. Kara, C. Kisten, R. Kisten, D. Koeberg, G. Koen, S. Kruger, C. Langson, J. Lillah, H. Lorgat, K. Majola, M. Majola, V. Malgas, A. Mali, M. Malie, Glenton Miller, K. Miller, C. Moodaley, W. O'Connor, G. Paul, C. Paulsen, A.D. Peters, M. Philander, G. Piedt, T. Pono, D. Reid, L. Renze, R. Rogers, N. Sain, C. Sampson, J. Sandan, F. Sarrahwitz, J. Smith, A. Snyman, P. Snyman, J. Vaghmaria, M. van Eck, E. van Heerden, D. van Vuuren, E. van Vuuren, M. Wicks.

Khaya Majola (front) was succeeded as captain by Richard Dollie (behind) in the last season of SACB cricket.

LEFT TO RIGHT *Zakie Hendricks, Alex Douglas going out to bat with Bravo Jacobs, Maurice Wilson.*

In the last, violent decade of apartheid sports fields were often the venues for mass funerals and rallies rather than sport over weekends. The burial of 14 victims of police action, Queenstown, 1985.

Chapter 30

SPORT PART *of the* COMMUNITY

KHAYA MAJOLA NEVER WAVERED from the non-racial sport cause once he committed himself to playing in SACBOC. He turned down numerous offers to play for establishment clubs, as well as a scholarship in Johannesburg. He remained firmly rooted in his home turf of New Brighton, where feelings between African sportspeople on different sides of the growing divide could be very strong. 'There were times when people chased each other around with knives,' Khaya recalled.[1]

After the local African sportspeople went over to non-racial sport, they soon became locked into conflict with the authorities. The cricketers were 'kicked out' of the facilities at the Woolfson Stadium and the New Brighton Oval and went to play on the veld in Veeplaats, which even today has a look of desolation about it. The Bantu Administration Board ruled that only 'Bantus' could play on facilities financed from its Bantu Revenue Account. The authorities also put a spanner in the works in various other ways — such as preventing journalists on the state-run Radio Xhosa from reporting on non-racial sport.[2]

Nevertheless, KWARU did excellently in the SA Cup competition after crossing over to SARU, reaching the inter-provincial rugby final in only their second season. When the team again made the final in 1975, the match was planned for the Adcock Stadium in Korsten. The authorities informed KWARU that as Africans wishing to play in a coloured area, they needed special permits. KWARU refused to apply. The national SARU started considering venues elsewhere as time was running out. Dan Qeqe remembers, 'We asked them, let us play the final here even if it is on the doldrums.'[3] One of the remarkable episodes in the history of non-racial sport followed. Dan and a team of volunteers started building a ground from scratch out at Veeplaats, even though there were only two to three weeks to go to the big match. They worked day and night, clearing stones and broken glass, drawing the chalk lines, putting up posts and a rudimentary pavilion. A rope around the field had to serve as the stadium fence. Six thousand people turned up and waited patiently to pay. 'No one jumped over the wire.' The game went ahead and the biggest crowd and gate-takings yet (R11 578) for a SARU final were recorded. Again in 1976, 20 000 people filled the 'people's' stadium for the SA Cup Final between KWARU and Tygerberg. The ground was named the Dan Qeqe Stadium in honour of the indefatigable Qeqe. He recalls that this was a 'thrilling period' where people stood together and 'great, entertaining' rugby of the highest quality was played.[4] KWARU was consistently one of the strongest provincial teams and Ebrahim Rassool, Minister for Economic Affairs in the Western Cape government, remembers the special aura around this team of Africans when they came to take on Western Province at the Athlone Stadium in Cape Town. 'There was always a buzz and for us it gave meaning to the non-racial struggles.'[5]

Non-racial sports leaders and players now also started being routinely harassed and threatened. The case of the Watson brothers who became *causes célèbres* when they turned their backs on whites-only rugby to play in the townships under KWARU, is a graphic example. Soon after the Soweto uprisings in 1976, Cheeky, a Junior Springbok on the verge of selection for South Africa, Valence, flank for Eastern

Province, and six other white players turned out in a match between KWARU and Grahamstown-based South Eastern Districts Rugby Union (SEDRU) at Dan Qeqe Stadium. The Minister of Sport threatened that they would be arrested if they went ahead and they were threatened with suspension by Danie Craven. One of the brothers was taken to security police headquarters and told: 'Go back and tell your brothers that ... they're not such fucking heroes that they can get away with anything. If you betray your kind, you'll get what's coming to you.'[6] The players decided to go ahead anyway, avoiding road blocks at all the main entrances to the townships and 'a mass of armoured vehicles' at the stadium. Ten thousand people were present and an excited 'pandemonium broke out as they approached'. Cheeky Watson scored two tries as KWARU beat SEDRU 23-14 and after that the brothers became icons of the non-racial sports struggle.[7]

The rugby match forever changed the lives of the Watsons. Branded as 'white kaffirs', the brothers were shunned, harassed and victimised by the white community and the police. Several attempts were made on their lives and the family home was burned down. They, in turn, deepened their commitment, eventually joining the underground struggle of the ANC.

Cheeky was quoted as saying, 'The pressures on us have been tremendous. We all realise we have given up our careers as white players and even the chance of Springbok colours. But we are now serving a far greater cause.'[8]

Non-racial sportspeople who were not African faced arrest for entering a township without permits. This made the mixed membership of the New Brighton-based United Cricket Club and the stance of the Jordaan family and other coloured members all the more significant. They were sometimes angry when EPCA clubs refused to come into the township or expected to be met at the entrance and escorted in. 'Eventually, we told them to find their own way to our grounds, just like in any other club,' Maxwell Jordaan recalls.[9]

Non-racial sports leaders such as Hassan Howa and M.N. Pather were denied passports to travel abroad and non-racial organisations were discriminated against by local authorities in the allocation of facilities. Sympathetic teachers were threatened with dismissal, transfers and the non-payment of salaries.[10] Then there were the security police, who were particularly vicious in Port Elizabeth as later testimony to the Truth and Reconciliation Commission and the murders of Steve Biko, Matthew Goniwe, Sisphiwe Mthimkulu and the PEBCO Three showed.

KWARU founder, Mono Badela, had to leave town for his own safety and in 1977 Dan Qeqe himself was arrested after 'defending' school children held by the police in the aftermath of the youth uprisings of 1976.[11] 'I was there at Algoa police station and Colonel Goosen, head of the local security police, said to me, "Kom".' Dan remembers, 'No one came close to you if you were followed by the Special Branch of the time. It was only your family. Those chaps were vicious. They didn't even care for a king's son. They were the kings of the country.'[12]

In 1978, shortly after Biko's death, newspapers reported that Yusuf Lorgat had resigned from the EPCA, the provincial Council on Sport and the football board after the security police twice visited his house. At the time the EPCU was threatening to sue the EPCA and others for calling it a 'racist body'.[13] Lorgat remained active, but clearly the pressure was intense.

The situation was deteriorating and sportspeople were coming much more directly into the firing line. From now on it would not be unusual for the non-racial SACOS and its affiliates to be banned from calling meetings and for its officials to be harassed, detained or imprisoned without trial.[14] Dan and his colleagues in New Brighton were among those on a collision course with the state. In the past, the sports leaders were pillars of middle class respectability and restraint. For example, Wilson Ximiya, A.Z. Lamani, Sidima Dwesi, Mr Mpondo and Qeqe himself served on the local Administration Board. But after Soweto these boards, for long derided as 'toy telephones', lost all legitimacy, particularly after the apartheid government promulgated the Black Local Authorities Act to put black local government on a new footing. The local boards were given greater powers than before, but the overall outcome was to tighten control over urban Africans, increase the cost of local administration and confirm the exclusion of Africans from government's 'reform' programme dealing with representation at the national level.[15]

Dan and his colleagues decided to withdraw from the Administration Boards. They stopped attending meetings and lost their positions. While 'unfortunately some like Dwesi and Mpondo [from the old African sports boards] went back,' Qeqe now became a member of the Action Committee which rejected the new Community Council system.[16] He was detained for the first time by the police soon afterwards. In 1981, he and Mono Badela were among the PEBCO leaders banned by the government.[17] This was a clear sign that after a decade and a half of brutal repression and banning of opposition, the local sportspeople were once again openly synchronising their activities with the goals of the banned liberation movements.

The Bantu Administration Boards became hated symbols of apartheid authority in the 1980s, yet both Khaya Majola and his mother Milase ended up working for them. After teaching for three years, Khaya joined the Bantu Administration Board as a recreation officer in 1977, remaining in this position until 1991. His mother worked under him as a social worker, running the local youth centre, which was burned down during the 1976 uprisings.[18] She was still active after 30 years in the Girl Guide movement, serving on

Cheeky Watson next to the touchline with his Spring Rose team-mates, including Khaya Majola (front right).

the national headquarters council. In 1976 she won a bursary to travel to Guiding events in England, Wales and Switzerland.[19] In 1987 she was chosen as one of four delegates to represent South Africa at the World Girl Guides Conference in Kenya.[20]

Khaya and his wife Cynthia Nondumo, whose father 'Gqaps' used to play cricket for Hard Catch, were married according to traditional rites, and their first child, Eric Vukile (literally, Eric has risen), was born in 1980.[21] They lived in a new house at KwaDwesi on the road to Uitenhage, named after a local sports figure and community councillor.

With his new job, Khaya was involved full-time in sport. Cynthia recalls that when they got married Khaya made it clear that she came third in his list of priorities: cricket was number one and rugby number two. Later, she laughs, when they moved to Johannesburg where there was no rugby, she was elevated to number two.[22]

According to Cynthia, the enthusiasm demonstrated by the ladies' sections in Milase's time no longer existed by the 1980s. Khaya would try to encourage some of his friends to bring their families to cricket, but she found she was usually alone, and this is how she ended up scoring. Every Sunday she was at cricket.[23]

Was it not a contradiction that he worked for these local authorities while being such a strong supporter of non-racial sport? Was he not compromised or attacked from within his own community? According to Khaya, the opposite was true. People recognised that he was able to get facilities for non-

racial sport which it would not otherwise have been able to secure. And he was able to become a full-time sports organiser, helping township sport to stay on its feet. 'I ended up doing virtually everything for United and Spring Rose – from organising practices, getting the grounds ready, coaching and picking teams to fetching players and playing.'[24] He was on the executive of both clubs and also represented KWARU as a scrum-half. Unlike Danie Gerber, the famous Springbok centre who also worked as a sports officer for Ibhayi and was at one stage chased out of the township, Khaya's credentials were not in doubt. Working for the council was seen to be different from standing for election in the apartheid local authorities.

Referring to the deepening struggles after 1976, Khaya commented, 'Politically, I must be honest, my struggle was to do well in sport. I was not a political activist. But we were part of the community and attended events.'[25] That was an understatement.

Non-racial sports groups were a valuable base for the emerging civic and trade union structures in the late 1970s and early 1980s. People like Dan Qeqe, in particular, provided material support which allowed struggle organisations to mobilise in the communities. By the mid-1980s, at the height of the States of Emergency, as brutal state repression and killings (such as the Langa massacres and the disappearances of the PEBCO Three) increased, the sports groups' efforts had become fused with the political struggle. A pamphlet in the Majola family album gives an example of this.

It is a funeral programme for four 'Apartheid Victims', including Sikhumbuzo Xatasi ('burnt to death') and nine-year old Zithobele Mabona. Seven speakers are listed: people from the Port Elizabeth Women's Organisation (PEWO), the Port Elizabeth Black Civics Organisation (PEBCO), the MACWUSA trade union, the IYY youth organisation, the United Democratic Front (UDF) and, finally, 'Spring Rose (on sport): Cde D.D. Qeqe'. At the bottom are the words, 'When will they stop this killing? An injury to one is an injury to all.'[26] As president of KWARU, a South African Rugby Union national selector and prominent community spokesperson, Dan was at the height of his influence in the late 1970s and early 1980s.[27]

Often the Casspirs, would park at the grounds and 'sit there and watch us. On the day Madiba came out of jail, they were at Woolfson while we were playing.'

The Dan Qeqe Stadium and township sports fields throughout the country became venues for mass funerals, and often sports events were cancelled over weekends to allow these funerals to take place.[28] One of the biggest such events was the funeral of the Cradock Four in July 1985. Thirty thousand people streamed to this Karoo town to bury Matthew Goniwe and three comrades brutally murdered and burnt by the security police. It became one of the landmark events of the mass struggles of that decade and the regime responded by declaring a State of Emergency the next day. One of the officiating ministers was the sports activist, Reverend Arnold Stofile, who became premier of the Eastern Cape province. He had just returned from a trip to New Zealand where he played a leading part in torpedo-ing the proposed All Blacks tour to South Africa. Also present were Greg Fredericks of Border (now a senior official in the Department of Sport) and Khaya Majola himself. Here was a cameo showing where non-racial sport stood in the unfolding drama in the country.

The Majola family was affected acutely by the growing conflicts caused by apartheid. In 1976, Mongezi participated in the anti-Afrikaans protests at Kwazakhele High and was unable to write exams that year. He had to change schools, eventually enrolling at Uitenhage High.[29] Brother Tozie was expelled from Fort Hare University for political reasons. Back in Port Elizabeth, where he played for United B in the EPCA premier league and was selected as 12th man for Eastern Province, Tozie joined the ANC underground. When their cell was discovered Tozie and his six comrades, including Phaki Ximiya and Vusi Pikoli, the Spring Rose centre, had to go into exile. One of those he worked closest with, Sizwe Kondile, later disappeared and was killed in mysterious circumstances. Kondile played flank for Easterns and was the son of ex-Springbok number eight, Dumile. Tozie became a commander in Mkonto we Sizwe (Spear of the Nation), the military wing of the ANC. It was nearly 15 years before he was reunited with the family.[30]

Danny Jordaan recalled how sporting groups were often forced to operate in those dangerous times, when people were routinely being arrested and killed:

You would be batting. An incoming batsman would bring you a note. It would have a message. 'Tozie needs a place to stay. Have a room ready for him in Gelvandale tonight.' You destroy the note, carry on batting and tonight you must have got a place ready. Secrecy was so important. People's lives depended on it. That's how close sport and the struggle became in the 1980s.[31]

United and the other township clubs also had to get used to playing their matches under the gaze of the security forces. Often the yellow-painted Casspirs, the armoured vehicles synonymous with apartheid brutality and control, would park at the grounds and 'sit there and watch us'. Gerald remembers that sometimes the players would 'sit with them and ask, why are you doing it?' And, 'On the Sunday Madiba came out of jail, they were at Woolfson while we were playing.'[32]

Given these circumstances, it was hardly surprising that Majola and other non-racial cricketers took the stand they did. In a 1989 interview he urged sportspeople not to exclude themselves from the 'activities of the community', saying, 'There is no way you can divorce yourself from being a cricketer and an ordinary person.'[33]

THE STORY OF TOZIE MAJOLA

In the photo of the Eastern Province team for the match against Western Province (below), Tozie Majola is sitting in the front row (right). His better-known sporting brothers, Khaya and Gerald – as well as Danny Jordaan – are also there. Tozie's story from 1978 to 1994 is an amazing one, shared by thousands of South Africans whose lives were disrupted and who left their country to continue the struggle against apartheid.

He came into contact with the ANC in Swaziland, while visiting his mother's sister. They met Comrade Stanley Mabizela and told him, 'We've got a problem. Things are not right at home. And we are sitting there. We are doing nothing about it. We want to do something.' He gave them tasks to do, collecting information on what was happening inside.[34] Then they were instructed to link up with the legendary Chris Hani in Lesotho. Underground operations in the Eastern Cape were being directed from Lesotho under Hani. 'So we went up to Lesotho and met Chris there in Lesotho and discussed with him. Then we started moving in and out between South Africa and Lesotho. We got training in Lesotho, but we were still here [in Port Elizabeth] working.'

After three years of working underground like this, Tozie's cell was discovered in 1980. How this happened is 'still a mystery, we still want to know what happened. Suddenly we had to leave the country. Otherwise there was no way of us surviving.' Dan Qeqe offered them shelter on his brother's

farm in King Williams Town. On the way they became fearful of being discovered, and decided to continue their journey. After eight days they got safely to Lesotho where they were met by a worried Chris Hani who had received reports of certain cells being uncovered by the police.

Tozie stayed in Lesotho until 1981, creating a 'legend' or new identity, which would allow him to get official permission to stay in the country from the Lesotho Interior Ministry. But when his comrade and friend Sizwe Kondile disappeared, 'Chris said you can't stay here. You are the next target. You'd better leave Lesotho.' Tozie left his comrades behind and was sent to Tanzania, where he worked on the underground Radio Freedom and at the Solomon Mhlangu Freedom College at Mazimbu, named after a young cadre who had been hanged by the regime. After that he was sent to Cuba for four years between 1982 and 1986, where he studied electrical engineering.

Tozie is reluctant to go into details about his training in Cuba. However, it was not the usual MK training. He was one of only a few South Africans deployed with the Cuban forces when they were sent to Angola to support the beleaguered MPLA government against the invading South African Defence Force. The defeat of the SADF at Cuito Cuanavale by Cuban-led forces in May 1988 changed the balance of power in Southern Africa and hastened the independence of Namibia. Among his tasks was that of

The new-look EPCA team which competed in the Howa Bowl, with three Majola brothers in it, January 1978. (Back row, left to right): Faghme Abrahams, Haroon Lorgat, Vernon Malgas, Tsepo Kadi, Danny Jordaan, Mongezi Majola. (Middle row) Ronnie Haynes (manager/coach), Wilbur Fischer, Manilal Kara. (Front row) Thembisile Bleki, Khaya Majola, Sydney Kruger, Tozie Majola (12th man).

Tozie Majola (front left) poses proudly with ANC leaders during their inspection tour of the Hugo Nkabinda camp in Uganda in the early 1990s. Treasurer General, Thomas Nkobi is back left, Secretary General, Alfred Nzo is in the centre of the back row and MK Commander, Joe Modise is second right.

Tozie Majola in his military uniform.

Camp Commander: Tozie Majola at the ANC's Hugo Nkabinde camp in Uganda, early 1990s.

interpreter to the Cubans, and monitoring South African radio broadcasts in Afrikaans. He worked with the Cubans throughout their campaign until 1989 when 'we had to withdraw'. As part of the Namibian settlement that paved the way for independence, agreement was reached that all foreign forces would leave Angola.

The young man from Port Elizabeth now embarked on the next stage of his odyssey; he was sent via Tanzania to Uganda 'to open a new camp'. Under pressure from the apartheid regime, frontline states like Mozambique, Swaziland, Zambia, Angola and Tanzania were being pressured to stop harbouring ANC freedom fighters. The ANC was forced to open a rear base in Uganda where President Museveni was willing to provide support. For Tozie the five years in Uganda between 1989 and 1994 were the most challenging of all his exile experiences. 'It was a hell of an experience,' he recalls. When he arrived in Uganda, there were only 152 MK cadres there. However, the numbers rapidly swelled to more than

2 000, making it the biggest camp outside South Africa. He was second-in-command from 1989, before becoming commander in 1993.

It was the time of the political transition, the suspension of the armed struggle and the return of exiles. In many ways, the cadres in Uganda became suspended in a no-man's-land. The ANC was refocusing on the move home and on overcoming the pressures of re-establishing a legal presence in South Africa. Thus there was only minimal financial and logistical support forthcoming from ANC headquarters. Food was scarce and the camp leadership had to barter goods for vegetables. 'We did not even have dispirins,' he remembers. Communications were poor and by the time of the historic democratic elections in April 1994, conditions in the camp were desperate. There were fears of an armed revolt. Tozie went to Kampala to contact home and was told to hold the situation. He was blunt with the top brass. 'I told them straight, don't expect that I'll take up arms and shoot

A proud Tozie Majola (back, second left), under a photograph of Oliver Tambo, surveys the scene as Nelson and Winnie Mandela are welcomed to the Hugo Nkabinde camp in Uganda.

people ... You'll find me dead. I won't shoot them. I won't. If they do something, you will find me dead with my administration.' He went back to the camp and after an all-night discussion with his troops, order was maintained. Two weeks later they got the message that they were coming back to South Africa.

It was a tough time and at some stage the cadres felt 'disowned' by the ANC. The family did not know what had happened to Tozie until a photo of Nelson Mandela visiting the camps appeared in *City Press*, with Tozie in it. 'For the first time ever we knew he was alive,' Gerald remembers. It was a huge relief.[35]

When Tozie returned for Chris Hani's funeral in March 1993, his family tried to persuade him not to go back. Mpho, Tozie's wife, who had also been a cadre in the camp, had told them the details. Khaya said it was Tozie's decision, but Milase was adamant: '... my mother was just saying, you are not going back there. And I listened to my mother.

I must be honest. I mean, I wanted to stay.' But he resisted the temptation. The example that motivated him to remain at his post was the revered Oliver Tambo. When Tambo visited the camp in March 1993, a few weeks before his death, he was already very frail. President Museveni said that 'OR', as he was affectionately known, must not sleep in the camp, but he turned down the offer of other accommodation. He told Museveni, 'I'm sleeping here with my kids. If my kids can stay in these conditions, I'm going to sleep with them, and he slept there.' The last thing Tambo told Tozie was, 'Please take care of these kids.' Tozie says he and his comrades today understand that the ANC wanted a trained back-up force in case 'things go bad', but it was tough.

Tozie Majola is now a major in the new South African National Defence Force, based in the SO2 operations planning unit of Group 6 Command in his home town, Port Elizabeth. He is only slightly wistful when he observes that his sports career was sacrificed for the freedom struggle.

DOUBLE STANDARDS

Divisions increased as South Africa became more polarised after the 1976 Soweto uprisings and slid into virtual civil war in the 1980s. This was not only between black and white, but also within black communities themselves. Attitudes hardened and gave rise to an increasingly ideologically-driven approach to sport.

The old conservative approach of 'playing the game' regardless of wider factors came under huge strain. After participating in 'normal cricket' in 1976/77, Bravo Jacobs was reported to have said he was returning to the EPCA because of the paternalism of whites in the EPCU. He said he was treated as a 'coloured' player, who had to 'sit in the lounge of the clubhouse waiting for the proffered lift [home] while the white owner of the car was quaffing beer with the rest of the team-mates in the club bar ... I could not go in there because they were scared of losing their licence.'[36]

The reasons for returning to the EPCA were not always because of dissatisfaction with the white cricket set-up. Cricketers felt ostracised as their former team-mates and communities shunned them. The SACOS Double Standards Resolution (DSR) prevented members from playing with 'defectors', even if this was in another code. So, during winter, many cricketers found themselves barred from their soccer and hockey clubs. Garth Cuddumbey summed up the dilemma, 'I was very happy with Pioneers during my one-and-a-half seasons with them, but I had to think of my future. I cannot even watch non-racial sport at the moment.'[37]

The non-collaboration policy of SACOS had the effect not only of showing up the limitations of apartheid reforms, but also helped to draw clear lines between those in or collaborating with the system and those against it.

In 1979 SACOS prohibited its members from sending their children to private 'white' schools or from using so-called 'international' hotels, which had permits to serve black guests. In addition, SACOS boycotted the black ethnic-based universities or 'bush colleges' created under apartheid and banned dealings with the Urban Foundation, which was a government-supported private sector project to improve living conditions in black urban areas.[38]

One of the most celebrated DSR cases in Port Elizabeth was the EPCA's suspension of Haroon Lorgat and the Good Hope Club in 1985. Lorgat, a SACOS Sportsmen of the Year finalist in 1984, was due to play for Eastern Province A against Eastern Province B in the national Benson and Hedges limited-overs competition the day after his wedding. However, on the Thursday before the wedding, several players demanded that he withdraw because the wedding was being held in the Feathermarket Hall in contravention of the SACOS policy forbidding the use of public facilities which required a permit. When Lorgat then withdrew, four of his Good Hope team-mates followed in sympathy, with the full support of the club which had the biggest membership in the EPCA. Lorgat's brother Yusuf, whose presence at the wedding further complicated the matter as he was the president of the EPCA, said that 'a SACOS rule had been inadvertently transgressed'. The player himself remained disciplined. He said there was no ill-feeling and 'everyone was prepared to accept the consequences of disciplinary action – whatever they may be'.[39] Others were not as calm. When the EPCA pardoned its president, but suspended Lorgat and Good Hope for 18 months, a furore erupted. While the club executive and certain players were banned for the full period, the remaining players would be free to join other clubs in the next season. Outraged club president, Dr Ismail Jakoet, who became head of the South African Institute for Drug Free Sport, said the decision was 'completely unjust and irregular' and that the club was perturbed by the 'many inconsistencies displayed by the EPCA officials'.[40] Lorgat missed the rest of Eastern Province's games that season, but the suspension was eventually overturned.

This was one of many cases in which the intensifying ideological struggles accompanying the last decades of apartheid rule increasingly affected the sport and the private domain of sportspeople, some of whom became disillusioned with what they saw as the over-politicisation of sport by SACOS. But with hindsight, most would probably agree that it successfully drew a clear line at a time that the apartheid rulers were trying to sell the lifting of petty apartheid restrictions as major reform. Raymond Uren, in fact, feels the DSR was 'the big thing' that enabled the non-racial sport organisations to survive.[41]

Devdas Govindjee, who played for the EPCA between 1968 and 1984, was one of those who joined the exodus to the EPCU for a while, but returned to the fold later. However, rather than subscribe to the ban on parents sending their children to 'white' private schools, he gave up playing in the mid-1980s. When relaxations in apartheid policy were eased to allow black children to attend some formerly whites-only schools, Devdas and his wife Urmila decided to send their son, Uvinash, to the St George's Preparatory School so that he could get a better education. Today, Uvinash is a law lecturer at the University of Port Elizabeth and the Govindjees do not regret the decision.[42]

Married to the game. ABOVE *Haroon and Farah Lorgat's wedding led to a cricket row.*
BELOW *Cricket and rugby teammates celebrate the wedding of Mongezi Gerald Majola and Honey Mfunifo
at the Order of Ethiopia's Bennett Mizeki Church, Port Elizabeth, 1988.*

The scars from these intra-sport and intra-community disagreements from this period between those who held out and those who were seen to have compromised are still sometimes visible in tensions within the coloured and Indian communities.

The ultimate flaw in this principled SACOS approach was that it doomed the overwhelming majority of African sportsmen to the category of collaborators. For example, the South African National Football Association (SANFA) was seen as a government stooge body and the players in its National Professional Soccer League as 'sell-outs', and the Tennis Association of South Africa (TASA) refused to have dealings with the Soweto-based black Tennis Foundation because of the support it received from the Urban Foundation. This was at a time when

African communities were bearing the brunt of apartheid and leading the broad struggle against it.[43]

Even a sympathetic historian from within the ranks has said that the organisation eventually ended up 'playing detective to its membership' rather than building a mass base. This, together with the fact that it aligned itself more with 'workerist' trade unions and the black-consciousness-supporting National Forum rather than the United Democratic Front (UDF) and other Charterist organisations which recognised the leadership of the ANC, led to the inevitable demise of SACOS. Eventually, it was superseded by the more broad-based National Sports Congress as the major sports organisation of the oppressed. The South African Cricket Board also switched its allegiance in this process.[44]

A STORY THAT NEEDS TO BE TOLD

One of the contradictions that caused the downfall of SACOS was that it was predominantly based in coloured and Indian Group Areas, as defined by apartheid laws. Despite admirable policies and brave struggles to overcome the racial divisions entrenched by apartheid, SACOS was not able either to draw large numbers of African sportspeople or always overcome existing bias against them.

According to Khaya Majola, racism was an issue within the non-racial cricket board as well:

Year after year United would win the club trophy, yet there would seldom be more than one player chosen [besides Khaya who had become a permanent fixture]. It was almost as if there was a quota.[45]

He felt several African players who never got the chance to play for Eastern Province were worthy of higher honours. They included Nkululeko Tundube, Brian Nonganga, a left-arm seamer and right-hand bat who had also played for the national African team and always did well, another good all-rounder Hambile Njenje and a team-mate from the first Passmore Week side, Pilot Mashicila. Khaya believes his brother Gerald should have got a chance much earlier too.[46] After being selected for Eastern Province's senior team and SA Schools (SACOS) in both rugby and cricket in 1979, Gerald played for a long time in the B side before he was selected again in 1984. He did study for three years in Cape Town, but the long exclusion was resented by the brothers. Once in the team, Gerald Majola established himself as a key player, being selected for the SACB national team. He scored a century and five fifties in 33 matches (average 22) with a top score of 117 against Transvaal in the 1986/87 season.

Staying with the racial issue within the non-racial EPCA, Khaya said in an interview for this book:

I don't know how we deal with this in the book, but it must be said. The biggest feeling I have looking back is how we as African cricketers were always regarded as marginal. We had to play twice as well as anyone to get recognition.[47]

Khaya could not hide the hurt that he was vice-captain under four different captains for 12 seasons before he was given the Eastern Province captaincy. First there was Wilbur Fischer in 1977/78, followed by Bravo Jacobs (1978-1981), Zakie Hendricks (1981-1982) and Jeff Frans (1982-1986). Once, when Frans missed some matches, Steven Draai was put in his place temporarily. Another time, when it was feared Frans would have to sit out because of the illness of his daughter in the 1984/85 season,

Ranie Hendricks was appointed.[48] 'All this time I was vice-captain,' said Khaya.

According to Majola, 'there was this racism' in and around the team, even to the extent of Africans being referred to as 'kaffirs'. One top player in particular was 'bad news'. Sitting around having drinks there would be these jokes, 'Give Khaya orange juice kind-of-thing.' The private hurt was exacerbated by incidents like the occasion he had to sneak in the back way at the Himalaya Hotel in Durban when the team arrived to check in because there wasn't the necessary permit for him.

After practices were moved from the traditional venue at Adcock, he sometimes had to walk long distances to get to them. 'These things hurt,' he said.

The fact that he ever became captain he credited to Jeff Frans, someone who Khaya had great respect for as a player and person. 'Jeff told me a whole season before that he was going to step down so I could get my turn, and he stuck to his word even though we won the Bowl.'

According to Khaya, Frans was also responsible for Eastern Province giving other African players opportunities at a higher level as well. 'He told the hierarchy bluntly that if they wanted Eastern Province to do better they should put more United players in.'[49]

The statistics support the fact that Frans gave Khaya's career a push. In eight seasons before Frans became captain, Majola did not bowl more than 41 overs or pass seven wickets a season, except once, in the Bowl-winning 1978/79 summer when his figures were 45.5 overs and 16 wickets. After playing only one game in 1982/83, he was given 122 and 155.2 overs by Frans in the next two seasons and he rewarded his captain with 14 and 22 wickets respectively. Thereafter he took off as a strike bowler, with 155 wickets in his last six seasons, to go from being a good SACB player to one of the best ever. Even if the retirement of first-choice spinner Devdas Govindjee is factored in here, these figures do tell a story.

When asked, Khaya was not inclined to single out any EPCA administrators as deserving credit.

The essence of Khaya's views were also conveyed in an impassioned contribution to the Transformation Monitoring Committee in Port Elizabeth in December 1998. Contesting the perceived hesitation of Robbie Muzzell and other white administrators to embrace cricket transformation fully, he spoke with feeling about how he as an African cricketer had known discrimination, not only under apartheid but also within the non-racial sports movement in the 1970s and 1980s.[50]

But he stressed that, although this story needs to be put on the record, the achievements and goals of the non-racial sports movement were admirable, and that there were good times and many fine people who were examples of how people should behave:

I had lots of great times in my 17 seasons with EP. We were a poor province and often travelled by kombi. There would be the inevitable jokes and team spirit. Also staying with people, I would be warmly received. That was when I also saw how well-respected my father was. We'd arrive at our destination, with people waiting to put us up in ones and twos. There would be those who say they'd like me to stay with them because they knew Eric, or had played against him, or watched him...[51]

Besides Jeff Frans, a regular room-mate, who was a captain and team-mate who 'showed over and over again that he had confidence in you', Khaya spoke warmly about people like Garth Cuddumbey and Richard Dolley. Danny Jordaan became an 'inseparable' friend. Whenever Danny was in town, he'd be in touch straight away. Gerald Majola concurs with this analysis of discrimination suffered by African players. There was definitely an 'unwritten quota clause in Eastern Province cricket' in those days, he says.[52] This marginalisation is further underlined by the fact that only eight of the ninety cricketers selected for the EPCA between 1971 and 1991 were African – and only nine out of 450 players in the top SACBOC competition during the same period.

The only African cricketer to play for another province was all-rounder Duncan Stamper, who was selected for one game for Transvaal in 1977/78. He scored a 42 and returned bowling figures of 24-8-45-1. Besides Stamper, not a single African player was selected for any of the other three A Section provinces in the 19 seasons of first-class cricket described here. Of the eight Eastern Province African players, Thembisile Bleki played one match as a replacement and Archie Mali two. Besides Khaya Majola's record 85 appearances, the total caps for the others were Gerald Majola 33, Tsepo Kadi 16, Thembisile Pono 15, Mandisi Mali 13 and Thoba Williams ten. Brian Nonganga played in the limited-overs side, but not the three-day team.

An analysis of the statistics of Tsepo Kadi provide the same conclusions as those reached by the Majola brothers above. A perennial replacement, his 16 matches stretched over 15 seasons from 1975/76. His first-class career was a bits-and-pieces, stop-start affair, yet he achieved the most remarkable results as the table below shows.

1975/76, one match, 19-0-57-2, average 28.50, best bowling 2/39.

1977/78, four matches, 90-29-219-13, average 16.84, best bowling 6/32.

1978/79, one match, 11-3-16-2, average 8.00, best bowling 2/10.

1979/80, three matches, 43-10-72-7, average 10.28, best bowling 3/17.

1980/81, no matches.

1981/82, one match, 17-4-67-3, average 22.33, best bowling 3/64.

1982/83, no matches.

1983/84, no matches.

1984/85, no matches.

1985/86, one match, 12-4-39-2, average 19.50, best bowling 2/37.

1986/87, no matches.

1987/88, no matches.

1988/89, two matches, 55-22-120-8, average 15.00, best bowling 6/31.

1989/90, three matches, 66-17-160-6, average 26.66, best bowling 4/36.[53]

Clearly this was a strike bowler out of the top drawer. Kadi's career figures, despite limited opportunities, take some beating in terms of consistency and quality: 331 overs, 89 maidens, 750 runs, 43 wickets, average 17.44, best bowling 6/31. If ever someone deserved the designation of 'Mr Reliable' it was this lanky speedster. He does appear to have been under-utilised, even considering that the formidable Jeff Frans and Steven Draai were the opening strike force for many years.

In South Africa things are often more complex and contradictory than they seem. The testimony of the Majola brothers shows that this was also the case with non-racial sport in the 1970s and 1980s.

SACOS and its affiliates had an enviable record of struggle, sacrifice and bravery. There is great pride in what it achieved and stood for, also among the African sportspeople who joined. But ultimately its ultra-pure standards and hands-off approach to the mass politics of the 1980s, together with its lack of a mass base in the African areas, caused it to implode. No one, however, can deny the gallant role it played in the isolation of apartheid sport with its principled non-collaboration approach during a crucial period in South Africa's history.

*'Olympics of the oppressed': Footballer Adeeb Abrahams lights the flame to open
the second SACOS Festival, Athlone Stadium, Cape Town, March 1988.*

Chapter 31

'OLYMPICS *of the* OPPRESSED'

B Y THE EARLY 1980s SOUTH AFRICAN society was more polarised than ever before. The Tricameral Parliament, intended to co-opt the coloured and Indian communities as allies of apartheid while keeping the mass of African people disenfranchised, came into being but led only to mass mobilisation and greater resistance. Unable to meet or contain popular demands, the apartheid government embarked on the road of open repression, including States of Emergency, bannings and extra-legal terror in the form of assassinations and harassment.

As the political situation deteriorated, the establishment South African Cricket Union decided to give up on its approach of gentle persuasion to get back into international cricket. The approach became one of aggressively buying overseas players and challenging the international cricket establishment, with the help of the National Party government which provided tax cuts and other support. The era of rebel tours, master-minded by Joe Pamensky, former national captain Ali Bacher, and a new generation of financially-connected Johannesburg-based administrators got underway.[1]

The non-racial sports movement on the other hand deepened its non-collaborationist stance and openly supported the mass struggles. However, with cricket opportunities and standards weakened by the ideological emphasis and virtual civil war that was unfolding, SACB and SACOS started selecting national teams as an incentive to their players. These were similar to the special invitation matches SACBOC had organised in the 1970s

The first of these events was the SACOS Festival held in Athlone in Cape Town in October 1982. Twenty-one affiliates of SACOS participated in this 'people's festival of sport'. Rugby was a notable exception. In each of the 21 codes a SACOS team, the 'best representative national team', was selected to take on the second-stringers in the form of a President's team.

According to SACOS president Morgan Naidoo, the festival was a high point in the decade of the organisation's existence:

Whilst individual non-racial sports codes have persevered in promoting the game against a climate of adversity, preoccupation with more fundamental issues governing sports in the country has virtually sapped us of any initiative towards staging sports activities under a singly co-ordinated effort. Today ... we cannot help but be proud that at long last a significant milestone has been achieved.[2]

The SACOS cricket team was effectively the representative SACB national team, the first to be selected by non-racial cricketers since the 1958 SACBOC 'tests' against the Kenya Asians 24 years earlier.

Khaya Majola was included, together with provincial team-mate, Jeff Frans. The rest of the side consisted of the two Natalians, Enver Mall and Mustapha Khan, and no less than seven Western Province players, namely Charlie van Schalkwyk (captain), Braima Isaacs, Neil Fortune, Munsoor Abdullah, Saait Magiet, Armien Jabaar and Vincent Barnes.[3]

As also happened in baseball, softball and both professional and amateur soccer, the second-stringers in the President's team, led by Transvaal veteran Aboo Manack, won the 50-overs-a-side match comfortably by seven wickets. The SACOS XI were 111 for six wickets before the captain, Charles van Schalkwyk, and

Armien Jabaar took the total to 173 for six in the allotted overs. Majola made second top score of 29, sharing a 37-run partnership in 36 minutes with the hard-hitting Saait Magiet. The President's XI replied with 174 for three, to win with just under five overs to spare. There were six Eastern Province players in the President's XI. Khaya's provincial colleagues, Haroon Lorgat, with a top score of 60, Garth Cuddumbey, Devdas Govindjee and Steven Draai, were among the top performers.[4]

At the end of the 1985/86 season, SACB started its own end-of-season invitation fixtures in a bid to halt sagging morale and a decline in standards. In the first of these matches, Eastern Province, as Howa Bowl champions, played the Rest of South Africa (SACB) under Mustapha Khan in Lenasia in April 1986. In a high-scoring match, the Rest batted first totalling 400 for seven declared. Saaiet Magiet (128) and Yacoob Omar (104) top scored. Khaya bagged both their wickets in finishing with an analysis of 22-7-105-3. Opening the batting with Garth Cuddumbey, he then scored 67 runs, as Eastern Province went on to knock up a total of 346 all out. A partnership of just under 100 with younger brother Mongezi, who came in at number three, remains one of the sweetest memories of his career. Khaya remembered: 'It was great playing like this against the top players in the country. I cried when Gerald went out (for 48). Partly it was pride at what we'd achieved. Partly sadness that he missed his half-century.' The match ended in a tame draw with the Rest on 286 for four in the second innings. Haroon Lorgat with top score of 85 and match figures of 49-15-135-3 was another who starred for Eastern Province. Yacoob Omar was nominated as Man of the Match, Saaiet Magiet best batsman, Vincent Barnes best bowler and André Peters best fielder.[5]

In November 1987, a SACB team was selected to play a President's XI in a special three-day match at the Green Point Stadium in Cape Town to commemorate the tenth anniversary of SACB.

The SACB line-up in this match, the only three-day game ever played by a SACB representative side, was Yacoob Omar (Natal), Seraj Gabriels (Western Province), Mongezi Majola (EP), Achmat Dinath (Transvaal), Munier Saleh (Transvaal, who replaced the originally-selected Steven Draai), Haroon Lorgat (EP), Khaya Majola (EP), Saaiet Magiet (Western Province) captain, Abdulhack Manack (Transvaal), wicketkeeper Yasien Begg (Transvaal) and Vincent Barnes (Western Province).[6]

Barnes took 13 wickets for 56 runs as the SACB team won a low scoring game. Magiet also starred again with top score of 75 not out. The wicket was a 'green mamba' and the teams agreed to use an adjacent strip after the first day. SACB scored 180 and 79 to which the President's XI could reply with only 152 and 50.

The match was a disappointment. After it finished in two days a day-night fixture between Western Province and the Rest of South Africa was hastily arranged at the University of the Western Cape. Ismail Behardien hit 63 in 92 balls to take Western Province to a winning 174 total. Manack took three for 27, but then the Rest capitulated to 87 all out.[7]

In 1988, the second SACOS Festival, dubbed the 'Olympics of the Oppressed', was organised. Cape Town was the venue again and the event was bigger and better than the one in 1982. Torch-carrying soccer star Adeeb Abrahams lit the flame at the Athlone Stadium to mark the opening of these alternative games. Political and community leaders gave support and for once there was good sponsorship by companies such as Adidas, who provided the athletes with 'high quality outfits', Warner Lambert, SA Preserving and the Wembley Group.[8] The 'Olympics' were poorly reported, but a special book was published to record the event. In it, SACOS's position was restated:

The Festival is a celebration of the perseverance and resourcefulness of the struggling people of South Africa. In the face of racist tyranny and oppression we maintain our dignity and determination in the struggle for equality in sport and equality in society. The Festival symbolises the unity of the oppressed in building a new nation based on equality and justice.[9]

Khaya Majola replaced Saait Magiet as captain of the national side for this game. Newcomers Stuart Hendricks, Ismail Behardien, Faiek Davids and Randall Cupido, who replaced Yasien Begg as wicketkeeper, were included. All were from Western Province. Only five members of the 1987 side were picked again, namely opening batsman Gabriels, all-rounder Haroon Lorgat, the opening bowlers Barnes, and Manack and Majola. However, Khan and Munsoor Abdullah, who played in the 1982 Festival, were recalled too.

As in the 1982 Festival, this was a one-day 50-overs match. The President's XI batted first and were restricted to 145 for nine. Only André Peters and Mongezi Majola topped 20 runs. Khaya Majola was the best bowler with 7-1-15-3. The SACOS XI passed the score comfortably, with Faiek Davids on 40 not out, to win by six wickets.[10]

The SACB planned to organise a further match during the 1988/89 season. However, the Board was unable to get sponsors and the match had to be cancelled.[11]

The last SACB team was picked in 1991. It played two back-to-back limited-overs matches against a Border Invitation XI on 1 and 2 March. The national team comfortably won both matches. In the first 45-over day-night game, it hit a healthy 239 for three to win by 61 runs. In the second game of 50 overs the next day, SACB easily reached the Invitation XI target, scoring 186 for three in 36 overs. This was due mainly to the contributions of the rising stars of the new generation, Ismail 'Miley' Behardien and Faiek Davids. They made hay with scores of 42 and 80 not out, and 63 not out and 36 not out respectively. The new caps André Peters (40), Nazeem White (32 not out) and Imraan Munshi (23, 33 and two for 32) also weighed in. The veterans Saait Magiet, who was captain, and Khaya Majola did not get to bat, but both turned their arms over. Majola's figures in the second match were 10-5-12-1.[12]

Two things indicated that the times were changing. Firstly, the game was played at the main stadium of the Border SACU side, Buffalo Park, and the Amatola Sun casino and hotel group were the sponsors, which would have been unthinkable in the old 'double standards' period. Buffalo Park season ticket holders and chalet owners belonging to the rival SACU were, however, told that 'they will have to pay for admission'. The prices were a royal R2 and R6 per person. A second sign of changing times was the presence of SACB patron, Walter Sisulu, as guest of honour. Sisulu was an icon of the struggle and one of the famous Rivonia trialists who had been released from prison in 1989 after 26 years in jail with Nelson Mandela. He presented the team with their SACB colours in an emotional ceremony.

These seven special invitation games (including the unofficial one at UWC in 1987) were the closest Khaya came to playing a test match under the non-racial board. In 1988, he was quoted in the *South* newspaper as saying he still cherished the dream of playing in an international match under SACB. But it was not to be. With his dream fading, he started devoting more time to coaching. When the new decade arrived, Majola was planning a R40 000 development programme in the Eastern Province sponsored by Volkswagen and Firestone.[13]

By now he had become an icon of the non-racial sports struggle. This was reflected in 1988, when he was voted the SACOS Sports Star of the Year, as well as the EPCA

Mongezi (left) and Khaya Majola. The only brothers and the only Africans to represent SACOS/SACB, wearing their national blazers.

Sportsman of the Year. His achievements were lauded in a series of newspaper articles in the alternative press, which stressed his place as a sporting role-model in a country traumatised by apartheid and virtual civil war.

The *SACOS Bulletin* said the award, ahead of football star, Duncan Crowie, reflected not only Majola's sporting ability, but also 'his commitment to the struggle of the oppressed people in South Africa, his dedication to the underprivileged sportspersons and his personal spirit of sacrifice'.[14]

The Indicator from Lenasia described him as a major figure who had 'sacrificed potential fame and riches in "normal" sport to help a politically aware organisation'.[15]

Majola dedicated his Sportsman of the Year trophy to ANC leader Raymond Mhlaba, then still languishing in jail after a quarter of a century in prison with Nelson Mandela. He said Mhlaba had 'played in the era of my father, but because of his dedication to the struggle he did not get anything'. Majola visited Mhlaba in jail while in Cape Town for a match against Western Province to tell him of the dedication and they were able to have 'a long talk'.[16]

In 1990, when the rebel English team led by Mike Gatting arrived in South Africa, Khaya and other non-racial cricketers joined mass protests against the tour. It was a radical Khaya Majola who attacked SACU's Ali Bacher, his coaching programme and the rebel tours. He was quoted as saying that if Bacher tried to come to New Brighton he would be necklaced.[17]

Little did he guess then that in a short while the whole political climate would change and he would be sharing an office with the selfsame Bacher.

SOUTH AFRICAN CRICKET BOARD REPRESENTATIVES, 1982-1991[18]

Abdullah, Munsoor (WP)
  1982, 1988
Barnes, Vincent (WP)
  1982, 1987, 1988, 1991
Begg, Yasien (Transvaal)
  1987, 1991 wicketkeeper
Behardien, Ismail (WP)
  1988, 1991
Cupido, Randall (WP)
  1988
Davids, Faiek (WP)
  1988, 1991

Dinath, Ahmed (Transvaal)
  1987
Fortune, Neil (WP) 1982
Frans, Jeff (EP) 1982
Gabriels, Seraj (WP)
  1987, 1988
Hendricks, Stuart (WP)
  1988
Isaacs, Ebrahim (WP)
  1982 wicketkeeper
Jabaar, Armien (WP)
  1982

Khan, Mustapha (Natal)
  1982, 1988
Lorgat, Haroon (EP)
  1987, 1988, 1991
Magiet, Saait (WP)
  1982, 1987 captain,
  1991 captain
Majola, Khaya (EP) 1982,
  1987, 1988 (captain), 1991
Majola, Mongezi Gerald (EP)
  1987
Mall, Enver (Natal) 1982

Manack, Abdulhack
  (Transvaal) 1987, 1988,
  1991
Munshi, Imraan (Transvaal)
  1991
Omar, Yacoob (Natal) 1987
Peters, André (EP) 1991
Saleh, Munier (Transvaal)
  1987
Van Schalkwyk, Charles
  (WP) 1982 captain
White, Nazeem (WP) 1991

TOUR PROTEST . . . Protesters hold up placards outside the De Beers Stadium on Saturday demanding the end of the rebel England cricket tour.

Tour demo ends in township riot

TOP LEFT *(left to right) Gavin Watson, Khaya Majola, Peter Hain, Ronnie Pillay and Cheeky Watson, Port Elizabeth, December 1989.*
ABOVE *Khaya Majola dedicated his SACOS Sports Star of the year to Raymond Mhlaba. Here they are with Silas Nkanunu (left) and Sam Ramsamy (second left).*
LEFT *The protests against the rebel cricket tour in 1990 heralded in a new era for cricket.*

SOUTH AFRICAN CRICKET BOARD/ SOUTH AFRICAN COUNCIL ON SPORT
SCORECARDS, 1982-1991

SOUTH AFRICAN COUNCIL ON SPORT XI vs PRESIDENT'S XI

Played at Turfhall Park, Cape Town, 10 October 1982[19]. **Result:** President's XI won by 7 wickets.

Sacos XI

E. Mall	b Draai	4
E. Isaacs	b Draai	6
N. Fortune	c Abrahams b Govindjee	28
M. Abdullah	c Cuddumbey b Gabriels	18
K. Majola	c Abrahams b Manack	29
S. Magiet	c Manack b Gabriels	13
C. van Schalkwyk	not out	32
A. Jabaar	not out	23
Extras		7
Total (for 6 wickets in 50 overs)		173

President's XI

R. Musson	lbw M. Khan	19
G. B. Cuddumbey	c Majola b M. Khan	41
H. Lorgat	not out	60
O. Visser	b S. Magiet	21
D. Govindjee	not out	13
Extras		15
Total (for 3 wickets in 42.5 overs)		174

President's XI

	O	M	R	W
E. Govender	6	2	9	0
D. Govindjee	7	0	17	1
S. Draai	6	3	40	2
S. Gabriels	9	3	31	2
H. Lorgat	4	1	18	0
A. Manack	5	0	19	1
I. Hendricks	9	1	19	0

Sacos XI

	O	M	R	W
V. Barnes	9	1	27	0
J. Frans	7,2	2	27	0
A. Jabaar	9	1	38	0
M. Khan	10	4	18	2
K. Majola	2	0	15	0
S. Magiet	8	0	34	1

The SACOS XI, 1982, the first national side of the SACB era, pictured in Cape Town with SACB and SACOS officials. (Back row, left to right) Morgan Naidoo, Charlie van Schalkwyk (captain), Enver Mall, Eddie Harris, Abe Adams, M.N. Pather, Saait Magiet, Neil Fortune, Munsoor Abdullah, Hassan Howa. (Front row) Armien Jabaar, Ebrahim Isaacs, Jeff Frans, Khaya Majola, Mustapha Khan, Vincent Barnes.

EASTERN PROVINCE vs REST OF SOUTH AFRICA (SACBOC)

Played at Lenasia Stadium, Johannesburg, 5, 6, 7 April 1986[20]. **Result:** Match drawn.

Rest of SACBOC

Y. Omar	lbw K. Majola	104	c Cuddumbey b Dolley		46
S. Gabriels	c Abrahams b J.Frans	3	b J. Frans		14
M. Saleh	b Lorgat	19	not out		101
A. Dinath	b Lorgat	20			
M. Abdullah	c E. Frans b K. Majola	13	b Lorgat		31
Y. Thomas	lbw A. Frans	87	c Abrahams b A. Frans		35
S. Magiet	st Abrahams b K. Majola	128	not out		37
M. Khan	not out	6			
Y. Begg	not out	6			
Extras		14	Extras		22
Total (for 7 wickets dec in 82 overs)		400	(for 4 wickets in 77.2 overs)		286

Eastern Province

G.B. Cuddumbey	c Begg b Barnes	18
K. Majola	b Barnes	67
M. Majola	c Omar b Magiet	48
H. Lorgat	c Manack b Gabriels	85
A.D. Peters	c Magiet b Thomas	30
C. Kisten	c Begg b Thomas	5
A. Frans	c Barnes b Gabriels	1
F. Abrahams	c Barnes b Gabriels	24
R. Dolley	b Barnes	24
J. Frans	b Barnes	4
E. Frans	not out	9
Extras		31
Total (95.2 overs)		346

Eastern Province

	O	M	R	W	O	M	R	W
E. Frans	6	0	37	0	–	–	–	–
J. Frans	8	2	17	1	9	4	20	1
H. Lorgat	21	7	73	2	28	8	62	1
A. Frans	15	0	95	1	11	1	53	1
K. Majola	22	7	105	3	5	1	25	0
R. Dolley	10	1	59	0	18.2	2	87	1
A. Peters	–	–	–	–	2	0	6	0
G. Cuddumbey	–	–	–	–	2	0	9	0
M. Majola	–	–	–	–	2	1	2	0

Rest of SACBOC

	O	M	R	W
V. Barnes	23.2	4	76	4
A. Manack	10	0	40	0
S. Gabriels	20	1	51	3
M. Khan	11	1	31	0
S. Magiet	9	0	47	1
Y. Thomas	16	2	43	2
Y. Omar	6	2	27	0

SOUTH AFRICAN CRICKET BOARD XI vs PRESIDENT'S XI

Played at Green Point Stadium, Cape Town, 14, 15, 16 November 1987[21]. **Result:** SACB XI won by 57 runs.

SACB XI

Y. Omar	c White b Frans	15	c Peters b Khan		18
S. Gabriels	b Ramnarain	11	c White b Frans		5
M. Majola	b Frans	4	c Khan b Frans		7
A. Dinath	c White b Ramnarain	14	b Frans		2
M. Saleh	b Davids	10	c Hendricks b Khan		11
H. Lorgat	b Ramnarain	2	c Peters b Frans		8
K. Majola	lbw le Roux	17	c Peters b Frans		3
S. Magiet	not out	75	c le Roux b Khan		4
A. A. Manack	c Khan b Edwards	9	b Khan		0
Y. Begg	b Davids	4	run out		12
V. A. Barnes	c Khan b Davids	2	not out		0
Extras		17	Extras		9
Total (65.4 overs)		180	Total (34 overs)		79

President's XI

S. Hendricks	c K. Majola b Lorgat	34	lbw Manack		1
G.B. Cuddumbey	c Begg b Barnes	3	lbw Barnes		1
I. Behardien	b Gabriels	30	c Magiet b Manack		1
A.D. Peters	c K. Majola b Gabriels	11	lbw Barnes		1
N. Edwards	c Saleh b Gabriels	18	c Magiet b Barnes		0
F. Davids	b Barnes	18	lbw b Barnes		7
N. White	c M. Majola b Barnes	8	not out		15
M. Khan	lbw Barnes	12	c Lorgat b Manack		4
T. le Roux	b Barnes	0	c M. Majola b Barnes		10
V. Frans	b Barnes	3	c Dinath b Barnes		5
N. Ramnarain	not out	2	c and b Barnes		0
Extras		13	Extras		4
Total (53.2 overs)		152	Total (20 overs)		50

President's XI

	O	M	R	W	O	M	R	W
N. Ramnarain	19	7	32	3	6	4	5	0
V. Frans	9	2	26	2	16	4	30	5
F. Davids	13.4	5	32	3	–	–	–	–
T. Le Roux	14	1	38	1	–	–	–	–
N. Edwards	10	5	35	1	–	–	–	–
M. Khan	–	–	–	–	12	0	35	4
	–	–	–	–				

SACB XI

	O	M	R	W	O	M	R	W
V. Barnes	17.2	6	33	6	10	3	23	7
A. A. Manack	8	1	30	0	10	3	23	3
M. Lorgat	16	3	38	1	–	–	–	–
S. Magiet	2	1	7	0	–	–	–	–
S. Gabriels	10	1	31	3	–	–	–	–

REST OF SOUTH AFRICA vs WESTERN PROVINCE

Day-night match **played at** University of the Western Cape, 13 November 1987[22]. **Result:** WP won by 87 runs.

Western Province

S. Hendricks	c Begg b Le Roux	18
S. Gabriels	b A. H. Manack	4
I. Behardien	st Begg b K.Majola	62
S. Conrad	c A. H. Manack b K. Majola	15
C. Martin	b Le Roux	8
D. Kemp	c M. Majola b A. H. Manack	36
S. Magiet	b A. H. Manack	7
G. Miller	run out	0
N. White	not out	1
R. February	not out	5
Extras		18
Total (for 8 wickets in 45 overs)		174

Rest of South Africa

Y. Omar	lbw Magiet	8
G. Cuddembey	c Behardien b barnes	2
M. Majola	c Behardien b Miller	7
A. Dinath	c Martin b Miller	12
H. Lorgat	b Magiet	5
K. Majola	run out	0
A. H. Manack	c Kemp b Gabriels	6
M. Khan	c Barnes b Conrad	18
Y. Begg	c Magiet b Gabriels	1
T. Le Roux	b Conrad	16
V. Frans	not out	1
Extras		11
Total (33.4 overs)		87

Rest of South Africa

	O	M	R	W
V. Frans	6	0	33	0
A. H. Manack	9	2	27	3
H. Lorgat	9	3	14	0
T. Le Roux	9	1	37	2
K. Majola	7	0	20	2
M. Khan	5	0	25	0

Western Province

	O	M	R	W
V. A. Barnes	5	0	7	1
R. February	5	2	4	0
S. Magiet	4	2	5	2
G. Miller	9	2	24	2
S. Gabriels	8	0	25	2
S. Conrad	2.4	0	11	2

The Rest of South Africa team for the hastily arranged match against Western Province, 1987. (Back row, left to right) Ahmed Dinath, Trevor le Roux, Abdulhack Manack, Vernon Frans, Jacob Omar, Neil Edwards, André Peters. (Front row) Garth Cuddumbey, Yasien Begg, Haroon Lorgat, S.K. Reddy (SACB), Mustapha Khan, Yusuf Lorgat (SACB), Khaya Majola, Mongezi Majola.

SOUTH AFRICAN COUNCIL ON SPORT XI vs PRESIDENT'S XI

Played at Rockland's Ground, Mitchell's Plain, 4 April 1988[23]. **Result:** SACB XI won by 6 wickets.

President's XI

G.B.Cuddumbey	b Manack	7
N. Moodaley	b Gabriels	8
M. Majola	b Barnes	21
A. Peters	b K. Majola	39
S. Conrad	run out	6
N. Miller	c.and b K. Majola	16
D. Kemp	b Manack	6
R. Dolley	c and b K. Majola	0
N. White	not out	3
R. February	run out	9
N. Ramnarain	not out	2
Extras		27
Total (for 9 wickets)		145

SACOS XI

S. Hendricks	b February	11
S. Gabriels	b Miller	10
I. Behardien	run out	28
M. Abdullah	c and b Ramnarain	18
H. Lorgat	not out	18
F. Davids	not out	40
Extras		21
Total (for 4 wickets)		148

SACOS XI

	O	M	R	W
V. Barnes	7	2	27	1
A. A. Manack	7	3	12	2
M. Khan	7	1	20	0
S. Gabriels	3	0	13	1
H. Lorgat	4	0	29	0
K. Majola	7	1	15	3

President's XI

	O	M	R	W
N. Ramnarain	6	0	28	1
R. February	4.3	0	21	1
N. Miller	6	0	30	1
K. Dolley	7	0	13	0
S. Conrad	7	0	33	0

*All-rounder Saait Magiet, captain of the national side in 1987 and 1991,
described as the best SACB player of his time by Khaya Majola.*

SOUTH AFRICAN CRICKET BOARD XI vs BORDER INVITATION XI
Played at Buffalo Park, East London, 1 March 1991[24]. **Result:** SACB XI won by 61 runs.

SACB XI

Munshi	b Dindar	23
Peters	b Dindar	60
Behardien	c sub b Dindar	42
White	not out	32
Davids	not out	63
Extras		19
Total (for 3 wickets in 45 overs)		239

Border Invitation XI

Viljoen	c Begg b Manack	6
Chellan	c White b Manack	15
Japhtha	c Behardien b Magiet	23
Abrahams	c Begg b Lorgat	16
Govender	b Lorgat	9
Thomas	b Davids	46
Moodaley	c Munshi b Magiet	17
Dindar	not out	14
Dolley	not out	5
Extras		27
Total (for 7 wickets in 45 overs)		178

Border Invitation XI

	O	M	R	W
Ramnarain	9	2	42	0
Jasson	8	1	42	0
Dindar	9	0	34	3
Dolley	9	2	33	0
Abrahams	9	0	51	0
Chellan	1	0	16	0

SACB XI

	O	M	R	W
Manack	8	1	25	2
Barnes	8	1	33	0
Majola	9	2	24	0
Lorgat	9	2	25	2
Magiet	5	1	23	2
Davids	4	0	16	1
Peters	1	1	0	0
Behardien	1	0	15	0

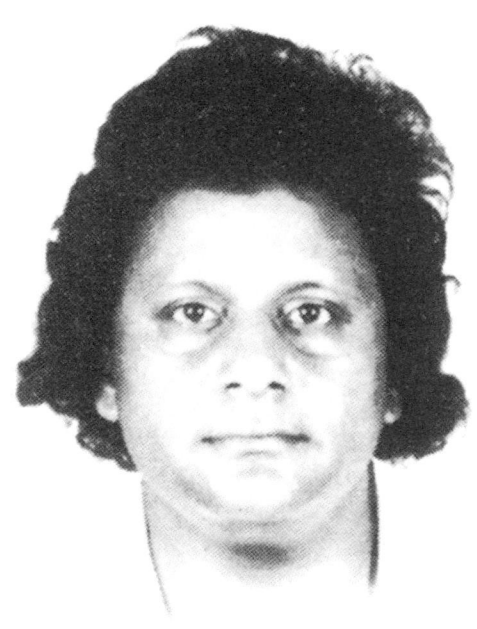

Krish Mackerdhuj, SACB president, 1984–1991.

SOUTH AFRICAN CRICKET BOARD XI vs BORDER INVITATION XI

Played at Buffalo Park, East London, 2 March 1991[25]. **Result:** SACB XI won by 7 wickets.

Border Invitation XI

Viljoen	c Behardien b Magiet	41
Chellan	c Munshi b Lorgat	36
Selani	c Behardien b Munshi	21
Manack	c Majola b Munshi	3
Abrahams	c sub b Majola	32
Thomas	run out	2
Dindar	b Manack	6
Dolley	lbw b Manack	0
Japhta	run out	1
Moodaley	not out	9
Jasson	c Begg b Davids	4
Extras		27
Total (48.3 overs)		182

SA Board XI

Munshi	c Japhta b Manack	33
Peters	c Chellan b Jasson	12
Behardien	not out	80
White	c Dolley b Jasson	8
Davids	not out	36
Extras		17
Total (for 3 wickets in 36 overs)		186

SA Board XI

	O	M	R	W
Manack	10	1	36	2
Barnes	3	0	22	0
Majola	10	5	12	1
Lorgat	10	2	34	1
Munshi	10	0	31	2
Magiet	5	1	24	1
Davids	0.3	0	5	1

Border Invitation XI

	O	M	R	W
Dindar	5	0	29	0
Jasson	10	0	57	2
Dolley	6	1	57	0
Manack	6	1	25	1
Abrahams	8	0	34	0

SACB patron, Walter Sisulu, imprisoned for 26 years, presented the SACB team with their colours in 1991. Here he is pictured with (left to right) Vido Mgadla (Border Cricket Board), Steve Tshwete and Qobs Qoboshiyana.

Part Seven

THE MAJOLA BROTHERS AND THE UNITED CRICKET BOARD (1990s-2000s)

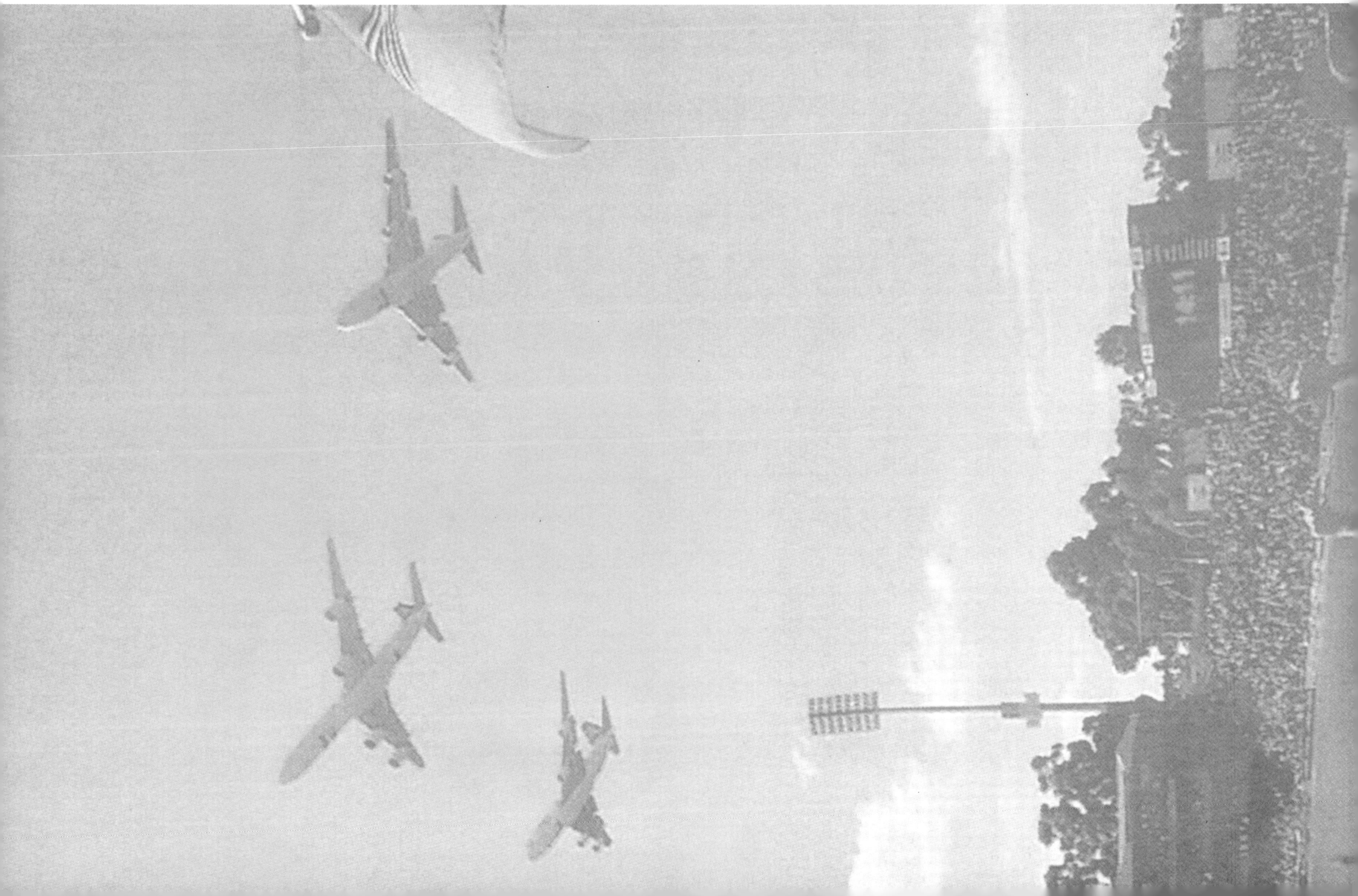

Thumbs up for unity. Ali Bacher, Krish Mackerdhuj and Khaya Majola celebrate the announcement that a single non-racial cricket body would be formed.

Chapter 32

UNITY

———————— ◖▮◗ ————————

T HE ONSET OF THE 1990s brought dramatic change to hundreds of millions of people throughout the world, including South Africans. Khaya Majola was one of those whose life took unexpected new turns in the new decade.

In 1989 the Berlin Wall came down, the Soviet Union collapsed and the Cold War ended. A new era in world politics began. Similarly, in South Africa, the regime realised that it was impossible to preserve apartheid without the total collapse of the country. Under pressure from the liberation movement headed by the ANC, the minority government agreed to unban the ANC, PAC and other groups and enter into negotiations with them. Nelson Mandela walked through the prison doors to freedom. On 27 April 1994 the first democratic elections were held. Two weeks later Mandela became President, signalling one of the most remarkable turnabouts in the political history of the 20th century.

Developments in cricket mirrored the changes taking place on the broad political front. In January 1990 SACU brought out to South Africa another rebel English touring side led by Mike Gatting. Mass protests against the rebel tour took place, inspired by the newly formed National Sports Congress which was in the process of supplanting SACOS as the national co-ordinating body.[1] SACU realised it was moving towards a dead-end. It acknowledged, 'In the present political climate, tours are counterproductive to the medium- to long-term aims of SACU and to the wider interests of South Africa as a whole.'[2] The tour was brought to an early end and the SACU sought to negotiate with the SACB, through the offices of the NSC and ANC. The ANC's Steve Tshwete, who later became the first Minister of Sport in democratic South Africa, acted as mediator, very quickly acquiring the nickname 'Mr Fixit'.[3]

On 4 August 1990 the non-racial SACB agreed to enter into discussions with SACU. The first formal meeting between the two organisations took place on 8 September in Durban. At a follow-up meeting in Port Elizabeth on 16 December SACU and SACB issued a joint declaration stating *inter alia* their intention to form 'one non-racial democratic controlling body under a single constitution' and to 'contribute through cricket to a just society in South Africa'.[4] The two bodies set up a national steering committee to drive the unification process.

At the Port Elizabeth meeting, the national steering committee also decided 'to administer and share, with immediate effect, the resources within the development field'. After the next joint meeting in January 1991, SACB announced that Khaya Majola had been appointed to start work with Ali Bacher on a national development project from 1 February 1991.[5] One year to the day after the unbannings of political organisations, the young all-rounder from the Eastern Province reported to the Wanderers for duty and took guard at the crease to face his next big challenge.

Khaya recalls how this major change in his life happened: 'EPCA president, Ronnie Pillay, one of the top administrators on the SACB executive, came to me one day and said, "Khaya, we want you to go and work in Johannesburg." When the purpose of the job was explained, I didn't even hesitate. I only asked about the salary details later.'[6]

(Left to right) Krish Mackerdhuj, Geoff Dakin, Ali Bacher and Steve Tshwete
at Lord's when the announcement was made in July 1991 that South Africa had been admitted
to the International Cricket Council.

Last meeting of the South African Cricket Board (SACB) before it became part of the new UCBSA, Durban, February 1991. (Back row, left to right)
Prem Brijlal, Rushdi Magiet, Errol Haynes, Logan Naidoo, Solomon Pango, Krish Pillay, Shaid Wadvalla, Cassim Suleman.
(Middle row) Goolam Karrim, Krish Reddy, Gordon Spadonie, Peter Heeger, Henry Paulse, P. Naicker, Wilfie Diedricks,
Khaya Majola, Cassim Docrat, Sagren Naidoo. (Front row) Barney Leendertz, Yusuf Lorgat, Ronnie Pillay,
Krish Mackerdhuj (president), Percy Sonn, S.K. Reddy, Dougie Maku. (Absent) Simon Swiegelaar.

South Africa celebrates a surprise win over Australia in Christchurch, New Zealand, during the 1992 World Cup. Steve Tshwete hugs South African captain Kepler Wessels. Tshwete famously shed tears on this occasion, symbolising the huge turnabouts that were happening as South Africa moved to democracy.

Khaya Majola's appointment as joint Director of Development with Ali Bacher was an important preparatory step towards unity.

In the meantime, the national steering committee had instructed the provinces to prepare the foundations for unity by May 1991 so that formal national unity and a new organisation could be established by mid-June. And, indeed, the new United Cricket Board of South Africa celebrated its formation at a glittering banquet in the Sandton Sun Hotel that month, attended by a galaxy of international cricketing stars including Garfield Sobers, Sunil Gavaskar, Bob Cowper and George Mann. The doyen of British cricket writers, E.W. Swanton, was guest of honour. Walter Sisulu, Steve Tshwete and Sam Ramsamy sat at the high tables, reflecting the amazing turnaround that had occurred in a very short period.[7] For the first time since the first recorded game of cricket was played on the Green Point Common in Cape Town in 1808, all South African cricketers were united under one body.

Events continued to move at speed. Within a month South Africa was admitted to the International Cricket Council, after Nelson Mandela had lobbied certain members personally, and in November 1991 South Africa toured India for the first time. Jonty Rhodes's swallow dive to run out Inzamam-ul-Haq during the World Cup early in 1992 firmly established a united South African cricket set-up as an exciting new brand both at home and internationally. The story of unity, and its many subtexts, will be dealt with in greater detail in the forthcoming Official History of South African Cricket.[8]

273

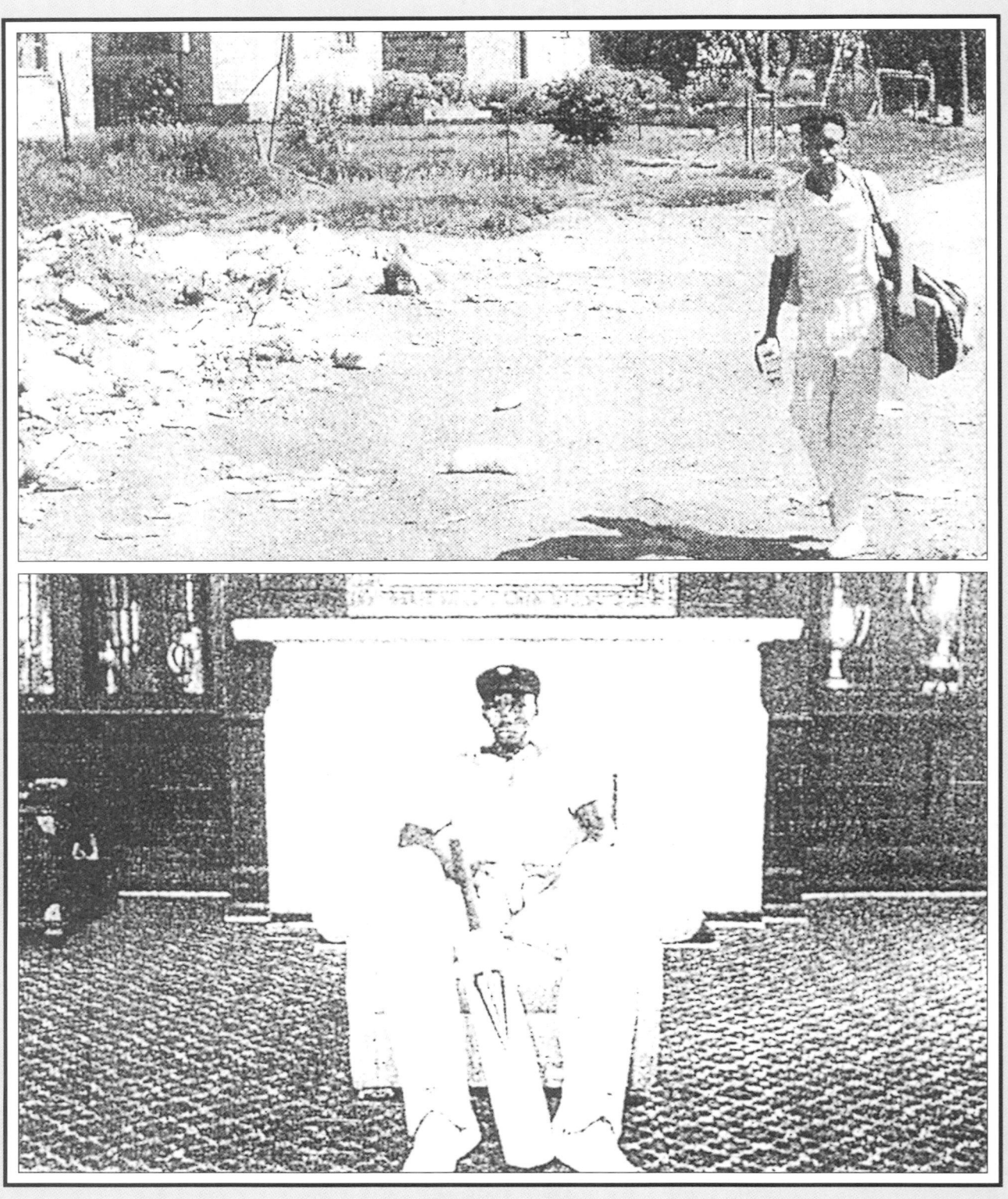

Opening of the doors. Arnold Somndaka from Soweto pictured at the formerly whites-only Wanderers Club, signifying the opportunities that unity and the development programme brought young cricketers.

Chapter 33

IN CHARGE *of the* DEVELOPMENT PROGRAMME

———————————— ◉ ————————————

KHAYA MAJOLA REMEMBERED ARRIVING for his new job at the current UCB headquarters, based at the Wanderers Club in Johannesburg. 'I was shy. I didn't know what to expect.' With winter ahead, he had no idea what the job would actually entail. However, he knew he would cope. 'If it's [about] a game of cricket I'd be able to handle it, that was my attitude. In a short space of time I was in the gear of what we were expected to do.'[1]

Life was not easy in the first few months. Majola had to get to know his new environment. The children came up to Johannesburg with him and needed looking after. His wife Cynthia remained in Port Elizabeth until a new job could be organised for her.

Khaya acknowledged that Ali Bacher helped ease him into the new position. What was it like working together after the conflict and polarisation of the preceding decade? 'Well, number one, you can imagine, we are coming from two different sides of the kraal. It wasn't easy to trust one another. One can't even doubt that.'[2]

But they soon settled down into a working relationship, which those close to them say had its ups and downs, but became a close connection over ten years. As Khaya put it, 'Ali has his strengths and weaknesses, and I have my strengths and weaknesses and together we must go forward.'[3]

Majola and Bacher were appointed as joint directors of development to start with, but Bacher was *de facto* the person in charge. This was confirmed when he was appointed as managing director of the new United Cricket Board. Majola became the UCB Director of Development. Other senior appointments to follow included Imtiaz Patel as director of professional cricket, Brian Basson as director of umpiring, and Ian Smith as director of finance. The former West Indies batting legend, Conrad Hunte, a long-time ally of SACU, and Hoosain Ayob, a prominent SACBOC player who had joined SACU, were part of the development team. Essentially, it was the old SACU office, plus Khaya. There was a feeling initially on his part that he was 'pushed down', instead of having the same status as Bacher.[4]

Majola recalled that by 1991 the development programmes in the black townships, started by SACU from 1987 onwards, were in trouble, given the political volatility of the period and the feelings generated by the rebel tours. The SACU programmes were mainly in the Gauteng area, particularly Alexandra, Soweto and Mamelodi. According to Majola, the first task was to win the confidence of local communities. 'People were not prepared to join Dr Bacher unless I came in … people were not prepared to talk to him, so he had to come with me to ease off the pressure, which was a lot at the beginning … I had to revive the area here [to start with].'[5]

Cultures of cricket. Greg Hayes, Border cricket development manager, participates in a beer-drinking ritual during a function in one of the province's rural villages.

Within a short time, the two new allies were able to expand the development programme throughout the country. The political support previously lacking was now there from the ANC and NSC. In addition, Ali Bacher astutely used the opportunities provided by the transition from the old to the new to reposition himself personally in the new dispensation. He made available offices at the UCB for Sam Ramsamy, the kingpin of South African sport, on his return from exile, and readily started working with Ramsamy, Steve Tshwete and non-racial heavyweights like Mluleki George and Mthobi Tyamzashe. Unlike most administrators from the old establishment, who remained defensive and politically bemused, Bacher quickly changed tack and exploited the opportunities provided by a situation based on the need for mutual accommodation among the top leadership.

Business also enthusiastically supported the UCB development programme. It was an attractive proposition for those keen to buy into the changing political dispensation and expand their markets with investments in the black townships. The Bakers mini-cricket programme soon became one of the main ways of marketing the new unity in cricket. Its administrators were seen to be ahead of other sports like rugby.[6]

Khaya's file of newsclippings shows the hectic dawn-to-dusk pace at which he and Bacher set out on their new mission: trips to the local townships with the NSC to reposition development; a deal with Score Furnishers to teach teachers to coach; plans to spread beyond Gauteng to Natal, Border and the Eastern and Western Cape; a visit to East London for a clinic at N.U. 7, Mdantsane; a cricket day for 1 000 children in Lenasia; getting the most talented young players ready for the national Plascon Academy; arranging for Clive Lloyd and other international stars to coach in the townships; and working with the British government to build new fields and distribute equipment to rural communities in Oudtshoorn and Alice, where he once studied.[7]

One of the areas the development programme started concentrating on was New Brighton. The UCB contributed R1 million to the upgrade of the Dan Qeqe Stadium, and the American civil rights campaigner Jesse Jackson persuaded the Ford Motor Company to give an extra R150 000. In December 1993, England A played against an Eastern Province team at the stadium. Dan Qeqe, a father figure for Khaya, was now, at the age of 65, enjoying the acknowledgement for many years of hard work. He was a member of the Port Elizabeth Transitional Local Council, as well as the development committees of the Eastern Province rugby and cricket boards. At the 1994 SAB/Lions of St Croix Eastern Province Sportsman of the Year function he was given a special merit award for his services to sport.[8] Dan's neighbour and old friend, Milase Majola, was also enjoying recognition in her sunset years. In 1994 she was given the Woman of the Year Award by the Union of Jewish Women for her life-long commitment to social work and the Girl Guide movement. The next year she was a finalist for the mayor's Citizen of the Year Award. The family remained close-knit. Tozie was back from exile, and Milase was revelling in the success of her sons.[9]

In his new home area, Khaya Majola started helping at the Soweto Cricket Club, taking them to third place in the premier league. Laurence Mvumvu recalled how Majola 'assembled old cricketers' at George Langa's home and exhorted them to get involved 'or else cricket will die'. He went with the Soweto CC on a tour of Britain and generally 'the boys tried their utmost to please him. He had an executive, but he was the leader,' Mvumvu concluded.[10]

Cynthia Majola remembers the 'sleep-overs', when the whole Soweto team would bunk down in their house in Bramley near the Wanderers. 'I knew when he phoned to say "What can I buy for you?" that something would be afoot and that soon two kombi-loads of cricketers would be descending on us. They loved *umngqusho* and that's when Laurence Mvumvu taught me how to cook pap.'[11]

Looking back at the nine years in his job as director of development for the United Cricket Board, Khaya reflected:

It is unbelievable how it has moved from '91 to now ... You know, when you work, at times you want to see whether you have achieved something. If there's something that I really cherish it is the work that I have put in ...'[12]

He reeled off the gains. In nine years hundreds of pitches had been laid throughout the country, over 200 schools assisted with equipment, coaching and facilities, and over 20 000 children per year had been introduced to cricket through the Bakers programme. He pointed to Makhaya Ntini and the 39 black cricketers who played first-class cricket in the 1999/2000 season, as well as youngsters such as Jacques Kallis and Mark Boucher who were now stars and had come out of the Plascon Academy. And who would have thought then that Pakistan would play at Ntselamanzi? Khaya mused. There was a carnival atmosphere at this village near Alice, in the heartland of African cricket in the Eastern Cape, when the Minister of Sport opened the new ground on 20 December 1994 and the first international match took place there. He is very proud of the gains cricket has made in the rural areas.

'Ali has his strengths and weaknesses and I have my strengths and weaknesses, and together we must go forward.'

Graeme Pollock teaches a young mini-cricketer how to bat during the Millennium Festival held at Newlands in 2000.

Khaya Majola (left) with Brian Lara (right) at a Bakers Mini-Cricket event. Pankie Mangisa (centre) looks on.

Clive Lloyd, one of the first international stars to lend support, with Khaya Majola, Ali Bacher and Imtiaz Patel.

Shane Warne with Khaya Majola in Mitchell's Plain, Cape Town.

Foot soldiers of development. Khaya Majola with the UCB youth and development team, 1997. (Back row, left to right)
Wally Nel, Leonard Rajagapaul, Aubrey Litseho, Donald Tono Mle, Niels Momberg, Rushdie Magiet, Richard Elms.
(Front row) Conrad Hunte, Hoosain Ayob, Imtiaz Patel, Giuliana Bland, Khaya Majola, Greg Hayes, Jeremy Fredricks.

Senior coaching academy at the Wanderers, Johannesburg, 11-14 September 1992. (Back row, left to right) H. Ayob (organiser, UCBSA), C. Henderson
(Boland), S. Pollock (Natal), M. Venter (EP), K. Venter (OFS), C. Kolisang (OFS), P. Radley (OFS), L. Koen (EP), G. Murgatroyd (Namibia),
H. Manack (Tvl), K. Mahuwa (EP), A. Pollock (Tvl). (Middle row) V. Vermeulen (Tvl), B. White (Tvl), B. Schultz (EP), D. McHelm (WP),
G. Liebenberg (OFS), S. Palframan (Natal), A. Meyer (WP), M. Vandrau (Tvl), R. Lyle (Natal), R. Veenstra (Natal). (Front row) D. Phaka, K. Majola,
R. Jackman, M. Garda, C. Hunte (coach, West Indies), V. van der Bijl (academy director), A. Kourie (coach, Tvl), S. Chotia (coach, Tvl),
I. Patel (organiser TCB), G. Munari (organiser, UCBSA). (Absent) E. Stewart (Natal), H. Ackerman (coach, WP).

The development programme of the UCB, described by former ICC president, Clyde Walcott, as 'the best of its kind in world cricket, both in terms of its scope and excellence',[13] had developed an impressive momentum since the early days. In 1999, the budget was R21 million per year. There was a dedicated team of 40 administrators around the country backing up Majola and the head office, where Niels Momberg served as the development officer and Fuad Waggie as schools co-ordinator. Each province had its own development manager. Khaya commented that the support and loyalty he got from throughout the country was 'unbelievable'.[14]

A whole range of development activities was run from Khaya's office, including an annual development conference to set targets and assess progress, an annual tour of a particular province by development managers, and an annual mini-cricket seminar.

Niels Momberg from the UCB office explained why Khaya initiated the seminar for the mini-cricket coaches:

He feels the Bakers mini-cricket people haven't really got a lot of perks. The coaches can go to national weeks and aspire to become provincial and national junior coaches … so what we do is once a year have a seminar at a central venue where we get seven or eight people from each province. Everybody drives there. Then for three days we discuss mini-cricket. Where we come from. What we're doing right. What we're doing wrong. Where we can improve. They're all teachers. We try and give them some more skills to improve the programme.[15]

According to those close to them, Ali Bacher left development to Khaya as time went on. Everything ended up being run by him. Ali didn't have anything to do with it.[16]

Ali Bacher is a legend in cricket. Besides being a marketer *par excellence*, he also has an outstanding record of delivery as an administrator. His recipe for success, according to someone who worked closely with him, is that 'he gets up earlier than anyone else'.[17] He is known for his shuffling early morning runs when he mentally draws up lists of things to do, and he 'actions well'. Many people have become accustomed to his early morning calls. But it is also common knowledge that Bacher has a quaint, if not outdated, management style. His approach at times exasperated both UCB officials and senior employees working under him, who found that they did not always have clearly delegated tasks and responsibilities, and would get information on a 'need to know' basis. They described his style as individualistic and keeping-it-close-to-the-chest. This led to strong undercurrents, and sometimes clashes. Ali would make decisions, for example regarding the make-up of provincial competitions, which Khaya and others

Khaya Majola (left) with his friend and colleague, Hoosain Ayob, now ICC Development Director for Africa, and Miss South Africa, Basetsane Makgalemela.

would then subtly have to undo.[18] Frustration levels among the directors were often high. When Imtiaz Patel resigned as director of professional cricket in 1999 to pursue a career in television, it was common knowledge that his differences with his one-time mentor played a big part in his decision.[19]

While Ali Bacher had run the old establishment SACU's affairs almost single-handedly for many years, there was a great deal of resistance to this approach in the new UCB dispensation. There was a strong desire to make him more accountable to the elected officials and some felt that the former SACB leaders like Krish Mackerdhuj erred in not making this clear from the beginning.

However, Majola and Bacher nevertheless developed a very close relationship. Niels Momberg commented:

I think they've got a very interesting relationship. I can only talk from Khaya's side. I don't know how Ali perceives it, if he's actually aware of everything that goes on. Khaya would say things like 'It's time for him to go,' but I think he has a lot of respect for Ali. He has — it might even be more than that — a definite connection. There's a bond, a definite bond. You can't get away from that. I can pick it up. And he might say, 'Well, it's not so,' but there is a connection there. Khaya has grown out of sight in the last ten years, which Ali has recognised. I'm not sure he's recognised how far and how big he has grown [though].[20]

Indeed, Majola had grown very big in South African cricket by 2000. Although still occupying his original senior UCB administrative position, he was also a major actor in the behind-the-scenes manoeuvres regarding national developments in cricket.

Khaya Majola and colleagues in the UCB Transformation Monitoring Committee.
(Back, left to right) Ashwin Desai, Ray Mali, André Odendaal, Imtiaz Patel and
Maxwell Jordaan. (Front) Dr R.A.M. Salojee and Khaya Majola.
Johannesburg, 22 July 2000.

Chapter 34

TRANSFORMATION TOP
of the AGENDA

———————————— ◉ ————————————

URING THE MID-1990s complaints began surfacing about glass ceilings and a lack of thoroughgoing change in cricket. Many felt that while development was being trumpeted, black cricketers were making little headway at the elite provincial and national playing levels. Also, despite the fact that administrators from the SACB were politically in charge, in practice the old establishment officials were still running the show and acting as gate-keepers, reproducing old power relations and ways of thinking, with neutral-sounding 'merit' arguments often the justification.[1]

Calls were made for transformation on a more fundamental level in cricket. These calls were replicating the broader demands for delivery and change after the 'rainbow nation' euphoria that accompanied the advent of democracy and Nelson Mandela's ascension to the presidency. Despite the heady new atmosphere in the country, there were strong feelings within the black majority that concrete change was slow in coming. While expectations were high, the delivery of new homes, schools and economic opportunities for those who suffered under apartheid proved more difficult for the new government. From 1996 onwards there was a clamour for transformation to be speeded up. It was on this platform of transformation and delivery that Thabo Mbeki became President in 1999 after the ANC romped home with over 60 percent of the vote in the country's second democratic election.[2]

Recognising the pressures for more fundamental change, the UCB initiated a series of national 'visioning' workshops where feelings could be gauged and new strategies could be developed for cricket. These workshops, held in every province over a period of 18 months, were likened to cricket's Truth and Reconciliation Commission. In emotive, charged sessions cricketers from vastly different backgrounds and pasts spoke openly about their angers, hurts and wishes for the future. The process culminated in a National Vision Conference held in Johannesburg on 13-15 November 1998.[3] More than 120 delegates adopted the Transformation Charter and a Pledge to the Nation, which committed the UCB to operating with a 'new culture and ethos' in an 'African context' so that cricket could become a dynamic reflection of South Africa's young democracy.[4]

The Transformation Charter covered ten main strategic areas or 'thrusts' for the future, with 'Redress and Representivity' being the key one.

A Transformation Monitoring Committee (TMC) was formed to ensure implementation of the new vision for cricket. Part of its task was to help draft practical three-year 'business plans' in each of the ten strategic areas identified.[5]

At a National Development Conference held in May 1999 the broad target of 50/50 representation at all levels of cricket within three years was set. They applied to every aspect of the game, from players to scorers, umpires, groundspeople, administrators and employees. Exceptions were the elite first-class and international playing level, where the initial targets were lower (although the expectation was that the progress at the base levels would also increasingly be reflected here as well).[6]

Duplicating the national TMC process, provinces also set up Provincial Monitoring Committees and developed their own strategies.

The goals were now clearly set and transformation became the guiding thrust in cricket.

Whereas in the past the emphasis was more on the 'development' of black cricketers on the margins without addressing power relations, representation and the culture of cricket at the centre, transformation stood for thorough-going change at every level of the UCB and the game.

Another way of explaining transformation is that it was about repositioning and growing South African cricket in an optimal way in the new, 21st-century financial and political environments.

An often overlooked fact is that transformation involved a sophisticated process of change management. It was about ensuring the future sustainability of the game in a complex environment. The UCB had to emphasise repeatedly that it was not anti-merit or anti-standards but directly about maximising resources and promoting merit.[7]

With a self-conscious focus on redressing historical imbalances in place, progress on the playing level was almost immediate. The target was 22 first-class players for the first season in 1999/2000. Many argued this was not 'practical' but it was easily surpassed with a figure of 39 players, some of whom were at the top of the averages.

At grassroots level, several formerly black clubs won provincial league competitions, including Yorkshire CC from Galeshewe in Kimberley.

Progress at the top administration level was rapid too. In the first year of the transformation programme, the UCB could point to Wilson Ngobese as the new head groundsman at Kingsmead, Rushdi Magiet as the new national selection convenor and Ray Mali as the first African president of a province.

These figures indicated not only quantitative change but also the emergence of a new institutional culture in the UCB and cricket. With new power relations came new imaginations and ways of doing things, which will impact hugely on the game down the line.[8]

Not everyone understood or supported the new transformation directions. This led to several public controversies. Scarcely a fortnight after the National Vision Conference, the selectors picked an all-white South African team, an anomaly highlighted by the fact that the West Indies were the opponents. Nelson Mandela cancelled his proposed visit to the Wanderers.[9] Then, at the public launch of the Transformation Charter at Newlands in January 1999, UCB president, Raymond White, caused an uproar when he deviated from the Pledge of the Nation to add his own (conservative) riders.[10] Leading administrators blundered again in November 1999 when they selected an all-white Gauteng/Northerns combination to play England in an invitation match. The Minister of Sport went on the attack and the Transformation Monitoring Committee called this 'dinosaur thinking'. The TMC said the UCB had to be held to account; if the officials in charge could not lead transformation, they should step down.[11]

The TMC played an active part in the transformation debates, helping to establish an unambiguous transformation agenda and discourse about change within the UCB. It also regularly emphasised the need for effective change management strategies and the importance of working on changing old mindsets if any transformation process was to be successful in a qualitative way. TMC interventions, reports to the UCB, analyses of media attitudes to cricket transformation and productivity in driving the 'recording the full history of South African cricket' thrust, all underlined these points.[12]

Khaya Majola was a key figure in the National Vision Seminar, pushing particularly hard for the UCB to address the empowerment of black African cricketers. Together with his brother Gerald, Julius Majola and Sidima Mooi from Eastern Province, he argued forcefully for an Africanisation clause in the Transformation Charter. After a passionate debate, the wording was changed, but the substance was retained in the key 'Representivity and Redress' principle.[13] As Ray Mali put it, 'We are done with talking, promises and waiting – we want to see results now!'[14]

African cricketers who had always been the stepchildren on the South African cricket scene were finally staking their claim in unambiguous ways. They were now able to do this because of the radically changed power relations in society generally, and because the issues being raised in the broader debates about change in the country were being echoed in cricket as well.

Majola, as well as the other UCB director most concerned with transformation issues, Imtiaz Patel, were among those appointed to the TMC. Other members included the veteran anti-apartheid activist and ANC member of the National Council of Provinces, Dr R.A.M. Salojee; the Durban-based social activist and journalist, Dr Ashwin Desai; senior Department of Sport official, Maxwell Jordaan, who was a close friend and ex-club-mate of Khaya at United; the

Geoffrey Toyana pictured with his father, former SA African XI wicketkeeper, Gus Toyana, was left out of the Invitation XI to play England.

Ray White, forced to resign as president of the UCB in 2000.

veteran administrator from the Border, Ray Mali, who had earlier played together with other family members for Dan Qeqe's Fort Beaufort Club in Port Elizabeth; and the chairperson, Professor André Odendaal.[15]

The Transformation Charter and the appointment of the TMC put the issue of transformation at the top of the South African cricket agenda. Some top administrators were uncomfortable with this new emphasis – and probably hoped it would subside after the usual public relations value had been extracted by the UCB. But they were to discover that the momentum of change could not be halted or ignored. The issue was no longer the development of people on the margins to bring them into the 'traditional' structures, but the examination and restructuring of power relations at every level of cricket.[16]

Majola revelled in the work and debates with like-minded people in the TMC and his consummate networking skills were particularly valuable. After nearly a decade at cricket's HQ he was in the middle of all development-related initiatives and connected to the people that mattered throughout the country. It also became common knowledge that during elections and the periodic UCB crises, such as the selection of all-white teams, when the old school types were busy shooting themselves in the foot, he would be the inside contact for concerned politicians and administrators alike. Those who regularly sought Majola's advice and views

included the Minister of Sport, Steve Tshwete, and top officials of the National Sports Council (NSC). In the absence of a thoroughly representative cricket set-up these informal networks carried a great deal of weight. After backroom caucusing and lobbying important decisions would often be carried in formal meetings, even if the officials there tended to be conservatively inclined.

The power of the transformation lobby was shown when the out-of-step Ray White was forced to resign in January 2000. Gerald Majola drew up a memorandum demanding that he step down, which many thought was intemperate and had no chance of success. But the brothers got to work and when the memo was leaked to the press, things started to unravel.

The newspapers picked up the story and ran with it. On the Saturday morning, Ray White was asked to recuse himself so that the UCB council could discuss the issue. He went to his house nearby to await the outcome. By the end of the morning he was gone. The council voted unanimously for him to stand down.[17]

Ray White's forced resignation showed that there was no longer space for those who equivocated about transformation. It led to a fundamental power shift in cricket and Khaya Majola, the cog around which the African cricket lobby revolved, was now perhaps the most powerful behind-the-scenes actor in South African cricket.

Hamba ngoxolo Ndlovu! *A page from Cynthia Majola's family album. Khaya being visited in hospital by the national team.*
(Left to right) Makhaya Ntini, Hansie Cronjé, Allan Donald, Shaun Pollock and Goolam Raja (manager).

Chapter 35

'THERE WILL NOT BE ANOTHER KHAYA'

A ROUND SEPTEMBER 1998, WHEN the transformation process to which he was so committed was reaching a climax, Khaya Majola suddenly felt ill. He had abdominal pains and was losing blood. X-rays at the Brenthurst Clinic indicated a large growth. Cancer of the colon was diagnosed.

Surgery followed, and it was found the cancer had spread. He was given 12 months to live. Then chemotherapy sessions kept the pain at bay, but this came with complications: ulcers, weight loss, bowel function impairment, 'colour changes', and an immune system that became increasingly prone to infections.[1] He hoped the gruelling treatment would be successful and despite being seriously ill he showed his mental toughness, insisting, for example, on driving alone to Centurion in January 2000 to attend a TMC meeting on the same day he had undergone treatment.

But slowly the ugly disease was winning its battle.

On 9 June 2000, Ali Bacher told the author that things looked bad: 'Khaya could see a whole lot of tumours on the screen without the doctor having to explain. He has got a few months left, at most. He knows that. But he is still quietly determined.'

Coming back from sabbatical in the USA in mid-2000, the author decided it was urgent that Khaya's story should be told. Khaya was thrilled. 'I'd love that,' he said.

The first interview for *The Story of an African Game* took place in his office at the UCB on 3 July. He looked weak. He could feel the tumour in his stomach with his hands. Did he want to go ahead? 'I want this as much as you do,' he said. But after an hour he was drained. Willing hands helped him onto cushions from an upstairs couch, laid out on the floor of his office, so he could rest. He was in pain as he curled up. 'This is like torture. Shouldn't I just shoot myself and get it over with?' Ian Smith gave him support. 'He is old school, but we have become very close since I've got sick,' Khaya told me later.

Niels Momberg said, 'Last Monday was the first time I saw that despite his courage his body was giving up.' He'd insisted on going to Bloemfontein for the annual seminar of mini-cricket coaches. After an 08.30 opening speech, he was so drained that he fell asleep soon afterwards. His colleagues persuaded him to go home and put him on the next flight back to Johannesburg.

Before, he had had difficulty sleeping. Now he needed to sleep. After an hour and a half he woke. He wanted to continue, but it was too much. He asked Ian Smith to take him to hospital.

Was it going to be the last time?

Fortunately it was not. He went through periods when he felt stronger. Other times, he felt very weak as the cancer ate away at him.

Still he attended the meeting of the TMC at the Johannesburg airport on 22 July. His colleagues minuted their respect for his courage. The TMC also took the group photo which it had not thought of doing until these moments of hard realisation.

Vukile Majola (right), who played rugby for the Gauteng Eagles and cricket for Christian Brothers College, with Makhaya Ntini, who was also at the funeral.

Cynthia and Khaya Majola during the Soweto Cricket Club tour of Britain in the mid-1990s.

On 26 August I phoned Khaya at home. It was a Saturday. After coming out of hospital for a check-up that morning, he and his son Vukile had gone to Pretoria to fetch his brother Tozie. People had been visiting. As usual, he was looking forward. He explained that Eastern Province had provisionally agreed to this book being launched the following March at a function at St George's Park.

But after that the end came quickly. Cynthia Majola recalls, 'On the Sunday, Doctor Nyoka came to visit and found him to be seriously ill.' Khaya maintained a brave face. He told Cynthia that the late uTata George (the legendary cricketer George Langa) and another Soweto veteran, uTata Yamaphi were calling him, but he was ducking and diving because he was still too young. They should call their peer Tata [Laurence] Mvumvu instead, he joked. He asked her to bathe him and cut his nails. He requested his friends Cola and Kedi to sleep over that night, but they promised gently to visit again the next day instead. He wanted to go to work on the Monday morning, but Cynthia sensed something was wrong. He battled to talk and his eyes were yellow. Vukile, Niels Momberg and Ian Smith took him to hospital. Vukile sat at the top of the bed and daughter Siphokazi at his feet, lovingly wiping his perspiring body from time to time. The pastor at the local St Catherine's Anglican church, Lynne Wyngaard, and Reverend Mandla Gamede of the Methodist church offered prayers. When the latter had finished he annointed him ('wamqaba ngeoil') and Khaya said 'enkosi mfundisi' and went to sleep. 'Vuki and Siphokazi tried to wake him and call him, but it was all over,' Cynthia remembers with great feeling. The time was around midday on Monday 28 August 2000.[2]

Imtiaz Patel phoned me at lunchtime to convey the news. I was sitting at the keyboards typing out this story. A spring sun was streaming in through the window.

I immediately got down to writing an obituary. It was deliberately economical, not overstating the case. It was run by the *Cape Argus*, and the new e channels of *Cricinfo*, before appearing in various UCB publications.[3]

The obituary described Khaya Majola as 'one of South Africa's leading cricketers in the 1970s and 1980s, and one of the country's top cricket administrators during the 1990s'. His positions and development successes, family background and playing statistics were summarised: 17 seasons of first-class cricket, 87 matches, 65 catches, 2 826 runs, 219 wickets.

One of the country's foremost cricket writers, Peter Robinson, commented, 'I had no idea about those details.' Like other black sportsmen, Khaya would have got a few lines about development and what a nice person he was if the obituary had not been written. People 'from the other side', even those with the important profiles, were still invisible. Without covering his 'previous' life, or having Krish Reddy's statistics, the essence would have been missing. The exclusions of the past would have been reproduced. The power of the pen – and its ability to empower or negate.

Among the many tributes to Khaya Majola was a motion in parliament mourning 'the loss to the entire nation'; this was followed by one noting the 23rd anniversary of the death of Steve Biko.[4] ANC spokesperson Smuts Ngonyama said, 'The ANC dips its revolutionary banner in honour of this fallen hero.'[5] 'Majola was a sports legend and an uncompromising agent of change,' added sports minister Ngconde Balfour.[6] Peter Hain, now British Minister for Africa, praised his enormous contribution and said, 'There will never be another Khaya and it is a tribute to him that it is no longer necessary for there to be one.'[7] Devdas Govindjee wrote, ' … from the fields of Lovedale College in Alice, through to the turf at Dan Qeqe Stadium, the New Brighton Oval and the Adcock Stadium, his bootmarks will remain indelible – a reminder of a great ambassador for sport.'[8] Ali Bacher, Majola's colleague for nearly ten years, said he was one of the most remarkable men he knew and added, 'He believed in using cricket to bring both whites and blacks together.'[9]

A memorial service was held in Johannesburg at the St Catherine's Anglican Church, where friends such as Chris Day were also congregants, and was followed by the funeral in New Brighton.

Cricketers from across the spectrum came to the St Catherine's service. When people 'doubted our skills in cricket', said Lawrence Mvumvu from the Soweto Cricket Club, 'Khaya was there'.[10]

Majola's body was taken home to New Brighton. As in the case of his father before him, who also died young, thousands came to say farewell in heart-warming African style. Notables present included the Minister of Sport, Ngconde Balfour, Mayor Nceba Faku, national ANC political figures like Smuts Ngonyama and Linda Mti, Dennis Neer and Saki Macozoma, the national cricket and rugby presidents, Percy Sonn and Silas Nkanunu, national captain Shaun Pollock, with Mark Boucher and Makhaya Ntini and hundreds of local sportspeople.[11]

They came wave after wave to pay their respects, standing around the coffin. Spring Rose RFC in their green blazers, were there, as was a more eclectic and laid-back Soweto CC, with claret red blazers and dark glasses.

The choirs and officiating ministers reflected Khaya's two worlds – Port Elizabeth and Johannesburg. The local choir, with strong rolling voices but dressed conservatively in black and white uniforms restrained against the zippy, gospel, toe-tapping, finger-clicking, side-stepping brothers from the city of gold. Mcebisi Xundu, the well-known local struggle priest, who buried Goniwe and many others, was quiet and understated in the Anglican style, handsome and strong-looking even with the pigment mark across his face. Counterpoised to him was the charismatic 'Americanised'

Siphokazi Majola and friend.

energy of Reverend Gamede, who explained with sweeping gestures and a great, dramatic voice how Khaya welcomed the end, chased away the devil and passed from this world.

Uncle Dan Qeqe wore the green and gold of SARFU. In the audience the green of Spring Rose and the seemingly chest-size badges of 'the Blues', Orientals, were everywhere in view, a reminder of a long tradition of sport. In front sat the Oliphants and the Majolas, all in black, united as a family, with Cynthia and Milase in the centre.[12]

Khaya Majola's significance to cricket was – and remains – huge. During the high-point of apartheid oppression, when it was said that Africans did not play the game of cricket, he was one of the few African cricketers with a profile large enough to prove that this was a lie. He was central in keeping alive a fragile tradition at a time when apartheid pushed African cricket to its lowest ebb.

He and the Eastern Cape cricketers were also symbols of those African cricketers who openly aligned themselves with the liberation struggle and non-racialism, rather than allow themselves to be identified with the ethnic policies and narrow politics of the apartheid state.

In his speech at the funeral, Danny Jordaan pointed out that Majola never wavered from the commitment to the struggle for freedom in South Africa, even if it meant jeopardising a promising career and returning to the matting wickets and poor facilities in the townships. He said Khaya always remained true to where he had come from. His life reminded Danny of the old gospel spiritual, 'I ain't gonna let no one turn me 'round'. When Khaya came back from England in 1974, he had the choice of playing on fancy fields or the choice of playing at Veeplaats and Zwide, where 'one snick is four'. He chose the gravel, and still always managed to look graceful driving off the front foot. His answer when it counted, in relation to community and country, was: I ain't gonna let no one turn me 'round.

Then, in the 1990s, as a key figure in consolidating cricket unity, the development programme and the transformation process, Majola became the cog around which the project of reconstituting African influence in cricket revolved. He was also one of the few in the UCB who epitomised unity, and who was recognised and liked across the spectrum.

The deep mix of the funeral procession attested to this unity in practice.[13]

Gerald Majola at Newlands.

Chapter 36

CEO *of the* UNITED CRICKET BOARD

———————————⬤———————————

WITHIN MONTHS OF KHAYA Majola's passing, his younger brother Gerald became Chief Executive Officer of the United Cricket Board, taking over the day-to-day running of the game in South Africa from Ali Bacher.

Wearied by transformation politics and looking to go out on top after nearly a decade in charge, Bacher got his chance when South Africa was awarded the ICC World Cup 2003. With his international reputation and his ability to organise, he was, for the UCB, the obvious candidate for the World Cup CEO position.

For a while, some felt that Bacher should continue to do both jobs. Ray White, who had not got on particularly well with him, preferred this arrangement to a so-called transformation candidate.[1]

But the change lobby in the UCB was not to be denied. They insisted that a new CEO had to be appointed. While he had shown himself to be a master string-puller, Bacher's style had made him many enemies. The days of a 'whitey' running the show single-handedly were over. Who to succeed the legend then, for whether you liked him or not Bacher had become a legend, almost single-handedly directing South African cricket for a decade? It had to be someone with a pedigree. After an advertising and interview process led nowhere, Percy Sonn and his team turned again to the Eastern Cape — and the Majola family.[2]

Gerald was approached to take the job, but he was reluctant to accept. He had been instrumental in getting Ray White to resign, and as a UCB council member and national selector, he had also called for a black successor to Ali Bacher. This could be seen as a conflict of interest situation, he said. But the UCB wanted him. He asked Nelson Mandela and others for advice. The great man phoned on the day he was celebrating his tenth wedding anniversary. 'It was a Sunday … four o' clock. I'll never forget. His first words were, "*Molo nyana*" (Hello son). He said you would not have been asked had you not been good enough. "Just go out there and do it for us." '[3]

Gerald initially did not discuss the issue with Khaya, who was six years older and 'became like a father to me' after Eric's early death. Khaya was his younger brother's mentor. 'I thought he would want to apply.' As a senior administrator at the UCB, Khaya would, by right, have aspired to the CEO position. Both he and Gerald, in fact, felt that he should have become joint CEO way back in 1991, that he had been cheated out of this in some way. Now, to complicate matters further, Khaya was seriously ill, but still working with a business-as-usual attitude.

Khaya, a master in networking, was aware of the approaches to Gerald. He was 'cross' that Gerald had not confided in him. 'Why you keep things away from me?' he asked in slang language. They discussed the matter and Khaya persuaded Gerald to give it a shot.[4]

The announcement was made early in October 2000, only a few weeks after Khaya's death. Gerald, supported by his family network, felt ready. 'When I got home my mum and Boet Dan and them were all there.' They said a prayer and 'did all the traditional things', like give advice. The Oliphants gave him a chair.[5] Later he went to the ancestral home in KwaZulu-Natal as well. There he was given a goat-hide wrist adornment for protection by the ancestors.

NEW MILLENNIUM

Gerald Majola's first day at office was on 2 January 2001 in Cape Town. He had to attend the traditional New Year's test at Newlands, one of the highlights of the South African cricketing calendar.

This January fixture was more special than usual because it marked the start of the first cricket test match of the new millennium. The opponents were Sri Lanka, deceptively frail looking physically, but with a line-up of greats — Jayasuriya the left-handed destroyer of fast bowling, the classical strokemaker De Silva, the once-in-a-generation Muralitharan and the intelligent left-handed opening bowler with the long name, Warnakulasuriya Patabendige Ushantha Joseph Chaminda Vaas.

The historic ground oozed atmosphere. The colourful crowd squeezed in, breaking attendance figures for that summer. One could feel the expectancy of a new year, a new day, a new game. The first ball on the first morning of a test match is always special. The banter and banners swirled like playground waves across the green-carpeted outfield.

South Africa won in three days by a massive innings and 229 runs, their biggest winning margin ever. The way was paved by gigantic performances from Man of the Match Shaun Pollock, batting centurion Daryll Cullinan, all-rounders Mark Boucher and Lance Klusener, and rookie new ball bowler, Mfuneko Ngam. Called in to replace the injured Alan Donald, Ngam caused havoc against the slight-built Sri Lankan batsmen, taking three wickets in each innings. His match figures were 21.2-4-62-6.[6]

Garth le Roux led the praises from the bowling stars of yesteryear. Ngam was the 'silent assassin' rather than the hackneyed 'black thunder', an epithet given to him by the media in a tired comparison with 'white wighting', Alan Donald. Was this not the ghost of Michael Holding? The crowd oohed and aahed as batsmen played late and the ball thudded into the gloves of a diminutive wicketkeeper going up. All ten wickets in the Sri Lankan first innings were caught, seven in the behind-the-wicket cordon.

It was the first time that South Africa fielded three black players in a test, a fact not even realised by those choosing the team. Ngam's presence in the bowling line-up alongside Makhaya Ntini, who was enjoying a glorious summer, made it seem run of the mill to see a test team with African faces.

Earlier, Ntini and Ngam had taken eight wickets against Sri Lanka, in the same week that Breyton Paulse and Chester Williams scored five tries for the rugby Springboks against the Barbarians at Cardiff Arms Park.

Up in the pavilion, in the President's Suite, something similarly new was happening.

Gerald Majola's first tasks in his new job gave some indication of where his priorities lay. He started the day with a breakfast meeting with the Transformation Monitoring Committee, assuring them that transformation would be central to his plans.[7] Then he visited the dressing room for a chat to the team before the game.

'Cricket is our [primary] product and our national team is what we sell to the public,' he told them. His concern was excellence and a winning team. His view was that, 'No irresponsible experimentation and tampering with the magic formula of winning can be tolerated. There is no margin for error. We need every part of the system geared towards providing the short-term and long-term support our national team needs.'[8] Moreover, he promised to make better communications between the players and his office a priority.

In the UCB box in the President's Pavilion a chattering of voices speaking away unselfconsciously in Xhosa could be heard. Mr Mvinjelwa from Umtata and Advocate Ngumbela, doyen of the Fort Beaufort *Macal eGusha* cricket weeks, were sitting with Ray Mali. The excitable comment-a-minute Advocate, who is not an advocate, was not your traditional President's Suite stiff-upper-lip guest. Majola respectfully greeted Archbishop Njongonkulu Ndungane in Xhosa. Like his predecessor Desmond Tutu, this ex-Lovedalian is a cricket fan who regularly watches at Newlands. Later, opposition party leader, Bantu Holomisa, a very good rugby player in his day, dropped by. The new cricket power-holders were also there: Haroon Lorgat, Tim Khumalo, Henry Paulse, Max Jordaan, Mtutuzeli Nyoka with his wife, Mula, and others.

Percy Sonn made an aside to Gerald, only partly in jest: 'Be careful, all the guys who can shoulder you out of a job are here.'

Sitting at table number one at lunch time with the new CEO were Nelson Mandela's ex-director general, Professor Jakes Gerwel, ex-Robben Islander and now Judge, Dikgang Moseneke, the chair of the TMC, and a top black business figure linked to a new cellphone company. It was noticeable, this changing of the guard at the CEO's table.

After two great balls by Ngam, one missing the stumps by a hair's breadth, the other hitting Russel Arnold, Gerald noticed that Ntini was exhorting him on loudly – in Xhosa – from 30 yards away.

One sensed this is how the institutional culture of cricket will change. At Newlands, on the second day of the new millennium, were clear signs that the new century would be very different from the one that had just passed.

SOMETHING OF A CALLING

Gerald Majola had to learn quickly. After an early visit to Australia, he was off to the Caribbean in April 2001. It was noticeable that he had a good rapport with Gregory Shillingford and other West Indian officials. He said he felt close to them. They understood what it was about to have a black skin in a white world.[9]

Majola and his entourage of South African administrators were escorted by police, sirens blaring, through the streets of Bridgetown, Barbados to the famous Kensington Oval for the fifth limited-overs international. After the informality of the Recreation Ground in St John's, Antigua, where Andy Roberts watched in a casual checked shirt, with short sleeves showing arms like sledge hammers, one could feel the formality of 'history' at the Oval.

In Barbados, a British colony for an uninterrupted 340 years with the third oldest parliament in the world, cricket and status went hand in hand. Two prime ministers and a string of faces from cricket's hall of fame were in the box that day.

Sir Gary Sobers himself. Besides him, Clyde Walcott and Everton Weekes, Wes Hall, Charlie Griffith, Lance Gibbs and Desmond Haynes. Three generations all there in the flesh. One recalled the image of two cricket-loving fathers watching their children play street games in dusty New Brighton 40 years before. Could Eric Majola and Wilson Ximiya, who named his first-born Walcott Weekes Phakamile Ximiya, and another one Sobers, ever have dreamed in those deep apartheid days that one of their boys would go to the Caribbean one day as the head of South African cricket?

Gerald was four months into his tenure as CEO of the UCB. Unbeknown to those of us following the tour, he was dealing at the same time with the dagga-smoking incident that would soon become a public drama. In an interview in his room at the Savannah Hotel, a stone's throw from the white sands of a tropical beach and a short walk to the rusted guns of the old British Fort, which guards the sea entrance to the city, Majola admitted that he could not quite believe that he was in the Caribbean as CEO. He recalled that the club

second team had been called the 'West Indians'. As children, he reflected, the Wes Halls and Gordon Greenidges were 'our heroes, more than the Pollocks'.[10]

Majola felt South Africans could learn from the West Indians, with their distinctive cricketing style and support base. This would mean recognising cultural differences. For example, while some complained about the incessant play of the band in Port Elizabeth, black supporters loved this. He wanted to see taverners, with their township connections, run liquor and food stalls, where sheep heads would be available in township style. He foresaw free tickets for mothers of the Bakers mini-cricket players and concerts with jazz greats like Jimmy Dludlu to get black spectators to fork out that R50 entrance fee, which they would otherwise think was not worthwhile.[11] Majola felt destiny had handed him the job and it was one for which he was qualified. It was his 'calling'. Some bigger hand had a role in this. He said it was almost as if his whole training and upbringing had prepared him for it. He could also feel Eric's presence. Often, when faced with challenges, 'the first person I go to is my father's grave … I always speak to him and say what do I do?' For Gerald it was almost as if his achievement was on behalf of Eric, whose progress had been frustrated under the 'old regime'.[12]

He was not intimidated by the job. 'It's something I like doing,' he said. Management was not new to him and he had always been a hands-on person. He had nearly two decades of involvement with Firestone and Sanlam in the corporate world. He had also started his own business and was establishing himself in it. Moreover, ever since he had played cricket, he had been an organiser. That was the nature of cricket in the townships. 'One person will run a club, drive everything, like Boet Dan and old Mr Ximiya,' who had been like a grandfather to him. At United, Danny Jordaan and Khaya had 'held the club together'. At Spring Rose Gerald had fulfilled that function. He had been a driving force at the club for ten years while they had gone from the lowest division to the premier league in the new united rugby set-up. In cricket, Gerald was often in charge of entertainment. Or he had to get balls. 'I'd go anywhere to ask for bucks. Sometimes it would be the butcher's shop that would be approached. Other times we'd buy balls that were stolen from sports shops in the city.[13]

'I've always been part of it. And all of us shared responsibilities,' he said. At home, although younger than Khaya, he found that both Khaya and his mother 'would phone him first' when a problem needed to be sorted out. All these things had prepared him for this job. Although he would have preferred

Milase and Gerald Majola unveiling a plaque in memory of Khaya Majola, St George's Park, Port Elizabeth, December 2000.

another two or three years of experience as a UCB councillor and national selector, he felt ready for the challenge.[14]

One sensed three important character traits in the new CEO. He had a strong sense of roots, the self-confidence of a life-long cricket disciple, and an innate belief and confidence about an inclusive future for South African cricket.

THE NEW AGENDA

Majola made it clear from the start that he was his own man and would not be trying to imitate Ali Bacher.[15] In fact his very first task was to try to professionalise the somewhat chaotic office Bacher had left behind. There were some multi-million rand contracts struck verbally without the paperwork to verify or explain them. (One of these was to cause Gerald headaches for months.) Staff did not have job descriptions. He started with one-on-ones with all staff and began to restructure the office. Aware of Khaya and Imtiaz

Patel's problems under the previous incumbent, he made a point of giving his directors more power and clear lines of responsibility.

Two years after he assumed the CEO position, the UCB was certified as the first sports organisation in the country run according to the internationally recognised ISO 9000 principles for good corporate governance.[16]

These initiatives were an indication of his goal that, 'We must corporatise the UCB and run it as a business.' It was rapidly becoming clear that South African cricket could not afford a bloated professional structure with around 170 professionals. Virtually all the provinces were in major debt, pointing to the long-term unsustainablity of the current structure. The solution was 'strategic and sustainable business initiatives understood and supported by all our stakeholders'.[17]

His vision was to have a well-run organisation, the top team in the world, a game that was transforming and relevant

Gerald Majola welcoming Steve Waugh and the Australian team to South Africa, 2002.

to the new democratic context in South Africa and an inclusive non-racialism where everyone had a place.

By June 2001, at the annual Transformation Review Conference at Kwa Maritane, a private game lodge, he was settled and ready to spell out his vision and agenda to the 150 key cricket stakeholders present.

Majola received a standing ovation and those present agreed it was the moment that his leadership was announced and endorsed. It was noticeable that while he emphasised ongoing change and the need for redress, he also challenged the UCB to go beyond old, fixed attitudes. He said there were still people 'limiting our future by hanging on to past views and mindsets'. In addition to spreading the game through development, he wanted limited resources to be used on 'centres of excellence'. And while leadership was becoming more representative, people who had a bias for action and delivery were needed at the top. Finally, while

quotas were important, he looked forward to the time when provinces had outgrown the need for them.[18]

Staked out here was essentially a middle-of-the-road position. It was a cricket-orientated, inclusive, flexible approach. 'Our sport has become inclusive and must stay that [way]. There is no place for those discrediting our administrators and players, and sowing division and discontent.' Cricket, moreover, stood for values that were essential for the maintenance of 'the very fabric of our society'. These included integrity and fairness, sophistication and mastery, good manners, discipline and honesty, and personal accountability and focus.[19]

Here was a basic reiteration of the values of the game, passed down to him by his parents and their peers in New Brighton – and indeed the generations before, going back to the 19th century mission-educated pioneers – even if it under emphasised power relations and ideological issues.

The ICC World Cup 2003 in South Africa was the best organised so far, but the team performed poorly, raising questions about players and administrators.

Chapter 37

FACING *the* BOUNCERS

———————————— ◖ ————————————

THIS BOOK IS NOT THE place to offer a comprehensive assessment of the progress of South African cricket under Majola in the dramatic period from 2001 to the ICC World Cup 2003, the first to be held in South Africa and the continent, but predictably the bouncers were soon flying.

The first came in April 2001 during the tour to the Caribbean. Several South African players and the physiotherapist, Craig Smith, smoked dagga at the Jolly Harbour resort after the series-clinching test victory in Antigua. The tour committee imposed a R10 000 fine and gave the players a severe reprimand. The UCB decided not to publicise the matter or take further disciplinary action but the news was leaked to the press, allegedly by one of the culprits' team-mates. Majola released the full details when approached, but the question was raised, why had he not revealed the story earlier, or acted more strictly?[1]

The summer of 2001/02 was expected to be a big one for South African cricket. The much-awaited away and home series against Australia loomed. Expectations were high that South Africa would avenge the famous tie against Australia in the 1999 World Cup, when the Proteas were eliminated at the semi-final stage. The heart-stopping run out muddle at Edgbaston between an incomparably dominant Klusener and Donald still preyed on South African minds. Local optimism was buoyed by the team's string of good performances under new captain, Shaun Pollock, who had taken over from Hansie Cronjé after the sensational 'Hansiegate' match-fixing disclosures of 2000. However, all was not well within the camp. There were strong below-the-surface problems within a team and management described by some as 'paranoid' after the Cronjé affair, and which was uncomfortable with the necessary process of transformation.[2]

The summer kicked off with a visit from the Indian team. South Africa comfortably defeated the perennially poor tourists, but not before an international furore had erupted. During the second test match in Port Elizabeth, match referee Mike Denness took action against six Indian players. The Board of Control in India demanded that Denness be replaced. It said its team would not play in the final test if he remained in charge. This amounted to a challenge to ICC authority and highlighted long-simmering differences between 'white' ICC members and Jagmohan Dalmiya who was increasingly flexing the muscles of his billion-strong cricket-mad country within the international body. The UCB agreed to the Indian request to remove Denness. The outcome was that the ICC downgraded the match to unofficial status. Denness's removal made some sense in terms of UCB contractual obligations and global cricket dynamics, but it infuriated the establishment and media. Majola called a press conference at which Denness was supposed to explain, but he was prevented by ICC rules from saying anything. The scene more or less descended into farce, contributing to a sense of chaos and administrative bungling.[3]

Once in Australia, the underlying tensions and divisions in South African cricket burst into the open. After defeat in the first test in Adelaide, Patrick Compton and others in the media blamed Makhaya Ntini's inclusion and the broader transformation agenda for South Africa's woes.[4] Journalists were being fed confidential information from inside the camp, promoting the image of an interfering and unknowledgeable new black cricket leadership. A complete breakdown in relationship between coach and selection convenor made the situation worse.[5]

297

Matters came to a head during the third test in Sydney. UCB president Percy Sonn vetoed the exclusion of Justin Ontong from the side and overturned a decision by the tour selectors to include Jacques Rudolph. All hell broke loose and the ensuing public spat damaged the reputation of South African cricket.[6] The CEO hastened to Australia and the press reported that, 'His arrival coincided with a lift in morale and an improvement in communication … '[7] But the damage could have been avoided and the question was asked why Majola's office had been closed over Christmas, and why the whole issue had not been better managed in the first place.

The cracks opened further under the pressure of a test series whitewash by a great Australian team. Gerald Majola faced two new, but related crises. Daryll Cullinan, brought in to strengthen the batting in the home leg of the series, held a gun to Majola's head: he would refuse to play unless he was given a long-term contract. Majola refused to bow to what he regarded as blackmail. Cullinan withdrew at the last moment. Debate raged, but the volatile Cullinan came out of the issue with his image tarnished and eventually apologised.[8]

Then came a fork of lightning from within UCB leadership ranks. Gauteng cricket president and boyhood neighbour of the Majolas in Port Elizabeth, Mtutuzeli Nyoka, added to the pressure when he called Majola's claim that transformation was going well 'buffoonery'. His fellow provincial presidents issued a statement strongly disassociating themselves from his views and actions. They expressed their full confidence in Majola and the position he had articulated. Nyoka resigned all his UCB positions.[9]

To make matters worse, Eastern Province cricket was being torn apart by an impasse over transformation and lines of authority. The dispute showed a worrying split along racial lines. The UCB intervened in an attempt to stabilise the situation. It instructed its provincial affiliate to meet ten conditions or face radical intervention. Long-standing president Flip Potgieter resigned in an attempt to bring calm, but the impasse continued. With the World Cup looming and a semi-final scheduled for St George's Park, the UCB decided to step in. Majola was instructed by council to put Eastern Province cricket under judicial management. The UCB made application to the High Court and Raymond Uren and Kevin Helm were appointed as temporary administrators, replacing the dysfunctional executive. The messy situation in Majola's home province saw him on opposing sides to family member, Julius Majola, and some other African administrators, and it was compounded by their efforts to get the ANC's provincial and national leadership involved.[10]

Percy Sonn, president of the UCB, 2000-2003.

The end of the season came with a general sense of crisis hanging over South African cricket. Gerald Majola and the UCB leadership acted to stabilise the situation. Majola explained that after the Australian series, 'It was a state of emergency, and we had to move fast … It was not a time to pussyfoot around the issues. The performance of the national team is paramount to all we do.'[11] Several steps were taken in an attempt to calm the situation.

The first was to get rid of both the coach and the convenor of selectors. The second was to set up a National Cricket Committee of specialists, including former players who had been among the main critics, whose task was to advise council on playing affairs. A new convenor and coach were appointed and this new team started the rebuilding process with an emphasis on professionalism and broad consultation. Furthermore, Majola brought in a team of communication experts to help the UCB develop a consistent strategy. The cricket media, which had in many ways overreached itself in criticising the UCB during the summer, leading to a political backlash among black South Africans, reacted well to these initiatives.[12]

The next step for Majola was to tackle the deeper structural issues facing cricket. He pushed for two changes here. Firstly, a change in emphasis regarding transformation. Secondly, the restructuring of the administration of cricket to ensure financial sustainability and a strength-versus-strength system in a smaller domestic competition. He picked up resistance on both counts.

While the UCB council agreed to restructure into a professional and amateur wing, the smaller provincial affiliates were not prepared to see themselves downscaled into secondary 'amateur' cricket structures. The unsustainability of having eleven professional teams, with the associated high costs, was recognised but a decision on the matter was deferred until after the World Cup in 2003.[13]

More controversial was Majola's position on transformation and, in particular, the quota system. By July 2002 the three-year plan for transformation adopted in 1999 had run its course. A strategy for the next phase was needed. With the broad three-year targets having been met, Majola pushed for the more politicised external 'monitoring' process to be superseded by one more operationally driven and managed from within by the UCB. He argued that a new progressive leadership had been created in the UCB and that the CEO and the organisation rather than an independent TMC should now drive the process. Moreover, the emotive issue of quotas should be dropped and the UCB should instead quietly regulate itself. While there were mixed feelings in the TMC and PMCs and among ex-Board cricketers, both the TMC and the annual UCB transformation review conference held in Kievietskroon near Pretoria in July 2002 endorsed the plans.[14] It was felt that the new CEO needed to be given the reins to impress his style and lead effectively.

However, while Majola and the UCB were confidently plotting new paths in the new post-democracy environments, they underestimated the impact the Kievietskroon 'quotas' decision would have. Cricket was running ahead of broader trends and thinking. The government, under pressure to deliver in practical terms to a constituency which if anything had grown more marginalised in employment terms since 1994, was emphasising redress and equity in the broader terrain. While this was also the goal of the UCB, using a more understated approach, it was out of kilter with the broader discourse. The Minister of Sport, stung by the fact that the UCB had not consulted him (although he had been invited to the conference), went on the attack saying this was a betrayal of the broad national transformation project. The erroneous impression was created that the UCB believed that transformation was something of the past. The issue was politicised in a way that painted cricket into a corner. While the UCB policy was, in fact, that cricket and societal transformation needed to be on-going and would take generations to accomplish, the populist response was to pigeon-hole it as a white-controlled game that was going against key national strategies.[15]

The Minister set up a commission of enquiry to look into the affairs of cricket. The UCB co-operated with the commission, although it suspected that the Commission was little more than a big stick to put the organisation in its place. The outcome was negative for both sides. The commission criticised the UCB although it did acknowledge in the small print that cricket had made great progress with transformation.[16] A vengeful UCB president Percy Sonn in turn made public UCB minutes of discussions with the Minister in which he was reported to have said that he 'didn't give a shit' about Jacques Kallis and other white players.[17]

Both the Minister and the UCB ended up with egg on their faces from this very public spat.[18] When the 2002/03 season started, passions were still high. But with the World Cup looming, the country closed ranks and started preparing for the big event.

The ICC World Cup 2003 was a magnificent all-round success for the country. It was acknowledged to have been the biggest and best so far. ICC president, Malcolm Gray, declared, 'The world has been watching and, Southern Africa, you have delivered.'[19]

From the spectacular opening ceremony at Newlands through to the final 43 days later, South Africa was marketed to billions abroad. The arrangements, it was agreed, had gone off smoothly. None of the political dramas over Zimbabwe, security issues at a time of heightened sensitivity preceding the US-led invasion of Iraq, or the small matter of the host nation being eliminated before the Super Six stage could detract from this overall success.[20]

Nevertheless, the early exit of the hosts was not what the UCB needed. One of Gerald Majola's goals was to make South Africa number one and he had said he wanted to be judged on his performance. Victory would have brought unprecedented unity and confidence and put to bed many of the pre-World Cup strains. But now the questions would re-emerge. The critics popped out of the woodwork again. Pat Symcox, given his chance to play a role as a selector and member of the National Cricket Committee, resigned, failing either to share responsibility or to behave professionally in committee.[21] In his post-mortem, the influential journalist Peter Robinson, no friend of transformation, pointed the finger at Majola and others at the top.[22]

Percy Sonn, in many ways highly competent, had neutralised himself by once too often over-imbibing and being egotistical and earthily impolitic. The press reported that he was so intoxicated at one game that 'he almost fell out of his trousers'. At the final ceremony, he was humiliatingly booed at a packed Wanderers. He deserved censure, but this was a gesture that said as much about old white mentalities in sport as his reported social excesses.[23] It was Ellis Park rugby stadium in the early 1990s all over again, *sans* the singing of the old anthem and the waving of the old flag.

The captain and coach, inescapably, had to take responsibility for calculating for a tie rather than the one run more needed for victory against Sri Lanka. Shaun Pollock was forced to step down in favour of a youthful Graeme Smith.[24]

Majola was quoted as saying, 'I don't think we've failed. We're all disappointed, but we won't make excuses. It was third time unlucky. The World Cup is the one event that seems to keep evading us.'[25] 'Really?' asked Robinson. If the CEO suggested the World Cup was not a failure, then 'how does the UCB measure failure?' He said there was a credibility gap between 'those who administer South African cricket and those who play it'. He criticised Majola for 'ill considered' and 'unnecessary' judgements. He commented, 'If Majola is to keep his job, he needs to consider seriously who has his ear.' Finally, his performance as CEO needed to be examined along with the captain and coach.[26]

Majola was not entirely unjustified in calling it 'third time unlucky'. Cruelly, the outcome for South Africa came down, yet again, to one ball, for the third World Cup out of four. But South Africa could not blame anyone but themselves for not progressing further. As Frank Duckworth, a member of the Royal Statistical Society, and Tony Lewis from the University of the West of England became the subject of serious conversation in shebeens and townships, Majola had to contemplate the questions that would come bouncing back again after the World Cup, rather than being able to consolidate his authority on the back of a historic home victory

An SABC/Markinor poll found that 57 percent of urban residents expected South Africa to win, against only 18 percent who believed the overwhelming favourites Australia would take the trophy.[27] The expectation of victory was always too high. Now there was a chance again for the doubters to speak: too little transformation, too much transformation, not professional and private sector orientated enough, too much focus on the corporates and not enough on the 'little person', and so on.

Still, the absence of general hysteria following the early exit in the World Cup was a good sign that South Africans were maturing, and it is undeniable that great progress has been made. As Graeme Pollock pointed out, South Africa was still after all the official world number one team in test cricket, and number two in one-day cricket.[28]

While content to take responsibility for the playing and administrative shortcomings during the World Cup, Majola was in no mood to submit meekly to some of the criticism. The *Financial Mail* came out blaming management weaknesses and cricket's new black leadership. It said, 'This generation of cricket's off-field leaders have done little to build on the legacy they inherited from the past decade and, in some ways, have undermined it.'[29] This was a clear reference to the post-Bacher era. Majola responded with uncharacteristic directness. He said the *Financial Mail's* position was that South Africa's failure 'on and off the field' was due to transformation and the 'new personnel at the helm of cricket', but:

> The legacy of the past decade is something the UCB would prefer not to replicate — 'Hansiegate', a shameful lack of black participation at administrative and playing levels, implicit and explicit racism in a divided sport, unsatisfactory financial and management systems, lack of transparency at all levels of administration, and unsustainable and inconsistent flow of quality players into the national and provincial set-up. What a proud legacy!
>
> South African cricket stepped into the international limelight after decades of isolation, with 11 white knights leading the charge with gung-ho and plenty of team effort to make up for their lack of super stars. But the reality of representing a transformed society soon set in, and the need for wider racial representivity brought cracks to the espirit de corp.[30]

Political columnist Max du Preez was one of the few who provided a supporting argument. According to him, the problem lay more within the heads of white cricketers than with cricket's new black leadership. The black players had been the stars in the World Cup team. On the other hand, the white players, previously imperiously confident about their skills and knowledge, were now reflecting the anxieties and uncertainties of a broader white population in a time of rapid loss of power. They had lost confidence and were uncertain, two of the greatest handicaps in top level sport.[31]

Majola further countered the *Financial Mail's* attack by pointing to the changing face of South African cricket and some of the progress made since Dr Bacher's departure in January 2001. He said that the UCB's quest for professionalism and sustainability based on transformation had been nothing short of remarkable:

- A three-year strategic business plan in place, when before there was none. Cricket has a collective vision in place, rather than a set of individual ambitions.
- An honest and transparent partnership between the CEO's office and the General Council has been established, ensuring good corporate governance and accountability.

Nelson Mandela shaking hands with Jonty Rhodes during the ICC World Cup 2003.
Shaun Pollock, who lost the captaincy soon afterwards, and Gerald Majola look on.

- *Proper systems have been established that are backed by policy and doc-umented procedures. These systems will soon enjoy ISO 9 000 accreditation – a first for South African sport.*
- *A zero-based budgeting approach has been implemented in order to get a proper handle on finances, and ensure the effective allocation of resources in the interest of cricket development.*
- *A participative management approach has been implemented and there has been a marked improvement in employees' sense of ownership, com-mitment and empowerment.*
- *Advisory committees have been installed to provide input on technical and management issues, such as coaching, selection and marketing.[32]*

Majola concluded by pointing out that the current UCB leadership had put South African cricket on 'a strong foundation that allows it to meet the demands of modern professional sport, whilst adhering to the principles of playing and developing the game in a transforming society'. The basis for future success was 'transformation coupled with sustainability'.

The challenges for South African cricket are daunting, but Gerald Majola is confident he can succeed. As a schoolboy from New Brighton, his favourite saying on racial issues after being expelled from Kwazakhele High during the upris-ings of 1976 was, 'I like black tea with sugar but no milk.'[33] Today he is a mature cricket leader with a universal vision and he is comfortable at the many levels on which he has to operate. His goals have remained consistent. To make South Africa number one with the new young team for the new era. To grow the game in the black communities. To run cricket professionally and to bring the people of South Africa together through the game.

In order to succeed he will have to show he can manage and balance complexity and contradiction.

And, as he seeks to lead cricket into the future, Majola will continue to draw on the century of cricket tradition, the life experiences of 40 years in New Brighton and the support of a family confident about what is right and what is wrong.

sa
Sports illustrated

Shooting Tiger down
He ain't **no legend** yet!

Sport's most hated woman
The *real* **Tonya Harding** story

Endangered species
Spotted a **mean tighthead** lately?

Your babe or the box?
How to press the right buttons

Ntini & Ngam

From **goats** to the **Gabba!**

Triathlete Dominique ...
want to change her tyre? ▶

WIN a R200 000 Isuzu 4x4

The times have changed!

302

Chapter 38

THE GAINS *of* UNITY

———————————— ● ————————————

CRICKET IN AFRICAN COMMUNITIES was on its way to extinction by the end of the apartheid era. The numbers were as low as they had ever been. There were neither the schools to be nurseries for the future, nor the facilities and resources to sustain the game in comfortable ways. Nor was the climate of poverty and seething anger in the townships conducive for it to become an aspect of everyday life. Cricket was virtually disconnected from its roots. Conditions were not conducive to growth. It was no longer an organic part of local and popular culture.

Africans had virtually no profile and had more or less disappeared off the radar screen of establishment cricket. After the old racial South African African Cricket Board (SAACB) was swallowed up by the 'mixed' South African Cricket Union (SACU) as part of the 'normal cricket' agreement in 1977, no African official was on the new SACU executive. There were only two other black faces, Rashid Varachia (president) and Frank Brache, brother-in-law of Basil D'Oliveira. No African club played in a provincial first league. In the 14 years after the formal end of the colour bar, only Rodney Malamba, son of the legendary Ben, played A Section cricket for Natal under SACU. The only other signs of life were the still-segregated Passmore Schools Cricket Week and the Langa Cricket Club in Cape Town patronised by John Passmore, which also took to hockey thanks to the efforts of Bob Woolmer.[1]

The situation was not that much better in the ranks of the non-racial South African Cricket Board (SACB). Africans did not have a great numerical presence. Only nine of the approximately 450 cricketers who played first-class cricket under the board between 1971 and 1991 were African. When the SACB held its last council meeting in 1991, three out of 25 administrators attending were Africans.

Nevertheless, the 'struggle' location and goals of the SACB ensured that Africans were people with a 'voice' rather than convenient luggage bearers. They were able to be assertive and have high profiles. Khaya Majola's appointment as captain of the national team and his 1988 SACOS Sportsperson of the Year award were indications of this.

In any case, as the formation of the National Sports Congress in the late 1980s demonstrated, Africans – drawing on the strength of the ANC and Mass Democratic Movement which were in the vanguard of the burgeoning national movement for freedom – started assuming the leadership roles that history would demand of them. The African sportspeople of the Eastern Cape became a core part of the non-racial sports project and helped give it content and direction.

AFRICAN SPORT REVIVED 'UPON THE ARRIVAL OF ENLIGHTENMENT'

Political democracy and the relative normalisation of the sporting environment that followed dramatically increased the opportunities for African sportspeople in South Africa, and indeed all South African sportspeople.

Today opportunities exist that were unheard of before. Sixty thousand children are introduced to the game each year through the Bakers mini-cricket programme.[2] During the World Cup, PPC cement built its one thousandth concrete pitch in poor communities since 1995.[3] The World Cup Legacy project led to an investment of R25 million in 50 more stadiums in townships around the country. Whereas in the 1960s there were fewer than 20 African schools catering for cricket, today the MTN schools project supports 223 schools in its efforts 'to create new cricket schools or centres of excellence in the townships'. Today the UCB also organises no fewer than 11 national (mainly youth) tournaments each year.[4]

In order to promote transformation and redress continuing inequalities, the UCB in May 1999 set targets of 50/50 representivity in all teams below the elite first-class and national levels within three years. Gerald Majola's 'Transformation Report' for the 2002/03 season summarised the gains since then. 1 089 black players out of a total of 2 106 participated in the various UCB tournaments in that season, including under-13 to under-19 and the Women and Country District Weeks. This amounted to 52 percent black players, and Africans constituted 40 percent of the total. Blacks also represented 70 percent of management, with black Africans comprising 38 percent. Black umpires were in the majority (53 percent) and a record number of 37 African umpires participated.[5]

The figures for the under-19 week, now named after Khaya Majola, were 91 black players out of 178, or 51 percent of the total. In December 1999, Thami Tsolekile became the first African captain of the Coca Cola South African Schools XI. When South Africa reached the under-19 World Cup finals in New Zealand in 2002, the team had a black captain, Hashim Amla, and eight out of the 11 members of the team were black.[6]

The transformation process since 1999 has also shattered the glass ceilings that previously existed at the elite first-class level. The old minimum number of one black player per team was changed in May 1999 to two, three and four for each of the succeeding seasons. From a number that could be counted on one hand in 1991, the total of black first-class cricketers spiralled from 26 out of 132 in 1998/99 to 39 out of 142 in 1999/2000 to 51 out of 157 in 2000/01 to 66 in 2001/02 and 86 out of 212 in the 2002/03 season.[7]

The number of African cricketers representing their provinces had grown to 15 by the 2000/01 season. Gauteng was the province which showed the most progress. Six players got a chance, namely Walter Masimula, Geoffrey Toyana, Johnson Mafa, Sonnyboy Letshela, Solly Ndima and Nicholas Mataboge.[8]

Going hand-in-hand with the increase in numbers has been a change in the roles of and attitudes towards black first-class players. Earlier African players were used as fillers, coming in at the tail even when picked as batsmen. An infamous statement by one top provincial coach to another

regarding quotas – 'If I play my two garden boys, you must play yours'[9] – summed up the initial scepticism that greeted the new entrants. Now there is a pool of good black (including African) players and confidence that they fully deserved their places. In January 2002 the *Sunday Times* carried an uncharacteristically flattering review of the transformation 'success story' at provincial level. It pointed out that at that stage of the season no fewer than seven of the top 12 bowlers in the Standard Bank Cup limited-overs competition were black. In the Super Sport four-day series, three of the 13 batsmen averaging over 50 were black, with 11 others sitting on the respectable average of 30 or over. The newspaper concluded, 'What the numbers prove is what advocates of transformation have always argued, that people of talent from disadvantaged backgrounds – not that all players of colour come from such backgrounds – need only opportunities.'[10]

Halfway through the season black players were topping the first-class tables in both batting and bowling. Herschelle Gibbs averaged 44.33 and Ashwell Prince and Ahmed Amla also came in above 40. Henry Williams with 42 wickets was leading the bowling averages and Robin Petersen, Garnett Kruger, Makhaya Ntini and Paul Adams all claimed more than 20 wickets.[11] Behind the wicket, Thami Tsolekile set a new Standard Bank Cup record of eight stumpings.

The UCB's statistics for 2002/03 confirmed the progress at the top levels. In the one-day and three-day UCB Bowl competitions, the second tier of provincial cricket, 119 (or 54 percent) of the 219 players were black. In the senior Standard Bank Cup and the Super Sport Series, the figures were 86 and 84 out of 212 respectively.[12] This amounted to over 40 percent of the total compared to the 15 percent four seasons before. The growing base was also demonstrated by the six black players who regularly played for the South African A team during the season. The South African team that won the Africa Cup tournament held in Lusaka in 2002 had eight black representatives.[13] In the final against Botswana, Monde Zondeki took five wickets for five runs.

One of the highlights of the season was the innings of 106 runs by Enoch Nkwe of the Soweto Cricket Club in his debut for Gauteng against Easterns, the first first-class century by an African player in the UCB competitions.[14] (The only previous official first-class century by an African player was Gerald Majola's 117 for the EPCA in the 1986/87 season.)

At the top national level, five black players, including two Africans, were selected for the 2003 World Cup team, whereas only one black player had played in the previous

ABOVE LEFT *Victor Mpitsang.* ABOVE CENTRE *Mfuneko Ngam.* ABOVE RIGHT *Monde Zondeki.*

three World Cups. He was Omar Henry, current national selection convenor, who made his test and World Cup debut in 1992 aged 40. Between 1991 and the end of the 1994/95 season, Henry was the only black player out of the total of 34 selected for South Africa. Between that season and 2000/01, nine out of the 33 caps were black. They included Makhaya Ntini, who made his debut in the 1997/98 season, followed by Victor Mpitsang, who toured New Zealand in 1998/99, and Mfuneko Ngam who played against New Zealand and Sri Lanka in 2000/01 before being injured. In the 2001/02 season seven black players — Gibbs, Ntini, Ontong, Langeveldt, Telemachus, Adams and Prince — played for the test and one-day teams, heralding a new level of involvement for black players at the highest level. Among the host of young black players knocking at the door of the senior team are batsmen Lungile 'Loots' Bosman of Griqualand West and wicketkeeper and hockey international,

Thami Tsolekile of Western Province, both of whom have put in good performances for the South African A team.

In February 2003, Makhaya Ntini broke into the top ten of the PriceWaterhouseCoopers world rankings for the first time. He was also the top South African wicket-taker in the World Cup with ten wickets at 17.60 and became only the ninth South African to reach 100 test wickets against Bangladesh soon afterwards.[15]

Ten years after cricket unity and political democracy which brought to an end more than a century of division and discrimination, the scenario in South African cricket has changed dramatically.

The formerly excluded black cricketers have made great progress both on and off the playing fields. Part of the success achieved in opening up the game is owed to the existence of an already established tradition of cricket in the black communities of the Eastern and Western Cape.

ABOVE *The South African players celebrate the dismissal of an English batsman in the 2000 CricInfo Women's Cricekt World Cup match played at BIL Oval, Lincoln, New Zealand. South Africa defeated England by five wickets.*
BELOW *In the same match, Sarah Collyer of England in action as Daleen Terblanche of South Africa watches.*

As Peter Roebuck, writing in *The Cricketer* in 1998 commented, it is only in parts of the country 'that the game had to be introduced rather than merely revived upon the arrival of enlightenment'.[16]

No one can gainsay the massive progress that has been made in a relatively short time. Black players are reasonably represented at every level for the first time, and there are also, incidentally, more white first-class players now than ten years ago, and cricketers are earning more money than ever before.[17]

South Africa is part of the global cricket community for the first time. By the end of the 2002/03 season, it had played exactly 100 test matches and 283 one-day internationals and participated in four World Cups in the 12 years since admittance to the ICC in 1991. (Compare this with the 172 tests and no one-day internationals played by the whites-only Springboks in the 102 years between 1889 and 1990.)[18]

Cricket has become a significant industry. The UCB's income in 2002 was R196 million[19] and the World Cup was budgeted to bring in an income of R400 million. Gerald Majola claims amongst his successes a recently negotiated TV deal worth $60 million for TV broadcast rights in Asia.[20]

On the broader sporting front, South Africa now participates in the Olympics, World Championships, Commonwealth Games and other top competitions. In 1996, Josiah Thugwane won gold in the marathon, the most symbolic Olympic race of all, showing how those who were excluded before are wasting no time in gaining the centre stage. South Africa won the Rugby World Cup in 1995 and the Africa Cup of Nations in soccer the following year. National captain, Lucas Radebe, Benni McCarthy and other footballers playing abroad are worth tens of millions of rand. Multiple world boxing champion Baby Jake Matlala is admired across the old divides as a national icon. Times have changed.

WOMEN BREAKING NEW GROUND

As this book has shown, women have been an integral part of the game since the formation of the very first clubs and inter-town contests in the 1880s. Although women have been pigeon-holed into gender roles, they have never been completely contained by Victorian and African patriarchal mindsets, as the 1950s photograph of African women playing touch rugby with men at St George's Strand in revealing costumes demonstrates (see Chapter 13).

In the past decade, women have started to make their mark in cricket. Kedi Tshoma, vice-president of the Soweto Cricket Club, was one of the pioneers in the development programme in the Gauteng townships. She was the most visible face of a legion of women coaches who formed the backbone of the programme. Her work was recognised when she received a President's Award for Sport in 2002.

Today more than 9 000 women from 1 109 schools and 269 clubs play cricket in South Africa.[21]

The UCB recognises women cricketers as part of the high priority 'targeted groups' earmarked for 'accelerated advancement because of historical imbalances', together with black African and disabled cricketers.[22]

According to the UCB, 'Women's cricket is being systematically revived in South Africa ... after a long period of being dormant.' Girls today participate actively on a large scale in mixed teams in the Baker's mini-cricket programme. The sport is also becoming increasingly popular in girls' schools. Tara Weinburg, who at the age of 15 has played for Western Province under-19, is currently engaged in a battle with the posh Westerford School in Cape Town to allow her to play in the school teams with boys. The untenable position of the school is allegedly that if she plays she will be denying a boy the opportunity to play. The matter may end up in the Constitutional Court.[23] In KwaZulu-Natal, which in many ways leads the way in breaking old moulds, Johmari Logtenberg became the first girl to play for a boys' provincial team. She competed in the under-13 primary schools tournament in East London in 2001/02 and was later made captain.[24] Six of her team-mates were black children. In the 2002 under-19 national girls cricket tournament, 61 black players participated. The majority were Africans.[25]

The South African Women's Cricket Association was established in 1996, replacing the dormant whites-only South Africa and Rhodesia Women's Cricket Association (formed in 1952). After a pilot tournament involving four of the five founding provinces, a formal inter-provincial tournament was started in the 1996/97 season, followed by a similar under-19 competition. SAWCA affiliated via the United Cricket Board to the International Women's Cricket Council (IWCC), and started competing internationally.[26]

In 1997 the first women's national side after democracy was selected to tour Britain and Ireland. Later that year South Africa reached the quarter finals of the World Cup played in India. In the 2001 World Cup in New Zealand, South Africa reached the semi-finals. South Africa is now ranked number three in the world, and has been awarded the 2005 Women's World Cup, giving women's cricket a major boost.[27]

An African batsman, Nolubabalo Ndzundzu from Border has made the national side, paving the way for the future.[28]

Women are moving into key positions in cricket. Elise Lombard is the CEO of the Northerns Cricket Union. Insiders have described her as probably the best provincial CEO in the country. Nomsa Chabeli and Bangu Masisi were the marketing and public relations directors for the well-organised World Cup 2003, impressing with their professionalism. Thandi Orleyn is on the executive of the Gauteng Cricket Union. The daughter of a former team-mate of Eric Majola, she is another example of cricketers from the Eastern Cape steeped in the game. Nomonde Majola, only daughter of Milase and Eric, is herself the teacher in charge of sport ('not netball') at Seyisi Primary School in New Brighton, right next door to the Woolfson Stadium.[29]

More than 50 percent of South African television viewers who follow cricket are women. With local trends likely to follow the United States' model of equity in state funding for sport, which turned women's football in the US into an instant international brand, the UCB needs to do more to promote the women's game. In its efforts to ensure the survival of club cricket, Western Province, for example, intends creating local cricket growth points whereby clubs will be rewarded financially and otherwise for an integrated approach, which includes youth and women's sections, thereby attempting to restore 'family' involvement and interest in cricket.[30]

In 2002, the ICC and the women's IWCC decided to amalgamate, bringing men and women cricketers under one global co-ordinating body. This will be seen in future as having been an important step forward, although currently it means very little in practice given the invisibility of women cricketers, the pervasive male 'rugger bugger' culture of cricket and the huge disparities that exist worldwide in terms of socio-economic indicators between the sexes.

During a keynote speech on diversity at a World Cup banquet in Johannesburg, the great West Indian cricketer and president of the West Indies Cricket Board, Wes Hall, warned cricket to revisit its patriarchal values and old ways. He said that out of 1 100 graduates per annum in Barbados, 800 were women. In his negotiations with companies the board was trying to involve in cricket, he found that women directors were increasingly responsible for business decisions relating to cricket.[31] Wes Hall's enthusiasm is still unusual among those in the upper echelons of the game, but it must have helped to get people thinking. Patriarchal attitudes also still dominate in the UCB with regard to women's cricket, but Max Jordaan, UCB director of amateur cricket, is a champion for the cause.

Women will play an increasing role in cricket in future because it makes financial, and common, sense.

NEW LEADERSHIPS IN SPORT

In the short time of one decade, the foundations for a new sporting future in South Africa have been laid. The Eastern Cape, soaked in a century of sporting tradition, is playing a leading role in the sporting renewal underway.

Eastern Cape administrators like Makhenkhesi Stofile, Silas Nkanunu, Dan Qeqe, Gideon Sam, Mthobi Tyamzashe and Mluleki George were in the forefront as South Africa moved from the old era of apartheid and mass struggles to the single framework of unity and open political activity.

The sports leadership of the 'New South Africa' after 1994 came largely from the Eastern Cape. Steve Tshwete from Peelton and Ngconde Balfour from Ntselamanzi became the first two Ministers of Sport. Mluleki George headed the powerful National Sports Congress (NSC), later National Olympic and Sports Congress (NOSC). Silas Nkanunu became president of the unified South African Rugby Football Union (SARFU), following Danie Craven, Ebrahim Patel and the blunt Louis Luyt, who indicted Nelson Mandela before the Constitutional Court, thus harming the sport and dissipating the feel-good effects of the World Cup. Mveleli Ncula, who attended Healdtown and Lovedale, became CEO of SARFU. Danny Jordaan, Khaya Majola's bosom friend and team-mate for United and, sometimes, Eastern Province, became CEO of the South African Football Association (SAFA) and joint head of the South African bid for the FIFA World Cup 2006. Mthobi Tyamzashe chairs the South African board of boxing. Gideon Sam became president of swimming, manager of the rugby Springboks and chairman of the South African Sports Commission. Mvuso Mbebe, currently in charge of sports programmes on the national broadcaster, SABC TV, belongs to a younger generation, but has also made a significant impact. A whole cadre of second level leaders like Zola Dunywa, Greg Fredericks, Allister Coetzee, Erroll Heyns, Solomon Pango, Max Jordaan and Songezo Nayo flowed into important support positions. Detractors, lacking historical insight, claimed that a 'Xhosa nostra' was in charge of South African sport.[32]

The far-reaching changes that have occurred are nowhere more clearly reflected than in the new leadership of South African cricket. In 2003, the president and the CEO were black. So were four out of the eight members of the executive committee, 11 out of 18 members of council (including six Africans), six out of nine provincial presidents, three out of five selectors and well over half the UCB office staff.[33]

TOP *Nozuko Masiba, Western Province girls under-19 captain, with WPCA vice-president, Sadick Emeran, Paul Adams and USSASA cricket president, Ghoosain Abrahams, 2003.* CENTRE *Johmari Logtenberg captained the previously boys-only Natal under-13 team in 2002.* BOTTOM LEFT *Nolubabalo Ndzundzu was selected for South Africa in the Women's World Cup in New Zealand in 2000.* BOTTOM RIGHT *Thami Tsolekile, double South African hockey and cricket international is among those who head a list of test aspirants. Here he is pictured with Paul Adams (front) and H.D. Ackerman (back).*

Black people are also now involved in cricket in ways that were inconceivable before. For example, Ray Mali only recently became the first provincial president, Thabo Moseki the first provincial CEO, Wilson Ngobese the grounds curator at Kingsmead (rather than the traditional barefoot assistant) and Thandi Orleyn is a woman on a provincial executive committee.

The old non-racial South African Cricket Board leadership, together with a new generation of African administrators, have established a new hegemony in South African cricket and are effectively leading the game today.

Many of the new generation cricket administrators come from Port Elizabeth and the Eastern Cape. Ray Mali, from Fort Beaufort, who played for the club of the same name in Port Elizabeth in the days of Eric Majola, is the most senior African official apart from Majola. He is favoured by many to become the first African president of the United Cricket Board. Involved with cricket for more than 50 years, he worked the scoreboard at St George's Park as a child. His father, a good cricketer himself, built a net in his yard at Korsten, where the children of the African and coloured neighbours came to test their skills.[34]

Several members of the United Club in Port Elizabeth in the time of the Majola brothers have made it into the national administration ranks besides them. The late Sydney Mgengo became a member of the Western Province Cricket Association Executive; Douglas Maku is a national selector and served on the UCB executive committee; Mtutuzeli Nyoka became first African president of Gauteng cricket, also serving on the UCB executive; Max Jordaan took over as director of amateur cricket at the UCB from Khaya Majola; Phaki Ximiya has risen to the Border executive committee and the national schools selection panel. Among those who remained in Port Elizabeth, Julius Majola and Sidima Mooi have served on various Eastern Province cricket structures.

Other prominent cricket personalities with Eastern Cape links include national selector Haroon Lorgat, and UCB council member Peter Bacela from King Williams Town, who played in the national team in 1975. Bacela qualified as a teacher at Healdtown before working for the South African Broadcasting Corporation for 30 years. Western Province cricket administrator and one-time UCB executive committee member Solomon Makosana is Cape Town born and bred, but he learned the game from migrant workers in the Strand and later studied at Healdtown.[35]

Gabriel 'Oupa' Nkagisang, manager of cricket and hockey at Potchefstroom University, Reuben Tseladimitlwa, president

of the Soweto Cricket Club, and Tim Khumalo from Bloemfontein are current UCB council members who reflect the emergence of cricket leaders from outside the traditional Eastern Cape area.

Khumalo, who is the Free State government's fleet manager, has had a fascinating journey into cricket. He was born in Springs on the East Rand, where his father was a nurse on the gold mines. His uncle Judas Ndlovu, predictably nicknamed 'Iscariot', played for the national team in the 1950s and was in the combined SA Haque team that beat a powerful white Transvaal Invitation side in 1961. Tim's family played soccer, cricket and rugby, and the tradition was continued when Mr Khumalo senior was transferred to Welkom in the Free State. Every year the mine would deduct 50 cents from staff salaries to buy the children a Christmas gift. The parents were asked for suggestions. Tim remembers that his present ideas were always a bat or a racquet or some other piece of sports equipment.[36] He recalls that while the Nguni-speakers played cricket, football was the only game for the Sotho miners. His heroes were mine-based athletes like Humphrey 'Ghost' Khozi, sprinter Motsapi Moorosi, William 'Rex' Mogoregi and the cyclist Sam Ramabodu.

After school, Tim Khumalo qualified as a teacher at Thaba Nchu and returned to Welkom to teach. But by then the mines had made the cricket clubs for miners only. His brother who worked on the mines 'pursued his career', but Tim had to give up the game because there were no leagues or facilities outside of the mines. During the Black Consciousness period of the 1970s he became involved in the political struggle, joining the Azanian People's Organisation (AZAPO) along with Mosiuoa Lekota, nicknamed 'Terror' because of his skills as a football striker. After teaching in Welkom for 12 years, Khumalo lost his job and was 'in and out of jail' over the next decade. After the normalisation of politics in the 1990s he became prominent in the ANC, got a government position and returned to cricket via administration.[37]

Those who were invisible before are now in the forefront. They are taking centre stage in a way the old players and administrators would scarcely have believed possible in South Africa.

And as this happens, cricket, in intent if not already in practice, is becoming a game for all, as envisaged by the UCB. The latest opinion surveys have confirmed it is now the second most popular sport after soccer in South Africa, and the only one 'enjoyed equally by men and women'.[38]

New leaderships. United Cricket Board of South Africa General Council 2002/03. (Back row, left to right) Brandon Foot, Logan Naidoo,
Oupa Ngakisang, Cassim Suleman, Henry Paulse, Peter Bacela, Tim Khumalo, Ahmed Jinnah, Mohamed Jajbhay, Arnold Block.
(Front row) Charlie Robinson, Gerald Majola, Robbie Kurz, Percy Sonn (president), John Blair, Ray Mali.

Reuben Tselamiditlwa (right), president of the Soweto Cricket Club, pictured next to the
Thames in London with Vukile Majola during the club's mid-1990s tour to Britain.

A photo essay on a Macal' eGusha (Sides of a Sheep) tournament by one of South Africa's top social documentary photographers, Mike Hutchins, 2002.

Chapter 39

LIKE CRICKET PLAYED *in* HEAVEN

———————————◗———————————

THE *AMACALA EGUSHA* (Sides of a Sheep) tournaments held every year at Christmas time in the Eastern Cape are the prime examples today of the long, distinct, living tradition of African cricket. They originated in the 19th century, and were still healthy in the 1950s, as we saw in Chapter 15. Today, after more than a hundred years, they remain an integral part of the annual Christmas/New Year social life and festivities of certain Eastern Cape communities.

According to Peter Bacela, head of the Border Villages Cricket Association, there are 12 of these village cricket boards in existence in the areas around King Williams Town.[1] They include the Mbeka-Mkupa Board and the Zondeki Cricket Union mentioned earlier in the reports of the 1950s. Samuel Zondeki, the great-grandfather of South Africa's World Cup debutant, Monde Zondeki, started the Zondeki Cricket Union way back in 1939.[2]

Like the other boards, the ZCU consists of six village teams who compete in the local Christmas tournament. The ZCU then picks a composite team to play in a knockout competition against the other unions. In order to encourage the game, the venue for these knockout games changes regularly. No town- or city-based teams are allowed to participate. In addition to the King Williams Town district, there are also boards and tournaments around Alice and Fort Beaufort, the largest and best known being the Ngumbela Tournament at Healdtown.[3]

This unique rural cricket tradition produced Makhaya Ntini, who became the first African player to play for South Africa in official test matches in the 1997/98 season. Ntini was first spotted playing at Mdingi village near King Williams Town, on a bumpy outfield with cows grazing, before the UCB gave him a cricket bursary to attend Dale College with its equally long but different sports tradition.

Ntini is often described as the prime product of the cricket development programme. This is true only to a point. His first memories of the game, he has noted, were 'probably quite early because cricket is not just a "white" game where I live'.[4] His uncle, Lungile Makula, played for the Border African team in the 1960s. Zimasile Mbatani, who became the national captain, and a familiar voice to many as a radio and TV commentator, played with Makula and remembers him as a 'very good cricketer'.[5] Makhaya Ntini is thus as much a product of this 100-year-old cricket tradition as of the development programme. When the hard-working Border development coaches arrived in Mdingi, his life took a new direction and he was sent to Dale College. He still remembers that time, when, aged 14, he first played with '… my ripped T-shirt and the broken takkies that slapped a bit when I ran up'.[6]

The pace bowling sensation Mfuneko Ngam, who so impressed on his debut for South Africa against New Zealand in 2000, but has now been laid low by persistent injuries possibly related to malnourishment as a child, also comes from these rural cricket areas. He grew up in Middledrift, the same area where Eric Majola and the Wide Awake CC members from Port Elizabeth regularly played over Christmas. He remembers that as a ten-year-old, 'We tried to play a bit with sticks at school.' But he only really started playing the game when he went to the city as a teenager for his schooling.[7]

Ntini, Ngam, Zondeki and other current city-based players and stars like Thami Tsolekile, the hockey international, and Western Province and South Africa A team wicketkeeper-batsman, still make the trek back to the rural areas to play in the *Macal' eGusha* tournaments. In an echo of Gordon Qumza's lamentations from the 1950s, Tsolekile was fined by his province in 2000 for missing provincial practices so that he could play in these games. Fresh from initiation school, where he had spent several weeks in the 'bush' with 15 peer group members, Tsolekile explained that he had not wanted to miss the event as Mr Ngumbela was his uncle and he had played in four or five tournaments already.[8]

According to Ntini, 'we play these games ... that last for six days until the 31st, then the trophies are won and the best team is picked'. The trophy is a sheep or goat, maybe a cow. 'It gets roasted and everybody eats together... It's party time, the whole thing. And those pitches can be dangerous,' adds Ngam. They 'just lay a mat on the ground' and play.[9]

The strength of this long tradition of cricket in certain African communities has only been recognised properly in the past few years. This has had two important outcomes. Firstly, it has put paid to the now outdated apartheid-rooted notion that Africans were 'discovered' and introduced to the game in the last 20 years. Secondly, it has persuaded the UCB to focus more resources on development in the traditional cricket-playing areas in future, particularly Border, Eastern Province and the two bastions of cricket in coloured communities, Western Province and Boland. Rather than randomly spreading new investments across the whole country, the UCB has decided on a more focused approach on the areas where a tradition of cricket already exists.[10]

Mr Ngumbela's Fort Beaufort tournament now gets UCB support, and the Border Village Cricket Association has been admitted to the South African Country Districts Week. The aim is that the region becomes a focus for unearthing talent and developing excellence from the traditional cricket-playing communities in the surrounding areas.[11] Among the

World Cup Legacy Projects are an Amacala eGusha Oval at Masingata village near King Williams Town, a Sport School of Excellence at Fort Hare University in Alice, and facilities at Ntselamanzi, Healdtown, Pirie and Middledrift in the old cricket heartland.[12]

Every game and every country has a certain distinguishing romance attached to it, derived from the special way it is played or the special atmosphere that it creates. The village greens in England and the Maidans in India, the spectators in the trees and the steel bands in Antigua, the telling formality of the Long Room in Barbados, and the great crowds at Eden Gardens and Melbourne are all distinctive in a home-grown way. Among South Africa's special inheritances is *Macal' eGusha*.

In recommending the photograph for the cover of this book, the publisher suggested to the author that it was particularly appropriate because, 'It looks like cricket being played in heaven.' The educated gestures of the bodies, ballet-like in the open-air idyll of mountain-meeting-sky evoke the most romantic and timeless images and aspects of the game; they are not specific to place, or specific to 'race', but universal.

This is so partly because of the skill of the observer behind the lens. It is also partly because the story of the African game has always been linked to the broader development and 'language' of world cricket.

OPPOSITE, TOP AND BOTTOM *An African rural cricket tradition. From a photographic essay
on an Amacala eGusha tournament, 2002, by Paul Weinberg.*

Part Eight

THE LEGACY OF 150 YEARS AND THE FUTURE

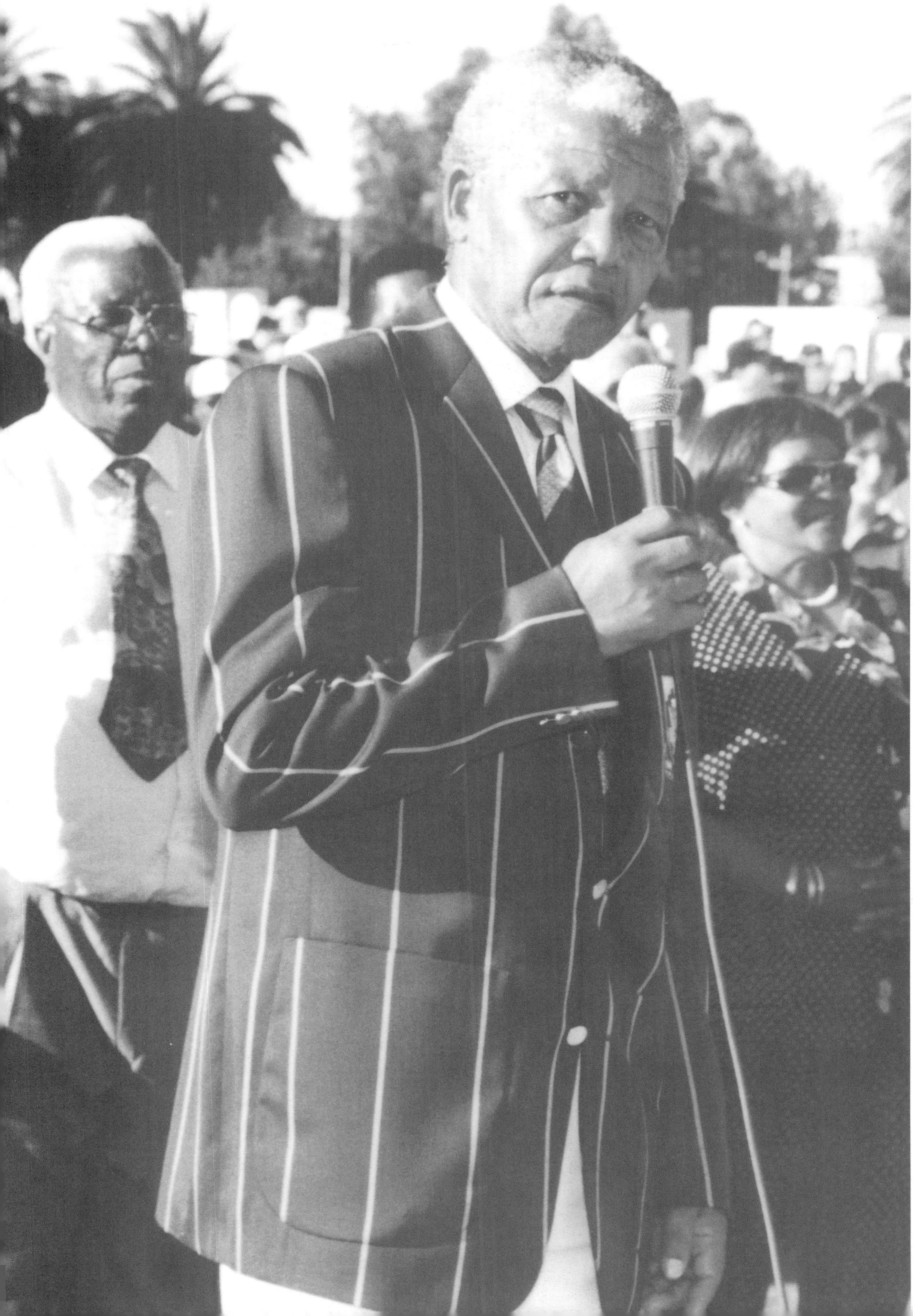

Chapter 40

STEREOTYPES HIT *for a* SIX

———————————— ◉ ————————————

THE HISTORY OUTLINED IN *STORY OF AN AFRICAN GAME* shows that, contrary to conventional wisdom, black people in the Eastern Cape were among the pioneers of cricket in South Africa, and have been playing the game for over 150 years. Decades before Johannesburg was founded in 1885 on the bare Highveld – or the Wanderers Stadium was built, or King Edward School, St John's College or Jeppe Boys High were established – the game was being learnt in the mission schools and black players were starting their own clubs. In 1884, before the great gold rush commenced, the first inter-town tournament of Eastern Cape teams was held.

It is comparable to other international examples, including the well-documented case of the pioneering Parsi cricketers in Bombay, India, who took up the game early on and started playing competitively from 1877.[1] It is not an exaggeration to compare the nurseries of Zonnebloem and Lovedale Colleges with the 'Indian Eton', Mayo College, or Queens Royal College in Trinidad, where C.L.R. James was educated, or Royal College, Colombo or any of the numerous other well-known schools in the colonies based on the British public school model.

From the time that Nathaniel Umhalla studied and played in Britain in the 1860s black people also followed international developments and sought to link up to them. The support for the British team in 1888/89 and the attempts to raise an Anglo-African team for a tour in the same year were only the first signs of the aspiration to be part of the world game and its development.

When the Champion CC surprised the Alberts Club in King Williams Town in 1885, and when the Malay XVIII played against W.W. Read's 1892 English touring team they showed clearly that, given the opportunity, black cricketers could rise to the same standards as any others.

And, when the Bantu Board resolved in the 1930s to seek international fixtures and individual black sportsmen started travelling abroad to compete at the top levels in the 1950s, they were giving notice of a determination to stand up to prevailing racism and exclusion.

The 1950s brought a new upbeat mood and Eric Majola was one of the symbols and pin-up boys of his self-confidently urban and cosmopolitan generation. In sport, he and people like Jake Tuli represented what Dolly Rathebe did for song, the *Drum* generation for writing, the *King Kong* musical for the stage, and Mandela and Tambo for politics. Spoken of in the same breath as Keith Oxlee and the great Cliff Morgan of Wales, Majola represented for black sportsmen of his generation a new-found confidence and belief that they could hold their own at every level.

In 2000, when the government of the Eastern Cape drew up a list of the most influential people of the century in their province, Eric Majola was in the top 100, together with famous politicians, religious leaders, writers, actors and educationists.[2]

We now also know that national cricket organisations for black people have existed for one hundred years, and that early organisational developments were sophisticated and closely followed the white examples. Between 1903 and 1974 the different black bodies in South Africa organised on a regular basis around 70 national tournaments at an average of one a year. When the African Board met in Queenstown in 1967, it was its 33rd annual general meeting since its formation in 1932.

THAT "LAST MAN IN" FEELING.

A long cricket tradition. ABOVE *A cricket cartoon from the 1930s.*
RIGHT *An advertisement from the 1930s.*

The story of the Majola family reveals a grounding in the game and culture that is as deep as any to be found anywhere. And this family is not unique. From Umhalla in the 1860s to Paul Xiniwe in the 1880s and 1890s, to Hamilton Masiza and Piet Gwele in the first half of the 20th century and other Port Elizabeth 'locals', like Johnson Marwanqa, F.H.M. Zwide, Walton Ntshekisa, Wilson Ximiya, Pat Cossie, Dan Qeqe, Ray Mali, Thoba Williams, Thembisile Pono and Tsepo Kadi, there has been an unbroken thread of commitment and service to the game and the community.

Let us also recognise the historical inaccuracy of the endlessly touted point that Dr Bacher and the white establishment's development programme introduced Africans in the townships to cricket from 1986 onwards. As we saw in Chapter 7, there were ten clubs in Johannesburg in the 1890s and 42 teams playing every Sunday in the African leagues in 1932. More than 30 years before the development programme reached Soweto and Alexandra townships, Orlando Brotherly CC won the league in Johannesburg and Try Again CC were flying the flag for Alex.[3]

Notions that black people have no real culture of cricket are quite simply incorrect; they are outdated assumptions rooted in apartheid power relations and racist thinking. The way African cricketers have been seen in the past has had more to do with the prejudices and ignorance of the dominant classes than the actual situations that prevailed.

Is Yours a "Sykes."

George Headley, the famous Jamaican batsman, made a score of 344 not out using a Sykes bat.

On March 16, 1932 he sent the following cable to Messrs. Wm. Sykes, Ltd.,:—

"Bats highly appreciated helped considerably my success against Lord Tennyson's team. Scored 723 runs with one bat."

To encourage Bantu cricket in South Africa, Messrs. Sykes have presented two first quality bats to the N.R.C. Cricket League for competition under the following rules:—

One bat for the player making the best batting average during the 1932–1933 Season, it being understood that the player shall not have played in less than eight matches.

One bat to be presented for the best bowling average, the player to have bowled not less than 50 overs during the season.

In addition, Messrs. Sykes, will present a new bat to any member of the N.R.C. Cricket League who makes a score of 100 runs or more, using a Sykes bat in a recognised match, provided the score is certified by the captain of the team and the secretary of the League.

The face of the future. The 2001 under-13 South African Invitation team celebrating before their departure for England.

Third-generation batsman and rugby fly-half. Allister Majola, pictured here with his father
Gerald in 2002, represents Gauteng province in both cricket and rugby in his age group.

Cricket and its connections. Steve Tshwete (front right) with Ali Bacher (left),
Khaya Majola (back) and an unidentified fellow spectator.

Chapter 41

THE CRICKET *and* MISSION SCHOOL LEGACY

———————————————— ◖ ————————————————

HE AMERICAN HISTORIAN PROFESSOR Chuck Korr from the University of Missouri completed a PhD on English history during the period of Cromwell, but changed course and ended up writing books on West Ham United Football Club and the Baseball Players Union in the United States.[1] He is now completing a study on the role of sport in the Robben Island Maximum Security Prison during the Mandela years.

Sport was very important to the political prisoners. Together with political and formal education, it provided a means of maintaining control of their lives. They petitioned to be allowed to play sport and, after at first being refused permission, they started various sports clubs and co-ordinated the Robben Island General Recreation Committee from the late 1960s onwards. Boxes and boxes of minute books and records were kept by the ex-prisoners[2] and one of the things that has struck Professor Korr most forcefully is the old fashioned, almost Victorian, 'fair play' language and ethos of sport revealed in the documents.[3]

Korr has pointed to the seeming contradiction of revolutionaries committed to an armed and highly ideological struggle which borrowed heavily from socialist and anti-colonial discourses, talking so seriously in the 'conservative' language of sport. What was the explanation?

The answer, of course, lies partly in the enduring influence and remarkable resilience of the missionary tradition of the 19th century, with its strong Victorian roots and emphasis on sport. From Nelson Mandela (Healdtown and Fort Hare) and Thabo Mbeki (Lovedale College) downwards, many of the 'Islanders' and new leaders of South Africa received their schooling in the old mission colleges of the Eastern Cape. And the disciplines and values inculcated there continued to inform their outlooks despite the abnormal conditions that overtook them and the new paths they followed.

The first secretary of the Robben Island General Recreation Committee was Steve Vukile Tshwete from Peelton in the Eastern Cape, a 'rural commuter suburb' started as a mission station in 1845, and one-time home to Dr Walter Benson Rubusana, first president of the Border Native Cricket Union and one of the honorary vice-presidents elected by the ANC at its inaugural meeting. Tshwete was a keen rugby player and became first Minister of Sport after democracy. It was he who brokered cricket unity and engineered South Africa's entry into world cricket in 1991.[4] One of Tshwete's fellow prisoners was Ben Tengimfene, school principal and later president of the Border Cricket Board, a gentleman of the old school.[5]

Steve Tshwete, it has come to light, was also a father figure to the fourth African cricketer to represent South Africa, Monde Zondeki, whose selection ahead of a creaking Alan Donald during the World Cup ended that great cricketer's international career. The young fast bowler grew up in the Tshwete household in Peelton and Lusaka (during the exile years). As we have seen, his great-grandfather, Samuel Zondeki, was the founder of the Zondeki Cricket Union, started in 1939 and still going strong today as part of the *Macal'eGusha* tradition (see Chapter 15).[6]

ABOVE LEFT TO RIGHT *Isaiah Bud Mbelle, first secretary of the South African Coloured Cricket Board and secretary-general of the SANNC, 1917–1919. Dr Walter Benson Rubasana, president of Border Native Cricket Union and one of the founding vice-presidents of the SANNC in 1912. Andrew Frank Pendla, president of the Eastern Province Bantu Cricket Union and the Cape African National Congress, 1930s.*

Cricket was the product of a particular African adaptability combined with the influence of the mission schools and their first generation products – as was the ANC, born at more or less the same time and led by and large by the same people who were at the helm in sport. There are remarkable continuities between the 'first generation' activists of the 1860s to 1880s and sport and politics today. As people have become more visible post-1994, these lineages have surfaced more clearly. They reveal the gritty integrity and remarkable wholeness and resilience of the 19th century black intellectual tradition and inheritance.

Steve Tshwete's successor as Minister of Sport, Ngconde Balfour, comes from Ntselamanzi near Lovedale. He is related to Noyi Balfour, a contemporary of Rev Tiyo Soga at Lovedale, who was one of the first contributors to the *Ikwezi* newspaper started by the missionaries in the 1840s.[7] In 1884 the first three batsmen in the Gaika Imperial team from 'Lovedale Station' were Balfours, and in the late 1950s, Magadu Balfour, Ngconde's father, was playing for the Fight Again Cricket Club in Ntselamanzi.[8]

The captain of the Conquerors Cricket Club in Ntselamanzi in 1952 was Benson K. Bokwe, no doubt related in some way to one of the earliest black Lovedale luminaries, the composer, minister and teacher, John Knox Bokwe. John Knox Bokwe was the father of Dr Roseberry Bokwe, patron of one of the cricket weeks at Middledrift, and of Frieda Bokwe, the first African woman to graduate from university in South Africa, who married Professor Z.K. Matthews, originator of the Freedom Charter, one-time head of Fort Hare University and later Botswana's ambassador to the

United Nations. J.K.'s grandson is current deputy minister Joe Matthews, and his great-granddaughter is Naledi Pandor, former university lecturer and a chairperson of the National Council of Provinces in Parliament.[9]

The secretary of the Lovedale Cricket Club in the 1930s was the well-known writer and academic, Professor A.C. Jordan, father of Pallo Jordan, a member of Nelson Mandela's first cabinet.[10]

The linkages go on and on. Tumi Plaatje-Molefe, former first lady of the North West Province, is the granddaughter of the famous writer and activist, Sol Plaatje, who was the brother-in-law of the first secretary of the South African Coloured Cricket Board, and the father of Halley Plaatje, first secretary of the South African Bantu Rugby Board in the 1930s.

Bangu Masisi, the public relations director for the ICC World Cup 2003, is a descendant of Reverend Joel Goronyane, a prominent politician in the Becoana Mutual Improvement Association before Union, and a member of the Rolong elite in Thaba Nchu whose cricket playing exploits were described in Chapter 5. Under the Land Restitution Act, she will be inheriting land which was taken from the family during the apartheid years.[11]

Another well-known politician from Thaba Nchu was Dr James Moroka, president of the ANC in the early 1950s, who was a patron of the South African Bantu Cricket Board. A member of the Rolong royal family, Dr Moroka would have been related to Samuel Moroka, who was among the first students at Zonnebloem College in the late 1850s and the young Moroka who was playing cricket for the college in the 1890s.[12]

ABOVE LEFT *ANC presidents, Dr James Moroka (patron South African Bantu Cricket Union) and Chief Albert Lutuli (executive member of the South African Football Association) were both prominent in sport as well.* ABOVE RIGHT *Lovedale alumni: current Minister of Sport, Ngconde Balfour, and President Thabo Mbeki.*

The exploits of the cricket team from Edendale mission station near Pietermaritzburg in Natal in the 1890s were mentioned earlier. Members of the prominent mission-educated Kholwa family, the Msimangs, represented this team. This family produced ANC leaders Richard and Selby Msimang and, later, Mavuso Msimang, who went into exile and currently heads the South African National Parks as CEO.[13]

Respected ANC president and Nobel Peace Prize winner, Chief Albert Lutuli, who in the 1930s served on the South African Football Association executive under D.M. Denelane (for 20 years also an official of the South African Cricket Board), was another such product from KwaZulu-Natal. Chief Lutuli's uncle was Martin Lutuli, first president of the Natal Native Congress. One of his grandchildren is Lindiwe Gadd, CEO of the Freedom Park heritage project.[14]

The Sishubas from Oxkraal and Kamastone near Queenstown – John Alfred and Isaiah Goda Sishuba – were close political allies of John Tengo Jabavu around the beginning of the last century. The letters that Prime Ministers of the day wrote in their own hand to court the Sishubas have been preserved in the National Library. Descendants today include a member of the Nelson Mandela National Museum Council and the first team rugby captain of the well-known Queens College in Queenstown.[15] As it happens, the great-great-grandson of Reverend Jonas Goduka, cricket enthusiast, leading light in Herschel and founder of the Ethiopian Church around 1900, is the captain of the college's second rugby team.[16]

S.E.K. Mqhayi, the 19th century South African Native Congress activist and renowned 'poet of the people' who left

an indelible impression on a young Nelson Mandela,[17] is the grandfather of current UNISA vice-chancellor, Barney Pityana, and former director general of foreign affairs, Sipho Pityana.

Scratch the surface and the deep-rootedness and durability of the struggle-linked, mission tradition of public intellectuals (excluded from the institutions of white domination) will reveal itself. Many other prominent South Africans have direct connections back to that first generation of literate politicians who started the first proto-nationalist organisations and displayed a healthy obsession with cricket.

The development of sport has always been an organic part of broader social and political developments in South Africa. This book confirms this.

The remarkable fact that more than half of all the African matrics in South Africa until as late as the 1940s came from the handful of colleges in the Ciskei that constituted the cricket heartland helps in no small measure to explain the close intellectual, political and sporting linkages over the years.[18]

This linkage was nowhere as strong as in the late 19th century when Africans set out to form the first modern political organisations and claim their space in the new colonial system. Cricket and the ANC had the same parents and they more or less shared birthdays. The composition of the renowned Native and Coloured Delegation that went to Britain in 1909 to protest the colour-bar constitution of the new Union of South Africa (Chapter 5) and the appointment of the early cricket and rugby administrator, Isaiah Bud Mbelle, as Secretary-General of the South African Native National Congress (later ANC), clearly demonstrated this link.[19]

Professor Jakes Gerwel, chairperson of the United Cricket Board's ICC World Cup 2003 Policy Committee, speaking in another capacity to the Oxford Union, declared that the achievement of democracy in South Africa was in a real sense a vindication of the universal vision and views of that first generation of mission people and the generations of political activists who followed. He said their political and intellectual arguments over time had a 'consistent thread of rationality' running through them, which in a sense 'predetermined the eventual outcome' in South Africa.[20]

When current Border Cricket president and member of the UCB executive Ray Mali was a student at Lovedale in 1959, Chris Hani and Archbishop Njongonkulu Ndungane sat in the desks alongside him. Thabo Mbeki, son of the cultured Govan and Epainette, was also at the school at the time. Mbeki too must have watched and been forced to play cricket at some stage. But he was expelled after a student demonstration and propelled into the world of revolutionary politics. By that time cricket had ceased to be an avenue for advancement and prestige and such quaint pastimes were being overtaken by bigger issues.

Exile and the tumult and violence of apartheid may have disconnected the political elite from their long association with cricket, but they have not broken the remarkable resilience of that 'old world' tradition that underlays it and thus the possibilities of the game's reconnection with the black educated classes in the normalising educational and social environments of 21st-century South Africa are good.

The footprints of 150 years of cricket are everywhere visible. The game has become a social institution with its own particular African culture and idiom. It has inscribed itself into the landscape of the country and the consciousness of the people, their language and their ways, particularly in Port Elizabeth and what Ray Mali has called the 'black cricket belt of the Border', stretching from Fort Beaufort through Alice and Middledrift to King Williams Town.[21]

Cricket sayings have become part of the Xhosa language. When a spectator shouts '*Khwelebedini*', it is an exhortation to

Ex-Robben Islander, school principal and president of the Border Cricket Board, Ben Tengimfene, with Ngconde Balfour (left) and Trevor Manual (right) during protests against the Gatting rebel tour, 1990.

'step onto the bed and hit the ball'. '*Yagqoboza nakwu Gwele*' is an excuse for a dropped catch or a misfield – sometimes the ball burst through the hands of the great 'Oom Piet' Gwele himself, people say. From the bumpy fields of the old 'locations' and the rural cow-patches has also come the saying, '*Ndithi betha lase Java phezu kokhuko lwase Yokohama*'. This goes back to the time when balls were made of rubber, produced in Java, and the mats came from Yokohama. It means hit the ball from Java on the mat from Yokohama.[22]

Cattle have played a central role in Xhosa economic life and culture, so it is inevitable that they would feature in cricket's folklore as well. The beautifully descriptive '*ziimpondo zenkomo*' ('it is the horns of a cow') became another way of saying 'it is a six'.[23]

At the inter-provincial tournament in Port Elizabeth in December 1956, the Natal opening batsman, Japhta Mahanjana, also known as 'Super', batted out a famous draw against his province of origin, North Eastern Transvaal, giving rise to the saying, '*Yi draw Mahanjana*' ('It is a Mahanjana draw'). North Easterns were captained by Mahanjana's brother, Julius, who was also the national captain. He set Natal a target of 245 runs in four hours. They decided to play defensively for a draw from the outset. There was 'no love lost' between Japhta and the opponents, with whom he often played during vacations at home. A draw would also deny them a place in the final of the tournament.

This extraordinary scene followed: *This was payback time for [Japhta] Super [Mahanjana]. Qangule and [he] opened the batting. Super batted with his short handle, a practice he adopted when he intended to 'get his eye in' and play conservatively. The short handle, he said, allowed him to play closer to his body. He changed to long handle once he had his eye in and intended to 'play some big shots'. [He] had the ability to use the long handle and perfected the stance of standing upright, his bat poised baseball style in a manner that Clive Rice made famous some three decades later This time Super stayed loyal to the short handle. The partnership lasted an hour and ten minutes, and was worth just ten runs, when Qangule was out. Gqabasa joined Mahanjana and Natal played out the rest of the match without losing another wicket. Throughout the innings Japhta stood in a forward defensive position before the ball was bowled, bat in front of his pad. If the bowler changed his length he would move forward or back towards his wicket. The crowd in Port Elizabeth, used to extravagant stroke-play, had never witnessed anything like it, and began chanting 'yi draw Mahanjana'.*[24]

As with Boycott in Yorkshire, batting defensively for a draw became linked to a name in the lexicon of yet another of the world's many languages.

Besides these Xhosa cricket idioms, the game has also contributed to popular culture via poetry and song. For example, when Champion Cricket Club from King Williams Town became the first inter-town winners in 1884, at a time when Xhosa literature was still in its infancy and people started making the transition from traditional oral praise poetry to formal written poetry, an excited supporter

ABANTSUNDU   TIVE OP

Ngxatshoke Qonce!

HEKE CHAMPION!

Champion'! Nkanzi ebekiweyo yakulo
    Ndlambe nakulo Ntiade,
Azi ubu ncetywe nganqua ube uzibutumele
    aje;
Bekunguziwana ukuba wena apa uwela ngo-
    ntantato,
Kuba lamanzi e-Qonce kuwe asuk' abe bu-
    buti.
Ucacante waya wafun' indlela 'kulo Gomp' e-
    Monti,
Apo ibula enfegi uye wayidla kona;
Gqwi, teudalela waya wel' ebalakisini e-Rini,
Apo unkatwaya waqoshelisa amadinala.
Akurumanga kubuy' ubuyelelo noko nbusel'
    ukp' etafezi,
Kub' impondo ube ungekazisukuli zombini;
Bayaqala e-Bayi akwaaek' izitya kub' iyiso-
    polo,
Bera ngawe selu uandis' amawa ezanta' ema
    Xambeni.
Ude wenjeoj' oku gxebe nbuz' uzonde utoni-
    na,
Abakuzelelanga yilina oko ubuse Monti ezi-
    bukweni?
Ukuba lomhlab' uwumeleyo nakub' ungase-
    wako,
Usaziwa noko nkuba 'yaytk' ingumhlaba ka
    Ntiade.
Mand' onesikwa kwabasezanta' ema Silamse-
    ni,
Nowase balakisini ebongile nje akafumana-
    ng' enze,
Etelele ngokwesel' ennuqamlezweni wahleka
    nje naye,
Ibisey' ikufihla amehlo kuba naye enziwe isi-
    qwala.
Akwabi ndandizaleiw' e-Meliman Tawala,
Ndaba nam ndapefumlelwa ngomoya we-
    mbongi;
Kuba nam' ngenamhla ngendigwentselela
    ndibonga,
Koko hay' lesto ukuba mbi ukuvelel' emlu-
    ngwini.

                                A.B.C.

exclaimed in the manner of the *Mbongi* or praise singer, '*Ngxatshoke Qonce! Heke Champion*'. The poem was printed in the *Imvo Zabantsundu* newspaper.[25] The animated participation of spectators, men, women and children, over the years was often commented on in reports.

There has always been wide community participation and the games became part of local culture. In Langa township in Cape Town, the streets in one of its new extensions bear the names of cricketers. Examples are Malamba St, Mama St, Ndlwana St and Mshumpela St. There is also a Rubusana Street and a Washington Street.[26]

In 1977, the prisoners on Robben Island wrote the following letter to the prison authorities:
Due to the long duration of cricket matches/practices and the fact that the main soccer/rugby field is most of the playing time occupied by other games, it has become difficult for cricket matches/practices to take place. Application is hereby made to have a cricketing practising pitch erected near the soccer/rugby pitch. It will require three or four poles and a covering net or mesh fence.[27]

The letter was sent on behalf of the Majola Cricket Union. If ever proof was needed that the game had African roots or that the Majola family were symbols of their community and their generations, this was it.

Cricket is an African game in a real sense. In fact, looking at international comparisons, it is not an exaggeration to say that the Africans of the Eastern Cape and the Muslims of the Western Cape and the Indian communities in Natal and Gauteng have an internalised tradition of cricket and love for the game of their former colonial masters which equals that of any other ex-subjects including those in Asia, the Caribbean and Australia.[28]

Given new life since democracy and boosted by the World Cup 2003, cricket is rapidly becoming part of national popular culture once again.

The old cricket establishment was comfortably part of the system of white domination.

Chapter 42

CHAINS *that* STILL
BIND US

---◉---

NEWLANDS WAS A GLORIOUS PLACE to be during the ICC World Cup 2003. The five 40-metre-high floodlight pylons, installed years ago to ensure the highest TV quality for this very occasion, created almost surreal colours in the balmy-dark February evenings. High on the mountain, roving TV cameras were mounted on the King's Blockhouse to give a billion viewers post-card-pretty pictures of Cape Town. Devil's Peak took on eerie countenances as rolling mist and changing light played with night-time feelings.

The crowd was delightfully energetic. Nearly 12 000 turned up for Kenya versus Canada. The generous applause for the visiting teams reflected an unusual oneness and contented maturity among South Africans, salted by the contestations and anxieties accompanying change.

Some 500 people squeezed onto the VIP lists for the opening ceremony and match. The A team was up in the usual place in the President's Suite. President Mbeki was expected to be accompanied by President Obassanjo of Nigeria, but this did not materialise. The overflow was accommodated on the pavilion of the Western Province Cricket Club. The 'Province Club', as it is known, is still seen by some as an anachronism and relic from the past. There was a time – in the days of W.H. Milton (who barred Krom Hendricks from the 1894 South African team) – when it ran cricket in the city. The other clubs rallied to form a provincial association so authority could be shared. But even today, in an age of egalitarianism, the WPCC still enjoys special privileges with its own pavilion at Newlands, like the MCC at Lord's, the institution it imitated.

The members in 'The Club' know their cricket, but during one of the matches, I discovered that some of them were still, as in Milton's day, only grudgingly hospitable. My wife and I needed to take a break. We waited until the end of the over before we got up – I'd been to Cambridge, so I knew the drill. Inside the clubhouse, a breathless member accosted me: 'Excuse me, Professor, it's totally unacceptable that you people move around like you do in those front seats.' I was taken aback. She continued, 'The coloured man with the thin moustache who shook your hand should not have been walking around during overs; it's just not good enough, you know. There are rules at cricket.'

George van Oord from Ravensmead, roughly-hewn and working class, was dressed in a zebra-striped shirt matching the World Cup logo, which his wife, Cynthia, had made. Gerald Njengele and soft-spoken Cyril Ntshidi, involved in the new R2 million stadium upgrade in Khayalitsha, one of 25 World Cup 'Legacy' projects, were sitting next to Mohamed Ebrahim and his guest. They were among the few people with tanned faces in view. I had no idea who the irate member could have been talking about, nor did I really care. The thought passed through my mind, 'While some were learning their etiquette in a cucumber-sandwich world, these guys were playing cricket without change rooms or pavilions.' But I remained silent. I was an ambassador of sorts and this was the World Cup.

Perhaps it was the occasion. Perhaps it was the place. But not even the headiness of Newlands during the World Cup could mask the clash of cultures and the struggles over power and change happening in cricket and a country in transition.

The next time it was England versus Pakistan. The selfsame Njengele, son of a 'Bantu Springbok' who partnered Eric Majola at half-back in the 1950s, and himself a school principal and member of two provincial executives, was sitting nearby with another colleague and friend of ours, a very well-intentioned person who works hard for the game but is sometimes baffled and frustrated by the sociological complexities of the changes in cricket. We talked about cricket and *The Story of an African Game*, which was nearing completion.

Njengele absorbed the story of Nathaniel Umhalla at Zonnebloem with relish. 'Okay. So maybe some blacks were playing in the 1860s, but where are they now,' asked our sceptical friend. He was uncomprehending: if black people made the claims they made, why were they still so like orphans in cricket. Gerald was immediately excited that some could be so confident in their views, and yet so blind. Here were colleagues, both soaked in the traditions of sport, but the fault lines that open up so easily along the racial divides were showing themselves again.

But the question posed is precisely the one that must be dealt with in this concluding part of *The Story of an African Game*, as it touches on the essence of the whole debate about cricket and change in South Africa.

UNDERSTANDING WHERE WE COME FROM

So why, if there is this rich history, are black cricketers still so invisible, and struggling to find acceptance?

The explanation lies in the system that the white minority imposed with guileless force on this country and the mentality this system engendered.

We need to remind ourselves where we have come from.

In the 'old' South Africa, black people were denied political representation, barred from certain jobs and from buying property, forced to live in designated areas, given an education that prepared them for servitude rather than enlightenment. A phalanx of laws rigidly controlled black settlement, movement and labour in order to create wealth for the white minority and secure their racialised system of domination. Eventually there were more than 300 laws controlling the lives of black people from the cradle (segregated hospitals) to the grave (separate cemetries).[1] The aspirations of the black middle class were battered and went into decline. It is hardly surprising, then, that their sport, including cricket, should suffer the same decline.

In the industrialised countries of Europe and North America, women and the working classes were gradually incorporated into the expanding political systems until, by the middle of the 20th century the social — or at least stable — democracies of Europe and North America were in place. The substantial black middle class that emerged from the mission schools of the 19th century was not incorporated into the evolving South African society in the same way from 1910 when South Africa became a modern state. Rather than an opening up or a progression, there followed a systematic assault on the social, economic and political rights of black South Africans. They were not citizens but subjects.

English-speaking South Africans and cricketers were active agents of apartheid and exclusion, though they are often not willing to admit this. The old explanation that it was the fault of the crude Afrikaners and an apartheid system they were not responsible for no longer stands, and is itself inherently racist. The cricket establishment may sometimes have voiced liberal positions, but it always operated comfortably within the system of white domination. There is no getting away from this.[2]

Racism and discrimination in cricket go back to the very beginning, in South Africa and the rest of the colonial world. The British exported the game around the world as an integral part of the process of colonial conquest. It was the Victorians, with a superiority complex unequalled in the 19th century (some say until the rise of the Nazis) who invented what later became known as sports apartheid. The exclusion of the 'inferior races' in sport was part of British attitudes and values of superiority.

After all, it was William Milton, big shot at the WPCC and the WPCU, working in tandem with Cecil John Rhodes himself, who prevented the 'impudent' Krom Hendricks from going to England in 1894, creating the firm precedent of a colour line at international level.

It was the South African Cricket Association which of its own volition, refused, to let blacks play in its Currie Cup competition from 1890 until 1977, and which protested

against the great Ranjitsinhji and Duleepsinhji playing against them for England.[3]

The culture of segregation in South African cricket until the mid-20th century was typical of a broader international pattern. When a young Pele rocked to super stardom at the 1958 football World Cup finals, he was the only player from the great Brazilian mix who was not white, something that is difficult to believe after witnessing the colourful style and composition of a marvellous Brazilian team at the latest World Cup in Korea and Japan. Similarly, Willie O'Ree became the first black professional ice hockey star in the United States only in 1959, and for many years black quarter-backs and coaches were frowned upon in the grid-iron leagues. In cricket, George Headley became captain of the West Indies for a single test in 1948, the year institutionalised apartheid was codified in South Africa, but black cricketers had to wait until 1959 before Frank Worrell was given an extended run as captain of the West Indies after a concerted public campaign.[4] It is interesting to note that this was also the time that the non-racial sports movement was being formed in South Africa to challenge apartheid sport; when Eric Majola had become a new-style sports star and others like the golfer Papwa Sewgolum and Basil D'Oliveira headed abroad in search of opportunities.

Decolonisation and the changing global context of the 1960s brought about a shift in attitudes. British power and old colonial values were overtaken and increasingly seen as part of a repressive past. Instead of moving with the 'winds of change', white South Africa tried to deepen and extend apartheid. The National Party government withdrew South Africa from the Commonwealth, banned the main black political organisations and intensified apartheid social engineering with large-scale forced removals. The Sharpeville massacre of March 1960 and the imprisonment of thousands that followed heralded in a new period of open repression that saw Nelson Mandela being sent to prison for 27 years.

As the freedom struggle and international opinion against apartheid intensified, white Afrikaans- and English-speaking South Africans increasingly shared the same political viewpoints and retreated into the same laager in order to protect racial privilege.

This was well reflected in the 1966 General Election. With apartheid at its pinnacle, the majority of English-speaking voters voted for rather than against the 'Nats' for the first time.

Cricket icons like Eric Rowan and Jackie McGlew, (the latter stood as a National Party candidate at one stage) were among the active supporters of South Africa's 'traditional way of life'.[5]

It was against this background that cricket grew in popularity among Afrikaners in the 1960s and 1970s. It was also in this context that the white Springboks discarded the colonial 'gentlemen' image of the past and with a muscular energy (typified by the ebullient Eddie Barlow) started thumping the 'Poms' and Aussies they had shown such deference to before.

So rigid were the boundaries between black and white by the 1960s that even the more enlightened white cricket administrators, like John Passmore, admitted that they did not even know that blacks played cricket until the D'Oliveira affair blew up in 1968 and threatened their 'traditional' way of playing.[6]

Louis Duffus, doyen of cricket writing in South Africa, showed the kind of attitudes that prevailed at the time when he offered his wisdom on the D'Oliveira affair. He said both D'Oliveira, 'for so long a dagger directed at the heart of South African cricket', and others should have been aware of the laws of the land, and respected them. 'The law of the land says you drive on the left. D'Oliveira was told to come out and drive on the right.' Duffus continued, 'Was it to be expected that the South African government would change its policy for a cricketer? England knew the law when a much greater cricketer, K.S. Duleepsinhji, could have been chosen for his country.

He was not selected and nothing was said about it ... Because of one cricketer the great players produced in this country and the game itself have both been victimised.'[7]

Duffus also claimed with confidence in his biography, published in 1969, 'The indigenous African does not readily take to cricket but he is prepared to play soccer all year round.'[8] He was transmitting pure apartheid thinking.

Cricketers comfortably endorsed the explanation in the official *South African Year Book*, which could claim, as late as 1977, that:

It is only comparatively recently that the Black people have shown a marked increase in what may be called modern sporting activities. For centuries they found their recreation in traditional activities, such as hunting and tribal dances. It was the White nation, with its European background and tradition, which participated in the recognised sports ...[9]

This thinking, so prevalent in sports circles for many years, is what gives rise to the kind of question posed to me at Newlands, referred to earlier in this chapter: if blacks have been playing since the 1860s, where are black players now?

Once black people were under the boot, or out of sight, the myth that they preferred dancing around naked to playing games such as cricket and rugby followed easily.

Perceptions developed to fit the exclusions that the apartheid system enforced in practice. These easy 'truths' helped justify the status quo. They made apartheid and inequality seem natural.

Defending the apartheid system in the 1970s, Springbok rugby captain Hannes Marais said, 'The Coloured population do not seem very interested in sport. They do not play much rugby and cricket.'[10]

In the same vein, Dawie de Villiers, former Springbok rugby captain and cabinet minister, declared confidently in 1980: 'Don't forget that the Blacks have really known western sports [only] for the last ten years. [Therefore], they have naturally not yet reached the same standard.'[11]

Rugby legend Uli Schmidt drew from the same colonial and racist myth when he declared in 1994 that rugby [and cricket] were not natural games for black people to play. 'It is not in their culture,' he said. 'They should play soccer.'[12]

In the 1970s, as SACA tried to engineer opportunities to get South Africa re-admitted to international cricket, its leaders, Jack Cheetham, Boon Wallace and Billy Woodin, stuck timidly to the parameters laid out by the National Party government.

Supported by the English-speaking businesses establishment, including the Argus Group and Harry Oppenheimer, SACA formed a close alliance with Minister Punt Janson

Dr Verwoerd at the cricket. Newlands, MCC tour, 1964/65. TOP *Pictured with officials.*
BOTTOM *With the captain of South Africa, Trevor Goddard (left) and his English counterpart M.J.K. Smith (right).*

333

and the Nationalists to counter the growing non-racial sports movement.[13]

Except for a brief walk-off and petition by the players during a Rest of South Africa versus Transvaal match at Newlands in 1971 when a tour to Australia hung in the balance, SACA and its cricketers loyally abided by government policy and stood by the regime to counter the 'onslaught' against South Africa. (Incidentally, the Transvaal dressing room was split seven to four on the protest.)[14]

During the 1980s, a younger generation of business-connected administrators, including Joe Pamensky, Ali Bacher and Geoff Dakin, worked closely with P.W. Botha's government to get tax subsidies of over 80 percent for rebel tours intended to circumvent sanctions against apartheid. This co-operation gave credence to 'Total Onslaught' theory, according to which a godless communism was intent on destroying 'western civilisation' in South Africa, and the tours were seen as coups in a generally gloomy foreign policy environment by the government and its supporters.[15]

Those opposing apartheid were demonised. When Nelson Mandela and his comrades were arrested at Rivonia, the *Sunday Times* printed a front page photograph pointing out the 'terrorists' and 'communists' headquarters. The cricket media went along with these typifications. Those cricketers opposing racial sport were described as being 'troublemakers', 'hotheaded', unreasonable agitators, 'not having the interests of the game at heart' and worse.

It is uncanny how this media discourse reproduced itself in a changed context after the transition to democracy in the 1990s with reference to sports transformation, without any great self-examination occurring.

In the 1970s, newspapers were white-owned and newsrooms were staffed almost exclusively by whites. A black journalist remembered that white cricket writers showed 'as much interest in covering the non-racial game as an arts correspondent in Iceland would have had in covering a *korfbal* tournament in South Africa'.[16]

When SACBOC and Lancashire League cricket star Dik Abed sought accreditation as a journalist to watch the 1970 Australian test match at Newlands, he was refused entry to the press box. A separate table was set up for him in front of the 'Non-White' enclosure.[17]

After the SACB secretary Ahmed Mangera had rebuffed overtures from Ali Bacher in 1985, *Sunday Times* and *Business Day* journalist Sy Lerman described him as an 'intransigent, lightweight' who would one day disappear 'as unlamented as

the system he fights tooth and nail'. Moreover, 'As a cricket administrator and personality, Mangera pales into insignificance behind Bacher, and he hides his inadequacy by shielding behind apartheid.'[18]

Most white cricket writers uncritically supported rebel tours and the old system. Some actively worked for the SACU in public relations capacities.

'Total Onslaught' drew whites tightly together into a laager. Education, censorship and the army galvanised them into the defence of the minority regime and the system. At school they learned a whites-only history. Colin Bundy, former vice-chancellor at Wits and now principal of the School of Oriental and African Studies in London, reviewed C.J. Joubert's *History for Standard 10* in 1986. It was then in the twelfth impression of the third edition. Bundy described it as 'history as negation':

C.J. Joubert's most striking achievement is the fifty-page chapter on the 'Political, Social and Economic Development of the Non-Whites'. Three black politicians are mentioned: Mahatma Gandhi, Tom Schwartz and Kaiser Matanzima. There is no reference to Abdurahman, Dube, Kadalie or Plaatje; no hint of Tabata, Lutuli, Sobukwe, Mandela or Biko. There is no word on the ANC, the ICU, PAC — or any other black political organisation; there is no echo of any black political resistance. No blood is shed on these pages: no Bulhoek, or Bondelswarts, no Sharpeville, or Langa, or Soweto ... This text book is to education what the black hole is to matter: a kind of anti-knowledge. It does not so much distort the past as maim and amputate it. It would not even be necessary to mention this ideological farrago, this toxic waste product of apartheid, were it not for the fact that it is solemnly offered and taught as history to scores of thousands of young South Africans every year.[19]

This is the type of history that informed the world view of young cricketers in South Africa before they went to practice in the afternoon. Behind it lay the mentality that could contend with such confidence that black people had no cricket history.

For a century, as the feature writer James Lawton pointed out, the English-speaking cricket establishment was happy to tolerate blacks at the plush Wanderers, and in their cricket clubs and grounds, but they had to know their place:

There have always been black boys at the Wanderers, of course ... They operated the water sprinklers nourishing the cricket and hockey fields, they worked in the kitchens and the dressing rooms, handed fresh towels and soap to the members and, if they were very presentable, very smart, they might just graduate to carrying tray-fulls of gin and tonic and whisky soda out onto the shaded terraces.[20]

White people lived comfortably in their segregated world. They put black spectators in separate enclosures at the Wanderers, Newlands and elsewhere.[21]

While the cricketers were sometimes ostensibly liberal (and this should not be assumed), they were comfortable with the system.

The cricket of the whites-only SACA institutionalised racism – like the school system, courts, press, Boy Scouts and other arms of society. The sport of cricket, therefore, was drenched in the substance and prejudices of colonialism and apartheid. Today, the language or discourse of cricket still draws significantly from these learned ideas and experiences.

HOW RACISM REPRODUCES ITSELF IN CRICKET TODAY

Racist Victorian and apartheid ideas, originating in the social Darwinism of the 19th-century Victorians, are still widely prevalent in cricket. They are transmitted and reproduced (often subconsciously) in many forms in the media and by top players and cricket lovers in the old establishment. This acts as a bar to progress and change. They need to be talked about, understood and challenged.

The first warning sign is when inequalities and discrimination are phrased in term of naturalness. As was shown in Chapter 3, the Victorians perceived themselves to be superior people sitting at the head of the evolutionary chain, which had at its base the apes and the dark races they had conquered.

The pseudo-scientific typification of black people as almost part of nature followed. The 'noble savage', exemplified by the Zulu in many British novels, was a natural athlete full of a threatening sexual energy. So when Hylton Ackerman agrees that 'black players have a naturally lithe physique, which makes them better suited to bowling than batting', he is feeding right into this old discourse.[22] The natural next step is to talk, as he did, about Hashim Amla being 'my Graeme Pollock'. Blacks, like the working class professionals of old in the class society of England, must be bowlers. Whites, like the gentlemen in England, are the batsmen. Ackerman's good batsman had to have a white role model.

The media of the 1990s consistently tapped into this imagery in relation to Makhaya Ntini. The report by Mark Smit of *Business Day* after Ntini took a match-winning career-best six for 66 against New Zealand in 2000 has been used as an example by media analysts:

On successive days of the Bloemfontein test against New Zealand, Smit managed to omit any reference to skill in reporting on Makhaya Ntini's match-winning performance. Under the headline, 'Ntini bowls the Kiwis over', Smit's first reference to Ntini was in the twelfth paragraph: 'Ntini justified all the faith placed in him by Rushdie Magiet and his national selectors by proving his fitness in the most emphatic fashion'. On the next day, Smit described Ntini as 'endlessly eager'.[23]

It took a long time before this fine player, now in the top ten on the PriceWaterhouseCoopers world rankings, was acknowledged for his subtleness, skill and discipline in cricket.

When the great Clive Lloyd is uncomfortable with the tag 'calypso cricketers' to describe West Indian teams, it is because he has experienced the assumptions that black cricketers are not deliberate, technical and studiously intelligent in their application of the game, but somehow given over to natural impulses and raw behaviour.[24]

'Natural' physical differences soon translate into 'natural' cultural differences in the colonial mind. In 2003, believe it or not, Martin Crowe, the New Zealand batting specialist, showed just how entrenched old racial stereotypes are when he stated that 'traditionally, not many Maoris make good cricketers because they don't have the patience or temperament to play through a whole day, leave alone a test match'. He had to apologise.[25] In the same year, the Australian cricketer Darren Lehmann was banned for three games for calling the Sri Lankans 'black cunts'.[26]

The formal language of cricket entrenches these notions of the inferior or dangerous 'other'. That deceptive wrong-arm ball that turns the opposite way to what you are led to believe is officially called the 'Chinaman'. Generations of young South Africans were taught that a sneaky delivery that kept low was a 'coolie creeper'. In 1999 Brian McMillan told a Western Province bowler within hearing range of KwaZulu-Natal batsman Ashraf Mall to bowl a 'coolie creeper'. The British colonial inheritance was speaking directly here. According to Desai *et al*, quoting Valentine Daniel, 'coolie' was a mixed Gujarati and Tamil term referring to a servant in India. In the imperial context, it acquired the added connotation that had 'to do with a denial of personhood and suggestions of someone devoid of morals'.[27] Unfortunately, rather than thinking about the issue, or being humble enough to find out why it gave offence, McMillan said he had used a 'cricketing term' and dismissed the brouhaha that followed as 'a load of crap'.[28]

It is no surprise, as Dr Helen Moffett points out, that Pakistani cricketers are currently getting the worst press of all. After the Cold War, and especially after September 11,

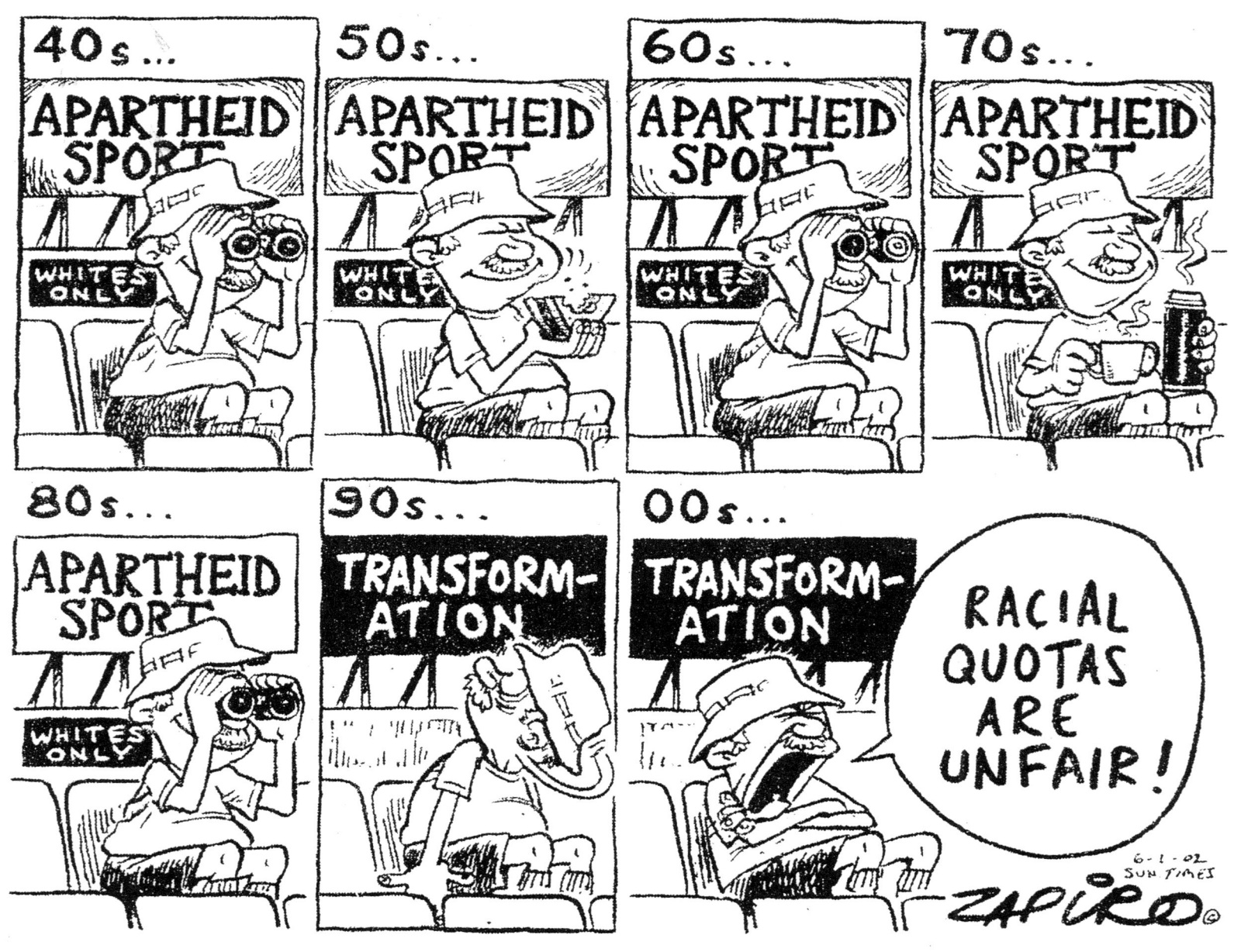

A searing portrayal of white hypocrisy in relation to cricket quotas by award-winning cartoonist, Zapiro, 2002.

the notion of Islam as the dangerous oriental 'other' has grown in western minds.[29] And at a time when India, with its long line of 'wily' spinners, is increasingly staking a claim for the global leadership of the game of the colonial masters, the perceived treachery of Jagmohan Dalmiya is almost unbearable for some to stomach.[30]

It is necessary, in a time of change from apartheid to democracy and its respect for human dignity, to think carefully about language. The observations that top cricketers and 'experts' on television make on television are not neutral or objective, but drawn from a values pool suffused with hundreds of years of history, power and prejudice.

They often promote disempowering stereotypes. Paul Adams, with his wildly unorthodox bowling action, which got him the nickname '*Gogga*' (insect), is one of those who has suffered. Certain commentators have revelled in an alleged looseness. 'There is his loose ball for the over,' is a phrase listeners have heard repeated endlessly. None thought to analyse his statistics closely until John Young showed that Adams's progress in test and one-day cricket matched the best bowlers of his variety since Grimmett in the 1930s.[31]

In the current South African context the debates around cricket 'cultures', transformation, quotas, merit and excellence all betray the still unhealthy dependence on old attitudes and assumptions.

Many former cricketers, like the outspoken Ray Jennings, continue to talk unquestioningly about blacks not having a cricket culture and of whites being victimised and turned into modern-day D'Oliveiras by cricket transformation.[32]

Many cricketers, including world-class all-rounder and former national captain, Shaun Pollock, talk without a hint of irony of the 'cricket culture' that blacks have to learn before they can progress properly. The point they never consider is that South Africa's cricket culture has been built on the foundations of extreme prejudice and notions of cultural superiority and it is, therefore, they who perhaps have to learn a new cricket culture and way of doing things.[33]

For many, cricket transformation and change to redress the inequalities of the past automatically go with the assumptions that it is anti-merit or 'anti-standards'. Journalists contend glibly, 'The bloodless revolution has brought a system that excludes excellence.'[34] Defining themselves as 'cricket purists', they contend 'merit should be the only criterion for selection'. Even if transformation at its heart is about moving from a race-based system where people were excluded merely because of their colour to one which maximises excellence, this discourse immediately pigeonholes it as being 'unfair' and patently promoting mediocrity.

The protectors of 'merit' become the very (white) people who ran and underpinned the racist system of the past, and in many cases still secretly believe in it. When former stars like Clive Rice, Pat Symcox, Fanie de Villiers and Kepler Wessels call for 'experts', or former test players to take over, it effectively implies a perpetuation of the old ways.[35]

These people in their denial or blankness of past realities feed the myth that racial inequalities in cricket evolved naturally. They bolster the old arguments that divisions existed because black people were not interested in the game or were not suited to it psychologically, emotionally and physically.

The argument that it will take time is another sign of an attitude that says, 'Watch out, this is our game.'

When Clive Rice rails against 'quotas' and suggests cricketers should break away from the United Cricket Board, his own comfortable career in a whites-only quota set-up is conveniently ignored. As former English professional Peter Roebuck put it during the Ontong affair in Australia in 2002, it was not appropriate for white South Africans to be 'trotting out the old mantras about choosing sides on their merit':

It is hardly appropriate for South Africans to say anything about that. The time for huffing and puffing came 25 years ago when black cricketers were restricted to their own Bantu league.'[36]

When people like Rice say transformation is all 'politics in sport' he forgets that politics shaped his opportunities and politics enabled him to meet Mother Theresa and hold up a white dove in front of tens of thousands of Indian spectators at Eden Gardens, Calcutta, as captain of South Africa in 1991.

Historical illiteracy and amnesia underlies another variant of the old apartheid myths: the past is past and the playing fields are now equal, so what is the fuss about? Many young players who we take as our role models would agree with 22-year-old national captain Graeme Smith, who stated without any self-doubt at the national cricket indaba at Kievietskroon in 2002: 'We are young. These things happened before our time. We don't want to carry around the baggage of the past. We recognise people just as cricketers. I have Ashwell Prince around to dinner at my home, no problem. Let's just get on with the game, full stop.'[37] While this has always been the end goal of the nonracial sports struggle — and it is good to see how racial and generational attitudes have changed — the reality is that the past is still very much with us, and it will take more than a few dinners and some nice guys to redress it.

Graeme Smith is no doubt well-meaning, but we cannot escape or ignore our history.

A whole mentality lies behind the opposition to cricket and broader transformation and the inability to see that the negative impact of the past needs to be addressed actively rather than ignored, wished away or rubbished. This mentality enables whites somehow still to feel the aggrieved party, despite them having blatantly supported and benefited from apartheid in the past.

Instead of Nuremburg, South Africa, thankfully, got Mandela in 1994, but one of the negative outcomes of this transition has been the space it has given the former oppressors to normalise and externalise the past. Many have adopted the kind of attitude that 'apartheid had nothing to do with me', which is one step away from saying that apartheid was not bad.

And so, hey presto — current dysfunctionalities and problems are once again the fault of those who were oppressed. The victims of the past again became the 'problems' of the present.

Many white South Africans complain endlessly with what some commentators have called an 'inconsolable pessimism', about Mbeki, about the ANC, about the country going to the dogs, and about transformation in sport, without recognising their own roles and culpabilities in the past.

Why is it that white South Africans and cricketers can still be so smugly unseeing?

In a recent Steve Biko Memorial Lecture, Professor Ndjabulo Ndebele, Rector of the University of Cape Town and one of this country's finest thinkers, argued that it is because whites themselves are still trapped in a consciousness which he called 'whiteness', stemming from the power they took for granted as a racial aristocracy in the past. He argues that this power and the apartheid culture to which it was linked 'became both a private and public condition', defining a whole 'cultural sensibility'. Whites were entitled to 'land, air, water, beast, and each and every black body'.

In its crudest form, as when Steve Biko was murdered, or as manifested in Truth and Reconcilliation Commission revelations, this racial consciousness meant that:

... the treatment of black people ceases to be a moral concern. Speaking harshly to a black person; stamping with both feet on the head or chest of a black body; roasting a black body over flames to obliterate evidence of murder (not because murder was wrong, but because it was an irritating embarrassment); dismembering the black body by tying wire round its ankles and dragging it behind a bakkie; whipping black school children; handing to 'an illiterate [black] mother presenting her ailing infant for treatment ... a death certificate in order that the [white]

doctor should not be disturbed in the night. These are things one who is white, in South Africa, can do from time to time to black bodies, in the total scheme of things.[38]

Professor Ndebele says the expression of this subconsciousness of innate superiority showed itself in various ways 'from the crude to the sophisticated' and it still exists throughout the educational, religious, cultural and business leadership of this country, 'caught in the culture of "whiteness" they built'. For Ndebele,

the quest for a new white humanity will begin to emerge from a voluntary engagement, by those caught in the culture of whiteness of their own making, with the ethical and moral implications of being situated at the interface between inherited, problematic privilege, on the one hand, and on the other, the blinding sterility at the centre of the 'heart of whiteness'.[39]

There is a message here for cricket. It is time to acknowledge that the old white cricket establishment has a deeply racist inheritance; people who complain at the drop of a hat on the right wing of the cricket spectrum and who thrived under the old system would do well to recognise the beams in their own eyes before they criticise the new dispensation in cricket.

There are many well-meaning cricketers across the racial spectrum who have moved with the times, but old attitudes still unhealthily permeate South African cricket, muddling debates and holding back transformation aimed at redressing historical inequalities in the process.

The latest example of this consciousness of 'whiteness' and historical denial and 'history as negation' in cricket is one of the new cricket books that appeared on the market during the World Cup. Written by Luke Alfred, deputy sports editor of the *Sunday Times*, the book, *Testing Times*, deals with South African cricket between 1947 and 1963. The subtitle is *The Story of the Men who made South African Cricket*.[40] The only black South African mentioned is Dennis Brutus who appears on the last page. President Nasser of Egypt is among the fortunate few black international figures to get a mention. Black people are invisible in this seamless and natural story, which casts in heroic mould those who severed the game from its imperial connections and gave it a 'South African' character. Their game took place in a sanitised space; it was apparently above politics — except now and again.

At three minutes before noon on the morning of 16 December 1949, the 'Dingaan's Day' holiday celebrating the defeat of the Zulu in battle, the Australian and SA XI teams playing at Kingsmead 'lined up facing the main grandstand, waiting for the peal of noon bells signalling the doors of the

[new] Voortrekker Monument in Pretoria were about to be opened'. We are told by a naïve Alfred that for the first time 'cricket, so long played in splendid isolation, was being dragged into the political realm'.[41]

The period covered by the book coincides exactly with the entrenchment of apartheid, but only passing, indirect reference is made to broader developments at the beginning and end of chapters. Cricket was a sanitised game played in a vacuum. Telegrams from National Party Prime Ministers and ministers are merely incidental. The first British anti-apartheid demonstrators are noted and fade off the page without any indication of what the white Springboks thought about the issues, or how they were implicated or not.[42]

In 1956/57, 'precise instructions' were given to Peter May and his MCC team 'to keep away from political issues at all costs'. When manager Freddie Brown tossed a consignment of Archbishop Trevor Huddleston's famous anti-apartheid tract, *Naught for Your Comfort*, into the Bay of Biscay on the journey to South Africa, the author finds he was not being politically subjective or malicious. He 'simply did what he thought best'.[43]

Black agency does not exist in Alfred's book. The implication is clear. Black South Africans were not among those who 'made' South African cricket. The possibility that it might have been Basil D'Oliveira's non-racial South African team of the 1950s rather than the whites-only Springboks who laid the foundations for the future does not even get a consideration. Not one South African black cricketer is even mentioned, nor is there any explanation for this.

It would be funny, if it was not so damaging, this amnesia and avoidance of a truth that all South Africans lived. The next step from here is to criticise the present cricket set-up as 'Third World', as Luke Alfred did recently in his column. His writing is typical of a whole spectrum of (still dominant) South African sports journalism which perpetuates old historical narratives that not only put whites at the centre of cricket's history, but also absolves them from any responsibility for the past by portraying them as being as much victims of an unreasonable Afrikaner nationalist government as of the non-racial bodies of the black cricketers. In this way, the marginal role of the people disadvantaged by apartheid is perpetuated.

Archbishop Desmond Tutu has said that those whites who do not acknowledge any sense of guilt or injustice about the past are 'in a sense worse off' than those who do:

Apart from the hurt that it causes to those who suffered, the denial by so many white South Africans even that they benefited from apartheid is a crippling, self-inflicted blow to their capacity to enjoy change and appropriate the fruits of change.[44]

An acknowledgement of the past and a humility about it should be the starting points in any discussion about South African cricket's future.

The cricket feats of great players like Graeme Pollock, Eddie Barlow and Barry Richards can be acknowledged without losing sight of the social context in which the game was played.

In a poignant moment at the historic 1998 UCB transformation conference, grey-haired Henry Metembo from Free State said one of the biggest frustrations in life for him was that the younger generation would not believe that he had actually played cricket decades before. He wanted to be able to point to the bookshelf and say, 'Look there.' Hopefully, Henry Metembo's plea will be heard now that the UCB has made the proper recording of South Africa's cricket history a priority.

President Thabo Mbeki has also emphasised the importance of reinserting people into the national narrative and helping to empower the 'invisible' African whose cultures, customs, beliefs and histories had been systematically destroyed over the centuries. At the launch of the Freedom Park heritage project on 16 June 2002, he quoted novelist Ben Okri to make the point:

He was born invisible. His mother was invisible too, and that was why she could see him. His people lived contented lives, working on the farms, under the familiar sunlight. Their lives stretched back into the invisible centuries and all that had come down from those differently coloured ages were legends and rich traditions, unwritten and therefore remembered. They were remembered because they were lived...

It was in the books that he first learnt of his invisibility. He searched for himself and his people in all the history books he read and discovered to his youthful astonishment that he didn't exist. This troubled him so much that he resolved, as soon as he was old enough, to leave his land and find the people who did exist, to see what they looked like...

He travelled the seas, saying little, and when anyone asked him why he journeyed and what his destination was, he always gave two answers. One answer was for the ear of the questioner. The second answer was for his own heart. The first answer went like this: 'I don't know why I am travelling. I don't know where I am going.' And the second answer went like this. 'I am travelling to know why I am invisible. My quest is for the secret of visibility.'

Those who worked with him in those years saw him as a simple man. Actually, they didn't see him at all.[45]

The saliency of those words for South Africa and for cricket cannot be overstated.

Chapter 43

THE FUTURE *and its* INSPIRATIONS

THE POLITICS AND ECONOMICS of colonialism and apartheid meant that Africans were the most oppressed, impoverished and excluded sector of South African society. The advent of democracy means that Africans will take the lead in future.

The growth and future health of cricket in South Africa lies in its ability to spread into the African market. This sector of the population constitutes nearly 80 percent of the population in South Africa, but still only a small percentage of the cricket-playing population. A recent survey used by the South African Rugby Football Union (SARFU) clearly delineated the sports markets of the future. Of the total number of South African children in the 7-15 age group in 1999, 3.3 million were black African, 360 000 white, 323 000 coloured and 84 000 Indian.[1] If cricket could get ten percent of this market to participate in the game, it would be well on the way to becoming truly national in character.

In the 1998 Transformation Charter, the UCB made 'Redress and Representivity' along the above lines a key goal for the future:

Our historic and moral duty is to ensure that cricket grows and flourishes amongst the truly disadvantaged of society, with the recognition that the majority of the disadvantaged come from our black African communities. This involves a commitment to develop potential among our black African people at all levels of the game. This programme reaffirms our mission to bring cricket to all the people of South Africa and facilitate a culture of non-racialism.[2].

The last point is both interesting and significant. The design of colonialism and apartheid was to pigeonhole and partition people into racial ghettos and mindsets. But, the basic defence of black people to racial oppression, as Nelson Mandela demonstrated, was to assert a universal vision and a broad humanity.

Non-racialism has always underpinned the broader struggle for freedom and it is inscribed as a key principle into the new constitution of South Africa for that reason. Progressive voices in cricket have also always echoed the broader universal political demands and vision from the start. Indeed, one of the greatest legacies of the Majola family and the Eastern Cape cricketers is their contribution to non-racialism. They were following in the footsteps of Umhalla, Jabavu, Rubusana and others who from the outset stood up to discrimination and self-confidently saw themselves as part of a wider national and international community.

In the 1970s and 1980s, when apartheid sport was trying to buy its way out of trouble with its multinational policy and rebel tours, new opportunities beckoned for African sportsmen. Lennox Mlonzi and the Transvaal-based national cricket leadership bought into the ethnic co-option strategy of the apartheid rulers. One of the most important legacies left by the Eastern Cape cricketers and the Majolas was their decision to take a contrary line. They rejected links with apartheid sport and aligned themselves unambiguously with the project of the liberation movement and the non-racial SACBOC and SACB. The bottom line was equal opportunities and full citizenship rights for all South Africans. In this, they gave content to the concept of non-racialism, even if conditions were not favourable at the time and there were consequently practical flaws because of restraints imposed by apartheid laws. Rugby fans have

ABOVE AND OPPOSITE *Media reflecting cricket's new markets, 2003.*

testified how there was a 'mystique' about KWARU and its African players when the team turned out in areas designated 'coloured', and this was heightened when the Watson brothers played. Eastern Cape people kept the vision alive.[3]

In the last few years there has been some contestation in cricket about the most appropriate philosophies and policies for the future, but the dominant position is still firmly non-racial and inclusive. Whether or not this tradition maintains itself will be one of the questions resolved in future debates within the new black leadership of cricket. The outcome will be influenced by trends within the broader movement for change, particularly in the governing ANC.

Regardless of differing strategic views, transformation, which aims to redress the historic marginalisation of black and African cricketers, remains the core of the UCB's vision for the future. As Gerald Majola has reiterated, it will remain an ongoing priority in future. The broad socio-economic inequalities arising from apartheid will take generations to eliminate, and cricket needs to remain an active agent for change, or it will stagnate.

Nevertheless, it is inescapable that huge progress has been made in making cricket a rooted national game. Opinion surveys have shown that it is now the second most popular sport in the new South Africa after soccer. The latest Markinor survey also reveals that cricket is the only sport enjoyed equally by men and women readers.[4]

City Press, a Sunday newspaper with predominantly black readers, said in an editorial after South Africa crashed out of the ICC World Cup 2003, ' ... cricket has become our pride and one of the fastest growing sports in the country. What makes it more unique is that it cuts across all racial lines'. The newspaper commented that there would inevitably be questions. 'The most important thing now, however, is to look to the future and stop the perpetual mourning.'[5]

In the letters columns, *City Press* readers confirmed the growth of cricket as a national game in the new environment of democracy. Itumeleng Mosipha from Rustenburg wrote:

It seems lately the game of cricket has grown into the hearts of black South Africans. In the townships and shebeens the main topic of discussion was not about whether Maroka Swallows might win the league, but whether the Duckworth Lewis system was necessary in cricket. I was in awe as my fellow black brothers were talking about a sport that has been played for whites and dominated by whites for a long time.[6]

Daphne Moloi of Germiston underlined the growing support for the game amongst all sectors of the population. He said, 'Being a black man in South Africa I always thought cricket was for whites; they even played for five straight days wearing white clothes!' But, he continued, he had discovered that cricket was actually a very nice game, and it was 'very painful for us to be kicked out of the World Cup'.[7]

These are all signs that South African cricket is at last healing itself and becoming accessible to everyone in South Africa.

Gerald Majola was 11 years old when his father died. He was six years the junior of a big brother who starred on the fields in the 1970s and 1980s and helped direct the game in new directions in the 1990s.

Today he sits in the CEO's office at the UCB headquarters at the Wanderers Club in Johannesburg. On the walls are photos of his father, mother and brother. In a real sense, he has based his vision on the efforts and principles they, and the generations before them, have struggled for. Majola typifies a middle class respectability and determination that has found its place. The sense of family, the awareness of roots, the neat dress, the suave manners, the ability to communicate across barriers, and even a shiny black Lexus GS 300 are reflections of this.

The photographs are about much more than just family. The respect accorded to the Majolas in African sport is also related to what they have stood for. As teachers and respected community figures, Eric and Milase were quintessential representatives of a long sports tradition based on valuing education, upholding decent values and combining individual self-respect and community-consciousness in a confident African-rooted identity, even as a

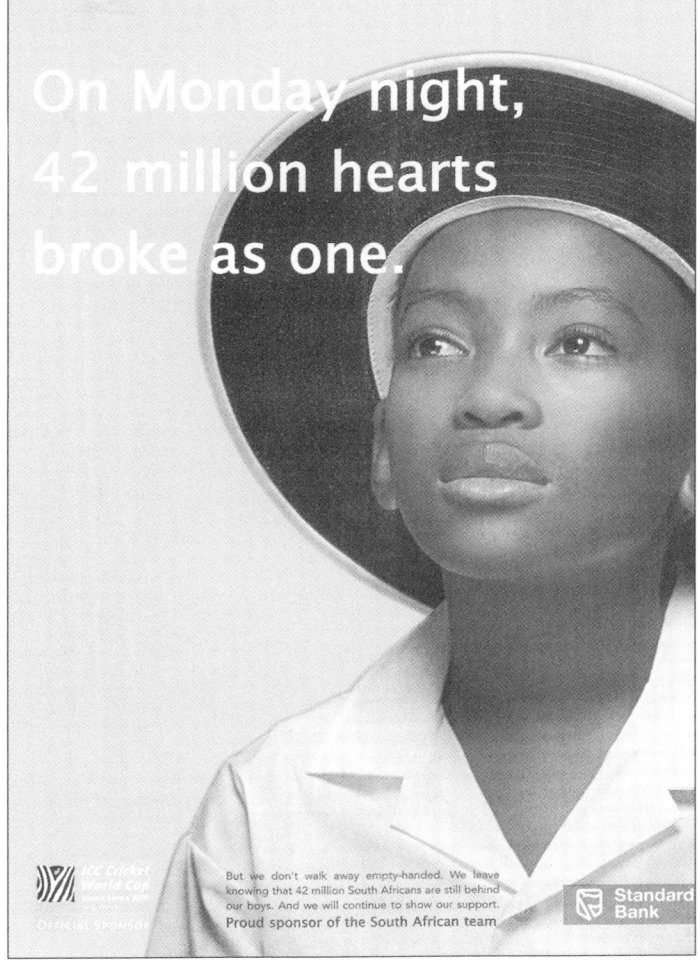

vicious and racist system sought to break down black advancement and dignity. When the Robben Island prisoners formed a Majola Cricket Union in 1977, they were acknowledging this family as representatives of a tradition.

While Majola is non-racial in outlook, another defining characteristic of the man at the helm of the UCB is his self-confident African identity. Often when one phones him, the voicemail will switch on to the following recitation in Zulu:

Ndlovu, Gatyeni, uboya benyathi buyasongwa buyasombuluka, ung-wenyama, intsizwa yakwa Mpongo nakwa zingelwayo.[8]

These are the clan praises of the Majolas from the Ndlovu (or Elephant) clan on his father's side. Derived from images in nature, they explain the identity and characteristics of the family. The Ndlovus, it is said, are slippery and elusive, like a skin which unravels whenever you try to roll it up.

Drawing on his Hlubi Zulu heritage, Majola invariably wears an *isiphandla* around his wrist. This is a band of dried goat skin from an animal that has been offered to the ancestors. 'You keep a piece' and the ancestors 'are now with you'.[9]

On the other side of Majola's study at the UCB, above a comfortable sofa, hangs a hefty wooden picture frame holding three portraits which reflect more contemporary identities and

goals. And they acknowledge the context in which the above-mentioned individual, family and community struggles took place. On the left is Nelson Mandela and on the right Thabo Mbeki. In the middle is Martin Luther King.

Majola is quoted by the *Evening Post* as saying that these three people represented 'my pursuit of my ideals. King's vision of non-racialism, Mr Mandela's statesmanship as a remarkable conciliator and Mr Mbeki's thrust for delivery on the needs of the nation'.

For Majola, the latter is currently the most relevant 'of my three icons' because he emphasises the need to 'bring sustainable delivery to our ideals ... What President Mbeki is telling us is simple: good proposals and nice sounding words are not enough. We need action. We need to deliver.'[10]

The construction of identity is never without contradiction, but the portraits on the wall at the Wanderers tell a story of a game going into the future aware of the past. The struggle in South Africa has brought vindication for the generations that went before. The spirit of Nathaniel Cyril Umhalla, who walked out to bat amidst the bunting, tents and refreshment stalls in Queenstown in 1870, seeking only to be treated like all other citizens and lovers of cricket, can rest at last.

REFERENCES

Detailed references are provided in order to validate the hitherto unrecognised history in *The Story of an African Game*, and in order to point future researchers in the direction of useful sources. The full details of publications are given when they are first referred to. Thereafter, the references are abbreviated. As far as possible, newspaper references include the title of the specific article used. However, this was not always possible; for example, in the case of the 1930s material, only the general newspaper reference was noted during the author's original research.

INTRODUCTION

1 Peter Abrahams, *The Coyaba Chronicles: Reflections on the black experience in the twentieth century* (David Philip, Cape Town, 2000), p. 182.
2 See A. Desai, V. Padayachee, K. Reddy and G. Vahed, *Blacks in whites, A century of cricket struggles in KwaZulu-Natal* (University of Natal Press, Pietermaritzburg, 2002), chapter 1, for a fuller discussion on the issue of race, class and ethnicity in cricket.
3 *Ibid.*, p. 4.

Part One

THE MAKING OF A UNIQUE CRICKET TRADITION (1850s-1900s)

Chapter 1 A GAME FOR PRINCES

1 This chapter relies heavily on seminal historical works on the Xhosa in the mid-1800s by two authors. They are N. Mostert, *Frontiers, The epic of South Africa's creation and the tragedy of the Xhosa people* (Pimlico, London, 1993 edition) and Janet Hodgson's MA thesis on Zonnebloem College and various writings emanating from it. The reference here is from Mostert, p. 1193. Another important work on the cattle-killing episode is J.B. Peires, *The dead will arise* (Ravan Press, Johannesburg, 1989).
2 N. Mostert, *Frontiers*, pp. 1177-1179.
3 *Ibid.*, p. 1181.
4 *Ibid.*, pp. 1193-1194.
5 *Ibid.*, p. 1187.
6 *Ibid.*, p. 1222.
7 *Ibid.*, p. 1229.
8 J. Hodgson, *Princess Emma* (A.D. Donker, Craighall, 1987), p. 46.
9 J. Hodgson, 'Cape Town as a cradle of black writing' in C.C. Saunders, H. Phillips and E. van Heyningen (eds.), *Studies in the history of Cape Town*, vol. 4 (UCT, 1981), p. 14.
10 *Ibid.*, p. 9.
11 J. Hodgson, 'A history of Zonnebloem College, 1858-1870. A study in church and society' (unpublished MA thesis, UCT, 1979), pp. 8-10.
12 J. Hodgson, *Princess Emma*, pp. 50-51.
13 J. Hodgson, 'Cape Town as a cradle of black writing', p. 11.
14 J. Hodgson, *Princess Emma*, pp. 51-52.
15 *Ibid.*, p. 54.
16 *Ibid.*, p. 53.
17 Hodgson, 'History of Zonnebloem College', p. 453.
18 A.C. Parker, *The Springboks, 1891-1970* (Cassell, London, 1970), p. 2.
19 D. Mc Intyre, *The Diocesan College, Rondebosch, South Africa, A history of 'Bishops'* (Juta, Cape Town, 1950), p. 20.
20 J. Hodgson, 'History of Zonnebloem College', p. 453.
21 J. Hodgson, 'Cape Town as a cradle of black writing', p. 17.
22 *Ibid.*, pp. 17-18.
23 J. Hodgson, 'Zonnebloem College and Cape Town, 1858-1870 in C.C. Saunders (ed.), *Studies in the history of Cape Town* (UCT, 1979), p. 10; J. Hodgson, 'History of Zonnebloem College, p. 82.
24 A. Odendaal, 'African political mobilisation in the Eastern Cape, 1880-1910' (unpublished DPhil dissertation, Cambridge University, 1983), p. 14.
25 J. Hodgson, 'History of Zonnebloem College', p. 76.
26 'Grand cricket match', *Queenstown Free Press*, 4 November 1870. My thanks to Janet Hodgson for giving me this reference in 1981.
27 *Ibid.*
28 *Ibid.*
29 *Ibid.*
30 *Ibid.* See also *Queenstown Free Press*, 8 March 1875 for a match between St Mark's and the Bolotwa mission.
31 J. Hodgson, 'History of Zonnebloem College', pp. 82-83. For a biography of Nathaniel Umhalla see S.E.K. Mqhayi, *U So-Gqumahashe* (Lovedale Press, Lovedale, 1921).
32 'Ibola e-Monti', *Isigidimi sama Xhosa*, 15 October 1883.
33 'Cricket – Native Champion vs Alberts', *Cape Mercury*, 3 March 1885.
34 'Cricket' *Cape Mercury*, 24 March 1885; 'Amangesi nabantsundu', *Imvo Zabantsundu*, 23 March 1885.

35 'An Anglo-African team', *Imvo Zabantsundu*, 25 October 1888.
36 'Ibala labadlali', *Imvo Zabantsundu*, 13 October 1892; 'Idinala ye Frontier', *Imvo Zabantsundu*, 21 November 1894.
37 See, for example, N. Cardus, *Autobiography* (Collins and the Book Club, London, 1947); A. Ross, 'The presence of Ranji' in R. Guha, *The Picador book of cricket* (Picador, London, 2001), pp. 410-412; and J. Young, 'Pitch Report', *Mail & Guardian*, 7 March 2003.
38 N. Cardus, *Autobiography*, p. 170.
39 Quoted in C.C. Saunders, 'Through the eyes of an African: The diary of Nathaniel Umhala', *Quarterly Bulletin of the South African Library*, vol. xxxiv, no. 1 (1979), p. 29. According to Chief Phatekile Holomisa, head of CONTRALESA, the organisation representing traditional chiefs in South Africa, the term 'Chief' is a colonial construct and a more correct and appropriate word would be 'Lord', as used in England.

Chapter 2 MISSIONARIES AND THE GENTLEMEN CRICKETERS OF THE 1800s

1 See A. Odendaal, 'African political mobilisation', chapter 1.
2 R. Archer and A. Bouillon, *The South African Game. Sport and racism* (Zed Press, London, 1982), p. 26.
3 See, for example, St Matthew's S.P.G.Mission Keiskamma Hoek, 'Visit of the Lord Bishop of Grahamstown and a short account of the mission, May 1884' (Lovedale Mission Press, Lovedale, 1884), p. 8; C. Bundy, *The rise and fall of the South African peasantry* (Heineman, London, 1979), pp. 40-43; A. Odendaal, 'African political mobilisation', p. 15.
4 A. Odendaal, 'African political mobilisation', p. 14.
5 H. Calderwod, 'Caffres and Caffre missions', pp. 210-211, quoted in D. Williams, *Umfundisi, A biography of Tiyo Soga, 1829-1971* (Lovedale Press, Lovedale, 1978), p. 82.
6 Quoted in R. Guha (ed.), *The Picador book of cricket*, p. 3; R.H.W. Shepherd, *Lovedale South Africa, The story of a century, 1841-1941* (Lovedale, 1940), p. 508.
7 A.F. Hattersley, *An Illustrated Social History of South Africa* (Cape Town, 1969), p. 221.
8 Bishop Henry Cotterell, 'Journal of the Bishop of Grahamstown in a visitation of the Kaffrarian missions in September and October 1860' (London, 1861) The date of the entry is 27 September 1860. I am grateful to Michael Berning for this reference.
9 *The Kaffir Express*, 1 December 1870, p. 4.
10 Cape Archives, NA 467, Ecclesiastical 1875-1890, J. Buchanan to C. Brownlee, 21 June 1877.
11 'Umdlalo webola', *Isigidimi sama Xhosa*, 1 March 1884.
12 'Ibala labadlali', *Imvo Zabantsundu*, 8 October 1891. Healdtown is commonly referred to as Healdtown College but the formal designation is Healdtown Institution.
13 'Umdlalo we krikiti', *Isigidimi sama Xhosa*, 15 March 1884.
14 'The late Date Kwashu', *Imvo Zabantsundu*, 16 March 1926.
15 *Grahamstown Journal*, 11 June 1853. My thanks to George Hofmeyr for this reference. It comes from his rough notes for the PhD dissertation on King Williams Town.
16 G.S. Hofmeyr, 'King Williams Town and the Xhosa, 1854-1921 (The role of a frontier capital during the high commissionership of Sir George Grey)' (unpublished MA dissertation, University of Cape Town, 1981), pp. 58-9.
17 A.F. Hattersley (ed.), *John Sheddon Dobie South African Journal, 1826-6*, Van Riebeeck Society, first series, no. 26 (Cape Town, 1945), p. 46.
18 See, for example, J.T. Jabavu to the editor, *Isigidimi sama Xhosa*, 1 May 1879, 1 February 1880 and 1 July 1880.
19 I.W.W. Citashe to the editor, *Isigidimi sama Xhosa*, 1 June 1882. The translation of this quote is from A.S. Gerard, *Four African literatures, Xhosa, Sotho, Zulu, Amharic* (Berkley, California University Press, 1971). Citashe and Wauchope were two names, used by the same person. Hoho was the mountain stronghold where the Ngqika Chief, Sandile, was killed in 1878.
20 See A. Odendaal, 'African political mobilisation', chapter 2.
21 J.M. Coetzee, *Stranger Shores, Essays 1986-1999* (Seeker and Warburg, London, 2001) p. 340, quoting Mostert, *Frontiers*, p. 1257.
22 See, for example, A. Odendaal, 'African political mobilisation', chapter 5.
23 Quoted in R. Christiansen, *The Visitors, Culture shock in nineteenth-century Britain* (Chatto and Windus, London, 2000), p. 179. I am grateful to John Young for this reference. His readings and generous comments helped sharpen my insights in this work.
24 On this see B.Willan, 'An African in Kimberley: Sol T. Plaatje, 1894-8' in S. Marks and R. Rathbone (eds.), *Industrialisation and Social Change in South Africa, African Class Formation, Culture and Consciousness, 1870-1930* (London, 1982), pp. 250-2 and A. Odendaal, 'South Africa's black Victorians: Sport and society in South Africa in the 19th century' in J.A. Mangan (ed.), *Pleasure, Profit and Proselytism: British Culture and sport at home and abroad, 1700-1914* (Frank Cass, London, 1988) chapter 11.
25 Editorial notes, *Imvo Zabantsundu*, 28 February 1889.
26 B. Willan, 'An African in Kimberley', pp. 248-9.
27 'Umanyano nge mfundo', *Isigidimi sama Xhosa*, 1 February 1884.
28 'A sound mind in a sound body', *APO*, 15 January 1910.
29 R. Archer and A. Boullion, *The South African game*, p. 115.
30 V.S. Naipul, 'The Caribbean flavour' in R. Gua (ed.), *The Picador Book of Cricket*, p. 433.
31 *Ibid.*, pp. 433-4. His book is a cricket classic: C.L.R. James, *Beyond a boundary* (Serpent's Tail, London, 2000).
32 N. Mandela, *Long walk to freedom, the autobiography of Nelson Mandela* (Abacus, London, 1995), p. 44.

Chapter 3 FIRST CLUBS AND COMPETITIONS

1 T. Chesterfield and J. McGlew, *South Africa's cricket captains* (Zebra Press, Cape Town, 2003), pp. 1-2.
2 R. Archer and A. Boullion, *The South African game*, pp. 22-24.
3 'Iziqingata neziqingata', *Imvo Zabantsundu*, 10 June 1897.
4 'Imidlalo eKomani', *Imvo Zabantsundu*, 16 July 1907.
5 *Imvo Zabantsundu*, 2 January 1894, p. 2.
6 Y. Agerdien, 'South End United Club' (Typewritten article to celebrate club's 75th anniversary), Yunus Agerdien papers in André Odendaal Collection. See also Y[usuf] Agerdien, A. George and S. Hendricks, *South End, As we knew it*.
7 *Ibid*.
8 The orginal founding date given was 1843, but researchers have recently revised this. See R. Isherwood to A. Odendaal, 17 April 2003; the website http://stgeorgespark.upe.ac.za/newspaper1html; and S. Levy, 'PECC, The first club in southern Africa' (Journal of the Port Elizabeth Historical Society, December 1979), p. 103.
9 A. Odendaal, 'African political mobilisation', pp. 62-63.
10 'To-day's telegrams', *Imvo Zabantsundu*, 27 April 1897.
11 'Ibandla le Tiyopia', *Isigidimi sama Xhosa*, 1 October 1884.
12 'Umanyano lwasebenzi', *Imvo Zabantsundu*, 5 November 1891.
13 'Imbumba yomfo ka Gaba', *Isigidimi sama Xhosa*, 1 November 1882 and 'Imbumba yamanyama', *Isigidimi sama Xhosa*, 1 March 1884.
14 'Umdlalo we cricket e-Bhayi', *Imvo Zabantsundu*, 16 March 1885; 'I-bala le cricket', *Imvo Zabantsundu*, 8 July 1883; 'Ibala labadlali', *Imvo Zabantsundu*, 1 December 1884, 29 December 1884, 11 May 1885, 6 September 1888 and 7 January 1889.
15 'Ukuzigcobisa – Port Elizabeth', *Imvo Zabantsundu*, 5 October 1898.
16 'Pakathi kwama Silamsi nododana oluntsundu lwase Tinara', *Isigidimi sama Xhosa*, 1 March 1884.
17 Paper read by Elijah Makiwane to the United Missionary Conference, *Imvo Zabantsundu*, 19 July 1888.
18 'Ibola e-Monti', *Isigidimi sama Xhosa*, 15 October 1883.
19 'King Williams Town NCC vs E. London NCC', *Isigidimi sama Xhosa*, 16 January 1884. For a profile of Rubusana, see T. Karis and G. Carter, *From protest to challenge: A documentary history of African politics in South Africa, 1882-1964*, vol. 4 (Hoover Institution Press, Stanford, 1977), pp. 134-5.
20 'King Williams Town NCC vs East London NCC', *Isigidimi sama Xhosa*, 16 January 1884.
21 Umdlalo we krikiti', *Isigidimi sama Xhosa*, 1 February 1884. See also Nathaniel Umhalla's reply 'H.J. Malgas nebanda lase bola lase Qonce', *Isigidimi sama Xhosa*, 1 March 1884.
22 'Umdlalo we krikiti', *Isigidimi sama Xhosa*, 16 January 1884, 1 May 1884 and 2 June 1884.
23 'Pakati kwama silamsi nododana ointsundu lwase Tinara', *Isigidimi sama Xhosa*, 1 March 1884; 'Newlands C.C. vs Gaika C.C.', *Isigidimi sama Xhosa*, 2 June 1884.
24 'Heald Town vs Fort Beaufort', *Isigidimi sama Xhosa*, 16 January 1884; 'Umdlalo we krikiti', *Isigidimi sama Xhosa*, 15 April 1884.
25 'Eze bola', *Isigidimi sama Xhosa*, 15 August 1884; *Isigidimi sama Xhosa*, 16 June 1884; 'Kubadlali bola', *Isigidimi sama Xhosa*, 1 November 1884.
26 'Editorial notes', *Isigidimi sama Xhosa*, 15 October 1883.
27 For a fuller description of the newspaper's establishment see, A. Odendaal, 'African political mobilisation', pp. 103-115.
28 'Editorial notes', *Imvo Zabantsundu*, 3 November 1884.
29 See, for example, 'Ukuzigcobisa', *Imvo Zabantsundu*, 21 August 1898 and 11 September 1899; 'Ibala labadlali', *Imvo Zabantsundu*, 18 February 1897.
30 See, for example, 'Ibali laba dlali', *Imvo Zabantsundu*, 23 November 1887.
31 'Ixesha le bhola, 1889', *Imvo Zabantsundu*, 17 October 1889. See also *Imvo Zabantsundu*, 6 September 1895 and 25 June 1896, p. 1.
32 Quoted in *Imvo Zabantsundu*, 22 December 1884.
33 'Ezababaleli', *Imvo Zabantsundu*, 3 November 1884.
34 'Editorial notes', *Imvo Zabantsundu*, 3 November 1884.
35 'Ibala le cricket', *Imvo Zabantsundu*, 19 January 1885.
36 *Ibid*.; 'Native cricket matches', *Cape Mercury*, 15 January 1885.
37 'Native cricket matches', *Cape Mercury*, 15 January 1885.
38 S.C. Caple, *The Springboks at cricket, England versus South Africa, 1888-1960* (Littlebury and Co, Worcester, 1960), p. 10.
39 W.M. Luckin, *The history of South African cricket, including the scores of all important matches since 1878* (W.I. Horton, Johannesburg, 1915), p. 19; 'Cricket tournament', *Cape Mercury*, 3 January 1885. The four teams participating were Port Elizabeth, King Williams Town, Kimberley and Cape Town.
40 I.D. Difford, *The history of South African rugby football, 1875-1932* (The Specialty Press, Wynberg, 1933), p. 14. The same four centres as in cricket participated.
41 'Native cricket matches', *Cape Mercury*, 15 January 1885.
42 'Cricket – Native Champion vs Alberts', *Cape Mercury*, 3 March 1885.
43 *Ibid*.
44 'Editorial notes', *Imvo Zabantsundu*, 9 March 1885.
45 Quoted in *Imvo Zabantsundu*, 9 March 1885.
46 *Ibid*.
47 'Notes', *Cape Mercury*, 3 March 1885.
48 'Editorial notes', *Imvo Zabantsundu*, 9 March 1885.
49 'Cricket' *Cape Mercury*, 24 March 1885; 'Amangesi nabantsundu', *Imvo Zabantsundu*, 23 March 1885.
50 'Editorial notes', *Imvo Zabantsundu*, 2 March 1885.
51 'Natives and cricket', *Imvo Zabantsundu*, 9 March 1885.
52 'Notes', *Imvo Zabantsundu*, 23 March 1885.
53 A. Odendaal, 'African political mobilisation', pp. 57, 64, 291-2; 'Natives and hotels', *Imvo Zabantsundu*, 13 June 1894; 'Ukuzigcobisa isazisokubadlali', *Izwi Labantu*, 17 September 1901.

54 A. Odendaal, 'African political mobilisation', pp. 63-4, 288.
55 *Ibid*., pp. 284-8.
56 *Ibid*., pp. 158-9, 291-2.
57 'Izimiselo ze kroki', *Isigidimi sama Xhosa*, 16 June 1884. See also tennis report in *Isigidimi sama Xhosa*, 1 May 1884.
58 Report in *APO*, 24 May 1909.
59 'Amangesi nabantsundu', *Imvo Zabantsundu*, 30 March 1885.
60 'Editorial notes', *Imvo Zabantsundu*, 30 March 1885.
61 *Ibid*.
62 'Ibala laba dlali', *Imvo Zabantsundu*, 21 December 1887.
63 W.M. Luckin, *History of South African cricket*, p. 18.
64 'Editorial notes', *Imvo Zabantsundu*, 16 February 1885; 'Ibola e Komani', *Imvo Zabantsundu*, 9 December 1885; 'Ibala labadlali', *Imvo Zabantsundu*, 21 December 1887; 'Blacks vs whites', *Imvo Zabantsundu*, 18 October 1888; 'Ibala labadlali', *Imvo Zabantsundu*, 8 October 1891. See also 'I-bala le cricket', *Imvo Zabantsundu*, 3 June 1885; 'Ibala labadlali', *Imvo Zabantsundu*, 27 October 1886, 23 November 1887 and 28 May 1896.
65 'Umdlala we bhola', *Isigidimi sama Xhosa*, 16 February 1884.
66 'Ibala le bhola, *Imvo Zabantsundu*, 4 January 1889.
67 S.J. Reddy and B. Bansda (eds.), *South African Cricket Almanack 1969*, p. 62.
68 'Umanyano lwabasebenzi', *Imvo Zabantsundu*, 5 November 1891.
69 'An Anglo-African team', *Imvo Zabantsundu*, 25 October 1888.
70 Luckin, *History of South African cricket*, pp. 15-19.
71 See reports in *Imvo Zabantsundu*, 21 January 1887.
72 See reports in *Imvo Zabantsundu*, 5 February 1891 and 12 March 1891.
73 'Notes on current events', *Imvo Zabantsundu*, 4 October 1888.
74 Sarah Baartman's remains were returned to South Africa for reburial by the *Musee de la Homme* in Paris in 2003 and a significant literature has emerged around her.
75 'Notes on current events', *Imvo Zabantsundu*, 4 October 1888.
76 'Editorial notes', *Imvo Zabantsundu*, 3 November 1884.
77 See, for example, 'Notes of current events', *Imvo Zabantsundu*, 4 October 1888; 'Correspondence', *Imvo Zabantsundu*, 11 October 1888; 'Abadlali abantsundu e England', *Imvo Zabantsundu*, 11 October 1888; 'Correspondence', *Imvo Zabantsundu*, 18 October 1888; 'The Anglo-African team', *Imvo Zabantsundu*, 20 December 1888.
78 A.A. Thompson, 'Bat, ball and boomerang' in R. Gua (ed.), *The Picador book of cricket*, pp. 229-237.
79 Christansen, *The visitors*, p. 170. See his description of the tour in chapter 5.
80 R. Guha, *A corner of a foreign field, The Indian history of a British sport* (Picador, London, 2002), pp. 14, 32.
81 'N. Cricketer to the Editor', *Imvo Zabantsundu*, 11 October 1888.
82 J. Winch, assisted by M. Patel, *Playing the games, The unification of South African sport* (unpublished manuscript, 2000), p. 12.
83 For a report of the tour and life in Port Elizabeth in the 1880s, see M. McCord, *The calling of Katie Makanya* (David Philip, Cape Town, 2000), chapters 2 and 4.
84 See match reports, *Imvo Zabantsundu*, 21 January 1887.
85 See match reports, *Imvo Zabantsundu*, 12 March 1891.
86 Cape Archives, 3/KWT 2/1/1/10/9, Bennie Tele, secretary to Town Clerk, King Williams Town, 27 September 1892.
87 Cape Archives, 3/KWT, 2/1/2/62, P. Xiniwe to Mayor and Councillors, King Williams Town, 15 November 1892, and other letters.
88 See tournament report, *Imvo Zabantsundu*, 5 January 1893.
89 'Notice', *Imvo Zabantsundu*, 8 February 1899.
90 For further details see *Imvo Zabantsundu*, 19 July 1910.
91 Ibala labadlali, *Imvo Zabantsundu*, 17 December 1891 and 14 January 1897.
92 'Ibala labadlali – Ibhola eBhayi', *Imvo Zabantsundu*, 18 January 1888.
93 *Ibid*.
94 'Ibala labadlali', *Imvo Zabantsundu*, 21 January 1897.
95 'Ibala labadlali', *Imvo Zabantsundu*, 24 October 1894; Ibala lebhola', *Izwi Labantu*, 12 November 1901.
96 *Izwi Labantu*, 15 September 1908 and other cuttings in the André Odendaal Collection.
97 Luckin, *History of South African cricket*, p. 31.
98 'Ibala labadlali', *Imvo Zabantsundu*, 2 July 1896.
99 'Ibala labadlali', *Imvo Zabantsundu*, 24 October 1894.
100 *Imvo Zabantsundu*, 10 December 1891, p. 3.
101 See report in *Izwi Labantu*, 22 September 1908. See also report of the 1901 meeting, 'Ibala lebhola', *Izwi Labantu*, 12 November 1901.
102 'Native cricket tourney', *Izwi Labantu*, 7 January 1909; 'Unyadala we qakamba', *Izwi Labantu*, 14 January 1909.
103 See reports in *Izwi Labantu*, 16 January 1910.
104 'I tumente e Cumakala', *Izwi Labantu*, 14 January 1909; 'Notice', *Imvo Zabantsundu*, 26 December 1911.
105 See, for example, 'Ibala labadlali', *Imvo Zabantsundu*, 6 February 1890 and 3 April 1890; reports in *Imvo Zabantsundu*, 7 January 1901, 14 May 1907, 30 July 1907 and 6 August 1907; reports in *Izwi Labantu*, 26 August 1902, 6 March 1906, 29 October 1907, 12 November 1907, 26 November 1907 and 14 January 1908.
106 'Ibala labadlali', *Imvo Zabantsundu*, 11 April 1889.
107 'Ibala labadlali', *Imvo Zabantsundu*, 28 May 1896.
108 See report in *Imvo Zabantsundu*, 22 January 1900.
109 'Ezase Qonce', *Imvo Zabantsundu*, 1895.
110 'Imidlalo', *Imvo Zabantsundu*, 20 October 1908; *Imvo Zabantsundu*, 26 January 1909.
111 'Ibala', *Imvo Zabatsundu*, 12 April 1888.
112 'E Komani' *Imvo Zabantsundu*, 20 April 1898.
113 J. Peires, ' "Facta non verba": Towards a history of black rugby' (paper presented at the History Workshop, University of the Witwatersrand, 1981), p. 1. A version of this paper also appeared in *Work in Progress*, April 1981. P. Dobson, *Rugby in South Africa* p. 201.

114 'Black rugby in Port Elizabeth', n.p., in B. Ngozi, 'History and development of non-white rugby in South Africa' (unpublished sourcebook).
115 A. Odendaal, 'African political mobilisation', p. 42.
116 'Port Elizabeth black rugby', 'Black rugby in Port Elizabeth', 'Orientals Rugby Football Club' and 'History of Spring Rose Rugby Football Club', n.p., in B. Ngozi, 'History and development of non-white rugby in South Africa' (unpublished sourcebook, n.d.).
117 'Indaba', *Imvo Zabantsundu*, 29 May 1899.
118 For details of the EPNRU see 'Ibala lomdlala', *Izwi Labantu*, 12 June 1906; 'Iqakamba', *Izwi Labantu*, 30 April 1907; Eastern Province Native Rugby Union, *Izwi Labantu*, 28 May 1907.
119 *Izwi Labantu*, 23 March 1909.
120 'Eastern Province Coloured Rugby Union', *APO*, 19 October 1912.
121 'PE footballers and the fishing boat disaster', *APO*, 2 November 1912.
122 *APO*, 3 May 1913.
123 A. Booley, *Forgotten Heroes, History of black rugby, 1882-1992* (Independent Newspaper Holdings Limited, Cape Town, 1998), pp. 71-74.

Part Two
SOUTH AFRICAN COLOURED CRICKET BOARD (1890s-1910s)

Chapter 4 CRICKET BECOMES A NATIONAL GAME

1 See, for example, 'Kwa Mzilikazi', *Imvo Zabantsundu*, 4 September 1899; 'Kwa Mzilikazi', *Imvo Zabantsundu*, 2 July 1901.
2 For a detailed discussion of the social life and activities of the black elite in Kimberley see B. Willan, 'An African in Kimberley' in Marks and Rathbone (eds.), *Industrialisation and Social Change*, chapter 9 and B. Willan, *Sol Plaatje: A Biography* (London and Johannesburg, 1984), chapter 2.
3 'Ezase Bloemfontein', *Imvo Zabantsundu*, 8 and 15 November 1893.
4 B. Willan, 'An African in Kimberley' in Marks and Rathbone (eds.), *Industrialisation and Social Change*, p. 241.
5 *Ibid*, pp. 238, 251-2, 257.
6 *Ibid*, p. 252.
7 *Ibid.*, pp. 251-2.
8 *Ibid.*, p. 251.
9 *Ibid.*, pp. 251, 257.
10 *Ibid.*, pp. 252, 258.
11 See, for example, 'Kimberley', *APO*, 19 October 1912.
12 A.F. Hattersley, *Social History*, p. 115.
13 See 'Here come the developers', *Cape Times*, 3 October 2002.
14 A. Odendaal, *Cricket in Isolation: The politics of race and cricket in South Africa* (Cape Town, 1977), p. 324.
15 The work hangs at the offices of the South African Rugby Football Board at the Sports Science Institute in Newlands, Cape Town.
16 Interview with Achmat Davids, Cape Town, 27 January 1995.
17 M. Galant, 'A history of Western Province cricket', (People's History Project, Department of History, University of the Western Cape, 1987), p. 2.
18 'Our history', Ottomans Cricket Club souvenir brochure, 115th anniversary, 1882-1997, Ghatam-al Quran, 14 December 1997, Jamiah Mosque, Cape Town. (Based on an article by A. Adams, *Muslim News*, 11 December 1981).
19 J. Winch, assisted by M. Patel, *Playing the games*, p. 14.
20 *Ibid.*, p. 13.
21 *Ibid.*
22 W.M. Luckin, *History of South African cricket*, pp. 517-518; A. Odendaal, *Cricket in Isolation*, p. 325.
23 E. Rosenthal, 'The "D'Oliveira" incident of the 1890s', undated Cape Times article in André Odendaal Collection.
24 *Ibid.* Luckin and writers who have used him as a source have referred to Samoodien, but I believe that Samsodien, as quoted by Rosenthal, is the correct name.
25 *Ibid.*
26 A. Odendaal, *Cricket in Isolation*, p. 325.
27 P.F. Warner, *The M.C.C. in South Africa* (Cape Town, 1906), p. 2.
28 B. Willan, *An African in Kimberley*, pp. 253-4.
29 P.F. Warner, *Cricket in many climes* (London, William Heineman, 1900), pp. 191-2.
30 Report in *The Friend*, 31 March 1909.
31 Personal communication Saait Magiet, May 2003; P. Dobson, *Rugby in South Africa*, pp. 171-2.
32 A. Grundlingh, A. Odendaal and B. Spies, *Beyond the tryline, Rugby and South African society* (Ravan Press, Johannesburg, 1995), pp. 29-30.
33 'Cape District Cricket Union', *APO*, 16 November 1912.
34 'Concerning clubs in the Peninsula', *APO*, 11 February 1911.
35 'Cricket', *APO*, 1 July 1911. For a profile of Abdurahman see M. Adhikari (ed.), *Dr A Abdurahman: A biographical memoir by J. H. Rynard* (Friends of the National Library of South Africa in association with District Six Museum), Cape Town, 2002, pp. 9-17.
36 'W.P. Cricket Board', *APO*, 16 November 1912.
37 Grundlingh, Odendaal and Spies, *Beyond the tryline*, pp. 30-31; R.E. van der Ross, 'The political and social history of the Cape coloured people, 1880-1970' (unpublished manuscript, Institute for Historical Research, University of the Western Cape), part 3, pp. 618, 622.
38 'Ibala labadlali', *Imvo Zabantsundu*, 19 December 1894.
39 'Ibala labadlali', *Imvo Zabantsundu*, 27 December 1895.
40 'Zonnebloem College', *APO*, 24 September 1910.
41 'E Kapa', *Imvo Zabantsundu*, 5 December 1898 and 'E Kapa', *Imvo Zabantsundu*, 8 February 1899.
42 S. Field, (ed.), *Lost communities, living memories: Remembering the forced removals in Cape Town* (David Philip, Cape Town, 2001), p. 17-18.
43 Cape Archives, NA 428: H. Adams Lowe to Port Captain and Doc Superintendent, Table Bay Harbour Board, 3 August 1904, plus attached correspondence.
44 'Umnyadala we qakamba , e-Kapa', *Imvo Zabantsundu*, 14 January 1908.
45 For details see Cape Archives NA 636, File number 2207: Memorandum by J. Jones, 'Re: cricketers ejected from the native location Uitvlugt', 9 January 1904, and attached correspondence.
46 'For inquiry', *South African News*, 6 January 1904.
47 S. Field, *Lost communities*, p. 18.
48 Desai et al, *Blacks in whites*, p. 125.
49 *Imvo Zabantsundu*, 5 April 1893, p. 2.
50 Desai et al, *Blacks in whites*, p. 126.
51 J. Hodgson, 'History of Zonnebloem College', note 35, chapter 11.
52 Match report, *Inkanyiso Yase Natal*, 5 January 1894. See also Desai et al, *Blacks in whites*, p. 126, quoting Gordon Mears.
53 Desai et al, *Blacks in whites*, pp. 127-129.
54 *Ibid.*, chapter 2.
55 A. Odendaal, *Vukani Bantu! The beginnings of black protest politics in South Africa to 1912* (David Philip, Cape Town and Barnes and Noble, Totowa, New Jersey, 1984), pp. 19-20.
56 *Ibid.*, p. 20.
57 A. Odendaal, *Cricket in isolation*, p. 307.
58 *Berliner Missionsberichte*, 1894, p. 291. My thanks to Dr Werner van der Merwe for this reference.
59 Desai et al, *Blacks in whites*, p. 110; A. Odendaal, *Cricket in isolation*, p. 328.
60 'Ibala labadlali', *Imvo Zabantsundu*, 7 January 1897.
61 *Ibid*
62 'Ibala labadlali', *Imvo Zabantsundu*, 13 January 1898.
63 'E Transvaal', *Imvo Zabantsundu*, 31 October 1898.
64 'Ibala labadlali', *Imvo Zabantsundu*, 13 January 1898.
65 'Ukuziugcobisa', *Imvo Zabantsundu*, 15 March 1899.
66 *Indian Opinion*, 6 March 1909, p. 104.
67 *Indian Opinion*, 4 May 1912, quoted in Desai et al, *Blacks in Whites*, p. 6. See also *Imvo Zabantsundu*, 2 August 1910.
68 See, for example, the detailed scorecards in 'Iqakamba', *Izwi Labantu*, 3 December 1907, 11 July 1907 and 14 January 1908.
69 'Klipspruit location (Johannesburg)', *Izwi Labantu*, undated cutting from André Odendaal Collection.
70 *Tsala ea Becoana*, 30 December 1911, p. 2.
71 'Transvaal Coloured Cricket Union', *APO*, 20 November 1911.
72 See report in *Imvo Zabantsundu*, 6 February 1890; 'Ibala labadlali', *Imvo Zabantsundu*, 25 April 1894.
73 'Imprisoning cricketers', *Imvo Zabantsundu*, 28 November 1894.
74 'The Free State native cricket business', *Imvo Zabantsundu*, 5 December 1894.
75 'Ikrikiti', *Imvo Zabantsundu*, 19 April 1899.
76 'Ukuzigcobisa', *Imvo Zabantsundu*, 10 December 1900.
77 South African Native Affairs Commission, Evidence of J.W. Hancock (Inspector of Locations), ORC, 22 September 1904, p. 393.
78 'Imidlalo', *Izwi Labantu*, 22 October 1907.
79 'Sport', *APO*, 9 April 1910.
80 *The Friend*, 16 April 1909.
81 National Archives, Pretoria, 1/33 N.A. 765 Correspondence files F130 1907-1911: Resident Magistrate Bethulie, OFS, to Acting Secretary for Native Affairs, 16 February 1911.
82 See report, *Izwi Labantu*, 6 February 1906.
83 'Colour and sports', *Tsala ea Batho*, 19 August 1911.
84 *Ibid.*

Chapter 5 THE FORMATION OF NATIONAL CRICKET AND RUGBY BOARDS

1 I.D. Difford, *History of South African rugby*, pp. 27-28; A.C. Parker, *W.P. cricket 100 not-out* (WPCU, Cape Town, 1990), pp. 7-8. For a profile of Frames see I.D. Difford, p. 703.
2 T. Partridge and F. Heydenrych (eds.), *The 1990 Protea Cricket Annual of South Africa*, p. 32.
3 B. Bassano, *South Africa in international cricket, 1888-1970* (Chameleon, East London, 1990), p. 13.
4 I.D. Difford, *History of South African rugby*, p. 215.
5 C. Merrett, 'A political and cultural history of South African cricket' (unpublished manuscript, 2000), p. 7.
6 D. Kelly, 'A Historical Survey of East African Cricket', *The Cricket Quarterly II* (1964), pp. 4-10, and J. Ferguson, 'Cricket in Nigeria', *The Cricket Quarterly IV* (1966), pp. 225, 233-238.
7 J. Morris, *The Spectacle of Empire: Style, Effect and the Pax Britannica* (London, 1982), chapter 8.
8 Quoted in Archer and Bouillon, *The South African Game*, p. 18. For more on Afrikaners and cricket see A. Odendaal, 'Turning history on its head, Some perspectives on Afrikaners and cricket' in C. Day (ed.), *Cricket ... Developing winners, A 10th birthday celebration of the United Cricket Board of South Africa's 'Development for all in the game for all'*, pp. 29-32.
9 A. Odendaal, 'South Africa's black Victorians', pp. 202-3.
10 J. Winch, assisted by M. Patel, *Playing the games*, p. 15.
11 See R. Barker, 'The Demon against England' in Gua (ed.), *The Picador book of cricket*, pp. 301-317.
12 J. Winch, assisted by M. Patel, *Playing the games*, p. 14.
13 *Ibid.*, p. 16.
14 *Ibid.*, pp. 16-7.
15 *Ibid.*, p. 17.
16 For a profile of Milton, see I.D. Difford, *History of South African rugby*, p. 704.
17 J. Winch, assisted by M. Patel, *Playing the games*, pp. 18-20.

18 For example, 'An oppressive municipality', *Imvo Zabantsundu*, 25 November 1897; Cape Archives 3/KWT, 4/1/95: Memorandum from town clerk to borough ranger and forester, King Williams Town, 6 September 1911; Cape Archives, NA 636, file no. 2207, statement by J. Jones, 'Re: cricketers ejected from native location, Uitvlugt', 9 January 1904.

19 'Editorial notes', *Imvo Zabantsundu*, 30 March 1885.

20 R. Magengelele, Secretary, Native Cricket Club, Stutterheim to Mayor and Councillors, 18 October 1897 and R. Mc. N. Plaatjes, Treasurer, to Mayor and Councillors, 2 November 1897, quoted in *Imvo Zabantsundu*, 25 November 1897.

21 'A Native Farmer', Upper Kabousie, Stutterheim to the editor, *Imvo Zabantsundu*, 12 November 1897, quoted in *Imvo Zabantsundu*, 25 November, 1897.

22 G.19-1909 Blue Book on Native Affairs 1908, p. 25.

23 *Ibid.*, p. 52.

24 B. Willan, 'An African in Kimberley', pp. 251-2.

25 'Ibala labadlali', *Imvo Zabantsundu*, 26 August 1897.

26 J. Comaroff and B. Willan, with S. Molema and A. Reed (eds.), *The Mafeking diary of Sol T. Plaatje* (David Philip, Cape Town, 1998), p. 11.

27 B. Willan, *An African in Kimberley*, p. 244; and T. Karis and GM. Gerhart (eds.), *From protest to challenge: A documentary history of African politics in South Africa*, vol. 4, p. 12 (Stanford, 1977).

28 B. Willan, *An African in Kimberley*, pp. 253-4.

29 'A Rhodes Cup', *Imvo Zabantsundu*, 29 July 1897.

30 'Ibala labadlali', *Imvo Zabantsundu*, 26 August 1897.

31 B. Willan, *An African in Kimberley*, p. 257.

32 Grundlingh, Odendaal and Spies, *Beyond the Tryline*, p. 38-39. (For a profile of D.J. Lenders, see *APO*, 13 January 1912.)

33 B. Willan, *An African in Kimberley*, pp. 250-1, 257; P. Dobson, *Rugby in South Africa*, p. 169.

34 D. Harris to I. Bud Mbelle, 1 November 1897, reproduced in *Imvo Zabantsundu*, 2 December 1897.

35 D. Oakes (ed.), *Readers Digest illustrated history of South Africa: The real story* (Readers Digest, Cape Town, 2nd edition, 1989), p. 174.

36 'A Barnato Trophy', *Imvo Zabantsundu*, 2 December 1897.

37 Grundlingh, Odendaal and Spies, *Beyond the Tryline*, p. 39.

38 P. Dobson, *Rugby in South Africa: A history, 1861-1988* (South African Rugby Board, Cape Town, 1989), pp. 168-170; Grundlingh, Odendaal and Spies, *Beyond the Tryline*, p. 41-2.

39 'Itumente e Rini', *Imvo Zabantsundu*, 7 November 1898.

40 *Ibid.*

41 *Ibid.*

42 W.W. Mjokozeli to the sports editor, 8 November 1898 and 'Makaya Akude' to the editor, 9 November 1898 in *Imvo Zabantsundu*, 14 November 1898.

43 'Ukuzigcobisa', *Imvo Zabantsundu*, 14 November 1898.

44 'Itumente e Rini', *Imvo Zabantsundu*, 7 November 1898.

45 'Ukuzigcobisa' and '"Imvo" special wires', *Imvo Zabantsundu*, 12 January 1899.

46 *Ibid.* Town and region (or province as we understand it today) were used interchangeably in the early reports, underlining the newness of the process of selecting representative regional teams.

47 'Ukuzigcobisa', *Imvo Zabantsundu*, 21 August 1899.

48 See notice in *Izwi Labantu*, 21 October 1902.

49 See 'Iqakamba' *Imvo Zabantsundu*, 18 November, 1902 and 'Barnato Trophy tournament', *Imvo Zabantsundu*, 4 December, 1902.

50 'Barnato Board', *Imvo Zabantsundu*, 11 March 1903.

51 *South African Coloured Cricket Board Rules*, in the Krish Reddy Collection

52 *Ibid.*

53 A.E. Docrat, 'A new era in South African cricket', *South African Non-European Cricket Almanack 1953/54*, p. 83.

54 'Presentation of Barnato Cup', *APO*, 23 April 1910.

55 *Ibid.*

56 *Diamond Fields Advertiser*, 12 November 1895, p. 6 and 14 November 1895, p. 6.

57 *APO*, 10 August 1912, p. 11.

58 Annual report by R. Sullaphan, Secretary and Treasurer, Durban and District Indian Cricket Union, 9 August 1913, in Krish Reddy Collection.

59 'Bowling and batting averages of all the participants in the Barnato Cup Tournament 1913, compiled by Mr E. J. Choonoo, who acted as the official scorer of Natal' in Krish Reddy Collection; 'Barnato Cup tournament', *APO*, 19 April 1913.

60 Grundlingh, Odendaal and Spies, *Beyond the Tryline*, pp. 41-42.

61 A. Odendaal, *Vukani Bantu!* p. 153.

62 *Ibid.*, chapters 9-11.

63 *Ibid.*, p. 216.

64 Karis and Gerhart (eds.), *From protest to challenge*, vol. 4, p. 12.

Part Three

SOUTH AFRICAN BANTU CRICKET BOARD (1920s-1950s)

Chapter 6 AFRICAN CRICKETERS GO THEIR OWN WAY

1 A. Odendaal, *Cricket in Isloation*, pp. 329-331.

2 *Umteteli wa Bantu*, 16 January 1932. The Orpen Cup, named after the liberal politician, J.M. Orpen, was started in 1918.

3 T.D. Mweli Skota (ed.), *The African yearly register (Being an illustrated national biographical dictionary (who's who) of black folks in Africa)*, (Johannesburg, 1931), p. 187.

4 *Umteteli wa Bantu*, 16 January 1932.

5 *Ibid.*; D.M. Denelane, 'A short history of the Bantu Cricket Board', SACBOC souvenir programme, 2nd Biennial Inter-Race Tournament, 1953.

6 Mweli Skota, *The African yearly register*, p. 247; 'Great reception to H.R.H. Prince George', *Umteteli wa Bantu*, 24 February 1934.

7 *Ibid.*, p. 187.

8 R.R. Molapo, 'Sports, festivals and popular politics: Aspects of social and popular culture in Langa township, 1945-70' (MA dissertation, UCT, 1994), p. 42. See also M. Wilson and A. Mafeje, *Langa: A study of social groups in an African township* (Cape Town, Oxford University Press, 1973), pp. 114-5.

9 B.P.B. Cossie, 'Western Province (Bantu) Cricket Union, A historical sketch of the Union', in S.J. Reddy and B. Bansda (eds.), *South African Non-European Cricket Almanack, 1953/54*, p. 117.

10 *Umteteli wa Bantu*, 24 December 1932.

11 *Umteteli wa Bantu*, 31 December 1932.

12 'S.A. Bantu cricket tournament', *Umteteli wa Bantu*, 16 December 1933.

13 *Umteteli wa Bantu*, 31 December 1932.

14 *Umteteli wa Bantu*, 30 December 1933.

15 *Umteteli wa Bantu*, 14 October 1933, p. 15.

16 *Umteteli wa Bantu*, 6 January 1934.

17 *Umteteli wa Bantu*, 26 December 1933.

18 *The Sun*, 19 January 1934, p. 8.

19 *Umteteli wa Bantu*, 13 January 1934, p. 4.

20 *Umteteli wa Bantu*, 6 January 1934, p. 14.

21 *Umteteli wa Bantu*, 14 October 1933, p. 15.

Chapter 7 CRICKET IN THE PROVINCES

1 *Umteteli wa Bantu*, 2 January 1932 and 2 April 1932.

2 *Umteteli wa Bantu*, 9 February 1932 and 26 November 1932.

3 B.P.B. Cossie, 'Western Province (Bantu) Cricket Union', in S.J. Reddy and B. Bansda (eds.), *South African Non-European Cricket Almanack 1953/54*, p. 117. See also 'Iqakamba eKapa', *Umteteli wa Bantu*, 21 January 1933.

4 *Umteteli wa Bantu*, 19 November 1932, p. 13.

5 *Umteteli wa Bantu*, 30 January 1932.

6 *Umteteli wa Bantu*, 2 January 1932, 26 November 1932 and 23 December 1933.

7 See H. Bradford, *A taste of freedom, The ICU in rural South Africa, 1924-1930* (Ravan Press, Johannesburg 1987), p. 91. The index has further references to Kroonstad.

8 *Umteteli wa Bantu*, 13 February 1932, p. 9.

9 Desai et al, *Blacks in whites*, pp. 147-8.

10 *Umteteli wa Bantu*, 19 November 1932.

11 See, for example, 'Mine boys!', *Umteteli wa Bantu*, 14 January 1933, p. 14.

12 Karis and Carter, *From protest to challenge*, vol. 4, p. 151.

13 See, for example, *Umteteli wa Bantu*, 13 February 1932, p. 9 and C. Badenhorst, 'Mines, missionaries and the municipality: Organised African sport and recreation in Johannesburg, c1920-1950' (PhD thesis, Queens University, Kingston, 1992), pp. 167, 203-204.

14 Badenhorst, 'Mines, missionaries and the municipality', pp. 229-230.

15 For more details on the BSC and BMSC see *Ibid.*, chapters 4 and 5.

16 E. Sisulu, *Walter and Albertina Sisulu, In our lifetime* (David Philip, Cape Town, 2002), p. 71.

17 'The Board and the Transvaal team', *Umteteli wa Bantu*, 30 January 1937.

Chapter 8 GOLDEN PROVINCE OF THE 1930s AND 1940s

1 A. Odendaal, *Cricket in Isolation*, p. 309.

2 See, for example, *Umteteli wa Bantu*, 31 December 1932 and 2 December 1933, p. 17.

3 S.J. Reddy and B. Bansda (eds), *South African Non-European Cricket Almanack, 1953/54*, pp. 45-49.

4 C. Day (ed.), *Cricket … Developing winners, A 10th birthday celebration of the United Cricket Board of South Africa's "Development for all in the game for all"' * p. 20.

5 See S.J. Reddy and B. Bansda (eds.), *South African Non-European Cricket Almanack, 1954/55*, p. 57 for a contemporary profile of Roro.

6 C. Day (ed.), *Developing winners*, p. 20.

7 S.J. Reddy and B. Bansda (eds.), *South African Non-European Cricket Almanack, 1953/54*, p. 45.

8 *Ibid.*, pp. 46, 48.

9 'Personalities you may know', *Imvo Zabantsundu*, 1 March 1952.

10 R. Mali, 'The black cricket belt of the Border' in C. Day (ed.), *Developing winners*, p. 36.

11 'Father of African cricket honoured', *Imvo Zabantsundu*, 13 March 1954.

12 ' "Oom Piet" Gwele faces sticky wicket as cricket season opens', *African Sports*, September 1953, p. 4 and ' "Oom Piet" goes out to a "no-ball" despite magnificent defence', *African Sports*, November 1953, p. 8.

13 'Transvaal honours P.S.A. Gwele', S.J. Reddy and B. Bansda (eds.). *South African Non-European Cricket Almanack, 1953/54*, pp. 48-50; 'Father of African cricket honoured', *Imvo Zabantsundu*, 13 March 1954.

14 Quoted in Archer and Boullion, *South African game*, pp. 115-116.

15 *Ibid.*, pp. 115, 117.

16 *Umteteli wa Bantu*, 10 April 1937, p. 19.

Chapter 9 ONGOING RUGBY AND CRICKET CONNECTIONS

1 Grundlingh, Odendaal and Spies, *Beyond the Tryline*, pp. 44-5.

2 M. Rall, *Peaceable warrior, The life and times of Sol T. Plaatjie* (Solomon Plaatje Educational Trust, Kimberley, 2003), pp. 223, 285-6.

3 P. Dobson, *Rugby in South Africa*, pp. 202-3.

4 Grundlingh, Odendaal and Spies, *Beyond the Tryline*, p. 47.

5   'Eastern Province retains trophy at 14th inter-provincial tourney', *African Sports*, August 1953, pp. 1, 13-4.
6   B. Ngozi, *Unpublished Sourcebook*, reports from *Umteteli wa Bantu*, 2 June 1940 and 8 June 1940; and 'Arrangements from East London tourney', n.p. The quote is from the first source.
7   B. Ngozi, *Unpublished Sourcebook*, 'Opening of tournament', undated cutting, n.p.

Chapter 10 SACBOC AND THE MOVES TOWARDS NON-RACIALISM, 1947-1959

1   A. Odendaal, *Cricket in Isloation*, pp. 330-1.
2   Hassan Howa quote in Odendaal, *Cricket in Isolation*, p. 390; Grundlingh, A. Odendaal and Spies, *Beyond the Tryline*, pp. 30-31. The SAICCB later changed its name to the South African Coloured Cricket Association (SACCA).
3   For biographical details of Christopher, see Desai et al, *Blacks in whites*, especially p. 112. See also A. Odendaal, 'South Africa's long road to the Cricket World Cup' in *Official souvenir brochure, ICC World Cup 2003, South Africa, February 8- March 23*, pp. 128-133.
4   For details see A. Odendaal, *Cricket in Isolation*, pp. 331-2.
5   South African Indian Cricket Union, tournament brochure, 1947, p. 27.
6   A. Odendaal, *Vukani Bantu!*, pp. 240-1; S. Forman and A. Odendaal (eds.), *A trumpet from the housetops! The selected writings of Lionel Forman* (Zed Books, London, 1992), chapter 5.
7   *Cricket Souvenir*, December 1951.
8   *Cricket Souvenir*, December 1951, p. 4.
9   C. De Broglio, *South Africa, Racism in sport*, (IDAF, London, 1970), introduction.
10   C. Greyvenstein, *The Fighters: A pictorial history of SA boxing from 1881*, (Don Nelson, Cape Town, 1981), pp. 416-417.
11   See, for example, 'CAF snubs an African legend', *Cape Argus*, 9 April 2003; J. Wantza to editor, *Cape Times*, (unpublished); J. Wantza to president, SARFU, 29 January 2003.
12   C. De Broglio, *South Africa*, p. 6.
13   S.J. Reddy and B. Bansda (eds.), *South African Cricket Almanack 1969*, pp. 97-118.
14   A. Odendaal, 'From De Beers to SFW', *South African Cricketer*, February 1976.
15   *Ibid.*
16   Programme for 8th annual Coca Cola Khaya Majola Cricket Week, Vaal Triangle, 17-21 December 2001 (inside cover and loose insert entitled 'Khaya Majola and the rich legacy he left South African cricket').

Part Four

ERIC MAJOLA AND THE BLACK SPRINGBOKS OF THE 1950s

Chapter 11 CLAN

1   Interviews with Milase Majola, New Brighton, 2 July 2000 and telephonically, 5 January 2001.
2   Interview with Skumbuzo Oliphant, New Brighton, 29 October 2002.
3   Interviews with Milase Majola, New Brighton, 2 July 2000 and telephonically, 5 January 2001.
4   *Ibid.*
5   Interview with Dan Qeqe, New Brighton, 2 July 2000.
6   *Ibid.*
7   *Ibid.*
8   Interview with Milase Majola, New Brighton, 2 July 2000.
9   Interview with Gerald Majola, New Brighton, 2 July 2000.
10   Speech at museum's workshop re: Red Location and South End Museum projects, Port Elizabeth, 2001.
11   A national competition to decide on a design for a freedom memorial in Red Location was held in 2000 and a winner was announced, but it seems little progress has been made since then.

Chapter 12 COMMUNITY

1   For this early history, see A. Odendaal, 'African political mobilisation', pp. 198-9; G. Baines, *The Shadow of the City: A history of New Brighton, Port Elizabeth, 1903-1953* (self-published, 2001), chapter 3.
2   T. Lodge, *Black Politics in South Africa since 1945* (Ravan Press, Johannesburg, 1985), p. 85.
3   J. Matyu, *Shadows of the past. Memories of Jabavu Road New Brighton* (Kwela Books, Cape Town, 1996), p. 1.
4   T. Lodge, *Black Politics in South Africa*, pp. 48-9.
5   J. Matyu, *Shadows of the past*, pp. 3-4.
6   T. Lodge, *Black Politics in South Africa*, p. 48. For a more detailed analysis see G. Baines, *The Shadow of the City*, chapter 1.
7   T. Lodge, *Black Politics in South Africa*, pp. 49-50.
8   *Ibid.*, p. 52.
9   Ibid., pp. 44, 46-7, 54; G. Baines, *The Shadow of the City*, pp. 288-295.
10   Interview with Ray Mali, Cape Town, 31 October 2000.
11   L. Callinicos, *The world that made Mandela*, (STE Publishers, 2000), p. 155 .
12   R. Mhlaba (narrated to T. Mufamadi), *Raymond Mhlaba's personal memoirs: Reminiscing from Rwanda and Uganda* (HSRC and Robben Island Museum, 2001), pp. 53, 61.
13   *Ibid.*, pp. 69, 96-97.
14   *Ibid.*, pp. 41-45, 80-81.
15   See, for example, J. Cherry, 'The making of an African working class – Port Elizabeth 1925-1963' (MA dissertation, Rhodes University, 1992); R. Davies, D. O'Meara and S. Dlamini, *The struggle for South Africa, A reference guide to movements, organisations and institutions* (Zed Books, London, 1984), pp. 359-361; M. Murray, *South Africa; Time of agony, time of destiny. The upsurge of popular protest* (Verso, London, 1987), pp. 276-287.

Chapter 13 CLUBS

1   Interview with Dan Qeqe, New Brighton, 2 July 2000.
2   G. Baines, *Shadow of the City*, p. 258.
3   *Ibid.*
4   *Ibid.*, pp. 258-259.
5   *Izwi Labantu*, 15 September 1907 and other cuttings in André Odendaal Collection.
6   Spring Rose Rugby Football Club, 90 years commemorative brochure, 1907-1997; Booley, *Forgotten Heroes*, pp. 115-6.
7   *Ibid.*
8   'Imidlalo – Iqakamba e Bhai', *Umteteli wa Bantu*, 28 January 1928.
9   'Stars of the Bantu cricket world', *Umteteli wa Bantu*, 3 February 1934.
10   'New Brighton Cricket Club looms as strongest in Union' and 'Cricket fever grows in Port Elizabeth', *African Sports*, October 1953.
11   ' "Big four" of African cricket', *African Sports*, January 1954, pp. 19-20.
12   *Ibid.*, p. 19; Dan Qeqe interview, New Brighton, 29 October 2002.
13   Interview with Dan Qeqe, New Brighton, 2 July 2000.
14   ' "Big four" of African cricket', *African Sports*, January 1954, p. 19.
15   *Ibid.*
16   Interview with Dan Qeqe, New Brighton, 29 October 2002.
17   Interview with Ray Mali, Cape Town, 31 October 2000.
18   'New Brighton Cricket Club wins championship', *Imvo Zabantsundu*, 21 February 1959.
19   Interview with Milase Majola, New Brighton, 2 July 2000.
20   Personal communication, Peggy Mali, Cape Town, 8 February 2003.
21   See 'Lifetime of dedication lauded', *Port Elizabeth Express*, 17 August 1994; 'Guiding light in all her words and deeds', *Guiding (UK), A national training magazine*, February 1988, p. 39.
22   Milase Majola interview, New Brighton, 29 October 2002.
23   St Matthew's S.P.G. Mission, Keiskama Hoek, Visit of the Lord Bishop of Grahamstown and a short account of the mission, May, 1884, p. 10.
24   A. Mager, *Gender and the making of a South African Bantustan, A social history of the Ciskei, 1945-1959* (David Philip, Cape Town, 1999), p. 201.
25   Interview with Milase Majola, New Brighton, 29 October 2002.
26   B.A. Pauw, *The second generation: A study of the family among the urbanised Bantu in East London* (Cape Town, Oxford University Press, 1987), pp. 44-5.
27   Molapo, 'Sports, festivals and popular politics', p. 42.
28   *Ibid.*
29   'A message from netball', Spring Rose Rugby Football Club, 90 years commemorative brochure, 1907-1997, p. 9.
30   Personal communication, Khonaye Penxa, 6 January 2001.
31   Interview with Milase Majola, New Brighton, 2 July 2000.
32   Interview with Khaya Majola, Johannesburg, 3 July 2000. While this interview, quoted regularly in the rest of the book, indicates a single date and place, information provided by Khaya Majola in a number of follow-up telephone conversations (as well as a further meeting) with the author before Majola's death less than two months later are also included under it.
33   Interview with Milase Majola, New Brighton, 2 July 2000.
34   Interview with Tozie Majola, New Brighton, 2 July 2000.
35   Interview with Milase Majola, New Brighton, 2 July 2000; interview with Khaya Majola, Johannesburg, 3 July 2000.
36   Interview with Milase Majola, New Brighton, 2 July 2000.
37   Personal communication, Khonaye Penxa, 6 January 2001.
38   *Ibid.*

Chapter 14 CHRISTMAS IN THE CITY

1   S.J. Reddy and B. Bansda (eds.), *South African Non-European Cricket Almanack, 1954/55*, p. 35.
2   S.J. Reddy and B. Bansda (eds.), *South African Non-European Cricket Almanack, 1953/54*, p. 138.
3   'Big four', *African Sports*, January 1954, pp. 19-20.
4   No complete lists of the tournaments up to 1974/75 exist, but from 1958/59 onwards Eastern Province were winners several times.
5   'Low scores characterised national cricket tournament', *Imvo Zabantsundu*, 10 January 1959.
6   Africana Library, Kimberley: H.M. Masiza, President, Griqualand West Bantu Cricket Board, and Mr Mahunga, Secretary, to Chairman of the Location Committee and Manager of the Native Affairs Department, 17 October 1950.
7   'Big four', *African Sports*, January 1954, p. 19.
8   See cricket report, *Imvo Zabantsundu*, 10 January 1953.
9   S.J. Reddy and B. Bansda (eds.), *South African Non-European Cricket Almanack 1953/54*, pp. 133-4.
10   Desai et al, *Blacks in Whites*, p. 151.
11   'Mines cricket union makes sticky wicket for North Eastern Bantu CU', *African Sports*, November 1953, p. 5.
12   'An appeal to all lovers of cricket', *African Sports*, January 1954, p. 19.
13   ' "Oom Piet" Gwele faces sticky wicket', *African Sports*, September 1954, p. 4.
14   'An appeal to all lovers of cricket', *African Sports*, January 1954, p. 19.
15   ' "Oom Piet" Gwele faces sticky wicket', *African Sports*, September 1954, p. 4.
16   *Ibid.*
17   *Ibid.*, pp. 4, 14 and 'Enterprising cricket marks the opening of Transvaal season', *African Sports*, November 1953, pp. 5-10.
18   See P. Cossie's report of the 1952 tournament in S.J. Reddy and B. Bansda (eds.), *South African Non-European Cricket Almanack 1953/54*, pp. 117-122. Like Wilson Ximiya, Pat Cossie deserves a study of his own as a long-standing player and administrator within a changing social and political context.

19 Fuller profiles of these individuals will be included in the forthcoming official history of South African cricket.
20 K. Reddy to A. Odendaal, 4 March 2002, with E. Majola tournament statistics.
21 Interview with Dan Qeqe, New Brighton, 29 October 2002.
22 See 'EP reveals her superiority to SA Bantu provinces', *Imvo Zabantsundu*, 17 January 1959.
23 A number of reports, written by Gordon Qumza, appeared in *Imvo Zabantsundu* in January and February 1959. It is likely that there are reports for every one of the more than 20 inter-provincial tournaments held, even if not in such detail.
24 'Border is a queer province', *Imvo Zabantsundu*, 14 February 1959.
25 'Comment on Border team' and 'Border must find batsmen for next tournament', *Imvo Zabantsundu*, 24 January 1954.
26 'Transkei will have to get rid of much of the dead wood', *Imvo Zabantsundu*, 31 January 1959.
27 'Both Transvaals were disappointing', *Imvo Zabantsundu*, 14 February 1959.
28 'Sports talk: I don't blame the poor players', *Imvo Zabantsundu*, 21 February 1959.
29 *Ibid.*
30 'Transvaal's flop in running cricket tournament', *Imvo Zabantsundu*, 10 January 1959; 'Low scores', *Imvo Zabantsundu*, 10 January 1959; 'Why did Board allow Transvaal to run tourney', *Imvo Zabantsundu*, 21 February 1959.
31 'Comment on Border team', *Imvo Zabantsundu*, 24 January 1959.
32 'Rowdy cricket meeting', *Imvo Zabantsundu*, 10 January 1959.
33 *Ibid.*

Chapter 15 CHRISTMAS IN THE COUNTRY

1 Interview with Milase Majola, Port Elizabeth, 2 July 2000.
2 Interview with Dan Qeqe, Port Elizabeth, 2 July 2000.
3 *Ibid.*
4 C.S. Morgan, 'Africans village green cricket festival', *Evening Post*, 23 January 1954. My thanks to Bob Edgar for this reference, and those from *Imvo Zabantsundu* below, which have enabled me to draw together the fascinating details on the rural cricket connections in this chapter.
5 M. Wilson and A. Mafeje, *Langa: A study of social groups in an African township* (Oxford University Press, Cape Town, 1973), pp. 114-126. See also B.A. Pauw, *The second generation: A study of the family amongst the urbanised Bantu in East London* (Oxford University Press, Cape Town, 1987), pp. 172-3.
6 Wilson and Mafeje, *Langa*, pp. 116-7.
7 Personal communication, Gerald Majola, August 2002; personal communication, Dan Qeqe, 26 February 2001.
8 'Cricket tourneys in "village green" ', *Imvo Zabantsundu*, 1 January 1955.
9 *Ibid.*; 'Village tourneys not serving any good', *Imvo Zabantsundu*, 19 December 1959.
10 'Village tourneys not serving any good', *Imvo Zabantsundu*, 19 December 1959.
11 See 'Doing it all for "Papa Steve" ', *Sunday Times*, 5 January 2003; 'Cricket tourneys in "village green" ', *Imvo Zabantsundu*, 1 January 1955.
12 *Ibid.*
13 *Ibid.*
14 'Village tourneys not serving any good', *Imvo Zabantsundu*, 19 December 1959.
15 See, for example, 'Obscene practices', *Imvo Zabantsundu*, 30 July 1891; C.S. Morgan, 'Africans' village green cricket festival', *Evening Post*, 23 January 1954.
16 'Village tourneys not serving any good', *Imvo Zabantsundu*, 19 December 1959.
17 *Ibid.*

Chapter 16 CRICKET CO-OPERATION

1 Biographical notes by N.P. Umley, n.d.; personal communication, Devdas Govindjee, 24 March 2003.
2 Interview with Dan Qeqe, New Brighton, 29 October 2002.
3 *Cricket Souvenir*, no. 1, December 1950.
4 S.J. Reddy and B. Bansda (eds.), *South African Non-European Cricket Almanack 1954/55*, p. 32. Another sports publication was *The Clarion*, published in Durban in 1948/49. On San Reddy see 'Good news', *Fair Lady*, 28 April 1999.
5 'Bouquets and brickbats', *African Sports*, January 1954, p. 20.
6 S.J. Reddy and B. Bansda (eds.), *South African Non-European Cricket Almanack 1954/55*, p. 32.
7 'Western Province opens tour in grand style', *African Sports*, January 1954, p. 23.
8 S.J. Reddy and B. Bansda (eds.), *South African Non-European Cricket Almanack 1954/55*, pp. 16-22.
9 N.P. Umley, 'Harmony and mutual trust exist' in SACBOC souvenir programme, first inter-provincial cricket tournament, Johannesburg, 26 December 1961 to 7 January 1962.
10 N.P. Umley, 'Welcome message' in Eastern Province Cricket Federation, The official souvenir brochure, Kenya Asian cricket tour of South Africa, 1956.
11 *Ibid.*, p. 21.
12 *Ibid.* and interview with Devdas Govindjee, Port Elizabeth, 28 October 2002.
13 S.J. Reddy and B. Bansda (eds.), *South African Cricket Almanack 1969*, pp. 104-5.
14 *Ibid.*, pp. 97-106.

Chapter 17 CRICKET SPRINGBOK

1 'S.A. Bantus win on first innings', *The Leader*, undated cutting in Reddy papers, André Odendaal Collection; S.J. Reddy and K. Bandsda (eds.), *South African Cricket Almanack 1969*, p. 121.
2 See S.J. Reddy and K. Bandsda (eds.), *South African Non-European Cricket Almanack 1954/55*, p. 57 for a contemporary profile of Roro.
3 'Natalspruit Mecca of sports' in SACBOC, souvenir programme, North Zone vs South Zone, Johannesburg, 21 to 23 April, 1973.
4 Yusuf Garda personal communication, 20 February 2003.

5 On this dispute see, Sol D. Royeppen, 'SA Barnato Board', *The Leader*, undated cutting in Reddy papers, André Odendaal Collection.
6 S.J. Reddy and B. Bansda (eds.), *South African Non-European Cricket Almanack 1953/54*, pp. 133-4.
7 *Ibid.*
8 K. Reddy, 'A feat unrivalled: 10 for 57 and all that' (unpublished article, 2002).
9 He apparently withdrew because he was unhappy with the selection process and Eastern Province administration issues. See *Imvo Zabantsundu*, 29 January 1955.
10 S.J. Reddy and B. Bansda (eds.), *South African Cricket Almanack 1969*, pp. 120, 125.
11 Desai et al, *Blacks in Whites*, pp. 152-3.
12 K. Reddy, '1956 – the year of Ben Malamba' (unpublished article, 2002).
13 K.Reddy, 'George Langa – "Ouboetie", the ever reliable' (unpublished article, 2002).
14 These statistics were drawn up from the *South African Non-European Cricket Almanack*, but were full of mistakes. My thanks to Krish Reddy for helping with the corrections.

Chapter 18 RUGBY STAR

1 Photograph and caption, *Imvo Zabantsundu*, 17 January 1959.
2 F.L. Erasmus quoted in *Weekend World*, 4 July 1971.
3 Unsourced cutting in André Odendaal Collection.
4 Booley, *Forgotten Heroes*, pp. 109, 125.
5 Personal communication, Mogammed Galant, Montagu Springs, July 2000.
6 *Ibid.*
7 Omar Henry made the point without prompting while watching a warm-up match for the World Cup 2003 on the same ground on 6 February 2003.
8 Booley, *Forgotten Heroes*, p. 20.
9 *Ibid.*, p. 102.
10 *Champs! The Official South African Rugby Football Union Magazine, Collector's Edition 2000*, p. 78.
11 Booley, *Forgotten Heroes*, pp. 104-5; Grundlingh, Odendaal and Spies, *Beyond the Tryline*, p. 55.
12 'Eastern Province retains trophy at 14th inter-provincial tourney', *African Sports*, August 1953, pp. 1, 14.
13 Interview with Dan Qeqe, New Brighton, 2 July 2000.
14 'Special branch spied on rugby players', *New Age*, 12 July 1956.
15 *Champs! The Official South African Rugby Football Union Magazine, Collector's Edition 2000*, pp. 78, 97-106.

Part Five

KHAYA MAJOLA AND NEW DIRECTIONS FOR SOUTH AFRICAN CRICKETERS (1960s-1970s)

Chapter 19 AFRICANS ON THEIR OWN AGAIN

1 A. Odendaal, *Cricket in isolation*, p. 314; M. Allie, *More than a game*, pp. 22-24.
2 See report in *Imvo Zabantsundu*, 18 February 1961. My thanks to Junior Tengo Sokhanyile for this and various other cuttings listed here, which he has found in the course of his research for am MA dissertation on the history of African cricket in the Western Province. The information has enabled me to get a much better understanding of the SAACB in the 1960s.
3 SACBOC souvenir programme, second inter-provincial tournament, Port Elizabeth, 1963/64.
4 'Harmony …' in SACBOC souvenir programme, first inter-provincial tournament, Johannesburg, 1961/62; EPCA, secretarial report for the 10th AGM, Alabama Hotel, Port Elizabeth, 20 September, 1970; SACBOC souvenir programme, second inter-provincial tournament, Port Elizabeth, 1963/64.
5 SACBOC souvenir programme, first inter-provincial tournament, Johannesburg, 1961/62.
6 See *Imvo Zabantsundu*, 11 March 1961.
7 See *Imvo Zabantsundu*, 16 December 1961.
8 SACBOC souvenir programme, first inter-provincial tournament, Johannesburg, 1961/62.
9 'Anomalies in Bantu cricket', *Imvo Zabantsundu*, 12 January 1963.
10 *Ibid.*
11 SACBOC souvenir programme, second inter-provincial tournament, Port Elizabeth, 1963/64.
12 See report of the tournament in S.J. Reddy and B. Bansda (eds.), *South African Cricket Almanack 1969*, pp. 25-26.
13 EPCA, secretarial report for the 10th AGM, Alabama Hotel, Port Elizabeth, 20 September 1970.
14 SAACB, 33rd AGM held on 25-26 March, Johannesburg, the secretarial report and review for the seasons 1965/66/67; J.T. Sokhanyile notes.
15 A. Odendaal *Cricket in Isolation*, p. 315.
16 SAACB, 33rd AGM held on 25-26 March, Johannesburg, presidential address by H.M. Butshingi and the secretarial report and review for the seasons 1965/66/67 by Lennox Lindelo Mlonzi.
17 SAACB, the secretarial report and review for the seasons 1965/66/67 by Lennox Lindelo Mlonzi, p. 4.
18 *Ibid.*
19 A.A. Dunjwa, 'History of black cricket South Africa. Period 1947-1990' (unpublished article, September 1990); interview with Ashton Dunjwa, East London, 30 October 2002.
20 Compare names on letterheads of the following SAACB correspondence: L.L. Mlonzi, general secretary, to all affiliated provinces and committee members – AGM, 7 March 1967 and L.L. Mlonzi to all secretaries – invitation to annual tournament, 7 July 1969.
21 A.A. Dunjwa, 'History of black cricket South Africa. Period 1947-1990' (unpublished article, September 1990).

22 C. Merrett, 'A political and cultural history of South African cricket' (unpublished manuscript, 2000).
23 Ibid.
24 Information regarding result from Krish Reddy.
25 A. A. Dunjwa, 'History of black cricket in South Africa. Period 1947-1990' (unpublished article, September 1990); interview with Ashton Dunjwa, East London, 30 October 2002. See also C. Day (ed.), Developing winners, p. 36.
26 'Test cancelled writes Sotewu', Imvo Zabantsundu, 30 March 1968.
27 Personal communication, Gerald Majola, 2003.
28 'The match of the century', souvenir brochure, 21 and 22 January 1967, p. 11.
29 SAACB, Minutes of the AGM held at the Centenary Hall, New Brighton, Port Elizabeth, 6 April 1969.
30 Interview with Dan Qeqe, New Brighton, 2 July 2002.
31 Interview with Ray Mali, Cape Town, 31 October 2000.
32 'Coloureds dominate the two trial matches', Post, 3 December 1967; 'Coloured provincial team has good win', Evening Post, 29 November 1967.
33 'A shocker as African XI tumbles', undated Post cutting from Devdas Govindjee scrapbook; EP Herald, 3 December 1969.
34 S.J. Reddy and B. Bansda (eds.), South African Cricket Almanack 1969, p. 63.
35 Ibid.
36 SAACB, Minutes of the AGM held at the Centenary Hall, New Brighton, Port Elizabeth, 6 April 1969.

Chapter 20 NEW ALLIANCES AND OPPORTUNITIES

1   On the D'Oliveira affair and its aftermath see B. D'Oliveira, D'Oliveira, An Autobiography (Collins, London, 1968); B. D'Oliveira, Time to declare, An autobiography (MacMillan, Johannesburg, 1980); E.W. Swanton (ed.), The Cricketer (Winter Annual, 1968/9); Wisden Cricketers Almanack 1969; P. Hain, Don't play with apartheid: The background to the Stop The Seventy Tour campaign (George Allen and Unwin, London, 1971).
2   A. Odendaal, Cricket in Isolation, pp. 11, 25; M. Allie, More than a game, pp. 92-93.
3   SAACB, Minutes of the AGM held at the Centenary Hall, New Brighton, Port Elizabeth, 6 April 1969.
4   Souvenir brochure, Nuffield Cricket Week, Pietermaritzburg, 12-17 January 1959.
5   A. Odendaal, Cricket in Isolation, p. 318.
6   Interview with Khaya Majola, Johannesburg, 3 July 2000.
7   'First South African African schoolboys cricket tournament', SACA annual report, 1970/71, presented by J.E. Cheetham, president, and S.H. Martin, secretary, p. 7.
8   T. Mazwai, 'A new Majola hits the headlines', Evening Post, undated cutting in the Majola Collection.
9   Personal communication, Saki Macozoma, 2000.
10 Interview with Khaya Majola, Johannesburg, 3 July 2000.
11 Interview with Tozie Majola, New Brighton, 2 July 2000.
12 Interview with Khaya Majola, Johannesburg, 3 July 2000.
13 Ibid.
14 A. Odendaal, Cricket in Isolation, pp. 318-9.
15 'First South African African schoolboys cricket tournament', SACA annual report, 1970/71, presented by J.E. Cheetham, president, and S.H. Martin, secretary, pp. 6-7.
16 Personal communication, Khonaye Penxa, 6 January 2000.
17 'First South African African schoolboys cricket tournament', SACA annual report, 1970/71, presented by J.E. Cheetham, president, and S.H. Martin, secretary, pp. 6-7.
18 J.T. Sokhanyile research notes.
19 Ibid.
20 A. Odendaal, Cricket in Isolation, pp. 318-9; interview with Khaya Majola, Johannesburg, 3 July 2000.
21 T. Mazwai, 'A new Majola hits the headlines', Evening Post, undated cutting in the Majola Collection.
22 A. Odendaal, Cricket in Isolation, p. 319; C. Merrett, 'A political and cultural history of South African cricket' (unpublished manuscript, 2000); J. Young (ed.), Langa Cricket Club – 21 years, 1976-1997, pp. 11-12.

Chapter 21 LOVEDALE TRADITIONS BATTERED BUT INTACT

1   A. Mager, Gender and the making of a South African Bantustan, A social history of Ciskei, 1945-1959 (David Philip, Cape Town, 1999), p. 196.
2   R. Archer and A. Boullion, South African game, p. 115.
3   Ibid.
4   Ibid.
5   My thanks to Bob Edgar for this information.
6   A. Mager, Gender and the making of a South African Bantustan, p. 212.
7   Interview with Ray Mali, Cape Town, 9 February 2003.
8   Interview with Raymond Uren, Johannesburg, 23 March 2003.
9   N. Jabavu, The ochre people, Scenes from a South African life (John Murray, London, 1963), pp. 89-90.
60 Ibid., pp. 90-91.
61 S. Mngqikana to R. Suttner, 27 February 2003; interview with Ray Mali, Cape Town, 9 February 2003; interview with Krish Mackerdhuj, Johannesburg, 23 March 2003.
12 Interview with Mveleli Ncula, London, 22 November 2002.
13 Ibid.
14 Personal communication, Solomon Makhosana, March 2003.
15 Interview with Raymond Uren and Krish Mackerdhuj, Johannesburg, 23 March 2003.
16 Interview with Makhenkhesi Stofile, Johannesburg, 30 August 2000.

17 T. Mazwai, 'A new Majola hits the headlines', Evening Post, undated cutting in the Majola Collection.
18 Chris Day speech at memorial service for Khaya Majola, St Catherine's Anglican Church, Johannesburg, 30 August 2000.
19 Ibid.

Chapter 22 PART OF THE 'SYSTEM'

1   T. Mazwai, 'A new Majola hits the headlines', Evening Post, undated cutting in the Majola Collection.
2   Interview with Khaya Majola, Johannesburg, 3 July 2000.
3   A. Odendaal, Cricket in Isolation, pp. 27-28.
4   Ibid., pp. 13-14, 21. New research by Bruce Murray and Basil D'Oliveira's biographer, Peter Oborne, will explore the support received by SACA in English cricket circles.
5   A. Odendaal, Cricket in Isolation, p. 316.
6   Ibid.
7   Interview with Tim Khumalo, Cape Town, 8 February 2003.
8   J.T. Sokanyile research material.
9   Personal communication, Tsepo Kadi, 5 July 2001.
10 'Fund for African sport', Rand Daily Mail, 24 October 1973; 'Swart sportfonds...', Die Burger, 24 October 1973.
11 EPCU Bantu Liaison Committee, 'Report to the meeting of delegates of provincial action committees for the development of African cricket, to be held in Johannesburg on Sunday 17 August 1975' in report submitted to the South African Cricket Association of the activities during the 1974/75 season of the action committees established in the provincial cricket unions for the furtherance of African cricket.
12 Ibid.
13 'Appoint black envoys, says Ciskei aide', Cape Times, 12 February 1971; 'Integration a failure, says Ciskeian official', Cape Times, 26 July 1973; 'City Ciskei citizens to celebrate', Cape Times, 12 October 1973; 'New Transkei envoy', Daily Dispatch, 7 October 1975.
14 Address given by Mr J. T. Passmore, Trustee SACA Fund, to delegates to AGM of SACA, 22 September 1973, on the subject of 'The development of African cricket in South Africa'.
15 Ibid.
16 Ibid.
17 Interview with Khaya Majola, Johannesburg, 3 July 2000.
18 See cuttings in Majola subject file, EP Herald archives, Port Elzabeth, especially articles of 13 January 1973 and 27 January 1973.

Chapter 23 DERRICK ROBINS AND INTERNATIONAL CONTACTS

1   For a background to the attempts by the National Party to find policies that could ward off isolation without undermining apartheid policy, see Gert Kotze, Sport en politiek (Makro, Pretoria, 1978), pp. 89-100, 118-124; 'Government policy since 1948', Politics in Sport, Information publication, DSG/SARS, no. 176, 13 September 1969.
2   G.A. Chettle (ed.), South African Cricket Annual 1974, pp. 222-224.
3   The author interviewed him at his house in the 1970s.
4   D. Wilson with S. Thorpe, Mad Jack, An Autobiography (The Kingswood Press, London, 1992), p. 147.
5   See the articles covering the match in Rand Daily Mail, 19-23 October 1973.
6   D. Wilson, Mad Jack, p. 147.
7   G.A. Chettle (ed.), South African Cricket Annual 1974, pp. 164-5.
8   Ibid., p. 7.
9   D. Wilson, Mad Jack, p. 147.
10 G.A. Chettle (ed.), South African Cricket Annual 1974, p. 163.
11 'Habane, Majola talented', Rand Daily Mail, 22 October 1973.
12 'One day the blacks will beat us - Robins', Rand Daily Mail, 22 October 1973.
13 Interview with Khaya Majola, Johannesburg, 3 July 2000.
14 'Habane, Majola talented', Rand Daily Mail, 22 October 1973.
15 'Soweto game sets SA on new path', Rand Daily Mail, 20 October 1973.
16 Rand Daily Mail, 2 October 1973, p. 1.
17 'Ali Bacher to retire', Rand Daily Mail, 23 October 1973.
18 'NUSAS-sport', Dissent, The NUSAS Newsletter, vol. 4, no. 29, October/November 1973, n.p.
19 'Robins XI blacks rebuked by Curry', Rand Daily Mail, 22 October 1973.
20 'NUSAS-sport', Dissent, The NUSAS Newsletter, vol. 4, no. 29, October/November 1973, n.p.
21 Reports in EP Herald, 25 February 1974 and 20 March 1974.
22 I. Hobbs report, Supplement to Daily Dispatch, 12 July 1974.
23 Interview with Khaya Majola, Johannesburg, 3 July 2000.
24 I. Hobbs report, Supplement to Daily Dispatch, 12 July 1974.
25 'Majola's no to major tourney shocked the cricket world', Evening Post, 14 May 1987.
26 I. Hobbs report, Supplement to Daily Dispatch, 12 July 1974.
27 Ibid.
28 'Khaya dreams of being a Springbok', Weekend World, 11 July 1974.
29 Ibid.
30 Ibid.
31 Rand Daily Mail, 18 July 1972.
32 Interview with Peter Bacela, 19 January 2002; J. Winch, Cricket's rich heritage: A history of Rhodesian and Zimbabwean cricket, 1890-1982, p. 130; D. Wilson, Mad Jack, pp. 148-150; 'First mixed tour abroad', The Star, 29 January 1975.
33 D. Heesom (ed.), The 1976 Protea Cricket Annual of South Africa, p. 126.
34 G.A. Chettle (ed.), South African Cricket Annual 1975, p. 187.

35   D. Heesom (ed.), *The 1977 Protea Cricket Annual of South Africa*, p. 247.
36   D. Wilson, *Mad Jack*, pp. 148-150.
37   These scorecards and player lists are the first to be drawn up for SABCB and SAACB, but they are still provisional and incomplete, drawn from a variety of sources, most already listed above. They will be refined further through additional research and work with professional statisticians.

Part Six

NON RACIAL STRUGGLES (1970s-1991)

Chapter 24 BREAKAWAY FROM THE AFRICAN BOARD

1   C. Roberts, *SACOS, 1973-1988, 15 years of sports resistance* (self-published, Durban, 1988), pp. 16-18.
2   Minutes, South African Council on Sport, Biennial Conference, Hotel Himalaya, Durban, 12 October 1975, pp. 12-18.
3   For details of the growth of the non-racial sports movement and the international anti-apartheid sports campaigns see, R.E. Lapchick, *The politics of race and international sport: the case of South Africa* (Connecticut, Greenwood Press, 1975); P. Hain, *Don't play with apartheid*; J. Brickhill, *Race against race, South Africa's 'multinational' sports fraud* (IDAF, London, 1975); R. Archer and A. Boullion, *The South African Game*.
4   Interview with Milase Majola, Port Elizabeth, 2 July 2000.
5   'Nearly 6 000 mourn sports star', *Evening Post*, 28 June 1971; *Weekend World*, July 1971, undated cutting in Majola Collection.
6   Funeral programme, 26 June 1971.
7   *Weekend World*, July 1971, undated cutting in Majola Collection.
8   *Ibid.*; 'Nearly 6 000 mourn sports star', *Evening Post*, 28 June 1971.
9   n.a., 'Rugby in the Eastern Cape: A history', *Work in Progress*, no. 17, April 1981, pp. 2-3.
10   See, for example, *EP Herald*, 17 January 1973.
11   EPCA, Secretarial report, Season 1972-73, p. 6.
12   Minutes, EPCA AGM, 10 September 1972, p. 3.
13   Interview with Ray Mali, 31 October 2000.
14   Interview with Khaya Majola, Johannesburg, 3 July 2000. From the time that Queenstown participated in the first Barnato Tournament in 1898, there were several African cricket and rugby provincial associations with Queenstown as the main base over the years, and the names used included North Eastern Districts, Midlands Frontier and Komani and Districts. More research is needed to clarify the different designations, periods and linkages.
15   Interview with Dan Qeqe, New Brighton, 2 July 2000.
16   K. Reddy, 'SACBOC and SACB first-class matches and records, 1971-1991' (draft manuscript); undated cutting in scrapbook, Devdas Govindjee Collection.
17   Interview with Khaya Majola, Johannesburg, 3 July 2000; 'Sportswide' by Lennie Kleintjies, *The Argus*, 18 December 1988.
18   'Majola's no to major tourney shocked the world', *Evening Post*, 14 May 1987.
19   G.A. Chettle (ed.), *South African Cricket Annual 1974*, pp. 222-4.

Chapter 25 UPDATING WISDEN'S RECORDS

1   For the various trophy winners see, K. Reddy, 'SACBOC/SACB cricket' in C. Bryden (ed.), *South African Cricket Annual 2002*, pp. 528-9.
2   K. Reddy, 'SACBOC and SACB first-class matches and records, 1971-1991' (draft manuscript) and K. Reddy, 'Career records of SACBOC/SACB cricketers who played three-day matches, 1956/57 to 1990/1991' (draft manuscript). These full scorecards of the 220-plus first-class games, and the individual career records going with them, will appear in A. Odendaal, K. Reddy and C. Merrett (eds.), *The Official History of South African Cricket*, 1808-2003 (forthcoming). See also C. Bryden (ed.), *South African Cricket Annual 2002*, pp. 543-555.
3   R. Isherwood to A. Odendaal, 1 May 2003, quoting interview by R. Eyre with A. Bacher, 21 January 1997.

Chapter 26 DOLLY AND A TIME OF OPTIMISM

1   EPCA, Minutes of the 9th AGM, Alabama Hotel, Port Elizabeth, 21 September 1969; EPCA, Notice of meeting and secretarial report for the 10th AGM, Alabama Hotel, Port Elizabeth, 20 September, 1970.
2   See, for example, EPCA, Minutes of the AGM, 10 September 1972; souvenir programme for SACBOC zonal inter-provincial tournament, Zone B, Port Elizabeth, 26-31 December 1974; EPCA, Season 1974/75, Annual reports and constitution, 15th AGM, Alabama Hotel, 24 August 1975.
3   EPCA, Secretarial report, Season 1972/73.
4   *Ibid.*, pp. 4-5; souvenir programme and scoresheet, South African invitation cricket XI versus Eastern Province, Adcock Stadium, Port Elizabeth, 25-26 November 1972.
5   S.J. Reddy (ed.), *Cricket Annual '73-'74*, p. 9.
6   EPCA, Secretarial report, Season 1972/73; K. Reddy (ed.), *Cricket Annual '73-'74*, p. 9.
7   See 'Message from Hassan Howa' in SACBOC souvenir programme. North Zone vs South Zone, Lenasia Stadium, Johannesburg, 21-23 April 1973.
8   'Howa plan stumped by ICC', *The Argus*, 3 August 1974.
9   *Ibid.*
10   'Dik Abed makes a call to Griffiths' and 'Griffiths visa refusal may hit tour' (undated cuttings, scrapbook, S.J. Reddy Collection).
11   'Griffith unlikely to come to South Africa', *The Argus*, 31 August 1971; 'Row if Dolly coaches coloureds only', *Sunday Express*, 5 September, 1971.

12   Personal communication, Sadick Emeran, 2001.
13   SACBOC, Biennial General Meeting, 13-14 September 1975, 'Mini-test' report, n.p.
14   'Transvaal lashing for "aggressive" Rohan', *Sunday Times Extra*, 14 September 1975.
15   *Cape Times*, 18 December 1974.
16   For scores and photo see S.J. Reddy, *Cricket Annual '73-'74*, p. 16.
17   'Basil the brain', *Post*, 3 December 1972.
18   *Post*, 11 March 1975.
19   Hassan Howa, 'Historic developments' in SACBOC souvenir programme, North Zone vs South Zone, Lenasia Stadium, Johannesburg, 21-23 April 1973.
20   *Ibid.*
21   EPCA, Treasurer's financial statement 1972/73.
22   See scorecard enclosed in documents for EPCA AGM, 9 September 1973.
23   SACBOC, Biennial General Meeting, 13-14 September 1975, scorecards in match reports, n.p.
24   SACBOC, Biennial General Meeting, 13-14 September 1975, 'Mini-test' report, n.p.
25   SACBOC, Biennial General Meeting, 13-14 September 1975, Minutes, p. 6.
26   SACBOC, Recording clerk's interim report reviewing season 1975-76, 2 October 1976, pp. 5, 34-35.
27   The individual first-class statistics mentioned in this chapter and chapter 29 are borrowed from Krish Reddy's above-mentioned, 'Career records of SACBOC/SACB cricketers who played three-day matches, 1956/57 to 1990/91'. Footnotes are not provided every time.
28   Interim Secretary's Report of SACBOC, 2 March 1976, p. 6.
29   D. Govindjee, 'Down EP's memory lane', *Evening Post*, 27 October 1983.
30   See, for example, 'Howa gives some straight answers', *Drum*, 8 March, 1973.
31   'Varachia no stranger to top post' (undated cutting, Andre Odendaal Collection); 'Howa loses election', *The Argus*, 15 September 1975.
32   See, for example, 'Howa hits back at Varachia', *Cape Times*, 18 December 1974.
33   Undated article by Bob Waller, (scrapbook, S.J. Reddy Collection); *Cape Times*, 18 December 1974.

Chapter 27 'NORMAL CRICKET' DISRUPTIONS

1   'Mixed cricket', *Daily Despatch*, 19 January 1976; A. Odendaal, *Cricket in Isolation*, pp. 41-43.
2   See A. Odendaal, *Cricket in Isolation*, chapter 3.
3   Interview with Khaya Majola, Johannesburg, 3 July 2003.
4   See A. Odendaal, *Cricket in Isolation*, chapter 4.
5   *Ibid.*, p. 59.
6   *Ibid.*, pp. 64-65.
7   Interview with Khaya Majola, Johannesburg, 3 July 2000.
8   See 'Split in cricket club', *Evening Post*, 29 October 1976; H. Lorgat to Secretary, Regents Sports Club, 1 November 1977 (scrapbook, Haroon Lorgat Collection).
9   'Varachia lays it on the line', *Cape Herald*, 12 December 1977.
10   'New cricket body formed', *Cape Herald*, 15 November 1977; M. Allie, *More than a Game*, pp. 143-4.
11   A. Odendaal, *Cricket in Isolation*, p. 65.

Chapter 28 UNITED WE STAND

1   *EPCOS Sportsperson 1988* (Newsletter).
2   'Majola in dashing form', *EP Herald*, 22 November 1976; 'Another century for Khaya Majola', *EP Herald*, 13 December 1976.
3   'Title for United as Regents barred', *Cape Herald*, 21 March 1978; 'EPCA league ends sadly', *Evening Post*, 26 March 1978.
4   'Majola's role of honour', *Cape Herald*, 17 January 1978; 'Mongezi Majola in fine form', *EP Herald*, 16 January 1978; 'Schoolboy saves United rout', *Evening Post*, 28 February 1978.
5   Interview with Gerald Majola, Spier, Stellenbosch, 16 March 2003.
6   See also chapters 30 and 38 below.
7   'Match off after incident on field', *Evening Post*, 10 March 1981; 'Fists fly on field', *Cape Herald*, 14 March 1981.
8   'EP stars for night cricket at Wolfson' and 'Night cricket proves to be a great success' (undated cuttings, scrapbook, Haroon Lorgat Collection).
9   Danny Jordaan speech at funeral of Khaya Majola, Centenary Hall, Port Elizabeth, 2 September 2000.
10   'Majola dominates', *Evening Post*, 15 January 1991.
11   'Captain courageous', *The Indicator*, 24 February 1989.

Chapter 29 THE HOWA BOWL

1   'SACB faces first test', *Cape Herald*, 22 November 1977. I am grateful to Haroon Lorgat for allowing me to use his scrapbooks, which greatly helped with this chapter.
2   'New WP caps for EP game', *Evening Post*, 24 November 1977.
3   'Bowlers on top in EP-WP game', *Evening Post*, 28 November 1977; 'Poor showing by EP batsmen', *Evening Post*, 29 November 1977; 'Slow batting as EP go down in Cape Town', *EP Herald*, 29 November 1977.
4   'Strong Natal side plays at Adcock', *EP Herald*, 23 December 1977.
5   'A and B teams play', *EP Herald*, 13 December 1977.
6   'Strong Natal side at Adcock', *EP Herald* 23 December 1977; 'Tough prospect for EP team', *Evening Post*, 23 December 1979. On Aurora see C. Merrett, 'Aurora; The challenge of non-racial cricket to the apartheid state in the mid-1970s', *The International Journal of the History of Sport*, vol. 18, no. 14, December 2001, pp. 95-122.
7   'Fighting knock by Pono', *Evening Post*, 29 December 1977; 'EP lose golden opportunity', *Evening Post*, 30 December, 1977; 'Natal win by 72 runs', *EP Herald*, 29 November 1977.
8   'Transvaal no match for EP', *Evening Post*, 3 January 1978.

9   *SACOS Sport, Cape Town, Festival '82*, pp. 32-33.
10 'EP's great find – Haroon Lorgat', *Cape Herald*, 14 January 1978; 'EP XI out to do better', *Evening Post*, 30 December 1977; 'Keen to make amends', *Evening Post*, 30 December 1978.
12 'The mighty have fallen', *Cape Herald*, 24 January 1978.
12 M. Allie, *More than a game*, p. 145.
13 'Players to register with EPCA', *Evening Post*, 5 January 1978.
14 'Five changes in EPCA XI', *EP Herald*, 24 December 1978.
15 *Ibid.*
16 'EP are SA Cricket Board champions', *EP Herald*, 21 March 1979.
17 'Drama as EP XI walk off', *Evening Post*, 24 January 1983; 'EP cricket team walks off in Howa Bowl game', *EP Herald*, 24 January 1983.
18 'EP's win was a highlight', *Evening Post*, 27 March 1985.
19 'Blame for EP defeat lies with selectors', *Evening Post*, 27 January 1982.
20 'A rebirth in popular interest in cricket', *Evening Post*, 24 January 1985.
21 'Match is tied as WP Board collapse', *Argus*, 19 November 1984; 'Utter bore followed by thrilling tie', *Cape Herald*, 24 November 1984.
22 'Win by EP puts grip on Bowl', *Evening Post*, 22 January 1985.
23 Interview with Khaya Majola, Johannesburg, 3 July 2000.
24 'EP's win a highlight', *Evening Post*, 27 March 1985; K. Reddy, 'Career records of SACBOC/SACB cricketers who played three-day matches, 1956/57 to 1990/91'.
25 Interview with Gerald Majola, Savannah Hotel, Bridgetown, Barbados, 10 May 2001.
26 *Argus*, 20 January 1986.
27 *Cape Times*, 21 January 1986.
28 *Evening Post*, 3 April 1986.
29 'Title shared as rain ends cricket final', *Cape Times*, 26 March, 1984.
30 C. Bryden (ed.), *Protea Assurance SA Cricket Annual 1996*, pp. 9, 486.
31 K. Reddy, 'SACBOC and SACB first-class matches and records, 1971-1991'; K. Reddy, 'Career records of SACBOC/SACB cricketers who played three-day matches, 1956/57 to 1990/1991'.
32 C. Bryden (ed.), *Mutual and Federal SA Cricket Annual 2001*, p. 493; D. Govindjee, 'Majola a worthy ambassador for cricket', *EP Herald*, 1 September 2000.
33 Interview with Khaya Majola, Johannesburg, 3 July 2000.
34 K. Reddy, 'SACBOC and SACB first-class matches and records, 1971-1991'; personal observations; and match reports by Michael Doman and Devdas Govindjee, namely 'EP does it again', *Cape Herald*, 23 November 1985 and 'Apalling wicket for Board game', *Evening Post* (undated cutting in Haroon Lorgat Collection).
35 M. Allie, *'More than a game'*, p. 146.
36 Interview with Khaya Majola, Johannesburg, 3 July 2000.
37 *Ibid.*
38 Mustupha Khan's career records are 245 wickets at 14.94 and 2 269 runs at 19.22.
39 M. Allie, *More than a game*, pp. 146-147.
40 List drawn from K. Reddy, 'SACBOC and SACB first-class matches and records, 1971-1991'.
41 *Ibid.* See list of SACBOC/SACB players.

Chapter 30 SPORT PART OF THE COMMUNITY

1   Interview with Khaya Majola, Johannesburg, 3 July 2000; *Argus*, 18 December 1988.
2   n.a., 'Rugby in the Eastern Cape: A history', *Work in Progress*, no. 17, April 1981, p. 3.
3   Interview with Dan Qeqe, New Brighton, 29 October 2002.
4   *Ibid.*
5   Personal communication, Ebrahim Rasool, 2001.
6   K. Williamson, *Brothers to us: The story of a remarkable family's fight against apartheid*, (Penguin Books, Ringwood, Australia, 1998, 2nd edition), pp. 32-34.
7   *Ibid.*, pp. 37-40.
8   *Ibid.*, p. 44.
9   'More SACOS men on "New Brighton" charges', *SACOS Bulletin*, vol. 1, no. 6, September/October 1983; personal communication, Maxwell Jordaan, 2001.
10 A. Odendaal, 'Stop padding up to apartheid', *Campus Sport*, January 1986, p. 16. A version of this article was also prepared for *NUSAS Review* (1987), but the edition was banned before it could appear.
11 See report, *EP Herald*, 17 October 1977.
12 Interview with Dan Qeqe, New Brighton, 29 October 2002.
13 'Sports boss quits "after SB visits"', *Cape Herald*, 27 May 1978.
14 A. Odendaal, 'Stop padding up to apartheid', *Campus Sport*, January 1986.
15 See A. Odendaal, 'Resistance, reform and repression in South Africa in the 1980s' in *Beyond the Barricades, Popular resistance in South Africa in the 1980s, Photographs by twenty South African photographers* (Kliptown Books, London, 1989).
16 Interview with Dan Qeqe, New Brighton, 29 October 2002.
17 n.a., 'Rugby in the Eastern Cape: a history', *Work in Progress*, no. 17, April 1981, pp. 3-4.
18 'Her business is children', *Umso*, March 1984, p. 2.
19 'Guiding light in all her words and deeds', *Guiding (UK)*, February 1988, p. 39; 'Motivation for woman of the year – 1994', J. Roberts, Regional Commissioner, Girl Guides, Eastern Cape, July 1994.
20 'Lifetime of dedication lauded', *Port Elizabeth Express*, 17 August 1994.
21 Interview with Cynthia Majola, Johannesburg, 16 April 2003.
22 Video interview with Cynthia Majola, screened at UCB dinner for 10th anniversary of the development programme, Johannesburg, March 2002.
23 Interview with Cynthia Majola, Johannesburg, 16 April 2003.
24 Interview with Khaya Majola, Johannesburg, 3 July 2000.
25 *Ibid.*
26 Pamphlet, Majola family papers.
27 For a biographical profile of Dan Dumile Qeqe, see 'Dan still in the firing line after life-long struggle', *Port Elizabeth Express*, 26 October 1994.

28 A. Odendaal, 'Stop padding up to apartheid', *Campus Sport*, January 1986.
29 Interview with Gerald Majola, Savannah Hotel, Bridgetown, Barbados, 10 May 2001.
30 Interview with Gerald Majola, Spier, Stellenbosch, 16 March 2003; interview with Tozie Majola, New Brighton, 2 July 2000.
31 Speech at funeral of Khaya Majola, Centenary Hall, New Brighton, 2 September 2000.
32 Personal communication, Gerald Majola, August 2002.
33 'Majola's mission', *South*, 30 November 1989.
34 Interview with Tozie Majola, New Brighton, 2 July 2000. This block is based on this interview. See also Mabizela's obituary, *Sunday Times*, 27 April 2003.
35 Interview with Gerald Majola, Spier, Stellenbosch, 16 March 2003.
36 'Bravo's in the fold', *Cape Herald*, 15 November 1977.
37 'Seven quit PECU clubs', *Cape Herald*, 17 January 1978.
38 Roberts, *SACOS, 1973-1988*, pp. 30-31.
39 'Sport rumpus over wedding', *Weekend Post*, 9 November 1985; 'Five "wedding" cricketers await discipline', *EP Herald*, 11 February 1985; 'Bowled by a wedding', *Evening Post*, 14 February 1985; 'Wedding bells tolled trouble', *Probe*, March 1985, p. 37.
40 'Buzz over Good Hope suspension', *Weekend Post*, 2 March 1985; 'Good Hope club banned', *Evening Post*, 28 February 1985; 'EP club banned for 18 months', *Cape Herald*, 9 March 1985.
41 Interview with Raymond Uren, Johannesburg, 23 March 2003.
42 Interview with Devdas Govindjee, Port Elizabeth, 28 October 2002.
43 See Roberts, *SACOS, 1973-1988*, pp. 33-36.
44 *Ibid.*, pp. 50-51, 62-66; 'UDF to SACOS: Build a mass sport movement', *New Era*, November 1987; A. Odendaal, 'NOSC: The sports movement of the future' (Cape Town, 1990); C. Roberts, *South Africa's struggle for Olympic legitimacy: From apartheid to international recognition* (Township Publishing Co-operative, Cape Town, 1991), pp. 7-9.
45 Interview with Khaya Majola, Johannesburg, 3 July 2000.
46 *Ibid.*
47 *Ibid.*
48 'Lack of organization calls for rethinking', *Evening Post*, 8 November 1984.
49 Interview with Khaya Majola, Johannesburg, 3 July 2000.
50 Personal notes and observations, Port Elizabeth, 11 December 1998.
51 Interview with Khaya Majola, Johannesburg, 3 July 2000.
52 Interview with Gerald Majola, Savannah Hotel, Bridgetown, Barbados, 10 May 2001.
53 Extracted from K. Reddy, 'Career records of SACBOC/SACB cricketers who played three-day matches, 1956/57 to 1990/91'.

Chapter 31 'OLYMPICS OF THE OPPRESSED'

1   On the rebel tours see, for example, SACOS 5th Bi-ennial report, Cape Town, 19-20 March 1983, pp. 74-82; E. Litchfield (ed.), *The 1982 Protea Cricket Annual of South Africa*, pp. 11-12, 81-83; C. Harte, *Cricket rebels* (QB Books, Sydney, 1985); C. Harte, *Two tours and a Pollock: the Australian cricketers in South Africa, 1985-87* (Sports Marketing, Adelaide, 1988).
2   Message from Morgan Naidoo, President, South African Council on Sport, *SACOS Sport, Cape Town, Festival '82*, p. 1.
3   'Cricket board teams', (undated Cape Herald cutting, scrapbook, Haroon Lorgat Collection).
4   'Easy for President's team', *The Argus*, 11 October 1982; 'Lorgat innings sets up victory', *Cape Times*, 11 October 1982.
5   Interview with Khaya Majola, Johannesburg, 3 July 2000; 'Slight edge for SA XI over EP', *Evening Post*, 7 April 1986; 'Saleh makes fine century', *Evening Post*, 8 April 1986.
6   K. Reddy, 'SACBOC and SACB first-class matches and records, 1971-1991'.
7   'I'm all right Jack … but what a farce!', *The Indicator*, 27 November 1987.
8   *SACOSPORT, Festival '88 (A commemorative volume)* (Buchu Books, Cape Town, 1988), pp. 12-13.
9   *Ibid.*, p. 8.
10 *Ibid.*, p. 67.
11 Personal communication, K. Reddy, April 2003.
12 'Cricket talent on view', *Daily Dispatch*, 1 March 1991, and match reports 2 and 4 March 1991.
13 'Majola's mission', *South*, 30 November 1989.
14 'Khaya Majola – SACOS sportsperson of the year', *SACOS Sport*, May 1989.
15 'Captain courageous', *The Indicator*, 24 February 1989.
16 'Majola's mission', *South*, 30 November 1989.
17 Address to UCB National Vision Conference dinner, 4 November 1998, videoed by the United Cricket Board.
18 The list is drawn from newspaper and other sources, and it includes both one-day and three-day games.
19 'Easy for President's team', *The Argus*, 11 October 1982; 'Lorgat innings sets up victory', *Cape Times*, 11 October 1982; 'Manack's men triumph', *Cape Herald*, (undated cutting in Haroon Lorgat Collection).
20 K. Reddy, 'SACBOC and SACB first-class matches and records, 1971-1991'.
21 *Ibid.*
22 M. Allie to A. Odendaal, 12 March 2003.
23 *SACOSPORT, Festival '88*, p. 67.
24 *Daily Dispatch*, 2 March 1991.
25 *Daily Dispatch*, 4 March 1991.

Part Seven

THE MAJOLA BROTHERS AND THE
UNITED CRICKET BOARD (1990s-2000s)

Chapter 32 UNITY

1   See, for example, A. Odendaal, 'Die rebelletoer: Nee', *Vrye Weekblad*, 12 January 1990; 'Tour demo ends in township riot', *Cape Times*, 29 January 1990.
2   M. Allie, *More than a Game*, p. 186.
3   See M. Bose, *Sporting colours, Sport and politics in South Africa* (Robson Books, London, 1994), chapters 8, 12; 'Bacher soothes rugby nerves', *The Star*, 3 February 1991.
4   M. Allie, *More than a Game*, p. 187.
5   'Cricket's Berlin Wall crashes down and Mr Majola comes to town', *Sunday Star*, 3 February 1991; 'Twee beheerliggame snoer eerste keer kragte saam', *Beeld*, 1 February 1991.
6   Interview with Khaya Majola, Johannesburg, 3 July 2000.
7   'New innings for SA cricket', *Weekly Mail*, 28 June 1991; T. Partridge and F. Heydenrych (eds.), *The 1991 Protea Assurance Cricket Annual of South Africa*, p. 21.
8   'Mandela goes in to bat for World Cup play', *Business Day*, 24 September 1991; 'SA krieket eenparig terug uit isolasie', *Beeld*, 24 October 1991; M. Bose, *Sporting colours*, pp. 232-243. On South Africa's admission to world cricket from 1991 onwards see, C. Bryden, *Return of the prodigals, South Africa's cricketing comeback* (Sunday Times and Jonathan Ball, Johannesburg, 1996); C. Bryden, *The story of South African cricket, 1991-1996* (Royston Lamond International, Cape Town); *How's that? On tour with South Africa in India, the World Cup and the West Indies* (The Argus souvenir, Struik, Cape Town, 1992).

Chapter 33 IN CHARGE OF THE DEVELOPMENT PROGRAMME

1   Interview with Khaya Majola, Johannesburg, 3 July 2000.
2   *Ibid.*
3   Quoted in C. Day (ed.), *Developing winners*, p. 10.
4   Interview with Khaya Majola, Johannesburg, 3 July 2000.
5   *Ibid.* See also 'Good news for cricket', *New Nation*, 8 February 1991.
6   'Another long, but exhilarating day', *Business Day*, 8 February 1991.
7   See, for example, 'Youngsters will benefit from grassroots level approach', *Indaba*, 4 April 1991; 'New innings for SA cricket', *Weekly Mail*, 4 July 1991; 'Lloyd to coach in SA', *The Citizen*, 17 July 1991; 'Kenyan for SA academy', *City Press*, 8 September 1991; 'Britain donates more gear', *City Press*, 26 October 1992.
8   L. Barnes, 'Dan still in the firing line after a life-long struggle', *Port Elizabeth Express*, 26 October 1994.
9   'Woman of the year', *Port Elizabeth Express*, 31 August 1994; 'Salute to a guiding light in East Cape', *Evening Post*, 31 August 1994; 'Youth's guiding light', *EP Herald*, 27 February 1995.
10 Speech by Lawrence Mvumvu, memorial service for Khaya Majola at St Catherine's Anglican church, Johannesburg, 30 August 2000.
11 Interview with Cynthia Majola, Johannesburg, 16 April 2003.
12 Interview with Khaya Majola, Johannesburg, 3 July 2000.
13 Quoted in C. Day (ed.), *Developing winners*, p. 70.
14 Interview with Khaya Majola, Johannesburg, 3 July 2000; UCB brochure, 'The development programme of the United Cricket Board of South Africa', 1996.
15 Interview with Niels Momberg, Johannesburg, 3 July 2000.
16 *Ibid.*
17 Personal communication, Imtiaz Patel, 23 March 2003.
18 Interview with Niels Momberg, Johannesburg, 3 July 2000.
19 He is at time of writing Director of Enterprises and Production at SuperSport, the leading sports television channel in Africa.
20 Interview with Niels Momberg, Johannesburg, 3 July 2000.

Chapter 34 TRANSFORMATION TOP OF THE AGENDA

1   See A. Odendaal, 'Planning for a 21st-century game: The UCB and cricket transformation, 1998-2002' in C. Bryden (ed.), *Mutual and Federal SA Cricket Annual 2002*, pp. 33-37.
2   'Rethinking the basics: The process of drafting the Charter' in Transformation Monitoring Committee first report to UCBSA, July 1999, pp. 3-4.
3   See UCB videos on this process and the 1998 National Vision Conference to get a sense of the feelings vented by the cricket constituency. The process was driven by Imtiaz Patel of the UCB, together with Gideon Steyn of RGA Consulting.
4   See Transformation Monitoring Committee first report to the UCBSA, July 1999, pp. 6-10 for full details of the Transformation Charter, Pledge to the Nation and the ten Transformation Thrusts identified at the National Vision Conference.
5   See Transformation Monitoring Committee second report to the UCBSA, January 2000, part 2.
6   'Blueprint for the implementation of development targets as agreed upon at the Development Conference held at the Riverside Sun, Vanderbijl Park on 28-29 May 1999', Appendix E in Transformation Monitoring Committee first report to the UCBSA, July 1999. See also pp. 17-18 and Appendix C for the database on South African Cricket that was developed to monitor progress.
7   A. Odendaal, 'Planning for a 21st-century game', p. 34.
8   *Ibid.*, pp. 34-5; Transformation Monitoring Committee third report to the UCBSA, July, 2000, vol. 1, pp. 5-9.
9   This was at the instigation of Khaya Majola who communicated with Jannie Momberg MP and others; personal communication, Niels Momberg, May 2003.

10 Statement by the UCBSA Transformation Monitoring Committee, 4 January 1999 in Transformation Monitoring Committee first report to the UCBSA, July 1999, Appendix B.
11 See statement by the Minister of Sport and Recreation, Ngconde Balfour, on the announcement of the Gauteng/Northerns Combined XI to play England at CenturionPark, 17 November 1999; press statement by André Odendaal, Chairperson, Transformation Monitoring Committee, 18 November 1999; 'Sonn tells off Ali Bacher', *Cape Argus*, 19 November 1999.
12 A. Odendaal, 'Planning for a 21st-century game', p. 35. For two examples see L. Steenveld, 'Newspaper coverage of selected cricket transformation issues' in Transformation Monitoring Committee second report to UCBSA, July 2000, and 'Conversations with the South African media' in 'Background to the transformation process in South African cricket' (Media package for Australian and South African journalists visiting Robben Island on 5 March 2002 as guests of the Transformation Monitoring Committee of the UCB for function in honour of Mr Gerald Majola, CEO).
13 Personal observations and notes, UCB National Vision Conference, Johannesburg, 13-15 November 1998.
14 *Ibid.*
15 Transformation Monitoring Committee first report to UCBSA, July 1999, p. 5. Later Chris Day, Ahmed Jinnah and Mtutuzeli Nyoka became members as well.
16 *Ibid.*, pp. 15-16; A. Odendaal, 'Planning for a 21st-century game', pp. 33-35.
17 M.G. Majola to R. White, 1 January 2000; 'Bid to oust UCB chief', *Cape Argus*, 21 January 2000; press release from A. Bacher, Managing Director, UCB, 22 January 2002; 'I'm not a racist says cricket-lover Majola' (undated cutting, Khaya Majola Collection).

Chapter 35 'THERE WILL NEVER BE ANOTHER KHAYA'

1   Dr Mtutuzeli Nyoka's speech at the funeral of Khaya Majola, Centenary Hall, New Brighton, 2 September 2000.
2   Telephonic interview with Cynthia Majola, 28 April 2003.
3   See, for example, A. Odendaal's obituary of Khaya Majola in *Cape Argus*, 30 August 2000; funeral programme, 2 September 2000; UCBSA diary 2001; and programme for 8th annual Coca Cola Khaya Majola Cricket Week, Vaal Triangle, 17-21 December 2001 (inside cover and loose insert). For other obituaries and profiles, see C. Barron, 'Cricket boss set ball rolling in townships', *Sunday Times*, 3 September 2000; D. Govindjee, 'Majola proved a worthy ambassador for cricket', *EP Herald*, 1 September 2000; C. Day, 'Khaya Majola player, patriot and pioneer' in C. Day (ed.), *Developing winners*, pp. 10-13.
4   Republic of South Africa, Minutes of proceedings of National Assembly, Tuesday 12 September 2000, No.s 49 – 2000, p. 665.
5   'Minute's silence for "fallen hero" Khaya', *Sowetan*, 28 August 2000.
6   Untitled and undated cutting, Cynthia Majola album.
7   P. Hain to A. Bacher, 30 August 2000.
8   'Majola proved worthy ambassador for cricket', *EP Herald*, 1 September 2000.
9   'UCB's popular Majola dies', *Evening Post*, 28 August 2000 and 'Condolences pour in for late Majola', *Citizen*, 29 August 2000.
10 Speech by Lawrence Mvumvu, memorial service for Khaya Majola at St Catherine's Anglican Church, Johannesburg, 30 August 2000.
11 'Touching tributes paid at funeral to Majola', *Weekend Post*, 2 September 2000; 'Majola honoured by top leaders at memorial service', *EP Herald*, 4 September 2000.
12 See videos by Matshoba Mzwandile, 'The memorial service of the late Eldridge Khaya Majola', 31 August 2000 and 'The funeral service of the late Eldridge Khaya Majola', 2 September 2000.
13 Speech at funeral service of Khaya Majola by Danny Jordaan, Centenary Hall, New Brighton, 2 September 2000.

Chapter 36 CEO OF THE UNITED CRICKET BOARD

1   R. White to all members of the General Council, 23 November 1999; T. Khumalo to president UCB, n.d.; F. Potgieter, to president UCB, 6 December 1999.
2   'Majolas to bat for South Africa', *Sunday Argus*, 26 August 2000; 'New CEO keen to end quotas', *Business Day*, 6 October 2000.
3   Interview with Gerald Majola, Savannah Hotel, Bridgetown, Barbados, 10 May 2001.
4   *Ibid.*
5   Personal communication, 6 October 2000.
6   C. Bryden (ed.), *Mutual and Federal SA Cricket Annual 2001*, pp. 85-88. See also 'Ngam's folks never realised they had a "gem" in the family', *Cape Times*, 12 January 2001; 'Ntini, Ngam transform SA cricket', *Cape Times*, 11 December 2000.
7   Minutes of UCB Transformation Monitoring Committee meeting, Cape Town, 2 January 2001.
8   M. Doman, 'Majola's vision for success' in C. Bryden (ed.), *Mutual and Federal SA Cricket Annual 2001*, p. 40.
9   Interview with Gerald Majola, Savannah Hotel, Bridgetown, Barbados, 10 May 2001.
10 *Ibid.*
11 *Ibid.*
12 *Ibid.*
13 *Ibid.*
14 *Ibid.*
15 'Oos-Kapenaar neem leisels by Ali Bacher oor', *Die Burger* (undated cutting in Majola Collection); 'New cricket CEO keen to end quotas', *Business Day*, 6 October 2000.
16 These issues were raised openly at UCB General Council meetings in 2001. G. Majola, 'Batting for a transformed future', March 2003 (published in *Financial Mail*, 21 March 2003).
17 UCB, 'Personal vision', Gerald Majola, 13 June 2001.
18 *Ibid.*
19 *Ibid.*

Chapter 37 FACING THE BOUNCERS

1   See C. Bryden, *Herschelle, A biography* (Spearhead, Cape Town, 2002), chapter 17.
2   UCB, convenor of selectors report to the CEO of the UCB, 19 January 2002.
3   'Cricket crisis over rebel test', *Cape Argus*, 23 November 2001; M. Bose, *A history of Indian cricket*, p. 470; C. Bryden, *Herschelle, A Biography*, pp. 181-3; C. Bryden (ed.), *Mutual and Federal South African Cricket Annual 2002*, p. 11.
4   *Cape Times*, 7 January 2003; *The Star*, 10 January 2003; *Cape Times*, 4 February 2003; *Cape Argus*, 10 February 2002.
5   UCB, convenor of selectors report to the CEO of the UCB, 19 January 2002. See also 'Secret of Protea revival', *Cape Argus*, 10 February 2002.
6   'Cricket greats slam Sonn', *Cape Times*, 3 January 2002; C. Bryden, *Herschelle, A biography*, pp. 184-7.
7   C. Bryden (ed.), *Mutual and Federal South African Cricket Annual 2002*, p. 9.
8   'Cullinan's unexpected exit could prove a silver lining for SA cricket' and 'Darryl still hopes for win-win outcome', *Sunday Times*, 10 March 2002.
9   C. Bryden (ed.), *Mutual and Federal South African Cricket Annual 2002*, p. 413.
10 UCB, 'The state of affairs of the Eastern Province Cricket Board', report to UCB Council, July 2002.
11 UCB, 'Majola two years in office' (internal media release), March 2003.
12 'The lily-livered journos and the lily-white team', *Independent on Saturday*, 5 January 2001; 'UCB invites 35 "brains" to Indaba', UCB media release, 9 April 2002; 'Eight wise men named to help get South Africa back on track', *Sunday Independent*, 28 April 2002; 'Pollock emerges from think tank "a lot happier" ', *Cape Times*, 24 April 2002.
13 'SA cricket on sticky wicket', *Sunday Times*, 10 November 2002; C. Bryden (ed.), *Mutual and Federal South African Cricket Annual 2002*, p. 9.
14 'Giving transformation a winning edge', *Sunday Independent*, 14 July 2002; 'Spirit of unity had cricket boss in tears of joy', *Sunday Times*, 14 July 2002; Transformation Monitoring Committee sixth and final report to the UCBSA, presented at the UCB National Consolidation Conference, Kievietskroon, 5-7 July 2002.
15 'SA cricket bowls itself a bouncer', *City Press*, 14 July 2002; 'ANCYL now in favour of World Cup', *Sowetan*, 11 November 2002.
16 'Balfour: we must look at bigger goal', *Saturday Argus*, 13 July 2002; Transformation in cricket, Report submitted to the Honourable Minister of Sport and Recreation, Mr N. Balfour, presented by J. Smith (chairman) et al, 16 October 2002.
17 'Balfour clears air over row', *City Press*, 10 November 2002.
18 See, for example, 'Balfour stop your loose cannons', *Sunday Sun*, 11 August 2003; 'Minister sê hy sal nie bedank al eis mense dat sy op moet rol', *Die Burger*, 6 November 2002; 'Not everyone believes Balfour is on the wrong foot', *Cape Argus*, 6 November 2002.
19 *The Star*, 24 March 2003, p. 1; 'WB-lof vir SA nadat Aussies Indië oorrompel', *Beeld*, 24 March 2003.
20 See, for example, 'WB-krieketsukses wys SA moet sokker in 2010 aanbied', *Die Burger*, 26 March 2003; 'Even before the World Cup is over South Africa has won', *The Star*, 17 March 2003.
21 'Symcox was not forced out', *Weekend Argus*, 9 March 2003.
22 'The end of an era', *Pitch Report*, 7 March 2003.
23 Reports on the final in *The Star* and *Beeld*, 24 March 2003, pp. 1-2; 'Omstrede Sonn dalk op pad uit', *Die Burger*, 28 March 2003.
24 'Smith's meteoric rise to the top', *Cape Times*, 17 March 2003; 'Krieket-tragedie', *Rapport*, 9 March 2003.
25 'They said it…', *City Press*, 9 March 2003.
26 'The end of an era', *Pitch Report*, 7 March 2003. See also 'Forward defensive strategy puts SA cricket on the back foot', *Sunday Times*, 23 March 2003.
27 'Proteas disappointed urban majority', *City Press*, 30 March 2003.
28 Graeme Pollock column, *Rapport*, 9 March 2003.
29 'Account for it', *Financial Mail*, 7 March 2003.
30 G. Majola, 'Batting for a transformed future', March 2003. (Reply to *Financial Mail*, 21 March 2003.)
31 M. du Preez, 'Sports heroes stuck in the past', *The Star* (undated cutting, March 2003).
32 G. Majola, 'Batting for a transformed future', March 2003.
33 Comment made during G. Majola speech, Kwa Maritane, 13 June 2001.

Chapter 38 THE GAINS OF UNITY

1   On Rodney Malamba and the Langa club, see J. Young (ed.), *Langa Cricket Club – 21 years, 1976-1997*.
2   Cricket and nation building, Report by the United Cricket Board of South Africa to the Parliamentary Portfolio Committee on Sport, 11 September 2001, p. 5.
3   See C. Day (ed.), *Developing winners*, p. 58, for details of the PPC programme.
4   *Ibid.*, p. 50.
5   Transformation: 2002/3 season, Interim report by Gerald Majola, CEO, to UCBSA General Council, 1 February 2003.
6   Transformation Monitoring Committee second report to the UCBSA, January 2000, p. 7.
7   *Ibid.*; A. Odendaal, 'Planning for a 21st-century game', p. 34.
8   Transformation Monitoring Committee fifth report to the UCBSA, June 2001, vol 1; 'Changing face of Gauteng cricket', *Saturday Argus*, 13 January 2002.
9   A. Colquhoun, 'To quota or not to quota', *The Big Issue*, vol. 9, no. 67, February 2003, p. 20.
10 'Quota bar vaulted with ease', *Sunday Times*, 27 January 2002.
11 Transformation Monitoring Committee third report to the UCBSA, July 2000, p. 9.
12 Transformation: 2002/3 season, Interim report by Gerald Majola, CEO, to UCBSA General Council, 1 February 2003.
13 *Ibid.*
14 J. Carlin, 'The winds of change', *SA Sports Illustrated*, April 2003, p. 55.

15 J. Young, 'Blame white insecurity not dud black cricketers', *Sunday Times*, 13 January 2002; 'Wat nou?', *Rapport*, 9 March 2003; 'Why Prince is no surprise', *Argus*, 5 March 2002; 'Knocking on keeper's door', *Sunday Times*, 23 March 2003.
16 P. Roebuck, 'Dark star', *The Cricketer*, March 1998.
17 It is ironic, given white suspicions of change, that it is only since democracy and unity that Afrikaans-speakers have been given greater opportunities to represent their country at cricket. For the changing historical relationship between Afrikaners and cricket, and Afrikaners and English-speaking whites, see A. Odendaal, 'Turning history on its head, Some perspectives on Afrikaners and cricket' in C. Day (ed.), *Developing Winners*, pp. 29-32.
18 R. Isherwood to A. Odendaal, 12 April 2003.
19 UCBSA Annual Report 2002, financial statements.
20 UCB, 'Majola 2 years in office' (internal media release), March 2003.
21 See 'A profile of Kedi Tshoma' in C. Day (ed.) *Developing winners*, pp. 33-4; UCBSA, 'Cricket and nation-building', p. 12.
22 Transformation policy of the UCBSA, adopted by the General Council of the UCBSA on 13 September, 2002, p. 11.
23 Personal communication, John Weinburg, Cape Town, 2002.
24 Desai et al, *Blacks in whites*, photograph and caption between pp. 234-5.
25 G. Majola, CEO, interim report, 'Transformation: 2002/3 season'.
26 C. Bryden (ed.), *Protea Assurance South African Cricket Annual 1996*, p. 495. For the early history of women's cricket in South Africa see E.W. Swanton (ed.), *Barclays World of Cricket, The game from A-Z* (Collins Publishers, London, 1980), pp. 348-9. For SARFU's attempts to broaden the base of rugby to include women, see full-page advertising supplement, *Cape Argus*, 22 April 2003.
27 UCBSA Annual Report 2002, p. 26; UCBSA, 'Cricket and nation-building', p. 12.
28 C. Day (ed.), *Developing winners*.
29 Interview with Gerald Majola, Spier, Stellenbosch, 16 March 2003.
30 Nabeal Dien presentation to WPCA executive committee, January 2003.
31 Keynote address, ICC World Cup 2003 banquet, Sandton Convention Centre, Johannesburg, 21 March 2003. For the recent changing notions of men and masculinity in South Africa, see R. Morrell, *From boys to gentlemen: settler masculinity in Natal, 1880-1920* (Unisa, Pretoria, 2001); R. Morrell (ed.) *Changing men in Southern Africa* (University of Natal Press, Scottsville, 2001).
32 For the use of this term see, for example, discussion regarding the Klein Karoo Kunstefees in *Rapport*, 6 April 2003.
33 Interview with Gerald Majola, Spier, Stellenbosch, 16 March 2003.
34 Interview with Ray Mali, East London, 30 October 2002.
35 Personal communication, 2000. One of Makhosana's cricket mentors at the Lwandle migrant workers' hostel was Arthur Jacobs who, as a 'squatter leader' from the informal settlements, became one of the leading figures on the Cape Town City Council after 1994.
36 Interview with Tim Khumalo, Newlands, 9 February 2003.
37 *Ibid.*
38 'Soccer 1, cricket 2, rugby 3', *Sunday Times*, 6 April 2003.

Chapter 39 LIKE CRICKET PLAYED IN HEAVEN

1   Interview with Peter Bacela, Johannesburg, 19 January 2002.
2   'Doing it all for "Papa Steve" ', *Sunday Times*, 5 January 2003.
3   *Ibid.*; interview with Peter Bacela, Johannesburg, 19 January 2002.
4   *SA Sports Illustrated*, February 2001, p. 43.
5   'The voice behind the scenes', *SA Cricket Action*, April 2001, p. 44.
6   *SA Sports Illustrated*, February 2001, p. 43.
7   *Ibid.*
8. Personal observation, WPCA executive committee meetings.
9   *SA Sports Illustrated*, February 2001, pp. 44-45.
10 Ray Mali, chairperson of the UCB Development Committee, is a strong proponent of this approach.
11 Personal communication, Gerald Majola, March 2003.
12 Transformation policy of the United Cricket Board of South Africa. Adopted by the General Council of the UCBSA on 13 September, 2002, pp. 28-29.

Part Eight
THE LEGACY OF 150 YEARS AND THE FUTURE

Chapter 40 STEREOTYPES HIT FOR A SIX

1   Guha, *A corner of a foreign field*, pp. 12-20; M. Bose, *A history of Indian cricket*, chapter 2.
2   'Let us walk in your golden footprints – God bless Africa', (Province of the Eastern Cape, Footprints Certificates, 15 December 2001).
3   'Enterprising cricket marks the opening of the Transvaal season, *African Sports*, November 1953, p. 5 and 'Presentation of cricket trophies', *African Sports*, September 1953, p. 4.

Chapter 41 THE CRICKET AND MISSION SCHOOL LEGACY

1   C.P. Korr, *West Ham United, The making of a football club* (University of Illinois Press, Urbana and Chicago, 1986); C.P. Korr, 'The end of baseball as we knew it', *The player's union, 1960-81* (University of Illinois Press, Urbana and Chicago, 2002).
2   See Robben Island General Recreation Committee papers, UWC Robben Island Mayibuye Archives, catalogue no. 8.

3   Presentation to United States African Studies Assocation Annual Conference, Washington DC, 8 December 2002.

4   See the tributes to Steve Tshwete in *South African Sports Action*, no. 17, June 2002.

5   Ben Tengimfene was a mentor and father-figure to me, Ngconde Balfour and other NSC activists during the heady circa 1990 period, and it was my pleasure as director of Robben Island Museum to host him on the island when he expressed a wish to visit his place of incarceration again. Unfortunately, he passed away shortly before this book was published.

6   'Doing it all for "Papa Steve"', *Sunday Times*, 5 January 2003.

7   A.C. Jordan, *Towards an African literature, The emergence of literary form in Xhosa*, Perspectives on Southern Africa, 6 (University of California Press, Berkeley, 1973), pp. 38, 44-51; A.S. Gerard. *Four African literatures, Xhosa, Sotho, Zulu, Amharic* (California University Press, Berkely, 1971), p. 30.

8   'Ibala le cricket', *Imvo Zabantsundu*, 29 December 1884; personal communication, Ray Mali, 9 February 2003.

9   'Iqakamba kwa Ntselamanzi', *Imvo Zabantsundu*, 24 January 1953; A. Odendaal, *Vukani Bantu!*, pp. 174, 184, 268. The above *Imvo* report also mentioned that Chief David Maqoma, whose forefathers were imprisoned on Robben Island and studied and played cricket at Zonnebloem in the mid-1800s, lived in the district and was a keen follower of cricket.

10   Personal communication, Bob Edgar, 2001.

11   A. Odendaal, *Vukani Bantu!*, pp. 21, 109, 116, 168, 170, 173, 178, 201-2, 232, 265, 270; personal communication, Bangu Masisi, Johannesburg, 23 March 2003.

12   J.T. Sokhanyile research notes; chapter 1 above; 'Ibala labadlali', *Imvo Zabantsundu*, 27 December 1895. J.H. Hofmeyr was a co-patron of the SABCB together with Dr Moroka in the late 1930s.

13   Richard Msimang was one of the founders of the ANC and a prominent soccer administrator. See profile in Karis and Carter, *From protest to challenge*, vol. 4, p. 106.

14   A. Odendaal, *Vukani Bantu!*, p. 59.

15   *Ibid.*, pp. 84, 193, 263.

16   *Ibid.*, pp. 24, 84, 99.

17   N. Mandela, *Long walk to freedom, The autobiography of Nelson Mandela* (Abacus, London, 1996 reprint), pp. 47-50.

18   A. Mager, *Gender and the making of a South African Bantustan*, p. 197.

19   For the political role of the cricket-linked people in establishing a new national movement, see A. Odendaal, *Vukani Bantu!*, chapters 9-11.

20   Quoted in C. Bundy, 'New nation, new history? Constructing the past in South Africa' (unpublished paper, SOAS, 2002). For more on the resilience of this struggle-linked intellectual tradition and intellectual trends in the post-colonial dispensation, see A. Odendaal, 'Heritage and the arrival of post-colonial history in South Africa' (paper presented to the US African Studies Association Conference, Washington DC, 5-8 December 2003.)

21   R. Mali, 'The black cricket belt of the Border' in C. Day (ed.), *Developing winners*, p. 36.

22   *Ibid.*, pp. 35-36.

23   My thanks to John Young and Morgan Mfobo for bringing this saying to my attention. It was confirmed by Ray Mali, personal communication, 1 May 2003.

24   Desai et al, *Blacks in whites*, pp. 154-5.

25   'Ngxatshoke Qonce! Heke Champion!', *Imvo Zabantsundu*, 12 January 1885.

26   My thanks to Junior Sokhanyile for this information.

27   Quoted in C. Roberts, *Sport in chains* (Township Publishing Cooperative, Cape Town, 1994), p. 17.

28   While I have touched on comparative experiences and developments in the former British colonies in this book, this topic, as it relates to South Africa, still awaits serious research.

Chapter 42   CHAINS THAT STILL BIND US

1   See A. Odendaal, 'Resistance, reform and repression in South Africa in the 1980s' in *Beyond the Barricades: Popular resistance in South Africa in the 1980s* (Aperture Press, New York and Kliptown Books, London, 1989), pp. 125-6.

2   See chapter 5 above.

3   T. Chesterfield and J. McGlew, *South Africa's cricket captains*, pp. 6-7, 12-13, 140-1.

4   C.L.R. James, *Beyond a boundary*, chapter 18; A. Grimshaw (ed.), *C.L.R. James, Cricket* (Allison and Busby, London, 1989), pp. 101-2, 255-270. Cricket was an integral part of early nationalist strivings in the colonies. In the West Indies it grew and became perhaps the primary way to 'invent ourselves as a people, as a nation' in the 20th century. But in South Africa it declined and became distanced from the growth of national identity because of apartheid. See, for example, J. Young, 'It's not just cricket' (honours essay, UCT, 1994); S. Berry, 'One of the most profound cricket books there has been', *Wisden Cricket Monthly* (June 1998, John Young Collection).

5   A. Odendaal, 'Turning history on its head, Some perspectives on Afrikaners and cricket' in C. Day (ed.). *Developing winners*, pp. 29-32.

6   Address given by Mr J.T. Passmore, Trustee SACA Fund, to delegates to AGM of SACA, 22 September 1973, on the subject of 'Development of African cricket in South Africa'.

7   L. Duffus, *Play abandoned* (Howard Timmins, Cape Town, 1969), pp. 172-3.

8   *Ibid.*, p. 177.

9   R. Archer and A. Boullion, *The South African game*, pp. 8-9.

10   P. Dobson, *Rugby in South Africa*, p. 167.

11   R. Archer and A. Boullion, *The South African Game*, p. 8.

12   'SA blacks not made to play rugby, says Ullie', *Cape Times*, 26 October 1994.

13   See chapter 22 above.

14   M. Procter, *Cricket Buccaneer* (Don Nelson, Cape Town, 1974), p. 25.

15   A. Odendaal, 'Stop padding up to apartheid', *Campus Sports*, January 1986, pp. 17-18.

16   M. Allie, *More than a game*, p. 160.

17   *Ibid.*, p. 58.

18   *Ibid.*, p. 165.

19   C. Bundy, *Re-making the past, New perspectives in South African history* (UCT, Cape Town, 1977), p. 69.

20   'Why this boy is a happy Wanderer', *Daily Express*, 29 April 1991.

21   See, for example, A. Khota, *Across the great divide, Transvaal cricket's joys, struggles and triumphs* (Gauteng Cricket Board, Johannesburg, 2003). p. 8.

22   'Black bats: Why are no black bats coming through', *SA Cricket Action*, May/June 2001, p. 53.

23   Quoted in UCB Transformation Monitoring Committee, Conversations with the South African Media, 5 March 2002.

24   C. Goodwin, *West Indians at the wicket* (Macmillan, London, 1986), Foreword by Clive Lloyd.

25   'Newsregister', *Wisden Cricket Monthly*, March 2003, p. 15.

26   Lehmann's ban kept him out of the first match in the ICC World Cup 2003. See newsclippings in ICC World Cup 2003 files, Andre Odendaal Collection.

27   Desai et al, *Blacks in Whites*, pp. 396, 409-410.

28   For a discussion on this issue, as well as the media attitudes it generated, see L. Steenveld, Department of Journalism and Media Studies, Rhodes university, 'Newspaper coverage of selected cricket transformation issues', pp. 24-36 in UCB Transformation Monitoring Committee, Second report to the UCBSA, January 2000.

29   Presentation on cricket and culture to coincide with opening of exhibition on the science of cricket, MTN Science Centre, Canal Walk, Cape Town, 2 March 2002.

30   M. Bose's *A history of Indian cricket* deals with Dalmiya and the changing power relations. pp. 469-470.

31   J. Young, 'Gogga, one of the best spinners of all time', *Cape Argus*, 15 March 2003.

32   F. Ryan, 'Give Polly and Ford more say – Jennings', Sapa, 25 February 2002. 'N. Momberg to C. Suliman', 25 February 2002; input by Ray Jennings, UCB Transformation Monitoring Committee meeting with stakeholders in Easterns Cricket Union, 22 November 2000. See UCB Transformation Monitoring Committee, fourth report to the UCB, January 2001, pp. 19-20.

33   Pollock articulated this commonly used argument at the seminar organised by the UCB with the national team to discuss transformation, Johannesburg, 20-21 September 1999. For a report of the seminar see, Transformation Monitoring Committee, second report to the UCBSA, January 2000, pp. 9-11.

34   C. Bryden article, *Sunday Times*, 12 August 2001, quoted in UCB Transformation Monitoring Committee, 'Conversations with the South African cricket media', 5 March 2002.

35   See, for example, 'Rice points fingers at bungling officials', *Cape Times*, 31 December 2001; Editorial and 'Cricket greats slam Sonn', *Cape Times*, 3 January 2002; Editorial, *Sunday Tribune*, 6 January 2002; 'SA cricket at crossroads', *Sunday Times*, 6 January 2002; K. Wessels, 'Krieket se toerbestuur toon hy is nie opgewasse vir probleme', *Die Burger*, 11 January 2002; 'Can South Africa afford to be cavalier about winning', *Weekend Argus*, 12 February 2002.

36   Quoted in *The Star*, 2 February 2002.

37   Graeme Smith, supported by players like Ashwell Prince, spoke along these lines at the UCB Consolidation Conference, Kievietskroon, Pretoria, 5-7 July 2002, in arguing for doing away with 'quotas'. The way in which black players internalise old 'fair play', 'merit' and anti-transformation arguments, often as a result of subtle peer pressure, is not dealt with here, but needs further analysis. For one account of how black sports stars 'put up and shut up' in rugby in the 1990s, see M. Keohane, *Chester: A biography of courage* (Don Nelson, Cape Town, 2002).

38   N.S. Ndebele, 'Iph'indlela? Finding our way into the future, The first Steve Biko Memorial Lecture, UCT, 2000 (Skotaville, Braamfontein, 2001). pp. 5-6.

39   *Ibid.*

40   L. Alfred, *Testing times, The men who made South African cricket* (Spearhead, Cape Town, 2003).

41   *Ibid.*, pp. 56-7.

42   *Ibid.*, pp. 98, 147, 168.

43   *Ibid.*, p. 124

44   'Whites didn't use TRC – Tutu', *Citizen*, 22 February 2003. On the reconciliation debate, see also, J. Qwelane column, *Sunday Sun*, 18 May 2003.

45   Address by the President of South Africa, Mr Thabo Mbeki, at the occasion of the launch of Freedom Park, Pretoria, 16 June 2002.

Chapter 43   THE FUTURE AND ITS INSPIRATIONS

1   Supplement, *Cape Times*, 14 June 2002.

2   Transformation Charter in Transformation Monitoring Committee, first report to the UCBSA, July 1999, pp. 8-10.

3   Personal communication, Ebrahim Rasool, 2001.

4   'Soccer 1, cricket 2, rugby 3', *Sunday Times*, 6 April 2003.

5   'There's life after the World Cup', *City Press*, 9 March 2003. See also 'How Tendulkar became a Zulu', *Sowetan*, 27 March 2003.

6   'Interest in cricket is high among blacks', *City Press*, 9 March 2003.

7   'Cricket had me spellbound', *City Press*, 9 March 2003.

8   Interview with Gerald Majola, Spier, Stellenbosch, 16 March 2003. One of South Africa's new national orders, the Order of the Companions of O.R. Tambo, for foreign nationals who have distinguished themselves in support of South Africa, is reported to have as its symbol 'the mole snake, or *majola*, which visits babies when they are born to prepare them for a successful adult life'. (*Cape Times*, 31 May 2002).

9   *Ibid.*

10   'Majola reflects on state of SA cricket', *Evening Post*, undated cutting in Majola Collection; 'Majola 2 years in office', internal UCB media release, received 17 March 2003.

NOTES *on* AUTHOR *and* BIBLIOGRAPHY

THE STORY OF AN AFRICAN GAME is the culmination of more than 25 years of research by Professor André Odendaal, a professional historian, writer and former first-class cricketer who has trodden an unusual path in cricket. It is also part of a new genre of cricket writing that seeks to broaden the story of South African cricket beyond the old colonial, whites-only narratives and the traditional 'elegant cover drive' and 'mesmerising googly' school of cricket writing.

The son of an Afrikaner father, André Odendaal was born on 4 May 1954 in Queenstown, and was the first of eight generations in the family to play cricket. He went to school at Queens College, a well-known cricket nursery, and captained the Border provincial team at the national Nuffield Schools Week. Contemporaries included Ken McEwan, Ivor Foulkes and Ian Greig, and he was coached by a succession of Sussex coaches, including Alan Oakman, John Langridge, Mike Buss and former Queenian, Tony Greig.

He wrote his first sports articles for the *Dagbreek and Landstem* newspaper as a schoolboy. One of the subjects was Tony Greig, then contemplating his move to English cricket.

Odendaal's tertiary education was at Stellenbosch University (1974-1978). He played cricket for a strong Stellenbosch team that was coached by Eddie Barlow and included players such as Peter Kirsten, Garth Le Roux, Kepler Wessels and Adrian Kuiper. He was captain in his final year, leading Stellenbosch to the Western Province Cricket Union league title. At the South African Universities cricket week in 1975 he was voted best fielder. He played for Western Province Colts and was twelfth man for Western Province B.

Besides completing BA, BA Honours *(cum laude)* and MA History *(cum laude)* degrees, Odendaal also edited the university magazine, became assistant editor of the *South African Cricketer* magazine (1975) and wrote two books on cricket, which he published himself, while still a student.

The first of these was *God's Forgotten Cricketers: Profiles of leading South African players* (1976). It contained chapters on the black cricketers Baboo Ebrahim, Tiffie Barnes and Edward Habane, at a time when the gallery of the famous still included only whites. A proposed introductory chapter on the broader cricketing context developed into his second book, *Cricket in Isolation: The politics of race and cricket in South Africa* (1977). The book called for 'mixed' sport at a time when apartheid seemed immovable. It took the author on a journey that led him to challenge the sporting and political status quo in South Africa and join the liberation struggle.

While preparing these books, Odendaal began research on the early history of black cricket in South Africa. The starting points for information were senior cricket administrators, important record-keepers of SACBOC cricket history, such as Syd J. Reddy, Chummy Mayet, Cliff Adams and Yunus Agerdien, and the brochures and correspondence of the various cricket boards. The *South African Non-European Cricket Almanack* in 1953/54 and 1954/55 and its successor, *South African Cricket Almanack* in 1969, all three edited by S.J. Reddy and Domodar Damoo 'Bennie' Bansda, were especially important, being in effect the official histories of black and non-racial cricket. Here black cricketers told the story from their own perspective. Until the first years of the 21st century, virtually every attempt at writing about the history of black cricket has been based on these sources.

Odendaal's first history articles appeared in the *South African Cricketer*. They included 'From de Beers to S.F.W.: 80 years of non-European cricket' (February 1976) and 'John Passmore on African cricket' (February 1977). *Cricket in Isolation* included chapters entitled 'SACBOC: Its origins and development' (written jointly with Syd Reddy, the eminent *Almanack* editor mentioned above) and 'The Africans: Cinderella cricketers'. The latter chapter was perhaps the first attempt to write an overview history of African cricket. However, it was very superficial and, as the title suggests, it reproduced the stereotypes of Africans as cricketers without any real history. The following sentence taken from this chapter underlines the point: 'Early records are virtually non-existent, so it is difficult to determine exactly when Africans took to playing cricket …' (p. 305).

Between 1978 and 1983, the author embarked on his MA and doctoral dissertations on the beginnings of black protest politics in South Africa, which led him to discover that there were indeed numerous records about the origins of African cricket. In the earliest, still-untapped 19th-century African-language newspapers, which formed the basis of his research, he came across regular reports which showed a highly developed cricket culture among Africans in the Eastern Cape from the 1880s onwards. Newspapers like *Isigidimi sama Xhosa* (known as the 'Kaffir Express' in English), *Imvo Zabantsundu* (Native Opinion), *Izwi Labantu* (Voice of the People) and the *APO* carried almost weekly news reports on cricket.

This was still more or less unknown at the time and Odendaal started publicizing the history in a series of articles and chapters in books. The first appeared in the *South African Cricketer* in 1983 as 'Some forgotten cricket history' (Winter 1983), and 'Gold, diamonds and cricket in the early days' followed early in 1984. His DPhil dissertation at Cambridge University, *African political mobilization in the Eastern Cape, 1880-1912* (Cambridge, 1983) included reference to the early cricket as an integral part of the wider political awakening of the time. In 1985, he expanded on the story in a chapter on South Africa (with Louis Duffus and Michael Owen-Smith) in a prestigious volume, *The Barclays World of cricket: The game from A-Z* (Collins London, 2nd edition, 1985), edited by E.W. Swanton.

Odendaal's first published academic work on this early cricket history was 'South Africa's black Victorians: Sport and society in South Africa in the 19th century' in J.A. Mangan (ed.), *Pleasure, profit and proselytism: British culture and sport at home and abroad, 1700-1914* (Cass, London, 1988). It was also published in *Africa Perspective*, New Series (1/7/8) 1989 and *The societies of Southern Africa in the 19th and 20th centuries*, Volume 15 (collected seminar papers no. 38, University of London, Institute of Commonwealth Studies, 1990), and presented as a paper to academic audiences at *inter alia* Warwick University, the Institute for Commonwealth Studies in London, the University of the Western Cape, the annual American Sociological Association Conference (1988) and the Wits History Workshop (1990).

The new historical perspectives provided by Odendaal in *Cricket in Isolation* and 'The black Victorians' helped reshape perceptions about black cricket history and have been widely quoted in academic and popular histories. Examples of those who have borrowed from these sources include R. Archer and A. Boullion, *The South African Game: Sport and Racism* (Zed Press, London, 1983); B. Crowley, *Cricket's exiles: The saga of South African cricket* (Don Nelson, Cape Town, 1983); M. Galant, 'A history of Western Province cricket' (People's History Project, Department of History, University of the Western Cape, 1987); A. Ball, 'It's not just cricket' (BA Hons. dissertation, UCT, 1987); M. Bose, *Sporting colours: Sport and politics in South Africa* (Robson Books, London, 1994); J. Nauright, *Sport, cultures and identities in South Africa* (David Philip, Cape Town, 1998); D. Booth, *The race game: sport and politics in South Africa* (Frank Cass, London, 1998); C. Merrett and J. Nauright, 'South Africa' in B. Stoddart and K.A.P. Sandiforth (eds.), *The Imperial Game: Cricket, culture and society* (Manchester University Press, Studies in Imperialism, 1998); and the soon-to-be-published doctoral dissertation on the history of football in South Africa by American scholar Peter Aleghi, 'Laduma! Soccer, politics and society in South Africa, 1910-1976'.

The new perspectives also seeped into journalism and popular writing, for example, B. Crowley, 'A History of South African cricket - Part I: Colonialism, racism and imperialism, 1790-1914', *The Cricketer International*, January 1994 and K. Reddy (ed. and comp.), *The other side: A miscellany of cricket in Natal* (KwaZulu-Natal Cricket Union, 1999), especially the section on 'SACB: A historical perspective'. See also K. Reddy, 'Playing the game: The early days (Part I)' in *Bear Facts*, the official magazine of the Border Cricket Board, November 1999. Various cricket bodies have also started taking over the material, as in A. Odendaal's 'Jabavu saw cricket as a route to advancement' in *100 years of Border cricket* (centenary brochure, Border Cricket Board, 1996) and 'Some forgotten South African cricket history' in J. Young (ed.), *Langa Cricket Club, 21 years – 1976-1997*.

After completing his doctorate at Cambridge University, André Odendaal joined the University of South Africa and then the University of the Western Cape, where he worked for 13 years. His book *Vukani Bantu! The Beginnings of Black Protest Politics in South Africa to 1912* (David Philip, Cape Town, and Barnes and Noble, Totowa, New Jersey) appeared in 1984. Reviewers described *Vukani Bantu!* as a pioneering study on the origins of African nationalism and the pre-history of the ANC. It was awarded third place in the Sanlam Prize for Literature in 1985.

Odendaal's career as an academic historian went parallel with his role as a first-class cricketer and anti-apartheid sports activist. At Cambridge University (1979-1983) he was awarded his blue for cricket. He played for Combined Universities against the West Indies and Sri Lankan touring sides. A highlight in England was his 61 on debut against Leicestershire and his Man-of-the-Match 74 at Edgbaston against a Warwickshire attack which included internationals Bob Willis, Gladstone Small and Dilip Doshi, and the South African all-rounder, Anton Ferreira.

Returning to South Africa for research during his Cambridge studies, Odendaal played first-class cricket for Boland in the 1980/81 and 1981/82 seasons. Under the captaincy of Eddie Barlow, Boland won the B Section Trophy and reached the semi-finals of the Datsun Shield competition. Odendaal top-scored with 42 when Boland surprised the A Section Eastern Province team in the quarter-finals.

As the struggle against apartheid intensified, Odendaal decided in 1983 that he could no longer be part of the establishment set-up in sport. He left the South African Cricket Union (SACU) to join the non-racial SACOS-affiliated South African Cricket Board (SACB). He was the only white first-class cricketer to join the non-racial Board during the apartheid years.

He represented Transvaal in SACB's Howa Bowl and Benson & Hedges competitions in the 1984/85 season and played one game for Western Province in 1985/86. Together with Omar Henry, he is perhaps the only cricketer who played first-class cricket in England and under both boards in South Africa. He also had the distinction of captaining United Cricket Club to the 'double' in the non-racial Western Province Cricket Board's premier leagues. While still a player he was elected onto the last executive committee of the WPCB, together with the current Minister of Sport, Ngconde Balfour.

During the 1980s he became active in the anti-apartheid struggle, *inter alia* via sport, United Democratic Front Area Committees and the National Education Crisis Committee. He attended the historic Dakar Conference in Senegal between the ANC and Afrikaners in 1987. In 1989 he visited Cuba briefly, undergoing training in underground intelligence work. He supported the emergence of the National Sports Congress (NSC) in the late 1980s, and was part of a delegation of non-racial sports officials who visited Harare in 1989. He was active in the campaigns against the Gatting rebel cricket tour, attended the national launch of the NSC and was elected onto the NSC Western Cape Executive Committee in 1990. He helped develop early NSC proposals for multi-purpose sports centres and was also involved in the formation of the Cape Town Sports Commission. He continued to write on sport during this period, but with a more contemporary focus for alternative media such as *Up Front, Nusas Review, South, New Era* and *Vryeweekblad*.

In the 1990s Professor Odendaal played a leading role in the cultural and heritage sectors in South Africa. He was responsible for planning and establishing the pioneering Mayibuye Centre for History and Culture in South Africa based at the University of the Western Cape. Under his leadership, the Mayibuye Centre built up a unique multimedia archive on apartheid and the struggle for freedom, consisting of over 70 000 photographs, 2 000 film and video productions, 1 000 oral history tapes and over 250 collections of personal and organisational documents. The archive included valuable sports-related collections, such as those of SANROC, the South African Cricket Board, Western Province Cricket Board and Western Province Football Board.

As a member (and later head) of the secretariat of the ANC's Commission for Museums, Monuments and Heraldry in the early 1990s he lobbied for change in museums and helped shape new national strategies and agendas. After the 1994 elections, he was one of 23 people appointed to the Arts and Culture Task Group (ACTAG) by the new minister to advise on cultural policies for a democratic South Africa. Professor Odendaal was also a member of committees responsible for drafting new heritage legislation, namely the new Archives Act and the first draft of the Heritage Resources Bill. He also served on the boards of the Arts and Culture Trust of the President, the South African Museum, the South African Cultural History Museum and the District Six Museum Foundation, and was actively involved in planning and establishing the Robben Island Museum in December 1996. He was appointed its first director, and during his tenure Robben Island became a World Heritage Site and one of the premier tourism and heritage destinations in South Africa.

Professor Odendaal continued to write. His historical essay on 'Resistance, reform and repression in South Africa in the 1980s' accompanied the photographic book, *Beyond the barricades; Popular resistance in South Africa in the 1980s* (Aperture Press, New York and Kliptown Books, London, 1989), which featured the work of 20 South African social documentary photographers from the Afrapix collective. He had three more books published in the early 1990s. The first was *A Trumpet from the housetops: The selected writings of Lionel Forman* (Zed Press, London, Ohio University Press, USA and David Philip, Cape Town, 1992), which he edited together with Sadie Forman. The next was *Liberation Chabalala and other stories: The world of Alex La Guma* (Mayibuye Books, 1993), edited with Roger Field. In 1995 he co-authored '*Beyond the Tryline: Rugby and South African society*' with Albert Grundlingh and Burridge Spies. This book attempted to locate rugby in its historical and social context and was published by Ravan Press to coincide with the Rugby World Cup.

As Mayibuye Centre director and joint series editor of the Mayibuye History and Literature Series with Barry Feinberg, he oversaw the publication and re-publication of 85 books dealing with the history of apartheid and the struggle by the Centre in the 1990s.

After cricket unity in 1991, Odendaal became a member of the first executive committee of the Western Province Cricket Association (WPCA), a position he still fills today. From November 1998 to July 2002 he was the chairperson of the United Cricket Board of South Africa's Transformation Monitoring Committee (TMC), responsible for overseeing the implementation of the three-year transformation plans of the UCB following the adoption of the historic Transformation Charter at the end of 1998. In this capacity, he served on the Council of the United Cricket Board and the UCB's ICC World Cup 2003 Policy Committee.

The aim of transformation was to bring about thoroughgoing change at every level of the UCB and South African cricket, and the TMC played a pivotal role in challenging old apartheid-rooted power relations, representations and cultures of cricket, and reshaping the cricket agenda in South Africa.

The UCB and TMC identified 'recording the full history of South African cricket' as one of its ten transformation priorities. It was concerned that black cricketers were still mere footnotes in the story of the game in South Africa. They had no real history, it was assumed by some. If this was so, then how could they be taken seriously as people who could meaningfully contribute and lead in the present? The UCB's Transformation Charter, therefore, emphasised that it should be a priority to 'acknowledge, record and respect' the achievements of black cricketers over the past century 'recognising our diversity as a source of strength in the process'.

The TMC was given the task of promoting this history thrust. As TMC chairperson and a trained historian, Odendaal enthusiastically drove the process.

Spurred on by the TMC, various provinces started history projects which could help change old perceptions of the past, including the Khaya Majola Room at St George's Park, recognition ceremonies during international matches in Port Elizabeth and Kimberley, a 'Night of the Legends' function and game for ex-players in Lenasia and a 'Night of the Stars' function organised by the Northerns Cricket Union in Pretoria. Odendaal, Ashwin Desai, Chris Day and other TMC members contributed pieces to various newspapers and publications, including columns in the *Daily News*, a weekly six-part series on black cricket history in the *Sowetan* newspaper, an historical overview in the official ICC World Cup 2003 brochure and articles in a range of UCB publications and brochures, including C. Day (ed.), *Cricket ... Developing winners* (UCB, 2002). The history initiatives became one of the most productive areas of the TMC's work.

As a result of the above-mentioned developments and the changing cricket focus since 1998, a whole new genre of post-colonial cricket history has emerged in South Africa.

Several major cricket histories have appeared recently and more are on the way. The first was the audio-visual *Iqakamba* (Hard ball) in 1999,

a nationally-screened R2 million, four-part television documentary series, by Junaid Ahmed and Primemedia, with active inputs from the TMC. The documentary used *Cricket in Isolation* as a guideline for the script on the early history, and Odendaal acted as an historical adviser and commentator. He has also given support in one way or another to nearly every one of the projects that followed, starting with the illustrated 375-page book, *More than a Game: History of the Western Province Cricket Board, 1959-1991* by Mogamad Allie (2001). Published by the WPCA in 2001 at a cost of over R500 000, this handsome book went far beyond the usual run-of-the-mill cricket brochures and publications. The proactive KwaZulu-Natal Cricket Union published *The other side: A miscellany of cricket in Natal'*, compiled by Krish Reddy in 1999. It followed this with Dr Ashwin Desai, Dr Goolam Vahed, Professor Vishnu Padayachee and Krish Reddy's path-breaking *Blacks in whites: A century of cricket struggles in KwaZulu-Natal* (Natal University Press, 2002). This superbly researched and analytical work produced by professional social scientists set new standards in cricket history writing, showing a depth of research and (often self-critical) details and insights previously absent from cricket histories. In March 2003, Aslam Khota edited *Across the divide: Transvaal cricket's joys, struggles and triumphs*, a 149-page compilation of regional cricket history published by the Gauteng Cricket Board. In the latest project, Junior Tengo Sokhanyile has started a dissertation on the history of African cricket in the Western Province for a MA degree at the University of the Western Cape. The former Langa Cricket Club captain and president, who is named after J.T. Jabavu, is being supported by the Western Province Cricket Association

These new histories are challenging and inverting old paradigms and understandings, giving shape to an emerging new institutional culture of cricket in this country, one that is South African (in an African context) rather than rooted in outdated Victorian and apartheid mythologies and power relations.

They show that, far from being insignificant, the cricketers who played on the wrong side of the colour line in the past had deep cricket cultures and were often the ones sowing the seeds for the future, and that it is their energies and imaginations which will, in fact, largely influence and shape the way forward. These new works have helped break down old stereotypes and allowed cricket to re-imagine the past and shape dynamic new understandings and identities.

The story of African cricket was shamefully neglected in the past. Even the old *South African Non-European Cricket Almanack* unwittingly perpetuated this marginalisation. The magazine, *African Sports*, reviewing the 1953 edition said the *Almanack* was a great step forward for black cricketers, but there were still major omissions. 'Unfortunately little is written about Bantu cricket', the magazine commented, and expressed the wish that the *Almanack* would eventually be 'on par in literature and accuracy with the illustrious *Wisden* and *Playfair*', (*African Sports*, January 1954, p. 18).

The Story of an African Game, part of the new wave of history, reveals a deeply-rooted and rich history that will hopefully surprise and encourage even the most enthusiastic believers in black agency in South African cricket. If the book in any way helps redress the massive exclusions and ignorance of the past it will have been a success. It does not claim to tell the whole history of African cricket, but is simply one narrative from a particular perspective. As noted earlier, there are still many untapped sources available and many histories that need to be written. The author hopes that the new leads given here will encourage more such research, resulting in deeper insights and understandings of the past.

Following *The Story of an African Game* is the UCB-sanctioned two-volume *Official History of South African Cricket, 1808-2003*, edited by André Odendaal, Krish Reddy and Christopher Merrett. Due to be published in 2004, it is intended as a companion volume to this one, dealing with the broader cricket context. It will include test cricket and the organisational histories of the ten different organisations who claimed to be 'national' and used the title 'South African' during the days of segregation and division.

The Story of an African Game has been part of a long intellectual journey. In many ways it marks the completion of that chapter started by the undergraduate editor of *Cricket in Isolation* in 1975. Over the past three decades, André Odendaal has played an important role in helping to reappraise South African history, both in the broader societal and narrower cricket and sporting sense. In March 2002 he was awarded the President's Award for Sport in the Lifetime Achievement category, together with several icons of the sport's struggle, namely Sam Ramsamy, Steve Tshwete, Joe Ebrahim, Cheeky Watson, Makhenkesi Stofile, Raymond Uren, Kedi Tshoma and Mthobi Tyamzashe. He is now a full-time researcher and writer, and is an Honorary Professor in History and Heritage Studies at the University of the Western Cape.

Professor Odendaal can be contacted at andreodendaal@absamail.co.za.
Telephone: (021) 762 4475.
Fax: (021) 762 1883.

INDEX

PHOTOGRAPHIC CREDITS

First published in 2003 in southern Africa
by David Philip Publishers,
an imprint of New Africa Books (Pty) Ltd,
99 Garfield Road, Claremont 7700,
South Africa

© in text: André Odendaal – © in photography: As credited
© in published work: New Africa Books (Pty) Ltd

Every effort has been made to trace the copyright holders of photographs and other published documents including poems reproduced in this volume, and these have been credited accordingly. The publishers would, however, be grateful for any information that may lead to identifying the copyright holders of extracts and photographs not credited here.

ISBN 0-86486-638-0

PROJECT MANAGEMENT: Integrated Publishing Solutions
ART DIRECTOR: Peter Bosman – DESIGNER: Damian Gibbs
ASSISTANT EDITOR: Catherine Bothwell – PROOFREADER: John Young
INDEXER: Mary Lennox
REPRODUCTION BY MegaDigital, Cape Town
PRINTED AND BOUND BY ABC Press